Architectural Design of Multi–Agent Systems:
Technologies and Techniques

Hong Lin
University of Houston – Downtown, USA

INFORMATION SCIENCE REFERENCE

Hershey · New York

Acquisitions Editor:	Kristin Klinger
Development Editor:	Kristin Roth
Senior Managing Editor:	Jennifer Neidig
Managing Editor:	Sara Reed
Assistant Managing Editor:	Sharon Berger
Assistant Managing Editor:	Diane Huskinson
Copy Editor:	Toni Fitzgerald
Typesetter:	Jennifer Neidig
Cover Design:	Lisa Tosheff
Printed at:	Yurchak Printing Inc.

Published in the United States of America by
Information Science Reference (an imprint of IGI Global)
701 E. Chocolate Avenue, Suite 200
Hershey PA 17033
Tel: 717-533-8845
Fax: 717-533-8661
E-mail: cust@igi-pub.com
Web site: http://www.info-sci-ref.com

and in the United Kingdom by
Information Science Reference (an imprint of IGI Global)
3 Henrietta Street
Covent Garden
London WC2E 8LU
Tel: 44 20 7240 0856
Fax: 44 20 7379 0609
Web site: http://www.eurospanonline.com

Library of Congress Cataloging-in-Publication Data

Architectural design of multi-agent systems : technologies and techniques / Hong Lin, editor.
       p. cm.
   Summary: "This book is a compilation of advanced research results in architecture and modeling issues of multi-agent systems. It serves as a reference for research on system models, architectural design languages, methods and reasoning, module interface design, and design issues"--Provided by publisher.
   Includes bibliographical references and index.
   ISBN 978-1-59904-108-7 (hardcover) -- ISBN 978-1-59904-110-3 (ebook)
   1. Intelligent agents (Computer software) 2. Electronic data processing--Distributed processing. 3. Computer architecture. I. Lin, Hong, 1965-
QA76.76.I58A72 2007
006.3--dc22
                              2006039663
British Cataloguing in Publication Data

A Cataloguing in Publication record for this book is available from the British Library.

All work contributed to this book set is new, previously-unpublished material. The views expressed in this book are those of the authors, but not necessarily of the publisher.

Table of Contents

Section I
Fundamentals of Multi-Agent System Modeling

Chapter I

Towards Agent-Oriented Conceptualization and Implementation / *Pratik K. Biswas*............................ 1

Chapter II

Concurrent Programming with Multi-Agents and the Chemical Abstract Machine / *Wanli Ma,*
Dat Tran, Dharmendra Sharma, Hong Lin, and Mary Anderson... 26

Chapter III

Coalition Formation Among Agents in Complex Problems Based on a Combinatorial Auction
Perspective / *Hiromitsu Hattori, Tadachika Ozono, and Toramatsu Shintani*....................................... 48

Chapter IV

A Gentle Introduction to Fuzzy Logic and Its Applications to Intelligent Agents Design /
Andre de Korvin, Plamen Simeonov, and Hong Lin 61

Section II
Agent-Oriented System Design

Chapter V

Component Agent Systems: Building a Mobile Agent Architecture That You Can Reuse /
Paulo Marques and Luís Silva.. 95

Chapter VI

Designing a Foundation for Mobile Agents in Peer-to-Peer Networks / *Daniel Lübke and*
Jorge Marx Gómez... 115

Section III
Agent-Based Intelligent Systems

Section IV
Applications of Multi-Agent Systems

Detailed Table of Contents

Section I
Fundamentals of Multi-Agent System Modeling

Chapter I

Towards Agent-Oriented Conceptualization and Implementation / *Pratik K. Biswas*........................... 1

This chapter provides an in-depth analysis of agent concept and compares it to conventional program-ming models such as object-oriented design. It defines agent models and proposes a high-level method-ology for agent-oriented analysis and design. It also looks at the heart of agent-oriented programming and outlines its advantages over traditional approaches to distributed computing and interoperability. It reviews the Foundation for Intelligent Physical Agents (FIPA)-compliant infrastructure for building agent-based systems and suggests a multi-agent systems framework that merges this infrastructure with the emerging Java 2 Enterprise Edition (J2EE) technologies.

Chapter II

Concurrent Programming with Multi-Agents and the Chemical Abstract Machine / *Wanli Ma,
Dat Tran, Dharmendra Sharma, Hong Lin, and Mary Anderson*... 26

A framework, MACH (multi-agent extended chemical abstract machine), for specifying autonomous agents using the chemical reaction metaphor is developed. Temporal logic is used to reason the prop-erties of the specified system. This chapter focuses on the design, implementation and verification of MACH. The aim on MACH is to develop a reactive programming language based on an interactive computational model.

Combinatorial auction metaphor is used to develop a scheme for coordinating agents in solving complex problems. A ombinatorial auction for scheduling is formalized as an MIP (mixed integer programming) problem, which integrates the constraints on items and bids to express complex problems. This integration solves the trade-off between the computation time to find the solution and the expressiveness to represent a scheduling problem.

This chapter presents a gentle introduction to fuzzy logic and discusses its applications to multi-agent systems. The purpose of this chapter is to present the key properties of fuzzy logic and adaptive nets and demonstrate how to use these, separately and in combination, to design intelligent systems.

Section II
Agent-Oriented System Design

This chapter proposes component-based mobile agent systems to overcome the limitations of traditional platform-based approach for developing mobile agents and demonstrate the effectiveness of their method by two case studies, viz., the JAMES platform, a traditional mobile agent platform specially tailored for network management; and M&M, a component-based system for agent-enabling applications. It also presents a bird's-eye perspective on the last 15 years of mobile agent systems research is presented along with an outlook on the future of the technology.

This chapter presents an effort to develop a common platform and framework for developing mobile agents that operate on a peer-to-peer network and contain the logic of the network services. By deploying mobile agents who can travel between network nodes to a large P2P network, one could embrace the peer-to-peer technology and use it for all kinds of services, like anonymizing network traffic, distributed storage of documents, replicating contents of heavily accessed Internet sites, trading of information, and so forth. For many of these things, there are solutions available, but by using a common framework and moving the logic into the agents, there is the opportunity to access all kinds of information through a common API, which guarantees extensibility and widespread use.

This chapter develops some algorithms to support dynamic multi-agent scheduling decisions in a network management scenario. The algorithms are developed using functional decomposition strategy, and an experiment has been done and shown promising results.

This chapter introduces a Scalable fault tolerant Agent Grooming Environment (SAGE) for creating distributed, intelligent and autonomous entities that are encapsulated as agents. SAGE has a decentralized fault tolerant architecture that provides tools for runtime agent management, directory facilitation, monitoring and editing messages exchange between agents, and a built-in mechanism to program the agent behavior and their capabilities. SAGE can be used to develop applications in a number of areas, such as e-health, e-government, and e-science.

This chapter presents methodologies and technologies of agent-based grid computing from various aspects and demonstrates that agent-based computing is a promising solution to bring a scalable, robust, thus tractable grid. This chapter firstly reviews backgrounds for multi-agent system, agent-based computing, and Grid computing. Research challenges and issues are characterized and identified together with possible solutions. After the investigation of current research efforts of agent-based grid computing, future research trends are presented and studied.

This chapter studies multi-agent based IT security approach (MAITS) as a holistic solution to the increasing needs of securing computer systems. In this approach, each specialist task for security requirements is modeled as a specialist agent, which has the ability of learning, reasoning, decision making, and an agent interface that enables inter-agent communications.

Section III
Agent-Based Intelligent Systems

Chapter XI

This chapter describes a methodology for modeling expert problem-solving knowledge that supports ontology import and development, teaching-based agent development, and agent-based problem solving. The methodology is applicable to a wide variety of domains and has been successfully used in the military domain.

Chapter XII

This chapter concludes three perspectives on multi-agent reinforcement learning (MARL): (i) cooperative MARL, which performs mutual interaction between cooperative agents, (ii) equilibrium-based MARL, which focuses on equilibrium solutions among gaming agents, and (iii) best-response MARL which suggests a no-regret policy against other competitive agents. Then, the authors present a general framework of MARL that combines all the three perspectives in order to assist readers to understand the intricate relationships between different perspectives. Furthermore, a negotiation-based MARL algorithm based on meta-equilibrium is presented that can interact with cooperative agents, games with gaming agents, and provides the best response to other competitive agents.

Chapter XIII

This chapter presents recent research of the authors on critiquing-based recommendation and a comparison between standard and recent proposals of recommendation based on critiquing. Their work leads to conversational recommender agents that facilitate user navigation through a product space.

Chapter XIV

Case-based recommender systems can learn about user preferences over time and automatically suggest products that fit these preferences. In this chapter, such a system, called CASIS, is presented. In CASIS, an approach inspired by swarm intelligence is applied to a case-based recommender system in the tourism domain and experiment results are shown that using the proposed metaphor the system always return some recommendation to the user, avoiding the user's disappointment.

Section IV
Applications of Multi-Agent Systems

Chapter XV

This chapter develops a multi-agent system that enables the effective formation and management of an optimal supply chain. By means of active communications among internal agents, the multi-agent system for optimal supply chain management makes it possible to quickly respond to the production environment changes such as the machine failure or outage of outsourcing companies and the delivery delay of suppliers.

Chapter XVI

This chapter presents an architecture for an agent-based electronic health record system (ABEHRS) to provide health information access and retrieval among different medical services facilities. The agent-system's behaviors are analyzed using the simulation approach and the mathematical modeling approach. The key concept promoted by ABEHRS is to allow patient health records to autonomously move through the computer network uniting scattered and distributed data into one consistent and complete data set or patient health record.

Chapter XVII

This chapter presents a control framework, which is able to control an autonomous robot in complex real-world tasks. The key features of the framework are a hybrid control paradigm, which incorporates reactive, planning, and reasoning capabilities, a flexible software architecture, and the capability for detecting internal failures in the robot and self-healing. The framework was successfully deployed in the domain of robotic soccer and service robots.

Chapter XVIII

This chapter discusses the use of multi-agent systems to develop virtual reality training systems and describe the system architecture of a multi-agent system for risk management (RiskMan) to help train police officers to handle high-risk situations. RiskMan has been developed using a high-level scripting language of a game engine, Unreal Tournament 2004. The system integrates a simulation agent, trainee agent, communication agent, interface agent, and scripted agents communicating using games technology.

Foreword

Multi-agent systems (MAS) have emerged as a new methodology to address the issues in organizing large-scale software systems. This methodology provides a conceptual model that helps maintaining constraints, a task conventional software engineering is unable to achieve. In recent years, MAS has been used in various areas in computer science and engineering and is becoming a versatile tool that addresses software engineering needs. It also extends the spectrum of computer science research and has drawn more and more attention to a wide range of areas from theoretical studies to practices.

An agent is a software entity that actively seeks ways to complete its tasks. Intelligent agents have the ability to gain knowledge through their problem-solving processes. The study of social behaviors of agents in cognitive science is an important part of the intelligent agent field. Software agents, on the other hand, focus on interaction and collaboration to achieve the goals in a context that changes in a usually unforeseen manner. The necessity of using agents arises from the complexity of large software systems, which bring about design issues that conventional software engineering technology fails to tackle. For instance, mobile agents were proposed to address the needs in the client/server model for the client to be able to migrate to the server side to perform the operation that passive message-passing mechanisms cannot handle efficiently. In a dynamic distributed system, agents with self-adjusting ability can simplify the system architectural design. The design of such a system may be exceedingly complicated in traditional software architecture frameworks or object-oriented modeling.

Agent-oriented modeling yields an unconventional approach to system design, including component definition and system integration. Different applications may impose various requirements on the design and lead to different types of agents. Autonomy is a distinguishing property of an agent. Autonomy entails the agent's capability to survive in a changing environment. An agent has the ability to sense the conditions and make decisions on how to react accordingly. Adaptability requires learning ability necessary for the agent to be able to adjust its decision-making according to past experience. Moreover, an agent-oriented design should address robustness—the system should be reliable when unexpected events occur.

According to their usages, agents can be classified as collaborative agents, interface agents, reactive agents, mobile agents, information agents, and so forth. In the design of large, complex real-life systems, an agent is an abstraction that helps the design of components that tackle different aspects of a problem. Each agent is designed in the most appropriate paradigm for solving its part of a problem. A multi-agent system is used to solve a complex problem that cannot be solved by any single entity of the system. The coordination of independent agents' behaviors is a central part of multi-agent system design. Multi-agent systems are often used to model loosely coupled distributed systems with decentralized control and data allocation. In these systems, communicating agents represent distributed expertise for problem solving. The agents have the ability to process local data efficiently and to communicate with other agents when necessary if the tasks that they are facing are beyond their domain knowledge. Multi-agent systems have been used in a wide spectrum of applications, such as e-commerce, e-learning, communication, data mining, simulation, robotics, transportation systems, and grid computing. It also initiated theoretical studies in specification and reasoning of MAS systems, languages, modeling methods, knowledge representation and processing, and cognitive sciences.

Multi-agent systems are often classified into two categories based on agents' characteristics: self-interested agents and cooperative agents. Self-interested agents are based on economic concepts in which an agent is assumed as a utility maximiser who always tries to maximize an appropriate utility function. This assumption is widely employed in micro-economics and game theory. Thus, researchers often use economic tools and game theory tools to model agents. Self-interested agents tend to close their private information and fail to react if no benefit is available. Cooperative agents are built so that they engage in behaving cooperatively.

Negotiation is one of the key research topics for multi-agent systems. Due to its nature, agents have to make an agreement and achieve consensus among themselves in order to cooperatively perform shared tasks. Negotiations are often modeled as interaction among self-interested agents. As a traditional result, the contract net protocol has been referred as the basic negotiation mechanism among self-interested negotiation. The contract net protocol is a simple task allocation protocol in which agents announce tasks, make bids, and award the tasks. Nowadays, researchers are trying to build more complex and sophisticated protocols based on auctions. Pareto optimality, incentive compatibility, and revenue optimality are crucial concepts to build such auction mechanisms.

As multi-agent system is a rapidly evolving area, promoting a worldwide exchange among scholars is crucial to helping researchers to rightly position their effort relative to the current trends. This book is one of the early attempts that aim to provide a resource to facilitate research and education endeavors in this area. This book covers a wide spectrum of topics and compiles research results from all around the world. The readers can find new advances in every aspect of current multi-agent systems research, such as mathematical logic, agent-oriented modeling, architectural design, coordination programming, knowledge engineering, machine learning, expert systems, communications, computer networks, parallel processing, grid computing, security, simulation, and robotics. The material in this book covers both theoretical and practical matters of MAS. The publication of this book will doubtlessly benefit the entire community of MAS research. Scientists who work in related areas can use this book as a reference of frontier research themes. University faculty can use this book as supplemental material that reflects trends in advanced research. Managers in industry can use these topics, especially the materials on applications, as a source to find solutions to engineering issues in complex systems.

Takayuki Ito & Chunsheng Yang
February 2007

Takayuki Ito *received a BE, ME, and doctor of engineering from the Nagoya Institute of Technology (1995, 1997, and 2000, respectively). From 1999-2001, he was a research fellow of the Japan Society for the Promotion of Science (JSPS). From 2000-2001, he was a visiting researcher at the University of Southern California Information Sciences Institute. From April 2001 to March 2003, he was an associate professor of Japan Advanced Institute of Science and Technology (JAIST). He joined Nagoya Institute of Technology as an associate professor of Graduate School of Engineering in April 2003. He is a founder of Wisdom Web Co., Ltd., on July 13, 2004. From 2005 to 2006, he is a visiting researcher at the Faculty of Arts and Sciences, division of engineering and applied science, Harvard University, and a visiting researcher at Sloan School of Management, Massachusetts Institute of Technology. He received the Best Paper Award of AAMAS 2006, the 2005 Best Paper Award from Japan Society for* Software Science and Technology, *the Best Paper Award in the 66th Annual Conference of Information Processing Society of Japan, and the Super Creator Award of 2004 IPA Exploratory Software Creation Projects. His main research interests include multi-agent systems, computational mechanism design, group decision support systems, and agent-mediated electronic commerce.*

Chunsheng Yang's *interests include data mining, case-based reasoning, network privacy and security, intelligent agent system, and multi-agent systems. After receiving his doctorate in September 1995 from National Hiroshima University in Japan, he worked at Fujitsu, Inc., in Japan, as a senior engineer. Since January 1998, he has been with the National Research Council Canada as a research* *officer. Dr. Yang has authored more than 30 papers and book chapters published in the referred journals and conference proceedings. He was the program co-chair for the 17th International Conference on Industry and Engineering Applications of Artificial Intelligence and Expert Systems.*

* * *

A person living at the beginning of the 21st century is surrounded by countless hardware and software artifacts. The mainframe computers of the classical era were designed to be shared by multiple users. The personal computers and the corresponding interactive programs assumed a ratio of approximately one user per computer. This was reflected in the interactive applications, which required the constant dialog between the user and the program. Since the turn of the millennium, the ratio had clearly turned to the favor of computers or computer-like devices (such as PDAs, programmable cell phones, or programmable embedded devices).

We cannot afford any more to pay individual attention to every hardware or software component. The only way out from this dilemma is to increase the autonomy of the individual software and hardware components, that is, to use autonomous agent technologies.

While originally proposed as a more flexible answer to the large, monolithic expert systems of the 1980's, autonomous agents have emerged as a discipline of their own, spawning a bewildering array of applications. From the agent-controlled spaceships to the agents participating in the stock market or in online auctions, agents are a regular part of our life. The implementation techniques vary from the highly formal, such as modal logic or partially observable Markov decision processes, to reactive, behavioral models, such as Brooks' subsumption architecture. Biologically inspired models, such as neural networks, swarm architectures, or models of flocking were applied with success in various agent applications.

In short, autonomous agents is a field of high vitality, a melting pot of the most advanced ideas from artificial intelligence, economics, game theory, robotics, simulation, linguistics, biology, and many other fields.

The current book provides the reader with a representative snapshot of the various currents of the field. It is a welcome and timely addition to the library of any developer or scientist who wants to get an understanding of the current frontiers of agent research. It can also serve as the basis for an advanced topics class in autonomous agents. While other books have concentrated on providing an undergraduate level introduction, this book maps the current frontiers of the agent research.

The chapters, written by experts from all over the world, show the diversity of applications and challenges faced by agent researchers. We cannot be but impressed by the range of applications discussed, from mobile robots to grid computing, from management of health care records to supply chain management. The major challenges of the agent field, such as the problems of collaboration, coalition formation, and security, are addressed in various chapters of the book. Finally, the reader will be able to grasp the underlying unity in diversity of the field, how the various techniques are contributing to hardware and software, which can pursue their goals more autonomously, thus become more performant and ultimately more useful to their human users.

Ladislau Bölöni
February 2007

Ladislau Bölöni *is an assistant professor at the School of Electrical Engineering and Computer Science of University of Central Florida. He received a PhD from the Department of Computer Sciences, Purdue University (May 2000). He received a Master of Science from the Department of Computer Sciences, Purdue University (1999) and a diploma engineer degree in computer engineering (Hon.) from the Technical University of Cluj-Napoca, Romania (1993). He received a fellowship from the Computer and Automation Research Institute of the Hungarian Academy of Sciences for the 1994-95 academic year. He is a senior member of IEEE, member of the Association for Computing Machinery (ACM), American Association for Artificial Intelligence (AAAI), and the Upsilon Pi Epsilon honorary society. His research interests include autonomous agents, Grid computing, and wireless networking.*

Preface

Agent-oriented design has become one of the most active areas in the field of software engineering. The agent concept provides a modeling paradigm for coping with the complexity of software systems. The design of multi-agent systems, however, remains a hard issue because conventional methods find it hard to capture the complex behavior patterns of agents in a multi-agent system. A multi-agent system model should be general enough to address common architectural issues and not be specific to design issues of a particular system. The architectural design of multi-agent systems is one of the most significant areas in the current literature. Research issues include system modeling and specification, specification languages, system derivation and reasoning, and domain-specific issues. Attempts have been made in software architecture, cognitive learning, very high-level languages, and distributed systems literature. Although great advances have been made in the study of architectural design of agent systems, its complexity and multi-disciplinary nature makes it a hard subject in the current technology suite. A compilation of current research results is needed to help bring this premature subject onto the next stage.

This book is an attempt to provide a compilation of current research results in multi-agent systems area that reflects the research trends and serves as a reference for further research. The book covers a wide spectrum of topics in multi-agent systems design, including fundamentals of multi-agent system theories, system models, formal methods and reasoning, knowledge management, and design issues pertaining to specific applications. The book will serve as both an overview on the current state of research on multi-agent systems and an in-depth exposure of theories and state-of-the-art design technologies. By publishing a collection of frontier research results in multi-agent systems, we aim to provide a comprehensive reference for scientists who work in artificial intelligence, programming methodology, software engineering, parallel/distributed computing, computer networking, security, and various research domains of multi-agent system applications.

The contributing authors of the chapters of this book have developed both theoretical and practical issues in multi-agent systems research. Their valuable scholarly work ensures both the breadth and the depth of the presentation of the current literature. The book's comprehensive coverage will help readers gain a bird's-eye view of the area and provide guidance for further research. The presentation of the frontier research results will also provide information on the limitation and current challenges when we use agent technology to reach a solution to problems under consideration, as well as on the benefits the agent systems can bring to the community.

The book is organized into four sections. Section I includes chapters that discuss fundamental theories for multi-agent systems; Section II focuses on agent-oriented design technologies of computer systems; Section III presents knowledge and artificial intelligence issues pertaining to agents; and Section IV covers applications of agent technology in various areas. We can find theoretical studies of agent-oriented modeling in Section I. In Chapter I, Dr. Pratik Biswas provides an in-depth analysis of agent concept and compares it to conventional programming models such as object-oriented design. In Chapter II, Dr. Wanli Ma, Dr. Dat Tran, Dr. Dharmendra Sharma, Dr. Hong Lin, and Ms. Mary Anderson develop a framework for specifying autonomous agents using the chemical reaction metaphor. Temporal logic is used to reason the properties of the specified system. In Chapter III, Dr. Hiromitsu Hattori, Dr. Tadachika Ozono, and Dr. Toramatsu Shintani use combinatorial auction metaphor to develop a scheme for coordinating agents in solving complex problems. In Chapter IV, Dr. Andre de Korvin, Dr. Plamen Simeonov, and Dr. Hong Lin present a gentle introduction to fuzzy logic and discuss its applications to multi-agent systems.

Section II contains valuable work in developing methodologies for agent-oriented system design. In Chapter V, Dr. Paulo Marques and Dr. Luís Silva propose component-based mobile agent systems to overcome the limitations of traditional platform-based approach for developing mobile agents and demonstrate the effectiveness of their method by two case studies. In Chapter VI, Mr. Daniel Lübke and Dr. Jorge Marx Gómez present an effort to develop a common platform and framework for developing mobile agents that operate on a peer-to-peer network and contain the logic of the network services. In Chapter VII, Dr. Luo Junzhou, Dr. Liu Bo, and Dr. Li Wei develop some algorithms to support dynamic multi-agent scheduling decisions in a network management scenario. The algorithms are developed using functional decomposition strategy, and an experiment has been done and shown promising results. In Chapter VIII, Dr. H. Farooq Ahmad, Dr. Hiroki Suguri, Dr. Arshad Ali, Ms. Amna Basharat, and Ms. Amina Tariq introduce a scalable, fault tolerant agent grooming environment (SAGE) for creating distributed, intelligent and autonomous entities that are encapsulated as agents. SAGE has a decentralized fault tolerant architecture that provides tools for runtime agent management, directory facilitation, monitoring and editing messages exchange between agents, and a built-in mechanism to program the agent behavior and their capabilities. SAGE can be used to develop applications in a number of areas, such as e-health, e-government, and e-science. In Chapter IX, Dr. Lizhe Wang presents methodologies and technologies of agent-based grid computing from various aspects and demonstrates that agent-based computing is a promising solution to bring a scalable, robust, thus tractable, grid. In Chapter X, Dr. Dharmendra Sharma, Dr. Wanli Ma, Dr. Dat Tran, Mr. Shuangzhe Liu, and Ms. Mary Anderson study multi-agent-based information technology (IT) security approach (MAITS) as a holistic solution to the increasing needs of securing computer systems. In their approach, each specialist task for security requirements is modeled as a specialist agent, which has the ability to learn, reason, and make decisions, and an agent interface that enables inter-agent communications.

Section III presents some significant work in the traditional area of agent technology—artificial intelligence. In Chapter XI, Dr. Michael Bowman describes a methodology for modeling expert problem-solving knowledge that supports ontology import and development, teaching-based agent development, and agent-based problem solving. The methodology is applicable to a wide variety of domains and has been successfully used in the military domain. In Chapter XII, Dr. Yang Gao, Mr. Hao Wang, and Dr. Ruili Wang present a general framework of multi-agent reinforcement learning (MARL), which combines three perspectives in order to assist readers to understand the intricate relationships between different perspectives, and a negotiation-based MARL algorithm that enables interaction among cooperative agents and gaming agents. In Chapter XIII, Dr. Maria Salamó, Dr. Barry Smyth, Mr. Kevin McCarthy, Mr. James Reilly, and Dr. Lorraine McGinty present their recent research on critiquing-based recommendation and a comparison between standard and recent proposals of recommendation based on critiquing. Their work leads to conversational recommender agents, which facilitate user navigation through a product space. In Chapter XIV, Ms. Fabiana Lorenzi, Ms. Daniela Scherer dos Santos, Ms. Denise de Oliveira, and Dr. Ana L. Bazzan present an approach inspired by swarm intelligence applied to a case-based recommender system in the tourism domain and show experiment results that, using the proposed metaphor, the system always return some recommendation to the user, avoiding the user's disappointment.

In Section IV, we can find exciting use of multi-agent systems in various application areas. In Chapter XV, Dr. Hyung Rim Choi, Dr. Hyun Soo Kim, Dr. Yong Sung Park, and Dr. Byung Joo Park develop a multi-agent system that enables the effective formation and management of an optimal supply chain. By means of active communications among internal agents, the multi-agent system for optimal supply chain management makes it possible to quickly respond to the production environment changes such as the machine failure or outage of outsourcing companies and the delivery delay of suppliers. In Chapter XVI, Mr. Ben Tse and Dr. Raman Paranjape present an architecture for an agent-based electronic health record system (ABEHRS) to provide health information access and retrieval among different medical services facilities. The agent-system's behaviors are analyzed using the simulation approach and the mathematical modeling approach. The key concept promoted by ABEHRS is to allow patient health records to autonomously move through the computer network uniting scattered and distributed data into one consistent and complete data set or patient health record. In Chapter XVII, Mr. Gordon Fraser, Mr. Gerald Steinbauer, Mr. Jörg Weber, and Dr. Franz Wotawa present a control framework that is able to control an autonomous robot in complex real-world tasks. The key features of the framework are a hybrid control paradigm that incorporates reactive, planning, and reasoning capabilities, a flexible software architecture, and the capability for detecting internal failures in the robot and self-healing. The framework was successfully deployed in the domain of robotic soccer and service robots. In Chapter XVIII, Dr. Manolya Kavakli, Dr. Nicolas Szilas, Mr. John Porte, and Mr. Iwan Kartiko discuss the use of multi-agent systems to develop virtual reality training systems and describe the system architecture of a multi-agent system for risk management (RiskMan) to help train police officers to handle high-risk situations.

All chapters included in this book are selected by the following review process: Authors who were interested in contributing a chapter submitted a proposal for review. Those authors whose proposals were selected were invited to prepare the full chapters to be reviewed on a double-blind review basis. Each chapter manuscript was reviewed by three reviewers. Authors of accepted chapter manuscripts were then asked to revise the manuscript to address the issues raised by reviewers. The chapters on which major revisions were deemed necessary went through another review to determine whether the suggested revisions had been performed accordingly. Through this review process, 18 out of 28 submitted manuscripts were selected to be included in this book.

Acknowledgment

The editor is grateful to the members of the international review board of this book for their valuable input to the quality of the submitted manuscripts and their constructive comments that guided the revisions of the manuscripts. Special thanks are given to Ms. Kristin Roth and Mr. Ross Miller of IGI Global for their assistance in the entire book editing process. Their meaningful advice and timely information ensured the smoothness of the procedure.

Hong Lin, Editor

International Review Board
(*in alphabetical order*)

Selma Azaiez, Université de Savoie, France
Ouahiba Azouaoui, Centre de Développement des Technologies Avancées, Algeria
Tomaz de Carvalho Barros, Universidade Federal de Pernambuco, Brazil
Jussara de França Barros, Universidad de Salamanca, Spain
Yang Cao, Athabasca University, Canada
Sergio Davalos, University of Washington – Tacoma, USA
Akbar Esfahanipour, McMaster University, Canada
Larbi Esmahi, Athabasca University, Canada
Tarek M. Hamdani, Université de Sfax, Tunisia
Shohreh Hashemi, University of Houston-Downtown, USA
Yen-Hung Hu, Hampton University, USA
Marc-Philippe Huget, University of Savoie, France
Robert Kleyle, Indiana University – Purdue University Indianapolis, USA
Long-Zhuang Li, Texas A&M University at Corpus Christi, USA
Fuhua Lin, Athabasca University, Canada
Kursheed Omer, University of Houston-Downtown, USA
Agnieszka Pieczynska, Wroclaw University of Technology, Poland
Yi Qian, University of Puerto Rico at Mayagüez, USA
Ongard Sirisaengtaksin, University of Houston-Downtown, USA
Utako Tanigawa, Itec International, *LLC, USA*
Hongxue Wang, Athabasca University, Canada
Zhigang Xiao, Alabama A&M University, USA
Menchun Xie, Wakayama National College of Technology, Japan
Chunsheng Yang, National Research Council Canada, Canada

Section I
Fundamentals of Multi-Agent System Modeling

Chapter I
Toward Agent–Oriented Conceptualization and Implementation

Pratik K. Biswas
Avaya Inc., USA

ABSTRACT

The desire to flexibly customize software, manage it efficiently, and empower it with intelligence has driven research and development-related efforts toward intelligent agents. The benefits in terms of rapid delivery, reduced costs, and enhanced productivity can be realized in the areas of systems and software engineering with the proliferation of this technology. Intelligent agents represent an alternate approach to distributed software engineering. Agent-oriented conceptualization provides a new paradigm for the design and development of these agent-based systems. This chapter extends and formalizes this agent-oriented modeling approach to the conceptualization process. It defines agent models and proposes a high-level methodology for agent-oriented analysis and design. It also looks at the heart of agent-oriented programming and outlines its advantages over traditional approaches to distributed computing and interoperability. The chapter includes analogies with the object-oriented methodologies and other existing agent-oriented methodologies wherever applicable. It reviews the Foundation of Intelligent Physical Agents-compliant infrastructure for building agent-based systems and suggests a multi-agent systems framework that merges this infrastructure with the emerging J2EE technologies. The chapter concludes with a case study and an insight to future challenges.

INTRODUCTION

Agent-based computing represents a novel *software engineering paradigm* that has emerged from merging two technologies (Odell & Burkhart, 1998), namely artificial intelligence (AI) and object-oriented distributed computing. Agent-based systems aim to strike a balance between artificial intelligence and computational utility.

Agents are *intelligent, autonomous, software components* capable of interacting with others within an application, attaining a common goal and thereby contributing to the resolution of some given problem. They are important because they inter-operate within modern applications like electronic commerce and information retrieval. *Multi-agent systems* (Biswas, 2005; Brazier, Keplicz, Jennings, & Treur, 1995; Brazier, Dunin-Keplicz, Jennings, & Treur, 1997; Jennings, 2001; Lind, 2000) are composed of a set of agents and are useful for the modeling and development of distributed information systems with synchronous or asynchronous component interactions. *Multi-agent systems (MAS)* differ from non-agent-based systems because agents are intended to be autonomous units of intelligent functionality who can interact with others through high-level protocols and languages.

A system can be successfully built and deployed if it has been properly conceptualized. Conceptualization requires an appropriate set of abstractions and a methodology for system specification, analysis, and design. However, many of our traditional ways of thinking about and designing software do not fit the multi-agent paradigm. In this chapter, we advocate an agent-oriented paradigm for conceptualizing the analysis and design of agent-based systems. The remainder of the chapter is organized as follows. In the second section, we provide motivations for this chapter. In the third section, we take a more detailed look at *intelligent agents*, their characteristics, capabilities and interactions. In the third section, we introduce the concept of *agent-oriented thinking*.

In the fourth section, we discuss *agent-oriented modeling*, define a new agent model, describe the steps involved in our approaches to *agent-oriented analysis* and *design*, and compare them with *object-oriented* methodologies. In the fifth section, we discuss *agent communication and mobility*, at the heart of *agent-oriented programming*, outline their advantages over traditional approaches to distributed computing, compare *agent-oriented programming* with *object-oriented programming*, and show why Java is the natural choice for its implementation. In the sixth section, we present a *Foundation of Intelligent Physical Agents (FIPA)-compliant platform* for building *agent-based systems* and then suggest a *multi-agent systems framework* using the *J2EE technologies* that can implement this platform. In the seventh section, we present a case study to illustrate the applicability of our methodology. In the next section, we compare our methodology with other existing *agent-oriented* methodologies. Finally, in the last section, we summarize our results and provide an insight to the future challenges. This chapter is an extension of the work presented in Biswas (2007).

MOTIVATIONS

Over the years, a wide range of software engineering paradigms have been devised (e.g., procedural programming, structured programming, declarative programming, object-oriented programming, design patterns, application frameworks, and component-ware) to deal with the increasing complexity of software applications. Although each successive development claims to make the engineering process easier, researchers continually strive for more efficient and powerful software engineering techniques, especially as solutions for ever more demanding applications are required.

Most real-world applications of today are significantly more complex than before as they contain many dynamically interacting components, each with its own thread of control. Most software engineering paradigms are unable to provide structures and techniques that make it easier to handle this complexity. Consequently a lot of research has now been directed toward treating *computation as a process of interactions*. Tools and technologies have been developed to understand, model, and implement systems in which interactions are the norm.

Furthermore, software development has now become a knowledge-intensive activity. Current software representations—from programming languages to specifications to requirements models—are *non-intentional*. They are meant to record the results of software work but not the process or the reasoning behind them. Thus there is a reason to develop a framework of software engineering that accounts for the intentional dimensions, namely intents and motivations, goals and reasons, alternatives, beliefs, and assumptions, in its methodologies.

Against this background, we'll argue that analyzing, designing, and implementing software as a *collection of interacting intelligent agents* represents a promising approach (Wooldridge & Jennings, 2000) to software engineering. An agent is an encapsulation of goals, know-how and resources. Agent-oriented techniques provide a natural way for modeling complex systems, by decomposing its problem space into autonomous agents and their interactions. Moreover, they enhance the reliability and reduce the cost and time-to-market of software applications by allowing their development through the assembly of a set of reusable software agents. In this chapter, we make a strong case for agent-oriented techniques for software engineering and advance our arguments by comparing their effectiveness against object-oriented methodologies.

BACKGROUND

In this section, we explain and clarify certain terminologies that are closely associated with *agent-oriented software engineering* (AOSE) and which we have used in describing our methodology.

Intelligent Agents

In this subsection, we discuss in detail about what people mean by the term *intelligent agent* when they use it often in the world of AI. An agent is an *assistant* that works on behalf of others (agents or humans). In its simplest form, an agent represents an *actor* and is thereby an embodiment of its *actions*. In AI, an *agent* refers to a software component that lives inside computer environments, operates continuously and autonomously, and cooperates with similar entities. An agent is associated with its mental state that can be composed of components like belief, capabilities, choices, and commitments. Wooldridge and Jennings (1995) have introduced *weak and strong notions of agencies*. They have used the *stronger notion of an agency* to imply "a computer system that, in addition to having some basic properties, can be either conceptualized or implemented using concepts that are more usually applied to humans."

The interactive nature of *multi-agent systems* calls for consensus on agent interfaces in order to support interoperability among agents coming from various sources. Foundation of Intelligent Physical Agents (FIPA) has developed standards (FIPA, 1998a; FIPA, 1998b; FIPA, 1998c; FIPA, 1998d; FIPA, 2003) for building interoperable agent-based systems.

Agent Characteristics

A characteristic is an intrinsic or physical property of an agent. The following are some common agent characteristics (Morreale, 1998; Wooldridge & Jennings, 1995):

- **Autonomy:** An agent can act on another's behalf without much guidance.
- **Communication:** An agent can communicate with other agents on a common topic of discourse by exchanging a sequence of messages in a speech-act-based language that others understand. The domain of discourse is described by its *ontology*.
- **Mobility:** An agent can migrate from one system to another in a pre-determined fashion or at its own discretion. Accordingly, agents can be *static* or *mobile*.
- **Learning:** An agent can have the ability to learn new information about the environment in which it is deployed and dynamically improve upon its own behavior.
- **Cooperation:** An agent can collaborate and cooperate with other agents or its user during its execution to minimize redundancy and to solve a common problem.

Of the five, the first two are considered by many to be the most basic agent characteristics, while the *second and third* together contribute toward another paradigm for distributed computing (also known as *agent-oriented programming*). We have used some of these characteristics to define our models.

Intelligence in Intelligent Agents

The intelligence in intelligent agents consists of its *mental state* (Shoham, 1993) and the underlying knowledge coupled with the problem solver, which can be artificially programmed through *reasoning, learning, planning, searching, other methods, or a combination of some of these techniques*. The *mental state* is sometimes captured through the BDI (*belief, desire, and intention*) model (Rao & Georgeff, 1995) or other similar mental components like *capabilities, choices, commitments,*

goals, and so forth (Shoham, 1993). The underlying knowledge may or may not be part of the agent structure but is always accessible to it.

Agent Capabilities

Intelligent agents have frequently been used in AI applications to *communicate, negotiate, move, reason, search, match, learn, predict, adapt, repair, sense, deliver, clone, and so forth*. These *atypical activities* often end up defining agent capabilities. It would be useful to remember some of these agent capabilities when we think about agents and designing agent-based applications.

Interaction Protocols

Agent *interactions* often fall under *typical patterns of behavior*, technically known as interaction protocols (IP) (FIPA 1998a). An agent can select a specific protocol to initiate an interaction. Typical patterns of behavior include *request-inform (FIPA-request), request-when-inform (FIPA-request-when), subscription, advertisement, broadcasting, brokering, and so forth. Brokering* may further include activities like *bidding, iterative bidding, recommending, recruiting, and so forth*. Again, these can be used as basic tools in conceptualizing agent interactions to build agent-based applications.

AGENT-ORIENTED THINKING

Thinking about thinking is often a complicated process. But sometimes it can be useful if we can think in advance about how we are going to solve certain problems in the future. This thinking process can be either *structured* or *unstructured* but seldom both simultaneously (Small, 1996).

With the *structured* approach, one would start with an overall plan for the proposed solution and work downward to sort out all the structural elements at an ever-increasing level of detail.

With *unstructured* thinking, one need not start with any fixed plan but might start anywhere and build up a plan for the solution from small, self-contained sub-plans that get fitted together as one thinks forward. *Agent-oriented thinking* often falls under the second category and works well in uncertain domains.

The idea behind *agent-oriented thinking* is to explore the applicability of the *agent paradigm* in conceptualizing a problem domain. In a very broad sense, it is about visualizing *actors* interacting with others in their environments for solving the given problem. An actor will act based on its perceptions. It may also realize that it has insufficient knowledge and seek that supplementary information elsewhere to conduct an activity. Actors, activities and their coordination will lead to the conception of scenarios, which will get stitched together as the thinking process gradually evolves toward the goal.

The key concepts in this thinking process are the actor, activity, and scenario. Accordingly, we define the following.

Definition 1: An actor is an entity (active) that performs some actions (fundamental units of behavior) based on its state (perceptions) and can interact with other entities (active or inactive) in the problem domain under consideration. An actor can play one or more roles. Note that our definition is different from the one used in Use Cases for UML (Fowler & Scott, 2001), which defines the actor as "a (one) role that the user plays with respect to the system."

Definition 2: An activity is a task that an actor needs to perform. An activity is composed of one or more actions. It provides a context for its constituent actions. An activity can be followed by another activity.

Definition 3: A scenario is a specification of a sequence of activities involving interacting actors.

Essentially there can be two approaches to think about agents, namely *actors to activities* and *activities to actors.*

Actors to Activities

In this strategy, we begin by thinking of an actor and thinking of that actor in a scenario. As we think of how this actor might act in this scenario, we begin to thrash out its roles and responsibilities, the underlying knowledge, ending up giving it a form, adding substance to the initial skeleton and developing a representation. New actors will be introduced to the scenario, which will interact with the first actor to trigger and initiate new activities. Interactions among actors may update their (actors') states (perceptions). Actors may need to adapt their activities. As the thinking process evolves, new scenarios, actors, activities, roles, and responsibilities will be introduced and the resulting interactions will be visualized, helping us to conceptualize a complete system. Figure 1 shows the process.

Activities to Actors

In this strategy, we begin with an activity, think of its cause, what it would take to implement this activity, its consequences, other activities it might trigger, changes in states (perceptions) that this might cause, adaptability to the changes, and so forth, eventually ending up giving it an expression. An actor is an embodiment of activities (Turchin, 1993). We conceptualize the actor, once we have thought enough about the activity. Likewise, the reaction to the activity will lead us to its (another) actor and so forth. This will help us develop a scenario. As the thinking progresses, new scenarios will get added, introducing new interactions with the existing scenarios, leading to new actors, activities, roles, and responsibilities, culminating in the conceptualization of a new system. For example, we can think of activities like searching and delivering, consider

Figure 1. Actors to activities

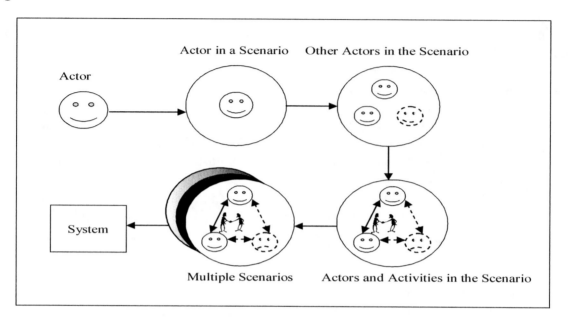

a search agent and a messenger agent, then think of a scenario where the search agent searches for some information on the net and communicates the information to the messenger agent, who acknowledges that message and then delivers that information to a subscribing customer. Figure 2 displays the process.

Agent-oriented thinking is vital to the analysis and design processes and can be considered as *part of* or *a precursor to agent-oriented modeling.*

AGENT-ORIENTED MODELING

In recent years, conceptual modeling has become very popular with AI practitioners for the design and implementation of knowledge-intensive software applications. A few (Bauer, Muller, & Odell, 2001; Biswas, 2005, 2007; Brazier et al., 1995; Brazier et al., 1997; Cossentino & Potts, 2002; DeLoach, Wood, & Sparkman, 2001; Elammari & Lalonde, 1999; Giunchiglia, Mylo-

poulos, & Perini, 2002; Jennings, 2001; Odell, Paranuk, & Bauer, 2000; Padgham & Winikoff, 2002; Wooldridge & Jennings, 1995; Wooldridge, 1997; Wooldridge, Jennings, & Kinny, 1999; Wooldridge & Jennings, 2000; Wooldridge, Jennings, & Kinny, 2000; Zambonelli & Jennings, 2003) have also been proposed for modeling agent behavior in distributed systems.

A *conceptual model* is an abstraction device that allows us to model natural data structures, independent of their physical organization. A conceptual model defines the rules according to which data needs to be structured. Structures often don't tell the whole story about semantics of the data and its usage. Activities need to be specified along with the structures.

Agent Model

We define *agent-oriented modeling* as a kind of conceptual modeling where we conceptualize most entities as agents, representing roles and

Figure 2. Activities to actors

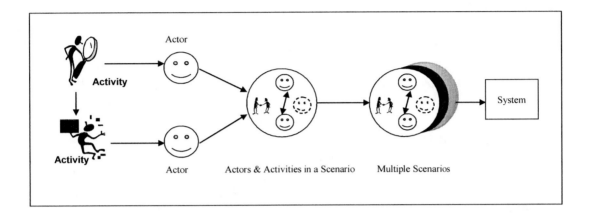

responsibilities. An agent's state is captured in its mental components. Its behavior is reflected in its ability to communicate on a common topic of discourse in a speech-act-based language, conduct interactions in a predetermined fashion, migrate from one system to another, learn from the available information, and adapt to the changes in its environment.

Definition 4: An agent model (AM) is a 2-tuple, defined as:

⟨A, I⟩, where

A is the set of all agent classes in the application domain and I is the set of all interactions among the agent classes in the domain.

The basic concepts in agent modeling are those of an *agent class* and *interaction (class)*.

An *agent class* represents the generic structure of an agent in the enterprise's realm of interest. An *agent class* is a collection of all agents that share the same attributes of the agent's mental state. An *agent* is instantiated by instantiating its mental state.

Definition 5: An agent class is a 10-tuple, defined as:

⟨IA$_I$, MC, KB, L, O, IP, CM, MM, IM, ACM⟩, where

IA$_I$ is the set of information attributes (name, location, destination, etc.), MC is the set of mental components used for defining the mental state of the agent, KB is union of the set of domain classes for its attributes (informational/mental) and the underlying knowledge-base that may or may not co-reside with itself but is always accessible to it for its decision making, L is the set (often singleton) of communication languages that it can communicate in, O is the set of ontologies (application domains) that it can converse about, IP is the set of all interaction protocols defining the types of interactions that it can participate in, CM is the set of methods (functions) for communication, MM is the set of methods for migration, IM is the set of intelligent methods for knowledge acquisition and reasoning, and ACM is the set all accessory methods required to accomplish specific roles and responsibilities. The set (CM∪MM∪IM∪ACM) defines the agent class's capabilities.

An agent's *mental state* at any given time can be seen as a collection of facts (belief), capabilities, and commitments (that is, mental components). Whenever an agent receives a message or executes a commitment, it may move to a new mental state. An agent's capabilities determine the *activities* that it can perform and is comprised of methods from the four types of method sets listed above.

A generic agent template, based on the above definition, may be comprised of its name, location, knowledge (belief), commitments, languages (for communication), ontology (dictionary on the domain of discourse), interaction protocols (identified patterns of behavior), and methods to communicate, migrate, and learn (capabilities).

An agent is associated with one or more roles. A *role* is defined as the functional or social part that an agent plays in a multi-agent environment in the context of agent systems. A *role* is a collection of responsibilities. A *responsibility* is a task that the agent needs to carry out to fulfill part of or its entire role.

Coordinated *interaction* among two or more agents is the core concept of multi-agent technology. Agents interact with each other in achieving a common goal. Interactions may involve a sequence of messages exchanged between two (or more) agents on some ongoing topic of discourse. They may or may not *update* agents' *mental states*. FIPA (FIPA, 2003) defines *interaction* as a specification of how stimuli are sent between agents to perform a specific task. Interaction can consist of three layers, that is, intent, protocol, and transport (Lind, 2000). Accordingly, we define *interaction* in the following way.

Definition 6: An interaction class is a 3-tuple, defined as:

⟨*IA₂, CA, TA⟩, where*

IA_2 *is the set of intent attributes (taxonomy, actors, etc.). Taxonomy can be co-ordination, cooperation, collaboration, competition, and so*

forth. (Parunak, Brueckner, Fleischer, & Odell, 2002). CA is the set of content attributes, that is, exchange details, speech acts, interaction protocol, knowledge, language, ontology, and so forth used in the associated interaction. TA is the set of transport attributes, that is, paradigm (client-server, peer-peer, etc.), mode (synchronous, asynchronous), architecture (store-forward, blackboard, etc.), and so forth. Note that every interaction need not have all the attributes. For a message-specific interaction, this definition can map easily to FIPA message structure for agent communication (FIPA, 1998a).

Agent Abstractions

Abstraction is the ability to create higher-level agent classes to hide unnecessary details during system design. In an agent model, we'll be primarily dealing with the three types of abstractions, namely, *generalization, aggregation,* and *cooperation.*

Generalization is an *organizational abstraction* mechanism that creates an agent class from its constituent classes that satisfy a *subclass-of* or *subtype-of* relationship to the generalized class. The inverse of generalization is known as specialization. The specialized agent class inherits the mental state of the generalized agent class.

Aggregation is also an *organizational abstraction* mechanism by which an agent class is constructed from its constituent agent classes that satisfy a *part-of* relationship to the aggregated form. Among other things, aggregation can also model a collection of roles.

Cooperation is, however, a *behavioral abstraction* mechanism that creates an organization (Jennings, 2001) or a society of cooperative agents or an agency from the constituent agent classes that satisfy a *collaborate-with* or *cooperate-with* or *coordinate-with* or *negotiate-with* relationship with other agents within the organization toward achieving a common goal.

Definition 7: An extended agent model (XAM) is a 10-tuple defined as:

⟨A, GC, AC, CS, B, G, C, IP, O, L⟩, where

A is the set of all agent classes in the application domain, GC is the set of all generalized classes, AC is the set of all aggregated classes, CS is the set of all cooperative societies (organizations), B is the set of all initial beliefs (knowledge-base), G is the set of goals (commitments) for all agents in the application domain, C is the set of all agent capabilities associated with the agent classes in the application, IP is the set of all possible interaction protocols indicating the types of interactions witnessed in the application, O is the set of all ontologies describing the various domains of discourses discussed in the agent interactions, and L is the set (often singleton) of all agent communication languages used in the system.

The model provides a way in describing *multi-agent systems* and sets the expectations for the analysis and design processes. Agent-oriented modeling begins with the analysis of the problem domain and ends with the design of the system for the proposed application. Next, we propose a *methodology for agent-oriented analysis and design* based on the above model.

Agent-Oriented Analysis

We define *agent-oriented analysis* (AOA) as the process that includes all activities for discovering, documenting, and maintaining a set of specifications for actors (roles), activities (responsibilities), and interactions for the design of an agent-based system. It may then primarily consist of the following four steps:

1. Study the scenario description and identify all the *possible actors* and *main activities*. For a start, look for off-the-shelf actors and activities (*agent capabilities*).

2. For each *actor*, determine its *roles*. It may be worth noting here that an actor may play multiple roles in the same or different contexts. For example, an airline agent may play the roles of an airline travel agent and an airline ticket coordinator. For each actor and each role, enlist all the possible *responsibilities*, based on the role definition and activities associated with the actor. Actors, roles, and responsibilities will help design the agent classes.

3. For each identified *activity*, analyze the *context* (*causes* and *consequences*) to determine all *interactions* (if any). It may be worthwhile to note here that agent interactions may often fall into typical patterns of behavior that have been previously identified and used in other applications. So the process may begin by looking for these patterns. For each *distinct interaction*, determine the *actors*, *exchange details*, the *typical pattern of behavior*, the *speech-acts* used for the communication, and the *associated knowledge*. This will help in designing the mental states of the agents and the ontology later.

4. Refine the analysis. For each actor and interaction, remove duplication and redundant information. In some cases, alter the interactions to make the communication/conversation more formal, meaningful, and generic.

Figure 3 illustrates our proposed approach for agent-oriented analysis.

We have compared our approach to agent-oriented analysis with object-oriented analysis (OOA) on the following criteria:

- **Basic units:** Fundamental entities under consideration
- **Expectations:** A set of anticipated specifications
- **Objective:** Goal toward which the process is directed

Figure 3. Proposed agent-oriented analysis concepts

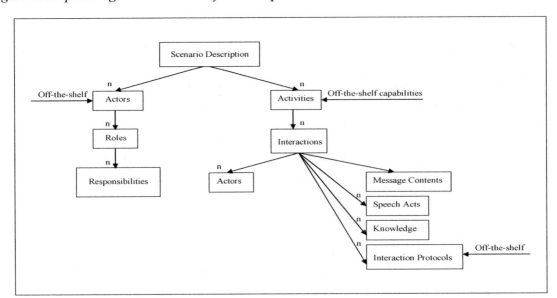

Table 1. Proposed AOA vs. OOA

Criteria	Proposed AOA	OOA
Basic units	Actors & activities	Objects & functions
Expectations	Goals, roles & responsibilities	Requirements
Objective	Agent model	Object model (sometimes - dynamic & functional models)
Dynamics	Agent interactions	User and system interactions
Information	Speech-act based messages	Unconstrained
Outputs	Actors, interactions, speech acts, interaction protocols, knowledge	Objects, attributes, functions, relationships, and states

- **Dynamics:** The activities and changes that characterize the process
- **Information exchanges:** Message types exchanged among fundamental entities
- **Outputs:** The information generated by the process

Table 1 illustrates the differences between the two approaches.

Diagrammatic Notation

We will use the following notations in the analysis phase (Figure 8).

- Circular face (☺) represents an *actor*
- Double arrow (⇄) represents an *interaction protocol*. Colorings are used to differentiate between interaction types

Agent-Oriented Design

We define *agent-oriented design* (AOD) as the process where the actors, activities, and interactions (outputs from agent-oriented analysis) are analyzed in order to produce an agent model that includes descriptions of the organization of the system (software architecture, agent classes and interfaces) and the internal structures of the agent classes and interactions, for the development/implementation of an agent-based system that can meet the application specifications. It may then primarily consist of the following six steps:

1. Design the various *agent classes* with their *mental states* from the analysis of the problem domain in the following ways:
    i. For each actor, from the analysis phase, design an agent class by starting with the *generic agent template* and customizing it, if necessary.
    ii. For each class, aggregate the associated *beliefs* (knowledge) and protocols (IP) from the specifics of all its interactions.
    iii. For each class aggregate the *commitments* from its responsibilities and the specifics of all its interactions.
    iv. For each class, add *accessory methods* (*capabilities*) to account for all its responsibilities.
    v. For each class, establish the *language* and *ontology* to be used for all its interactions.
2. Define the *agent interactions/interaction classes* (interfaces and message structures, if any). Select off-the-shelf interaction protocols, wherever applicable. Decide on which of these interactions would be *static* and which would be *mobile. An interaction would be considered mobile, if one of the participants needs to migrate to the location of the others to communicate locally so as to complete the interaction.*
3. Construct an *ontology* (ontologies) of the problem domain by aggregating domain-specific terms, used in all interactions and scenario descriptions.
4. Identify the organizational abstractions by *generalizing* and *aggregating agent classes* as necessary to form higher-level agent classes.

Figure 4. Proposed agent-oriented design concepts

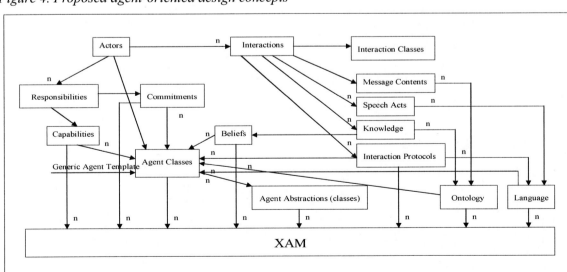

5. Identify the behavioral abstractions by determining the *cooperative societies* or organizations of collaborative agents.
6. Formulate the *XAM* for the application problem domain.

Figure 4 illustrates the proposed agent-oriented design approach.

We have compared our approach to agent-oriented design with object-oriented design (OOD) on the following criteria:

- **Basic unit:** Fundamental entity under consideration
- **Information:** Knowledge exchanged among fundamental entities
- **Generic class template:** Abstracted class structure applicable to all entities
- **Method type:** The procedures and techniques that are the characteristics of each basic unit
- **Message type:** The nature and substance of basic communication
- **Protocols:** Set of rules that would allow the basic units to coordinate with each other without ambiguity

- **Communication type:** Nature of communication
- **Knowledge specifications:** Particulars for knowledge representation
- **Abstractions:** Types of conceptualizations
- **Inheritance:** The nature of characteristics transmitted from parents to children
- **Outputs:** The results produced by the process

Table 2 illustrates the differences between the two approaches.

AGENT-ORIENTED PROGRAMMING

Once an agent-system has been adequately designed, it needs to be implemented. The agents, their mental states and their interactions would have to be programmed to build an application that accomplishes its goal. Yoav Shoham (1993) coined the term *agent-oriented programming* (AOP) to describe this new programming paradigm that is based on the cognitive view of com-

Table 2. Proposed AOD vs. OOD

Criteria	Proposed AOD	OOD
Basic Unit	Agent class	Object class
Information	Mental states	Object attributes
Generic Template	Constrained	Unconstrained
Method Type	Communication, mobility, reasoning, searching, learning (adapting), etc.	Mostly communication
Message Type	Speech-acts	Unconstrained
Protocol	Interaction protocol (IP)	Unconstrained
Communication Type	Static (remote) and mobile (local)	Mostly static
Knowledge Specs	Ontology for the domain	Data from database
Abstractions	Generalization, aggregation, cooperation	Generalization, aggregation, association
Inheritance	Mental states	Methods & attributes
Outputs	Agent classes & extended agent model (XAM)	Object Classes & abstractions

putation. It's a specialization of *object-oriented programming*, where basic computation consists of agents *informing, requesting, offering, accepting, rejecting, competing, and assisting* each other based on their own *belief, desire,* and *intentions.* Unlike the client-server mode of computing, this paradigm often involves light remote (static) and heavy local (mobile) communication. It is based primarily on two *agent characteristics*, namely *communication* and *mobility.*

Agent Communication

The *agent communication,* also known as the *agent-based messaging* paradigm (Labrou, Finin, & Peng, 1999), provides a universal messaging language with a consistent speech-act-based, uniform messaging interface for exchanging information, statically or dynamically, among software entities. Agent communication has the following advantages over the traditional *client-server* (RPC) based communication:

- De-centralized, peer-peer communication, as opposed to the traditional client-server roles
- Asynchronous exchange of messages
- Universal message-based language with speech-act-based interface
- Single method invocation for all types of message exchanges (FIPA)

Agent Communication Model

A simple model for agent communication works the following way. The communication involves at least two parties: a sending agent that generates the information and transmits it and a receiving agent that receives the message and uses the information.

The information that is exchanged between the communicating parties may be formally coded into a universally understood *agent communi-cation language (ACL)* with a speech act based interface. The sending agent on generating this ACL coded message string invokes the message method of the recipient and passes the string through it (FIPA framework). The receiving agent, on receiving this message, decodes the information and then performs the necessary actions. In case of a bi-directional communication, it may communicate the result back to the sender by reciprocating the same process.

Agent Communication Language

Agent communication, under this paradigm, is accomplished through the use of three components: ontology, content language, and agent communication language. *Ontology* enumerates the terms comprised by the application domain. The *content language* is used to combine terms in the ontology into meaningful sentences in the language as defined by the grammar. Sometimes the two are so tightly coupled that they become one. Finally, the *agent communication language* acts as a medium for exchanging dialogs among agents, containing sentences of the content language. It provides the outer encoding layer, which determines the type of agent interaction, identifies the network protocol with which to deliver the message, and supplies a speech act also known as *communicative act or performative.* The communicative act indicates whether the message is an assertion, a query, a command or any other acceptable speech form. ACLs range from some form of primitive communication to elaborated standards. Two of the most widely used ACLs are knowledge query manipulation language (KQML) and FIPA ACL (FIPA, 1998a). Knowledge interchange format (KIF) is often used as a content language with KQML. Likewise, semantic language (SL) is often used to represent the application domain, even though the FIPA ACL specification document does not make any commitment to a particular content language.

Agent Mobility

Mobility refers to an agent's ability or inability to move from one environment to another. Accordingly, an agent may be typed as *static* or *mobile*. If *static*, then the agent is unable to move to an environment different from its source of origin. An agent is *mobile* if it can move from host to host and adapt itself to a variety of host environments. A mobile agent is a software process that can transport its mental state, autonomously or otherwise, from one environment to another and still perform adequately in the new environment. OMG's (1997) mobile agent systems interoperability facilities specification (MASIF) provides specifications for agent migration. FIPA's agent management specifications have also been extended to cover for agent mobility (FIPA, 1998d).

Agent mobility has the following advantages over traditional forms of distributed computing:

- Shipment of program to the data source as opposed to data to program source
- Dynamic introduction and removal of services
- Introduction of customized software without any recompilation of client codes at run time
- Elimination of multiple method calls
- Local interaction within the same host
- Reduction of network load and latency
- Dynamic adaptation to new environments

Agent Mobility Model

A simple model for agent mobility works the following way. The source (host) initiates the transfer. The agent suspends its activities on the source, while the system captures the entire agent state and transfers it together with the code to the destination (host) following a predetermined itinerary or according to the agent's own determination. Once the agent is received at its new location, its state is automatically restored. The agent resumes its activities on the destination. On completion, it may or may not return to the host, as per its intentions.

Agent-Oriented Programming vs. Object-Oriented Programming

Table 3 illustrates the differences between Agent-oriented programming and object-oriented programming (OOP). It's a slight modification/extension of Shoham's (1993) table.

Agent-Oriented Programming and Java

Java* is the language of choice for agent-based systems, both for building platforms and applications. Java has several features that directly support implementation of static or mobile agents. Some of these are the following:

- Java's object serialization facilitates conversion and reconstruction of agents for their mobility
- Java's networking support, which includes sockets, URL communication, and RMI, help remote exchange of messages or codes
- Java's class loading model dynamically loads classes included in an application either locally or from another source
- Java's security management helps build secure agent-based systems
- Java's multi-threading allows agents to suspend/stop old threads on the source and start new ones on the destination
- Java's reflection mechanism allows other agents to query the mobile agent's interface on runtime
- Java's applets or servlets can facilitate launching of mobile codes
- Java's naming and directory services may provide yellow pages and help static agents find advertisers that can service their needs

Table 3. AOP VS OOP

Criteria	AOP	OOP
Basic Unit	Agent	Object
Unit state	Mental components	Unconstrained
Communication paradigm	Peer-peer	Client-server
Communication mode	Message passing	Message passing
Communication type	Local (mobile) + remote (static)	Mostly remote
API	Uniform method call	Unconstrained
Method constraints	Honesty, consistency, etc.	None
Message type	Speech Acts (ACL)	Unconstrained
Mobility	Autonomy and mobility-related metadata	No autonomy or mobility related meta data
Inheritance	Mental states	Methods and attributes
Intelligence	Intelligent operations	Not always present

or help mobile agents determine their next moves

Agent-oriented programming is about choosing a language of implementation and then implementing the static and mobile communication among the agents intelligently to build an application.

MULTI-AGENT SYSTEMS FRAMEWORK

In order for the theoretical concepts to be implemented, we need an intermediate layer of abstraction, whose fundamental components must provide for and manage the primitive resources of an agent. Developing an agent-based application becomes a much simpler task if we can have the underlying infrastructure that can support agent identity, autonomy, co-existence, communication, mobility, security, and lifecycle management. The *agent architecture*, supported by the *multi-agent systems* framework, implements the runtime environment for the domain-dependent roles of the agents.

Requirements

The *architectural drivers* for *agent-based applications* are a combination of its *functional and quality requirements* (Bass, Klein, & Bachmann, 2001) that shape its architecture. This subsection presents a set of core requirements for agent-based systems. A MAS framework must meet some or all of the following functional and quality requirements.

Functional requirements

- **Autonomy:** Agent-based systems should be automated and self-managed as far as possible. It should involve minimal manual interventions.
- **Interoperability:** Agent-based applications running on the different platforms must be able to interoperate with each other. Agents from one environment should be able to

communicate with agents from another. They should be able to migrate to other environments, as and when needed.

- **Distributed services:** Agent-based systems should provide a suite of distributed services to facilitate information processing. Application-specific network and system services, including communication, management, mobility, etc., may be provided by software agents themselves.
- **Reusability:** Agent-based systems could be developed by assembling off-the-shelf reusable software agents.
- **Cooperative task processing:** Agents must cooperate and collaborate with each other to solve common problems.

Quality requirements
- **Usability:** Agent-based systems should provide easy-to-understand, easy-to-use and easy-to-train interface for agents.
- **Scalability:** Agent-based systems should still be able to perform their tasks when the number of agents is increased. Agent architecture must support adaptive load balancing.
- **Modifiability:** Agent-based systems should be distributed. Agents could be modifiable without changing the existing functionality of the system.
- **Reliability:** Agent-based systems should be reliable. Mobile agents can be sent when the network connection is alive and return results when the connection is re-established, in case of a network failure.
- **Extensibility and adaptability:** Agents can be programmed to carry different task-specific processes, which extend the functionality of the network.
- **Security:** Agent-based systems should prevent unauthorized access from untrusted sources.

- **Performance:** Agent-based systems should accomplish their tasks in reasonable time (reasonable to the customer) without avoidable delays and in the least disruptive manner.

Next we provide a specific framework and platform that can meet the requirements for an agent architecture.

A FIPA Framework

In this subsection, we present an architectural overview of a FIPA-compliant agent management framework (FIPA, 1998b, 1998c). The framework provides an infrastructure for building agent-based systems. The salient features of this framework are:

- Means for agent identification.
- Means for user interaction.
- Support for co-existence of multiple agents and simultaneous execution.
- Local and remote communication (RMI/IIOP*).
- A subset (almost complete) of ACL grammar for basic messaging (message syntax) and a grammar and ontology for agent management.
- An interpreter for ACL and another for AMS grammar and ontology.
- A platform consisting of three standard FIPA-compliant management agents: *agent management system (AMS), directory facilitator (DF) and agent communication channel (ACC)*. The main role of AMS is agent management, that is, registration, authentication, and security. AMS has now been extended to provide support for mobility. DF is an agent, which helps other agents find appropriate partners for a particular conversation. ACC is a message routing agent, which delivers messages as requested by their senders.

- Asynchronous exchange of messages among the management agents, where the processing is accomplished through threading.
- A uniform messaging interface for each agent that is invoked via the remote *message* method. This method takes, as an input, a parameter of type string and is implemented with a queue (*store and forward architecture*) so that message delivery can overlap with message processing.
- Means for agent migration.
- Facilities for secure and trusted environment.
- De-centralized, peer-to-peer realization of software

Implementation of a system becomes easier if we have a generic platform that is compliant with the framework.

J2EE Platform

J2EE* technologies (Cattell & Inscore, 2001) facilitate the development and deployment of enterprise-level web applications. They support the component model of development, with tools and services for employing business logic in modular, reusable, and platform-independent components. J2EE platform provides a unified programming model and a standard set of APIs. In this subsection, we briefly describe the platform, the technologies behind the platform and the types of components it supports.

J2EE architecture comprises of four layers/ tiers, namely the *client tier, presentation tier, business logic tier,* and *database.* The client tier runs on a browser of the user's personal computer or may even be a standalone application or other processes. The presentation (Web) tier runs on a centralized server and services the client tier. *Java servlets* (JS), *Java server pages* (JSP) and regular *Java beans* can make up the Web tier. Servlets

act on the *request-response* model. The business logic tier handles the business rules of the applications, while the database provides basic storage and access to the organization's data. *Enterprise Java beans* (EJB) consisting of *entity* and *session beans, Java database connectivity* (JDBC), *Java transaction API* (JTA) and *Java message service* (JMS) are some of the technologies that make up these two layers. Besides, the platform also supports *remote method invocation* (RMI)/IIOP and *Java IDL* for communication services, *Java naming and directory information* (JNDI) for naming services, and *registration, authentication, security, lifecycle management,* and so forth, as part of its management services.

J2EE Platform for FIPA Framework

In this subsection, we suggest very broadly how the agent infrastructure, under the FIPA framework, can be mapped readily into the J2EE platform. *Agents* will map to the *presentation layer.* Domain agents can become servlets, standalone classes or simple java beans. Platform agents (AMS, DF and ACC) can be standalone classes or simple java beans with access and control over the management, naming (JNDI) and communication services (RMI, IIOP, etc.) of the J2EE platform. *Intelligence of agents* consisting of the *mental state, knowledge and intelligent operations* will map to the *business logic layer* and *database.* Entity beans can adequately capture the attributes of the mental state and session beans can perform tasks for an agent by executing complicated, intelligent (or otherwise) operations like reasoning, searching, learning, planning, communication, mobility, and so forth, or simply provide sessions associated with agents. The EJBs would provide the *persistent mental states* and *intelligent operations* that could be shared among a large pool of domain and platform agents. Figure 5 shows the FIPA-compliant J2EE platform for MAS framework.

Figure 5. FIPA integration into J2EE platform for MAS framework

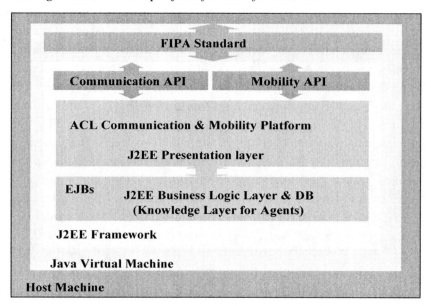

CASE STUDY

We present a case study from an information system application area to illustrate the usefulness of our methodology. We begin with a business scenario, apply agent-oriented analysis & design to develop an agent model and then provide a Java* based application architecture for the implementation of this scenario on a FIPA-compliant agent management platform.

Sense and Respond Business Scenario

The following represents a simplistic *sense & respond* business scenario from supply chain management (OR, 2002).

The supply chain manager of a company sends a request for *alert notification for order shortfall* to the customer manager. The customer manager tracks orders from customers for the various products that the company sells. As he senses a sudden reduction in the demand for a given product and realizes that its orders have dropped below a prefixed threshold value, he triggers an alert notification to the supply chain manager.

The supply chain manager quickly formulates his strategy. The strategy here involves coordination among production planning, demand forecasting, resource allocation, and inventory management. On re-evaluating his strategy, the supply chain manager sends out requests to the suppliers of the product to increase its production. The suppliers acknowledge the requests and confirm the increased production by responding to these requests (promise for production).

The supply chain manager then sends out requests to the sellers of the product to give special promotions on this item and sell it to the relevant buyers. The sellers acknowledge the requests and confirm the sell of this item through promotions by responding to these requests (promise for promotion).

In this way, a crisis situation is quickly averted by monitoring (sensing) the *drop in orders* and responding to it in real time.

Figure 6. Actors, roles & responsibilities for sense and respond business Scenario

Actors: Customer Manager, Supply Chain Manager, Supplier and Seller

Activities: Order tracking, Strategy formulation, Production increase, Promotion offering

Roles & Responsibilities:

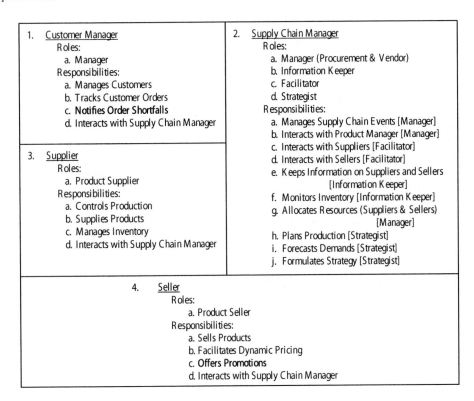

Agent-Oriented Analysis

We begin our modeling process with an agent-oriented analysis of the scenario.

Step 1, 2 & 4: actors, activities, roles and responsibilities (and refinement)

Based on the above scenario description, four actors and four main activities can be identified. Figure 6 is an enumeration of actors, activities and the actors' perceived roles and responsibilities:

Steps 3 & 4: Analysis of interactions (and refinement)

The analysis of the four activities yields three interactions of two distinct types. Each interaction has been analyzed in detail with exchanges, speech acts (within parenthesis), associated knowledge, and applicable protocols (IP) (see Figure 7 and Figure 8).

Agent-Oriented Design

Next, we design the agent classes, abstractions and XAM based on the above analysis (see Figure 9).

Figure 7. Analysis of interactions for sense & respond business scenario

1. <u>Supply Chain Manager ⇔ Customer Manager</u>
   Interactions & Speech Acts:
   a. The Supply Chain Manager requests the Customer Manager to send alert notification when he notices a reduction in the orders of a given product (request-when)
   b. The Customer Manager notifies the Supply Chain Manager when he notices a drop in order (agree & inform)
   Knowledge:
   a. Customer orders for a given item (product)
   b. Threshold (# of orders) for each item (product)
   Protocol:
   a. Request-when-Inform (FIPA-Request-when Protocol)
2. <u>Supply Chain Manager ⇔ Supplier { 1..n}</u>
   Interactions & Speech Acts:
   a. Supply Chain Manager requests Supplier(s) to increase production of the given item (request)
   b. Supplier(s) agree to increase production of the given item (product) and inform on completion (agree & inform)
   Knowledge:
   a. Requested Item (Product)
   b. Product Inventory
   c. List of related Suppliers
   Protocol:
   a. Request-Inform (FIPA-Request Protocol)
3. <u>Supply Chain Manager ⇔ Seller { 1..n}</u>
   Interaction & Speech Acts:
   a. Supply Chain Manager requests Seller(s) to offer promotion on the given item (product) and sell it to relevant buyers (request)
   b. Seller(s) agree to offer promotion on the given item (product) & sell it the relevant buyers and then inform when done (agree & inform)
   Knowledge:
   a. Requested Item (Product)
   b. Product Inventory
   c. List of related Sellers
   d. Terms of Promotion
   Protocol:
   a. Request-Inform (FIPA-Request Protocol)

Agent-Oriented Implementation

A Java*-based implementation of this scenario can easily reside on a FIPA-compliant agent management platform, (as discussed in the previous section). The agent models in Figure 10 and Figure 11, created through *Javadoc**, provide snapshots of the class hierarchies for the *SenseRespondScenario* application (Figure 9) and the *agentPlatform* framework that can support this application.

COMPARISON WITH EXISTING AOSE METHODOLOGIES

Recently, several methodologies have been proposed for AOSE, namely, DESIRE (Brazier et al.,

1997), GAIA (Wooldridge et al., 2000; Zambonelli et al., 2003), Multi-agent Systems Engineering Methodology (MaSE) (DeLoach et al., 2001), Tropos (Giunchiglia et al., 2002), PASSI (Cossentino & Potts, 2002), Prometheus (Padgham & Winikoff, 2002), AUML (Bauer et al., 2001; Odell, Paranuk, & Bauer, 2000). Several workshops have also been conducted in conjunction with *International Conferences on Autonomous Agents and Multi-agent Systems (AAMAS conferences)* on AOSE and AOIS (Agent-oriented Information Systems). Next, we look briefly at three of these existing methodologies, namely, GAIA, MaSE & AUML and compare them with ours.

GAIA (Wooldridge et al., 2000; Zambonelli et al., 2003) is a general methodology that supports both the micro-level (agent structure) and macro-level (agent society and organization structure)

Figure 8. An agent-oriented design for sense & respond business scenario

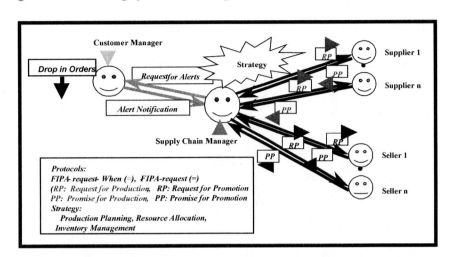

conceptualization for agent-based system development. GAIA analysis process identifies roles and interactions in two separate steps. Roles, in the *organization,* consist of four attributes: *responsibilities, permissions, activities,* and *protocols.* The output of the analysis phase, from the extended version of this methodology (Zambonelli et al., 2003), consists of an *environmental model,* a preliminary *roles model,* a preliminary *interactions model,* and a *set of organizational rules.* GAIA design process consists of three steps. In the first step, it maps roles into agent types and creates instances for each type. In the second step, it determines the *services model* for the fulfillment of roles. In the third step, it creates the *acquaintance model* to represent agent communications.

MaSE (DeLoach et al., 2001) methodology builds upon the work of many agent-based approaches for analyzing, designing, and building *multi-agent systems* and combines them into a complete end-to-end methodology. MaSE is similar to GAIA vis-à-vis generality and the application domain supported, but it supports automatic code generation through the MaSE tool. It requires agent interactions to be one-on-one. It consists of seven phases in a logical pipeline. In the first phase, it captures and orders goals. In the second phase, it applies *use cases* and *sequence*

diagrams. In the third phase, it refines roles. In the fourth phase, it maps roles into agent classes and creates a class diagram. In the fifth phase, it constructs conversations. In the sixth phase, it assembles agent classes into an agent architecture. In the final phase, it creates instances and models the application through deployment diagram.

AUML (agent unified modeling language) (Odell et al., 2000; Bauer et al., 2001) is based on UML (unified modeling language). It has extended UML to support the distinctive requirements of multi-agent systems. AUML provides tools for representing agent classes, specifying agent interaction protocols, representing the internal behavior of an agent, representing role specification, packages, templates with agent interfaces, and deployment diagrams indicating mobility. The essential elements of *protocol diagrams* are: agent roles, agent lifelines, threads of interactions, nested and interleaved protocols, extended semantics of UML messages, input and output parameters for nested protocols, and protocol templates.

Our analysis and design processes are based on our agent models. The steps involved and the specific activities in each step, of the analysis and design phases, differ from those of GAIA and MaSE. Our analysis and interpretations of actors,

Figure 9. An agent-oriented design for sense & respond business scenario

```
Agent Classes:
    1. Customer Manager (CM)
            Name: Customer Manager
            Knowledge: (B1) - Customer Orders for various products, Threshold for each product
            Capabilities: Communicate, Negotiate, Sense & Track (Monitor), Measure, Reason
            Commitment: Alert Supply Chain Manager on order shortfall
            Interaction Protocols: Request-when-Inform (FIPA-Request-when Protocol)
            Languages: ACL
            Ontology: Supply Chain Event Management (Terms: Alert, Order, Item, Production, Promotion)
    2. Supply Chain Manager (SCM)
            Name: Supply Chain Manager
            Knowledge: (B2) - Information on Suppliers, Information on Sellers, Product Inventory,
            Capabilities: Communicate, Negotiate, Search, Match, Reason, Plan, Allocate, Predict, Migrate
            (if necessary)
            Commitment: Sense and Respond to avoid order shortfalls
            Interaction Protocols: Request-when-Inform (FIPA-Request-when Protocol),
            Request-Inform (FIPA-Request Protocol)
            Languages: ACL
            Ontology: Supply Chain Event Management (Terms: Alert, Order, Item, Production, Promotion)
    3. Supplier (S1)
            Name: Supplier
            Knowledge: (B3) - Requested Product, Production Control, Product Inventory
            Capabilities: Communicate, Produce (Increase production), Measure, Control
            Commitment: Increase production of an item (product) on request
            Interaction Protocols: Request-Inform (FIPA-Request Protocol)
            Languages: ACL
            Ontology: Supply Chain Event Management (Terms: Alert, Order, Item, Production, Promotion)
    4. Seller (S2)
            Name: Seller
            Knowledge: (B4) - Requested Product, Product Inventory, Promotional Details
            Capabilities: Communicate, Calculate (price), Offer Promotion (Promote), Sell, Measure,
            Control
            Commitment: Sell an item (product) by offering promotion
            Interaction Protocols: Request-Inform (FIPA-Request Protocol)
            Languages: ACL
            Ontology: Supply Chain Event Management (Terms: Alert, Order, Item, Production, Promotion)
Generalized Agent Class: Manager (M), Specialized Agent Classes: CM, SCM
Aggregated Agent Class: SCM (Procurement and Vendor Manager, Information Keeper, Facilitator, Strategist)
Cooperative Society: Sense & Respond Value Enterprise (SARVE) - <SCM, S1, S2>
Extended Object Model (XAM):
        < {CM, SCM, S1, S2}, {M}, {SCM}, {SARVE}, {B1, B2, B3, B4}, {Sense & Respond, Alert
        Notification, Increase Production, Offer Promotion & Sell}, {Communicate, Negotiate, Migrate, Monitor,
        Reason, Negotiate, Search, Match, Predict, Plan, Allocate, Measure, Control, Produce, Calculate,
        Promote, Sell}, {Request-when-Inform, Request-Inform}, {Supply Chain Event Management}, {ACL}>
```

activities, interactions, and agent abstractions are mostly different from those of GAIA, MaSE, and AUML. Consequently, we have different structures for agents, interactions, and abstractions. Our modeling notation for the analysis phase is much simpler than AUML but doesn't cover all behavioral diagrams from UML. Unlike in MaSE, we start our analysis process by identifying actors,

activities, and interactions from the problem domain. We build up beliefs from the specifics of the interactions and activity contexts. We determine commitments by analyzing agent interactions and responsibilities. Commitments add up to the system goal. We do provide a MAS framework that merges the FIPA-compliant infrastructure with the emerging J2EE technologies.

Figure 10. An agent model for sense & respond business scenario

```
• class java.lang.Object
    • class SenseRespondScenario.Agent
        • class SenseRespondScenario.Manager
            • class SenseRespondScenario.CustomerManager
            • class SenseRespomdScenario.SupplyChainManager
        • class SenseRespondScenario.Supplier
```

Figure 11. An agent model for FIPA-compliant agent platform

```
• class java.lang.Object
    • class agentPlatform.AMSDescription
    • class agentPlatform.Agent (implements java.lang.Runnable)
        • class agentPlatform.AgentCommunicationChannel
        • class agentPlatform.AgentManagementSystem
        • class agentPlatform.DirectoryFacilitator
    • class agentPlatform.AgentMessage
    • class agentPlatform.Constraint
    • class agentPlatform.DfDescription
    • class agentPlatform.MessageContent
    • class agentPlatform.Service
```

CONCLUSION AND FUTURE CHALLENGES

In this chapter, we have tried to address the various issues that are associated with the *conceptualization and implementation* of agent-based systems. We have extended the paradigm of *agent-oriented conceptualization* and formalized the notion of agent-*oriented modeling*. We have proposed a simple, high-level methodology for agent-oriented analysis and design, based on our agent models. We have highlighted the differences between our methodology and the object-oriented approaches to conceptual modeling. We have discussed about the two main components of *agent-oriented programming*, namely, *communication* and *mobility*, outlined their advantages over traditional approaches to distributed computing, and compared AOP with OOP. We have also suggested a *multi-*

agent systems framework that merges the FIPA-compliant agent-development infrastructure with the emerging J2EE technologies to provide a platform for building agent-based applications. We have illustrated our methodology with a case study. We have also briefly described three of the existing methodologies for AOSE and compared these with ours.

Challenges remain in developing tools that can automate the processes of agent-oriented analysis and design for an application domain, based on the proposed methodology, as well as in extending the methodology to provide full lifecycle coverage for software and knowledge engineering. We do also envision that this merger of the FIPA framework with J2EE technologies may open up new frontiers for *agent architecture* that could then be commercially exploited to build new platforms and applications.

TRADEMARKS

Java, J2EE, and all Java-based trademarks are trademarks or registered trademarks of Sun Microsystems Inc.

IIOP is a registered trademark of the Object Management Group.

REFERENCES

Bass, L., Klein, M., & Bachmann, F. (2001, October 4). Quality attribute design primitives and the attribute driven design method. *Proceedings of 4th Conference on Product Family Engineering,* Bilbao, Spain.

Bauer, B., Muller, J. P., & Odell, J. (2001). Agent UML: A formalism for specifying multi-agent software systems. *International Journal of Software Engineering and Knowledge Engineering, 11*(3), 207-230.

Biswas, P. K. (2005, April 18-21). Architecting multi-agent systems with distributed sensor networks. *Proceedings of IEEE International Conference on Integration of Knowledge Intensive Multi-Agent Systems (KIMAS),* Waltham, MA.

Biswas, P. K. (2007). Towards an agent-oriented approach to conceptualization. *Applied Soft Computing J.* Retrieved from http://dx.doi.org/10.1016/j.asoc.2006.11.009

Brazier, F. M., Dunin-Keplicz, B. M., Jennings, N. R., & Treur, J. (1997). DESIRE: Modeling multi-agent systems in a compositional formal framework. *International Journal of Cooperative Information Systems, 6*(1), 67-94.

Brazier, F. M., Keplicz, B. D., Jennings N. R., & Treur, J. (1995, June 12-14). Formal specification of multi-agent systems: A real-world case. *Proceedings of the 1st International Conference on Multi-agent Systems (ICMAS '95),* San Francisco.

Cattell, R., & Inscore, J. (2001). *J2EE technology in practice.* Addison-Wesley.

Cossentino, M., & Potts, V. (2002, June 24-27). A CASE tool supported methodology for the design of multi-agent systems. *Proceedings of International Conference on Software Engineering Research and Practice (SERP'02),* Las Vegas, NV.

DeLoach, S. A., Wood, M. F., & Sparkman, C. H. (2001). Multi-agent systems engineering. *The International Journal of Software Engineering and Knowledge Engineering, 11*(3).

Elammari, M., & Lalonde, W. (1999). An agent-oriented methodology: High-level view and intermediate models. *Proceedings of AOIS Workshop,* Seattle, WA.

FIPA (1998a). *FIPA 97 specification Part 2: Agent communication language, Version 2.0.* Foundation for Intelligent Physical Agents. Retrieved from www.fipa.org

FIPA (1998b). *FIPA 97 specification Part 1: Agent management, Version 2.0.* Foundation for Intelligent Physical Agents. Retrieved from www.fipa.org

FIPA (1998c). FIPA *98 specification part 13: FIPA97 developers guide, Version 1.0.* Foundation for Intelligent Physical Agents. Retrieved from www.fipa.org

FIPA (1998d). FIPA *specification 11 V1.0: Agent management support for mobility specification.* Retrieved from www.fipa.org

FIPA (2003). *FIPA Methodology: Glossary rel. 1.0.* Retrieved from http://www.pa.icar.cnr.it/~cossentino/FIPAmeth/glossary.htm

Fowler, M., & Scott, K. (2001). *UML distilled* (2nd ed.). Addison-Wesley.

Giunchiglia, F., Mylopoulos, J., & Perini, A. (2002). The Tropos software development methodology: Processes, models and diagrams. *Proceedings of AOSE Workshop* (pp. 162-173). Retrieved from http://www.jamesodell.com/AOSE02-papers/aose02-23.pdf

Jennings, N. R. (2001). An agent-based approach for complex software systems. *Communications of the ACM*, 35-41.

Labrou, Y., Finin, T., & Peng, Y. (1999). Agent communication languages: The current landscape. *IEEE Intelligent Systems*, 45-52.

Lind, J. (2000). *General concepts of agents and multi-agent systems.* Retrieved from www.agentlab.de

Morreale, P. (1998, April). Agents on the move. *IEEE Spectrum.*

Odell, J., & Burkhart, R. (1998). *Beyond objects: Unleashing the power of adaptive agents.* Tutorial presented at OOPSLA, Vancouver, B.C.

Odell, J., Paranuk, H. V., & Bauer, B. (2000). Extending UML for agents. *Proceedings of the AOIS Workshop at the 17th National Conference on Artificial Intelligence* (pp. 3-17). Retrieved from http://www.jamesodell.com/extendingUML.pdf

OMG. (1997). *OMG mobile agent systems interoperability facilities specification (MASIF).* OMG TC Document ORBOS/97-10-05. Retrieved from http://www.camb.opengroup.org/RI/MAF

OR. (2002). Sense and respond business scenarios. *OR/MS Today*, April 2002. Retrieved from http://lionhrtpub.com/orms/orms-4-02/frvaluechain.html

Padgham, L., & Winikoff, M. (2002, July 15-19). Prometheus: A methodology for developing intelligent agents. *Proceedings of the 3rd AOSE Workshop at AAMAS'02*, Bologna, Italy. Retrieved from http://www.cs.rmit.edu.au/agents/Papers/oopsla02.pdf

Parunak, H., Brueckner, S., Fleischer, M., & Odell, J. (2002, July 15-19). Co-X: Defining what agents do together. *Proceedings of AAMAS '02,* Bologna, Italy.

Rao, A., & Georgeff, M. (1995). BDI agents: From theory to practice. *Proceedings of the 1st International Conference on Multi-Agent Systems (ICMAS 95)*, San Francisco.

Shoham, Y. (1993). Agent-oriented programming. *Journal of Artificial Intelligence, 60*(1), 51-92.

Small, P. (1996). *Lists, objects and intelligent agents.* Retrieved from www.obsolete.com/dug/sorcery/loops

Turchin, V. (1993). The cybernetic ontology of action. *Kybernetes, 22*(2), 10-30.

Wooldridge, M., & Jennings, N. R. (1995). Intelligent agents: Theory and practice. *The Knowledge Engineering Review, 10*(2), 115-152.

Wooldridge, M. (1997). Agent-based software engineering. *IEE Proceedings of Software Engineering 144* (pp. 26-37).

Wooldridge, M., & Jennings, N. R. (2000). Agent-oriented software engineering. In J Bradshaw (Ed.), *Handbook of agent technology.* AAAI/MIT Press.

Wooldridge, M., Jennings, N. R., & Kinny, D. (1999). Methodology for agent-oriented analysis and design. *Proceedings of the 3rd International conference on Autonomous Agents* (pp. 69-76).

Wooldridge, M., Jennings, N. R., & Kinny, D. (2000). The Gaia methodology for agent-oriented analysis and design. *Journal of Autonomous Agents and Multi-agent Systems, 3*(3), 285-312.

Zambonelli, F., & Jennings, N. R. (2003). Developing multi-agent systems: The Gaia methodology. *ACM Transactions on Software Engineering and Methodology, 12*(3), 317-370. Retrieved from http://www.ecs.soton.ac.uk/~nrj/download-files/tosem03.pdf

Chapter II
Concurrent Programming with Multi–Agents and the Chemical Abstract Machine

Wanli Ma
University of Canberra, Australia

Dat Tran
University of Canberra, Australia

Dharmendra Sharma
University of Canberra, Australia

Hong Lin
University of Houston – Downtown, USA

Mary Anderson
University of Canberra, Australia

ABSTRACT

In this chapter, we propose a new concurrent programming approach called MACH (multi-agent extended chemical abstract machine). MACH extends the chemical abstract machine with multiple coexisting agents. This paper focuses on the design, implementation, and verification of MACH. The aim of MACH is to develop a reactive programming language based on an interactive computational model, which we believe is the key to concurrent programming. We present MACH as a simple and efficient programming approach based on a sound theoretical background.

INTRODUCTION

Agent-based software engineering (ABSE) is a new area in software development. The basic idea of ABSE is to use agents as the building blocks for a software system, the same way that objects are the building blocks in object-oriented software engineering. ABSE promises a simplified and enhanced approach to construct complicated software systems. Stemming from the continuous and autonomous nature of agents and also the high level of abstraction and communication amongst the agents, it is especially for concurrent programming (we use concurrent programming to cover multiprogramming in a single computer, parallel programming, and distributed programming; we also use "parallel" and "distributed" interchangeably if there is no confusion). In the last couple of decades, a plethora of concurrent programming languages and models have been proposed; most extend the existing sequential programming languages with thread control facilities. However, parallel programming is still far more difficult than sequential programming. It is intuitive to assume use of multiple control threads for concurrency and that the difference between concurrent and sequential programming is the number of active control threads at a given time. In fact, the difference, realised by the research communities, is not in the *single thread* nature versus the *multi-thread with communications*, but in contrast, between a *functionality program* and a *reactive one* (Lamport, 1993).

A functionality program is the one that maps an input state (or data) into an output state. Traditionally, we explain a program in this way: It accepts some input data and then, according to the instructions of the program, produces the output data. The instructions are executed in a step-by-step manner. There may be some procedure and function calls, but, at any time instance, only a single control flow, which is also known as a *thread, exists*. The flow starts from an initial point, normally the first instruction of the main module of that program, and terminates at a stop point. Denotational semantics (Gordon, 1979; Stoy, 1977) is the formal description of this idea, where each program statement transfers the program from the state before its execution the state after it. The behaviour of the whole program is to map the initial state to a final state.

A reactive system emphasizes the interactions among the components of a program: Different parts of a program interact with each other in response to stimuli from the outside world. The *intrinsic property* of the systems is the *interactions among the components* rather than the coexisting execution flows (or multi-control-thread), although the latter can also be observed from the outside of the systems.

Multi-agent systems (MAS) stem from the fields of distributed computing and artificial intelligence (Stone & Veloso, 2000). According to Wooldridge and Jennings (Wooldridge & Jennings, 1995), if a piece of software has the characteristics of *autonomy, social ability, reactivity,* and *pro-activity*, it is an agent in weak notion. On top of these characteristics, if the software has further characteristics of *adaptability, mobility, veracity,* and *rationality*, it becomes an agent in strong notion. A MAS is a society of multiple coexisting agents. Each agent interacts with other agents and the environment. Together, with certain rules to coordinate and regulate individual behavior, they achieve the goal of the system. These agents have a high degree of autonomy, heterogeneity, and parallelism. The properties make them excellent candidates for building blocks of concurrent, including parallel and distributed, programming.

In this chapter, we propose a new programming paradigm called *MACH* (multi-agent extended chemical abstract machine). It is the further development of T-Cham (Ma, Johnson, & Brent, 1996a, 1996b), where we used transactions to extend the chemical abstract machine. Instead of transactions, MACH extends the chemical abstract machine (Cham) (Berry & Boudol, 1992; Boudol, 1993) with multiple agents (Bradshaw, 1997; Stone & Veloso, 2000; Wooldridge & Jennings, 1995). This allows MACH to conduct computations based on the chemical reaction metaphor where computation proceeds as a succession of chemical reactions in a tuple space, with the agents controlling the coordination of the elements in this tuple space. The combination of Cham and a multi-agent system creates an interactive and modular multi-paradigm programming language.

MACH uses tuple space (Gelernter & Carriero, 1992) as the environment context for agent communication. The coordination and communication of concurrent reactions among agents are based on the status of tuple spaces. On the other hand, *reaction rules* regulate agent behavior—when and which agents can perform. The processing (or performing) part, which is the internal operation of an agent, could be written in any programming language. Finally, a reaction rule also has its temporal logic interpretation (Ma, Krishnamurthy, & Orgun, 1994; Ma & Orgun, 1996; Ma, Orgun, & Johnson, 1998), which makes correctness proofs possible for a program.

Our novel contribution to the proposal is to seamlessly integrate tuple space, chemical abstract machine, MAS, and temporal logic together to provide a programming paradigm that emphasizes *simplicity, abstraction, efficiency*, and a sound *theoretical background*. The chemical reaction model makes it easy to express concurrent agent tasks in MACH. The explicit declaration of tuple space helps the optimisation of data (tuples) and task distribution, and hence the efficient execution of MACH programs. The temporal logic interpretation of reaction rules promotes program verification.

The rest of the chapter is organized as follows: we start with a discussion of the background which lays the foundation for MACH. This is followed by the answers to our motivation for developing MACH; next we show the style of the MACH language with common programming examples; then we work through temporal logic proofs of these programming examples; finally, we finish with a conclusion and future work.

BACKGROUND

This section studies the background technologies on which MACH is built. The GAMMA model (Banâtre & Métayer, 1990; Hankin, Métayer, & Sands, 1992) and the chemical abstract machine

(Berry & Boudol, 1992; Boudol, 1993) define a computation model with a set of transformation rules similar to a succession of chemical reactions, which drives the idea behind the chemical metaphor of Cham. Linda (Ahuja, Carriero, & Gelernter, 1986; Carriero & Gelernter, 1989) is a parallel programming paradigm based on language coordination, featuring the use of tuple spaces. Tuple space provides the environment for agents to play; it is the context where agents reside and also the space for agents to communicate and coordinate. Finally, the agents in a MAS (Bradshaw, 1997; Stone & Veloso, 2000; Wooldridge & Jennings, 1995) are the building blocks for a software system. We leave the introduction of temporal logic to a later section.

GAMMA Model and the Chemical Abstract Machine

The GAMMA (Banâtre, 1996; Banâtre, Coutant, & Métayer, 1988; Banâtre & Métayer, 1990, 1993) model is based on a multiset data structure. A *multiset* is a *set* except that there can be multiple occurrences of its elements. The computational model of GAMMA resembles a succession of chemical reactions in which some elements (a.k.a. molecules) of a multiset are consumed and then some new elements are produced, similar to the behaviours of molecules in chemical reactions. Cham (Berry & Boudol, 1992; Boudol, 1993) is a theoretical refinement of GAMMA. The rigid mathematical definitions of molecules, reactions, and reaction rules are given, and so are the structured molecules and their transformation rules.

The Linda Paradigm

Linda (Ahuja et al., 1986; Carriero & Gelernter, 1989; Carriero, Gelernter, Mattson, & Sherman, 1994) is the first coordination parallel programming paradigm based on a global tuple space. There are a few fully implemented Linda languages. The most popular one is C-Linda (Cohen

& Molinari, 1991). Coordination (Gelernter & Carriero, 1992) is the basic idea promoted by Linda. Linda provides a global shared tuple space to coordinate the activities of each individual programming language. A tuple space is a logically shared memory used for data exchange and synchronization control among the interactive components of a program. Accessing the tuples on the tuple space is in association manner. In MACH, we view the operations of the tuple space as the coordinator and communication media for agents.

Multi-Agent Systems (MAS)

The agent technology originated from artificial intelligence research and can be traced back to the actor model by Hewitt (1977) of 1970. The agent concept might be the one with the most diversity among the research communities. According to Bradshaw, a software agent is *"a software entity which functions continuously and autonomously in a particular environment"* (Bradshaw, 1997). Wooldridge and Jennings define agents by their characteristics: If a piece of software has the characteristics of autonomy, social ability, reactivity, and pro-activity, it is an agent in weak notion. On top of these characteristics, the software can have further characteristics of adaptability, mobility, veracity, and rationality. Nwana suggests that agent is an umbrella term, under which many different types of agents exist (Nwana, 1996). Almost every agent system consists of multiple agents. Multi-agent system technology is another way of talking about agents, although it tries to emphasize on multiple, perhaps distributed, agents and the communication amongst them. Stone wrote a good survey paper on agent communication to achieve the common goal (Stone & Veloso, 2000).

Using agents as the basic building blocks to construct complicated software systems was first suggested by Shoham in 1993 (Shoham, 1993). The phase "agent-oriented software engineering" was coined by Jennings and Wooldridge (Jennings, 2000; Wooldridge & Ciancarini, 2001). Charles Petrie suggested to use "agent-based software engineering" as a *"refinement of some aspect of AOSE, based upon our practice experience in agent building"* (Petrie, 2001).

MOTIVATION

The motivation behind MACH is to create an interactive concurrent programming paradigm. This section discusses our observations and our motivation.

Functionality vs. Interaction

A functionality program (a functionality program is distinct from a functional program based on λ calculus) is one that maps an input into an output. Functionality is the traditional way of thinking about the behaviour of a sequential program. A program starts from the starting point of the program with initial data and then halts at the ending point with the resulting data of this computation.

A reactive program emphasizes the interactions among the components of a program: different parts of a program interact with each other in response to the stimuli from the outside world. The phenomenon was noticed as early as the beginning days of concurrent programming and operating system design, which is why Dijkstra introduced the *dining philosophers* problem. However, it takes a very long time for computer scientists to accept the "new" idea in the parallel programming area; according to Lamport (Lamport, 1993): *"Computer scientists originally believed that the big leap was from sequentiality to concurrency. ... We have learned that, as far as formal methods are concerned, the real leap is from functional to reactive systems."* The honour of this discovery was credited to Harel and Pnueli (Harel & Pnueli, 1985).

The concepts of *sequential, concurrent, parallel,* or *distributed* should belong to the execution of a program on a particular computational resource instead of the program itself. At the programming language level, we should not focus on sequential, concurrent, parallel, or distributed programs but only *functional* and *interactive* programs.

Single Thread, Multi-Thread, and Non-Thread

Control flow and *control thread* are two different concepts in the description of a program. Control flow relates to a static program. It can be built on three basic constructs, *sequence, branch,* and *goto* (Dahl, Dijkstra, & Hoare, 1972). During execution, only one branch of a branch construct can be chosen at any time on a given set of data. The operation sequence of the execution of a program is unrolled by control thread. Control thread is a concept related to the execution of the program.

A sequentially executed program has only one control thread, which unrolls the control flows of a program, step by step, in a sequential manner. When the program goes to a parallel machine, it is possible to unroll the operations of a program in a parallel manner. Rather than having multi-threaded control in a parallel program, a different approach completely abandons the control part of a program: it consists of a number of autonomous actions, which are executed atomically and concurrently in a chaotic manner. It does not have any form of control, centralised or de-centralised. An action happens whenever its execution condition is satisfied.

The main idea behind non-control flow programs is *non-determinism*, which distinguishes this kind of programming paradigm from data flow model (Dennis, Gao, & Todd, 1984; Dennis & Misunas, 1975; Srini, 1986). No control flow at the programming language level means that a programmer can concentrate on the logical correctness of a program, rather than worry about the execution order.

Shared Memory vs. Distributed Memory and Memory Accessing

The concepts of *shared memory* and *distributed memory* originally come from computer architectures. There is an endless debate on which type of memory is superior (Carriero et al., 1994).

A third approach to access memory is *associatedly accessible* logical shared memory—tuple space. Tuples in a tuple space are accessed by pattern-matching on their content instead of their addresses. A tuple space provides a high level of accessible and distributed data. It avoids the scalability problem of a normal shared memory system and is easier to manage by programmers than a distributed memory system (Carriero et al., 1994; Zenith, 1991).

Debugging vs. Verification

Automatic program verification is a long-desired goal in the program development community. A great deal of achievement has been made in this area, some of which are becoming more mature and applicable to real applications. Clark, Grumberg and *et al* are a good example, they used a temporal logic model checking method to prove the correctness of a couple of IEEE communication protocol standards and found a few bugs in IEEE Futurebus+ standard (IEEE Standard 896.1-1991) (Clarke, Grumberg, & Long, 1993; Clarke, Grumberg, & Hiraishi, 1993). Given the fact that IEEE standards are carefully designed and well debugged by the *élite* of the related areas, bugs are still not avoidable. To conclude, we'd like to cite Dijkstra's famous words: "*Program testing can be quite effective for showing the presence of bugs, but is hopelessly inadequate for showing their absence*" (Dijkstra, 1976).

Why the Chemical Abstract Machine?

A quality computational model lays the foundation to design a programming language with good programmability. The chemical abstract machine was chosen as the computational model for MACH because it provides an easy and natural way to express the interactions among the components of a program—agents. Cham also has formal operational semantics, which is much easier to understand and implement on computer systems than declarative semantics, but both operational semantics and declarative semantics are important, and they play different roles in programming. Declarative is better for system verification (a proof system), and the operational semantics is better for implementation (code transformation).

Why Tuple Space?

Tuple space is logically shared memory used for data exchange and synchronization control among the interactive agents. It is the (logically) global environment, or global space, for agents to reside and interact. It provides the social environment for the agents. It is also the communication media for the agents to interact with each other. Tuple space shields the underlying computer system details from the logic presentation of the tuples.

Why a Multi-Agent Approach?

An agent is a piece of programming code that can run autonomously. The characteristics of autonomy, social ability, reactivity, and pro-activity can be further developed into the properties of *atomicity, consistency, isolation*, and *durability*, which are highly desirable for programming, implementation, and especially verification.

- **Atomicity:** An agent entity is regarded as an undividable single step operator, no matter how big it is.
- **Consistency and isolation:** An agent is a closed system and won't be affected by the changes of the context it is in.

- **Durability:** The effect of the agent operation, when it is committed, won't be rolled back. Durability is essential for the correctness of the multi-agent system and its efficient implementation.

An agent has two sets of behavior, internal and external. The internal behavior is the intrinsic operation of the agent. It consists of learning, reasoning, and decision-making ability. The external behavior is comprised of the communications and the reactions with other agents and the environment. It is observable behavior from outside of this agent.

For any agent, MACH requires a pre-condition and a post-condition to describe the external behavior of the agent. From BDI model (Rao, Anand, & Georgeff 1995; Wooldridge 2000) point of view, the behavior of an agent is driven by its *beliefs*, *desires*, and *intention*. According to Braubach, Pokahr, and Lamersdorf (2005), in programming term, the beliefs reflect the environment where the agent resides, the desires are the goals for the agent, and the intentions are the operational or executable plans of the agents. In MACH programming, the pre-condition captures part of the environment. When the condition meets, the agent starts to react. The post-condition describes the goals of the agent. And the intentions of the agent are programmed as the internal behavior of the agent.

In this chapter, we primarily concentrate on the external behaviors of agents. The tuple space is where the external behaviors can be observed and the agent activities can be coordinated. The coordinated activities of the involved agents achieve the goals of the system.

Why Theoretical Background?

Although mathematics and logic are the better way to achieve a correct program, most programmers are not comfortable with the rigid process of mathematical reasoning. People tend to use a natural and intuitional way to express their ideas. For example, people prefer *Venn Diagrams* (Cooke & Bez, 1984) over the mathematical definitions of set operations. When trying to provide formal semantics to the goals of agents, Winikoff, Padgham, Harland, and Thangarajah had the same observations (2002). They discussed the differences of declarative and procedure semantics and also argued that both are important. Perini, Pistore, Roveri, & Susi (2003) advocate a mixed approach, which interleaves formal and informal specification. The approach is to *"allow for lightweight usage of formal verification techniques, that are used as services in an 'informal' development methodology."* They suggested keeping informal visual modeling languages but interpreting them formally. Thus, a formal specification system can be derived from informal visual modeling.

Formal temporal logic semantics provide a means of correctness proof for MACH programs, but the proof system is separated from programming, or kept in the background. Formal verification to a program can be performed if needed. MACH programming notations serve as the Venn Diagrams in set theory, while the temporal logic interpretation of a MACH program is like the mathematical definitions, by which the reasoning is carried out.

PROGRAMMING WITH MACH

MACH uses agents as the building blocks for a program. This section shows through examples how these building blocks are put together to create the style of the MACH programming language.

The Producer-Consumer Problem

The producer produces one message, a string of at most MAX characters at one time, and the consumer consumes one message at another time.

Both producer and consumer are autonomous. The only constraint on them is the capacity of the repository where the messages are temporarily stored. We assume the capacity is N in our example. The producer will continue producing messages as long as the total message number is less then N, and the consumer will consume messages whenever they are available. The program is in Figure 1.

The first two lines define two constant MAX and N. They are substituted by 1024 and 100, respectively, before the program is passed to a compiler. There are two kinds of tuples in this program. They are token and msg. The number of tuple tokens denotes the current capacity of the message container in this example. If there are n $(0 < n \leq N)$ tokens currently in the tuple space, it means that the producer can still produce n messages without any consumption by the consumer. The tuple msgs simply hold the messages. At the very beginning, there are N tuple tokens and no msg.

The first reaction rule says that the agent prod consumes (thinking as occupies) one token tuple and generates one message msg. The reaction cannot happen if there are no tokens left. The second reaction rule says that the agent cons consumes one msg, and as the result of the consumption, one more token is available. Similarly, the consumption reaction could not happen if there is no msg currently in the tuple space.

The agent goal (agentgoals) section has a collection of pre- and post-conditions pairs for each agent described in the reaction rule section. A pre- and post-condition pair specifies that under the context of pre-conditions, an agent will be triggered to perform and achieve the goal described in the post-conditions. In the example, there are two agents: prod and cons. The pre- and post-condition pairs actually specify the population of token and msg in the tuple space before and after the execution of the agents.

Figure 1. MACH program of the producer-consumer problem

```
#define MAX    1024                -- the max length of a message
#define N      100                 -- the max number of messages

REACTIONS producer_consumer
      tuples
            boolean token;         -- a place-holder for a message
            char msg[MAX];         -- a message
      initialization
            [i:1..N]::token=1;
      reactionrules
            token leadsto msg by prod;    -- producer rule
            msg leadsto token by cons;    -- consumer rule
      agentgoals
            prod: |token|>0 // (|token|'=|token|-1)&&(|msg|'=|msg|+1);
            cons: |msg|>0 // (|token|'=|token|+1)&&(|msg|'=|msg|-1);
end

AGENT prod
#language C
#tuplein boolean token;
#tupleout char msg[];
      prod() {
            /* some C code writing messages to the msg tuple */
      }
end

AGENT cons
#language C
#tuplein char msg[];
#tupleout boolean token;
      cons() {
            /* some C code reading the content of the msg tuple */
      }
end
```

There is no termination section in this example because this is a non-terminating program. The termination section, led by keyword `termination`, if it exists, specifies the grand system goal that the multiple agents are collectively trying to achieve. Upon reaching this condition, all reactions are terminated. In other words, all agents together with their individual goals are aborted.

The Meeting Scheduler

We are to find the earliest common meeting time for a group of people. For the sake of brevity, we suppose that there are only three people, F, G, and H, in the group. Every person of the group suggests his/her earliest acceptable meeting time. Finally, the earliest common meeting time is reached. The program is in Figure 2.

In the program, the tuple `time` holds the current suggested time for the meeting. It will be changed by the persons *F, G,* and *H* according to their own agenda. The transaction `F_time` (resp. `G_time` and `H_time`) withdraws `time` and then checks it against his/her own agenda. If the `time` is an acceptable time, it remains unchanged and `F_changed` is set to FALSE; otherwise, a new `time` is put back into the tuple space and `F_changed` is set to TRUE. The common meeting time will be reached when `F_changed`, `G_changed`, and `H_changed` are all set to FALSE. More formally, the transaction `F_time` executes the function *f*:

f: int → int

The result of *f(t)* is the time acceptable for *F* to have the meeting according to the current suggestion *t*, that is, for any *t*, *f(t) ≥ t*, and *f(t)* is an acceptable time for *F* while any other time *r*, *t<r<f(t)*, is not acceptable; *g* and *h* are defined accordingly.

In fact, we can have a unique transaction `my_time` instead of `F_time`, `G_time`, and `H_time`. The transaction executes the function φ:

φ : {*F,G,H*} × *int → int*,
or   φ : {*F,G,H*} → (*int → int*).

If we apply φ to *F, G,* and *H*, we obtain φ(*F*) ≡ *f*, φ(*G*) ≡ *g*, and φ(*H*) ≡ *h*. We keep the different transactions, `F_time`, `G_time`, and `H_time`, in the thesis to simplify our proof in the fifth section. The result of the program in Figure 3 is the time u, which satisfies *u = f(u) = g(u) = h(u)*.

The Auction Problem

There is one item to be auctioned. To simplify the problem for explanation purpose, we assume that there are one auctioneer and three bidders. The auctioneer is known as A, and the three bidders are P, Q, and R. Each bidder has a price range for the item. The goal for a bidder is to acquire the item with a minimum price within its price range, and the goal for the auctioneer is to achieve the highest possible price for the item. The program is in Figure 3.

The current bidding price of the item is represented by tuple `price` in the tuple space. It is initialized to the auctioneer's minimum reserve price. Token `ticket` has to be obtained for an agent to bid. Supposing agent P obtained the token `ticket` and also the current `price`, it will check who updated the price last time and also if the current price is still within its acceptable price range. If the price was not updated by itself and is still lower than the maximum acceptable price, it will increase the price and then inject the updated tuple `price` back to the tuple space, together with a new tuple `update`. The tuple `update` has the information on P's action – bid or not. The auctioneer agent A checks the tuple `update`. If the last bidder agent did increase the price (`update.Updated==TURE`), agent A will turn the tuple into a `ticket` tuple and also preserve the name of the last bidding agent. The bidding process continues. If the `update` tuple indicated no action from the last bidding agent, it

Figure 2. MACH program of the meeting scheduler

```
REACTIONS meeting_scheduler
   tuples
        date time;
        boolean F_changed, G_changed, H_changed;
   initialization
        time=0; F_changed=G_changed=H_changed=true;
   reactionrules
        time, F_changed, !G_changed, !H_changed leadsto time, F_changed
                  by F_time when (G_changed==TRUE || H_changed==TRUE);
        time, G_changed, !F_changed, !H_changed leadsto time, G_changed
                  by G_time when (F_changed==TRUE || H_changed==TRUE);
        time, H_changed, !F_changed, !G_changed leadsto time, H_changed
                  by H_time when (F_changed==TRUE || G_changed==TRUE);
   termination
     on(F_changed==false&&G_changed==false&&H_changed==false) do output;
   agentgoals
        F_time: time=r // (time=r) && (F_changed==FALSE) ||
                                (time=f(r)) && (F_changed==TRUE)
        G_time: time=r // (time=r) && (G_changed==FALSE) ||
                                (time=g(r)) && (G_changed==TRUE)
        H_time: time=r // (time=r) && (H_changed==FALSE) ||
                                (time=h(r)) && (H_changed==TRUE)
end
AGENT F_time
#language X
#tuplein date time;
#tupleout Boolean F_changed, G_changed, H_changed;
        F_time() {
                /* calculating the earliest available time in language X*/
        }
end
/* AGENT G_time and AGENT H_time, similar to agent F_time */
```

remains unchanged in the tuple space. If the tuple space accumulates three update tuples, it means that none of them can be turned into a ticket tuple. In the other words, all three bidding agents have checked the price, and decided not to bid anymore. Thus, the bidding process terminates. The winning bidder is price.Bidder, and the final price for the item is price.Price.

Figure 3. MACH program of the auction problem

```
REACTIONS Auction
    tuples
        token price, ticket, update;
    initialization
            price.Price = TheReservedPrice;
    reactionrules
        ticket, price leadsto price, update by P;
        ticket, price leadsto price, update by Q;
        ticket, price leadsto price, update by R;
        update leadsto ticket by A when (update.Updated == TURE);
        termination
            (|update|==3) do output_price;
end


AGENT P
#language ObjectX
#tuplein price, ticket;
#tupleout price, update;
    P() {
        if (price.Price < P.MaxPrice and ticket.UpdatedBy != P) {
            price.Price += P.Inc; price.Bidder = P;
            update.Updated=TRUE; update.By = P;
        }
         else { update.Updated=Flase; update.By = P; }
end


/* AGENT Q and AGENT R are similar to AGENT P */


AGENT A
#language ObjectX
#tuplein update;
#tupleout ticket;
    A() {
        ticket.UpdatedBy = update.By;
    }
end
```

TOWARDS THE TEMPORAL LOGIC PROOF SYSTEM OF MACH

Temporal logics (Gotzhein, 1992; Harel & Pnueli, 1985; Lloyd, 1987; Manna & Pnueli, 1992; Rescher & Urquhart, 1971) are very useful tools to reason about temporal properties and especially suitable for modeling and reasoning about parallel and distributed applications. They are widely used in program specification and verification, even as programming languages on their own right (Orgun & Ma, 1994).

Temporal logics are useful in studying the *temporal properties*, which depend on time instants during computation, of programs. They can express the properties, such as safety, liveness, precedence, and response, in a natural and succinct way. There are many kinds of temporal logics: linear, branching, or interval time, discrete time or dense time, and so forth. Gotzhein's paper (1992) is a good introduction to temporal logics. In this chapter, we adopt Manna-Pnueli temporal logic (Manna & Pnueli, 1992), which is linear, discrete, and based on non-negative time with an original time point 0.

The temporal logic is based on the first-order (predicate) logic (Curry, 1963; Manna & Pnueli, 1992) with the extension of some temporal operators. Formulae from predicate logic are called *state formulae*, and so are *state predicate, state term,* and so on. A *temporal formula* is a state formula governed by *temporal operators*. We use the following temporal operators:

$$\Box, \Diamond, u, w$$

Their informal meanings are:

1. $\Box$ is *always* or *henceforth*. $\Box p$ says that p is TRUE from now on;
2. $\Diamond q$ means q will be TRUE *eventually*;
3. puq means p is TRUE and holds *until q* eventually becomes TRUE; and
4. w is called *weak until*—*pwq* means p is TRUE and holds *until q* eventually becomes TRUE or p holds forever if q cannot become TRUE.

The formal semantics of a temporal formula is defined on a model σ, which is a sequence of states $\sigma = s_0 s_1 s_2 s_3 \ldots$ along the time axis, where $s_i (i \geq 0)$ denotes the state at time instant i. We use m to stand for the set of models, that is, all possible sequences of states. While a state formula can be evaluated at any individual state of a sequence, a temporal formula should be evaluated on the sequences. Each state s_i can be considered as a collection of predicates that have the value TRUE at s_i, or equivalently, as a mapping between variables and boolean values.

If $(\sigma, j) \vDash p$, we say the model $\sigma \in m$ *satisfies p at position j*; if a formula p holds at position 0 of a model σ, that is, $(\sigma, 0) \vDash p$, we write $\sigma \vDash p$ and say that the model σ *satisfies* the formula p; and if a formula p is satisfied in every model $\sigma \in m$, it is *valid*, and we write $m \vDash p$, or $\vDash p$ for short.

Formally, supposing $\sigma = s_0 s_1 s_2 s_3 \ldots$, the meaning of temporal formulae is defined as follows (read *iff* as "if and only if"):

- $(\sigma, j) \vDash p$ *iff* p is TRUE in s_j if p is a state formula;
- $(\sigma, j) \vDash \neg p$ *iff* it is not the case that $(\sigma, j) \vDash p$;
- $(\sigma, j) \vDash p \wedge q$ *iff* $(\sigma, j) \vDash p$ and $(\sigma, j) \vDash q$;
- $(\sigma, j) \vDash \Box p$ *iff* $(\sigma, k) \vDash p$ for every $k \geq j$;
- $(\sigma, j) \vDash \Diamond p$ *iff* $(\sigma, k) \vDash p$ for some $k \geq j$;
- $(\sigma, j) \vDash puq$ *iff* there is a $k \geq j$, such that $(\sigma, k) \vDash q$, and for every $i, j \leq i < k$, $(\sigma, i) \vDash p$;
- $(\sigma, j) \vDash pwq$ *iff* $(\sigma, j) \vDash puq$ or $(\sigma, j) \vDash \Box p$.

The operators $\Box$, $\Diamond$, u, and w are not all independent. Actually, we can use w as the only primitive operator and define:

$$\Box p \equiv pw \text{ FALSE}$$
$$\Diamond p \equiv \neg \Box \neg p$$
$$puq \equiv pwq \wedge \Diamond q$$

A deductive system consists of a set of axioms, say A, and a set of rewriting rules, called *inference rules*, which govern the deductive process. In other words, a deductive process is defined in purely syntactical terms. We do not deal with the issue of the *completeness* and *soundness* of a deductive system in this paper. We refer readers to the related papers (Kröger, 1987; Leeuwen, 1990; Manna & Pnueli, 1992; Rescher & Urquhart, 1971). For a temporal formula p, if we can find a sequence of rewritings from the axioms by a limited number of the applications of inference rules that leads to p (reasoning by syntax), it is called a *theorem*, and we can also be sure that it is valid provided that the deductive system is sound, that is, it is based on sound inference rules. We write $A \vdash p$, or simply $\vdash p$, to mean that p can be proven in our deductive system from a given set of A.

Here we list some of temporal logic axioms and inference rules. For more details, we refer readers to the corresponding papers (Gotzhein, 1992; Manna & Pnueli, 1992). Supposing p and q are temporal logic formulae, we write:

$$p \leftrightarrow q \text{ for } \Box [(p \rightarrow q) \wedge (q \rightarrow p)]$$

and

$$p \Rightarrow q \text{ for } \Box (p \rightarrow q)$$

where $p \rightarrow q$ means $\neg p \vee q$. $p \Rightarrow q$ is actually a stronger version of logic implication, which is known as *entailment*.

Some of general axioms of temporal logic are:

A0	axioms and tautologies of underlying logic
A1	$\Box p \Rightarrow p$
A2	$p \Rightarrow \Diamond p$
A3	$\Box \Box p \leftrightarrow \Box p$
A4	$\Diamond \Diamond p \leftrightarrow \Diamond p$
A5	$\Diamond \Box p \leftrightarrow \Box \Diamond p$
A6	$\Box \Diamond \Box p \leftrightarrow \Diamond \Box p$
A7	$\Box p \rightarrow p$
A8	$\Box(p \rightarrow q) \Rightarrow (\Box q \rightarrow \Box p)$
A9	$\Box p \Rightarrow pwq$

Inference rules are:

1. **Generalization (GEN):** For a state formula p which does not have any temporal

logic operators (i.e., it is satisfied in every state):

$$\frac{p}{\Box p}$$

2. **Specialization (SPEC):** For a state formula p:

$$\frac{\Box p}{p}$$

3. **Modus Ponens (MP):** For any formula p_1, ... , p_n and q:

$$\frac{(p_1 \wedge ... \wedge p_n) \rightarrow q, p_1, ..., p_n}{q}$$

4. **Entailment modus ponens (EMP):** For any formula p_1, ... , p_n and q:

$$\frac{(p_1 \wedge ... \wedge p_n) \Rightarrow q, \Box p_1, ..., \Box p_n}{\Box q}$$

5. **Entailment transitivity (ET):** For any formula p, q, and r:

$$\frac{p \Rightarrow q, q \Rightarrow r}{p \Rightarrow r}$$

6. $\Diamond$**T:** For any formula p, q, and r:

$$\frac{p \Rightarrow \Diamond q, q \Rightarrow \Diamond r}{p \Rightarrow \Diamond r}$$

FROM A MACH PROGRAM TO ITS TEMPORAL LOGIC FORMULAE

The logic proof system for a program consists of three parts: *the uninterpreted logic part, the domain part,* and *the program part* (Manna & Pnueli, 1983). The uninterpreted logic part is the general underlying logic system, which is the temporal logic discussed in the previous section. The domain part restricts the proof system to the related domains, for example, the axioms and theorems about integers, strings, trees, and so forth. The program part of the proof system further restricts the proof system to the acceptable computation sequences of this program.

To represent the program part of the proof system in temporal logic notations, we recast MACH programs to a 4-tuple, $P = (T, S, R, I)$, where

- T is the set of all tuples (data) possibly appearing in the tuple space. It is specified in the `tuples` section of a MACH program.
- S is the set of all possible tuple space states. Its purpose is twofold. On the one hand, an element of S can assign values to tuples or the variables contained in the tuples. In other words, it maps variables to their domains. On the other hand, the element designates the tuples currently in a tuple space. For any tuple $t \in T$, the characteristic function $C(t)$ = TRUE if t is currently present in the tuple space; otherwise $C(t)$ = FALSE. For simplicity, we write just t itself for $C(t)$ whenever there is no ambiguity.
- R $(R \subseteq S*S)$ is the set of reaction rules. The elements of R come from the `reaction-rules` section of an agent.
- I $(I \in S)$: the initial state of the tuple space, which is specified by the initialization section of a MACH program, for example, $I =$ {token, token, token}

A MACH deductive system consists of a set of axioms and a set of inference rules. Axioms come from the general axioms of the uninterpreted temporal logic, domain axioms (including fairness properties, etc.), and the axioms from a given MACH program. For any reaction rule, say:

$x_1, x_2, ..., x_n$ leadsto $y_1, y_2, ..., y_m$ by *Agent_T* when $f(x_1, x_2, ..., x_n)$

supposing the pre-condition and post-condition

of *Agent_T* are p and q, that is:

{p} Agent_T {q}

and there are no repetitive elements among x_1, $x_2, ..., x_n$, we have

$$(\bigwedge_{i=1}^{n} |x_i| \geq 1) \wedge f(x_1, x_2, ...x_n) \wedge p \Rightarrow$$

$$\Diamond [(\bigwedge_{i=1}^{n} |x_i|^{-1}) \wedge (\bigwedge_{j=1}^{m} |y_i|^{+1}) \wedge q]$$

where $|x|$ denotes the number of x tuples currently in the tuple space, and $|x|^{-t}$ means the number of tuple x has decreased by t in comparison to the former state (i.e., the state corresponding to the left hand side of the reaction rules), while $|y|^{-t}$ means that the population of tuple y is increased by t.

The Producer-Consumer Problem

To prove the correctness of producer-consumer (the first part of the fourth section), we first convert its MACH program in Figure 1 to temporal logic formulae, which will be used as additional axioms of the "producer-consumer" deductive system. The axioms, referred as A_{pc}, are:

$(\sigma, 0) \vDash (|token| = n) \wedge (|msg| = 0)$
$|token| > 0 \Rightarrow \Diamond (|token|^{-1} \wedge |msg|^{+1})$
$|msg| > 0 \Rightarrow \Diamond (|msg|^{-1} \wedge |token|^{+1})$

For the sake of brevity, we use variable prod to denote the producing action and cons to denote the consuming action. Thus, $\Diamond$ prod asserts there will be a producing action, i.e., transaction prod will be committed, and $\Diamond$ cons stands for a consuming action in the future.

Two main properties of the producer-consumer problem are *reactivity*, which means there always are producing or consuming actions, $\Box(\Diamond prod \wedge \Diamond cons)$, and *liveness*—every produced message (by transaction prod) will be eventually consumed (by transaction cons), that is, *prod*

$\Rightarrow \Diamond cons$. The two properties can certainly be represented by assertions on tuples `token` and `msg`, but it is natural to reason on the actions of *prod* and *cons*.

$$|\,\texttt{token}\,| > 0 \Rightarrow \Diamond (\,|\,\texttt{token}\,|^{-1} \wedge |\,\texttt{msg}\,|^{+1}\,)$$

thus is written as

$$|\,\texttt{token}\,| > 0 \Rightarrow \Diamond prod \text{ and}$$
$$prod \Rightarrow \Diamond (\,|\,\texttt{token}\,|^{-1} \wedge |\,\texttt{msg}\,|^{+1}\,)$$

Besides, from A_{pc}, we can also have "*the total number of* `token`s *and* `msg`s *is n*" that is:

$$A_{pc} \vdash \Box(\,|\,\texttt{Token}\,| + |\,\texttt{Msg}\,| = n),$$

which is also called an *axiom* in the following proof for brevity. Thus, we have the new set of axioms (see Box 1).

We can obtain (pc.2) by a simple calculation:

$$(|\,\texttt{Token}\,| + |\,\texttt{Msg}\,| = n) \Rightarrow$$
$$(|\,\texttt{Token}\,| > 0 \vee |\,\texttt{Msg}\,| > 0) \Rightarrow$$
$$\Diamond prod \vee \Diamond cons$$

Theorem 1 (reactivity of producer-consumer) There will always be prod or cons actions, that is, $\Box (\Diamond prod \vee \Diamond cons)$.

Proof:

1	$\Box(\,|\,\texttt{Token}\,| + |\,\texttt{Msg}\,| = n)$	(pc.1)
2	$(\,|\,\texttt{Token}\,| + |\,\texttt{Msg}\,| = n) \Rightarrow$ $\Diamond prod \vee \Diamond cons$	(pc.2)
3	$\Box (\Diamond prod \vee \Diamond cons)$	EMP, 1, 2

Theorem 2 (liveness of producer-consumer) Every produced message will be eventually consumed, or, in other words, every prod action will be followed by a cons action. $prod \Rightarrow \Diamond cons$.

Proof:

1	$prod \Rightarrow \Diamond (\,|\,\texttt{Msg}\,| > 0\,)$	(pc.3)
2	$(\,|\,\texttt{Msg}\,| > 0\,) \Rightarrow \Diamond cons$	(pc.5)
3	$prod \Rightarrow \Diamond cons$	$\Diamond$T, 1, 2

The Meeting Scheduler Problem

The goal of meeting scheduler, in the above section, is to find the minimum u such that $u = f(u) = g(u) = h(u)$. After `time` $= u$, the tuples F _ changed, G _ changed, and H _ changed are all set to FALSE and the program terminates. Let F _ changed denote to F _ changed = TRUE and ¬F _ changed to F _ changed = FALSE, so do (¬)G _ changed and (¬)H _ changed. From the program (Figure 2), we get what is shown in Box 2.

The correctness of the program relies on (i) the

Box 1.

$\Box(\,|\,\texttt{Token}\,| + |\,\texttt{Msg}\,| = n)$	(pc.1)
$(\,|\,\texttt{Token}\,| + |\,\texttt{Msg}\,| = n) \Rightarrow \Diamond prod \vee \Diamond cons$	(pc.2)
$prod \Rightarrow \Diamond (\,|\,\texttt{Msg}\,| > 0\,)$	(pc.3)
$cons \Rightarrow \Diamond (\,|\,\texttt{Token}\,| > 0\,)$	(pc.4)
$(\,|\,\texttt{Msg}\,| > 0\,) \Rightarrow \Diamond cons$	(pc.5)
$(\,|\,\texttt{Token}\,| > 0\,) \Rightarrow \Diamond prod$	(pc.6)

Box 2.

$(\sigma, 0) \vDash$ `time` $= 0 \wedge$ `F_changed` $=$ TRUE $\wedge$ `F_changed` $=$ TRUE $\wedge$ `F_changed` $=$ TRUE (ms.0)

`time` $= r \wedge$ (`G_changed` $\vee$ `H_changed`) $\Rightarrow \Diamond$ $\left[\begin{array}{c} (\text{time} = r \wedge \neg \text{F\_changed}) \\ \vee \\ (\text{time} = f(r) \wedge \text{F\_changed}) \end{array}\right]$ (ms.1)

`time` $= r \wedge$ (`F_changed` $\vee$ `H_changed`) $\Rightarrow \Diamond$ $\left[\begin{array}{c} (\text{time} = r \wedge \neg \text{G\_changed}) \\ \vee \\ (\text{time} = g(r) \wedge \text{G\_changed}) \end{array}\right]$ (ms.2)

`time` $= r \wedge$ (`F_changed` $\vee$ `G_changed`) $\Rightarrow \Diamond$ $\left[\begin{array}{c} (\text{time} = r \wedge \neg \text{H\_changed}) \\ \vee \\ (\text{time} = h(r) \wedge \text{H\_changed}) \end{array}\right]$ (ms.3)

program will terminate, that is, $\Diamond TC$, and (ii) the value of `time` will reach the value of u.

In the proofs of the following results, we just show the main steps and omit some of the trivial derivations.

Lemma 1 (`time` *non-decreasing) The value of* `time` *is non-decreasing: (*`time` $= r) \Rightarrow \Diamond$ *(*`time` $\geq r$*).*

Proof: (See Box 3.)

Theorem 3 (u reached) The value of `time` *will eventually reach the value of u:* $\Diamond$*(*`time` $= u$*)*

Proof:

1. $(\sigma, 0) \vDash$ `time` $= 0$, (given, ms.0);
2. (`time` $= r) \Rightarrow \Diamond$ (`time` $\geq r$), (Lemma 1), it is the same as $(\sigma, i) \vDash$ `time` $= r$ *iff* (σ, j) $\vDash$ `time` $\geq r$, *for some j, j ≥ i;*
3. `time` is monotonic and increasing, while u is limited. A position k can be found, such that $(\sigma, k) \vDash$ (`time` $= u$);
4. From $A2$ ($p \Rightarrow \Diamond p$), we have $\Diamond$(`time` $= u$).

Theorem 4 (termination) The termination condition will be eventually reached: $\Diamond TC$.

Proof: (See Box 4.)

Box 3.

1. From (ms.1) - (ms.3), we can get:

$$
\left(
\begin{array}{c}
\texttt{time} = r \wedge (\texttt{G\_changed} \vee \texttt{H\_changed}) \\
\vee \\
\texttt{time} = r \wedge (\texttt{F\_changed} \vee \texttt{H\_changed}) \\
\vee \\
\texttt{time} = r \wedge (\texttt{F\_changed} \vee \texttt{G\_changed})
\end{array}
\right) \Rightarrow
$$

$$
\Diamond \left(
\begin{array}{c}
(\texttt{time} = r \wedge \neg \texttt{F\_changed}) \vee (\texttt{time} = f(r) \wedge \texttt{F\_changed}) \\
\vee \\
(\texttt{time} = r \wedge \neg \texttt{G\_changed}) \vee (\texttt{time} = g(r) \wedge \texttt{G\_changed}) \\
\vee \\
(\texttt{time} = r \wedge \neg \texttt{H\_changed}) \vee (\texttt{time} = h(r) \wedge \texttt{H\_changed})
\end{array}
\right) ;
$$

Formula 5.4.1

2. The left side of Formula 5.4.1 can be reduced to

   $(\texttt{time} = r) \wedge (\texttt{F\_changed} \vee \texttt{G\_changed} \vee \texttt{H\_changed})$;

3. From the right side Formula 5.4.1 and the tautology of $p \wedge q \to p$, we get

   $(\texttt{time} = r) \vee (\texttt{time} = f(r) \vee \texttt{time} = g(r) \vee \texttt{time} = h(r))$;

   According to the definition of the functions f, g, and h, we have $f(r) > r$, $g(r) > r$, and $h(r) > r$. Thus, the new right side of Formula 5.4.1 is:

   $(\texttt{time} \geq r)$;

4. Formula 5.4.1 becomes

   $[(\texttt{time} = r) \wedge (\texttt{F\_changed} \vee \texttt{G\_changed} \vee \texttt{H\_changed})] \Rightarrow \Diamond (\texttt{time} \geq r)$;   (5.4.2)

5. Before time u is reached, i.e., $\texttt{time} = r, 0 \leq r \leq u$ at least one of $\texttt{F\_changed}$, $\texttt{G\_changed}$, and $\texttt{H\_changed}$ will be true:

   $(\texttt{time} = r) \Rightarrow \Diamond (\texttt{F\_changed} \vee \texttt{G\_changed} \vee \texttt{H\_changed})$;   (5.4.3)

6. Applying tautology $(p \to q) \leftrightarrow (p \to p \wedge q)$ to Formula 5.4.3, and with the definition of "$\Rightarrow$",

   $(\texttt{time} = r) \Rightarrow \Diamond [(\texttt{time} = r) \wedge (\texttt{F\_changed} \vee \texttt{G\_changed} \vee \texttt{H\_changed})]$;   (5.4.4)

7. Applying $\Diamond T$ to Formula 5.4.2 and Formula 5.4.4, we can get

   $(\texttt{time} = r) \Rightarrow \Diamond (\texttt{time} \geq r)$.

Box 4.

1.

> $(\texttt{time} = r) \wedge (\texttt{G\_changed} \vee \texttt{H\_changed}) \Rightarrow$
> $\Diamond\,[(\texttt{time} = r \wedge \neg\texttt{F\_changed}) \vee (\texttt{time} = f(r) \wedge \texttt{F\_changed})]$ (given, ms.1);

2. Referring the reasoning in the proof of Theorem 4, we get:

$$(\texttt{time} = r) \Rightarrow \Diamond[(\texttt{time} = r \wedge \neg\texttt{F\_changed}) \vee (\texttt{time} = f(r) \wedge \texttt{F\_changed})];$$

3. Before u has been reached, i.e., $0 \le r < u$, from Lemma 1:

$$(\texttt{time} = r) \Rightarrow \Diamond\,(\texttt{time} = f(r) \wedge \texttt{F\_changed});$$

4. When $\texttt{time} = u$,

$$(\texttt{time} = u) \Rightarrow \Diamond(\texttt{time} = r \wedge \neg\texttt{F\_changed}),\ \text{i.e.,}\ (\texttt{time} = u) \Rightarrow \Diamond\neg\texttt{F\_changed};$$

5. The same reasoning can give us

$$(\texttt{time} = u) \Rightarrow \Diamond\neg\texttt{G\_changed} \wedge (\texttt{time} = u) \Rightarrow \Diamond\neg\texttt{H\_changed};$$

6. Put the three formulae together, we get

$$(\texttt{time} = u) \Rightarrow \Diamond(\neg\texttt{F\_changed} \wedge \neg\texttt{G\_changed} \wedge \neg\texttt{H\_changed});$$

7. From Theorem 5 and the rule of $\Diamond T$, we have

$$\Diamond(\neg\texttt{F\_changed} \wedge \neg\texttt{G\_changed} \wedge \neg\texttt{H\_changed});$$

The Auction Problem

The proof system for the auction problem is almost the same as that of the meeting scheduler problem. We start with the proof of *price non-decreasing*, *final price reached*, and then *bidding termination*. Due to the limit of the pages, we won't repeat the proof processes.

CONCLUSION AND FUTURE WORK

This chapter proposed a new programming language called *MACH* (multi-agent extended chemical abstract machine). It is based on the chemical abstract machine model with the extension of multiple agents. MACH can, on the one hand, take the advantage of the simplicity chemical abstract machine). It is based on the chemical abstract machine model with the extension of multiple agents. MACH can, on the one hand, take the advantage of the simplicity of Cham control structures, and, on the other hand, with the help of conventional programming languages, be efficiently implemented on current computer architectures. MACH is also carefully designed to meet the requirement of easy formal verification. MACH keeps the theoretical part of the language in background. It can be ignored, but it is there and ready to use. We expect that MACH can lead us to a new way of separating (i) the logic of a program from its implementation, (ii) correctness from efficiency, and (iii) the rigid formal reasoning aspect from a comfortable intuitive presentation, without heavy penalties on execution efficiency.

ACKNOWLEDGMENT

This research work is supported by the divisional grants from the *Division of Business, Law and Information Sciences, University of Canberra, Australia*, and the university grants from *University of Canberra, Australia*.

REFERENCES

Ahuja, S., Carriero, N., & Gelernter, D. (1986). Linda and friends. *IEEE Computer*, 26-34.

Banâtre, J. P. (1996). Parallel multiset processing: From explicit coordination to chemical reaction. In P. Ciancarini & C. Hankin (Eds.), *Coordination languages and models, first international conference, COORDINATION'96* (pp. 1-11). Springer-Verlag.

Banâtre, J. P., Coutant, A., & Métayer, D. L. (1988). A parallel machine for multiset transformation and its programming style. *Future Generation Computer System, 4*, 133-144.

Banâtre, J. P., & Métayer, D. L. (1990). The GAMMA model and its discipline of programming. *Science of Computer Programming, 15*, 55-77.

Banâtre, J. P., & Métayer, D. L. (1993). Programming by multiset transformation. *Communications ACM, 36*(1), 98-111.

Berry, G., & Boudol, G. (1992). The chemical abstract machine. *Theoretical Computer Science, 96*, 217-248.

Boudol, G. (1993). Some chemical abstract machines. In J. W. d. Bakker, W. P. d. Roever & G. Rozenberg (Eds.), *A decade of concurrency: Reflections and perspectives* (pp. 92-123). Springer-Verlag.

Bradshaw, J. M. (1997). An introduction to software agents. In J. M. Bradshaw (Ed.), *Software agents* (pp. 3-46). AAAI Press/The MIT Press.

Braubach, L., Pokahr, A., & Lamersdorf W. (2005). Jadex: A BDI Agent System Combining Middleware and Reasoning. In M. Klusch, R. Unland, & M. Calisti (Eds.), *Software agent-based applications, platforms and development kits*. Birkhäuser.

Carriero, N., & Gelernter, D. (1989). Linda in context. *Communication ACM, 32*(4), 444-458.

Carriero, N., Gelernter, D., Mattson, T., & Sherman, A. (1994). The Linda alternative to message-passing systems. *Parallel Computing, 20*, 632-655.

Clarke, E., Grumberg, O., & Long, D. (1993). Verification tools for finite-state concurrent systems. In J. W. de Bakker, W. P. d. Roever, & G. Rozenberg (Eds.), *A decade of concurrency: Reflections and perspectives* (pp. 125-175). Springer-Verlag.

Clarke, E. M., Grumberg, O., & Hiraishi, H. (1993). Verifying of the Futurebus+ cache coherence Protocol. In L. Claesen (Ed.), *Proceedings of the Eleventh International Symposium on Computer Hardware Description Languages and Their Applications.* North-Holland.

Cohen, R., & Molinari, B. (1991). Implementation of C-Linda for the AP1000. Proceedings of the 2nd ANU/Fujitsu CAP Workshop.

Cooke, D. J., & Bez, H. E. (1984). *Computer mathematics.* Cambridge: Cambridge University Press.

Curry, H. B. (1963). *Foundations of mathematical logic.* McGraw-Hill.

Dahl, O.-J., Dijkstra, E. W., & Hoare, C. A. R. (1972). *Structured programming.* Academic Press.

Dennis, J. B., Gao, G. R., & Todd, K. W. (1984). Modeling the weather with dataflow supercomputers. *IEEE Transactions on Computer, 33,* 592-603.

Dennis, J. B., & Misunas, D. P. (1975). A preliminary architecture for a basic dataflow processor. *Proceedings of 2nd Symposium on Computer Architectures* (pp. 126-132).

Dijkstra, E. W. (1976). *A discipline of programming.* Prentice-Hall.

Gelernter, D., & Carriero, N. (1992). Coordination languages and their significance. *Communication ACM, 35,* 96-107.

Gordon, M. J. C. (1979). *The denotational description of programming languages: An introduction.* Springer-Verlag.

Gotzhein, R. (1992). Temporal logic and application: A tutorial. *Computer Networks and ISDN Systems, 24,* 203-218.

Hankin, C., Métayer, D. L., & Sands, D. (1992). *A calculus of GAMMA programs.* Springer-Verlag.

Harel, D., & Pnueli, A. (1985). On the development of reactive systems. In K. R. Apt (Ed.), *Logics and models of concurrent systems* (pp. 477-498). Springer-Verlag.

Hewitt, C. (1977). Viewing control structures as patterns of passing messages. *Artificial Intelligence, 8*(3), 323-364.

Jennings, N. R. (2000). On agent-based software engineering. *Artificial Intelligence, 117,* 277-296.

Kröger, F. (1987). *Temporal logic of programs.* Springer-Verlag.

Lamport, L. (1993). Verification and specification of concurrent programs. In J. W. d. Bakker, W. P. d. Rover, & G. Rozenberg (Eds.), *A decade of concurrency: Reflections and perspectives* (pp. 347-374). Springer-Verlag.

Leeuwen, J. V. (1990). *Handbook of theoretical computer science: Formal models and semantics* (Vol. B). Elsevier, The MIT Press.

Lloyd, J. W. (1987). *Foundations of logic programming.* Springer Verlag.

Ma, W., Johnson, C. W., & Brent, R. P. (1996a). Concurrent programming in T-Cham. In K. Ramamohanarao (Ed.), *Proceedings of the 19th Australasian Computer Science Conference (ACSC'96),* (pp. 291-300).

Ma, W., Johnson, C. W., & Brent, R. P. (1996b). Programming with transactions and chemical abstract machine. In G.-J. Li, D. F. Hsu, S. Horiguchi, & B. Maggs (Eds.), *Proceedings of Second International Symposium on Parallel Architectures, Algorithms, and Networks (I-SPAN'96)* (pp. 562-564).

Ma, W., Krishnamurthy, E. V., & Orgun, M. A. (1994). On providing temporal semantics for the GAMMA programming Model. In C. B. Jay (Ed.), *CATS: Proceedings of computing: The Australian Theory Seminar* (pp. 121-132). Sydney, Australia: University of Technology.

Ma, W., & Orgun, M. (1996). Verifying multran programs with temporal logic. In M. Orgun & E. Ashcroft (Eds.), *Intensional programming I* (pp. 186-206). World-Scientific.

Ma, W., Orgun, M. A., & Johnson, C. W. (1998). Towards a temporal semantics for frame. *Proceedings SEKE'98, Tenth International Conference on Software Engineering and Knowledge Engineering* (pp. 44-51).

Manna, Z., & Pnueli, A. (1983). How to cook a temporal proof system for your pet language. *Proceedings of 10th Ann. ACM Symp. on Principles of Programming Language* (pp. 141-154).

Manna, Z., & Pnueli, A. (1992). *The temporal logic of reactive and concurrent systems: Specification.* Springer-Verlag.

Nwana, H. S. (1996). Software agents: An overview. *Knowledge Engineering Review, 11*(3), 1-40.

Orgun, M., & Ma, W. (1994). An overview of temporal and modal logic programming. In D. M. Gabbay & H. J. Ohlbach (Eds.), *The first international conference on temporal logic* (pp. 445-479). Springer-Verlag.

Perini, A., Pistore, M., Roveri, M., & Susi, A. (2003, 2004). *Agent-oriented modeling by interleaving formal and informal specification.* Paper presented at the 4th International Workshop on agent-oriented software engineering, (AOSE 2003), Melbourne, Australia (LNCS 2935).

Petrie, C. (2001). *Agent-based software engineering.* Paper presented at The First International Workshop on agent-oriented software engineering, (AOSE2000), (LNCS 1957).

Rao, A. S., & Georgeff, M. P. (1995). *BDI agents: From theory to practice.* Australian Artificial Intelligence Institute.

Rescher, N., & Urquhart, A. (1971). *Temporal logic.* Springer-Verlag.

Shoham, Y. (1993). Agent-oriented programming. *Artificial Intelligence, 60*(1), 51-92.

Srini, V. P. (1986). An architecture comparison of dataflow systems. *Computer,* 68-88.

Stone, P., & Veloso, M. M. (2000). Multiagent systems: A survey from a machine learning perspective. *Autonomous Robots, 8*(3), 345-383.

Stoy, J. E. (1977). *Denotational semantics: The Scott-Strachey approach to programming language theory.* The MIT Press.

Winikoff, M., Padgham, L., Harland, J., & Thangarajah, J. (2002, April 22-25). Declarative & procedural goals in intelligent agent systems. Paper presented at the *Proceedings of the 8th International Conference on Principles and Knowledge Representation and Reasoning (KR-02),* Toulouse, France.

Wooldridge, M. (2000). *Reasoning about rational agents.* Cambridge, MA: The MIT Press.

Wooldridge, M., & Ciancarini, P. (2001). *Agent-oriented software engineering: The sate of the art.* Paper presented at The First International Workshop on agent-oriented software engineering, (AOSE2000), (LNCS 1957).

Wooldridge, M., & Jennings, N. R. (1995). Intelligent agent: Theory and practice. *Knowledge Engineering Review, 10*(2), 115-152.

Zenith, S. E. (1991). A rationale for programming with ease. In J. P. Banâtre & D. L. Mètayer (Eds.), *Research directions in high-level parallel programming languages* (pp. 147-156). Springer-Verlag.

Chapter III
Coalition Formation Among Agents in Complex Problems Based on a Combinational Auction Perspective

Hiromitsu Hattori
Nagoya Institute of Technology, Japan

Tadachika Ozono
Nagoya Institute of Technology, Japan

Toramatsu Shintani
Nagoya Institute of Technology, Japan

ABSTRACT

This chapter focuses on a scheduling problem that considers various constraints as a complex real-world problem. Constraints on scheduling can be expressed as combinations of items (time slots) in a combinatorial auction. Agents bid for necessary combinations of time slots to satisfy users' preferences. We formalize a combinatorial auction for scheduling as an MIP (mixed integer programming) problem, which integrates the constraints on items and bids to express complex problems. This integration solves the trade-off between the computation time to find the solution and the expressiveness to represent a scheduling problem. This chapter presents a new formalization of a combinatorial auction with constraints. We have experimentally confirmed that our method can obtain a socially preferable schedule in practical time.

INTRODCUTION

Auctions have been studied in the field of electronic commerce (EC). Various studies on auctions have already been made, and many protocols and methods have been developed (Ito, Yokoo, Matsubara, & Iwasaki, 2005; Parkes & Kalagnanam, 2005; Sakurai, Yokoo, & Kamei, 2000). An auction also can be a promising method for coalition formation among agents. The purpose of our work is to apply auction protocols and methods developed in EC studies to a coalition formation.

We focus on a scheduling problem considering various constraints as a complex problem. This is because the scheduling problem is a kind of resource allocation problem, and combinatorial auction is compatible with kinds of resource allocation problem. We are currently attempting to construct a scheduling system based on multi-agents. In our system, each agent makes bids based on users' preferences on events. Agents must determine a consistent schedule by resolving conflicts among agents. To construct the system, we must propose appropriate problem formalization and methods for finding an optimal solution. In this chapter, we formalize a scheduling problem as a combinatorial auction. An appropriate schedule can be obtained by solving the winner determination problem in a combinatorial auction. A combinatorial auction protocol (Sandholm, 1999) is one of the most notable auction protocols for dealing with preferences over multiple items. The winner determination problem is one of determining the optimal allocation of items that can maximize the auctioneer's revenue. The winner determination problem is a complicated optimization problem, so it can be re-defined as a scheduling problem. When a scheduling problem is formalized as a constraint satisfaction problem (CSP), like in some existing studies (Tsuruta & Shintani, 2000), we need particular methods to relax over-constrained problems. On the other hand, because of the formalization as a combinatorial auction, we can obtain a socially preferable solution according to an economical rationality without having to use such particular methods.

The basic idea behind our formalization is that a scheduling is compared to an auction for winning time slots. This perspective is intuitively and easily understandable for users. In our formalization, a schedule can be represented as combinations of items (time slots) in a combinatorial auction. Agents bid for necessary combinations of time slots to satisfy users' preferences. In this chapter, we try to deal with various constraints, *for example*, the date and time, participants, the order of events, and the interval of events. The greater the variations of bids considering some constraints becomes, the more time-consuming the computation time for finding a solution becomes. Nevertheless, decreasing the number of bids reduces the expressiveness of representing a scheduling problem. Therefore, we formalize a combinatorial auction for scheduling as an MIP (mixed integer programming) problem, which integrates the constraints on items and bids to express complex problems. This integration solves the trade-off between the computation time to find a solution for a combinatorial auction and the expressiveness to represent a scheduling problem. We conducted experiments with limited discrepancy search (LDS) and MIP solver to confirm that our method is useful to obtain a semi-optimal schedule within practical time.

A combinatorial auction is appropriate for adjustment of time slots. Considering each time slot as an item, we can use a combinatorial auction protocol to effectively deal with events, each of which needs sequential multiple time slots. Without the dealing with combination of items, an agent might obtain multiple time slots that do not increase his/her utility by obtaining them simultaneously. For example, Rassenti, Smith, and Bulfin (1982) use a combinatorial auction protocol to determine arrival and departure times of airplanes. In this work, each time needs sequential multiple time slots. Because a combinatorial auction allows complementary preferences over multiple time slots to be explicitly represented, *that is*, sequential time slots are worthy and distributed ones are worthless, time slots can be efficiently allocated to each airplane.

The rest of this chapter is organized as follows. In the next section, we describe the outline of a combinatorial auction. In the third section, we propose our basic formalization that represents a scheduling problem as a combinatorial auction. In the fourth section, we describe the formalization based on an MIP. In the fifth section, we experimentally evaluate a scheduling based on our formalization and outline our multi-agent-based group scheduling system. Then, we discuss related work. Finally, we make some concluding remarks.

COMBINATORIAL AUCTION

In a combinatorial auction (Sandholm, 1999), bidders can bid on combinations of items. This allows the bidders to express their valuations of items instead of having to estimate others' valuations. The items are assigned in order to maximize the auctioneer's revenue. A combinatorial auction protocol can increase both the bidders' utility and the auctioneer's utility.

To find a revenue-maximizing allocation, the auctioneer must solve the winner determination problem (i.e., the problem of determining what items each bidder gets). Let G denote a set of items and A denote a set of bidders. The highest bid for a combination of items S is defined as:

$$\bar{b}(S) = \max_{i \in A} b_i(S) \qquad (0.1)$$

where $b_i(S)$ represents bidder i's bidding on the combination $S \subseteq G$. Then, the optimal allocation of items is the solution of the following formula:

$$\arg\max_{\chi} \sum_{S \in \chi} \bar{b}(S) \qquad (0.2)$$

where χ is defined as follows:

$$\chi = \{S \subseteq G \mid S \cap S' = \emptyset \ for\ every\ S, S' \in \chi\} \qquad (0.3)$$

Namely, χ is a set of allocations of items, and an identical item has never been in combinations included in χ.

SOLVING A SCHEDULING PROBLEM AS A COMBINATORIAL AUCTION

Definition of Scheduling Problem

We deal with a scheduling problem, which consists of several events (e.g., meeting scheduling, computer resource sharing, and others). During scheduling, it is necessary to adjust each agent's schedule, *that is*, agents must stagger the start and the end time of events or cancel some of them. For a scheduling, each agent declares constraints and a valuation for each event. We consider three constraints on each event: (1) a list of participants, (2) the length, and (3) the duration of an event. Namely, the start time of an event is not fixed.

In this chapter, each participant and resource (e.g., meeting room, classroom) is represented as r, and a set of them is represented as $R = \{r_1, r_2, \ldots\}$. For simplicity, the word "resource" is used to represent a participant (agent) and resource. The schedule of each resource consists of some time slots, each of which is a unit of the schedule. For example, when we assume one time slot means one hour in the real world, one day is represented as a set of 24 time slots. Each time slot is denoted as t_i. The time goes by in the increasing order of i, that is, t_1 is preceded by t_2. The j-th time slot of resource r_i is specially denoted by t_{ij}. Let T_j be a set of j-th time slots for all resources and $T_j\{r_1, r_1, r_k\}$ be a set of j-th time slots of resources r_1, $r_2, \ldots, r_k$.

Fixing event means that a certain agent, which is a host of an event, wins some required time slots. Assuming that a certain agent wants to hold a meeting with three other agents from 14:00 to 15:00, the host must win one time slot "14:00-15:00" of the others and the meeting room, simultaneously. That is to say, winning time slot t_{ij} means to purchase the right to restrict r_i during the duration t_{ij}. r_i's schedule E_i is denoted as follows:

$$E_i = \{e_{i1}, e_{i2}, ..., e_{in}\} (n \geq 0)$$
$$e_{ij} = (T_{ij}, R_{ij}, v_{ij}) \qquad (0.4)$$

where e_{ij} denotes each event and is distinguished by parameters, T_{ij}, R_{ij}, and v_{ij}. T_{ij} is a set of constraints on time and is represented using logic symbols; it includes the start time T_{ij}^0, the end time T_{ij}^1, and the length of the event, $T_{ij}^1 - T_{ij}^0$. For example, when the start time is between time-point t_a and t_b, the end time is between time-point t_c and t_d, and the length is between l_0 and l_1, the constraint on time is represented as:

$$T_{ij} = (t_a \leq T_{ij}^0 \leq t_b) \wedge (t_c \leq T_{ij}^1 \leq t_d)$$
$$\wedge (l_0 \leq T_{ij}^1 - T_{ij}^0 \leq l_1).$$

R_{ij} denotes a set of resources for e_{ij}; it is a subset of R, i.e., $R_{ij} \subseteq R$. v_{ij} is the valuation for e_{ij}.

In addition to constraints of each event, we deal with constraints among multiple events. To put it concretely, "number constraint" and "order constraint" is introduced. The number constraint is for selecting m events from n events. Given that E is a set of all events, the number constraint is represented as $|E_0'| = m$, $|E_0| = n$, and $E_0' \subseteq E_0 \subseteq E$. This constraint enables exclusivity among events to be expressed. The order constraint is for specifying an order and an interval between two events. For example, the order constraint $e_{i1} < e_{i2}$ means that the end time of e_{i1} is l slots ahead of the start time of e_{i2}.

Formalization of a Scheduling Problem as a Combinatorial Auction

In this section, we formalize the scheduling problem described in Section three as a combinatorial auction. A time slot is regarded as an item in an auction. A bid is placed for a set of time slots that is required by a certain event. Note that one event may generate multiple alternative sets of time slots. When an event requires two sequential time slots from t_{i0}, t_{i1}, and t_{i2}, for example, there are two possible alternatives, *that is*, $\{t_{i0}, t_{i1}\}$ and $\{t_{i1}, t_{i2}\}$. A set of alternative sets of time slots is denoted by $AT_{ij} = \{AT_{ij}^1, AT_{ij}^2, ..., AT_{ij}^k\}$, where AT_{ij}^k denotes the k-th alternative for e_{ij}. Since agents can bid for all possible combinations in a combinatorial auction, detailed preferences concerning the time and date of an event can be represented.

To represent the bid, possible combinations of items are enumerated and a valuation is allocated to each of them. A set of combinations of items, S_i, that agent r_i bids for is as follows:

$$S_i = \bigcup_{j|e_{ij} \in E_i} S_{ij} \qquad (0.5)$$
$$S_{ij} = \{S_{ij}^1, S_{ij}^2, ..., S_{ij}^k\}$$
$$S_{ij}^k = \left(\bigcup_{l|t_{il} \in AT_{ij}^k} T_{lR_j} \right) \cup \{d_{ij}\}$$

The event d_{ij} is a dummy item to express exclusivity among alternatives for identical events. S_{ij} is a set of alternatives for e_{ij}. A certain alternative S_{ij}^k consists of a dummy item and time slots for resources R_j which are restricted by S_{ij}^k. For instance, a certain event $e_{ij} = ((one\ slot\ from\ \{t_1, t_2\}), \{r_1, r_2\}, 100)$ generates a set of alternatives $\{\{t_{11}, t_{21}, d_{ij}\}, \{t_{12}, t_{22}, d_{ij}\}\}$. The allocation of the valuation enables various preferences to be represented. If an agent wants to hold an event e_{ij} earlier, it should set the difference in valuation between two bids, *that is*, a bidding price for $\{t_{11}, t_{21}, d_{ij}\}$ is 110 and for $\{t_{12}, t_{22}, d_{ij}\}$ is 100.

The final schedule is a solution of the following formula:

$$\arg \max_{\chi} \sum_{j|S_{ij} \in \chi} v_{ij} \qquad (0.6)$$

Here, χ is defined as follows:

$$\chi = \{S_{ij} \subseteq S_i \mid S_{ij} \cap S' = \\ \varnothing \text{ for every } S_{ij}, S' \in \chi\} \qquad (0.7)$$

The solution can be obtained by using various search techniques. In our work, we adopted the LDS (Harvey & Ginsberg, 1995) and used the algorithm described in Sakurai et al. (2000) because it can quickly search for a high-quality solution.

INTRODUCTION OF CONSTRAINTS TO COMBINATORIAL AUCTION

To represent the number and order constraint based on the formalization described in the previous section, we must enumerate all possible combinations that take such constraints into consideration. As a result, when we express detailed preferences, the computation time for obtaining an appropriate solution increases exponentially since there is a dramatic increase in the number of combinations of items. Therefore, another way to express constraints among multiple events, without having to enumerate combinations, is needed. In this section, we try to express a combinatorial auction as a mixed integer programming problem to avoid explosive increases in combinations of items.

Formalization of a Combinatorial Auction as an MIP Problem

First, we formalize a combinatorial auction as an MIP problem according to AndersonTenhunen, and Ygge *(2000)*. It is assumed that there are *m*

items denoted by $M = \{g_1, g_2, ..., g_m\}$ and *n* bids denoted by $B = \{b_1, b_2, ..., b_n\}$. The bid is denoted by $b_i = \langle S_i, p_i \rangle$, where S_i is a set of items and $S_i \subseteq M$; p_i is a bidding price for S_i and $p_i \geq 0$. The winner determination problem in a combinatorial auction can be formalized as follows:

$$\max \sum_{i=1}^{n} p_i x_i$$

$$\sum_{i|g_j \in S_i} x_i \leq 1, g_j \in M \qquad (0.8)$$

$$x_i \in \{0, 1\}$$

If b_i wins, $x_i = 1$, if not, $x_i = 0$. Namely, to obtain the solution, the agent should solve the above problem and regard b_i as a winning bid when $x_i = 1$.

Representation of Number Constraint

The number constraint is represented such that the number of winning bids must be $n'_0 (n'_0 \leq n_0)$ or less for a set of n_0 bids $B_0 \subseteq B$. The definition is given as:

$$\sum_{i|b_i \in B_0} x_i \leq n_0' \qquad (0.9)$$

The number constraint is useful for managing the exclusivity of bids that are generated from an identical event. The variation of bids for a certain event *e* is denoted as $B_e = \{b_{ei} \mid b_{ei} \text{ is a bid for event } e, b_{ei} \in B\}$. The number constraint for exclusivity is represented as follows:

$$\sum_{i|b_{ei} \in B_e} x_i + x_{B_e} = 1 \qquad (0.10)$$

Here, if all bids included in B_e do not win, $x_{B_e} = 1$, and if not, $x_{B_e} = 0$. Though it is possible to represent the constraint without x_{B_e}, *that is,*

$\sum_{i|b_{ei} \in B_e} x_i \leq 1$ is required in order to represent the order constraint.

Representation of Number Constraint

The order constraint is one for describing the order of multiple events and the interval between them. In this section, an example case regarding the order and interval between two events, e_1 and e_2, is given. It is assumed that $e_1 < e_2$; that is, the end time of e_1 is l slots ahead of the start time of e_2. B_{e_1} and B_{e_2} are a set of bids for events e_1 and e_2, respectively. Let $t_{b_i}^0$ be the start time of event e required by b_i and $t_{b_i}^1$ be its end time required by b_i.

$$f = -\sum_{i|b_i \in B_{e_1}} t_{b_i}^1 x_i + \sum_{i|b_i \in B_{e_2}} t_{b_i}^0 x_i \geq l \quad (0.11)$$

If either bid for both events does not win, equation will not be satisfied. For example, when a bid for e_1 wins the item and a bid for e_2 does not win:

$$-\sum_{i|b_i \in B_{e_1}} t_{b_i}^1 x_i \leq 0 \quad and \quad \sum_{i|b_i \in B_{e_2}} t_{b_i}^0 x_i = 0 \quad (0.12)$$

Accordingly, equation is not satisfied. To solve this problem, we use the following equation:

$$f + (\max\{t_{b_i}^1 \mid b_i \in B_{e_1}\} + l) x_{B_{e_2}} \geq l \quad (0.13)$$

Even if:

$$\sum_{i|b_i \in B_{e2}} t_{b_{ij}}^0 x_j = 0,$$

equation will be satisfied since $x_{B_{e_2}} = 1$ according to equation.

We can set the minimum interval l_{min} and maximum interval l_{max} by describing the interval between events as $l_{min} \leq f \leq l_{max}$. For instance, considering two events e_1 and e_2, which require one time slot from t_1, t_2, and t_3 and same participants, we represent the order constraint for these two events. Moreover, e_2 is preceded by e_1 and $l_{min} = 1$ *slot*. In this case, the constraint is described as follows:

$$-x_{11} - 2x_{12} - 3x_{13} + x_{21} + 2x_{22} + 3x_{23} + 4x_{B_{e_2}} \geq 1$$

$$\sum_{i|b_i \in B_{e_1}}^{3} x_{1i} \leq 1, \quad \sum_{i|b_i \in B_{e_2}}^{3} x_{2i} + x_{B_{e_2}} = 1$$

$x_{11}, x_{12}, x_{13} :$ *the variables for* e_1

$x_{21}, x_{22}, x_{23} :$ *the variables for* e_2

$$(0.14)$$

Formalization of a Combinatorial Auction with Constraints

A combinatorial auction can be formalized regarding some combinations of items and all constraints.

$$\max \sum_{i=1}^{n} p_i x_i$$

$$\sum_{i|t_j \in S_i} x_i \leq 1, t_j \in M = \{t_1, t_2, .., t_m\}$$

$$x_i \in \{0,1\}$$

$$c_{11}x_1 + ... + e_{1n}x_n + x_{n+1} = 1$$

$$c_{d1}x_1 + ... + e_{dn}x_n + x_{n+d} = 1$$

$$t_{11}x_1 + ... + t_{1n}x_n + t_{1n+1}x_{n+1} \geq l_1$$

$$...$$

$$t_{r1}x_1 + ... + t_{rn}x_n + t_{rn+1}x_{n+r} \geq l_r$$

$$c_{ij} = \begin{cases} 1 & b_i \in B_{e_i} \\ 0 & otherwise \end{cases}$$

$$t_{ij} = \begin{cases} t_{b_i}^1 & b_i \text{ is a bid for a precedent event} \\ t_{b_i}^0 & otherwise \end{cases}$$

$$(0.15)$$

Figure 1. A scheduling problem based on our formalization

	Bids for e_1 $[Be_1]$			Bids for e_2 $[Be_2]$					
	b_{11}	b_{12}	b_{13}	b_{21}	b_{22}	b_{23}	x_{Be_1}	x_{Be_2}	Const.
t_1	x_{11}			x_{21}					≤ 1
t_2		x_{12}			x_{22}				≤ 1
t_3			x_{13}			x_{23}			≤ 1
XOR	x_{11}	x_{12}	x_{13}				x_{Be_1}		$= 1$
				x_{21}	x_{22}	x_{23}		x_{Be_2}	$= 1$
Order	$-1 \cdot x_{11}$	$-2 \cdot x_{12}$	$-3 \cdot x_{13}$	$1 \cdot x_{21}$	$2 \cdot x_{22}$	$3 \cdot x_{23}$		$4 \cdot x_{Be_2}$	≥ 1

According to the above formalization, constraints on the number of items, exclusivity of bids, and the order of events can be represented. The purpose is to maximize the sum of the valuations of successful bids.

Figure 1 shows a simple example that represents a scheduling problem based on our formalization. In this example, we assume that there are events e_1 and e_2 ($e_1 < e_2$), each of which require one time slot from t_1, t_2, t_3. The variation of bids for events e_1 and e_2 are denoted as $B_{e_1} = \{b_{11}, b_{12}, b_{13}\}$ and $B_{e_2} = \{b_{21}, b_{22}, b_{23}\}$, respectively. Each of the columns indicates variables with respect to a bid excepting the two columns on the right. The first three rows (t_1, t_2, t_3) indicate the status of each time slot. For instance, variable x_{11} is required by bid b_{11}. Each of these three rows is constrained according to the formalization, that is "≤ 1". The forth and fifth rows (combined as row "*XOR*"), are used to deal with the number constraints, more specially exclusive. Here, the value of variables $x_{B_{e_2}}$ and $x_{B_{e_1}}$ is set according to equation, *that is*, if $x_{11} + x_{12} + x_{13} = 1$, $x_{B_{e_1}} = 0$. Thus, even if all the bids for event e_1 cannot win, the fourth row can satisfy the constraint. Here, according to equation, the coefficient of $x_{B_{e_2}}$ is the sum of the maximum number of time slots "3" and interval "1". Given

that b_{12} and b_{21} are accepted, the values of x_{11}, $x_{12}, x_{13}, x_{21}, x_{22}, x_{23}, x_{B_{e_1}}$, and $x_{B_{e_2}}$ can be set to 0, 1, 0, 1, 0, 0, 0, and 0, respectively. In this case, the order constraint is not satisfied, since $(-1 \times 0) + (-2 \times 1) + (-3 \times 0) + (1 \times 1) + (2 \times 0) + (3 \times 0) + (4 \times 0) \ngeq 1$. Thus, our formalization can represent that b_{12} and b_{21} are never accepted simultaneously. In the end, solving a scheduling problem comes down to finding the value of each variable that can satisfy all constraints, while the sum of valuations of successful bids must be maximized. To solve the problem represented in the form of a variable table like Figure 1, we use the MIP solver offered by GLPK (GNU Linear Programming Kit).

DISCUSSION

Formalization of a Combinatorial Auction with Constraints

Our scheduling method was experimentally evaluated in terms of the computation time, the valuation, and the satisfaction rate. Satisfaction rate means the ratio of won events to all desired events. The number of time slots per agent was set to 40 (the sum of normal working hours in a week).

The scheduling problem was generated randomly under uniform distribution. Though the number of participants and the length of every event were fixed, the start times were unfixed. But the possible time range in which an event could begin was constrained. In the problem-generation process, firstly, several private events were generated for each agent. Each private event could not be shared with other agents. The number of private events was set to 10. In this experiment, private events were not in conflict. Namely, if there was only one agent, it could determine a consistent schedule, including all its private events. Secondly, several events that were shared by multiple agents were generated. The number of events that were shared by two and three agents is 10; moreover, 10 events shared by agents of which the number was from 4 to 20 were randomly generated. Finally, the possible time range for the start time and the length of each event were set randomly. The length was determined according to the settled ratio, *that is*, [1:2:3] = ration [50%:33%:17%].

For each number of agents, we generated 10 problem instances where we varied the number of agents from 2 to 50. The problem was solved in two ways: using the LDS method based on the formalization described in the third section and using the MIP solver based on the formalization described in the fourth section. Because solving a problem by using an MIP solver takes a lot of time, the calculation was terminated 1,800 seconds (30 minutes) after. The best solution at that time was used.

The results of the experiments are shown in Figure 2, Figure 3, and Figure 4. All experiments were performed on a Power Mac G4 (PowerPC G4 1GHz, 512MB) with a program written in Java and C.

Figure 2 shows the computation time using LDS. This figure indicates that our method enables the largest problem to be solved in practical time. Although there are 50 agents in the largest problem, the computation time is about 210 seconds. This is sufficiently acceptable for use in practical scheduling systems.

Figure 3 shows the valuation using LDS, the MIP solver, and the LP (linear programming) solver, which can obtain an optimal solution. In our experiments, the MIP solver can achieve better than 95% of the optimal solution through LP. Since the solution is calculated within a real number in LP, a unit of the schedule would be divided in the solution, *for example*, "an event e_{ij} can be held during 2.5 time slots." Then, practically, it

Figure 2. Computation time over the number of agents using LDS

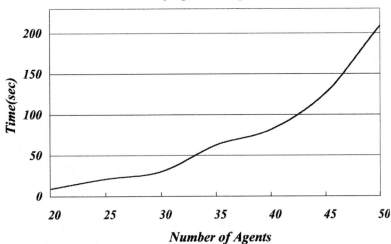

Figure 3. Valuation over number of agents (MIP: 1800 sec.)

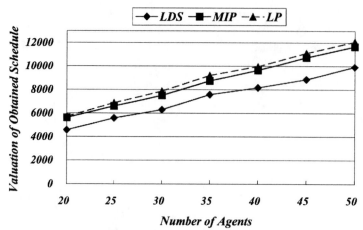

Figure 4. Satisfaction rate over number of agents (MIP: 1800 sec.)

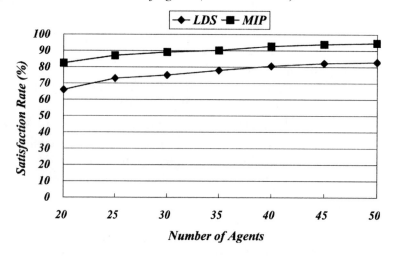

is impossible to use the solution obtained by LP. Generally, the valuation of possible optimal solutions is between the valuation of the MIP solution and LP solution. Therefore, we can consider that the MIP solution is almost optimal. Moreover, the LDS method can always achieve about 80% of the MIP solution. Figure 4 shows the satisfaction rate using the LDS method and MIP solver. As shown in this figure, the MIP solver can achieve a sufficient rate to use in practical scheduling. The LDS method can also achieve a high rate in all problem sets, but it is insufficient compared with

the rate using the MIP solver. In Figure 4, as the number of agents increases, the satisfaction rate rises. This is because the ratio of private events to all events is increased due to the fixed number of shared events.

The LDS method can find a solution with a small amount of effort compared with the MIP solver, but this solution is inadequate. However, the MIP solver performs well on the quality of the solution and the satisfaction rate. We think both methods can be practically used. We should select the method based on the purpose. If agents desire to obtain a semi-optimal solution, they should use the MIP solver. Moreover, if agents need to express detailed preferences to obtain more satisfactory solutions for his/her use, the MIP solver is the appropriate way. However, if semi-optimal solutions are not necessarily desired and high computation costs are to be avoided, agents can solve the problem by LDS. But we think that the waiting time for MIP solutions is not serious compared with the difficulty of solving the problem manually.

Implementation: Multi-Agent-Based Group Scheduling System

In this section, we present an outline of our scheduling management system. Our system, which is implemented using C and Apple Script, can support group and personal scheduling management. The scheduling function is based on our formalization. There are various potential methods of obtaining a schedule. Currently, we have adopted the MIP solver and the LDS method. Our system consists of an Apple iCal, which is a calendar application, one group agent, and some personal agents corresponding to each user as shown in Figure5. It is good for users, who want not to open their own private information, to implement a system as multi-agent-system because each personal agent keeps the information private and sends only required information automatically.

Our system can achieve scheduling based on the following steps: (1) A user inputs event information (e.g., the time and date, participants, event name, and contents of events) to his/her personal agent. (2) The personal agent describes the owner's requirement in a script based on COLS (COnstraint script Language for meeting Scheduling), which is described in Tsuruta and Shintani (2000). (3) Each personal agent sends the script to a group agent. Here, agents only send information that is required for scheduling (*i.e.*, the time and date, participants, and some constraints among events).

That is to say, agents do not send event names and content because users usually want to keep information private. (4) A group agent accepts information from personal agents and converts this based on our formalization. (5) A group agent determines a group schedule using the MIP solver and LDS method. (6) The obtained schedule is submitted to the group agent's calendar, which is shared by all users. In this step, each user is aware of the existence of events but does not know about the concrete content of each event. (7) Personal agents whose users hold events interact with other participants' personal agents to send detailed information, *that is*, event name, content, and other participants. (8) The participant's agent inputs obtained information to each user's calendar using Applescript. The user can view the schedule visually via iCal.

Related Work

Research on scheduling based on CSP includes studies by Abdennadher and Schlenker (1999), Bakker, Dikker, Tempelman, and Wognum (1993), and Hofe (1997), which focus on over-constrained CSPs. In their work, scheduling problems are formalized as centralized CSPs in which all variables and constraints are centralized in one process.

In Tsuruta and Shintani (2000), the scheduling problems are formalized as a distributed valued constraint satisfaction problem (DVCSP). In this formalization, the user's preferences are represented by some constraints and weight. However, they use an ad hoc constraint relaxation method for an over-constrained problem, therefore, the quality of solution cannot be guaranteed. In this chapter, we improve the expressiveness of users' preferences by representing them as bids for them and constraints on a schedule. Moreover, for constraint relaxation, our method is based on an economical rationality; *that is*, it is not ad hoc.

Research on a combinatorial auction introducing a linear programming problem includes works by Anderson et al. (2000) and Sandholm, Suri,

Figure 5. An architecture of multi-agent-based group scheduling system

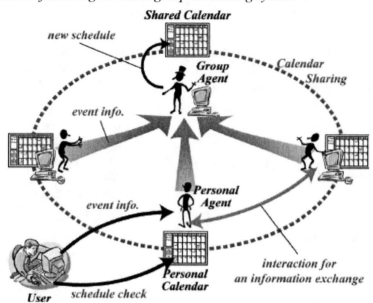

Gilpin, and Levine (2001). Anderson et al. (2000) say that the winner determination problem can be solved efficiently by using a wide-use LP solver. In Sandholm et al. (2001), a sophisticated search algorithm for determining the winners can solve the problem in short time. The algorithm solves the problem as an LP problem and narrows the search space by using a branch-and-bound search. On the other hand, in this chapter, the winner determination problem is considered as a mixed integer programming problem. Our formalization allows the constraints on bidding to be represented within the framework of a mixed integer programming problem. As a result, it was found that we can represent every detailed constraint on the events in the scheduling problem. Parkes and Ungar (2001) solve the winner determination problem based on the MIP formulation for train scheduling. Their work is close in spirit to ours. Since the formalization described in Parkes and Ungar (2001) is specialized in representing several constraints for train scheduling, *that is,* shared resources among agents are only the railway, each agent cannot express the resources

associated with the event by bids. On the other hand, since our formalization is more flexible, it can explicitly deal with events that require the participation of other agents.

Hunsberger and Grosz (2000) use a combinatorial auction protocol as a method for task allocation among agents. They use a combinatorial auction protocol for task planning. Namely, each agent places bids on possible tasks by considering the constraint on the date and time of each task. To determine the schedule, they use a search method that applies the algorithm described in (Sandholm et al., 2001). In contrast, for determining the schedule, we use an MIP that enables us to consider several types of constraints.

CONCLUSION

In this chapter, we formalized a scheduling problem considering many constraints as a combinatorial auction. Our contribution is that we represent each detailed constraint on events in scheduling by representing them as bids within the framework of the MIP problem. By solving the problem as a combinatorial auction, we were able to guarantee that the schedule we obtained was appropriate and that it did not include impossible events. Since many bids might be generated in a scheduling process in our basic formalization, the computation time tends to be long. Furthermore, by casting the scheduling problem as an instance of an MIP problem, we could represent various constraints without creating a combinatorial explosion in the number of bids and obtain an appropriate schedule in practical time. In this chapter, we applied the LDS method and the MIP solver to obtain a solution. We presented the experimental results and features of each method. We concluded that scheduling using the MIP solver based on our formalization is an efficient way of obtaining a semi-optimal schedule and solving the trade-off between the computation time to find a solution for a combinatorial auction and the expressiveness to represent a scheduling problem. Then, we showed the concept of implementation of a multi-agent-based scheduling system using our proposed method. Although in this chapter we have focused on group scheduling problems, the proposed method could be applied for kinds of allocation problems, such as a class allocation problem.

In this chapter, we do not consider each agent's budget. Thus, to win a desired event, a certain agent should bid at an expensively high price. One future direction of this study is how to allocate the budget to each agent at the initial state.

REFERENCES

Abdennadher, S., & Schlenker, H.(1999). Nurse scheduling using constraint logic programming. *Proceedings of the 11ᵗʰ Conference on Innovative Applications of Artificial Intelligence (IAAI-99)* (pp. 838-843).

Anderson, A., Tenhunen, M., & Ygge, F.(2000). Integer programming for combinatorial auction winner determination. *Proceedings of the 4ᵗʰ International Conference on Multi-Agent Systems (ICMAS2000)* (pp. 39-46).

Bakker, R.R., Dikker, F., Tempelman, F.,& Wognum, P. M. (1993). Diagnosing and solving over-determined constraint satisfaction problems. *Proceedings of the 13ᵗʰ International Joint Conference on Artificial Intelligence (IJCAI93)* (pp. 276-281).

Hofe, H. M. (1997). ConPlan/SIEDAplan: Personnel assignment as a problem of hierarchical constraint satisfaction. *Proceedings of the 3ʳᵈ International Conference on Practical Applications of Constraint Technologies* (pp. 257-272).

Harvey, W. D., & Ginsberg, M. L. (1995). Limited discrepancy search. *Proceedings of the 14ᵗʰ International Joint Conference on Artificial Intelligence (IJCAI-95)* (pp. 607-613).

Hunsberger, L., & Grosz, B. J. (2000). A combinatorial auction for collaborative planning. *Proceedings of the 4ᵗʰ International Conference on Multi-Agent Systems (ICMAS2000)* (pp. 151-158).

Ito, T., Yokoo, M., Matsubara, S., & Iwasaki, A. (2005). A new strategy proof greedy-allocation combinatorial auction protocol and its extension to open ascending auction protocol. *Proceedings of the 20ᵗʰ National Conference on Artificial Intelligence (AAAI-05)* (pp. 261-266).

Parkes, D. C., & Kalagnanam, J. (2005). Models for iterative multiattribute Vickrey auctions. *Management Science, 51,* 435-451.

Parkes, D. C., & Ungar, L. H. (2001). An auction-based method for decentralized train scheduling. *Proceedings of the 5th International Conference on Autonomous Agents (Agents-01)* (pp. 43-50).

Rassenti, S., Smith, V., & Bulfin, R. (1982). Combinatorial auction mechanism for airport time slot allocation. *Bell Journal of Economics, 13*(2), 402-417.

Sakurai, Y., Yokoo, M., & Kamei, K. (2000). An efficient approximate algorithm for winner determination in combinatorial auctions. *Second ACM Conference on Electronic Commerce.*

Sandholm, T. (1999). An algorithm for optimal winner determination in combinatorial auctions. *Proceedings of the 16th International Joint Conference on Artificial Intelligence (IJCAI-99)* (pp. 542-547).

Sandholm, T., Suri, S., Gilpin, A., & Levine, D. (2001). Cabob: A fast optimal algorithm for combinatorial auctions. *Proceedings of the 17th International Joint Conference on Artificial Intelligence (IJCAI-01)* (pp. 1102-1108).

Tsuruta, T., & Shintani, T. (2000). Scheduling meetings using distributed valued constraint satisfaction algorithm. *Proceedings of the 14th European Conference on Artificial Intelligence (ECAI-00)* (pp. 383-387).

Chapter IV
A Gentle Introduction to Fuzzy Logic and Its Applications to Intelligent Agents Design

Andre de Korvin
University of Houston – Downtown, USA

Plamen Simeonov
University of Houston – Downtown, USA

Hong Lin
University of Houston – Downtown, USA

ABSTRACT

The purpose of this chapter is to present the key properties of fuzzy logic and adaptive nets and demonstrate how to use these, separately and in combination, to design intelligent systems. The first section introduces the concept of fuzzy sets and their basic operations. The t and s norms are used to define a variety of possible intersections and unions. The next section shows two ways to estimate membership functions, polling experts, and using data to optimize parameters. Section three shows how any function can be extended to arguments that are fuzzy sets. Section four introduces fuzzy relations, fuzzy reasoning, and shows the first steps to be taken to design an intelligent system. The Mamdami model is defined in this section. Reinforcement-driven agents are discussed in section five. Sections six and seven establish the basic properties of adaptive nets and use these to define the Sugeno model. Finally, the last section discusses neuro-fuzzy systems in general. The solution to the inverted pendulum problem is given by use of fuzzy systems and also by the use of adaptive nets. The ANFIS and CANFIS architectures are defined.

BASIC CONCEPTS

Fuzzy Sets vs. Standard Sets

A standard set is a collection of objects. Underlining this concept is a specified universal set X. Thus, when a reference is made to a standard set A, one really refers to the subset A of X.

Example: Let $X = \{1, 2, 3, 4, 5, 6, 7\}$ and $A = \{4\}$. Here A is considered to be a subset of X consisting of one element, that is, the integer 4.

Each subset of X can be identified with a function defined on X, taking the value 1 on elements of the subset and the value 0 on the elements of X that are not in that subset.

Example: Let $X = \{1, 2, 3, 4, 5, 6, 7\}$. Let $A = \{3, 4, 5\}$. This set defines a function f on X with $f(x) = 1$ for $x = 3, 4, 5$ and $f(x) = 0$ for $x = 1, 2, 6, 7$. Conversely, if g is a function on X with $g(x) = 1$ for $x = 2, 5, 7$ and $g(x) = 0$ for $x = 1, 3, 4, 6$, then g defines the subset $A = \{2, 5, 7\}$.

A fuzzy subset of X generalizes the concept of standard set.

Definition: By a fuzzy subset of X, we mean a function from X into the interval [0, 1].

Example: Let $X = \{1, 2, 3, 4, 5, 6, 7\}$ and define a function g from X into [0, 1] as follows:

$g(1) = 0, g(2) = .4, g(3) = .8, g(4) = 1,$
$g(5) = .8, g(6) = .4, g(7) = 0$

Then, g defines a fuzzy subset of X. If we look back to the definition of a standard set, $f(x) = 1$ means x belongs to the (standard) subset A and $f(x) = 0$ means x does not belong to A. A similar interpretation holds for fuzzy subsets. In this example, $g(6) = .4$ means that on a scale of 0 to 1, 6 belongs .4 to the fuzzy subset defined by g.

The statement $g(1) = 0$ means that 1 does not belong at all to that subset and $g(4) = 1$ means that 4 belongs totally to that subset. The graph of g is shown on Figure 1.

The interpretation of g could be "The (fuzzy) set of numbers around 4." The integer 4 belongs totally to "Numbers around 4." The integers 1 and 7 are too removed "Numbers around 4," so they don't belong at all. The integers 2, 3, 5, 6 belong somewhat, 3 and 5 more than 2 and 6. The function g is referred to as "the membership function" of the set "Numbers around 4." The membership function of a standard set takes values in $\{0, 1\}$; the membership function of a fuzzy set is allowed to take values in [0, 1]. Thus standard sets constitute a special case of fuzzy sets.

The standard notation for the membership function of a fuzzy set A is μ_A. Thus, in our previous example:

$$\mu_{Numbers\ around\ 4}(x) = g(x), \quad x = 1, 2, 3, 4, 5, 6, 7.$$

Another standard notation is to express the set "Numbers around 4" by $.4/2 + .8/3 + 1/4 + .8/5 + .4/6$. The fact that 1 and 7 are missing from this expression indicates that the membership function on 1 and 7 is 0. In general:

$$A = \sum_{i=1}^{n} \alpha_i / x_i$$

indicates

$$\mu_A(x) = \sup_{x_i = x} \alpha_i.$$

Thus, $A = .8/x_1 + .4/x_2 + .2/x_1 + .9/x_2$ indicates $\mu_A(x_1) = .8$ and $\mu_A(x_2) = .9$.

The notation:

$$A = \int_{x \in X} \mu_A(x)/x$$

where μ_A is the membership function of A signifies that A is a fuzzy subset of X whose membership function is μ_A.

Figure 1.

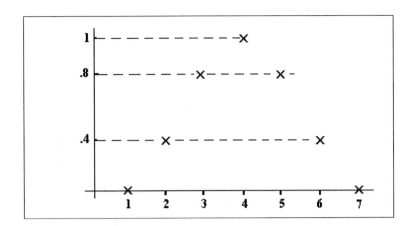

Example: Suppose we wanted to define the fuzzy set "Numbers around 4" when the universal set is $X = [1, 7]$. (Thus, we are not restricted to integers anymore.) We could set:

$$A = \int_{x \in [1,7]} e^{-100(x-4)^2} / x.$$

Note that 4 still has membership 1 in A while 1 and 7 have membership e^{-900} (i.e., very close to 0). If we wanted to have μ_A to come close to 0 on 1 and 7, close to .2 on 2 and 6, and close to .8 on 3 and 5 we could have set:

$$A = \int_{x \in [1,7]} e^{-c(x-4)^2} / x$$

and determine "the best c" by performing a least square fit. For different ways to apply versions of the least square fit algorithm we refer the reader to Hsia (1977), Sen and Srivasta (1990), and Strobach (1990).

Some Standard Membership Functions

The purpose of this section is to indicate some of the commonly used membership functions.

Figures 2 and 3 indicate the general shape of a membership function of sets of the form "Approximately *m*."

Figures 4 and 5 indicate the general shape of membership functions of the sets "More than *c*" and "Less than *c*," when the universal set X is the real line. Of course, variation in the shapes can easily be conceived.

For instance, Figure 6 could represent the fuzzy set "Over 50 years old." Being 40 years old or younger is too young to belong to that set. Being 50 years old or older is an age that totally belongs to that set, and being between 40 and 50 years old is to some extent in that set. Similarly, Figure 7 could represent "Earnings less than $40,000 a year."

It is, of course, important to *precisely* determine the membership functions for a specific problem. In a later section, we will indicate some ways to do this. In the next section, we use membership functions to motivate the definitions of commonly used operations on fuzzy sets. For methods based on steepest descent and pair-wise comparisons to estimate membership functions, see Bazaraa and Shetty (1979) and Saaty (1980).

Figure 2.

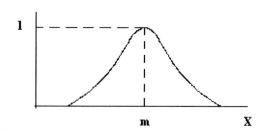

Figure 3.

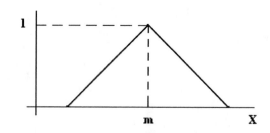

Figure 4.

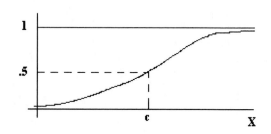

Figure 5.

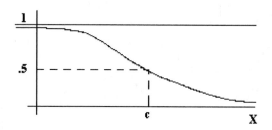

Figure 6.

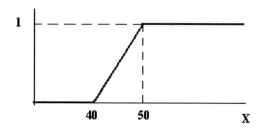

Figure 7.

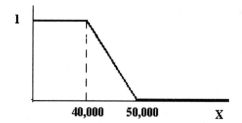

Operations on Fuzzy Sets

A common way to define meaningful operations on fuzzy sets is to look at standard sets, figure out what a specific operation does to the membership functions of these standard sets, and then perform the same operation on the membership functions of the fuzzy sets. The result should be some func-

tion from X into $[0, 1]$ which is the membership function of the resulting set. For example, if A and B are *standard* sets, then the corresponding membership functions of $A \cup B$ and $A \cap B$ are clearly $\mu_A \vee \mu_B$ and $\mu_A \wedge \mu_B$ where $\vee$ and $\wedge$ denote the max and the min operations, for example, $\mu_{A \cup B} = \mu_A \vee \mu_B$ and $\mu_{A \cap B} = \mu_A \wedge \mu_B$. Therefore, if A and B are *fuzzy* subsets of X, we can define $A \cup B$ and $A \cap B$ by defining their membership functions to be $\mu_A \vee \mu_B$ and $\mu_A \wedge \mu_B$, respectively.

Example: Let $X = \{1, 2, 3, 4\}$, $A = .8/1 + .2/2 + .7/3 + .5/4$, and $B = .5/1 + .4/2 + .6/3$. Then:

$A \cup B = .8/1 + .4/2 + .7/3 + .5/4$
$A \cap B = .5/1 + .2/2 + .6/3$

Similarly, the complement A' of a fuzzy subset A can be defined by its membership function:

$\mu_{A'} = 1 - \mu_A.$

t-norms, s-conorms, Negations

In this section we generalize the concepts of union, intersection, and complement of fuzzy subsets.

Definition: A t-norm is a mapping from $[0, 1]^2$ into $[0,1]$ satisfying:

1. $t(x, y) = t(y, x)$ (Commutative)
2. $t(t(x, y), z) = t(x, t(y, z))$ (Associative)
3. If $x \leq y$ and $z \leq w$, then $t(x, z) \leq t(y, w)$ (Monotone)
4. $t(0, x) = 0$, $t(1, x) = x$. (Boundary Conditions)

Definition: An s-conorm is a mapping from $[0, 1]^2$ into $[0, 1]$ satisfying (1), (2), and (3), and:

5. $s(0, x) = x$, $s(1, x) = 1$.

It is clear that the $\wedge$ operation is a t-norm and the $\vee$ operation is an s-conorm. Thus, t-norms and s-conorms may be used to generalize intersection and union of fuzzy subsets.

The union $A \cup B$ can be defined in terms of its membership function by:

$\mu_{A \cup B}(x) = s(\mu_A(x), \mu_B(x))$

and similarly:

$\mu_{A \cap B}(x) = t(\mu_A(x), \mu_B(x)).$

Examples of s and t maps: We have already stated $\wedge$ and $\vee$ as obvious examples. Other examples:

$$t_1(x, y) = xy, \quad t_2(x, y) = \left(\frac{1}{x^p} + \frac{1}{y^p} - 1 \right)^{-1/p}$$
$$p > 0$$

$$t_3(x, y) = \frac{xy}{x \vee y \vee p}, \quad p \in [0, 1],$$

and

$$s_1(x, y) = x + y - xy,$$

$$s_2(x, y) = 1 - \left(\left(\frac{1}{1-x} \right)^p + \left(\frac{1}{1-y} \right)^p - 1 \right)^{-1/p},$$
$$p > 0$$

$$s_3(x, y) = 1 - \frac{(1-x)(1-y)}{(1-x) \vee (1-y) \vee p}, \quad p \in [0, 1].$$

Many more examples of t-norms and s-conorms are available. For additional information on t and s norms we refer the readers to Butnatiu and Klement (1993) and Pedrycz and Gomidt (1998).

We should note that for every t-norm, one can define a "dual s-conorm" by:

$s(x, y) = 1 - t(1 - x, 1 - y).$

Definition: A negation is a map N from $[0, 1]$ to $[0, 1]$ satisfying:

1. N is non-increasing
2. $N(0) = 1$, $N(1) = 0$. (Boundary conditions)

The obvious standard negation is $N(x) = 1 - x$. A general family of negations is provided by:

$$N(x) = \frac{1-x}{1+\lambda x}, \quad \lambda > -1$$

and

$$N(x) = (1 - x^w)^{1/w}, \quad w > 0.$$

Obviously negations can be used to define the complement of a fuzzy set:

$$\mu_{A'}(x) = N(\mu_A(x)).$$

Numerous examples of connections such as and, or, negation and implication can be found in Pedrycz and Gomidt (1998) and Weber (1983).

CONSTRUCTION OF MEMBERSHIP FUNCTIONS

While a number of methods are available to construct membership functions in specific situations, we will outline only two methods.

Polling Experts

Assume one wants to determine the membership of a fuzzy term such as "large velocity." Of course this term has to be defined in known context (e.g., large velocity for Olympic runners or large velocity for supersonic planes, etc.). Some set of velocities say $\{v_1, v_2, ..., v_n\}$ is given to a panel of experts. On each velocity v_i, the panel is asked to give a yes or no answer to this question: Is a "large velocity" in the context at hand? If we have N experts and n_i of these experts state that v_i is large, the membership of v_i in "large velocity" is defined to be n_i/N. The expected shape of "large velocity" is given in Figure 8.

Figure 8.

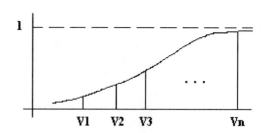

Using Data to Compute the Parameters

Many membership functions are defined through the use of parameters. For example, a function such as the one represented in Figure 8 may be defined as:

$$\mu_A(x) = \frac{1}{1 + e^{-cx}}$$

where c is a positive parameter. Other ways of defining this membership function could be:

$$\mu_A(x) = \frac{1}{1 + \left(\dfrac{x-\mu}{\sigma}\right)^2},$$

$$\mu_A(x) = e^{-1/2\left(\frac{x-\mu}{\sigma}\right)^2}, \quad \sigma > 0.$$

The last two examples define bell-shaped curves centered around μ. The membership function:

$$\mu_A(x) = \frac{1}{1 + e^{-a(x-c)}}, \quad a < 0$$

defines a curve such as the one shown in Figure 9.

The data is given as a set of points $\{(x_1, y_1), (x_2, y_2), ..., (x_n, y_n)\}$. Knowing the general parametric

Figure 9.

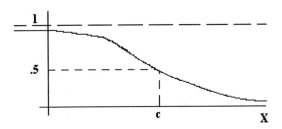

form of the membership function, the problem is to determine the values of the parameters that best fit the data. If the membership function has the form $\mu_A(\alpha, \beta, ..., x)$, where $\alpha, \beta, ...$ denote parameters, the problem then is to find the minimum of:

$$\sum_{i=1}^{n}\left(\mu_A(\alpha,\beta,...;x_i)-y_i\right)^2$$

as a function of the parameters $\alpha, \beta, ...$. There are many available methods to do that. Perhaps the most often used is the method of steepest descent (provided the partial derivatives exist). If such a method is used, different initial values should be tried to avoid landing on a local minima. Additional methods to determine membership functions containing parameters are presented in Jang, Sun, and Mizutani (1997).

THE EXTENSION PRINCIPLE

Let f be a function from the set X into the set Y. The function f is defined on elements of X and the value of f on each such element is an element of Y. The extension principle states that f can be extended so that it is defined on every fuzzy subset of X and the value of f on each such subset is a fuzzy subset of Y. The corresponding extension formula is simple to write down. If A is a fuzzy subset of X, $f(A)$ is defined as a fuzzy subset of Y through its membership function:

$$\mu_{f(A)}(y) = \sup_{x: f(x)=y} \mu_A(x).$$

We have to verify that this is indeed an extension of the original function f. Thus, if A is reduced to $\{x^*\}$, it is true that $f(A)$ reduces to $\{f(x^*)\}$. If A is reduced to $\{x^*\}$, then:

$$\mu_A(x) = \begin{cases} 1 & if \quad x = x^* \\ 0 & otherwise \end{cases}$$

and

$$\mu_{f(A)}(y) = \sup_{x: f(x)=y} \mu_A(x) = \begin{cases} 1 & if \quad y = f(x^*) \\ 0 & otherwise \end{cases}$$

So

$$\mu_{f(A)}(y) = \begin{cases} 1 & if \quad y = f(x^*) \\ 0 & if \quad y \neq f(x^*) \end{cases}$$

So, $f(A)$ reduces to $\{f(x^*)\}$.

In fact, more generally, if f is a function from $X_1 \times ... \times X_n$ to Y, f can be extended to fuzzy arguments by the formula:

$$\mu_{f(A_1,...,A_n)}(y) = \sup_{(x_1,...,x_n): f(x_1,...,x_n)=y} \{\mu_{A_1}(x_1) \wedge ... \wedge \mu_{A_n}(x_n)\}$$

Example: Consider a fuzzy subset of the reals given by $A = .1/-2 + .2/-1 + .5/1 + .7/2$ and the function $f(x) = x^2$. Then:

$$\mu_{f(A)}(4) = \sup_{x: x^2=4} \mu_A(x) = .1 \vee .7 = .7.$$

We will later show that the extension principle is a special case of the important compositional rule of inference.

THE MAMDAMI MODEL

Fuzzy Relations

Let X and Y be standard sets. A (fuzzy) relation is defined to be a function from $X \times Y$ into [0, 1]. A standard relation is, of course, defined to be any (standard) subset R of $X \times Y$ and, therefore, is a special case of fuzzy relation. The membership function of a standard relation is defined by:

$$\mu_R(x,y) = \begin{cases} 1 & if (x,y) \in R \\ 0 & otherwise. \end{cases}$$

If X and Y are finite sets, then a fuzzy relation is defined by a matrix with entries in [0, 1].

Example: Let $X = \{x_1, x_2, x_2\}$ and $Y = \{y_1, y_2\}$. Set $R(x_1, y_1) = .8$, $R(x_1, y_2) = .2$, $R(x_2, y_1) = .9$, $R(x_2, y_2) = .1$, $R(x_3, y_1) = .7$, $R(x_3, y_2) = .5$. Then, R defines the matrix:

$$R \leftrightarrow \begin{bmatrix} .8 & .2 \\ .9 & .1 \\ .7 & .5 \end{bmatrix}.$$

There are various ways to compose relations. We indicate here the one that is used most often, the Min-Max composition. If R is a relation from X to Y and S is a relation from Y to Z, we define:

$$R \circ S(x,z) = sup_{y \in Y}\{R(x,y) \wedge S(y,z)\}.$$

In the case when X, Y, and Z are finite sets, R and S are defined by matrices with elements in [0, 1], and $R \circ S$ is then defined by a matrix whose entries are obtained by matrix multiplication replacing $\times$ by $\wedge$ and + by *sup*.

Example: Let:

$$R \leftrightarrow \begin{bmatrix} .8 & .2 \\ .9 & .1 \\ .7 & .5 \end{bmatrix} \quad and \quad S \leftrightarrow \begin{bmatrix} .4 & .8 \\ .2 & .9 \end{bmatrix}.$$

Then:

$$R \circ S \leftrightarrow \begin{bmatrix} .4 & .8 \\ .4 & .8 \\ .4 & .7 \end{bmatrix}.$$

The Max-Min composition can be applied to the case where A is a fuzzy subset of X. Let R be a relation from X into Y.

Definition: The compositional rule of inference of A with R is defined to be:

$$A \circ R(y) = sup_{x \in X} \mu_A(x) \wedge R(x,y).$$

The extension principle discussed previously is a special case of the composition rule of inference. Let f be a function from the set X to the set Y. The equation $y = f(x)$ defines a relation from X into Y given by:

$$\mu_f(x,y) = \begin{cases} 1 & if \quad y = f(x) \\ 0 & otherwise. \end{cases}$$

Let A be a fuzzy subset of X. Then:

$$(A \circ \mu_f)(y) = sup_x \mu_A(x) \wedge \mu_f(x,y)$$
$$= sup_{x:f(x)=y} \mu_A(x).$$

The last term is $\mu_{f(A)}(y)$ as defined in the extension principle.

Remark: The Max-Min composition can be generalized by replacing Max by an *s*-conorm and Min by a *t*-norm in the case when X is finite.

The composition rule of inference is a key concept used in computations involving fuzzy sums. Another key concept, the projection of a fuzzy relation, is also needed. Let R be a fuzzy relation from X into Y.

Definition: The projection of R on X is defined by:

$$\mu_{R_X}(x) = sup_{y \in Y} \mu_R(x, y).$$

Of course the projection of R on Y, R_Y is similarly defined:

$$\mu_{R_Y}(y) = sup_{x \in X} \mu_R(x, y).$$

If we consider Figure 10 and the standard projection of the relation R defined by $(x, y) \in R$ if (x, y) is inside the closed contour C, then R_X should be the interval $[a, b]$. Applying the previous definition, if $x \in [a, b]$, then $\mu_{R_X}(x) = sup_y \mu_R(x, y) = 1$. If on the other hand $x \notin [a, b]$, then clearly $\mu_{R_X}(x) = 0$. Thus, R_X defines the interval $[a, b]$.

The last concept pertaining to relations is the concept of implication. Let A be a fuzzy subset of X and let B be a fuzzy subset of Y. There are a number of ways to define the relation $A \rightarrow B$ (reads "A implies B"). The implication $A \rightarrow B$ will be a fuzzy relation from X into Y. In general, $\mu_{A \rightarrow B}(x, y) = f(\mu_A(x), \mu_B(y))$, where f is a function from $[0, 1]^2$ into $[0, 1]$ satisfying some properties, which we do not list in this work. Common choices are $f(a, b) = a \wedge b$ or $f(a, b) = ab$. Two other common choices are:

$$\mu_{A \rightarrow B}(x, y) = (1 - \mu_A(x)) \vee \mu_B(y),$$
$$\mu_{A \rightarrow B}(x, y) = sup_{c \in [0,1]}\{c : \mu_A(x) \wedge c \leq \mu_B(y)\}.$$

The third choice coincides with the classical definition of implication when A and B are standard sets, that is, when μ_A and μ_B take values in $\{0, 1\}$. The last choice can be generalized by replacing $\wedge$ by any t-norm.

In this section we have defined three key concepts pertaining to fuzzy relations:

1. Compositional inference $A \circ R$
2. Projection R_X of R on X,
3. Implication $A \rightarrow B$ as a fuzzy relation from X to Y.

These three concepts will be used in describing the mechanism of fuzzy reasoning. These concepts were first introduced by Zadeh (1975a, 1975b) and are extensively discussed in Klir and Yuan (1995).

Fuzzy Reasoning

Assume that x and y are related by the formula $y = f(x)$, where f is some function. Assume moreover that it is known that $x = a$. What can we say about y? Clearly we would want to state that

Figure 10.

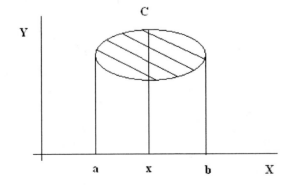

Figure 11.

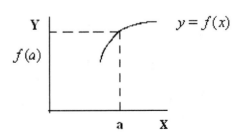

$y = f(a)$. There are three steps that lead to that conclusion:

1. Take the cylinder c_a based on a, which is just the vertical line going through the point $(a, 0)$. The membership function of that line can be written as:

$$\mu_{c_a}(x,y) = \mu_a(x) = \begin{cases} 1 & if \quad x = a, \\ 0 & otherwise. \end{cases}$$

2. Take the intersection of the line c_a with the graph of f. The membership function of that intersection is:

$$\mu_{c_a} \wedge \mu_f, \quad where$$

$$\mu_f(x,y) = \begin{cases} 1 & if \quad y = f(x), \\ 0 & otherwise. \end{cases}$$

3. Project that intersection on the y-axis.

We now generalize the three steps above to the situation where:

1. We know that x belongs to some fuzzy subset A' of X.
2. We have the relation $A \rightarrow B$ defined from X into Y.

Following the three steps outlined above:

1. Take the cylinder $c_{A'}$ based on A'. The membership of that cylinder is $\mu_{c_{A'}}(x,y) = \mu_{A'}(x)$.
2. The intersection I of $c_{A'}$ with $A \rightarrow B$ has membership function:

$$\mu_I(x,y) = \mu_{A'}(x) \wedge \mu_{A \rightarrow B}(x,y).$$

3. Project I on the y-axis. The projection B' is obtained by the projection operation that has been previously defined:

$$\mu_{B'}(y) = sup_x \, \mu_{A'}(x) \wedge \mu_{A \rightarrow B}(x,y).$$

Figure 12a.

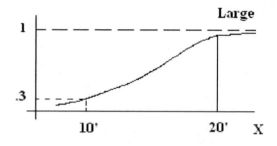

Figure 12b.

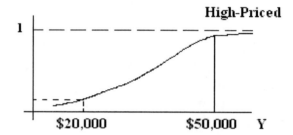

This is the formula of the compositional inference of A' with $A \rightarrow B$.

In summary, if the input is the fuzzy set A' and we know $A \rightarrow B$, the output set is given by $A' \circ (A \rightarrow B)$.

Example: Assume one has the following rule: If T is large, then V is high priced. The membership functions of large (L) and high priced (HP) are, of course, known and the general shapes are as shown in Figure 12(a) and Figure 12(b).

We would like to give meaning to the relation large$\rightarrow$high priced. We recall that the general method is to set $\mu_{L \rightarrow HP}(x,y) = f(\mu_L(x), \mu_{HP}(y))$ with a suitable function f. It was pointed out earlier that common choices for f are $f(a, b) = a \wedge b$ and $f(a, b) = ab$. We shall use $f(a, b) = a \wedge b$ in this example. Then, $\mu_{L \rightarrow HP}(x,y) = \mu_L(x) \wedge \mu_{HP}(y)$. Suppose that we know that T is 10. How high priced is the item? The answer is obtained by taking the compositional inference of 10 with large$\rightarrow$high priced. So if $A' = \{10\}$, then $B' = A' \circ (L \to HP)$, or if we identify any fuzzy set with its membership function, then:

$$B'(y) = sup_x \mu_{10}(x) \wedge \mu_{L \to HP}(x, y) =$$
$$(L \to HP)(10, y) = L(10) \wedge HP(y).$$

Let $L(10) = 3$. Then, $B'(y) = 3 \wedge HP(y)$. Had we used $f(a, b) = ab$, the answer would have been $3 \times HP(y)$. The two corresponding graphs are shown on Figure 13(a) and 13(b).

The interpretation of Figure 13(a) is that on a scale of 0 to 1, we believe .3 that an item of size 10 will be priced $20000 or higher. The interpretation of Figure 13(b) is similar except that $20000 is replaced by $50000.

Remark: The input does not have to be a singleton. The computation $A' \circ (A \to B)$ is defined for any fuzzy subset A' of X.

In reality, we almost never have only one rule as in the example above. In reality we have a set

Figure 13a.

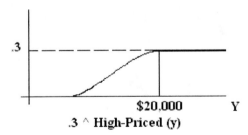

.3 ∧ **High-Priced (y)**

Figure 13b.

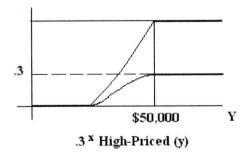

.3 × **High-Priced (y)**

of rules. For example, we may have $N > 1$ rules of the form:

R_i: If T_i is A_i, then V_i is B_i, $i = 1, ..., N$.

The T_i may or may not be all distinct. Each A_i is a fuzzy subset of the corresponding X_i. The same observation holds for V_i, and each B_i is a fuzzy subset of a Y_i. The input is T_1 is A'_1, T_2 is A_2, ..., T_N is A'_N, where A'_i is a fuzzy subset of X_i for each i. What is then the output set B'? The output of each rule, as we have previously discussed, is a fuzzy subset B'_i of Y_i. Thus, B' being the result of all of the N rules should be a fuzzy subset of $Y_1 \times Y_2 \times \cdots \times Y_N$. In fact, $B'(y_1, ..., y_N)$ is obtained by "aggregating" the $B_i'(y_i)$, that is:

$$\mu_{B'}(y_1,...,y_N) = A_{i=1}^N \mu_{B'_i}(y_i),$$

where A denotes the aggregation operation. There are a number of ways to select an aggregating operation. One of the most often used is the $\vee$ operation (recall that $\vee$ denotes the sup operation). Thus, the output obtained by applying the N rules given above is:

$$B' = \vee_{i=1}^N A'_i \circ (A_i \to B_i)$$

or if we define $\mu_{A_i \to B_i}(x_i, y_i)$ as $\mu_{A_i}(x_i) \wedge \mu_{B_i}(y_i)$ (as we did earlier), then:

$$\mu_{B'}(y_1,...,y_N) =$$

$$sup_{x_1,...,x_N}\{\mu_{A'_i}(x_i) \wedge \mu_{A_i}(x_i) \wedge \mu_{B_i}(y_i)\}.$$

We set $w_i = sup_{x_i} \mu_{A'_i}(x_i) \wedge \mu_{A_i}(x_i)$, $i = 1, ..., N$. The w_i can be interpreted as "the largest intersection of A'_i with A_i." It denotes the extent to which input A'_i matches the antecedent A_i and is called "the strength of rule R_i" (relative to input A'_i). Then:

$$\mu_{B'}(y_1,\ldots,y_N) = sup_i \left\{ w_i \wedge \mu_{B_i}(y_i) \right\}$$

The number $\mu_{B'}(y_1, \cdots, y_N)$ indicates on a scale 0 to 1 our belief that $(y_1, \cdots, y_N)$ is the multidimensional output given by the system of (fuzzy) rules.

Example: Consider the rules:

- If T_1 is large, then V_1 is high-priced.
- If T_2 is heavy, then V_2 is high-volume.
- It is understood that we have obtained the membership functions for large, high-priced, heavy, and high-volume. Suppose the input is $T_1 = 10'$ and $T_2 = 200$ lbs. The (fuzzy) output is then:

$$B'(price, volume) = \\ Large(10) \wedge \\ (Large \rightarrow High - Priced)(10, price) \\ \vee Heavy(200) \wedge \\ (Heavy \rightarrow High - Volume) \\ (200, volume),$$

where again fuzzy sets are identified with their membership functions. From now on, for convenience of notation, we will freely identify a set with its membership function. In our previous notation:

$$w_1 = sup_{x_1} \left\{ \mu_{10}(x_1) \wedge Large(x_1) \right\} = \\ Large(10),$$

$$w_2 = sup_{x_2} \left\{ \mu_{200}(x_2) \wedge Heavy(x_2) \right\} = \\ Heavy(200).$$

If as earlier we define:

$$(Large \rightarrow High - Priced)(x_1, y_1) = \\ Large(x_1) \wedge High - Priced(y_1)$$

and

$$(Heavy \rightarrow High - Volume)(x_2, y_2) = \\ Heavy(x_2) \wedge High - Volume(y_2),$$

then

$$B'(price, volume) = \\ \left\{ Large(10) \wedge High - Priced(price) \right\} \\ \vee \left\{ Heavy(200) \wedge High - \\ Volume(volume) \right\}.$$

An important case is the case when the set of fuzzy rules takes the form:

R_i: If T is A_i then V is B_i, $i = 1, ..., N$,

where A_i are all fuzzy subsets of X, and B_i are all fuzzy subsets of Y. If the input is $T = a$ where a is an element of X, then the fuzzy output given by this set of rules is:

$$B'(y) = \vee_{i=1}^{N} \left\{ A_i(a) \wedge B_i(y) \right\} \quad or$$
$$B'(y) = \vee_{i=1}^{N} \left\{ A_i(a) B_i(y) \right\}$$

depending if $(A_i \rightarrow B_i)(x, y)$ is defined as $A_i(x) \wedge B_i(y)$ or as a product $A_i(x)B_i(y)$. Figure 14(a) and Figure 14(b) show the output B' in these two cases when $N = 2$.

Some Generalizations

Suppose that we have N fuzzy rules where the i-th rule is of the form:

R_i: If $T_{i,1}$ is $A_{i,1}$ and ... T_{i,k_i} is A_{i,k_i} then V is B_i.

Assume the inputs are $V_{i,p}$ is $A'_{i,p}$, where $i = 1, 2, ..., N$ and $p = 1, 2, ..., k_i$. Assume also that all of the B_i are fuzzy subsets of Y. Then, the fuzzy output given by these rules is:

Figure 14a.

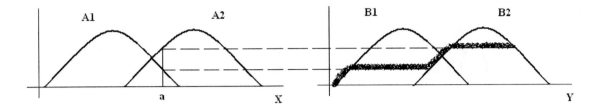

Figure 14b.

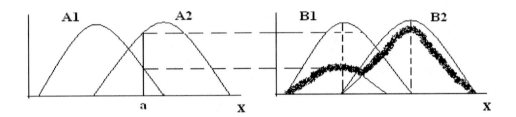

Figure 15.

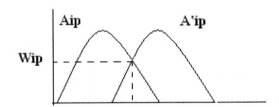

$$B'(y) = \vee_{i=1}^{N} w_i \wedge B_i(y) \quad or$$
$$B'(y) = \vee_{i=1}^{N} w_i B_i(y),$$

depending on how the composition and the implication relations are defined. The value w_i is the strength of the i-th rule (relative to the specified output) and:

$$w_i = \wedge_{p=1}^{k_i} w_{i,p},$$

where $w_{i,p}$ is the largest intersection of $A_{i,p}$ and $A'_{i,p}$, that is

$$w_{i,p} = sup_x \left\{ A_{i,p}(x) \wedge A'_{i,p}(x) \right\}.$$

The diagram in Figure 15 shows the largest intersection of two fuzzy sets.

At this point we are in a position to handle the fuzzy analogs of if-then rules. Many situations involve these types of rules. Some cases require more complex rules. We give two examples of such rules that can be converted to classical if-then statements.

Our first example involves if-then with exceptions. Suppose the i-th rule is:

R_i: If T is A_i, then V is B_i unless W is E_i.

Of course, it is assumed that the membership functions of A_i, B_i, and E_i are known. The rule can be converted to the following two rules:

1. If T is A_i and W is E_i^c, then V is B_i.
2. If T is A_i and W is E_i, then V is B_i^c.

Here, E_i^c and B_i^c denote the negations of E_i and B_i. Typically, the negations would be $1 - E_i$ and $1 - B_i$.

Our second example deals with the same case when modifiers are placed in front of the fuzzy values. For example, assume that the *i*-th rule is:

R_i: If *T* is very A_i, then *V* is somewhat B_i.

This could be: If *T* is very large, then *V* is somewhat high-priced. Often (but not always) very A_i is defined as A_i^2 and somewhat B_i is defined as $B_i^{1/2}$. The motivation for this definition is that $A_i^2 < A_i$ and $B_i^{1/2} > B_i$ when the range of the values is the open interval (0, 1). Thus it is harder to reach high membership for very A_i than for A_i and easier to reach high membership for somewhat B_i than for B_i.

Remark: The rule "If *T* is A_i, then *V* is B_i unless *W* is E_i" can also be replaced by the following three rules:

1.   If *T* is A_i and *W* is E_i^c, then *V* is B_i.
2.   If *T* is A_i and *W* is E_i, then *V* is B_i^c.
3.   If *T* is A_i and $W \equiv 1$, then *V* is B_i.

Rule (3) states that if we have no information about *W*, then *V* is B_i. Indeed, compare (3) with the rule "If *T* is A_i, then *V* is B_i." By rule (3) we have:

$$(A_i \wedge W \rightarrow B_i)(x, w, y) =$$
$$A_i(x) \wedge 1 \wedge B_i(y) =$$
$$A_i(x) \wedge B_i(y)$$

which is exactly $(A_i \rightarrow B_i)(x, y)$. Additional types of Mamdami rules are analyzed in Dogherty, Driankov, and Heffendorn (1993), Dubois and Prade (1992), and Yager (1984).

Defuzzification

Until now, we have had the following situation: There is a set of *N* fuzzy if-then rules and an input, fuzzy or not, for each variable in the antecedents of the rules. The generated output is fuzzy. Often it is necessary to pick a single element that best represents the fuzzy output *B'*. The reason that it is often necessary to do this is that some action needs to be performed, for example, what should the target speed be, or how far should one travel, or what price should be charged? Such decisions require a single value, not a fuzzy set. There are a number of ways to pick the best representative of *B'*; we indicate two ways.

Perhaps the most common way is to pick the "center of gravity" defined by B_i:

$$V_{CoG} = \frac{\int_Y B'(y)\,y\,dy}{\int_Y B'(y)\,dy}.$$

The second common way is to pick the mean value over the set over which *B'* is maximum:

$$V_{MoM} = \int_{Y'} y\,dy / \int_{Y'} dy,$$

where

$Y' = \{y : B'$ assumes a maximum value on $y\}$.

For the numerous methods of defuzzification, we refer the readers to Hellendoorn and Thomas (1993), Mabuchi (1993), and Yager and Filer (1993).

Application: Designing an Intelligent Agent

What precedes may be applied to design an intelligent agent. An intelligent agent is an entity that reacts to a changing environment. The environment changes may or may not be produced by the agent.

The working of an intelligent agent as sketched in Figure 16 is denoted as "fuzzy controller." This construction has been used in a large variety of situations where it is necessary to control some processes, for example, unmanned vehicles, chemical processes, balancing a pole on a mov-

Figure 16.

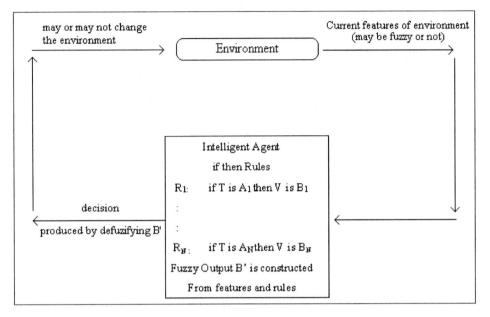

ing cart, and others. A somewhat typical rule for unmanned vehicle could be the following: If the error angle is small and positive and the obstacle is not close, then set the steering angle to slight right. Numerous articles dealing with fuzzy controllers can be found in the literature. We list here a few articles dealing with this important subject: Castro (1995), Mamdami (1977), Mamdami and Gaines (1981), Pedrycz (1994), and Tong (1985).

REINFORCEMENT-DRIVEN AGENT

The agent constructed at the end of section four interacts with the environment according to the (fuzzy) rules that were built into the agent. In some situations, it is not easy to construct appropriate rules; it is preferable to let the agent learn from the gain/losses that its action generates. The goal of this section is to show how such an agent may be constructed.

Adaline

The adaptive linear element (adaline) is the simplest example of an adaptive network. The basic components of an adaline are sketched in Figure 17.

The output is given by:

$$a = \sum_{i=1}^{n} w_i x_i + w_0$$

where the input is the vector $(x_1, x_2, ..., x_n)$ going through the parameters (often called weights) $w_1, w_2, ..., w_n$. In addition, an input of 1 is sent through w_0 (often called the bias). The output is then a linear combination of the x_i, with coefficients being the weights w_i, plus the bias. We also have a "training set." What this means is that for specified input vectors $(x_{1,p}, x_{2,p}, ..., x_{n,p})$, we want the system to produce the specified outputs t_p, respectively, $1 \leq p \leq Q$. Initially one assigns (usually small) random values to the weights and the bias. When the p-th input is applied to the

Figure 17.

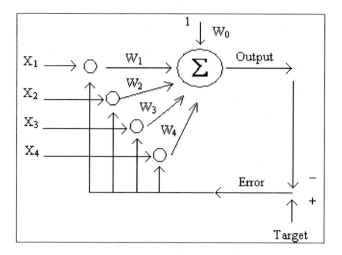

system, the output is, of course, not t_p but a_p. One defines the error for the p-th input by:

$$E_p = (t_p - a_p)^2.$$

Then,

$$\frac{\partial E_p}{\partial w_i} = -2(t_p - a_p)\frac{\partial a_p}{\partial w_i} = -2(t_p - a_p)x_{i,p}.$$

We would like to minimize E_p as a function of the weights and the bias. The weights and the bias are variables in a_p. A straightforward way to minimize E_p is to take small steps in the $w_1, ..., w_n$, w_0 space in the opposite direction to the gradient ∇E_p. The components of ∇E_p are precisely $\partial E_p/\partial w_i$, $i = 0, 1, ..., n$. Thus, if $w_1(0), ..., w_n(0), w_0(0)$ are the initial random values assigned and if $w_1(k), ..., w_n(k), w_0(k)$ are the values after the k-th iteration, the update for the $(k+1)$-th iteration is:

$$w(k+1) = w_i(k) + \eta(t_p - a_p)x_{i,p}, \quad i = 0,1,...,n$$

if the p-th input is presented at the $(k+1)$-th iteration. Here η denotes a small positive number (the step size). This can be rewritten as:

$$\Delta_p w_i(k) = \eta(t_p - a_p)x_{i,p}, \quad i = 0,1,...,n,$$

where $\Delta_p w_i(k)$ denotes the change in the i-th weight at iteration $k+1$ if the p-th input is presented. Intuitively, if $x_{i,p} > 0$ and the system is "underestimated" $(t_p - a_p > 0)$, then w_i is increased.

The adaline is then trained by presenting the inputs from the training set many times over and updating the weights as shown. Under some conditions it can be shown that the weights converge to some values so that specified inputs will result in specified outputs (or will come close to doing this). Adaline is probably the simplest example of a neural net. For comprehensive textbooks on the subject we like to mention Hagan, Demuth, and Beale (1995) and Haykin (1994).

The Reinforcement-Driven Agent

The reinforcement-driven agent attempts to predict the cumulative outcome of a state. If C_{t+1} denotes the cost (or benefit) of making some decision at time t, then the cumulative outcome at time t is defined as:

$$\sum_{k=t}^{m} C_{k+1}$$

if the agent tries to predict all the way to time m, where $m \geq t$. Let V_t be the predicted cumulative outcome at time t. The error made at time t is:

$$\sum_{k=t}^{m} C_{k+1} - V_t.$$

The above difference can be rewritten as:

$$\sum_{k=t}^{m} (C_{k+1} + V_{k+1} - V_k),$$

where V_{m+1} is defined to be 0. In order to minimize this error, it is desirable to minimize:

$$\frac{1}{2}(C_{t+1} + V_{t+1} - V_t)^2$$

at each t. If the predicted cumulative outcome V_t depends on some parameter vector w, then applying the steepest descend algorithm, w should be updated as follows:

$$w_{new} - w_{old} = -\alpha(C_{t+1} + V_{t+1} - V_t)(-\nabla V_t),$$

where α is a small positive number denoting the step size and ∇V_t denotes the gradient of V_t. The above formula is then rewritten as:

$$\Delta w_t = \alpha(C_{t+1} + V_{t+1} - V_t)\nabla V_t,$$

where Δw denotes the parameter vector change at time t.

What happens if we want to deal away with m? Our time horizon then becomes infinite, and $V_{m+1} = 0$ does not hold anymore. The cumulative outcome should not be defined as:

$$\sum_{k=t}^{\infty} C_{k+1},$$

since the above series may diverge. Instead, we define it as:

$$\sum_{k=0}^{\infty} \gamma^k C_{t+k+1},$$

where $0 < \gamma < 1$. The effect is to apply a discount γ to the cost/benefit with each increment of time from t on. Repeating the previous argument, to minimize the error on the predicted cumulative outcome at each step t, we change the parameter vector w as follows:

$$\Delta w_t = \alpha(C_{t+1} + \gamma V_{t+1} - V_t)\nabla V_t.$$

Recall the update given for the adaline was $\Delta_p w_{i,t} = \alpha(t_p - u_p)x_{i,p}$, where we identified η and α. Here again, t_p denotes the target when input p is presented and a_p is the output (activation).

We want to estimate V_t, that is, make at time t a prediction on what the cumulative outcome is. The two formulas above show that an adaline can be used to form such a prediction. We make the activation (output) be V_t. The error $t_p - a_p$ is then identified with $C_{t+1} + \gamma V_{t+1} - V_t$. Since:

$$V_t = a = \sum_{i=1}^{n} w_i x_i + w_0,$$

then

$$\nabla V_t = (x_1, ..., x_n, 1)^T.$$

Thus, the idea is to build an adaline that at each step t will change the weights treating $C_{t+1} + \gamma V_{t+1} - V_t$ as the error. The reinforcement driven agent can be constructed as shown in Figure 18.

The environment is at some state S_t (represented by some vector). An action is generated. The environment sends the appropriate cost/benefit generated by that action. The left adaline modifies appropriately its weights and sends the error to the right adaline, which similarly modifies its weights (using the same error) and then generates an appropriate action. The algorithm is as follows:

1. Record the current state vector S_t.
2. Record the output V_t of the left adaline using S_t as input.

Figure 18.

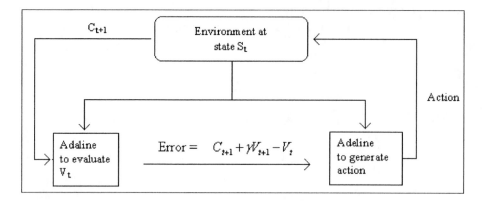

3. Select an action using the right adaline (see later for how to do this).
4. Record the resulting state S_{t+1} of the environment and the cost/benefit C_{t+1}.
5. Use the left adaline to record V_{t+1}.
6. Adjust the weights of the left adaline using $C_{t+1} + \gamma V_{t+1} - V_t$ as error.
7. Pass this error to the right adaline for similar weight updates. Then go to step 1 with S_t replaced by S_{t+1} and the updated weights for the two adalines.

The only information needed (in step 3) is how does the right adaline select an action. The right Adaline, as opposed to the left one, does not have one output but n outputs if we have n actions available. The diagram in Figure 19 summarizes the situation.

Suppose we want to maximize our reward. Then we want to increase the weights leading to high $C_{t+1} + \gamma V_{t+1}$ and decrease the weights leading to low $C_{t+1} + \gamma V_{t+1}$. The state S_t is a vector of dimension N. If action i ($1 \leq i \leq n$) is taken at time t, the change in weights is:

$$\Delta w_{l,j} = \alpha (C_{t+1} + \gamma V_{t+1} - V_t) x_{l,j},$$

where

$$x_{l,j} = \begin{cases} 1 & \text{if} \quad j = i \\ 0 & \text{if} \quad j \neq i \end{cases} \qquad l = 1, 2, \ldots, N.$$

Figure 19.

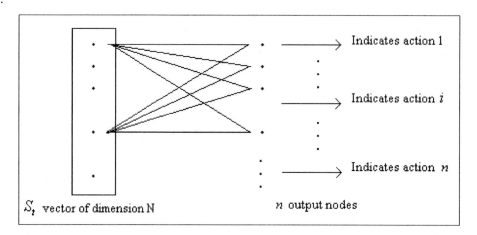

This update reinforces action, leading to high expected rewards. With this action only, links of S_t to the node corresponding to the action taken are updated. The other weights remain constant.

If we take the action corresponding to the node with highest activation, we run the risk of taking the "best action so far" and failing to explore other possibilities. If the output of the i-th node is t_i, we define the probability of taking the i-th action by:

$$p_i = e^{t_i/T} / \left(\sum_{j=1}^{n} e^{t_j/T} \right).$$

Initially, we set T to be high, which then forces the distribution $\{p_i\}$ to approximate the uniform distribution. Thus, initially we try every action with approximately equal probabilities. As we proceed, we slowly lower T, which will then put higher probabilities on actions that have higher outputs. Thus, initially we explore all actions, gradually learning the best response based on the feedback from the environment. The technique of introducing "a temperature T" is used in simulated annealing, a powerful approach in optimization problems. Reinforcement learning and the associated method of simulated annealing are discussed in Barto (1992), Berenji and Khedkar (1992), Hinton and Sejnowski (1986), and Ingber (1989).

A somewhat typical example where the reinforcement-driven agent could be used to learn the optimal path from an initial position to a final position. Suppose the cost of traveling from node i to node j is $c_{i,j}$. This problem can be converted to maximizing the benefit problem by introducing $b_{i,j} = -c_{i,j}$. For example, consider the graph in Figure 20.

If at time t we are at node c and choose to travel to node f, then in our previous notation C_{t+1} would be $b_{i,j}$ where i is the node c and j is the node f. The states are the nonterminal nodes, and they need to be represented as vertices. One could represent a by $(1,0,0,0,0,0)^T$, b by $(0,1,0,0,0,0)^T$, ..., f by $(0,0,0,0,0,1)^T$. The action set could be defined as {horizontal, up 1, down 1, up 2, down 2}. Thus, the action adaline could be represented as indicated on Figure 21.

At high "temperature T" state c would have probability 1/6 to be tried. Actions "up 1" and "down 1" will be explored. Eventually, if benefits of going up 1 were higher, the weight connecting c to "up 1" would be increased over the weight of c to "down 1." As the temperature T would be lowered, at state c the action "up 1" would be more and more favored.

It should be noted that the feedback from the environment need not be of the form $C_{t+1} = b_{i,j}$. It could, for example, be in the form "good" ($C_{t+1} = 1$), "OK" ($C_{t+1} = 0$), or "bad" ($C_{t+1} = -1$). In fact, in

Figure 20.

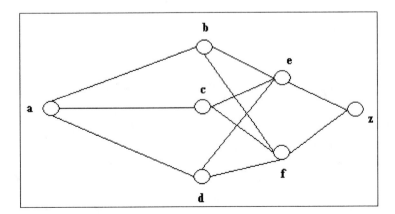

Figure 21.

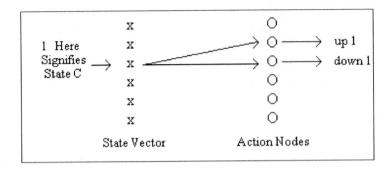

Figure 21, *c* could be connected to all of the action nodes provided that undefined actions (such as horizontal from *c*) would be given very negative benefits. In time, the system would learn that a horizontal move from *c* is inappropriate.

ADAPTIVE NETWORKS

The first type of agent that we defined was driven by fuzzy rules (the Mamdami model). It adapted to a changing environment by following flexible rules that allowed particular truth values. However, this type of agent performs as well (or as poorly) as the rules are realistic.

The second type of agent was reinforcement driven. It had to receive from the environment some type of evaluation of how good (or how bad) its response had been. That agent did not use built-in rules to operate.

Each of these agents has built-in weaknesses. The first is only as good as the rules under which it operates. It is not clear what the second type of agent is learning as it builds "appropriate responses" to situations.

The main goal in this section is to build an agent that combines the advantages of the two previous agents, that is, the user understands the rules under which the agent operates and the agent adapts the rules as it learns from its changing environment. To achieve this goal, we need to construct a more general methodology from the one used for the adaline. This will be the goal of

this section. In the next section we will define fuzzy rules in a somewhat different fashion from the Mamdami model. Finally, we will combine these two methodologies to obtain an adaptive neuro-fuzzy inference system.

Basic Architecture

We consider here a network with a number of nodes connected by directional links. Each node represents a processing unit. A subset of these nodes consists of *adaptive* nodes, that is, nodes whose output depends on some parameters. The diagram in Figure 22 illustrates such a setting.

In this example, the input is the vector (x_1, x_2, x_3) and the output is the vector (x_6, x_7, x_8). The square nodes, that is, node 4 and node 7, are adaptive. Each node represents some function. Node 4 represents a function involving the parameter *a*. Node 7 represents a function involving the parameter *b*. Each node's output is represented as $x_{l,k}$, where *l* denotes the layer and *k* represents the node's number. The input is layer 0 (L0), nodes 4 and 5 are layer 1 (L1), and nodes 6, 7, and 8 are in layer 2 (L2). Thus, node 4 outputs $x_{1,4}$ and node 6 outputs $x_{2,6}$. Specifically, we have the following process:

$$x_{1,4} = f_{1,4}(a, x_1, x_2, x_3),$$

$$x_{1,5} = f_{1,5}(x_1, x_2, x_3),$$

$$x_{2,6} = f_{2,6}(x_{1,4}, x_{1,5}),$$

Figure 22.

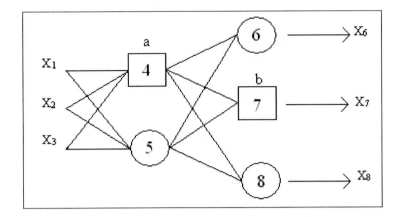

$$x_{2,7} = f_{2,7}(b, x_{1,4}, x_{1,5}),$$

$$x_{2,8} = f_{2,8}(x_{1,4}, x_{1,5}),$$

and of course $x_6 = x_{2,6}$, $x_7 = x_{2,7}$, and $x_8 = x_{2,8}$. The functions $f_{l,k}$ are known, the values of the parameters need to be determined.

Back-Propagation

The back-propagation method makes use of the chain rule for partial derivatives as well as the method of steepest descent.

Consider Figure 23 where $x_{l,i}$ is connected to $x_{p,j}$ in a number of steps. Assume x_{m_h}, i_h are the outputs of some intermediate nodes, and we have

the complete set of chains connecting $x_{l,i}$ to $x_{p,j}$. Then, the chain rule states:

$$\frac{\partial x_{p,j}}{\partial x_{l,i}} = \sum_{h=1}^{k} \frac{\partial x_{p,j}}{\partial x_{m_h, i_h}} \frac{\partial x_{m_h, i_h}}{\partial x_{l,i}}.$$

Let $N(l)$ denote the number of nodes at layer l. Thus, in Figure 22, $N(0) = 3$, $N(1) = 2$, $N(2) = 3$. Let L denote the output layer, $L = 2$ in Figure 22. The quantities $\varepsilon_{l,i}^{p} = \partial E_p / \partial x_{l,i}^{p}$ play a crucial role in the back-propagation method. Here, E_p denotes the output error when input p is presented. E_p is defined as:

$$E_p = \sum_{i=1}^{N(L)} \left(d_i^p - x_{L,i}^p \right)^2,$$

Figure 23.

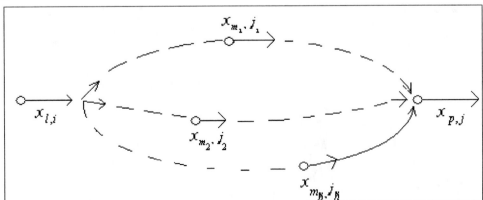

where d_i^p denotes the desired output at node i of the output layer and $x_{L,i}^p$ denotes the output actually obtained at that node. From now on, for the sake of making the notation less cumbersome, we will omit the index p. It will be understood that the quantities pertain to some input. Thus we will write:

$$E = \sum_{i=1}^{N(L)} \left(d_i - x_{L,i} \right)^2 .$$

In the long run we need to compute ∇E where the gradient of E is with respect to the parameters in the adaptive nodes. In Figure 22, $\nabla E = (\partial E/\partial a, \partial E/\partial b)$.

The method of steepest descend then determines the updates of the parameters by the rule:

Change in parameters $= -\eta \nabla E,$

where η is a small positive number. The algorithm is initiated by setting the parameters to some initial values. The quantities $\varepsilon_{l,j}$ are used to compute ∇E. Applying the chain rule mentioned earlier yields $\varepsilon_{l,i} (i = 1, ..., N(l))$ in terms of $\varepsilon_{l+1,j} (j = 1, ..., N(l+1))$. In other ways, we "back-propagate $\varepsilon_{l+1,j}$" to obtain $\varepsilon_{l,j}$. At the output layer we have:

$$\varepsilon_{L,i} = -2(d_i - x_{L,i}), \quad i = 1, ..., N(L).$$

At layer l we have:

$$\varepsilon_{l,i} = \frac{\partial E}{\partial x_{l,i}} = \sum_{m=1}^{N(l+1)} \frac{\partial E}{\partial x_{l+1,m}} \frac{\partial f_{l+1,m}}{\partial x_{l,i}} = \sum_{m=1}^{N(l+1)} \varepsilon_{l+1,m} \frac{\partial f_{l+1,m}}{\partial x_{l,i}}.$$

Note that we have implicitly assumed here that each node at level l connects to each note at level $l + 1$ (as is the case in Figure 22). We are also assuming that there is no loop in the graph.

Example: We apply the previous considerations to the graph in Figure 22. We obtain the following partial derivatives:

$$\varepsilon_{2,6} = -2(d_6 - x_{2,6}),$$
$$\varepsilon_{2,7} = -2(d_7 - x_{2,7}),$$
$$\varepsilon_{2,8} = -2(d_8 - x_{2,8}),$$
$$\varepsilon_{1,4} = \varepsilon_{2,6} \frac{\partial f_{2,6}}{\partial x_{1,4}} + \varepsilon_{2,7} \frac{\partial f_{2,7}}{\partial x_{1,4}} + \varepsilon_{2,8} \frac{\partial f_{2,8}}{\partial x_{1,4}},$$
$$\varepsilon_{1,5} = \varepsilon_{2,6} \frac{\partial f_{2,6}}{\partial x_{1,5}} + \varepsilon_{2,7} \frac{\partial f_{2,7}}{\partial x_{1,5}} + \varepsilon_{2,8} \frac{\partial f_{2,8}}{\partial x_{1,5}},$$

and finally,

$$\varepsilon_{0,1} = \varepsilon_{1,4} \frac{\partial f_{1,4}}{\partial x_1} + \varepsilon_{1,5} \frac{\partial f_{1,5}}{\partial x_1},$$
$$\varepsilon_{0,2} = \varepsilon_{1,4} \frac{\partial f_{1,4}}{\partial x_2} + \varepsilon_{1,5} \frac{\partial f_{1,5}}{\partial x_2},$$
$$\varepsilon_{0,3} = \varepsilon_{1,4} \frac{\partial f_{1,4}}{\partial x_3} + \varepsilon_{1,5} \frac{\partial f_{1,5}}{\partial x_3}.$$

We then compute ∇E:

$$\frac{\partial E}{\partial a} = \frac{\partial E}{\partial x_{1,4}} \frac{\partial f_{1,4}}{\partial a} = \varepsilon_{1,4} \frac{\partial f_{1,4}}{\partial a},$$
$$\frac{\partial E}{\partial b} = \frac{\partial E}{\partial x_{2,7}} \frac{\partial f_{2,7}}{\partial b} = \varepsilon_{2,7} \frac{\partial f_{2,7}}{\partial b}.$$

The change in a and b at each step is then given by:

$$\begin{bmatrix} \Delta a \\ \Delta b \end{bmatrix} = -\eta \nabla E.$$

Remark: For graphs having a loop, we introduce time and obtain recurrence relations allowing the computation of ∇E_i which denotes the gradient of the error at time i.

Figure 24.

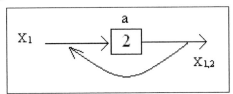

For example, for the diagram in Figure 24 using our previous notation we have $x_{1,2}^i = f_{1,2}(a, x_{1,2}^{i-1})$, where the superscript i denotes the time i. So if $E_i = (d_2 - x_{1,2}^i)^2$, then:

$$\frac{\partial E_i}{\partial a} = -2(d_2^i - x_{1,2}^i)\frac{\partial x_{1,2}^i}{\partial a}$$

and

$$\frac{\partial x_{1,2}^i}{\partial a} = \frac{\partial x_{1,2}^i}{\partial x_{1,2}^{i-1}}\frac{\partial x_{1,2}^{i-1}}{\partial a}.$$

If we set $u_i = \partial x_{1,2}^i / \partial a$ we have:

$$u_i = \frac{\partial f_{1,2}}{\partial x_{1,2}^{i-1}}u_{i-1}.$$

Therefore, the change in a at step i is given by $\Delta a = -\eta e_i u_i$, where $e_i = d_2^i - x_{1,2}^i$. The initial value u_0 is $\partial f_{1,2}/\partial x_{1,2}$ at the input point $(a_0, x_{1,2}^0)$. In this way we control the output to follow a time trajectory $d^1, d^2, ..., d^i, ...$. For additional information on adaptive nets, the reader is referred to Jang (1991).

THE SUGENO MODEL

This model is also known as the TSK model, as it was developed by Takagi, Sugeno, and Kang. Defuzification, a necessary step in the Mamdami model, is the step that consumes the most time. The Sugeno model bypasses the defuzzification step. A typical rule in the Sugeno model takes the form:

If x is A and y is B, then $z = f(x, y)$.

Example: Let X and Y denote the number of manufactured widget-1 and widget-2 and x and y denote the number of hours spent on making widget-1 and widget-2, respectively. A typical rule could look like this:

If x is high and y is low, then the cost per hour is $3x + 5y + 10$.

In practice, Sugeno-type rules work best when the input is not fuzzy but numerical. In fact, in many cases the inputs are the numbers x and y in the consequent. The function f is, of course, known and in many cases it is a linear function of the input variables. The diagram in Figure 25 illustrates a somewhat typical example of the inference process.

From the two diagrams we have $z_1 = p_1 x + q_1 y + r_1$ and $z_2 = p_2 x + q_2 y + r_2$, respectively. The value of z is then:

$$z = \frac{w_1 z_1 + w_2 z_2}{w_1 + w_2}.$$

Thus, the strength of each rule i is evaluated and the final output is of the form $\sum \overline{w}_i z_i$ or $\sum \overline{w}_i f_i(x_1, ..., x_p)$, where $\overline{w}_i$ denotes the normalized strength of rule i, f_i are specified functions in the consequent, and $x_1, ..., x_p$ are the input variables. The strength w_i is given by:

$$X_1(x_1) \wedge X_2(x_2) \wedge ... \wedge X_p(x_p) \quad or$$
$$X_1(x_1) X_2(x_2) \cdots X_p(x_p)$$

depending on whether we select the $\wedge$ or the product to be the t-norm. Thus, computing the output does not require defuzzification. All that is required is the computation of $\overline{w}_i$ for each new input.

Figure 25.

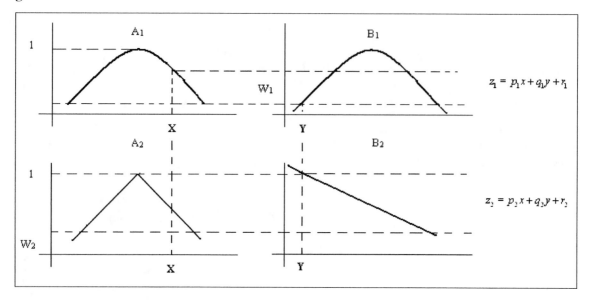

Figure 26.

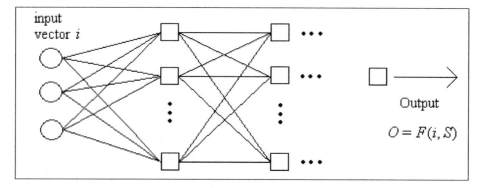

ADAPTIVE NEURO-FUZZY INFERENCE SYSTEMS

Hybrid Learning

Consider the situation sketched in Figure 26.

An input vector *i* goes through an adaptive net as defined earlier. Some of the nodes are adaptive, that is, depend on parameters, and other nodes may not be adaptive. For the sake of simplicity, assume the output *O* is a number (as opposed to a vector). The output depends on the input vector *i* and on

the parameters generated by the adaptive nodes. Let *S* be the set of these parameters. We then set $O = F(i, S)$, where *F* is a known function that we can obtain by forward propagation. Assume that $F(i, S)$ is a linear function of the parameters θ_1, ..., θ_n, and depends non-linearly on the parameters t_1, ..., t_p. We then can write:

$$O = F(i, S) = \sum_{k=1}^{n} \theta_k f_k(i, t_1, \ldots, t_p),$$

where the functions f_k depend on t_1, ..., t_p and the input *i* only (and not on θ_1, ..., θ_p). We assume that we have a training set, that is, a set of the form $\{(u_1, y_1), ..., (u_m, y_m)\}$ where each u_j denotes a specified input vector and y_j denotes the corresponding output. We then would like the following m equations to hold:

$$\sum_{k=1}^{n} \theta_k f_k(u_j, t_1, ..., t_p) = y_j, \quad j = 1, ..., m.$$

Let A be the $m \times n$ matrix whose (j, k) entry is $f_k(u_j, t_1, ..., t_p), j = 1, k = 1, ..., n$. The system of m equations above can be written in matrix form as $A\Theta = Y$, where:

$$\Theta = (\theta_1, ..., \theta_n)^T, \qquad Y = (y_1, ..., y_m)^T.$$

We need $m > n$ (i.e., we need sufficient amount of training data). Then it can be shown that the vector Θ that minimizes:

$$\| Y - A\Theta \|^2$$

is given by

$$\Theta = A^+ Y,$$

where A^+ is the pseudo-inverse of A. The pseudo-inverse matrix is obtained by the formula:

$$A^+ = (A^T A)^{-1} A^T$$

under some reasonable conditions, where A^T denotes the transpose of A. Note that if $m = n$ and A^{-1} exists, then $A^+ = A^{-1}$.

Now having the training set $\{(u_1, y_1), ..., (u_m, y_m)\}$, we compute the matrix A. The vector Y is determined. We the obtain the parameter vector Θ by the formula:

$$\Theta = (A^T A)^{-1} A^T Y.$$

The error is given by:

$$E = \sum_{j=1}^{m} \left(y_j - \sum_{k=1}^{m} \theta_k f_k(u_j, t_1, ..., t_p) \right)^2.$$

We then use the back-propagation to compute the partial derivatives $\varepsilon_{i,j}$ as explained earlier (see the second part of the sixth section). This leads to the update for $t = (t_1, ..., t_p)$:

$$\Delta t = -\eta \nabla E.$$

Remark: We could update $t_1, ..., t_p$ after each presentation of a single input u_j rather than using the cumulative error for all outputs, as we have done above. Of course, the process would start by assigning initial values to $t_1, ..., t_p$. Then $\theta_1, ..., \theta_n$ are computed using the pseudo-inverse of the matrix A. The process of alternating between the use of the pseudo-inverse and back-propagation would go on until some stopping criteria would be met.

Basic Architecture

Assume that we have two Sugeno-type rules of the form:

R_1: If X is A_1 and Y is B_1, then $z = f_1(x, y)$.

R_2: If X is A_2 and Y is B_2, then $z = f_2(x, y)$.

We can construct an adaptive net with five layers corresponding to these rules as shown on Figure 27.

The input layer is L0, layer L1 consists of adaptive nodes with parameters involved in the membership functions of A_1, A_2, B_1, and B_2. Layer L2 performs the t-norm operations $A_i(x) \wedge B_i(y)$ (or $A_i(x) B_i(y)$). Layer L3 normalizes the output L2 (which gives the strengths of the rules). Layer L4 takes inputs of the form $\overline{w}_i, x, y$ and produces outputs of the form $\overline{w}_i f_i(x, y)$. Finally, layer L5 produces $\sum \overline{w}_i f_i(x, y)$. This can be obviously generalized to any number of rules and any number of antecedents.

In most cases the functions f_i are linear. In the above example, $f_i(x, y) = p_i x + q_i y + r_i, i = 1, 2$. From now on we shall assume that this is the case.

Figure 27.

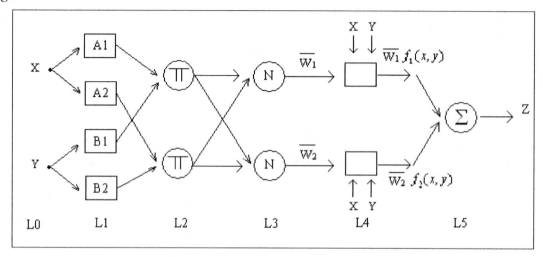

Training of the Net

Having a training set, we need to determine:

1. The parameters of the membership functions
2. The parameters (coefficients) of the linear functions f_i

The hybrid learning algorithm is the way to proceed. Consider a set of general rules of the form:

R_i: If X_1 is A_1 and ... X_i is A_i..., then $z = f_i(x_1, ..., x_K)$, $i = 1, ..., N$, where:

$$f_i(x_1, ..., x_K) = \sum_{j=1}^{K} p_{i,j} x_j + r_i, \quad i = 1, ..., N.$$

From previous considerations the output is:

$$\sum_{i=1}^{N} \overline{w}_i \left(\sum_{j=1}^{n} p_{i,j} x_j + r_i \right) = \sum_{i=1}^{N} \left(\sum_{j=1}^{K} (\overline{w}_i x_j) p_{i,j} + \overline{w}_i r_i \right),$$

where $\overline{w}_i$ denotes the normalized strength of the i-th rule. This shows that the output is linear in $p_{i,j}$ and r_i, $i = 1, ..., N$, $j = 1, ..., n$. Thus, the output is linear in the parameters of the consequent. We first initialize $p_{i,j}$, r_i, and the parameters found in the antecedents (i.e., the membership functions). We then adjust the values of $p_{i,j}$ and r_i using training data and the pseudo-inverse method and follow this up by back-propagation to adjust the membership functions.

Generalizing to Multiple Outputs

Assume now that we have rules that are more general and of the form:

If X is A_i and Y is B_j, then $z_1 = f_{i,1}(x, y)$ and $z_2 = f_{i,2}(x, y)$, $i = 1,2$, where $f_{i,j}(x, y) = p_{i,j} x + q_{i,j} y + r_{i,j}$, $j = 1,2$.

A possible architecture for such rules is shown in Figure 28.

In Figure 28, we have shown (for convenience) only the output z_1. The complete diagram would in addition have connections from the input (x, y) to

Figure 28.

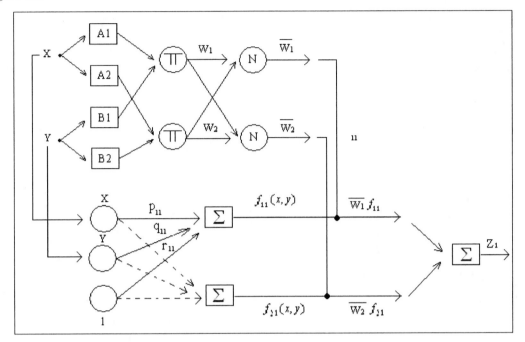

a second network with weights $p_{i,2}$, $q_{i,2}$, $r_{i,2}$. This network would, of course, have the same structure as the network shown in Figure 28. Again, for convenience we have labeled the weights $p_{1,1}$, $q_{1,1}$, and $r_{1,1}$ along the solid connections at the bottom, and the dotted connections have weights $p_{2,1}$, $q_{2,1}$, $r_{2,1}$ (not shown in the diagram). The two nets at the bottom of the diagram (only one of which is shown) can be used to learn the functions $f_{i,j}$, while back-propagating would determine the parameters of the membership functions of A_i and B_i ($i = 1,2$ in our example). The generalization to more than two rules and more than two variables in the antecedents is obvious.

This system allows the design of an intelligent agent where rules and data are seamlessly integrated. It also integrates into one-unit Sugeno rules and adaptive nets. It should be noted that:

1.   The architectures defined here are certainly not the only possible ones. For example, we could accomplish the same result by not having the two separate nets to learn the

functions $f_{i,j}$ but by having one adaptive net. In this case, we might not have linearity in $p_{i,j}$, $q_{i,j}$, and $r_{i,j}$, and hybrid learning would then not be applicable. The consequent and antecedent parameters would both be obtained by back-propagation.

2.   The functions $f_{i,j}$ might not be linear. In that case, the nets to learn the $f_{i,j}$ could be more complex than the adalines in Figure 28. In fact, it might be desirable to add another layer to these nets to gain the necessary flexibility.

We now give an example that demonstrates the use of fuzzy logic and neural nets to solve a problem that would be quite difficult to solve by use of a standard mathematical model.

Example: Stabilization of an inverted pendulum

Recent work on fuzzy controllers has shown a strong connection between fuzzy systems and neural nets. In fact, neuro-fuzzy systems combine the advantages of both approaches: thinking in terms of "common sense" rules and refining these rules through learning. It is well known that feed-forward neural nets with n inputs and m outputs and one hidden layer with sigmoid activation functions are universal approximators (i.e., any function on a compact subset of R^n can be approximated by such a net.) It is also well known that fuzzy input-output controllers based on multi-conditional antecedents are also universal approximators.

We demonstrate this equivalence by looking at the problem of stabilizing an inverted pendulum, a classical problem in fuzzy control. Many versions of this problem have been analyzed by many authors. We look at a simple version; see Yamakawa (1989). We will achieve stabilization by using an appropriate set of fuzzy rules and then by constructing an appropriate network.

The situation is as depicted in Figure 29. There are two input variable θ, the angle of the pole with the vertical, and θ', the rate of change of θ with time. The output variable is f, which drive the cart to move forward or backward.

The dynamical equations describing this system can be shown to be as follows:

$$\begin{cases} I\theta'' = VL\sin\theta - HL\cos\theta \\ V - mg = -mL(\theta''\sin\theta + \theta'^2\cos\theta) \\ H = mx'' + mL(\theta''\cos\theta - \theta'^2\sin\theta) \\ U - H = Mx'' \end{cases}$$

where:

L = half of the length of the pole P
x = position of the cart and x'' is the second derivative of x
H, V = horizontal and vertical force on the pivot of pole P
$I = mL^2/3$
m, M = masses of pendulum and vehicle

More complex versions of this problem involve bringing x to some position and two additional variables would then be involved: d and d' where d is the distance between x and x_0, and d' is its derivative. The goal is to bring (and keep) the pole P near the vertical position.

It is clear that it would be very awkward to achieve stabilization by using the non-linear dynamical system defined above. It is relatively easy to achieve this goal by using an appropriate fuzzy system of rules.

Figure 29.

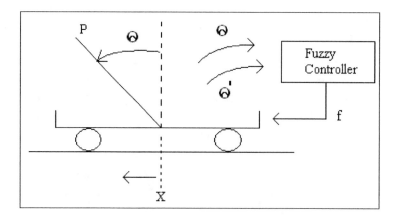

A standard approach to design a fuzzy system for problems of comparable complexity to the one we are considering is to use seven possible values for the variables involved. The seven values are: *NL* (negative large), *NM* (negative medium), *NS* (negative small), *AZ* (approximately zero), *PS* (positive small), *PM* (positive medium), and *PL* (positive large). Often these values are defined by simple triangular functions where (*PS, NS*), (*PM, NM*), and (*PL, NL*) are pairs of triangular functions symmetric, respectively, to the *y* axis and defined on appropriate ranges (depending on the specific problem). Typically some appropriate interval [−*a*, +*a*] is divided into six subintervals so each of the right boundaries of these subintervals marks the position where one triangle pears and the next triangle starts our. See Figure 30.

If the seven possible values for variables θ and θ' were used, there would be $7^2 = 49$ possible rules. If one wanted, in addition, to bring *x* to x_0, two additional variable *d* and *d'* would have to be used bringing the total number of possible rules to $7^4 = 2,401$. As is often the case in such problems, only a small subset of these rules is really needed (in this case around 20). In the Yamakawa simpler model (Yamakawa, 1989), the following chart sums up the rules needed:

θ'\θ	NM	NS	AZ	PS	PM
NS		NS		AZ	
AZ	NM		AZ		PM
PS		AZ		PS	

The entries in the middle of the table denote the output values (i.e., the values of *f*). These are common sense rules. For example, if θ' is *PS* and θ is *NS*, the direction in which θ changes tends to correct the situation θ being *NS*, so practically no corrective force needs to be applied, thus the value of *f* is *AZ*. A sensor feeds the numerical value of θ to the controller and successive measurements of θ define θ'. Then applying these rules and using defuzzification as previously discussed will define *f* to be applied at each interval of time. It should be noted that at each time no less than one and no more than two rules are fired. The inverted pendulum problem was one of the early problems treated as an application of fuzzy controllers.

We now look at the same problem and use neural nets to stabilize the position of pole *P* near the vertical. Assuming that θ takes on the values *NM, NS, AZ, PS,* and *PM* while θ' takes on the values *NS, AZ,* and *PS* and using the previous chart the possible values of *f* are given by Figure 31.

The network to be used is shown in Figure 32.

Consider a typical rule:

If θ is *NS* and θ' is *PS* then *f* is *AZ*

We assume the activation function for each neuron is a sigmoid. We use back-propagation to train this net. The above rule is one element of the training set. The antecedent generates the

Figure 30.

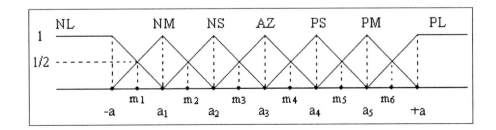

Figure 31.

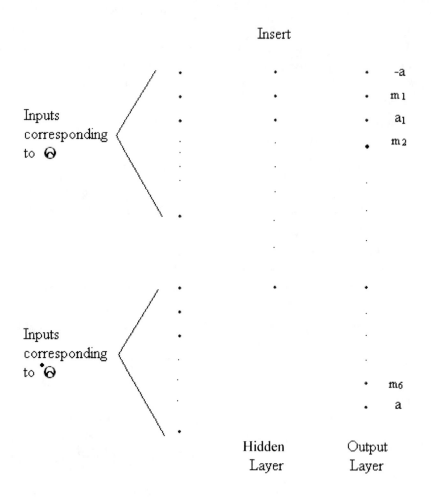

Figure 32.

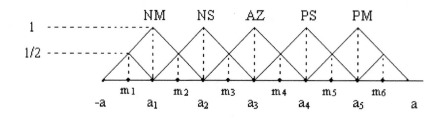

input, which is 1 on the node corresponding to *NS* (the fifth node in Figure 31) and ½ on the nodes corresponding to m_2 and m_3 (the fourth and sixth node in Figure 31). Similarly, we input 1 on the node in the θ' input corresponding to *PS* (i.e., on the node corresponding to a_4) and ½ on the nodes corresponding to m_4 and m_5. We require the output to be *AZ*, that is, we specify an output of 1 on the output layer corresponding to a_3 and ½ on the nodes corresponding to m_3 and m_4. We use all the rules to generate in this fashion the training set. When a new input is given, we interpret the (discrete) output as the membership function of the output by fitting some parameterized function (for example, a Gaussian membership) to the output.

The structures we have defined here are examples of the general ANFIS network (for scalar output) and CANFIS network (for vector output). These general structures are defined and discussed in Jang (1993); Kosko (1991); Mizutani, Jang, Nishio, Takagi, and Auslander (1994); Mizutani and Jang (1995); and Takagi (1991). Finally, in conclusion, we would like to state that standard fuzzy sets have been introduced in this chapter. Recent research has added "fuzzy sets of type 2" as a system of interest. For fuzzy sets of type 2, the value of the membership function at a point is itself a fuzzy subset of [0, 1] (rather than a point in [0, 1]). In some situations, it is more natural to consider rules involving such sets than to consider rules based on standard fuzzy sets. Many questions remain open in the context of fuzzy sets of type 2, and the reader is referred to the excellent book by J. M. Mendel for an extensive overview of this area (Mendel, 2001).

ACKNOWLEDGMENT

The authors are grateful to Mr. Fernando Fernandez, who has drawn all the figures of this chapter. Also, the authors received generous financial assistance from the department of computer and mathematical sciences in typesetting the chapter.

REFERENCES

Barto, A. G. (1992). Reinforcement learning and adaptive critic methods. In D. A. White and D. A. Sofge (Eds.), *Handbook of intelligent control: Neural, fuzzy, and adaptive approaches* (pp. 469-491). New York: Van Nostrand Reinhold.

Bazaraa, M., & Shetty, C. (1979). *Non-linear programming*. New York: John Wiley and Sons.

Berenji, H. R., & Khedkar, P. (1992). Learning and tuning fuzzy logic controllers through reinforcement. *IEEE Transactions on Neural Networks, 3*(5), 724-740.

Butnariu, D., & Klement, E. P. (1993). *Triangular norm based measures and games with fuzzy coalitions*. Dordrecht, Netherlands: Kluwer Academic Publishers.

Castro, J. (1995). Fuzzy logic controllers are universal approximators. *IEEE Trans. On Systems, Man, and Cybernetics, 25*(4), 629-635.

Dogherty, P., Driankov, D., & Heffendorn, H. (1993). Fuzzy if then unless rules and their implementation. *International Journal of Uncertainty, Fuzziness and Knowledge Based Systems 1*(2), 167-182.

Dubois, D. & Prade, H. (1992). Gradual inference rules in approximate reasoning. *Information Sciences, 61*, 103-122.

Hagan, M. T., Demuth, H. B., & Beale, M. (1995). *Neural network design*. Boston: PWS Publishing Company.

Haykin, S. (1994). *Neural networks: A comprehensive foundation*. Macmillan College Publishing.

Hellendoorn, H., & Thomas, C. (1993). Defuzzification in fuzzy controllers. *Journal of Intelligent and Fuzzy Systems, 1*(2), 109-123.

Hinton, G. E., & Sejnowski, T. S. (1986). Learning and relearning in boltzmann machines. In D. E. Rumerhart, J. L. Mclelland, and the PDP Research Group (Eds.). Parallel distributed processing (pp. 282-317). Cambridge, MA: MIT Press.

Hsia, T. C. (1977). *System identification: Least square methods*. D.C. Heath and Company.

Ingber, L. (1989). Very fast simulated re-annealing. *Mathematical and Computer Modeling, 12*(8), 967-973.

Jang, J. S. R. (1991). Fuzzy modeling using generalized neural networks and kalman filter algorithm. *Proceedings of the Ninth National Conference on Artificial Intelligence (AAAI-91)*, 762-767.

Jang, J. S. R. (1993). ANFIS: Adaptive network based fuzzy inference systems. *IEEE Transactions on Systems, Man, and Cybernetics, 23*(03), 665-685.

Jang, J. S. R., Sun, C. T., & Mizutani, E. (1997). *Neuro-fuzzy and soft computing*. NJ: Prentice Hall.

Klir, G. J. & Yuan, B. (1995). *Fuzzy sets and fuzzy logic. Theory and applications*. NJ: Prentice Hall.

Kosko, B. (1991). *Neural networks for signal processing*. NJ: Prentice Hall.

Mabuchi, S. (1993). A proposal for a defuzzification strategy by the concept of sensitivity analysis. *Fuzzy Sets and Systems, 55*(1), 1-14.

Mamdami, E. H. (1977). Applications of fuzzy logic to approximate reasoning using linguistic systems. *IEEE Trans. On Systems, Man, and Cybernetics, 26*(12), 1182-1191.

Mamdami, E. H., & Gaines, B. R. (Eds.). (1981). *Fuzzy reasoning and its applications*. London: Academic Press.

Mendel, J. M. (2001). *Uncertain rule-based fuzzy logic systems*. NJ: Prentice Hall.

Mizutani, E., & Jang, J. S. R. (1995). Coactive neural fuzzy modeling. *Proceedings of the International Conference on Neural Networks*, 760-765.

Mizutani, E., Jang, J. S. R., Nishio, K., Takagi, H., & Auslander, D. M. (1994). Coactive neural networks with adjustable fuzzy membership functions and their applications. *Proceedings of the International Conference on Fuzzy Logic and Neural Networks*, 581-582.

Pedrycz, W., & Gomidt, F. (1998). *An introduction to fuzzy sets analysis and design*. Cambridge, MA: The M.I.T. Press.

Saaty, T. L. (1980). *The analytic hierarchy process*. New York: McGraw Hill.

Sen, A., & Srivasta, M. (1990). *Regression analysis: Theory, methods, and applications*. London: Springer Verlag.

Strobach, P. (1990). *Linear prediction theory: A mathematical basis for adaptive systems*. London: Springer Verlag.

Takagi, H., & Hayashi, I. (1991). Nn-driven fuzzy reasoning. *Proceedings of the International Journal of Approximate Reasoning, 5*(3), 191-212.

Tong, R. M. (1985). An annotated bibliography of fuzzy control. In M. Sugeno (Ed.). *Industrial applications of fuzzy control* (pp. 249-269). New York: North Holland.

Weber, S. (1983). A general concept of fuzzy connections, negations and implications based on t-norms. *Fuzzy Sets and Systems 11*, 115-134.

Yager, R. (1984). Approximate reasoning as a basis for rule-based expert systems. *IEEE Trans. On Systems, Man, and Cybernetics, 14*(4), 636-643.

Yager, R., & Filer, D. P. (1993). On the issue of defuzzification and selection based on a fuzzy set. *Fuzzy Sets and Systems, 55*(3), 255-272.

Yamakawa, T. (1989). Stabilization of an inverted pendulum by a high speed logic controller hardware system. *Fuzzy Sets and Systems, 32*(2), 161-180.

Zadeh, L. A. (1975a). Fuzzy logic and approximate reasoning. *Synthese 30*(1), 407-428.

Zadeh, L. A. (1975b). The concept of a linguistic variable and its application to approximate reasoning i, ii, iii. *Information Sciences, 8*, 199-251; 9, 43-80.

Section II
Agent–Oriented System Design

Chapter V
Component Agent Systems:
Building a Mobile Agent Architecture That You Can Reuse

Paulo Marques
University of Coimbra, Portugal

Luís Silva
University of Coimbra, Portugal

ABSTRACT

One central problem preventing widespread adoption of mobile agents as a code structuring primitive is that current mainstream middleware implementations do not convey it simply as such. In fact, they force all the development to be centered on mobile agents, which has serious consequences in terms of software structuring and, in fact, technology adoption. This chapter discusses the main limitations of the traditional platform-based approach, proposing an alternative: component-based mobile agent systems. Two case studies are discussed: the JAMES platform, a traditional mobile agent platform specially tailored for network management, and M&M, a component-based system for agent-enabling applications. Finally, a bird's eye perspective on the last 15 years of mobile agent systems research is presented along with an outlook on the future of the technology. The authors hope that this chapter brings some enlightenment on the pearls and pitfalls surrounding this interesting technology and ways for avoiding them in the future.

INTRODUCTION

A mobile agent (Chess et al., 1994; White, 1996) is a simple, natural and logical extension of the remote distributed object concept. It is an object with an active thread of execution that is capable of migrating between different hosts and applications. By using mobile agents, the programmer is no longer confined to have static objects and perform remote invocations but can program the objects to move directly between applications. In itself, a mobile agent is just a programming abstraction: an active object that can move when needed. It is a structuring primitive, similar to the notion of class, remote object, or thread.

Two possible approaches for the deployment of mobile agents in distributed applications are:

a. To use a middleware platform that provides all the mechanisms and support for the execution of mobile agents. The basic characteristic of platform-based systems is that there is an infrastructure where all agents execute. This infrastructure typically corresponds to a daemon or service on top of which the agents are run. All agents co-exist on the same infrastructure. When the programmer develops an application, he is in fact modeling different mobile agents, which execute on the platform. Typically, this is done by extending a `MobileAgent` class or a similar construct. In fact, some of the mobile agents may not even be mobile but just static service agents interfacing with other functionalities of the system. Examples include, among others, the SOMA platform (Bellavista, Corradi, & Stefanelli, 1999), D'Agents (Kotz et al., 1997), Ajanta (Tripathi et al., 2002), Aglets (Aglets Project Homepage, 2006; Lange & Oshima, 1998), and JAMES (Silva et al., 1999). This is by far the most common approach.

b. An alternative approach is to provide the support for mobile agents as software components that can be more easily integrated in the development of applications. This approach is followed by the M&M project (Marques, 2003), described in this chapter.

In this chapter, we present the results of two major projects that have been conducted in our research group: JAMES and M&M.

The **JAMES** platform was developed in collaboration with SIEMENS and consisted of a traditional mobile agent platform especially optimized for network management applications. Our industrial partners used this platform to develop some mobile agent-based applications that were integrated into commercial products. These applications used mobile agents to perform management tasks (accounting, performance management, system monitoring, and detailed user profiling) that deal with very large amounts of data distributed over the nodes of GSM networks. With this project, we learned that this technology, when appropriately used, provides significant competitive advantages to distributed management applications.

The main motivation for the second project, M&M, was to facilitate the development process and the integration of mobile objects within ordinary applications. M&M abandoned the classic concept of mobile agent platforms as extensions of the operating system. Instead, this middleware is able to provide for agent mobility within application boundaries, rather than within system boundaries. Its objective was to demonstrate that it is possible to create an infrastructure such that the mobile agent concept can be leveraged into existing object-oriented languages in a simple and transparent way, without interfering in the manner in which the applications are normally structured. In order to achieve this goal, a component-oriented framework was devised and implemented, allowing programmers to use mobile agents as needed. Applications can still be developed using current object-oriented techniques but, by including certain components, they gain the ability to send, receive, and interact with agents. The component palette was implemented using the JavaBeans technology and was, furthermore, integrated with ActiveX (Box, 1997; Denning, 1997), allowing programmers from any programming language that supports COM/ActiveX to take advantage of this paradigm. To validate the soundness of the approach, a large number of applications have been implemented using M&M. Two application domains were of particular interest: agent-enabling web servers (Marques, Fonseca, Simões, Silva, & Silva, 2002a) and disconnected computing (Marques, Santos, Silva, & Silva, 2002b).

The rest of the chapter is organized as follows:

- In the **Background** section, a general introduction to platform-based systems for mobile agents is presented, followed by a case study: the JAMES platform;
- Then, in the **Component-Based Mobile Agent Systems** section, an alternative model is discussed, based on binary software components. In particular, it addresses some of limitations of the platform-based approach, presenting the M&M case study and its implications;
- The next section gives a **Bird's Eye Perspective** on the state of mobile agent technology;
- Finally, the last section presents the **Conclusion** and an outlook on the future of mobile agent technology.

BACKGROUND

Mobile Agent Platforms

The foundation for most platform-based systems is a server that sits on top of the operating system and where all agents execute. The platform is responsible for housing the agents and for providing every single feature needed by them and their surrounding environment (Delamaro, 2002; Marques, Simões, Silva, Boavida, & Gabriel, 2001). It provides functionalities like migration support, naming, security, inter-agent communication, agent tracking, persistence, external application gateways, platform management, and fault-tolerance. In fact, the agent platform plays the role of the "operating system of agents."

This list of supported features in an agent platform is by no means complete. Many application-specific domains have specific requirements. This leads to domain-specific implementations, having special features to address domain-specific requirements. Examples include: the JAMES platform (Silva et al., 1999), for telecommunication applications; aZIMAS (Arumugam, Helal, & Nalla, 2002) for supporting mobile agents in web servers; SOMA (Bellavista, 1999) for interoperability and integration with CORBA.

Figure 1 presents the typical architecture of such a system. As said, the operating system sits on the bottom. In the middle, there is the agent platform where all the agents execute. On the top, there are the agents belonging to all applications. This last point is especially important. Since all agents execute on top of the platform, usually all the agents from all applications can see each other. Although agents/applications can be divided into namespaces, as it happens in some platforms, and security permissions can be configured for proper access, in most cases the notion of application is quite weak or even inexistent.

In terms of programming model, in most platforms, the only support provided for application development is around the concept of mobile agent. Everything becomes a mobile agent, even entities that are conceptually services or gateways. Typically, inter-agent communication mechanisms are used to allow interactions between the different parts of the system. Some authors even refer to the concept of "whole application as a mobile agent" as the *fat-agent model* (Simões, Reis, Silva, & Boavida, 1999).

In Figure 2, this concept is illustrated. The developers have implemented two different applications, A and B, which in practice are just a set of mobile agents. True mobile agents are represented as white pawns. Black pawns represent static entities that are programmed as mobile agents due to the lack of proper infrastructure for application development. The interactions are fully based on inter-agent communication mechanisms. The concept of application is largely based on conventions about which agents communicate with

97

Figure 1. The mainstream mobile agent platform architecture

what. Interestingly, many times there is even the need to set up agents with special interfaces (and permissions) that are able to communicate with external applications via inter process communication (IPC) mechanisms. As strange as it seems, it is not uncommon for the only IPC mechanism available to provide integration with external entities to be a socket connection. It is also common for the agent platform to mediate all the access to operating system resources, especially if support for security is provided by the platform.

Developing distributed applications based on mobile agent systems has important advantages over the traditional client-server type of interactions. Mobile agents allow, among other things (Lange & Oshima, 1999), for: *reduced network traffic, easy software upgrading on-demand, easy introduction of new services in the network, higher robustness for the applications, support for disconnected computing, higher scalability, easy integration of vendor-proprietary systems,* and *higher responsiveness in the interactions with other systems.*

The JAMES Platform

In 1998, realizing the importance and advantages of using mobile agents in distributed systems, a consortium was setup for developing a mobile agent platform oriented for the development of applications in the field of telecommunication and network management. The project was called JAMES, and its partners were the University of Coimbra (Portugal), SIEMENS S.A. (Portugal), and SIEMENS AG (Germany); the being was implemented under the umbrella of a European Eureka Program (Σ!1921).

The JAMES platform provides the running environment for mobile agents. There is a distinc-

Figure 2. Applications on a standard agent platform are implemented as different mobile agents that map all the required functionality

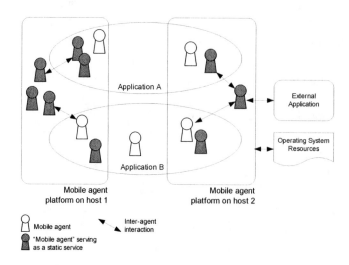

Figure 3. An overview of the JAMES platform

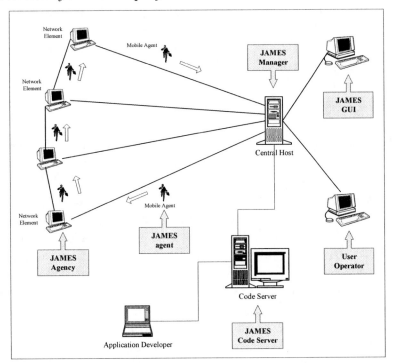

tion between the software environment that runs in the manager host and the software that executes in the network elements (NEs): the central host executes the JAMES manager while the nodes in the network run a JAMES agency. The agents are written by application programmers and execute on top of that platform. The JAMES system provides a programming interface that allows the full manipulation of mobile agents. Figure 3 presents a global snapshot of the system, with a special description of a possible scenario where the mobile agents will be used.

Every NE runs a Java virtual machine and executes a JAMES agency that enables the execution of the mobile agents. The JAMES agents will migrate through these machines of the network to access some data, execute some tasks, and produce reports that will be sent back to the JAMES manager. There is mechanism of authentication in the JAMES agencies to control the execution of agents and to avoid the intrusion of non-official

agents. The communication between the different machines is done through stream sockets. A special protocol was developed to transfer the agents across the machines in a robust way and is atomic to the occurrence of failures.

The application developer writes the applications that are based on a set of mobile agents. These applications are written in Java and should use the JAMES API for the control of mobility. After writing an application, the programmer should create a JAR with all the classes that make part of the mobile agent. This JAR file is placed in a JAMES code server. This server can be a different machine or in the same machine where the JAMES manager is executing. In both cases, it maintains a code directory with all the JAR files available and the mapping to the corresponding mobile agents.

The host machine that runs the JAMES manager is responsible for the whole management of the mobile agent system. It provides the interface to the end-user, together with a graphical user for the remote control and monitoring of agents, places, and applications. The JAMES GUI is the main tool for management and administration of the platform. With this interface, the user can manage all the agents and agencies in the system.

For lack of space we will not describe the inner details of the JAMES platform. However, in the following list we present the key features of our mobile agent system:

- Portability of the applications, through the use of the Java language;
- High-performance in mobility through the use of caching and prefetching techniques;
- Security mechanisms for code authentication;
- Resource control service to manage the use of underlying resources;
- An overview of the JAMES Platform (CPU, memory, disk and operating system resources);
- System monitoring;
- Fault-tolerance through the use of check-pointing and reconfiguration;
- Easy-to-use programming interface;
- Scalable execution of mobile agents, through the use of decentralized protocols;
- Easy customization of the software;
- "On-the-fly" software upgrading;
- Interoperation with classical network management protocols, like SNMP;
- Distributed management and easy configuration of the network;

The result of this platform was further exploited by the industrial partners that have developed some applications for performance management in telecommunications networks using mobile-agent technology and the JAMES platform.

COMPONENT-BASED MOBILE AGENT SYSTEMS

Introduction

Having completed the JAMES project, several important lessons were learned. Possibly the most important was that using a *mobile agent platform* as middleware seriously limits the acceptance of mobile agents as a structuring and programming paradigm. The problem is not the mobile agents by themselves but the use of monolithic platform for developing and deploying them. Platforms force the programmer to adopt a completely different development model from the one in mainstream use (object-oriented programming). When using an agent platform, the programmer is forced to center its development, its programming units, and its whole applications on the concept of agent. Although useful and relatively simple to implement, the use of platforms limit the acceptance of mobile agents as simple programming constructs (Kotz, Gray, & Rus, 2002).

In this section, we start by exploring how traditional mobile agent platforms limit the acceptance of mobile agents as a structuring primitive, and then we present M&M, an agent system specifically for overcoming those limitations.

Limitations of the Platform-Based Model

The reasons why the platform architecture limits the acceptance of the mobile agent paradigm can be seen from three perspectives: the programmer, the end-user, and the software infrastructure itself.

The Programmer

One fundamental aspect of the mobile agent paradigm is that, by itself, it does not provide more functionality than what is attainable with the traditional client/server model. One of the major advantages of the mobile agent paradigm is that *logically* (i.e., without considering its physical implementation), its functionalities as a whole and as a structuring primitive—*an active thread of execution that is able to migrate*—are particularly adapted for distributed computing (Papaioannou, 2000). Mobile agent technology, in itself, has no killer application (Chess et al., 1994; Kotz et al., 2002).

Taking this into consideration, a relevant question is: What strong reason can motivate a programmer to consider using mobile agents to develop its applications? After all, everything that can be attained by using mobile agents can be done using client/server. The most important reason, as discussed before, is that a mobile agent is a logical structuring primitive very adapted for distributed computing. Still, for it to be accepted, the price to be paid by the programmer cannot be too high. With traditional agent platforms, typically it is.

The problems include: the mobile agent concept is not readily available at the language level; the applications have to be centered on the mobile agents; and a complicated interface between the agents and the applications and operating system resources must be written. The programmers want to develop their applications as they currently do, by using object-oriented techniques, and by using mainstream APIs. Agents will typically play a small role on the application structuring. Current platforms force exactly the opposite. Instead of being middleware, agents are the *frontware*.

If one looks at history, it is easy to understand that the RPC success is due to its strong integration with structured programming environments. RPCs did not force programmers to abandon their programming languages, environments, and methodologies. On the contrary, RPCs embraced them. Understandably, if the RPC model had required completely different languages and methodologies, it would have failed. Programmers would have continued to use sockets. After all, everything that can be done using an RPC can

be done using a socket, granted that it is so with different degrees of difficulty. The argument also applies to RMI and its integration with object-oriented languages. Remote method invocation did not require different languages or environments but instead blended into existing systems. In both cases, developers started to use the new technologies because: (a) they were readily integrated at the language level and into their programming environments; (b) the applications could continue to be developed using the existing methodologies and only use the new technologies as needed; c) no workarounds were necessary for integrating with existing applications.

The point is that mobile agent technology should not necessarily force complete agent-based software design. It should be a complement to traditional object-oriented software development and easily available to use in ordinary distributed applications, along with other technologies.

The End-User

From the viewpoint of the user, if an application is going to make use of mobile agents, it is first necessary to install an agent platform. The security permissions given to the incoming agents must also be configured, and the proper hooks necessary to allow the communication between the agents and the application must be setup. While some of these tasks can be automated by using installation scripts, this entire setup package is too much of a burden.

Usually, the user is not concerned with mobile agents nor wants to configure and manage mobile agent platforms. The user is much more concerned with the applications than with the middleware they are using in the background. In the currently available mobile agent systems, the agents are central and widely visible. They are not the background middleware but the foreground applications.

Also, the term *mobile code* has very strong negative connotations, which makes the dissemination of mobile agent technology difficult. The user is afraid of installing a platform capable of receiving and executing code without its permission. This happens even though the existence of mobile code is present in technologies like Java, in particular in Applets, RMI, and JINI. The fundamental difference is that in those cases, the user is shielded from the middleware being used. In many cases, using mobile agents does not pose an increased security threat, especially if proper authentication and authorization mechanisms are in place. However, because the current agent platforms do not hide the middleware from the user, the risk associated with the technology is perceived as being higher than it is. This causes users to back away from applications that make use of mobile agents.

The Software Infrastructure

One final limitation of the platform-based approach lies in the architecture itself. Generally speaking, there are very few platforms that provide means for extensibility. Typically, the platform is a monolithic entity with a fixed set of functionalities. If it is necessary to provide new functionality, for instance, a new inter-agent communication mechanism, that functionality is directly coded into the platform. What this means is that if there are new requirements or features to be supported, it is necessary to recompile the whole platform and deploy it in the distributed infrastructure. This lack of support for system extensibility has several important consequences.

The first important consequence is management costs. As the name indicates, the *platform* is a software infrastructure that must be managed and attended at all times. Currently, when an operator deploys an agent-based application, it does not gain just one new application to administrate. Besides the application, it gains a full-blown agent platform to manage. This type of cost is not negligible. For instance, it is curious

to observe how sensitive the network management and telecommunications communities are to management costs, even though they are amongst the ones that can most benefit from the use of this technology (Picco, 1998; Simões, Rodrigues, Silva, & Boavida, 2002).

Another facet of the monolithic structure of the agent platform problem has to do with changing requirements. It is well known in the software industry that the requirements of applications are constantly changing. In fact, this knowledge has motivated a whole series of software methodologies that take this into account, as rapid development (McConnell, 1996) and eXtreme programming (Beck, 1999). In most of the current agent platforms, each time a feature is added or an error corrected, the software is recompiled, originating a new version. Although it is quite simple to upgrade an application based on mobile agents—it may be as simple as to kill the agents and send out new ones—the same does not happen to the agent infrastructure. When there is a new version of the agent infrastructure, it is necessary to manually redeploy it across the distributed environment.

Even though it is easy to devise code-on-demand solutions for the complete upgrade of agent platforms or to use server-initiated upgrades, as in the case of JAMES (Silva et al., 1999), most existing platforms do not provide for it. In many cases, the cost of redeploying the software across the infrastructure may be unacceptable. This is a second type of management cost that must be paid. In terms of deployment, it would be much more appealing to have an infrastructure where parts could be plugged in, plugged out, and reconfigured as necessary. Voyager (Glass, 1997), MOA (Milojicic, Chauhan, & la Forge, 1998), and gypsy (Lugmayr, 1999) provided the first experiments in this area, though, due to the monolithic architecture of most platforms, this type of solution is not readily available for them.

The M&M Agent System

The most distinctive characteristic of M&M is that there are no agent platforms. Instead, the agents arrive and depart directly from the applications they are part of. The agents exist and interact with the applications from the inside, along with the other application objects.

The applications become agent-enabled by incorporating well-defined binary software components into their code. These components give them the capability of sending, receiving, and interacting with mobile agents. The applications themselves are developed using the current best-practice software methods and become agent-enabled by integrating these "mobility components," that is, M&M framework components. We call this approach ACMAS—*application centric mobile agent systems*—since the applications are central and mobile agents are just part of the system playing specific roles.

The key idea is that the different functionality typically found on a monolithic agent platform is factored out as independent pluggable components that can be added or removed from the applications. No underlying agent platform is involved. In Figure 4, the approach is shown. Here, an application is being run on two different hosts. This application was built by using object-oriented programming and by incorporating generic components, like the ones that provide easy database connectivity or graphics toolkits, and mobility-related components, as the ones that provide migration support and agent tracking. Agents are able to migrate between applications by using the mobility-related components.

Comparing this model with the platform-based architecture, it is quite clear that the applications are no longer a set of agents. In this approach, when inside an application, an agent is just another object that has an associated thread of execution. The agents are just like any other objects of the application. Different applications incorporate the specific components necessary for their operation, executing them side-by-side. Another advantage of this approach is that agents can be specific to their applications, not having all the agents from all the applications coexisting together.

The M&M Component Palette

When developing an application by using the ACMAS approach, three different types of components are involved: generic third-party off-the-shelf components; application-specific components; and mobile agent-related components (see Figure 5):

Figure 4. The applications become agent-enabled by incorporating well-defined binary components

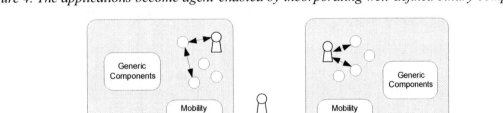

- **Third-party off-the-shelf components** are components that are commercially available from software makers. Currently, there is a large variety of components available for the most different things, like accessing databases, designing graphical user interfaces, messaging, and others. All these components can be used for building the applications without having to re-implement the required functionalities.

- **Domain-specific components** are modules that must be written in the context of the application domain being considered, providing functionalities not readily available off-the-shelf. For instance, while implementing a particular application, it may be necessary to write special parsers for extracting information from files or to write supporting services for allowing agents to monitor the hardware of a machine. These modules can be coded as components and incorporated into the application.

- **Mobile agent-related components** provide the basic needs in terms of mobile-agent infrastructure. These components provide the functionalities typically found in agent platforms: mobility support, inter-agent communication mechanisms, agent tracking, security, and others. The M&M component palette fits into this category.

When writing an application, the programmer assembles the necessary components and interconnects them by using programmatic glue. The application logic that mandates the execution of the program can be a separate module or be embedded in the wiring of the components. Typical examples of the former are backend database and transaction processing applications; examples of the latter are form-based applications for data entering and querying. The final application is the combination of components, wiring glue, and backend application logic.

When considering a component palette for supporting mobile agents, two different aspects

Figure 5. Applications are created by assembling the necessary components

Selection and wiring
of the necessary
components

Final Application

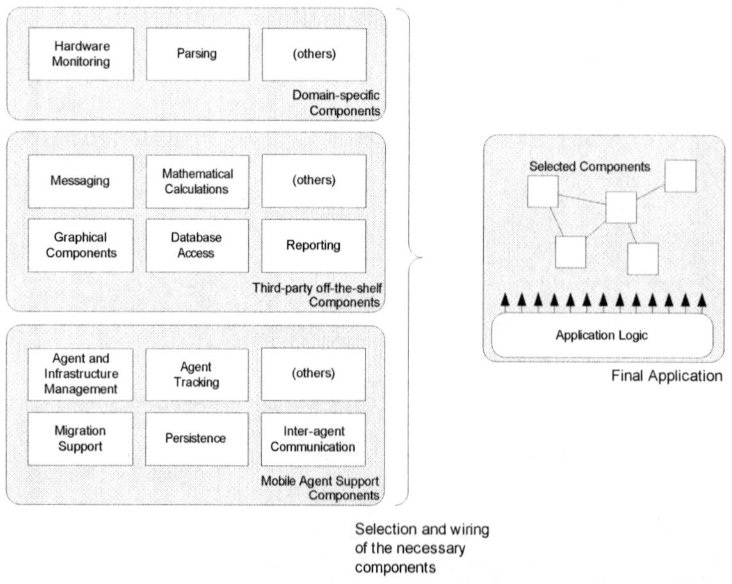

Table 1. Available components in the M&M component palette

Component(s)	Functionality
Mobility component	Provides the basic support for agent mobility, agent control, and monitoring. It incorporates an extensibility mechanism that allows other components to interact with the mobile agents.
Management components	Allows agents and the instantiated components to be monitored and controlled locally and remotely by applications and by administrative agents.
Agent tracking components	Allows the agents, local, and external applications to know the location of each agent in the distributed application.
Security component	Allows agents to safely execute inside the applications and for the applications to safely execute the agents. It is responsible for the provision of authentication and authorization services, and of monitoring and controlling what operations each agent is allowed to perform.
Local communication components	Supports message exchange between agents and applications or other agents, in the context of a single running application, using several paradigms (message passing and publisher-subscriber, both synchronously and asynchronously).
Global communication components	Allows the agents and the applications to exchange messages using several paradigms (message passing and publisher-subscriber, both synchronously and asynchronously), in the global context of a distributed application.
Disconnected computing components	Provides support for disconnected computing, allowing agents to be saved into persistent storage if they are not able to migrate to a disconnected device, and to migrate when the device comes back online. Persistent storage is also implemented as a separate component.
Web publishing components	Allows agents that migrate to a Web server to publish information and act as Web resources.

must be considered. On the one hand, there are components that are integrated into the application, giving it special abilities in terms of interacting with mobile agents. One example of this is a component that gives the application the ability to track the agents whenever they migrate.

On the other hand, when programming the mobile agents themselves, there are components that can be used for building them, for instance, a component that when included in a mobile agent gives it the ability to communicate with other mobile agents. Currently, the M&M framework supports both types.

Thus, when discussing the component palette of M&M, presented in Table 1, it is important to realize that there are components for including into the applications and components for including into agents. In fact, some of the components can even be used for both purposes (e.g., the client components of inter-agent communication).

Another important point is that sometimes the components do not implement the full functionality of a service and serve only as access points to certain functionalities. For instance, the client component for agent tracking connects to a network server that holds and updates the location of the agents. It should be noted that the M&M component list is by no means static or fixed. The M&M framework has well-defined interfaces that allow third-party developers to create new components and add them to the system and to upgrade existing components. In fact, M&M somewhat resembles a Lego system where new pieces can be created and fitted into the existing ones.

Figure 6 shows an application being created in a visual development tool and being agent-enabled by using M&M. On the left it is possible to see that the mobility component has been included; on the right, the properties of this component are shown; on the top, the M&M component palette is visible.

A detailed account of the M&M system and its implementation can be found in Marques (2003).

Consequences of Using a Component-Based Approach

Using a component-based approach for developing applications that use mobile agents has several important consequences. Some of these consequences are directly related to the characteristics of component technology, others are a product of the way M&M was designed. Some of the most important aspects are:

- **The users do not see agents or manage agent platforms:** As agents are sent back into the middleware instead of being "frontware," what the users ultimately see are applications and their interface. The adoption of a certain application is once again based on its perceived added value, not on the technology that it is using. Also, because users do not have to manage agents nor platforms, applications become conceptually simpler. No middleware infrastructure is explicitly visible to install and maintain. Although there are still distributed applications to install and manage, this is much easier than managing a separate infrastructure shared by a large number of distributed applications with different policies and requirements.
- **Tight integration with the end applications:** Since the agents can migrate from end-

Figure 6. Screen capture of the M&M component palette being used for developing a demonstration application

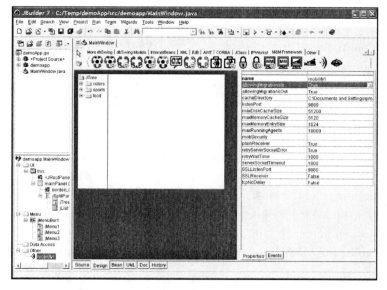

applications to end-applications, interacting with them from the inside, development becomes much more straightforward. There is no need to set up service agents, configure their policies, and devise workarounds based on IPCs. Once inside an application, a mobile agent is just a thread of execution that can access all the objects of that application, under proper security concerns. This contributes to better performance and scalability since the interaction with the applications does not have to go through the middlemen—the service agents.

- **Tight integration with existing programming environments:** For supporting mobile agents in an application, all the developer has to do is to include some of the components into the application and interconnect them. The applications can continue to be developed using object-oriented methodologies, having the necessary support for active migrating objects. By using M&M components in the applications, developers do not have to center all the development on the agents. Agents become just "one more" powerful distributed programming construct, as once advocated by Papaioannou (Papaioannou, 2000). What this means is that the development model is well integrated with current software development practices and environments. The path to using mobile agents in the applications becomes as smooth as using, for instance, remote method invocation.

- **Possibility of using visual development tools:** Software components are normally designed so that they can be manipulated visually. Instead of focusing on an API approach, components emphasize on well-defined visual entities with properties and interconnections that the programmer can configure visually. This can result in a large increase in productivity, a smoother learning curve, and a wider acceptance of a technology. By using a component-based

approach, M&M takes benefit of all these characteristics.

- **Support for any programming language:** It is possible to use a JavaBeans/ActiveX bridge to encapsulate JavaBeans components as ActiveX ones. Thus, in the Windows platform it is possible to use a JavaBeans component from any programming environment, as long as it supports COM/ActiveX. This was the approach taken in the M&M framework. By using such a bridge, it was possible to have applications written in several languages—Visual Basic, Visual C++, Java, and so forth—sending and receiving agents between them. Even though, from a research point of view, this might not seem so important, from an integration and acceptance point of view it is quite important: It is directly related to whether a technology gets to be used or not.

- **Security can be integrated into the application:** One of the valuable lessons learned when designing the Internet was the importance of the end-to-end argument in system design (Saltzer, Reed, & Clark, 1984). There is a fragile balance between what can be offered generically by an infrastructure and what should be left to the application design on the endpoints. In terms of security, this is especially important. In many cases, it is only at the end applications, and integrated with the application security policies and its enforcement, that it is possible to take sensible security decisions. By using components directly integrated into the applications, the security of the mobile agents of an application becomes integrated with the security policies of the application itself.

- **Only the necessary components are included in each application:** Because the developer is implementing its application and only using the necessary features of mobile code, only the required components that implement such features need to be included. What this means is that it is not necessary to have a gigantic platform that implements every possibly conceivable feature, because in the end many of these features are not used in most applications. By using specific components it is possible to build a software infrastructure that is much more adapted to the needs of each specific application.

- **Extensibility and constant evolution:** In the last section it was discussed how "changing requirements" are an important problem and how monolithic platforms are ill-equipped to deal with new features, new releases, and redeployment. By using a component-based approach, it is possible to continually implement new components, with new features and characteristics, without implying the rebuilding of a new version of "the platform." The component palette can always be augmented.

- **Reusability and robustness:** One of the acclaimed benefits of using components is their tendency to become more robust over time. As a component is more and more reused in different applications, more errors are discovered and corrected, leading to new and more robust versions. Because components are black boxes with well defined interfaces and functionalities, they are also easier to debug and correct. By using a component-based approach to implement a mobile agent framework, it is also possible to benefit from these advantages.

Overall many applications have been implemented using M&M accessing its usefulness, easy of use, and close integration with programming environments and software. In this context, two application domains were of particular interest: agent-enabling web servers and supporting disconnected computing.

- The M&M component framework allows any Web server that supports the *servlet specification* to send, receive, and use mobile agents. M&M provides a clean integration, requiring neither a custom-made Web server nor a special purpose agent platform. A full account of this exploration can be found in Marques et al. (2002a).

- Finally, supporting disconnected computing has allowed us to understand the current limitations of the framework in supporting very low-level operations. This account can be found in Marques et al. (2002b).

A BIRD'S EYE PERSPECTIVE

Over the years, there has been a huge proliferation of mobile agent platforms. In fact, already in 1999 there were 72 known platforms. Nevertheless, the technology is still far from common use by mainstream programmer and, oddly as it seems, there now seems to exist more agent platforms than mobile agent-based applications.

In the previous sections, we have discussed how the agent platform architecture seriously impairs the actual leverage of the mobile agent paradigm into real applications, by real programmers, to real users. The paradigm does not bring a "one order of magnitude" increase in functionality, and at the same time, the agent platform architecture imposes a too-high price to developers, users, systems administrators, and institutions that could make use of the technology. The road imposed by the platform architecture is not one of integration with existing tools and environments but one of complete conversion to a new architecture. This conversion is asked for without giving anything substantial enough in return, and imposing many limitations on what can be implemented and how.

About the Proliferation of Mobile Agent Platforms

In our view, the huge proliferation of mobile agent platforms is directly connected with two factors: (a) the monolithic nature of agent platforms; (b) the advent of the Java language.

When considering different application fields, each one has its specific requirements. For instance, in the network management area, an important requirement is integration with SNMP. In other domains, there are others. Because in most cases it is not possible to extend a generic agent platform to take into account the needs of a certain application domain, what has happened is that researchers, and in fact the industry, have developed many new agent platforms that try to address specific domains. The Java language made it extremely easy to develop basic infrastructures for object and thread mobility, and thus to experiment in this area. In most cases, these platforms were developed from scratch.

The problems with these platforms are: they are not reusable across domains (many times not even across problems in a single domain); they do not take into account results in research (e.g., how to properly implement agent tracking or fault-tolerance); and, because in many cases they are quite experimental, they lack the robustness needed to be usable in the real world. The result is the current huge number of platforms that are not used by anyone and a large disappointment with the mobile agent paradigm.

The Mobile Agent Community

Another important problem is that the mobile agent community is too biased on the platform architecture, and little concerned with its integration with existing systems and infrastructures. This strong bias is easy to observe in practice. For instance, when looking at standards for mobile agents systems such as MASIF (OMG, 2000),

from the Object Management Group, and FIPA (FIPA, 2000; FIPA, 2002), from the Foundation for Intelligent Physical Agents, it can be seen that the standardization effort was done around the concept of "agent platform", the platform on top of which all agents *should* execute. Neither alternative execution models nor any provisioning for integration with existing programming environments were considered.

Curiously, two of the most respected researchers in the area of intelligent agents—Nick Jennings and Michael Wooldridge—have long been arguing about the dangers of trying to leverage agents into the market. In the classic article *Software Engineering with Agents: Pitfalls and Pratfalls* (Wooldridge & Jennings, 1999), they examine what has been happening in the intelligent agent community. But, in fact, the observations also apply to the mobile agent community. Some of the key lessons from their experience are: "*You oversell agents,*" "*You ignore related technology,*" "*You ignore legacy,*" "*You obsess on infrastructure,*" and "*You see agents everywhere*". These are all relevant points if one wants to bring the mobile agent paradigm into real-world programming environments.

This view is somewhat supported by the success of Voyager (Glass, 1997) when compared with other agent infrastructures. Voyager is not a mobile agent platform but an ORB that, among other things, is also able to send and receive agents. Voyager does not force everything to be centered on agents, nor forces the applications to be agents. Applications are developed using ordinary methods and can use Voyager as an ordinary ORB. In practice, what has happened is that programmers who were using Voyager as a commercial ORB understood that they also had support for sending and receiving "active threads." Not having any prejudice, they started using this facility. Users continued to see applications as they always had, and system administrators did not gain complex agent platforms to manage.

Security

Security is traditionally singled out as the biggest problem facing mobile agents, and that prevented their dissemination as a paradigm. The idea of having arbitrary code that can execute on a host can be a scary one. There is the danger of resource stealing, denial-of-service attacks, data spying, and many other problems (Farmer, Guttman, & Swarup, 1996; Greenberg, Byington, & Harper, 1998).

Even so, although there are still some hard problems to be solved in a practical way, like the malicious host problem (Hohl, 1998) and proper resource control, security is probably one of the most active areas of research in mobile agent systems (e.g., Loureiro, 2001, contains an extensive survey on existing research on the topic).

When developing mobile agent applications, two different scenarios have to be considered. The first scenario consists of deploying an application that uses mobile agents in a closed environment. What this means is that it is possible to identify a central authority that controls all the nodes of the network where the agents are deployed. For example, a network operator may deploy an agent platform on its network, for being able to deliver new services in an easy and flexible way. Although different users, with different permissions, may create agents, the key point is that there is a central authority that is able to say who has what permissions and guarantee that nodes do not attack agents.

A completely different scenario is to have agents deployed in an open environment. In this picture, agents migrate to different nodes controlled by different authorities, possibly having very different goals. One classic example of this situation is an e-commerce application on the Internet. Different sites may deploy an agent platform, allowing agents to migrate to their nodes and query about products and prices, and even perform transactions on behalf of their owners. Here the sites will be competing against each other

for having the agents making the transactions on their places. There is no central authority, and each site may attack the agents, stealing information from them, or making them do operations that they were not supposed to do.

Although it may appear that deploying applications on closed environments is too restrictive, there is a large number of applications that are worth deploying in such setting. Examples include network management, telecommunication applications, software distribution and upgrading, parallel and distributed processing, and groupware. For such environments, the currently available solutions are well adapted and sufficient. In many cases, it is a matter of proper authentication and authorization mechanisms, associated with a public key infrastructure.

The key argument is that although a lot of research is still necessary for securely deploying agents in open environments, there is a multitude of applications that can be developed securely for existing computing infrastructures in closed environments. On closed environments, besides the psychological effect of having code that is able to migrate between hosts, there is no additional risk when compared with existing technologies. The risks are similar to having *rexec* daemons running on machines, or using code servers in Java RMI.

In our view, the argument that it is security that is preventing the deployment of mobile agent technology is a misguided one. Many applications can be developed securely; and considering distributed systems, there are many technologies that operate without any special security considerations. That lack of security has not prevented them from being developed or having a large user base. A classical example is SNMP.

Agent Languages: Could They Be the Solution?

Over the years, many researchers came up with new languages that express mobile processes and mobile computations directly (e.g., Visual Obliq,

Cardelli, 1995; Jocaml Conchon, & Fessant, 1999; Nomadic Pict & Wojciechowski, 1999). Although these languages integrate the mobile agent paradigm at the language level and are interesting in terms of the lessons learned in expressing new abstractions, they present the same generic problem as the platform architecture.

These languages force the programmers to use completely different programming paradigms and software structuring methodologies. At the same time, because using mobile agents does not bring any large increase in productivity nor enables anything important that cannot be achieved by classical means, programmers are not compelled to try out these new languages. In fact, it does not make much sense to ask developers to abandon proven development techniques and environments in favor of new languages that do not allow anything new or powerful, have not proven themselves, and force all the development to be centered on different abstractions.

The mobile agent technology should be available at the language level, but this means that the middleware should allow the creation, management, and integration with mobile entities directly, probably through an API at the same level than other programming libraries. It means that the programmer should be able to continue to use its current programming environments, languages, and development methodologies. When necessary, and only then, it should be able to create an active thread of execution that would be able to migrate and interact with the objects on different applications. This does not mean that all the development should be centered on the agents or that new languages are really necessary.

CONCLUSION

Mobile agent research is now almost 15 years old. Many valuable lessons have been learned in areas so diverse as persistence, resource allocation and control, tracking, state capture, security,

communication, coordination, and languages. Nevertheless, no killer application has emerged, and only a few commercial applications have been developed. Two standardization efforts were made and failed.

Although the mobile agent paradigm has not entered the realm of mainstream programming, the fact is that *mobile code* and *mobile state* are now mainstream programming techniques. This has happened not as most researchers would expect it to have, namely as mobile agents, but in many different and more subtle ways. Java RMI code servers are a standard mechanism in use. Java object serialization and .NET's Remoting mechanism, which are for everyday use, offer state mobility and also code mobility in certain circumstances. Remotely upgradeable software, ActiveX-enabled pages, and other forms of code and state mobility are now so common that we do not even think about them. Even mainstream undergraduate books like Coulouris, Dollimore, and Kindberg (2000) and Tanenbaum and Steen (2002) discuss code and state mobility, and even mobile agents, without any prejudice. Books that are not mobile agent-specific but are related to code mobility are available (Nelson, 1999). Mobile code and mobile state have entered the realm of distributed programming.

It is always hard and error prone to make predictions. But, quoting Kotz et. al., it is also our view that *"The future of mobile agents is not specifically as mobile agents"* (Kotz, 2002). We also do not believe that the future of mobile agents is connected to the use of agent platforms as we know them today. That belief arises from our experiences with the JAMES and M&M systems, as presented in this chapter.

In our view, the future of mobile agents will be a progressive integration of mobile agent concepts into existing development environments. This integration will be as readily available at the API level as object serialization and remote method invocation have become. The programmer will be able to derive from a base class and with no effort have an object that is able to move between applications. That class and that object will be ordinary ones among the hundreds or thousands used in any particular application. This evolution will probably occur as the development of object serialization APIs becomes more complete, powerful, and easy to use.

ACKNOWLEDGMENT

We would like to thank to all the students and researchers that over the years worked on the JAMES and M&M systems. Also, this investigation was partially supported by the Portuguese Research Agency – FCT, through the CISUC Research Center (R&D Unit 326/97).

REFERENCES

Aglets Project Homepage (2006). Retrieved April 27, 2006, from http://sourceforge.net/projects/aglets

Arumugam, S., Helal, A., & Nalla, A. (2002). aZIMAs: Web mobile agent system. *Proceedings of 6th International Conference on Mobile Agents (MA'02)* (LNCS 2535). Barcelona, Spain: Springer-Verlag.

Beck, K. (1999). *eXtreme programming explained: Embrace change*. Addison-Wesley.

Bellavista, P., Corradi, A., & Stefanelli, C. (1999). A secure and open mobile agent programming environment. *Proceedings of the 4th International Symposium on Autonomous Decentralized Systems (ISADS'99)*, Tokyo, Japan.

Box, D. (1997). *Essential COM*. Addison-Wesley.

Cardelli, L. (1995). A language with distributed scope. *Computing Systems Journal, 8*(1).

Chess, D., Grossof, B., Harrison, C., Levine, D., Parris, C., & Tsudik, G. (1994). *Mobile Agents: Are they are good idea? (RC19887)*. IBM Research.

Conchon S., & Fessant, F. (1999). Jocaml: Mobile agents for objective-caml. *Proceedings of the Joint Symposium on Agent Systems and Applications/Mobile Agents (ASA/MA'99),* Palm Springs, CA.

Coulouris, G., Dollimore, J., & Kindberg, T. (2000). *Distributed systems: Concepts and design* (3rd ed.). Addison-Wesley.

Delamaro, M., & Picco, G. (2002). Mobile code in .NET: A porting experience. *Proceedings of 6th International Conference on Mobile Agents (MA'02)* (LNCS 2535). Barcelona, Spain: Springer-Verlag.

Denning, A. (1997). *ActiveX controls inside out* (2nd ed.). Redmond, WA: Microsoft Press.

FIPA. (2000). *FIPA agent management support for mobility specification*. DC000087C. Geneva, Switzerland: Foundation for Intelligent Physical Agents.

FIPA. (2002). *FIPA abstract architecture specification*. SC00001L. Geneva, Switzerland: Foundation for Intelligent Physical Agents.

Farmer, W., Guttman, J., & Swarup, V. (1996). Security for mobile agents: Issues and requirements. *Proceedings of the 19th National Information Systems Security Conference (NISSC'96)*, Baltimore.

Glass, G. (1997). *ObjectSpace voyager core package technical overview*. ObjectSpace.

Greenberg, M., Byington, J., & Harper, D. (1998). Mobile agents and security. *IEEE Communications Magazine, 36*(7).

Gschwind, T., Feridun, M., & Pleisch, S. (1999). ADK: Building mobile agents for network and systems management from reusable components. *Proceedings of the Joint Symposium on Agent*

Systems and Applications/Mobile Agents (ASA/ MA'99), Palm Springs, CA.

Hohl, F. (1998). A model of attack of malicious hosts against mobile agents. In *Object-Oriented Technology, ECOOP'98 Workshop Reader / Proceedings of the 4th Workshop on Mobile Object Systems (MOS'98): Secure Internet Mobile Computations* (LNCS 1543). Brussels, Belgium: Springer-Verlag.

Kotz, D., Gray, R., Nog, S., Rus, D., Chawla, S., & Cybenko, G. (1997). AGENT TCL: Targeting the needs of mobile computers. *IEEE Internet Computing, 1*(4).

Kotz, D., Gray, R., & Rus, D. (2002). Future directions for mobile agent research. *IEEE Distributed Systems Online, 3*(8).

Lange, D., & Oshima, M. (1998). Mobile agents with Java: The Aglet API. *World Wide Web Journal,* (3).

Lange, D., & Oshima, M. (1999). Seven good reasons for mobile agents. *Communications of the ACM, 42*(3).

Loureiro, S. (2001). *Mobile code protection.* Unpublished doctoral dissertation, Institut Eurecom, ENST, Paris.

Lugmayr, W. (1999). *Gypsy: A component-oriented mobile agent system.* Unpublished doctoral dissertation, Technical University of Vienna, Austria.

Marques, P. (2003). *Component-based development of mobile agent systems.* Unpublished doctoral dissertation, Faculty of Sciences and Technology of the University of Coimbra, Portugal.

Marques, P., Fonseca, R., Simões, P., Silva, L., & Silva, J. (2002a). A component-based approach for integrating mobile agents into the existing Web infrastructure. In *Proceedings of the 2002 IEEE International Symposium on Applications*

and the Internet (SAINT'2002). Nara, Japan: IEEE Press.

Marques, P., Santos, P., Silva, L., & Silva, J. G. (2002b). Supporting disconnected computing in mobile agent systems. *Proceedings of the 14th International Conference on Parallel and Distributed Computing and Systems (PDCS2002).* Cambridge, MA.

Marques, P., Simões, P., Silva, L., Boavida, F., & Gabriel, J. (2001). Providing applications with mobile agent technology. *Proceedings of the 4th IEEE International Conference on Open Architectures and Network Programming (OpenArch'01),* Anchorage, AK.

McConnell, S. (1996). *Rapid development: Taming wild software schedules.* Redmond, WA: Microsoft Press.

Milojicic, D., Chauhan, D., & la Forge, W. (1998). Mobile objects and agents (MOA), design, implementation and lessons learned. *Proceedings of the 4th USENIX Conference on Object-Oriented Technologies (COOTS'98),* Santa Fe, NM.

Nelson, J. (1999). *Programming mobile objects with Java.* John Wiley & Sons.

OMG. (2000). *Mobile agent facility, version 1.0.* Formal/00-01-02: Object Management Group.

Papaioannou, T. (2000). *On the structuring of distributed systems: The argument for mobility.* Unpublished doctoral dissertation, Loughborough University, Leicestershire, UK.

Picco, G. (1998). *Understanding, evaluating, formalizing, and exploiting code mobility.* Unpublished doctoral dissertation, Politecnico di Torino, Italy.

Saltzer, J., Reed, D., & Clark, D. (1984). End-to-end arguments in system design. *ACM Transactions in Computer Systems, 2*(4).

Silva, L., Simões, P., Soares, G., Martins, P., Batista, V., Renato, C., et al. (1999). James: A platform of mobile agents for the management of telecommunication networks. *Proceedings of the 3rd International Workshop on Intelligent Agents for Telecommunication Applications (IATA'99)* (LNCS 1699). Stockholm, Sweden: Springer-Verlag .

Simões, P., Reis, R., Silva, L., & Boavida, F. (1999). Enabling mobile agent technology for legacy network management frameworks. *Proceedings of the 1999 International Conference on Software, Telecommunications and Computer Networks (SoftCOM1999),* FESB-Split, Split/Rijeka Croatia, Trieste/Venice, Italy.

Simões, P., Rodrigues, J., Silva, L., & Boavida, F. (2002). Distributed retrieval of management information: Is it about mobility, locality or distribution? *Proceedings of the 2002 IEEE/IFIP Network Operations and Management Symposium (NOMS2002),* Florence, Italy.

Tanenbaum, A., & Steen, M. (2002). *Distributed systems: Principles and paradigms.* Prentice Hall.

Tripathi, A., Karnik, N., Ahmed, T., Singh, R., Prakash, A., Kakani, V., et al. (2002). Design of the Ajanta system for mobile agent programming. *Journal of Systems and Software, 62*(2).

White, J. (1996). Telescript technology: Mobile agents. In J. Bradshaw (Ed.), *Software agents.* AAI/MIT Press.

Wojciechowski, P., & Sewell, P. (1999). Nomadic pict: Language and infrastructure design for mobile agents. *Proceedings of the Joint Symposium on Agent Systems and Applications/Mobile Agents (ASA/MA'99),* Palm Springs, CA.

Wooldridge, M., & Jennings, N. (1999). Software engineering with agents: Pitfalls and pratfalls. *IEEE Internet Computing, 3*(3).

Chapter VI
Designing a Foundation for Mobile Agents in Peer–to–Peer Networks

Daniel Lübke
Leibniz University Hannover, Germany

Jorge Marx Gómez
Oldenburg University, Germany

ABSTRACT

Within this chapter, we present the requirements and a possible conception of a framework, which provides a platform and starting point for the development of mobile agents in peer-to-peer networks. Peer-to-peer networks like Kazaa, Gnutella, and so forth have reached a widespread use on the Internet. By deploying mobile agents that can travel between network nodes to a large P2P network, one could embrace the peer-to-peer technology and use it for all kinds of services like making network traffic anonymous, distributing storage of documents, replicating contents of heavily accessed Internet sites, trading of information, and so forth. For many of these things there are solutions available, but by using a common framework and moving the logic into the agents, there is the opportunity to access all kinds of information through a common API, which guarantees extensibility and widespread use.

MOBILE AGENTS

A mobile agent is software that acts autonomously and can travel from one computing device to another (Di Stefano & Santoro, 2002). Essentially, an agent should act on behalf of its user and may complete tasks on nodes accessible to him. Agents are mobile, if their code can be transferred to other computers. The transfer includes the agent's state as well so that the agent resumes execution at the same state. There are several approaches and solutions for developing mobile agents available (W3C, 1996), but most of these are focusing on a very special kind of problem and none has reached widespread use in day-to-day applications.

This is remarkable because there were many who hoped that the use of agents would lead to a shift in programming paradigms. Despite the pending breakthrough, many possible scenarios, useful applications, and benefits are being discussed that hopefully will be realized in the future (e.g., see Chess, Harrison, & Kershenbaum, 1995, and Lange & Oshima, 1999).

To help mobile agents to become a widespread technology, we want to develop a common platform and framework, which makes the development of mobile agents as simple as possible while integrating a standard level of security into the system to allow normal users to maintain their computers' integrity. The agents shall operate on a peer-to-peer network and contain the logic of the network services. Thereby, the network can be extended by the simple means of deploying a new agent into the network. No software updates at the already deployed nodes are necessary (see Lübke & Marx Gómez, 2003).

REQUIREMENTS FOR THE FRAMEWORK

For being successful and widely deployed by all kind of users, the peer-to-peer network has to provide an infrastructure and a set of standards that allows:

- Easy deployment of mobile agents (auto-generated agents/code)
- The agents' owners to be identified by the system and the users
- The easy yet safe use of individual security policies for limiting the power of locally run agents

The given requirements are mainly motivated by the constraint of being operated by ordinary users. Since they are not developers, programming tasks must be hidden and technical details must be hidden by the application. Furthermore, there

are purely technically motivated requirements, allowing normal operation of mobile agents in peer-to-peer networks. The system must therefore also allow:

- Agents to be moved or copied between network nodes
- Agents to access contents of the node they are running on based on the security policies in effect
- The announcement and management of network nodes and their capabilities
- Agents to communicate with each other as long as the local security policies allow this

These requirements lead to the following decisions, which are outlined below.

Network Infrastructure

Relying on the Internet, the peer-to-peer network has to be based on the transmission control protocol/internet protocol (TCP/IP) protocol suite (Socolofsky & Kale, 1991). Because the agents' code and state has to be transferred intact, TCP connections will be used and not UDP datagrams, since TCP guarantees packets will be transmitted correctly by using checksums and acknowledgements. A container service, which manages all agent movements and the execution of mobile code, should bind to a specific port and wait for incoming connections. When this service is started, it has to locate neighbouring peers, announce its presence, and connect to neighbouring nodes.

The retrieval of these neighbour-lists are one of the problems peer-to-peer networks face because this is one point that is not easily done without centralized resources like a node-list.

The peer-to-peer client should first look if any other peer is available within the local area network. For example, this could be done by using the service location protocol (SLPv2) (Guttman, Perkins, Veizades, & Day, 1999) or local broadcasts. If no other peer is located, the client has to access central peer-lists. These could be distributed on many nodes of which at least one has to be known by the client. After connecting to the peer-to-peer network, the client should update its peer list so next time it can try all of these peers in the case no other local peers are available.

Platform Decision

To be able to transfer agents between every kind of network device, the agent has to be in a form that can be executed on as many computer architectures as possible. This can be achieved by transferring scripts, for example, source code, which can be interpreted or compiled on each target device.

However, the concept of the platform-independent Java™ (Sun Microsystems, 1995-2003c) architecture comes to mind because it addresses this problem and is widely used in mission critical systems, so that stability is presumably not a problem. The Java™ byte code can be executed on all computer and operating system architectures for which a Java™ Runtime Environment (JRE) (About.com, 2003) is available. Runtime environments are available for Windows™, Linux™, and most UNIX™ systems as well as for embedded systems (Sun Microsystems, 1995-2003b). Furthermore, based on Java™, the JXTA™ framework is available for realizing peer-to-peer applications. Furthermore, Java has successfully been used for mobile agent-related applications, that is, the Aglet framework (Lange & Oshima, 1998).

Security Issues

Because agents distributed via a peer-to-peer network essntially are untrusted code that might try to access data on a computer where they are not authorized to do so, some countermeasures have to be taken so that the agent is not capable of doing any harm to the user's data. By limiting the agents through Java™ security-managers, the container is able to control and monitor the agents' actions (Venners, 1997).

Furthermore, the user should be able to configure security policies, which can be different for every agent, which are run onto the user's node: The user could allow information retrieval only for agents from a specific user, limit the processor time of any agent, the use of network bandwidth, and so on. These security policies directly alter the sandbox and therefore influence the set of actions an agent is allowed to execute.

Because this is a very critical configuration issue, a simple and easy-to-use graphical user interface (GUI) has to be designed that allows the creation and management of security policies and the monitoring of the agents. New users should be guided and the default values should be very restricted.

For security reasons, all traffic between the clients should be encrypted and all transferred agents digitally signed by their respective owners. The most practical choices for encryption standards seem to be the OpenPGP (The Internet Society, 1998) standard and S/MIME (The Internet Society, 1999b) with X.509 (The Internet Society, 1999a) certificates.

OpenPGP has the advantage of relying itself on a distributed validation scheme: The Web of Trust, which can be used without any additional costs because each user can sign any key if he wants to show that that key actually belongs to the person it claims to belong to. The disadvantage is that one might not be able to verify if a signature is a trusted one because there is no direct or a too long path between one's key and the key to be validated.

X.509 certificates solve this issue by introducing a hierarchical model of certification. The drawback of this approach is that for trusted certificates a user has to use, trust, and often pay a certification authority (CA), which states that the key owner is actually the one whose name is in the certificate.

We settled on OpenPGP as its trust model integrates better into the peer-to-peer network.

To make traffic analysis harder for any potential attacker of the network, the clients should send dummy network traffic, which is configurable by the user. By sending dummy packages, which might be relayed by other nodes, an outside attacker should not be able to know or guess the source or destination of any data sent over the network.

PLATFORM DESIGN

Container Design

The main premise for the container's design was flexibility: Therefore, all parts of the system are specified by interfaces, which are implemented by corresponding implementations. These implementations are bound to the system by the use of factories.

This approach allowed us to experiment with different approaches for each design element.

The container has to provide functionality to accept, relocate, and execute the agents. Because of these complex requirements, the container design was split up into two main parts: the first part deals

with the network communication, including the transfer of agents, and the second part is responsible for the safe execution of the agents.

For implementing the network communication, a protocol specification has to be made: Our framework can integrate and address many peer-to-peer network protocols at a time. Furthermore, the network part has to locate and connect to other hosts of the peer-to-peer network as described above. Implementations can be registered at the system. For example, self-implemented protocols and standardized ones like JXTA can be integrated and used transparently for the agents.

If an agent is sent to the container, it is extracted from its Java™ archive (JAR) (Sun Microsystems, 1995-2003a), the signatures are checked for validity and then checked against the local security policies. If execution is permitted by the security policies, the agent will be passed on to the execution environment.

The execution environment will restore the transferred object representing the agent and limit its access to the local system by using Java™ security-managers. These deny agents direct access to local resources, like file operations. Therefore, other means have to be in place for the agents to access resources. This is possible by the use of an own abstraction layer centred around so-called resource providers. Since an agent must access resources via their correspondent provider, central security controls can be put in place. Resource-providers can manage access to all kind of resources, like local files, other currently executed agents, or databases. To be integrated into the container, all providers have to implement the interface Resource-provider, which defines methods for opening, reading, writing, and searching resources.

An agent can request a specific resource provider by asking the container. The resource the agent wishes to access is specified by a unique identifier. The container can decide to actually create a corresponding resource provider or reject the agent's request by returning a null reference.

Figure 1. Principle container design

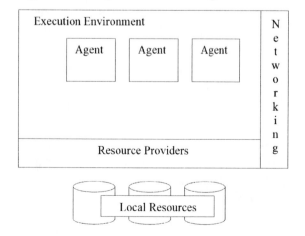

Basic Agent Class Design

All agents have to inherit the abstract base class agent. This class defines methods for saving the agent's object state, notification of changes in the execution environment, and passing a reference of the container to the agent.

The container reference can be used to request resource providers, relocate itself, and register new resource providers within the system, which are providing access to information handled by the agent itself. This allows agents to communicate directly with each other by self-defined protocols and interfaces; the resource abstraction proved to be very powerful in such cases.

To make relocation and generic object creation possible, the agent has to implement a default constructor without arguments, a save and corresponding restore method, and a start and stop method.

When the agent is relocated a new object will be created in the new execution environment using the default constructor. The saved object state is then restored by the container. It therefore calls the restore method. Afterwards the agent can be executed which is done by calling the start method.

If an agent has or wants to be relocated, it is stopped using the stop method. Then the agent's state will be saved by calling the save method. All resource providers will be closed by the container, so that the agent won't have to deal with that.

FRAMEWORK APPLICATIONS AND POSSIBLE IMPLEMENTATIONS

By using the proposed framework, many tasks can be realized within peer-to-peer networks without needing to alter the clients themselves (Lübke & Marx Gómez, 2004). Only special resources need to be published on the client-side. Possible scenarios and implementation sketches are given in this section.

Offline Applications

With the rise of new, small, and mobile devices connecting to the Internet, new applications are possible, like initiating searches for accommodation, traffic information, and so forth if someone is on the road. However, traffic and connection fees are still very high, so it is necessary to reduce the amount of data sent from and to the devices and the time the devices are connected to the network. Sometimes it is even necessary or likely that a device or another node is not connected all the time to the network, which is needed to accom-

Figure 2. Basic class design for the framework

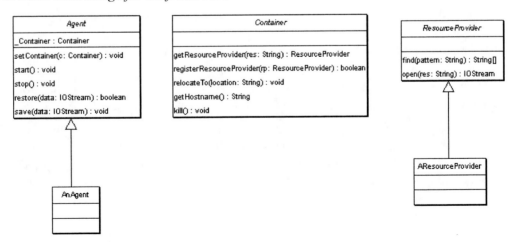

plish the tasks. In either case, mobile agents can be used to develop applications, where the initiating node does not need to be online all the time. Instead, the owner sends a mobile agent, which roams the network for the desired information. After all information is collected, there are two possible implementations, which are applicable under different scenarios:

- The agent waits on a node somewhere in the network until the initiating node comes online again. If the node, where the agent waits, goes down, the agent has to look for another node to wait. However, it might be too slow to do this, or for other reasons the node goes down without notifying the agent and all information is lost.

- The agent stops at a node, where a special resource provider is installed. This provider offers a persistent storage for agents. For example, it can offer 500 Kbytes to certified agents. This way, an agent may request a resource. Custom resource providers will then be used to provide the resource, if the security-policy for the agent allows the use of this resource type. The agent gets a reference to a resource object and can write its results to it. These results can be fetched by the initiating node via another agent or by special messages exchanged between the nodes. If the storage is always online, like it is provided by a service provider, this method is safer than the first one. However, it needs write access to resources, which may be a problem in public networks.

The advantages mobile agents have over traditional applications in this scenario is that connection fees are reduced by sending mobile agents to the network and disconnecting while the processing takes place. Furthermore, processing-intensive tasks can be moved from the mobile device with its limited resources to other nodes in the network.

Agent-Supported Download-Applications

File-sharing applications are quite popular today. However, they depend on searching the network via broadcasts and trusting the unauthenticated and invalidated results, which are coming back. Extending the methods used by Dunne (2001), it is possible to verify the results and only send them back using mobile agents, if they really match the search results or other given criteria. Therefore, agents can travel to the node, which offers a specific source file, read the data, and validate it. Afterward, it needs to send the data to its owner. This can be accomplished by giving an agent a unique job-number. When the agent is initiated, it receives this job-number. This number can be used by the agent to send the verified data to its owner's host-address, so that the owner's host is able to handle the incoming data. The agent may also encrypt the data sent back or try to send the data via different hosts so that the traffic is obscured to outside listeners.

The advantages of this approach over the traditional file-sharing networks are that data can be verified before downloading it, which can take lots of time. Furthermore, the agent may obfuscate the data before sending it to its user so that external parties cannot determine which data are being transferred.

Distributed Computing

There are some projects available offering clients that will run on all kinds of computers and will solve specific algorithmic problems. Examples for such applications are seti@home (seti@home, 2006), which will use the donated computing power for performing computational analysis of data to find signs of extraterrestrial life. Other projects are trying to find large prime numbers (psearch, n.d.) or are trying to crack encryption keys (Distributed Net, 2006).

DNA sequence problems and research in bio-informatics often need to analyse big data chunks with varying and newly implemented algorithms. The problem here is that the processing can take much processing power, which normally will be provided by computing clusters. However, many computers are available for word processing and so forth but spend most of the time doing nothing. By connecting these computers to a P2P network, which distributes varying algorithms and data to be processed via mobile agents, makes the otherwise unused computing power available without needing to install software on all nodes, which is quite burdensome and normally even very expensive. The agents can be easily modified for reflecting new algorithms or trying to experiment with different data. The advantages of using an existent P2P-network with mobile agent is that mobile agents can transparently make use of otherwise unused resources and that updates of the calculation algorithms or different targets can easily be carried out by writing and deploying a new agent without the need of user interaction.

Calendaring and Scheduling

Personal data are normally distributed all over different personal computers. Companies are normally trying to use groupware like Lotus Notes™ (IBM Software, n.d.) or Microsoft Exchange™ (Microsoft, 2006) to centralize these data to make appointments. However, in the private sector this is not possible because such solutions are impractical and too expensive. One could share personal calendars using file sharing networks or publishing such events on a personal Web page, but from a privacy point of view, these solutions are not good. The distributed security model allows the fine-grained control and specific views onto calendars and other personal data to different persons. This way, an agent sent by a friend may access the whole calendar while other persons do not see that a calendar is published at all. The agent may also have the knowledge

to access several calendars and check if an appointment is possible within a specific time-frame and to make suggestions based on that data. The advantages of mobile agents in this case are that access rights may be granted without publishing either the calendar or its existence to the public. Instead of mailing appointment recommendations, the process is automated because the agent can find time-slots, which are marked free for all participants.

CASE STUDY: ANONYMIZING DATA

Application's Focus

As part of the framework, a sample application was developed to show the functionality of the system. The sample application's purpose is to relay Web traffic through the P2P-network, thereby making web requests anonymous, issued by an ordinary web browser. This application is developed on top of the presented framework and consequently utilizes mobile agents for fulfilling the task. The agents therefore contain all the logic needed: Agents are spawned for each request, that is, each Web page, and roam the P2P-network to anonymously fetch the requested data for the user. The request is anonymous because the IP address seen by the Web server is a random one, depending from which host the mobile agent accesses the page.

Anonymizing Traffic

Today more and more people are using the Internet, especially the World Wide Web. Many things are conducted digitally, including e-commerce and information gathering. However, each packet of data sent in the Internet contains the sender's unique address. Because most computers are only used by one person at a time, the IP address not only correlates to the computer but also to the user.

This way it is possible to create user profiles by analyzing the generated traffic. For example, Web site operators are able to analyze logs and secret services are capable of capturing and analyzing networking traffic in central routing points. This practice conflicts with the right of privacy that citizens in modern democracies enjoy. To re-establish privacy in the digital era, traffic needs to be anonymized. This is often done by sending it randomly through the network, getting relayed at each computer it passes. Thereby the original source address can be obscured because each computer retransmits the packet and thereby places its IP address in the packet. By using encryption, this scheme can be used to hide the traffic's contents as well.

Systems working like this are called mixnets (Chaum, 1981). Mixnets are networks in which messages are routed randomly between the nodes to obscure the senders' original addresses to make traffic analysis harder. Since each node only knows from which other node a packet was received, the original sender is unknown.

However, issuing a request anonymously is not as difficult as returning the request's result anonymously as well, because for this the request's source needs to be known and therefore needs to be stored somewhere. We address this issue by holding a list of the nodes a request travelled along. To not comprise privacy, this list is initialized with random hosts.

Application Flow

The request from the Web browser is sent to the proxy-server, which is a node in the P2P-network at the same time. For each page the browser requests, a request-ID is generated. Afterward, the connection is saved with this ID. A new agent is spawned, which receives the request-ID and the uniform resource locator (URL) it should fetch. Upon start-up, the agent initializes a list of nodes it travelled to. This list contains a random-length initialization, which consists of valid host-names

in the P2P network. Since this list has only valid names and has a random length, the real origin of the agent cannot be determined by looking at this list.

The agent then proceeds by visiting a randomly chosen number of hosts. At each host, it adds the host name to its host list. On the last node, the agent issues the request for the URL it has to fetch. The data are stored within the payload reference, and the agent will go back its internal host-list, getting the previous host it has visited and requesting migration to that host. On each host, the agent will try to deliver the data. If this is successful, the request has been issued by that host and the agent has fulfilled its task.

If the resource could not be found, the agent travels back down the list until it reaches its origin. If one host is down, it will be skipped and the agent will proceed to the previous one in the list. This way, it does not matter if one host on the list is down, unless it is the originating node. If this happens, the agent will reach the list's end and will quit execution.

Anonymizing Agent

Every request is handed over from the proxy-server to an agent. The agent is responsible for fetching the data. For this, the agent initializes itself at the first start. During initialization, it constructs a faked initial travel-list for this agent to obscure the real owner. To get valid host-names, a list containing all neighbouring nodes is requested from the system. Names from this list are taken to put a random number of fake entries at the top of the list.

After the initialization is guaranteed, the agent determines if it is in forward or backward movement by looking at its payload data. If no payload is saved, the agent is in forward movement and checks if it has to go to further hosts. If it must, it chooses one random neighbour host, adds it to its list, and travels there. If the agent has to get the data, it requests it from the current node. After getting the data, the agent switches to backward movement.

In backward movement, the agent tries to deliver its data on the current host. This is done by requesting a resource with the given request ID. If this fails, the agent chooses the next host from its list and migrates there and proceeds. If the resource could be opened successfully, the agent writes its entire payload to that resource and terminates.

SUMMARY AND PERSPECTIVE

The creation of a flexible platform and a corresponding framework for mobile agents in peer-to-peer networks is being researched. Our goal is to achieve a level of abstraction that allows quick development of mobile agents, which then can be deployed to a hopefully large user base.

By using Java™, we can build upon a proven technology, which allows us a quick reference implementation of our ideas. We already have developed mobile agents, which are caring about anonymous communication by wandering between nodes within that network before sending a request. By doing this, the IP address of the sending computer cannot be associated with the user for whom the request is being made.

On top of this, eventually other services can be implemented, like information gathering agents, trading agents, and so forth. Other topics of interest include failover services, distributed storage, advanced security, and further application scenarios.

REFERENCES

About.com (2003). *Definition of Java runtime environment (JRE).* Retrieved April 27, 2006, from http://java.about.com/library/glossary/bldef-jre.htm

Chaw, D. L. (1981). Untraceable electronic mail, return addresses, and digital pseudonyms, *Communications of the ACM, 24*(2), 84-90.

Chess, D., Harrison, C., & Kershenbaum, A. (1995). *Mobile agents: Are they a good idea.* IBM Research Report RC 19887. Retrieved from http://mega.ist.utl.pt/~ic-arge/arge-96-97/artigos/mobile-ibm-7929.ps.gz

Di Stefano, A., & Santoro, C. (2002). *Locating mobile agents in a wide distributed environment.* Retrieved April 27, 2006, from http://www.cs.albany.edu/~mhc/Mobile/leena_Presentation1.ppt

Distributed Net. (2006). *Distributed net, node zero.* Retrieved April 27, 2006, from http://www.distributed.net/

Dunne, C. R. (2001). Using mobile agents for network resource discovery in peer-to-peer networks. *ACM SIGecom Exchanges, 2*(3), 1-9.

Guttman, E., Perkins, C., Veizades, J., & Day, M. (1999). *RFC 2608: Service location protocol, Version 2.* Retrieved April 27, 2006, from http://www.ietf.org/rfc/rfc2608.txt

IBM Software. (n.d.). *IBM Lotus Notes.* Retrieved April 27, 2006, from http://www.lotus.com/products/product4.nsf/wdocs/noteshomepage

Lange, D. B., & Oshima, M. (1998). Mobile agents with Java: The Aglet API. *World Wide Web (Journal), 1*(3), 111-121.

Lange, D. B., & Oshima, M. (1999). Seven good reasons for mobile agents. *Communications of the ACM, 42*(3), 88-89.

Lübke, D., & Marx Gómez, J. (2003). Designing a framework for mobile agents in peer-to-peer Networks. *Proceedings of SCI 2003.*

Lübke, D., & Marx Gómez, J. (2004). Applications for mobile agents in peer-to-peer-networks. *Proceedings of the 11th IEEE International Con-*

ference and Workshop on the Engineering of Computer-Based Systems.

Microsoft. (2006). *Microsoft exchange server.* Retrieved April 27, 2006, from http://www.microsoft.com/exchange/

psearch (n.d.). Retrieved April 27, 2006, from http://www.people.iup.edu/vmrf/

seti@home. (2006). *Seti@home project.* Retrieved April 27, 2006, from http://setiathome.ssl.berkeley.edu/

Socolofsky, T., & Kale, C. (1991). *A TCP/IP tutorial.* Retrieved April 27, 2006, from http://www.cis.ohio-state.edu/cgi-bin/rfc/rfc1180.html

Sun Microsystems. (1995-2003a). *JAR files.* Retrieved April 27, 2006, from http://java.sun.com/docs/books/tutorial/jar/index.html/

Sun Microsystems. (1995-2003b). *Java™ 2 platform.* Retrieved April 27, 2006, from http://java.sun.com/java2/whatis

Sun Microsystems. (1995-2003c). *The source for Java technology.* Retrieved April 27, 2006, from http://java.sun.com

The Internet Society. (1998). *RFC 2440: OpenPGP message format.* Retrieved April 27, 2006, from http://www.ietf.org/rfc/rfc2440.txt

The Internet Society. (1999a). *RFC 2459: Internet X.509 public key infrastructure, certificate and CRL profile.* Retrieved April 27, 2006, from http://www.ietf.org/rfc/rfc2459.txt

The Internet Society. (1999b). *RFC 2633: S/MIME version 3 message specification.* Retrieved April 27, 2006, from http://www.ietf.org/rfc/rfc2633.txt

Venners, B. (1997). *Java security: How to install the security manager and customize your security policy.* Retrieved April 27, 2006, from http://www.javaworld.com/javaworld/jw-11-1997/jw-11-hood.html

W3C (1996). *W3C: On mobile code.* Retrieved April 27, 2006, from http://www.w3.org/MobileCode/

Chapter VII
Dynamic Scheduling of Multi-Agent in Agent-Based Distributed Network Management

Luo Junzhou
Southeast University, China

Liu Bo
Southeast University, China

Li Wei
Southeast University, China

ABSTRACT

Agent technology has played an important role in distributed network management, and agent scheduling is an inevitable problem in a multi-agent system. This chapter introduces a network management scenario to support dynamic scheduling decisions. Some algorithms are proposed to decompose the whole network management task into several groups of sub-tasks. During the course of decomposition, different priorities are assigned to sub-tasks. Then, based on the priorities of these sub-tasks, a dynamic multi-agent scheduling algorithm based on dependences of sub-tasks is proposed. An experiment has been done with the decomposition algorithms, the results of which demonstrate the advantage of the algorithms. The performance test demonstrates that the competitive ratio of the dynamic scheduling algorithm is always smaller than that of the existing online scheduling algorithm, which indicates that the performance of the dynamic scheduling algorithm is better than the existing online scheduling algorithm. Finally, as an application example, the process of network stream management is presented. The authors hope that this scheduling method can give a new approach or suggestion for studying dynamic agents scheduling technology.

INTRODUCTION

Conventional network management is mostly based on the simple network management protocol (SNMP) and often runs in a centralized manner. The SNMP-based management systems give network administrators the flexibility of managing the whole network from a single place. When a manager needs a small amount of data from a small set of managed nodes, SNMP is a better choice, but when a large amount of MIB (managed information base) data is to be retrieved from multiple managed nodes, mobile agent based management is preferred (Kona, 2002). The increasing dependence on network management station makes network management station a bottleneck. The network management member in conventional network management manner runs short of adaptability to the changing environment and also lacks the ability of self-organization, so it can hardly manage with the more and more complex network management tasks. It is the properties of the intelligent agent, such as autonomy, mobility, and so forth (Buchanman, Naylor, & Scott, 2000) that makes it possible to solve the problems. The merits of using agent in network management are also discussed in another paper (Liu, Luo, & Li 2005). But when using agent technology in network management, problems arise: how to integrate the agent with the functions of network management and by what manner to assign tasks to multi-agents in large-scale network management task.

Agent scheduling in multi-agent system is an important factor influencing task execution efficiency. The traditional scheduling algorithm often assigns task to agents statically. The scheme or plan of task always has been established before execution in static scheduling methods. These static (offline) algorithms (Zhuang & Pande, 2003) generate output with complete knowledge of the entire input (job sequence). However, this assumption is often unrealistic in practical applications. Many of the algorithmic problems that arise in practice are online. A dynamic (online) algorithm (Albers, 2003) must generate output without knowledge of the entire input. Making good scheduling decisions requires a careful analysis of the relationships among tasks. Knowing the relationship among tasks, task dynamic decomposition can be achieved during agent dynamic scheduling.

BACKGROUND

In recent years, many researchers have interests in task decomposition and scheduling, especially in the area of distributed computing, the research area ranging from serial program decomposition (Luo, Huang, & Li, 1995) to program slicing (Morel, 2003). But in multi-agent-based large-scale network management task, if we adopt the method of program decomposition, there will be many sub-codes, which make it very complicated to create and assign agent; even if we reassemble the sub-codes, the integrality of network management function will be destroyed and the intelligent exertion of agent will be affected. So we propose a method of decomposing network management tasks into sub-tasks considering the dependences among sub-tasks. Then these small-scale tasks are assigned to multi-agents.

Some researchers take the scheduling problem into consideration integrated with agent migration itinerary. Singh and Pande (2002) proposed two strategies for agent migration. The first strategy: attempting to carry all the live definitions of variables from a given node when visited, the goal of which is to minimize the number of migrations; the second strategy: attempting to carry only those definitions that will be used in the destination node, it aims to minimize bandwidth consumption during a migration. These two strategies both have their merits, but neither of them can resolve the problems in dealing with tasks in large-scale complicated network management. Zhuang and Pande (2002) regarded minimal number of migrations (MNM) and minimal data transfer (MDT) as optimization metrics to schedule single-agent transfer route, but this method only concerned single-agent system. However, agent-based applications always are multi-agent system, and in such applications agents are required to migrate among all specified nodes efficiently to perform their own tasks. Of course, we can use "Dijkstra algorithm" to make the migration itinerary be the shortest one if the knowledge about the network is known ahead of schedule, but things are not easy as expected. Satoh (2002) states: "It is often difficult to dynamically generate an efficient itinerary among multiple nodes without having any knowledge of the network. Even if a smart agent can create an efficient itinerary based on its previous processing and the current environment, such an agent is not always be appropriate, because both the cost of discovering such an itinerary and the size of its program tend to be large" (p. 52). So, integrated migration itinerary with multi-agent scheduling is an open problem.

Another direction of agent scheduling is to design good task scheduling algorithm to decrease the make-span. Various approaches to design agent task scheduling algorithm exist. Clement and Durfee (1998) assumes that the response time of task in the task system is known and proposes a scheduling algorithm based on the rate of priority/response-time. Jones, Blake, and Archibald (2002) presented a task-scheduling algorithm for multi-agent systems suitable for environments with hard real-time deadlines. Zhang, Luh, and Santos (2004) proposed a price-based multi-agent scheduling. Most of these algorithms lack theoretical analysis and adaptability. For example, the algorithm presented by Clement and Durfee (1998) does not apply to the agents executing in the dynamic network because the state of the network has great influence on the response time. Hence, only a dynamic scheduling algorithm can adapt for agents running in the dynamic environment. Yang, Ma, and You (2002) proposed an online task scheduling algorithm and use competitive

theory to evaluate the number of agents. Yang et al.'s work is an advancement in task scheduling of multi-agents, but they simplify the running background of agent. They assume that the tasks executed by agents is simple, repeated, and parallel; once the sub-tasks are not parallel completely, the agent executing in the network will cost a large amount of time and network resources to weight each other, so this method is not adapted to complicated task system. In order to avoid wasting time and long waiting for other agents, we take the dependence relationship of sub-tasks into account.

Though there are many evaluation metrics for evaluating scheduling methods, such as MNM, MDT, make-span, deadlines, schedule completion time, agent utilization, throughput, availability, and reliability, scheduling completion time is the most important thing of concerned to us because scheduling completion time is closely related to task completion time, and task completion time is very import in network management. In this chapter, we mainly focus on the analysis of agent dynamic scheduling method. We analyze relationship among tasks and then discuss task decomposition algorithm. Then based on these analyses, a dependence-based dynamic scheduling algorithm (DDSA), which contains agent destination and dynamic online decomposition, is proposed. To objectively and fairly determine the approach of task allocation for agents, we take advantage of "competitive analysis" to analyze the performance of dynamic algorithm. Otherwise, a practical example of network stream management is introduced. At the end of the chapter, we provide a conclusion and look toward future research work.

TASK MANIPULATION PROCESS

Network management task can be requested by managed entities or be defined by users through WEB interface. Users can select managed entities in a topology graph of network or define the managed entities by specifying Internet protocol (IP) addresses. According to the management function of OSI (open system interconnection) (Pras, 1995), we define the following functions: MIB management, objects management, status management, condition management, critical value management, alert report, event report, log management, security report, workload monitor, and test management. Through MIB management, the MIB variables (Pras, 1995, pp. 67-69) about managed entities can be visited; objects management provides defining of managed content and scale; status management provides state query and includes condition management and critical value management; alert report, event report, log management, and security report can make the managed entities report the correlative information to manager; workload monitor function is responsible for monitoring the network traffic or the central processing unit (CPU) load; and test management provides the function of testing the state of managed entities. These functions are listed in the Web to users. Users select functions from list corresponding to the managed entities. Next, tasks are decomposed into groups of sub-tasks by decomposition algorithms. Then these sub-tasks are provided to an agent-scheduling module to work out the schedule of multi-agent.

If the code corresponding to some sub-tasks cannot be acquired directly from the code database, then the sub-tasks will be decomposed again. Finally, according to task schedule, agents will be created or recycled, assembled with management code, and dispatched to the target network node to perform a certain job. According to the function of agents, various agents are assembled with various functional codes. The processing flow is described in Figure 1.

In distributed network management, large-scale managed network is divided into some local domain. Every domain is autonomous to some extent, and there is an agent acting as "the agent organizer" (AO) to manage the agents running in its domain. During the course of task scheduling, some urgent or temporary task may be pushed to AO, so AO should have the ability to interact with task decomposition module online.

TASK ANALYSIS AND FORMALIZATION

According to the management framework defined by OSI, network management functions involve five functional areas (Pras, 1995): fault management; configuration management; performance management; accounting management; and se-

Figure 1. Task manipulation process

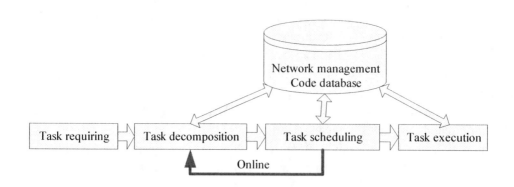

curity management. Most network management tasks can be decomposed into small management actions (sub-tasks). The identification and tracking of dependencies between the actions is important for task decomposition. We call actions that depend on other actions descendants, while actions on which other actions depend are termed antecedents. An action often plays both roles. There exist two types of dependencies: data dependence and control dependence. If in one task, action *B* needs results or variables of action *A*, then *A* should be added to the data antecedents set of *B*, and *A* should be executed before *B*. This relationship between actions is called data dependence. If in one certain task, action *B* and action *C* are descendants of action *A*, the result of action *A* decides that only one action (*B* or *C*) should be executed; then A should be added to the control antecedents set of *B* and *C*, and *A* should be executed before *B* and *C*. This relationship between actions is called control dependence.

Definition 1: Data antecedents set is denoted with *DDep*. Control antecedents set is denoted with *CDep*.

Definition 2: A control flow graph is a directed graph augmented with a unique entry node and a unique exit node such that each node in the graph has at most two groups of successors (Ferrante, Ottenstein, & Warren, 1987). In a control flow graph, there are two kinds of nodes, statement and branch statement. Branch statement has two groups of statements, true or false. A control flow graph contains the relationship of data and control dependences.

TASK DECOMPOSITION ALGORITHM

In our network management environment, network management task is produced in the form of control flow graph (CFG). A large-scale network management task is likely to consist of several control flow graphs, so we only need to consider how to decompose one control flow graph and how to find out the parallel network management actions.

CFG is a directed graph and a hierarchical structure. Therefore, using breadth first search (BFS) algorithm (Yan & Wu, 2000) to traverse the graph is just traversing the CFG layer by layer. The graph contains control dependence and data dependence, so a control antecedents set of every sub-task can be obtained by using a BFS algorithm traversing the directed graph (Algorithm 1) and the nodes in the graph are stored in the cycling queue simultaneously. The queue will be used in producing a data control antecedents set of the nodes in the graph (Algorithm 2). After the sub-task's control antecedents and data antecedents set are generated, the task can be decomposed into sub-tasks, which are endowed with different priorities on the basis of antecedents sets (Algorithm 3).

Algorithm 1: Traverse the task's CFG and produce the control antecedents set of sub-tasks.

Method: The directed graph is traversed using BFS algorithm, and every arc's property is inspected. If the arc's property is T or F, then the head node of the arc is the control dependence of the end node of the arc. If it is null, there is no dependence relationship existing.

Input: *CFG*

Output: *CDep, CQ* (*CDep* is a two-dimension array; for example, *CDep*[1][1] denotes that the first control antecedent of node 1. *CQ* is a cycling queue, which store the directed graph layer by layer.)

Algorithm description: Traverse the task *CFG* using *BFS* algorithm from the start node. Store the nodes into *CQ* during the course of traversing.

Figure 2. The course of decomposition

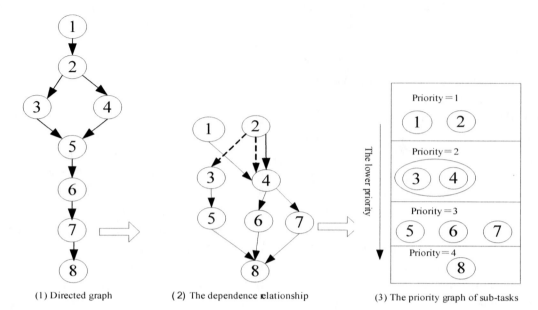

(1) Directed graph (2) The dependence relationship (3) The priority graph of sub-tasks

Algorithm 2: *CQ* is visited conversely, and the data antecedents set of every sub-task is produced.

Method: Every element in the *CQ* is visited from the end of the queue conversely. If some ancestor of this element is the element's data antecedent, then this node is added to the element's data antecedents set. All such ancestors are added to the element's data dependence.

Input: *CQ* (Cycling queue of the Algorithm 1 is input.)

Output: *DDep* (Data dependence set is output.)

Algorithm description: From the end of cycling queue, every node in the queue is visited one by one. For every node, to see whether there are those variables in its variable set that come from its ancestors' results, if there are such variables, the host node of the variables is added to its data antecedents set, otherwise not.

Algorithm 3: Every node in directed graph are visited, their priorities are produced according their control antecedents and data antecedents.

Method: Since control antecedents set and data antecedents set are already worked out by Algorithm 1 and Algorithm 2, the node whose control antecedents set and data antecedents set are both null can be executed at the same time with its ancestors. The nodes whose antecedents set are not null must be executed after the ancestors in their antecedents set being executed, but they can be executed in parallel with other nodes that have no relationship of dependence with them. As a result, we apply priority to manage the relationship of dependence.

Input: *CFG, CDep, DDep*

Output: *pri*[] (Every sub-task's priority is stored in *pri*[ ].)

Algorithm description: Judge every node in CFG; if one's control antecedents set and data antecedents set are both null, then get rid of this node and all the arcs whose arc-head is this node. Those nodes that have been visited make up a set with priority value being 1, hence, the directed graph turns into a new graph called DG2. Manipulate DG2 in the same way until every node is given a priority. The smaller the value of the priority is, the higher the node's priority is.

One example expressing the procedure of decomposition is shown in Figure 2.

Through Algorithm 1, we can know that node 2 is the control dependence of node 3 and node 4. Through Algorithm 2, data dependence sets are produced. The broken line denotes control dependence and the real line denotes data dependence in Figure 2 (2). Figure 2 (3) gives us the priority order of all the sub-tasks. Sub-task 1 and 2 can be executed in parallel. Because sub-task 2 is the control dependence of 3 and 4, only one sub-task of 3 and 4 will be executed. After the sub-tasks whose priorities are 2 are finished, sub-task 5, 6, and 7 can be executed in parallel. All these rules are the foundation of making scheduling for multi-agent.

DEPENDENCE-BASED DYNAMIC SCHEDULING APPROACH

In distributed network management system, tasks are executed by agents in distributed mode. Tasks are required dynamically and need to be manipulated dynamically. According to the characteristic of network management functions, some simple network management actions can be executed at real time, but when confronted with complicated management task, it requires task decomposition and multi-agents' cooperation. The priority graph is the final result of task decomposition process, which is the basis of scheduling. Scheduling the agents for the complicated tasks is the key problem we are concerned.

The Process of Agent Scheduling

Through decomposition, complicated tasks are decomposed into small network management sub-tasks with corresponding priorities. The destinations of these actions are distributed in-network. The network can be divided into several local domains. In every domain, we arrange an agent to act an agent organizer. When new sub-tasks

Figure 3. Agent organizer in network

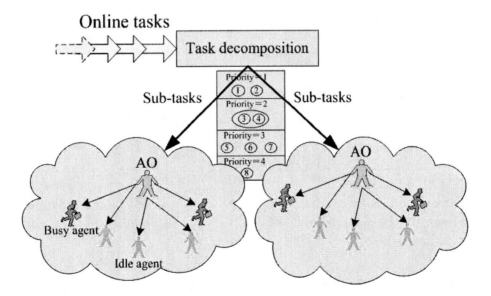

are produced, the agent organizer should organize the idle agent or create new agents to execute the tasks in its local domain. The function of agent organizer is shown in Figure 3.

We try to give a comprehensive study of the multi-agent scheduling problem with guaranteed performance over every sequence of events. Both dynamic scheduling and distributed network management require the algorithm deal with tasks with partial information, where only local information is known to the scheduler and data transfer is costly. If one is to suggest an algorithm, it only makes sense if one can compare this algorithm to alternatives and answer the fundamental question: "Which algorithm is better?" How to compare two dynamic algorithms, which is called "competitive analysis," was introduced by Sleator and Tarjan (1985). Thereafter, the competitive analysis theory has been further studied (Albers, 2003; Azar, 1998; Bartal, Fiat, & Yuval, 1992; Fiat & Mendel, 2000).

Assumption 1: A sequence of tasks must be scheduled on a set of agents so as to optimize time. Tasks arrive one by one and must be scheduled immediately without knowledge of future tasks.

Definition 3: Competitive ratio

In a competitive analysis, an online algorithm A is compared to an optimal offline algorithm. An optimal offline algorithm knows the entire request sequence in advance and can serve it with minimum cost. A competitive algorithm must perform well on all input sequences.

Given any input I, let $C_A(I)$ denote the cost incurred by online algorithm called A and let $OPT(I)$ denote the cost incurred by an optimal offline algorithm OPT. The algorithm A is called a − *competitive* if there is a constant c such that for all request sequences, $C_A(I) \leq \alpha \cdot C_{OPT}(I) + C$ and α is called competitive ratio (Albers, 2003).

$$\alpha = sup \frac{C_A(I)}{C_{OPT}(I)}.$$

The better an online algorithm approximates the optimal solution, the more competitive this algorithm is (Bartal et al., 1992).

The Dependence-Based Dynamic Scheduling Algorithm

While the task is decomposed and transferred to AO dynamically layer by layer, how to make AO give responses quickly is important for task scheduling. We consider the scheduling algorithm in one local domain. The optimization objective is to reduce the time occupied by scheduling algorithm for complicated network management task. AO is responsible for agent scheduling in its local domain. AO may have no knowledge of the future tasks, so the scheduling algorithm is online.

Let $a_1 = T(dispatching)$, $a_2 = T(disposing)$, $a_3 = T(cloning) + T(dispatching)$ and $p = a_2/a_1$, $q = a_3/a_1$. Suppose the requested task needs r agents in some local domain at some time, and the number of agents needed by the sub-tasks in the first layer is m, and C(cost) denotes the time of scheduling algorithm, then the dependence-based dynamic scheduling algorithm A is described as following:

1. Before one task comes, AO prepared (g) agents.
2. There are four instances:
   - If $g = m$, then (m) agents are dispatched; the rest ($r-m$) agents are prepared before their execution time. The scheduling algorithm cost is:

   $$C(I) = a_1 r$$

   - If $g < m$, then (g) agents are dispatched, and ($m-g$) agents need to be cloned; the rest ($r-m$) agents are prepared before their execution time. The scheduling algorithm cost is:

$$C(I) = a_1 r$$

- If $g > m$ and $r\text{-}m \geq g\text{-}m$, then m agents are dispatched, and $(g\text{-}m)$ agents can be used for the next layer sub-tasks; the rest $(r\text{-}g)$ agents are prepared before their execution time. The scheduling algorithm cost is:

$$C(I) = a_1 m + a_1 (g - m) + \\ a_1 (r - m - (g - m)) = a_1 r$$

- If $g > m$, and $r\text{-}m < g\text{-}m$, then m agents are dispatched, and the rest $(r\text{-}m)$ agents can be gotten from $(g\text{-}m)$ agents; the remainder $(g\text{-}r)$ agents are disposed. The scheduling algorithm cost is:

$$C(I) = a_1 m + a_1 (r - m) + \\ a_2 (g - r) = a_1 r + a_2 (g - r)$$

3. The algorithm is end.

Competitive Ratio Analysis

In one local domain, if a sub-task sequence is denoted with $I = (r_1, r_2, \cdots r_n)$, where r_i denotes the actual request number of agents on the ith time. $(m_1, m_2, \ldots m_n)$ is the nodes in the first layer of sub-task priority table corresponding to the sequence $(r_1, r_2, \ldots r_n)$. In the offline optimal scenario, (m_i) agents have been prepared before task r_i requested. So the offline optimal cost is:

$$C_{OPT}(I) = \sum_{i=1}^{n} (T(dispatching))m_i + \\ \sum_{i=1}^{n} (T(dispatching))(r_i - m_i) = a_1 \sum_{i=1}^{n} r_i$$

(1)

For the same request sequence, the number of agents prepared by DDSA A before ith time is g_i. Then the cost of DDSA is:

$$C_A(I) = a_1 \sum_{i=1}^{n} r_i + a_2 \sum_{\substack{i=1, g_i > m_i, \\ r_i - m_i < g_i - m_i}}^{n} (g_i - r_i) \\ + (a_3 - a_1) \sum_{i=1, g_i < m_i}^{n} (m_i - g_i)$$

(2)

From Definition 3, the definition of competitive ratio is:

$$\alpha = \sup \frac{C_A(I)}{C_{OPT}(I)};$$

now consider the supremum of α.

Theorem 1: The competitive ratio of DDSA A in local domain $[R_1, R_2]$ is $Max(\alpha_{M_2}, \alpha_{M_2})$.

Proof: Suppose the range of the number of agents requested in one local domain is $[R_1, R_2]$, denoted with LD($[R_1, R_2]$). R_1 is the lower bound and R_2 is the higher bound. $[M_1, M_2]$ is the corresponding range of the number of agents for the first layer of priority graph. Then two possible worst cases exist.

1. The request sequence is $I_{M_2} = (R_2, R_2 \ldots \ldots R_2)$ (every request has (M_2) requests in the first layer of priority graph). That is to say, every request r_i is R_2 and every priority graph's first layer requests (M_2) agents. But AO only prepares (M_1) agents. See Box A.
2. The request sequence is $I_{M_1} = (R_1, R_1 \ldots \ldots R_1)$ (every request has (M_1) requests in the first layer of priority graph). That is to say, every request r_i is R_1 and every priority graph's first layer requests (M_1) agents. But AO prepares (M_2) agents. See Box B.

If the first case is the worst case, then suppose there exists another case worse than the first case.

Box A.

$$C_A(I_{M_2}) = a_1 \sum_{i=1}^{n} R_2 + (a_3 - a_1) \sum_{i=1}^{n} (M_2 - M_1)$$

$$= a_1 R_2 n + (a_3 - a_1)(M_2 - M_1)n = [1 + (q-1)(\frac{M_2 - M_1}{R_2})]C_{OPT}(I_{M_2})$$

$$\Rightarrow \alpha_{M_2} = 1 + (q-1)(\frac{M_2 - M_1}{R_2})$$

Box B.

$$C_A(I_{M_1}) = a_1 \sum_{i=1}^{n} R_1 + a_2 \sum_{i=1}^{n} (M_2 - M_1)$$

$$= a_1 R_2 n + a_2 (M_2 - M_1)n = [1 + p(\frac{M_2 - M_1}{R_1})]C_{OPT}(I_{M_1})$$

$$\Rightarrow \alpha_{M_1} = 1 + p(\frac{M_2 - M_1}{R_1})$$

Let the number of the agents requested by the first layer of priority graph in the third case be M_2', but the number of agent prepared by AO be M_1'. Let the competitive ratio be α'. The requested range is $[M_1, M_2]$, so $M_2' \leq M_2$, $M_1' \geq M_1$. From the result of competitive ratio given in the first case, $\alpha' \leq \alpha_{M_2}$ can be gotten obviously. If the second case is the worst case, then $\alpha' \leq \alpha_{M_1}$ can be proved in the same way. Therefore, $Max(\alpha_{M_2}, \alpha_{M_1})$ is the supremum of competitive ratio of DDSA in LD($[R_1, R_2]$). When $(q-1)=p$, the competitive ratio is α_{M_1}. The proof is completed.

From the proof, we can see the ranges of LD have great effect on the competitive ratio.

Theorem 2: The competitive ratio of Yang et al.'s (2002) algorithm in LD$[R_1, R_2]$ is $Max(a_{R_2}, a_{R_1})$.

Proof: In Yang et al.'s algorithm, all agents needed by all tasks are dispatched in spit of their dependence relationship. With the same method in Theorem 2's proof, the supremum of the competitive ratio of Yang's algorithm can be got as $Max(a_{R_2}, a_{R_1})$, thereinto:

$$a_{R_2} = 1 + (q-1)(\frac{R_2 - R_1}{R_2})$$

and:

$$a_{R_1} = 1 + p(\frac{R_2 - R_1}{R_1}).$$

Obviously, for the same priority graph, $M_2 - M_1 \leq R_2 - R_1$, so the supremum of competitive ratio of DDSA is smaller than that of Yang et al.'s algorithm.

Adaptability Analysis

Since distributed network management is the direction of development, it is not adaptive for every case of network management. Chun, Cho, and Cho (2002) have used three methods of use agent to realize distributed network management: Peer-to-peer mobile agent method; roaming method; and clustering method. The response time has results similar to SNMP method and peer-to-peer mobile agent method. As network entities increase, the overall response time drastically increases by using SNMP polling method, by which network traffic and processing time have been caused. However, if managed entities are minor, SNMP polling method is better than any other methods. When the number of managed entities is increased to more than 30, the performance of agent methods is better than SNMP method and clustering method is better than roaming method (Chun, 2002).

The value of $(M_2 - M_1)$ is a direct proportion of the competitive ratio. In practical application, the less the $(M_2 - M_1)$ is, the less the competitive ratio is, so the local domain should be divided into as small a scale as possible it can be.

Because the existing dynamic scheduling method (Yang et al., 2002) doesn't consider the relationship of sub-tasks, the DDSA in this chapter use dependence relationship to reduce the required range from $[R_1, R_2]$ to $[M_1, M_2]$. If the task is simply parallel, then the performance of DDSA is the same as the existing dynamic scheduling method. However, if the task is composed of not only parallel sub-tasks but also serial sub-tasks, then $M_2 - M_1 \leq R_2 - R_1$, that is to say, DDSA will be more competitive than the existing method when used for complicated tasks.

TEST AND PERFORMANCE ANALYSIS

The efficiency of the network management task executed by multi-agent is most closely related to the efficiency of task decomposition and task scheduling. Three algorithms are used in task decomposition. Assume n is the number of nodes

in priority graph; the complexity of Algorithm 1 is $O(n)$, the complexity of Algorithm 2 is $O(n^2)$ at most, and the complexity of Algorithm 3 is $O(n)$. Compared with the algorithm in the reference (Zhuang & Pande, 2003), the complexity of these algorithms are smaller. Zhuang and Pande (2003) started their research from the point of view of optimizing single-agent migration path, but our research comes from considering multi-agent task allocation.

Task Decomposition Algorithm Tests

Let T denote network management task. Let n denote the number of sub-tasks. Let m denote the number of priority ranks. Assume the time of agent migration between any pair of network nodes is t_g.

Method 1: Assume n sub-tasks are assigned to a single agent, and suppose that the average execution time spending on one sub-task is:

$t_e = (\frac{t_1 + t_2 + \cdots + t_n}{n}, t_1, t_2 \ldots t_n$ is the time of executing every sub-task),

then agent migration times is n at least, and the total execution time is $nt_e + nt_g$ at least.

Method 2: Assume m priorities are given to n sub-tasks. Then n sub-tasks are divided into m groups. If one sub-task is dispatched to one agent, n agents are needed and agent migration times is n. Assume that the max execution time of sub-task is t_{max}, then the total execution time is: $mt_{max} + nt_g$. The goal of our optimization is to make the following formula true.

$$mt_{max} + nt_g < nt_e + nt_g$$
$$\Rightarrow \frac{m}{n} < \frac{t_e}{t_{max}} \qquad (3)$$

Figure 4. Task definition and its priority graph

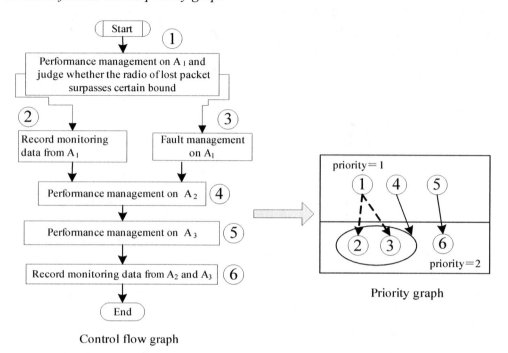

As we can see from formula (3), the less m and the more t_e and n, the nearer to the goal of optimization. In conclusion, task decomposition is adapted to the circumstance of a large scale of task (n is large), and when the difference of scale among sub-tasks is little (t_e is close to t_{max}), the optimization is performed well.

In order to verify the efficiency of the task decomposition algorithms, a network management task is defined in Figure 4: in 100M Ethernet, performance and fault management on server A_1, router A_2, and switcher A_3, and these equipments support SNMP. The performance and fault management include all of their sub-functions. We use Aglets' system of IBM as agent platform, tracking Aglet port by using Sniffer software to test data traffic.

Two types of agent dispatch methods are tested. One method is to assign all sub-tasks to a single agent called g_1, and g_1 executes each sub-task according to its itinerary. We calculate executing time by adding timer code to agent code and data

traffic by using Sniffer software at Aglet port. Another method is: First, the total task is decomposed into sub-tasks with different priorities. Second, the sub-tasks whose priorities are 1 are executed by multi-agent in parallel. The basic rule is that one agent is responsible for one sub-task. After the sub-tasks whose priorities ranked 1 are finished, the sub-tasks whose priorities being a rank of 2 will be executed according to the same rule until all sub-tasks are accomplished. Because sub-task 2 and 3 control depend on 1, the result of subtask 1 will decide if either 2 or 3 is executed. The total executing time of the task is recorded.

Test results: For method 1, the data traffic in method 1 is about 129M Bytes; for method 2 is about 85M Bytes. For method 1, the total executing time of the task is 16968ms, but for method 2 is 9151ms.

The total executing time in method 2 is far less than that in method 1, which answers the goal of optimization. Data traffic in network in method 2 is also less than that in method 1 because in method 1 only one agent executing the task needs to communicate with Aglet platform frequently, but in method 2 the communication traffic is decentralized into multi-agent in the network.

Dependence-Based Dynamic Scheduling Algorithm Tests

Three types of agent time have been involved in our system: time of cloning, time of dispatching, and time of disposing, so the influences of the time that are correlative with agents catch our attention. When the granularity of the sub-tasks increases, the response time of agent are tested. The experiments prove that when the load (the number of MIB variables) of agent increasing with 5, the time of cloning and disposing fluctuate at 16ms. When the load of agent increasing with 100, the time of dispatching fluctuate at 156ms. Therefore, we get $p = 0.103$, $q = 1.103$, and $(q - 1) = p$. According to the algorithm presented by Yang et al. (2002), the infimum of Yang's online algorithm is:

$$\alpha'_L = 1 + p(q-1)\frac{(R_2 - R_1)}{pR_2 + (q-1)R_1}$$

if:

$$g = \frac{(q-1)R_1R_2 + pR_1R_2}{pR_2 + (q-1)R_1}.$$

Because $(q - 1) = p$, then $\alpha'_L = \alpha_{R_2} = \alpha_{R_1}$. We can get the following conclusion:

The infimum of competitive ratio can be gotten when:

$$g = \frac{2R_1R_2}{R_2 + R_1} \qquad (4)$$

Method: Assume that the actions in this task are in one local domain; let AO prepare the agents according to formula (4), let the request range of agent numbers in the local domain vary from [30,30] to [30,100], and the time occupied by scheduling algorithm be calculated with timer code in the AO. A priority graph of a complicated large-scale network management task is presented in Figure 5.

Figure 5. A network management task and its priority graph

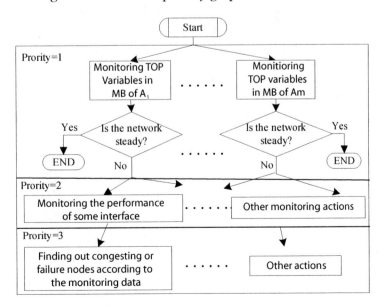

The main criterion of evaluation for dynamic scheduling algorithm is the time cost of scheduling algorithm. The time occupied by the algorithm can be computed in the experiment. According to the proof of competitive ratio in this chapter, the competitive ratio changes with the variety of range of local domain. For different ranges of local domain, we can compute the scheduling time. From the priority graph, we can see the range of local domain is three times of the range of number of agents requested by the first layer of the task priority graph. When the lower bound is 30 and the upper bounder increases with 30, Figure 6 presents the varieties of scheduling time of Yang's algorithm (without considering the relationship of sub-tasks) and our dynamic scheduling algorithm with the varieties of the range of request agents. As can be seen from the graph, when the range of local domain is [30,30], their scheduling time is equal to the time of the offline optimal algorithm. This result means that when the number of agents requested is exactly known, the algorithm becomes the offline optimal algorithm. With the range of local domain increasing, the scheduling time of two algorithms are increasing, but the scheduling time of DDSA is always less than that of Yang et al.'s online algorithm. These results indicate that the performance of DDSA is better than that of Yang's scheduling algorithm and the former is more close to OPT. So in the actual application, the less the range of local domain is, the better the allocation algorithm is.

APPLICATION TO NETWORK STREAM MANAGEMENT

To evaluate the effectiveness of dynamic scheduling, we developed a distributed network stream management system whose computational environment consisting of five sub-networks and each of the sub-networks has three managed elements distributed geographically. The purpose of the management system is to monitor some network data stream and to guarantee the steam be transferring fluently from data source to destination in the network. The network topology of experimental environment is shown in Figure 7.

Five sub-networks compose one local domain, and it has an agent organizer to perform the function of scheduling. In order to display the effectiveness of multi-agent scheduling, three data streams are designed in this system: a guaranteed stream and two disturbing data streams. The guaranteed stream is sent from one node in sub-network 1 to a data receiving node in sub-network 4. Two disturbing streams are sent from one node in sub-network 2 and sub-network 3 to a data receiving node in sub-network 4. In this system, we use three kinds of functional agents: monitoring agent, bottleneck searching agent, and configuring agent. The task is created by a manager and then submitted to AO. According the decomposed sub-tasks, AO dispatches two monitoring agents to stay on the data sending terminal and data receiving terminal. These two monitoring agents are responsible for collecting the characteristics of the data stream in its host. When disturbing streams have been started, the monitoring agent finds that the characteristics of the guaranteed stream in the data receiving terminal is not consistent with the characteristics of the guaranteed stream in the data sending terminal. This message of inconsistent state is then sent to AO. Also, AO dispatches an agent (bottleneck searching agent) to travel the nodes in the local domain to search the bottleneck node. As a result, four bottleneck nodes are found out: Router_2, Router_3, Router_4, and Router_5. These bottleneck nodes should be configured by a configuring agent to reserve certain bandwidth to the guaranteed stream. Because the bottleneck node is found dynamically, a scheduling configuring agent should be dynamic. Assume that the historical scale of required configuring agents is [1, 5], according to scheduling strategy:

Figure 6. Comparison of scheduling time with varieties of local domain range

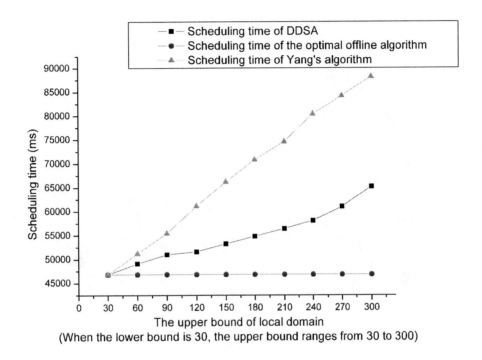

Figure 7. The network topology in the experiment

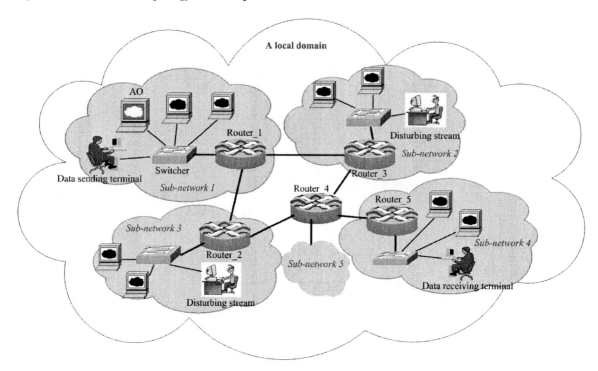

$$g = \frac{2R_1R_2}{R_2 + R_1} = \frac{2 \times 1 \times 5}{1+5} \approx 2 \, ,$$

so AO has prepared 2 configuring agents in advance to ensure that the scheduling algorithm is most close to the optimal scheduling algorithm for any required queue. Then configuring agents are dispatched to bottleneck nodes to execute the QoS configuration sub-task. Since this is only an example for application, the network is small-scale. In a real application, for example, the managed telecommunication network is large-scale and complicated and the number of agents required by managed entities is large, so the DDSA will work in such areas.

FUTURE TRENDS

The problem of scheduling tasks among distributed agents in the multi-agent systems has drawn much attention in recent years. Agent-based technology has been applied to various practical problems, and the agent scheduling problem has been widely studied by various methods, but different applications should be considered with different methods, because the scheduling efficiency will get better if we integrate the scheduling strategy with the characteristics of tasks with different background. Rapid growth in the Internet community and related business make network management become larger and more complicated, so how to make network manager manage the network efficiently and respond quickly and exactly becomes a critical issue. Effective dynamic scheduling for agents can manage with this issue for a certain degree. However, there are other influencing factors of the performance of task scheduling. The process of scheduling is actually a process of optimization, which includes the optimization for scheduling algorithm and the optimization for the process of executing. Because the network environment of agent execution is dynamic and changing, we try to optimize the scheduling process at the first step. Optimizing the process of task executing is complicated work, and many details need some specific optimization, but the collaboration of multi-agents will be helpful. So our future work will involve the rules contained by sub-tasks and the influence of collaboration strategies on the efficiency of task execution.

CONCLUSION

We have looked at the problem of agent scheduling in network management. The main contribution here is a mechanism of task decomposition and scheduling for multi-agents in distributed network management. Based on the analysis of dependence relationship between sub-tasks, some task decomposition algorithms and a dependence-based dynamic scheduling algorithm for agents are presented. In addition, the comparison with the existing online algorithm proves that DDSA is more optimal than the existing online algorithm. This work not only gives a new scheduling approach to the agents in network management but also can serve as a framework for further studies in other types of agent tasks.

ACKNOWLEDGMENTS

This work is supported by National Natural Science Foundation of China under Grants No. 90204009 and 90604004 and China Specialized Research Fund for the Doctoral Program of Higher Education under Grants No. 20030286014.

REFERENCES

Albers, S. (2003). Online algorithms: A survey. *Mathematical Programming, 97*(1), 3-26

Azar, Y. (1998). On-line load balancing. In A. Fiat & G. Woeginger (Eds.), *Online algorithms: The state of the art* (pp. 178-195). Springer.

Bartal, Y., Fiat, A., & Karloff, H. (1992). New algorithms for an ancient scheduling problem. *Proceedings of the 24th Ann. ACM Symposium on Theory of Computing* (pp. 51-58). Retrieved June 20, 2003, from http://portal.acm.org

Bartal Y., Fiat, A., & Rabani, Y. (1992). Competitive algorithms for distributed data management. *Proceedings of the 24th Annual ACM Symposium on Theory of Computing* (pp. 39-50). Retrieved March 20, 2003, from http://portal.acm.org

Buchanman, W.J., Naylor, M., & Scott, A.V. (2000). Enhancing network management using mobile agents. *The 7th IEEE International Conference and Workshop on the Engineering of Computer Based Systems* (pp. 218-228). Retrieved April 5, 2002, from http://ieeexplore.ieee.org

Chun, J. K., Cho, K. Y., & Cho, S. H. (2002). Network management based on pc communication platform with SNMP and mobile agents. *Proceedings of the 22nd International Conference on Distributed Computing Systems Workshops* (pp. 222-227). Retrieved May 16, 2003, from http://ieeexplore.ieee.org

Clement, B. J., & Durfee, E. H. (1998). Scheduling high-level tasks among cooperative agents. *International Conference on Multi Agent Systems* (pp. 96-103). Retrieved March 3, 2002, from http://ieeexplore.ieee.org

Ferrante J., Ottenstein K. J., & Warren J. D. (1987). The program dependence graph and its use in optimization. *ACM Transactions on Programming Languages and Systems, 9*(3), 319-349.

Fiat, A., & Mendel, M. (2000). Better algorithms for unfair metrical task systems and applications. *Proceedings of the 32nd Annual ACM Symposium on Theory of Computing* (pp. 725-734). Retrieved

June 20, 2003, from http://portal.acm.org

Jones, P. B., Blake, M. A., & Archibald, J. K. (2002). A real-time algorithm for task allocation. *IEEE International Symposium on Intelligent Control*, 672-677. Retrieved September 1, 2003, from http://ieeexplore.ieee.org

Kona, M. K., & Xu, C. Z. (2002). A framework for network management using mobile agents. *Proceeding of the International Parallel and Distributed Processing Symposium* (pp. 227-234). Retrieved October 15, 2002, from http://ieeexplore.ieee.org

Liu B., Luo J., & Li W. (2005). Multi-agent based network management task decomposition and scheduling. *The 19th International Conference on Advanced Information Networking and Applications* (pp. 41-46). Retrieved December 1, 2005, from http://ieeexplore.ieee.org

Luo, X., Huang, Z., & Li, L. (1995). A method for partitioning a sequential program into parallel tasks. *Journal of HarBin Institute of Technology, 27*(5), 46-50.

Morel, B., & Alexander, P. A. (2003). Slicing approach for parallel component adaptation. *The 10th IEEE International Conference and Workshop on the Engineering of Computer-Based Systems* (pp. 108-114). Retrieved May 20, 2003, from http://ieeexplore.ieee.org

Pras, A. (1995). *Network management architectures*. Unpublished doctoral dissertation, Netherlands: Centre for Telematics and Information Technology of the University of Twente.

Satoh, I. (2002). A framework for building reusable mobile agents for network management. *IEEE/IFIP Network Operations and Management Symposium* (pp. 51-64). Retrieved May 20, 2005, from http://ieeexplore.ieee.org

Singh, A., & Pande, S. (2002). Compiler optimizations for Java aglets in distributed data intensive applications. *The 17th ACM Symposium on Applied Computing, with a Neuro-Fuzzy Applications Track* (pp. 87-92). Retrieved March 20, 2003, from http://portal.acm.org

Sleator, D. D., & Tarjan, R. E. (1985). Amortized efficiency of list update and paging rules. *Communications of the ACM, 28*, 202-208.

Zhang, F., Luh, P.B., & Santos, E. Jr. (2004). Performance study of multi-agent scheduling and coordination framework for maintenance networks. In K. Deguchi (Ed.), *Sendai, Japan: Vol. 3. Proceedings of 2004 IEEE/RSJ International Conference on Intelligent Robots and Systems* (pp. 2390-2395). Sendai: Kyodo Printing Co.

Zhuang, X., & Pande, S. (2003). Compiler scheduling of mobile agents for minimizing overheads. *Proceedings of the 23rd International Conference on Distributed Computing Systems* (pp. 600-607). Retrieved September 1, 2003, from http://ieeexplore.ieee.org

Yan, W., & Wu, W. (Eds.). (2000). *Data structure*. Beijing, China: Tsinghua University Press.

Yang, X., Ma, W., & You, J. (2002). On the dynamic allocation of mobile Agents by on-line task scheduling. *The 16th Proceedings of the International Parallel and Distributed Processing Symposium* (pp. 217-224). Retrieved April 19, 2003, from http://ieeexplore.ieee.org

Chapter VIII
Scalable Fault Tolerant Agent Grooming Environment (SAGE)

H. Farooq Ahmad
Communication Technologies, Japan

Hiroki Suguri
Communication Technologies, Japan

Arshad Ali
NUST Institute of Information Technology, Pakistan

Amna Basharat
NUST Institute of Information Technology, Pakistan

Amina Tariq
NUST Institute of Information Technology, Pakistan

ABSTRACT

Multi-agent systems (MAS) advocate an agent-based approach to software engineering based on decomposing problems in terms of decentralized, autonomous agents that can engage in flexible, high-level interactions. This chapter introduces scalable fault tolerant agent grooming environment (SAGE), a second-generation Foundation for Intelligent Physical Agents (FIPA)-compliant multi-agent system developed at NIIT-Comtec, which provides an environment for creating distributed, intelligent, and autonomous entities that are encapsulated as agents. The chapter focuses on the highlight of SAGE, which is its decentralized fault-tolerant architecture that can be used to develop applications in a number of areas such as e-health, e-government, and e-science. In addition, SAGE architecture provides tools for runtime agent management, directory facilitation, monitoring, and editing messages exchange between agents. SAGE also provides a built-in mechanism to program agent behavior and their capabilities with the help of its autonomous agent architecture, which is the other major highlight of this chapter. The authors believe that the market for agent-based applications is growing rapidly, and SAGE can play a crucial role for future intelligent applications development.

INTRODUCTION

Multi-agent systems (MAS) are based on the idea that a cooperative working environment comprised of synergistic software components can cope with problems that are hard to solve using traditional centralized approach to computation (Jennings, 2000). Smaller software entities—software agents—with special capabilities (autonomous, reactive, pro-active, and social) are used instead to interact in a flexible and dynamic way to solve problems more efficiently.

MAS is a distributed paradigm that contains a community of social agents, which can act on behalf of their owners (Wooldridge, 2000). It is increasingly becoming an ubiquitous paradigm for the design and implementation of complex software applications as it can support distributed collaborative problem solving by having collections of agents that dynamically organize themselves. The improvements in the use of multi-agent technology in automation and manufacturing systems are fast adaptation to system reconfiguration (for example, addition or removal of resources, different organizational structures, etc.), re-use of code for other control applications, increase of flexibility and adaptation of the control application, and more optimised and modular software development.

Multi-agent systems have been developed for a variety of application domains, including electronic commerce, air traffic control, workflow management, transportation systems, and Web applications, among others. Critical importance of agent-oriented architectural concepts is being highlighted in the next-generation computing domains (Luck, McBurney, & Preist, 2002). Autonomic computing in particular views autonomic elements as agents and autonomic systems as multi-agent systems. The next-generation agent computing calls for the development of multi-agent systems developed on this very theme of autonomic computing, possessing the key characteristics of self-managing systems, namely self-healing, self-protecting, self-adapting, and self-optimising (Kephart & Chess, 2003). Our research focuses on the development of a next-generation multi-agent system called scalable fault tolerant agent grooming environment (SAGE) (Farooq Ahmad et al, 2003; Zaheer, Farooq Ahmad, Ali, & Suguri, 2005).

The vision of SAGE takes inspiration from the concept of autonomic computing, which originates directly from theoretical perspective of autonomous decentralized system (ADS) (Mori, 1993). ADS primarily relies on the principles of autonomous controllability and autonomous coordinability. These two properties assure online expansion, fault tolerance, and online maintenance of the system. They suggest that every "autonomous" subsystem requires an intelligence to manage itself and without directing to and being directed from the other subsystems and to coordinate with other subsystems. Based on this notion of ADS, each component of the multi-agent system is conceived to exhibit its own autonomic behavior, contributing to the overall autonomic behavior of the system (McCann & Huebscher, 2004). Particularly at the level of individual components of an MAS, well-established techniques, many of which fall under the rubric of fault tolerance, have led to the development of elements that rarely fail, which is one important aspect of being autonomic (Kephart & Chess, 2003). We describe below how we envision SAGE, as primarily a fault-tolerant agent environment complemented by well-defined agent architecture to facilitate the development of agent-based applications.

Twofold Approach Toward Next-Generation Computing

Autonomic computing is seen as a holistic vision that enables a computing system to "deliver much more automation than the sum of its individually self-managed parts" by various researchers (Koehler, Giblin, Gantenbein, & Hauser, 2003). Autonomic computing systems ought to self-configure, self-protect, self-heal, and self-optimize on both system and application level (Kephart & Chess, 2003). This two-level approach toward the synergy of autonomic computing has been adopted while conceiving the architecture of SAGE. At the system level, SAGE is designed with a decentralized architecture, scalability, and fault tolerance as its key design features, providing a strong base for incorporating the features of self-healing, self-protecting, and self-configuring behaviors.

The most famous and widely used FIPA-compliant platforms include Comtec-AP (Suguri, 1998), JADE (Bellifemine, Poggi, & Rimassi, 1999), FIPA-OS (Poslad, Buckle, & Hadingham, 2000), and Zeus (Nwana, Nduma, Lee, & Collis, 1999), which are first-generation FIPA-compliant MAS frameworks, implemented FIPA specifications to varying degrees. However, none of these systems was developed with the true vision of next-generation autonomic systems both at the system and application level. These systems also lack techniques to manage challenges faced by distributed systems. Existing architectures are centralized and use component replication or distribution, which have various shortcomings. These systems also lack fault tolerance, which is a key feature of high assurance (Farooq Ahmad, Sun, & Mori, 2001; Farooq Ahmad et al., 2003).

The MAS has moved into a new era, known as the second generation, where the problems faced in the era of the first generation are being tackled and resolved. Developers have emphasized developing high-performance multi-agent systems that are fault tolerant, scalable, secure, autonomous, and lightweight. SAGE has been developed at the NUST-Comtec labs as one of the next generation FIPA-compliant MAS and aims to overcome the problems inherent in first generation MASs. The highlight of SAGE is its decentralized system architecture (Farooq Ahmad, Suguri, Shafiq, & Ali, 2004; Ghafoor, Rehman, Khan, Farooq Ahmad, & Ali, 2004; Zaheer et al., 2005) coupled with

its hybrid agent architecture (Amina, Basharat, Farooq Ahmad, Ali, & Suguri, 2005), which provides a foundation for developing next generation autonomic systems and applications.

Objectives of the Chapter and Chapter Outline

The chapter serves to highlight the following areas of research in the development of SAGE:

- Describes the twofold approach toward next-generation computing systems and its mapping onto the current architecture of SAGE:
  o *Multi-agent system architecture:* A decentralized, fault tolerant, and autonomous multi-agent system architecture.
  o *Agent architecture (agent behavior subsystems):* Hybrid agent architecture.
- Delineates upon the decentralized system architecture of SAGE:
  o Discusses rational and the decentralized system level architecture of SAGE focusing on the virtual agent cluster methodology to achieve fault-tolerance of the agent management system.
- Discusses agent architecture of SAGE:
  o Presents the design of a generic agent architecture that incorporates the key features of autonomic systems.
  o Compare SAGE with first-generation MAS.

The chapter is organized as follows. The second section gives definitions of necessary background terminologies and discussion of the topic. The third section presents a detailed view of the system-level architecture of SAGE. The fourth section describes agent architecture of SAGE in detail with its design and implementation. The next section presents discussion on the future research opportunities and emerging trends. Overall discussion of the chapter and concluding remarks are presented in the final section.

BACKGROUND

Main contribution in autonomous agents comes from artificial intelligence, object-oriented programming, concurrent object-based systems and human-computer interface design (Jennings, Sycra, & Wooldridge, 1998). This section briefly addresses the main concepts associated with the agent-oriented paradigm that will assist the understanding of overall architecture of SAGE.

Distributed Computing and DAI

Traditionally, research into systems composed of multiple agents was carried out under the banner of distributed artificial intelligence (DAI) and has historically been divided into two main camps: distributed problem solving (DPS) and multi-agent systems. More recently, the term "multi-agent systems" has come to have a more general meaning and is now used to refer to all types of systems composed of multiple (semi-) autonomous components.

Distributed problem solving considers how a particular problem can be solved by a number of modules (nodes) that cooperate in dividing and sharing knowledge about the problem and its evolving solutions. In a pure DPS system, all interaction strategies are incorporated as an integral part of the system. In contrast, research in MAS is concerned with the behavior of a collection of possibly pre-existing autonomous agents aiming at solving a given problem. Jennings (1998) describes some reasons for the increasing interest in MAS research to include: the ability to provide robustness and efficiency; the ability to allow inter-operation of existing legacy systems; and the ability to solve problems in which data, expertise, or control is distributed.

Agents and Multi-Agent Systems

Two very primitive yet pertinent constituents of agent-oriented paradigm are agents and multi-agent systems. Agents can be defined as autonomous, problem-solving computational entities capable of effective operation in dynamic and open environments (Singh & Huhns, 2005; Wooldridge, 2002). Agents can be distinguished from objects (in the sense of object-oriented software) in that they are autonomous entities capable of exercising choice over their actions and interactions. Agents cannot, therefore, be directly invoked like objects. However, they may be constructed using object technology. Agents are often deployed in environments in which they interact and cooperate with other agents. Such environments are known as multi-agent systems.

Foundation for Intelligent Physical Agents

The Foundation for Intelligent Physical Agents (FIPA) is an Institute of Electrical and Electronics Engineers (IEEE) standards committee that promotes agent-based technology and interoperability. The core mission of FIPA is to facilitate the interoperation between agents across heterogeneous agent systems. To this purpose, FIPA has been working on specifications that range from agent platform architectures to support communicating agents, agent communication languages, and content languages for expressing messages and interaction protocols that expand the scope from single messages to complete transactions (FIPA, 2005).

FIPA Abstract Architecture

FIPA provides abstract architecture of a multi-agent system. Amongst the technology-oriented features of its abstract architecture include abstract entities for platform management (white and yellow pages), message transport, agent com-

Figure 1. FIPA platform

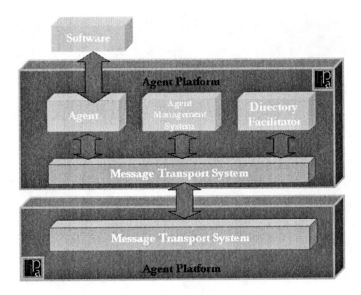

munication languages, content languages, and interaction protocols (dialogues, conversations). An overview of FIPA platform is shown in Figure 1 (FIPA, 2005).

FIPA Compliant Distributed Architecture

FIPA specifies distributed architecture for developing multi-agent sSystem frameworks. The generic model given by FIPA is presented in Figure 2, and a detailed description can be found at FIPA (2005).

Scope: Agent-Oriented Paradigm

The agent environment is a result of an approach that encompasses various phases in a layered manner as shown in Figure 3 inspired by the layered model given by HP Research Laboratories (Fonsecal, Griss, & Letsinger, 2001). The multi-agent system framework in the agent-oriented paradigm abstraction layer is the underlying language. Application framework and agent infrastructure are the primary tools for agent engineering. On top of this framework, the agent role is defined by developing autonomous agent architecture. The combination of the architecture and the framework enables development of various agents, which interact together to merge into agent society. This eventually leads to the development of complete agent environment.

Overall Abstract Architecture of SAGE

In the light of the complete vision of an agent-oriented paradigm, we have conceived the basic architecture of SAGE in accordance with the FIPA specifications. The system architecture consists of the mandatory components specified by FIPA as shown in Figure 4. Amongst these, prime components include:

- **AMS:** Agent management system exerts supervisory control over the agent platform and provides white page services. The main focus has been to make it fault tolerant.

Figure 2. FIPA-compliant distributed architecture

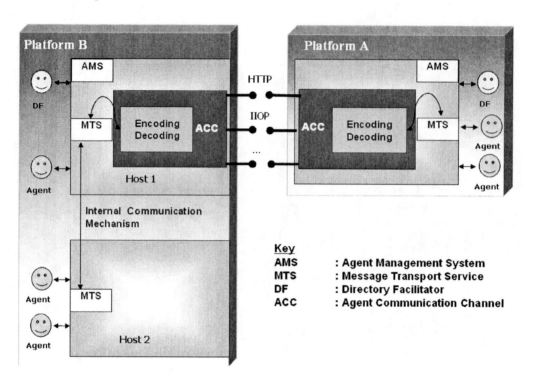

- **DF:** Directory facilitator provides yellow page services.
- **MTS:** Message transport service deals with the transportation of ACL messages among agents. Scalability is the most important design issue for MTS.

These three components have been included in the architecture as the main system level agents of SAGE.

- **VMA:** Visual management agent provides GUI, monitoring, and utility services. It also monitors and manages distributed environments.
- **Agent communication language facilitator:** Allows the exchange of messages with well-defined structured contents, represented in FIPA ACL.

- **Autonomous agent architecture:** The autonomous agent architecture is one of the most important components built on top of the system architecture, which aids in the development of autonomous entities.

SAGE: SYSTEM LEVEL DECENTRALIZED ARCHITECTURE

Rationale

In FIPA platforms, agents require some execution environment in which they can publish their service interfaces and can provide services to other agent. Such execution environment is called agent platform (AP). Any abnormal behavior of platform can have a negative impact on agents residing on that platform. Therefore, it is necessary to provide a suitable architecture for the AP,

Figure 3. Layered view of a complete agent oriented paradigm (Source: Fonsecal et al., 2001)

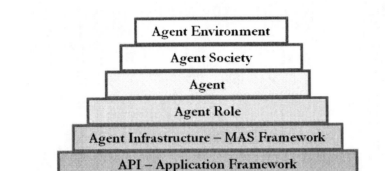

which should not only provide fault tolerance but also scalability features.

All the agents within MAS are managed by AMS, which is the mandatory supervisory authority of any AP. To be more scalable, a single agent platform can be distributed over several machines. In existing systems, AMS is centralized, that is, it exists on one machine. With centralized AMS, this infrastructure lacks fault tolerance, which is a key feature of high assurance. Absence of fault tolerance is the main reason for the small number of deployments of MAS. Failure of AMS leads towards abnormal behavior in the distributed platform. In this section, virtual agent cluster (VAC) methodology is presented, which strongly supports decentralized AMS to achieve fault tolerance in distributed AP.

Need and Importance of Fault Tolerant Agent Systems

One of the most important factors in any distributed application is the continuous service provision regardless of any failure. There is a need to improve the existing architecture of agent platforms to make these systems more effective and fault tolerant. There exist different concerns in quality of service, such as timeliness, reliabil-

ity, and fault tolerance for information service utilization and provision. A system is called a high-assurance system when heterogeneous and changing requirement levels of QoS are satisfied (Farooq Ahmad et al., 2001, 2003). High assurance of service provision in distributed multi agent systems is a key feature for its successful deployment. Several solutions have been proposed regarding the fault tolerance of individual application agents, but limited work is done on the fault tolerance of AP. This chapter primarily focuses on fault tolerance of distributed AP through decentralized architecture. Importance of the proposed architecture can be assessed by the fact that the same architecture supports scalability, fault detection, fault tolerance, fault recovery, and load sharing.

Related Work: Fault-Tolerant Architectures

A lot of work has been done on fault detection and fault tolerance of individual agents in multi-agent systems. Certain approaches provide solution of consistency problems amongst agent replicas. However, some address the solutions of maintaining agent cooperation. Let us have a brief look into the existing architectures.

Figure 4. Overall abstract architecture of SAGE

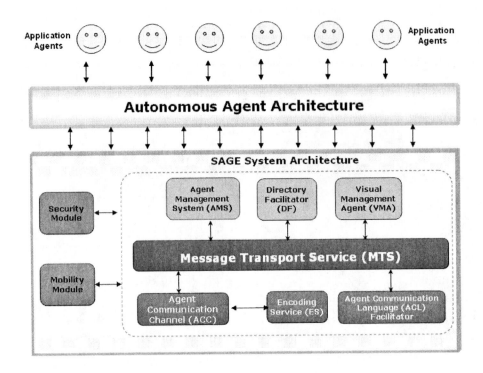

Peng and Deters (2005) and Klein and Dellarocas (1999) proposed exception handling by sending periodic events to agents to inspect their state. Exception handling requires periodic probing and is an overhead on the system. Event monitoring causes each agent to notify the event manager when trying to do some event.

Kumar, Cohen, and Levesque (2000) proposed a fault-tolerant architecture by integrating agents and brokers. It seems to be fault tolerant but mostly concentrates on the fault tolerance of brokerage team, not on individual agents. It also requires extra computing for the management of brokerage layers.

In Benno and Brazier (2003), integration of AgentScape with Dynamic Agent Replicated eXtension (DARX) is described. AgentsScape Operating System (AOS) handles the heterogeneity issues among agents of different multi-agent systems and DARX is used for the provision of fault tolerance. Integration of agent and object

servers makes it more complex. This integration handles only the failure of individual agents regardless of MAS.

In Bellifemine et al. (1999) and Vitaglione, Quarta, and Cortese (2002), Java agent development environment (JADE) is presented, which is one of the most commonly used FIPA compliant frameworks. JADE also supports distributed architecture, but its distributed architecture lacks fault tolerance because of its centralized registry. Distributed architecture uses a container-based approach. Its main container stores the registry information of all the agents that exist on other containers, running on separate hosts.

Proposed Solution: Fault-Tolerant System Architecture

The basic theme employed in developing our second-generation MAS is to move from a centralized to decentralized architecture. Instead of relying on the usual client/server paradigm traditionally used in existing architectures, a peer-to-peer (P2P) computing paradigm has been adapted to bring about this decentralization. This decentralized architecture has been designed within the distributed AP. Detailed proposed architecture of system can be seen in Figure 5.

Virtual Agent Cluster

Virtual agent cluster is an abstraction that encompasses all the machines over which a single AP is deployed. The concept of VAC is analogous to that of cluster computing. Just as in cluster computing, there exists a front-end processor that distributes the load among other machines within that cluster. Agent communication channel (ACC) plays the role of front-end processor in the current system. VAC provides scalable transparency among all the distributed machines. Each VAC has a global unique identification, normally an AP name. Each machine within VAC also has a unique ID, which not only helps in routing the messages but also avoids extra communication among different

machines. In Figure 5, machines 1, 2, and 3 are separate peers of an AP, and each peer runs with its own local registry and local instance of AMS. There also exist separate parallel communication layers among all distributed machines. These parallel layers avoid placing extra load on MTS communication layer and help the fault tolerance of system. All the peers are aware of each other's identity (location/name) within the same VAC.

AMS is distributed in such a way that failure of one instance does not affect its peer instances executing on peer machines. Agents registered with local AMS are kept in an active pool. Remote calls among all the peers within a VAC are done using Java remote method invocation (RMI). All the peer machines within the VAC send heartbeats (hello messages) to each other to check whether the peers are alive. These hello messages are either sent when a message is sent across the machines between different agents or by using dynamic probing policy. If any peer appears faulty, its information is removed from all the peer machines after performing a confirmation test.

Figure 5. Decentralized, fault-tolerant intra-system architecture of SAGE

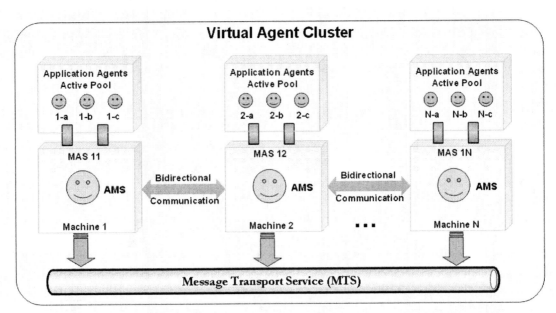

Synergy of VAC

The virtual agent cluster is designed to support dynamic synergy of platform peers (machines). As soon as more machines join the same VAC, they autonomously start working; as shown in Figure 5 and Figure 6, centralized management is shifted to decentralized control. Initially centralized registry failure causes the 100% failure of the system. But in proposed architecture, if any of the single machines running an instance of MAS fails, then the degree of fault tolerance depends upon the number of available machines in VAC. In existing systems, centralized AMS provides a single point of access to all distributed resources, which not only becomes bottleneck under heavy load conditions but also leads toward failure. Once a request for an agent arrives in a platform, it is transparently delivered to its recipient by using distributed message transport service (MTS). The process of locating an agent in a VAC was initially a problem. It was required to perform extensive search among all the machines, because VAC provides an abstraction of unique system. Creation of agents with transparent platform name restricts us to provide centralized access to all agents, which exist on different machines, as is the case with JADE. It may become bottleneck, and failure of centralized access may lead toward failure of the whole system. The above problem is solved by using the fully qualified agent name (FQAN) of the agents according to the following format:

Agentname:MachineID@VACID

Messages are delivered to MTS/ACC, which identifies the *MachineID* and sends the message directly to its recipients. FQAN of the agent by itself provides its exact location, that is, on which machine it exists. It avoids the extra broadcast or multicast communication over network. *MachineID* identifies its location and by resolving the machine ID its Internet protocol (IP) can be located. VAC ID identifies the platform in which it exists. This approach transparently accesses the agents, which either exist on local or any remote AP. Proposed FQAN format brings fault tolerance in distributed agent platform, provides better search mechanism across the platform, and enhances the message routing performance.

Characteristics of Decentralized Architecture

Following characteristics of system architecture enrich its behavior and increase its significance. Effectiveness of proposed architecture can be assessed by its characteristics. A brief overview of these characteristics follows:

- **Fault tolerance and recovery:** Decentralized system architecture brings fault tolerance in AP. Complete failure of a machine within AP is tolerated with the cooperation of its peer machines over which distributed AP is deployed.
- **Autonomy:** One of the most important aspects of the AP architecture is its autonomy. All peer machines autonomously provide services to their local application agents.
- **Application layering architecture for Intra-VAC:** AP works at application layer where it is further subdivided into different processing layers, as shown in Figure 7.
- **Application layering architecture for inter-VAC:** When two agents need to communicate with each other and both of them exist on different APs, they communicate through ACC, as shown in Figure 8. Despite the fact that these layers involve slight processing overhead, they also provide a standard way of communication and separation of concerns among the agents.
- **Load sharing:** One AP can be expanded on any number of machines. Each peer can execute different types of application agents rather than same agents.

Figure 6. Decentralized, fault tolerant inter-system architecture of SAGE

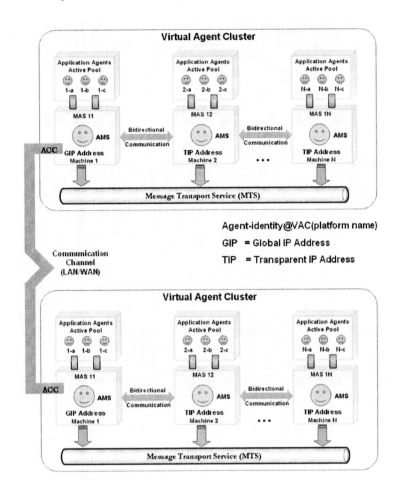

- **FIPA-compliancy:** It is worth mentioning that the above architecture does not compromise the FIPA-compliancy of the MAS framework.

Distributed Architecture of SAGE

The system has been distributed according to the VAC methodology. Its distributed architecture uses separate communication layers among system components and agents residing on separate peer machines (Zaheer et al., 2005). Application agents communicate on separate peers through MTS communication layer. But for the sake of remote management, separate communication layers among AMS, DF, and VMA are used. For example, if an AMS has to respond to its local agent with some information related to any application agent, which exists on remote peer, then it does not use MTS layer. Rather, it uses its own communication layer using RMI so that MTS should not be overloaded. Another reason for providing separate communication layers for system agents is to bring fault tolerance. In case of failure of any one-communication layer, others can be used to mask the failure. It

Figure 7. Intra-VAC layering architecture

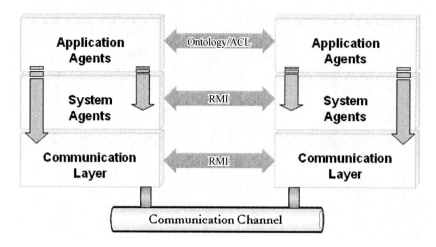

Figure 8. Inter-VAC layering architecture

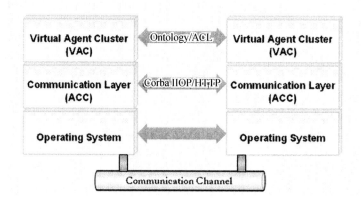

also avoids extra processing and delay for formulating ACL message and sending it through robust MTS.

Distributed architecture can be seen in Figure 9. RMI was selected, which supports object serialization implicitly as a communication mechanism among all system agents as well as for MTS, which sends messages to remote machines.

Motivations for Distribution

Motivations of distributing a single AP over multiple machines include covering a vast range of applications and also a long-distance coverage where same management policy is needed.

In addition, we wanted to avoid extra processing involved for interoperability between different platforms. For example, SAGE and JADE either require CORBA IIOP or HTTP interfaces to communicate with each other. But using decentralized architecture, a single platform can be distributed without using CORBA IIOP or HTTP.

Intelligent Dynamic Probing

Intelligent dynamic probing technique has been employed to facilitate fault detection. Although SAGE supports probing on demand, that is, whenever a message is transmitted on remote machines, the transmitting module looks for the failure, and if

Figure 9. Distributed system architecture of SAGE

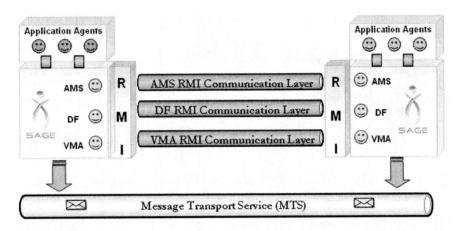

it finds any failure from remote machine it notifies to its local AMS. AMS performs failure detection by using its own communication layer. Initially, it tries to mask the failure, but if it finds severe failure, that is, the machine crashed, it notifies other machines in VAC to update their status. But probing on demand is performed only when a message is transmitted to an agent, which exists on another machine. Figure 10 shows the steps involved in probing on demand. The application agent on the leftmost machine tries to communicate via MTS with the application agent on the machine that has failed, marked as step 1. When MTS is unable to deliver the message, it raises an error and informs the sending MTS about it, shown as step 2. In step 3, probing on demand, the MTS of the unsuccessful sending machine notifies its AMS about the fault in form of an ACL message. AMS probes the peer machine via its own RMI layer. If the machine does not respond to the host, exception is raised, marked as step 4. In step 5, the AMS removes the entry of that machine from its local AMS and also from the other machines in the agent platform. Finally, the AMS notifies VMA to update the administrative GUI of AMS.

To keep up-to-date information at any instance, intelligent dynamic probing was incorporated in the system. In dynamic probing, every peer sends a "hello message" to the next adjacent peer machine as is done in mobile adhoc networks (MANETs). It not only detects the failure of any peer machine but also reduces the network traffic as shown in Figure 11 and Figure 12.

Dynamic probing shows very interesting results. See Figure 12 where it is compared with the Mesh probing architecture. It not only reduces the network communication cost but also reduces extra processing.

System Evaluation Using RBD Model

Reliability block diagram (RBD) is a static form of reliability analysis using inter-connected boxes (blocks) to show and analyze the effects of failure of any component in the system (RBD, 2000).

RBD Success and Failure Logic for SAGE

Since SAGE works in peer-to-peer architecture, it follows the parallel system paradigm in RBD as shown in Figure 13 and explained in Table 1.

Figure 10. Probing on demand

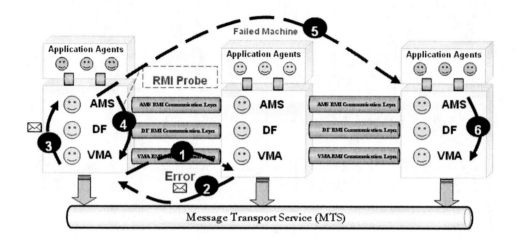

Figure 11. Dynamic probing

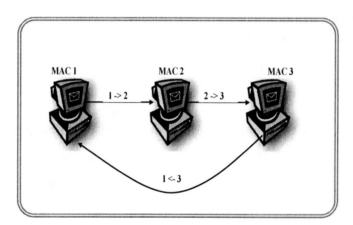

If it is assumed that the reliability of each machine is 0.5 i.e. 50%, Table 2 shows the success and failure logic of SAGE.

Success and Failure Analysis for SAGE

Graphically the success and failure logic of SAGE is shown in Figure 14 and Figure 15. Figure 14 clearly shows that increase of peers increases the success logic. It means that as a greater number of machines become part of distributed AP, there exists less chances of failure of complete system. Failure behavior of the system is presented in Figure 15. An increase in the number of machines decreases the failure logic of SAGE because with more machines there exists less chances of failure.

Figure 12. Improved results with probing using mesh vs. peer-to-peer technique

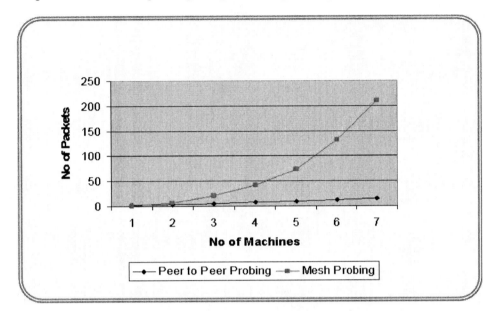

SAGE: AUTONOMOUS AGENT ARCHITECTURE

Rationale

Agent architectures are the fundamental engines underlying the autonomous components that support effective behavior in real-world, dynamic, and open environments. They specify how the agents can be decomposed into the construction of a set of component modules and how these modules should be made to interact. Architecture encompasses techniques and algorithms that support this methodology (Luck et al., 2002). In this section, we propose SAGE agent architecture that allows the programmer to develop autonomic agents, embedding them with domain specific capabilities.

Related Work: Agent Architectures

MAS frameworks attempt to provide programmer with reusable agent-oriented classes that share useful relationships. Comtec-AP, FIPA-OS, JADE, and Zeus provide agents as the unit of encapsulation for developing applications. These agents have core behavior subsystem that includes an execution process, ACL message interface agent behavior engine, and corresponding primitive processing objects (Fonsecal et al., 2001).

Literature classifies agent architectures into four main types based on their modular architecture and their interactions (Luck et al., 2002).

- Logic-based agent architecture
- Reactive agent architecture
- BDI agent architecture
- Layered (hybrid) agent architecture

Later in this section, we dilate upon the amalgamation of these types of architectures to achieve the hybrid agent architecture for SAGE.

Conceptualization of the Autonomic Agent Construction Model

SAGE supports interactive collections of agents called SAGE-Agents (SAgents), which we aim to

Figure 13. RBD model of SAGE

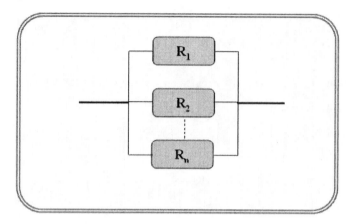

Table 1. Success and failure logic for SAGE

Success logic for SAGE
Reliability R = 1 – F
Failure logic for SAGE

Failure F = (1–R1) * (1–R2) * (1–R3) * (1–R4)* (1–R5) * (1–R6) * (1–R7) * (1–R8) * (1–R9) * (1–R10)
 	
    OR
        =   1 – R

Table 2. Success and failure logic for SAGE with individual peer's reliability 0.5

Success logic		
No. of Peers	R	F
1	0.500	0.500
2	0.750	0.250
3	0.875	0.125
4	0.9375	0.063
5	0.96875	0.031
6	0.984375	0.016
7	0.9921875	0.008
8	0.996093750	0.004
9	0.998046875	0.002
10	0.99902343750	0.001

Figure 14. Success model for SAGE

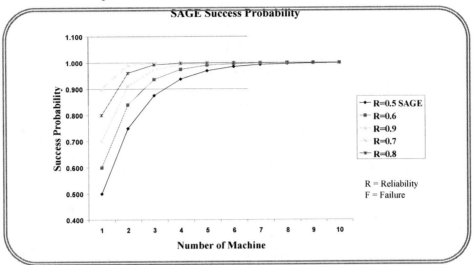

Figure 15. SAGE failure probability

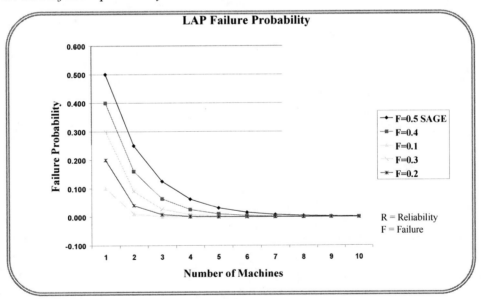

build as autonomic entities. We have proposed the conceptual autonomic agent architecture shown in Figure 16 that features a lower-level action framework consisting of sensors and effectors for interacting with the external environment. This lower level action framework works on top of a number of reactive, adaptive, and reasoning frameworks that dynamically model the SAgent itself and its environment.

Each SAgent may require assistance from other agents to achieve its goals. If so, it will be responsible for obtaining necessary resources

Figure 16. Conceptual framework proposed for autonomous agents

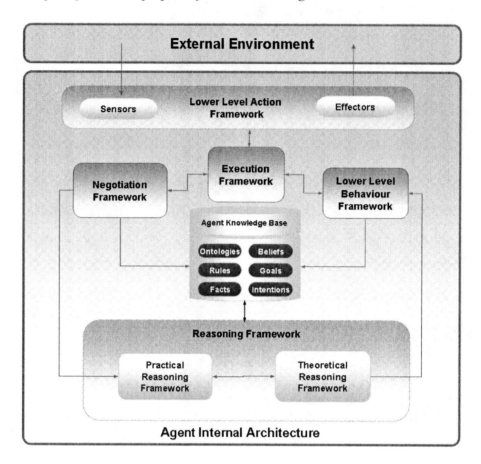

from other agents and for dealing with exception cases, such as the failure of a required resource. However, once an agent finds potential providers of an input service, it must negotiate with them to obtain that service. Thus, SAgents need flexible ways to express multi-attribute needs and capabilities, and they need mechanisms for deriving these expressions from human input or from computation. For embedding the capability of high-level negotiations within each Sagent, we have proposed a negotiation framework, which will provide built-in support for high-level agent conversations and will support the myriad interactions amongst the system entities.

We have conceptualized a lower-level behavior framework that will be responsible for providing set of actions needed commonly by every agent in an agent society. This framework also provides support for state-based modeling of agent simple behavior to define the complex agent behavior.

Design of the Autonomic Agent Construction Model for SAgents

Figure 17 shows the design model for the agent architecture of SAGE referenced on the conceptual architecture outlined in the previous section. The model consists of the following core sub-systems: (1) the action sub-engine, (2) the behavior sub-engine, (3) the reasoning sub-engine and (4) the learning sub-engine. These are the core components from which all SAgents can be built. The high-level interactions between the sub-engines are shown by the dotted lines. The practical reasoning sub-engine receives input from the communication controller (which in turn receives its input from the lower-level action subsystem) in the form of an ACL message and based on the reasoning (and processing by learning sub-engine) passes the decided action to be taken to the lower-level behavior controller. The action is then executed within the action sub-engine with the help of the execution controller. The interactions have been kept to a minimum so as to address the key factors of self-protection and complexity.

Conceived as a central repository in the conceptual architecture, the agent's knowledge base now takes the shape of separate repositories and data bases with the constituent sub-engines where necessary. For example, a message repository comes with the communication controller for storing messages, while a goal library and belief and plan repositories become part of the practical reasoning sub-engine to store the mentalistic concepts of the SAgents. In the following subsections, these sub-engines are discussed in detail.

Core Subsystems of the Agent Architecture

The behavior sub-engine theoretically consists of execution and communication controllers along with sensors and effectors. This system represents the agent's functional and non-functional capacities and skills ("know how"). The reasoning sub-engine is composed of a module for theoretical reasoning—theoretical reasoning controller and a module for practical reasoning, the practical reasoning controller, each with an associated database. Theoretical reasoning controller is responsible for agent reasoning that is based on its beliefs only, where as the practical reasoning controller represents the agent's reasoning about what it should do and consists of a high-level AI planning system.

The high-level interactions between the sub-engines are shown by the dotted lines. The reasoning sub-engine receives input from the communication controller (which in turn receives its input from the lower-level action subsystem) in the form of an ACL message and based on the reasoning passes the decided action to be taken to the lower-level behavior controller. The action is then executed within the action sub-engine with the help of the execution controller. The interactions have been kept to a minimum so as to address the key factors of self-protection and complexity.

The Action Sub-Engine

The unit of abstraction used to model sensors and effectors is termed "TaskUnit." TaskUnits provide the ability to perform lower level tasks to SAgents where various TaskUnits basically encapsulate the actual role an agent has to perform. A single TaskUnit represents a task or action that an agent can carry out. TaskUnits provide means for multiple threads of activity and provide lower-level functional and non-functional support to the SAgents. These are modeled as a user-level package, based on co-operative scheduling. The behavior sub-engine is responsible for their modeling and execution (Amina et al., 2005).

The Behavior Sub-Engine

The behavior sub-engine is equipped with controllers that control and monitor the execution of the TaskUnits and thus the overall agent behavior.

- **Execution controller:** The main objective of execution controller is to provide SAgents with a strong execution framework allowing them to carry out concurrent task execution both at inter- and intra-agent levels. A lightweight multitasking model has been

previously described for the core design of the execution controller in (Amina et al., 2005). The execution controller directly interacts with the behavior controller and the communication controller. It is responsible for scheduling of active agents tasks efficiently at the user level in a cooperative manner.

- **Lower-level behavior controller:** It is primarily responsible for controlling the interactions between the execution controller and the action sub-engine. The lower level

Figure 17. Autonomous agent architecture for SAGE

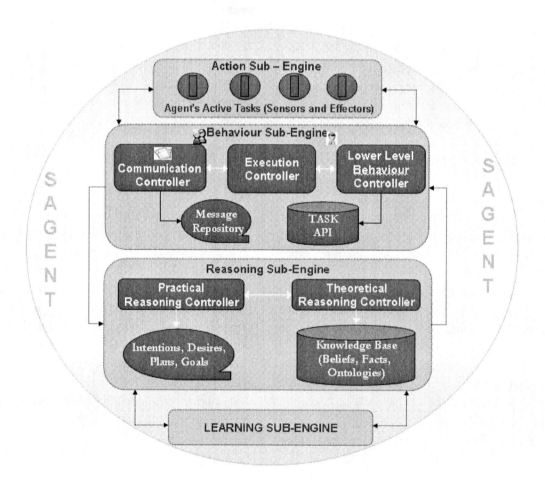

behavior controller is provided with a task API—a library of tasks that provides the agent programmer with a set of tasks that may be needed commonly by every agent in a society. We decompose the SAgents' role according to Figure 18, where agent role can be described by a set of complex tasks the SAgents can perform. Each of these complex tasks is accomplished when SAgents execute certain state-based tasks and may be involved in the execution of more than one lower-level agent tasks. These tasks cannot be decomposed further into simpler tasks and form the foundation of the agent behavior.

- **Communication controller:** All the communication in MASs may be viewed as a layered model depicted in Figure 19. Agents require high-level conversational support at the application layer on top of the underlying message transport infrastructure in order to enable high-level inter-agent interaction. At the application level they require a well-defined communication and content language in which they can exchange messages. They also require well-defined conversation patterns in the form of interaction protocols in order to engage in intelligible conversations.

Communication controller was designed to facilitate communication with other agents and software components as shown in Figure 20. FIPA-ACL has been implemented as part of the system framework of SAGE (Sana, Jamshed, Farooq Ahmad, Ali, & Suguri, 2005). The ACL message interface has been designed to provide a dynamic interface to the programmer to utilize the features of ACL module. The ACL message interface provides reusable TaskUnits for sending and receiving messages to save programmers from writing tedious and redundant code. The

prime purpose of the communication controller is to provide high-level conversation management support to the SAgents. A library of interaction protocols has been provided allowing SAgents to communicate in a one-to-one or one-to-many mode based on FIPA-interaction protocol library specifications (FIPA-IP, 2001).

An important component of the communication controller is the pattern matcher. The messages received through the execution controller are recognized and analysed through this before being passed onto the practical reasoning sub-engine for reasoning purposes. It also allows for message template building and customized message patterns for utilization in interaction protocols and for their semantic interpretation. Along with the communication controller, each SAgent has been provided with a central message repository that serves as a useful abstraction mechanism for storing messages and forwarding when needed or requested. The communication controller interacts with this message repository allowing messages to be sent and received when interaction protocols are used. The processing of the messages remains the responsibility of the owner and dependent on the domain.

Reasoning Sub-Engine

Reasoning sub-engine consists of theoretical reasoning controller and the practical reasoning controller designed to embed autonomy and intelligence into the agent.

The theoretical reasoning controller: Theoretical reasoning is the reasoning of the agents that is directed towards their beliefs, desires and intentions (Singh & Huhns, 2005). Theoretical reasoning controller was conceived for SAGE's agent architecture as shown in Figure 21, whose design was based on the concept of integrating

Figure 18. Composition of agent role in SAGE

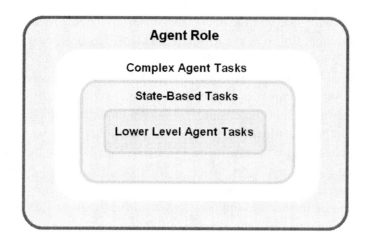

the agent architecture with a rule-based expert system.

Rule-based expert systems are well suited for the purpose of theoretical reasoning in SAGE agents because rules make a compact definition of behavior possible as described above. Also, there is an increasing trend of integrating multi-agent system with an expert system, which allows the building of such agents that have the capacity to "reason" using knowledge supplied in the form of declarative rules. Agent toolkits such as FIPA-OS, JADE, and JATLite have integrated expert systems to support complex reasoning (Pokahr, Braubach, & Lamersdorf, 2003). The expert system chosen for the design of theoretical reasoning controller for SAGE is the Java expert system shell (JESS) (Hill, 2002).

For SAGE, theoretical reasoning controller is designed as a built-in TaskUnit. This TaskUnit is designed to work in manner that, for each received message, it asserts a fact in the JESS engine that describes the message. This allows a JESS program to control sending or receiving messages and creating or destroying TaskUnits in response to the message received.

The practical reasoning controller: The belief-desire-intention (BDI) model (Rao & Georgeff, 1991, 1995) is seen as a preliminary means to provide a base for practical reasoning and thus self-adaptation. The relevance of the BDI model can be explained in terms of: i) Its philosophical grounds on intentionality and practical reasoning (Bratman, 1987); ii) Its elegant abstract logical semantics and different implementations, for example, IRMA and the PRS-like systems, including PRS and dMARS; and iii) Successful applications, that is, diagnosis for space shuttle, factory process control, and business process management as suggested in Hernandez, El Fallah-Seghrouchni, and Soldano (2004).

We have designed the BDI-based practical reasoning controller as composed of two sub-engines. The BDI-deliberation sub-engine includes a deliberation process (as shown in Figure 22) responsible for the analysis and processing of agent goals and beliefs. The deliberation process has been designed keeping in view all the factors and considerations mentioned in Dastani et al. (2003). Incoming messages, as well as internal events and new goals, serve as input to the deliberation

Figure 19. Layered communication model followed in SAGE

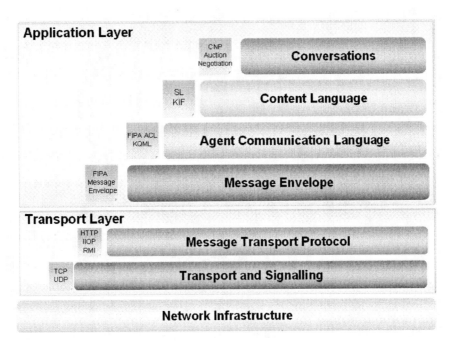

Figure 20. Design of communication controller

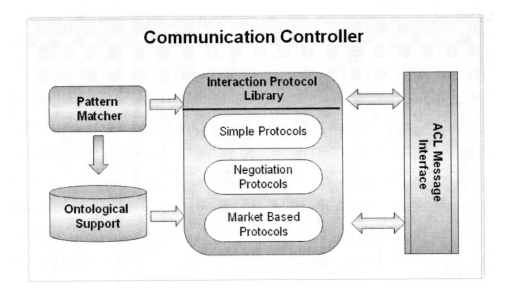

Figure 21. Design of theoretical reasoning controller

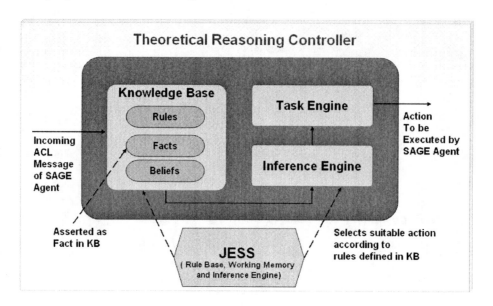

process. Based on the results of the deliberation process, these events are dispatched to already-running plans or to new plans instantiated from the plan library.

The Learning Sub-Engine

A key feature of autonomic entities is self-optimization, for which the ability to learn is a key element of agent behavior. Learning and optimization in multi-agent systems are challenging (Kephart & Chess, 2003).

Two main drawbacks of using the BDI model are highlighted in Hernandez et al. (2004), as 1) lack of MAS learning competencies, and 2) lack of explicit MAS functionality. In order to manage these deficiencies, a learning sub-engine cooperating with the Reasoning Sub-engine has been proposed as shown in Figure 23 based on the design of a learning agent suggested by Stuart Russell

and Peter Norvig (1995). At this stage, only the design has been conceived, and implementation of this module is in progress.

The BDI model, which is at the core of the practical reasoning sub-engine, will form the performance element of this architecture. It will be a challenging to incorporate learning techniques such as ILP, decision tress, and belief networks as has been suggested (Hernandez et al, 2004) to implement the learning process of the learning sub-engine shown in Figure 23.

At the end, it is important to mention that efforts are underway for developing real-world applications using SAGE. The conference planner application (Farooq Ahmad et al 2005; Omair et al., 2005) uses SAGE as the underlying agent middleware and utilizes the AgentWeb Gateway for interaction with the Web services (Suguri, Farooq Ahmad, Omair, & Ali, 2004).

Figure 22. Design of practical reasoning controller

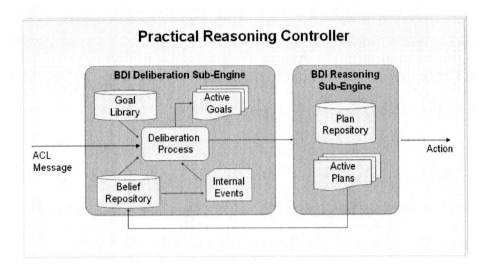

Figure 23. Proposed design model for the learning engine of SAGE agents

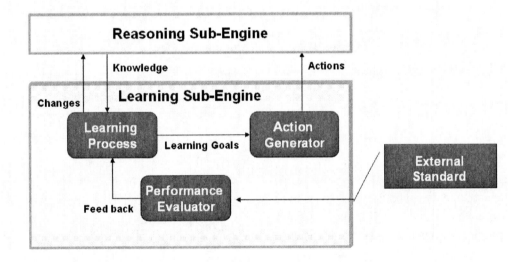

FUTURE RESEARCH DIRECTIONS

Alongside the development of the fault-tolerant AP and the autonomous agent architecture, work is proceeding in various directions. The synergy of the agent system with the grid and the Web services has already made its mark as discussed above. Some of the other key areas of target in current and future work research perspective are briefly described below:

- **Intra- and inter-platform mobility:** Our aim is to improve homogeneous intra-platform mobility in SAGE and to design and implement heterogeneous inter-platform mobility in FIPA-compliant MASs.
- **Security mechanisms:** Extensive work is going on for the provision of security mechanisms within agent platform.
- **SAGE-lite:** A major research direction is to make *"SAGE-lite,"* the lightweight agent platform for handheld devices.
- **Semantic interoperability:** To fully utilize agents in Web, interoperability between FIPA SL and OWL must be achieved (Sana et al., 2005).

CONCLUSION

Multi-agent systems are expected to grow in different distributed applications (Tesauro et al., 2004). The ideas presented in this chapter target some of the key challenges faced when developing autonomic systems and entities in the domain of FIPA-compliant multi-agent architectures.

The first aim of the chapter is to introduce assurance in agent platforms. High assurance using VAC brings fault tolerance and load balancing among different physical machines over which logical AP is distributed.

For the development of application agents, autonomic construction model is proposed, which is the second main highlight of this chapter. It

defines an agent structure with well-defined functional components that contribute toward their autonomic behavior.

With the fault-tolerant platform and autonomic architecture, we have laid the foundation for future researches, including mobility, security, ubiquity, and semantic interoperability.

ACKNOWLEDGMENT

The Authors would like to acknowledge the Higher Education Commission (HEC), Pakistan for its partial support and encouragement throughout this research work.

REFERENCES

Baratloo, A., et al. (1998, April 27-30). Filter fresh: Hot replication of Java RMI server objects. *Proceedings of 4ᵗʰ USENIX Conference on Object-Oriented Technologies and Systems (COOTS),* Santa Fe, NM.

Bellifemine, F., Poggi, A., & Rimassi, G. (1999). JADE: A FIPA-compliant agent framework. *Proceedings of Practical Applications of Intelligent Agents and Multi-Agents* (pp. 97-108).

Bergenti, F., Poggi, A., Rimassa, G., & Turci, P. (2000). *Middleware and programming support for agent systems.* Telecom Italia Labs.

DeLoach, S. A. (2001, May 28 - June 1). Specifying agent behavior as concurrent tasks: Defining the behavior of social agents. *Proceedings of the 5ᵗʰ Annual Conference on Autonomous Agents,* Montreal, Canada

Duvigneau, M., & Moldt, D. (2002, July). Concurrent architecture for a multi-agent platform. *Proceedings of the 3ʳᵈ International Workshop on Agent-Oriented Software Engineering (AOSE-2002),* Bologna, Italy.

Farooq Ahmad, H., Ali, A., Suguri, H., Abbas Khan, Z., & Rehman, M. U. (2003). Decentralized multi agent system: Basic thoughts. *Proceedings of 11ᵗʰ Assurance System Symposium* (pp. 9-14).

Farooq Ahmad, H., Iqbal, K., Ali, A., & Suguri, H. (2003). Autonomous distributed service system: Basic concepts and evaluation. *Proceedings of the 2ⁿᵈ International Workshop on Grid and Cooperative Computing, GCC 2003* (pp. 432-439).

Farooq Ahmad, H., Suguri, H., Ali, A., Malik, S., Mugal, M., Omair Shafiq, M., et al. (2005, July 25-29). Scalable fault tolerant Agent Grooming Environment: SAGE. *Proceedings of the 4ᵗʰ International Joint Conference on Autonomous Agents and Multiagent Systems (AAMAS) 2005*, The Netherlands.

Farooq Ahmad, H., Suguri, H., Omair Shafiq, M. & Ali, A. (2004, September). Autonomous distributed service system: Enabling Webs services communication with software agents. *Proceedings of 16ᵗʰ International Conference on commuters and Communication (ICCC 2004)*, Beijing, China.

Farooq Ahmad, H., Sun, G., & Mori, K. (2001). Autonomous information provision to achieve reliability for users and providers. *IEEE Proceedings of the 5ᵗʰ International Symposium on ADS (ISADS01)* (pp. 65-72).

Foundation for Intelligent Physical Agents. (n.d.) Retrieved from http://www.fipa.org/

Foundation for Intelligent Physical Agents. (2000). *Agent Management specification.* Retrieved from http://www.fipa.org/

Foundation for Intelligent Physical Agents. (2001). FIPA interaction protocol library, Retrieved from http://www.fipa.org/repository/ips.html

FIPA-OS. (n.d.) Retrieved from http://fipa-os.sourceforge.net/features.htm

Fonseca1, S. P., Griss, M. L., & Letsinger, R. (2001). *Agent behavior architectures, A MAS framework comparison* (Tech. Rep.HPL-2001-332). Hewlett-Packard Laboratories.

Ford, B., Hibler, M., Lepreau, J., Mccgrath, R., & Tullmann, P. (1999). Interface and execution models in the Fluke kernel. *Operating Systems Design and Implementation,* 101-115.

Ghafoor, A., Rehman, M.U., Abbas Khan, Z., Farooq Ahmad, H., & Ali, A. (2004). SAGE: Next Generation multi-agent system. *Proceedings of IEEE International Conference on Parallel and Distributed Processing Techniques and Applications (PDPTA'04)* (Vol. 1, pp. 139-145).

Guessoum, Z., & Briot, J. P. (1999). From active objects to autonomous agents. *IEEE Concurrency, 7*(3), 68-76.

Hernandez, G., El Fallah-Seghrouchni, A., & Soldano, H. (2004, January 6-7). Learning in BDI multi-agent systems. *Proceedings of 4ᵗʰ International Workshop on Computational Logic in Multi-Agent Systems (CLIMA IV)*, Florida.

Hill, F. (n.d.). *JESS- Java expert system shell.* Retrieved from http://herzberg.ca.sandia.gov/jess

Java. (1998). *Programming Java threads in the real world: A Java programmer's guide to threading architectures.* Retrieved from http://www.javaworld/jw-09-1998/jw-09-threads_p.html

Java Agent Development Framework. (1998). http://sharon.cselt.it/projects/jade

Jennings, N. R. (2000). On agent-based software engineering. *Artificial Intelligence, 117,* 277–296.

Jennings, N. R., Sycra, K., & Wooldridge, M. (1998). A roadmap of agent research and development. In M. Wooldridge (Ed.), *Autonomous agents and multi-agent systems* (pp. 275-306). Boston: Kluwer Academic Publisher.

Kephart, J. O., & Chess, D. M. (2003). The vision of autonomic computing. *Computer, 36*(1), 41-52.

Klein, M., & Dellarocas, C. (1999, May 1-5). Exception handling in agent systems. *Proceedings of the Third International Conference on Autonomous Agents*, Seattle, WA.

Koehler, J., Giblin, C., Gantenbein, D., & Hauser, R. (2003). *On autonomic computing architectures* (Research Report). IBM Research Zurich Research Laboratory.

Khalique, S., Jamshed, M., Farooq Ahmad, H., Ali, A., & Suguri, H. (2005, September). Significance of semantic language in multi agent systems. *Proceedings of 8th Pacific Rim Workshop on Agents and Multi-Agent Systems (PRIMA, 2005),* Kuala Lumpur, Malaysia.

Khan, Z. A., Farooq Ahmad, H., Ali, A., & Suguri, H. (2005, April 5-7). Decentralized architecture for fault tolerant multi agent system. *Proceedings of International Symposium on Autonomous Decentralized Systems*, China.

Kumar, S., Cohen, P. R., & Levesque, H. J. (2000, July). The adaptive agent architecture: Achieving fault-tolerance using persistent broker teams. *Proceedings of the 4th International Conference on Multi-Agent Systems (ICMAS 2000)*, Boston.

Luck, M., McBurney, P., & Preist, C. (2002). *Agent technology: Enabling next generation computing.* AgentLink, software report.

Mangina, E. (2002). *Review of software products for multi-agent systems.* AgentLink, software report 2002.

McCann, J. A., & Huebscher, M. C. (2004, October). Evaluation issues in autonomic computing. *Proceedings of the 3rd International Conference on Grid and Cooperative Computing (GCC).*

Mori, K. (1993). Autonomous decentralized systems: Concept, data field architecture and future trends. *Proceedings of the 1st International Symposium on Autonomous Decentralized Systems (ISADS93)* (pp. 28-34). IEEE.

Nwana, H., Nduma, D., Lee, L., & Collis, J. (1999). ZEUS: A toolkit for building distributed Multi-Agent Systems. *Artificial Intelligence Journal, 13*(1), 129-186.

Odell, J., Van Dyke, Parunak, H., & Bauer, B. (2001). Representing, agent interaction protocols in UML. *Proceedings of the 1st International Workshop, AOSE 2000 on Agent Oriented Software Engineering* (pp. 121-140).

Omair Shafiq, M., Ali, A., Tariq, A., Basharat, A., Farooq Ahmad, H., Suguri, H., et al. (2005). A distributed services based conference planner application using software agents, grid services and Web services. *Proceedings of the Fourth International Joint Conference On Autonomous Agents and Multi Agent Systems (AAMAS)* (pp. 137-138).

Overeinder, B., & Brazier, F. (2003). Fault tolerance in scalable agent support system: Integrating DARX in the agentscape framework. *Proceedings of the 3rd International Symposium on Cluster Computing and the Grid*, Tokyo, Japan.

Ousterhout, J. K. (1996). Why threads are a bad idea (for most purposes). *Proceedings of USENIX Technical Conference.*

Panti, M., et al. (2000). A FIPA compliant agent platform for federated information systems. Computer Science Department – University of Ancona – 60131- Ancona – Italy. *International Journal of Computer & Information Science*, RY Lee and H. Fouchal (eds.), *1*(3).

Peng Xu, E., & Deters, R. (2005). Fault-management for multi-agent systems. *Proceedings of SAINT 2005* (pp. 287-293).

Pokahr, L., Braubach, & Lamersdorf. (2003). Jadex: Implementing a BDI-Infrastructure for JADE Agents. *EXP: In search of innovation, 3*(3), 76-85.

Poslad, S., Buckle, P., & Hadingham, R. (2000). The FIPA-OS agent platform: Open source for open standards. *Proceedings of the 5th International Conference and Exhibition on the Practical Application of Intelligent Agents and Multi-Agents* (pp. 355-368).

Rao, & Georgeff, M. (1991). Modeling rational agents within a BDI architecture. *Proceedings of the Second International Conference on Principles of Knowledge Representation and Reasoning* (pp. 473-484).

Rao & Georgeff, M. (1995). BDI agents: From theory to practice. *Proceedings of the First International Conference on Multi-Agent Systems (ICMAS-95)* (pp. 312-319).

RBD. (2000). Retrieved from http://www.reliabilityblockdiagram.info/http://www.staff.brad.ac.uk/ckarazai/ReliabilityModelling/Reliability%20Block%20Diagrams.pdf

Russell, S. J., & Norvig, P. (1995). *Artificial intelligence, A modern approach.* NJ: Prentice-Hall.

Singh, M. P. & Huhns, M. N. (2005). *Service-oriented computing.* Wiley.

Stallings, W. (2000). *Operating systems: Internals and design principles* (4th ed). Alan Apt.

Suguri, H. (1998). Integrated meta media environment based on FIPA agent platform (in Japanese). *Proceedings of Symposium on Creative Software and E-Commerce Promotion* (pp. 279-282).

Suguri, H., Farooq Ahmad, H., Omair Shafiq, M., & Ali, A. (2004, October). Agent Web gateway -enabling service discovery and communication among software agents and Web services. *Proceedings of Third Joint Agent Workshops and Symposium (JAWS2004)*, Karuizawa, Japan.

Tariq., A., Amna, B., Farooq Ahmad, H., Ali, A., & Suguri, H. (2005, April 12). SAgents: Next generation autonomic entities for FIPA-compliant multi-agent system. *Proceedings of IADIS Virtual Multi Conference on Computer Science and Information Systems (MCCSIS 2005) under Intelligent Systems and Agents (ISA 2005)*.

Tariq, A., Basharat, A., Farooq Ahmad, H., Ali, A., & Suguri, H. (2005). A hybrid agent architecture for modeling autonomous agents in SAGE. *Proceedings of Sixth International Conference on Data Engineering and Automated Learning (IDEAL 2005)*, Brisbane, Australia.

Tesauro, G., Chess, D. M., Walsh, W. E., Das, R., Segal, A., Whalley, I., et al. (2004, July 19-23). A multi-agent systems approach to autonomic computing. *Proceedings of AAMAS '04.* New York.

Vitaglione, F., Quarta, E., & Cortese. (2002, July 16). Scalability and performance of JADE message transport system. *Proceedings of AAMAS Workshop on AgentCities*, Bologna, Italy. Retrieved from http://sharon.cselt.it/projects/jade

Wooldridge, M. J. (2002). *An introduction to multi-agent systems.* John Wiley & Sons.

APPENDIX A: SAGE GUIDE

SAGE along with documentation and sample application is available for download at http://sage.niit.edu.pk or http://www.comtec.co.jp/sage/.

APPENDIX B: GLOSSARY OF TERMS

ACL	Agent Communication Language
AMS	Agent Management System
B2B	Business to Business
CORBA	Common Object Resource Broker Architecture
DF	Directory Facilitator
FIPA	Foundation for Intelligent Physical Agents
GUI	Graphical User Interface
IDL	Interface Definition Language
IIOP	Internet Inter-ORB Protocol
JADE	Java Agent Development Framework
Java RMI	Java Remote Method Invocation
KQML	Knowledge Query Manipulation Language
MAS	Multi-Agent System
MTS	Message Transport Service
P2P	Peer to Peer
QoS	Quality of Service
SL	Semantic Language
TCP/IP	Transmission Control Protocol/ Internet Protocol
UDDI	Universal Description and Discovery Integration

Chapter IX
Toward Agent–Based Grid Computing

Lizhe Wang

Institute of Scientific Computing, Forschungszentrum Karlsruhe, Germany

ABSTRACT

This chapter discusses research issues related to agent-based Grid computing. Grid computing now becomes an innovative computing paradigm and helps build non-traditional computing infrastructures and applications. Multiple-agent systems and algorithms, on the other hand, mainly focus on solving corporative problems among multiple participants, mainly from theoretical aspects. It is thus a natural choice to combine these two key technologies together and benefit both research communities. This chapter first reviews background for multi-agent system, agent-based computing, and Grid computing. Research challenges and issues are characterized and identified together with possible solutions. After the investigation of current research efforts of agent-based Grid computing, future research trends are presented and studied.

INTRODUCTION

Grid computing (Foster, Kesselman, & Tuecke, 2001; Foster, 2002) is one of the most innovative aspects of computing techniques in recent years. Distinguished from conventional parallel and distributed computing, Grid computing mainly focuses on resources sharing among geographically distributed sites and the development of innovative, high-performance-oriented applications (Foster et al., 2001). Computational Grid can provide Grid users with pervasive and inexpensive access to a wide variety of resources.

Agent-based computing now becomes an important computing paradigm for software engineering. Capable of performing autonomous and intelligent actions in dynamic environments (Russell & Norvig, 2003), agent-based computing could be a promising solution in diverse application domains (Jennings & Wooldridge, 1998).

Communities of Grid computing and agent-based computing share the same properties: collaborating multiple independent components in an open distributed system to reach some goal, albeit from different perspectives (Foster, 2004). Some works developed in both communities independently can benefit each other. Furthermore, as both communities mature, some challenging research issues, such as architecture and infrastructure, scalability, and robusticity, are expected to get promising solutions.

The chapter is organized as follows: background of research fields of Grid computing and agent-based computing, for example, concepts, technologies, and applications, are investigated in the second section. The next section discusses how to bring an agent-based computing paradigm to the research field of Grid computing. Various technologies, methodologies, and use scenarios are examined and analyzed. The fourth section points out research challenges and future trends, and the fifth section concludes the chapter.

BACKGROUND

Grid Computing

What is the Grid?

In 1998, Foster and Kesselman defined computational Grid as follows (Foster, 2005):

A computational Grid is a hardware and software infrastructure that provides dependable, consistent, pervasive, and inexpensive access to high-end computational capabilities.

This definition of Grid focuses on the access to computing resources, data, and services on demand.

Foster, Kesselman, and Tuecke, in 2000, refined the definition of the Grid to address social and policy issues (Foster et al., 2001). They defined virtual organization (VO) as follows:

A set of individuals and/or institutions defined by such sharing rules form what we call a virtual organization.

Based on the concept of virtual organization, they redefined the concept of Grid as follows:

The real and specific problem that underlies the Grid concept is coordinated resource sharing and problem solving in dynamic, multi-institutional virtual organizations.

While Grid technologies have made great progress recently, there still remain technical problems to meet various requirements of QoS (qualities of service) when applications are executed on different types of platforms. To address the new challenges of Grid computing, the open Grid services architecture (OGSA) (Foster, Kesselman, & Tuecke, 2002) is proposed to evolve the current Grid infrastructure toward a Grid system architecture based on an integration of Grid and Web services concepts and technologies. OGSA defines:

- Grid service using a uniform exposed service semantics, and
- standard mechanisms for creating and naming Grid service instances.

It also supports:

- location transparency and multiple protocol bindings for service instances, and
- integration with underlying native platform facilities.

In order to provide users with the ability to access and manipulate the state of Grid service and promote evolution of Web service, WS-Resource framework (Czajkowski, Ferguson, & Foster 2003) is proposed to model stateful resources (Czajkowski et al., 2003). Stateful resource is defined in Foster, Jenning, and Kesselman (2004) to:

- Have a specific set of state data expressible as an extensible markup language (XML) document
- Have a well-defined lifecycle
- Be known to, and acted upon, by one or more Web services

Precisely, WS-Resource is defined in Czajkowski et al. (2003) as follows:

- A WS-Resource is composed of a Web service and a stateful resource
- A stateful resource is used in the execution of Web service message exchange
- WS-Resources can be created and destroyed
- The definition of a stateful resource can be associated with the interface description of a Web service to enable well-formed queries against the sate of a WS-Resource, and the state of the WS-Resource can be queried and modified via Web service message exchanges

What Makes Grid Computing Distinguished?

The driving ideas that stay behind Grid computing are not new. The concepts of employing various distributed resources for executing a single job has been proposed for several decades (Schopf & Nitzberg, 2003). Several similar computing paradigms exist; for example, network computing, heterogeneous computing, parallel distributed computing, and meta-computing. How does Grid computing distinguish from these computing paradigms? What makes Grid computing as a novel computing paradigm of modern days?

To identify Grid computing from traditional computing paradigms, three check points are examined as follows (Foster et al., 2002):

- Grid coordinates resources that are not subject to centralized control.

There are no central servers that administrate the system. Grid provides coordinated resource sharing and problem solving in dynamic, multi-institutional virtual organizations.

- Grid uses standard, open, general-purpose protocols and interfaces.

Protocols and interfaces, which are used in Grids for authentication, authorization, resource discovery, and access, are standard and open and acknowledged by international organizations, for example, W3C, GGF and OASIS.

- Grid delivers nontrivial qualities of service.

Grid provides dependable, consistent, pervasive, and inexpensive services. In other words, Grid implementations allow resource usage in a fashion with various QoS, for example, response time, throughput, security.

Layered Grid Architecture

To help develop complex Grid systems and software, a layered model is built to abstract the architecture of Grid systems. The description of Grid architecture is not to provide a complete enumeration of all required protocols (and services, APIs, SDKs) but rather to identify requirements for general classes of components (Foster et al., 2001; Foster et al., 2002).

In Foster et al. (2001) and Foster et al. (2002), a five-layer hourglass model is proposed to model Grid architecture (shown in Figure 1). Components within each layer share common characteristics and can be built on the capabilities and behaviors provided by any lower layers. For example, protocols at resource and connectivity layers are designed so that they can be implemented on top of a diverse range of resource types, defined at the fabric layer. On the other hand, they can be used to construct a wide range of global services

Figure 1. Hourglass model of grid architecture

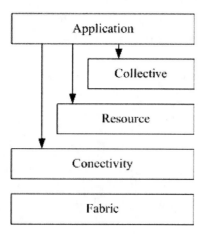

and application-specific behaviors at the collective layer. The detail of each layer is described as follows:

- **Fabric: Interfaces to local control.** The Grid fabric layer provides basic Grid protocols that enable Grid applications to share resources, which can be, for example, computational resources, storage systems, network resources, and sensors. Fabric components implement the local, resource-specific operations that occur on specific resources. These operations enable resource sharing operations at higher levels.
- **Connectivity: Communicating easily and securely.** The connectivity layer defines core communication and authentication protocols required for Grid-specific network transmission. Communication protocols enable the exchange of data between fabric layer resources. Authentication protocols provide cryptographically secured mechanisms for verifying the identity of users and resources.
- **Resource: Sharing single resources.** The resource layer builds communication and authentication protocols of the connectivity layer to define protocols (and APIs, SDKs) for the secured negotiation, initiation, moni-

toring, control, accounting, and payment of sharing operations on individual resources. Resource layer calls fabric layer functions to access and control local resources.
- **Collective: Coordinating multiple resources.** While the resource layer is focused on interactions with a single resource, the collective layer in the architecture contains protocols and services (and APIs, SDKs) that are not associated with any specific resource but rather interactions across collections of resources.
- **Application.** The application layer in the Grid architecture is comprised of the user applications that operate within a VO environment. Applications are constructed in terms of services defined at any other layers.

Another layered model (shown in Figure 2), community Grid model, is presented in Lee and Talia (2003). It contains the following layers:

- **Resource layer.** This layer consists of the hardware resources that underlie the Grid. These resources, such as computers, networks, data archives, instruments, and visualization devices, are distributed and heterogeneous.
- **Common infrastructure layer.** This layer consists of the software services and systems that virtualize the Grid. Community efforts such as NSF's Middleware Initiative (NMI), OGSA, and Globus Toolkit are included in this layer.
- **User-oriented middleware layer.** User-or application-oriented middleware layer contains software packages based on the common infrastructure. This software serves to enable applications to more productively use Grid resources. Examples of software, such as portals, application-level scheduling software, and community authentication, reside in this layer.

Figure 2. Community grid model

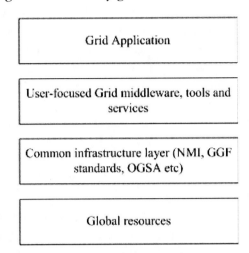

- **Grid applications layer.** Users and applications stay at the Grid application layer and access Grid resources and services with the help of various layers below.

Grid Applications

Grid applications need functionalities of computational Grids to access multiple types of resources shared in Grids. On the other hand, Grid computing needs various types of applications to develop, proceed, and evolve. This section reviews typical applications for computational Grids.

There may exist several ways to classify Grid applications. Here, three taxonomies are presented. In the early days of trid computing, the primary goal for applications using Grid was to access computing resources and data resources. In this stage, Grid computing is resource-centric. Therefore, Grid applications are initially categorized into the following classes based on how applications employ computing resources/data resources (Foster & Kesselman, 2005):

- **Distributed supercomputing.** Distributed supercomputing applications usually demand huge computing power, which cannot be fulfilled in a single site. This is the initial

reason of the I-WAY project (Foster et al., 1997), which are also the prototype and forerunner of Globus project. Examples of these applications include distributed interactive simulation (Brunett et al., 1998), which is a technique used for training and planning in the military, and accurate simulation of complex physical process, for example, cosmology (National Cosmology Grid, 1998).

- **High-throughput computing.** In high-throughput computing, a large number of independent or loosely coupled jobs are processed in Grids (Condor System, 1998), with the goal of maximizing the usage of computing resources. A typical example is Condor system (Condor System, 1998) and Condor-G system (Condor-G System, 2001).

- **On-demand computing.** On-demand applications use computing resources on Grids to meet short-term requirements, for example, to finish one intensive computational task in one hour. Requirements of these applications usually cannot conveniently be located in a local site. For example, a computer-enhanced MRI machine and scanning tunneling microscope developed at NCSA uses supercomputers for image processing (IPG Project, 1998).

- **Data-intensive computing.** Data-intensive applications focus on synthesizing information from huge datasets, for example, digital libraries, database, and raw data from scientific experiments. Some examples include Digital Sky Survey (Foster et al., 2001), high-energy physics experiments (Foster et al., 2002), and remote satellite observation (Foster et al., 2004).

As the concept of Grid computing evolves, the concept of service-oriented computing (SOA) has been accepted by Grid technologies, and collaborative applications becomes an important type of application for Grid computing. Current

Grid applications can be categorized based on various primary driving reasons of applications for using Grids (Allen, Goodale, Russell, Seidel, & Shalf, 2003):

- **Community-centric applications.** Some applications try to construct an environment where people or communities work together for certain collaborative objects. For example, Access Grid (2001) is a project that allows interactive video presentation and conferencing from many sites simultaneously.

- **Data-centric applications.** As discussed above, a lot of applications need to process huge amounts of data. Core tasks of these applications are to retrieve, mine, analyze, and visualize these data. Current applications range from particle to astrophysics experiments (Britton & Cass, 2005), which themselves generate several terabyte datasets each day.

- **Computation-centric applications.** These are the traditional high-performance computing applications, common in astrophysics (Allen et al., 2001), the automotive/aerospace industry (Lopez et al., 2000), and climate modeling (Earth System Grid, 2001). These applications would benefit from Grids considering huge computing resources shared in the Grid.

- **Interaction-centric applications.** Some applications require, or are enhanced by, real-time user interaction from users (Coveney, 2005). This interaction can be of many forms, ranging from decision-making to visualization.

Agent-Based Computing

Agents and Software Agents

An agent is anything that can perceive its environment through sensors and act upon that en-vironment through actuators (Russell & Norvig, 2003). Autonomy is the most essential feature, which differentiates the agent from other simple programs (Jennings & Wooldridge, 1998).

Software agent is a software entity that functions continuously and autonomously in a particular environment, often inhabited by other agents and processes (Shoham, 1997). The requirement for continuity and autonomy derives that an agent be able to carry out activities in a flexible and intelligent manner that is responsive to changes in the environment without requiring constant human guidance or intervention. Ideally, an agent that functions continuously in an environment over a long period of time would be able to learn from its experience. In addition, it is expected that an agent inhabits an environment with other agents and processes to be able to communicate and cooperate with them, and perhaps move from place to place when doing so (Bradshaw, 1997).

Software agents now emerge as an import computing paradigm and development technology for software engineering in many aspects, for example, intelligent user interface (Lieberman, 1997), electronic commerce (Nwana et al., 1998), business process management (Jennings et al., 2000), and digital libraries (Atkins et al., 1996).

There are mainly two agency models: the weak agency model and the strong agency model (Dennett, 1987). The weak agency model, which is defined by Wooldridge and Jennings (1995), is widely accepted. Accordingly, weak agency enjoys the following properties:

- **Autonomy:** Agents operate without the direct intervention of human or others, and have some kind of control over their actions and internal state (Castelfranchi, Miceli, & Cesta, 1992);
- **Social ability:** Agents interact with other agents (and possibly humans) via some kind of agent communication language (Genesereth & Ketchpel, 1994);

- **Reactivity:** Agents perceive their environment (which may be the physical world, a user via a graphical user interface, a collection of other agents, the Internet, or perhaps all of these combined) and respond in a timely fashion to changes that occur in it;
- **Pro-activeness:** Agents do not simply act in response to their environment, they are able to exhibit goal-directed behavior by taking the initiative.

Multi-Agent System

Multi-agent system (MAS) aims to provide both principles for construction of complex systems involving multiple agents and mechanisms for coordination of independent agents' behaviors (Stone & Veloso, 1997). Multi-agent system supports the scenario that one problem is divided into multiple sub-problems and solved by multiple agents with their interests and goals.

Multi-agent systems offer advantages over the alternatives as follows (Stone & Veloso, 1997):

- Some of the problem is distributed in nature and demands to be solved by multiple agents. Some examples emerge from e-business, e-science.
- Since multiple agents can work in parallel, multi-agent system, they thus can gain performance improvement from parallelizing works of different agents.
- As there is no central control of multi-agent system and tasks are executed by multiple agents, multi-agent system is more robust than the alternatives.
- Multi-agent system inherently offers the feather of modularity; it is easy to scale the system by including more agents

The following topics (Cao, 2001) are related to research on multi-agent system:

- **Knowledge representation**
  Knowledge representation is to represent knowledge of the external world and storing the information in the internal symbolic reasoning system.
- **Agent communication**
  Agents can interact with other agents. Agent communication language (ACL) describes "speech acts" in the form of message exchange (Wijngaards et al., 2002). KQML (Finin, Labrou, & Mayfield, 1997) is the one of first research efforts that tries to standardize ACL. FIPA (FIPA, 2005) recently provided standards for ACL and protocols (Dale & Mamdani, 2001).
- **Agent negotiation**
  Negotiation is the process by which two agents come to a mutually acceptable agreement on some concern (Cao, 2001).
- **Agent coordination**
  Agent coordination manages interactions and dependencies among activities (Malone, 1994). The coordination model is the formal framework where interactions of software agents can take place (Gelernter & Carriero, 1992).

AGENT-BASED GRID COMPUTING

Agent-Based Grid Computing: The Natural Choice

As discussed above, Grid computing makes efforts on resource sharing across multiple persons, institutions, and sites, thus problem solving with various resources shared in Grids. Therefore, new research challenges arise:

- **Site autonomy**
  Research institutes and persons of various virtual organizations prefer to keep their autonomy and share their resources based on some rules or agreements. Thus, users and

developers have to face the problem of solving problems across multiple administration domains while keeping the site autonomy.

- **Large-scale distribution**
  Computational Grid is a large-scale distributed system. It may contain geographically distributed resources that span departments, cities, and maybe countries. The large-scale distribution brings research issues, for example, robustness and scalability of the system.

- **Dynamic resource property**
  The Grid is a highly dynamic environment with concern for performance disturbance, resource competition, and dynamic availability of resources.

- **Heterogeneity**
  Resources in the Grid could have various software/hardware configurations, management policies, and access interfaces. Uniform solutions can be beyond consideration.

Although communities of Grid computing and agent-based computing focus on different goals and enjoy different features and methodologies, agent-based computing can be a promising solution to address issues discussed above:

- Multi-agent system, which by nature is distributed and can map distributed Grid resources. Agents in multi-agent system can collaborate to solve one problem across multiple resources or virtual organizations.
- Agent can behave on behalf of resources or institutions that join virtual organizations with some goals or interests. This helps keep the site autonomy.
- Agent can also represent Grid users, who are perhaps not familiar with complex Grid computing environment, to execute various tasks.
- As agents in the multi-agent system can have their own goals, knowledge representation,

and problem-solving strategies, heterogeneous resource properties can be treated with individual solutions by different agents.

- Intelligent agents can take actions to deal with the dynamic environment, which is the property of reactivity defined in the weak agency model.

On the other hand, Grid computing offers a great chance for agent-based computing community. In a long period of the past, research attention to agent community has been focused on theoretical models and algorithms for agent definition, communication, cooperation, and negotiation (Foster et al., 2004). A large number of algorithms and models have come to results. However, the key to justify agent-based computing is real applications, deployments, and robust infrastructure for achieving the available research results (Roure, 2005). Now, Internet-scale Grid brings a concrete infrastructure for agent models, algorithms, and real application deployments. This will change the fact that most of the results from agent community are simulation based. Concrete infrastructures and applications would also give birth to new research issues and activate agent community furthermore.

The Agent-Based Grid Computing and How It Works: Research Issues and Possible Solutions

This section discusses the main research topics of agent-based Grid computing and investigates the possible solutions for the research issues.

System Architecture

The first research topic is the system architecture for agent-based Grid computing. Multi-agent system and computational Grid are different in the system concept, design, and implementation. Current research on multi-agent system mainly focuses on the theoretical aspects, and some works are implemented only as prototypes. Grid computing, on the contrary, has concrete infrastructures and architectures as discussed in the section of background. It is therefore necessary to build an efficient, scalable and balanced system architecture for agent-based Grid computing.

It is quite straightforward to layer the multi-agent system on top of computational Grids. For example, multi-agent system can be employed as resource allocation and information dissemination. It is pointed out in Foster et al. (2004), however, this mechanism is not so efficient.

It is better to employ the service-oriented architecture for the agent-based Grid computing. A service can be deemed a network-enabled entity that can provide some functions through message exchange. In this sense, an agent can also be regarded as a service enabled by the multi-agent platform. Grid computing nowadays has evolved from the protocol-oriented computing paradigm to the service-oriented computing paradigm, which is defined and specified in the OGSA (open Grid service architecture). It is thus a promising choice to implement the agent with the Grid service and ship various algorithms from agent community to solve problems in the Grids, for example, virtual organization management and collaboration of multiple participants.

Service Composition and Negotiation

The next topic is naturally the collaboration of multiple agents that are implemented with Grid services. To build an efficient multi-agent system, a state-of-the-art implementation is unavoidable. Currently, computational Grids provide powerful service models: dynamic service and stateful service, which is discussed in the background section. Dynamic service can be created and destroyed dynamically (Foster, Kesselman, & Nick, 2002). The agents implemented with the dynamic service model can benefit from robustness and fault tolerance. The stateful service

model extends the common Web service model and contains the internal state, which can record the state of the services across multiple service invocations (Czajkowski et al., 2003).

On the Agent-Based Grid Computing: Case studies

One methodology to reach agent-based Grid computing is to build multi-agent system on top of Grid infrastructure. However, the solution is undesirable considering that a simple layering agent on Grids can only be reached via fine-grain intertwining of the two technologies (Forster et al., 2004). Various methodologies and levels of integration therefore should be investigated. This section examines the schemes in following case studies.

Resource Allocation in the Grid with Multi-Agent Learning Techniques

Galstyan, Czajkowski, and Lerman (2004) present their work on applying multi-agent learning techniques to the problem of resource allocation in the Grid from the perspective of learning and adaptation. In the work, users are modeled as rational, selfish agents who try to maximize their utilities. The agents have no prior knowledge about the resources and employ a simple reinforcement learning scheme to estimate the efficiency of different resources based on their past experience.

The Grid model used in the work is defined as follows:

- The Grid consists multiple resources; each resource is managed with local resource management system.
- Local resource management system maintains a local job queue. In the queue, a scheduling policy of FCFS (first come, first served) is employed.

- Each resource is characterized by its processing power, says *P*, which is defined as CPU time for completing the job.

Grid users, who generate jobs and submit them to Grid resources, are modeled as agents. Agents are selfish; in specific, agents want to minimize the user-centric metric, ρ_i, which is employed to describe job turn-around time:

$$\rho_i = \alpha_i T_w + (1 - \alpha_i) T_{exc}$$

where, T_w is the queue waiting time, T_{exc} is the job execution time normalized to the duration of the job, and α_i is the control parameter for balancing the two parameters.

There is no communication between agents. Agents can only get information of expected completion time when a job is submitted to a certain resource.

As indicated in the term of "reinforcement learning," agents use their past experience for resource selection. *Q*-learning (Watkins & Dayan, 1992) is a method adopted to incorporate reinforce learning: a *Q*-value indicates the efficiency of the resource in the past. For a new job, resource allocation is based on ε-greedy rule:

- With probability of $(1-\varepsilon)$, the agent chooses the resource with highest *Q*-value;
- With probability of ε, the agent chooses randomly and uniformly among other resources.

When the job is completed, the agent gets a reinforcement signal, computes the metric E_i and translates it to a reward r_i for resource *i*:

$$Q_{i,t+1} = Q_{i,t} + \alpha(r_i - Q_{i,t})$$
$$r_i = sign(\overline{\rho_i} - \rho_i)$$

where, ρ_i is the resource utility and $\overline{\rho_i}$ is the average resource utility for all submitted jobs.

ARMS: Agent-Based Resource Management System for Grid Computing

Agent-based resource management system (ARMS) is researched in Warwick University (Cao, Javis, & Asini, 2002) to address the challenges of scalability and adaptability of Grid computing. In this section, ARMS is investigated as a case study to analyze research issues of agent-based resource management for Grid computing.

Resource management in ARMS (Figure 3) is processed in hierarchy: local resource level and Grid (meta) level. ARMS brings the performance prediction toolkit (PACE) together with a scheduling algorithm designed to manage a local Grid resource. At the meta-level, each agent represents a local resource and cooperates with other agents.

ARMS architecture (shown in Figure 3) mainly contains the following components:

- **Grid users:** Grid users are in principle scientists and engineers who develop their applications and employ Grid resources.
- **Grid resources:** Grid resources are various resources shared in Grids and accessed by Grid users.
- **ARMS agents:** ARMS contains a number of homogeneous agents that are organized in hierarchy. Each agent represents a Grid resource at the Grid level thus serving as a service provider on behalf of the Grid resource.
- **ARMS PMA:** Performance monitor and advisor (PMA) is a special agent that is capable of modeling and simulating the performance of the system.

Agents in ARMS are structured in layers:

- **Communication layer:** Communication layer of each agent performs communication

Figure 3. ARMS architecture

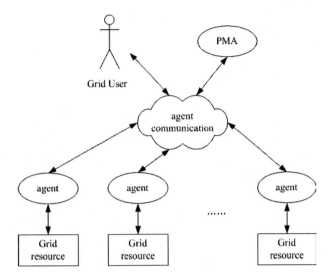

functions and serves as an interface to the external environment. Agents get the service information from the communication layer, which is required by coordination module and publishes its own service information via communication module.

- **Coordination layer:** Coordination layer focuses on taking strategies to coordinate with other agents. In the layer, there are four components:
  - *ACT manager:* Each agent uses an agent capability table (ACT) to store service information of other agents. The ACT manager controls the agent access to the ACT database.
  - *PACE evaluation engine:* A PACE evaluation engine is used to evaluate performance of resource allocation for an application. The engine gets service information from the communication layer and the ACT manager, together with the application performance model, generates a performance evaluation result.
  - *Scheduler:* Based on various results of performance prediction from the PACE

evaluation engine, the scheduler of agents allocate services (or resources) for applications.
  - *Matchmaker:* Matchmaker is responsible for comparing the scheduling results with the cost model of the application. The comparison results decide diverse agent behaviors.
- **Local management layer:** The local management layer functions as a local resource monitoring, scheduling, and application management.

Agent-Based Semantic Grid

Service-oriented computing (SOC) is an emerging computing paradigm that addresses research issues on loosely coupled, standard-based, and implementation-independent distributed computing (Papazoglou & Georgakopoulos, 2003).

A service is a function or software package that is well-defined, self-contained, and independent on the implementation, context, or state of other services. Services are described via standard service definition language, that is, WSDL, published with well-defined interfaces, and communicating with each other with implementation independent protocols, for example, SOA. In the service-oriented architecture, all resources are interfaced, implemented, or packaged with services.

SOA can help solve many research issues in loosely coupled, large-scale distributed systems, for example, application integration, workflow management, legacy codes support, and access to heterogeneous platforms (Papazoglou & van den Heuvel, 2005).

Architecture of service-oriented Grid computing is described in Figure 4. Grid resources are virtualized as Grid services and publish themselves in the service registry or index service. Service consumers look up index services and find desirable Grid services. After the negotiation with Grid service providers, service consumers can invoke Grid services via some protocols.

Semantic Grid aims to incorporate the advantages of the Grid, Semantic Web, and Web services (Geldof, 2004). Figure 5 schematically shows their relations (Geldof, 2004):

In the semantic Grid, agents are proposed to manage and execute semantic Grid services (Rana & Pouchard, 2005). According their roles in the semantic Grid environment, agents can be divided into three classes: service provider, service consumer, and community manager. An

implementation of this use scenario can be found in the materials microcharacterization collaboratory (MMC) project.

Another example is from myGrid project (myGrid, 2001), a collaboration work funded by the UK e-Science initiative. The myGrid project is designed as a development environment where collaborative distributed bioinformatics applications can be designed, developed, deployed, and executed. To meet this requirement, an abstract communication architecture is developed to map concrete communication technologies (Moreau, 2002).

CONOISE-G: Agent-Based Virtual Organization

Conoise-G (Conoise-G Project, 2005) is a project that focuses on the formation and operation of robust virtual organization (VO) in dynamic environments with multiple agents. It seeks to support robust and resilient VO formation and operation (Norman et al., 2004).

The Conoise-G architecture consists of multiple different agents classified as system agents and service provider agents according their functions. System agents are involved with VO formation and operation and service agents serve for the VO itself.

Figure 4. Service-oriented computing

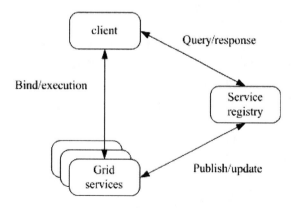

Figure 5. Semantic grid

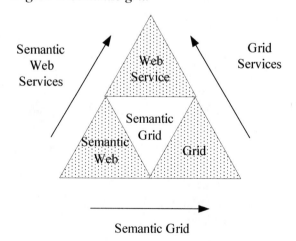

The VO formation process is described as follows. Service provider agents publish themselves to yellow page agents. A request agent on behalf of the Grid user poses a service request, then selects services required from yellow page agents. The quality agent and trust agent together with the clearing agent thus evaluate the service combinations and determine an optimal VO formation.

During the operational phase of VO, request agent, which now manages the VO, demands a QoS consultant agent to monitor various services involved in the VO formation. A policing agent, which can be invoked by any member of VO, is responsible for processing any dispute concerning service provision.

The Conoise-G system is FIPA (FIPA, 2005) compliant and implemented with JADE (JADE, 2005) platform. FIPA ACL messages are used in agent communication.

FUTURE TRENDS

As computational Grid evolves from protocol-oriented to service-oriented, research efforts are shifted to the semantic Grid, the semantic Grid services, and so on. To merge agent-based computing into this arising trend, various research aspects should be investigated:

- New service architecture should be carefully defined, providing autonomous behaviors of services. This work will accelerate the convergence of agent the Grid technologies. The architecture should include baseline interfaces and behaviors supporting dynamic and stateful services and a suite of higher-level interfaces (Foster et al., 2004). This service architecture should not be restricted for Grid computing. It can also benefit the advantages of state of the art from current distributed computing techniques, that is, e-science, P2P technique, and Web service.

- Agents can function for monitoring and evaluating services in the system. In case of troubles, intelligent agents can also detect problems and repair the system. This demands various algorithms and strategies brought from agent communities to Grids. It is promising to define the policies, rules, and conventions of Grid participants with existing results of agent community.

- Service composition and negotiation can also be handled by intelligent agents. Intelligent agents act as matchmaker and execute some economy-based algorithms for the optimal solution. Game theory is also of interest for this scenario.

- In the open dynamic distributed system, which contains multiple components, security-related issues require careful treatment. As discussed above, Grid services could be created dynamically and multiple Grid services can be combined into a meta-service. In this scenario, how to process issues of authentication, authorization of services, delegated service, and meta-service is a reach challenge. Furthermore, agents should be able to deal with different trust policies from multiple Grid services.

CONCLUSION

This chapter focuses on agent-based Grid computing, which introduces agent computing paradigm to the Grid community to address diverse research challenges. Related works in research fields of Grid computing and agent-based computing are investigated and discussed. Based on the introduction of background, the chapter presents methodologies and technologies of agent-based Grid computing from various aspects, for example, resource management, Grid economics, and virtual organization management. Although there are various research challenges as discussed in the fourth section, the chapter claims that agent-based computing is a promising solution to bring a scalable, robust, and thus tractable Grid.

REFERENCES

Access Grid. (2001). Retrieved from http://www.accessGrid.org/

Allen, G., Dramlitsch, T., et al. (2001). Supporting efficient execution in heterogeneous distributed computing environments with Cactus and Globus. *Proceedings of International Conference of Supercomputing.*

Allen G., Goodale T., Russell M., Seidel E., & Shalf, J. (2003). Classifying and enabling Grid applications. In F. Berman, G. Fox, & T. Hey (Eds.), *Grid computing: Making the global infrastructure a reality* (pp. 601-614). John &Wiley Press.

Atkins, D. E., et al. (1996). Toward inquiry-based education though interacting software agents. *IEEE Computer, 29*(5), 69-76.

Bradshaw, J. M. (1997). Introduction to software agents. In J. Bradshaw (Ed.), *Software agents.* Cambridge, MA: MIT Press.

Britton D., Cass A. J., et al. (2005). GridPP: Meeting the particle physics computing challenge. *Proceedings of UK e-Science All Hands Conference.*

Brown, M. C. (2005). *What is the semantic Grid.* Retrieved from http://www-128.ibm.com/developerworks/Grid/library/gr-semGrid/

Brunett, S., et al. (1998). Implementing distributed synthetic forces simulations in metacomputing environments. *Proceedings of IPPS/SPDP Heterogeneous Computing Workshop.*

Cao, J. (2001). *Agent-based resource management for Grid computing.* Unpublished doctoral dissertation, University of Warwick, Coventry, UK.

Cao, J., Javis, S. A., & Asini S. (2002). An agent-based resource management system for Grid computing. *Scientific Programming, 10*(2), 135-148.

Castelfranchi, C., Miceli, M., & Cesta, A. (1992). Dependence relations among autonomous agents. *Proceedings of the 3rd European Workshop on Modeling Autonomous Agents and Multi-Agent Worlds* (pp. 215-231). Amsterdam, The Netherlands: Elsevier Science Publishers.

Condor-G System. (2001). Retrieved from http://www.cs.wisc.edu/condor/condorg/

Condor System. (1998). Retrieved from http://www.cs.wisc.edu/condor/

Conoise-G project. (2005). Retrieved from http://www.conoise.org

Coveney, P. (2005). Simulated pore interactive computing environment (SPICE): Using Grid computing to understand DNA translocation across protein nanopores embedded in lipid membranes. *Proceedings of International Conference on Supercomputing.*

Czajkowski, K., Ferguson, D. F., Foster, I., et al. (2003). *The WS-resource framework.* Retrieved from http://www.globus.org

Dale, J., & Mamdani, E. (n.d.). Open standards for interoperating agent-based systems. *Software Focus, 2*(1), 1-8.

Dennett, D. C. (1987). *The intentional stance.* Cambridge, MA: MIT Press.

Earth System Grid. (2001). Retrieved from https://www.earthsystemGrid.org/http://e-science.ox.ac.uk/oesc/projects/test/projects.xml.ID=body.1_div.12

Finin, T., Labrou, Y., & Mayfield, J. (n.d.). KQML as an agent communication language. In J. Bradshaw (Ed.), *Software agents* (pp. 291-316). Cambridge, MA: MIT Press.

FIPA. (n.d.) *The Foundation for Intelligent Physical Agents.* Retrieved from http://www.fipa.org

Foster, I. (2002). *What is the Grid? A three point checklist.* GridToday.

Foster, I., Frey, J., Graham, S, & Tuecke, S. (2004). *Modeling stateful resources with Web services, Version 1.1.*

Foster, I., Geisler, J., et al. (1997). Software infrastructure for the I-WAY high performance distributed computing experiment. *Proceedings of IEEE Symposium on High Performance Distributed Computing* (pp. 562-571).

Foster, I., Jenning, M., & Kesselman, C. (2004). Brain meets brawn: Why Grid and agents need each other. *Proceedings of Autonomous Agents and Multi-Agent Systems.*

Foster, I., & Kesselman, C. (2005). *The Grid: Blueprint for a new computing infrastructure,* Morgan Kaufmann Publisher.

Foster, I., Kesselman, C., & Nick, J. M. (2002). Grid services for distributed system integration. *IEEE Computer, 35*(6), 37-46.

Foster, I., Kesselman, C., & Tuecke, S. (2001). The anatomy of the Grid. *International Journal of Supercomputer Applications, 15*(3).

Foster, I., Kesselman, C., & Tuecke, S. (2002). *The physiology of the Grid: An open Grid services architecture for distributed systems integration.* Open Grid Service Infrastructure WG, Global Grid Forum.

Galstyan, A, Czajkowski, K., & Lerman, K. (2004). Resource allocation in the Grid using reinforcement learning. *Proceedings of International Conference on Autonomous Agents and Multi-agent Systems.*

Geldof, M. (2004). *The semantic Grid: Will semantic Web and Grid go hand in hand?* Retrieved from http://www.semanticGrid.org/documents/Semantic%20Grid%20report%20public.pdf

Gelernter, D., & Carriero, N. Coordination languages and their significance. *Communications of the ACM, 35*(2), 96-107.

Genesereth, M. R., & Ketchpel, S. P. (1994). Software agents. *Communications of the ACM, 37*(7), 48-53.

IPG project (1998). Retrieved from http://www.ipg.nasa.gov/

JADE – Java Agent DEvelopment Framework. (n.d.) Retrieved from http://jade.tilab.com/

Jennings, N. R., et al. (2000). Autonomous agents for business process management. *International Journal of Applied Artificial Intelligence, 14*(2), 145-189.

Jennings, N. R., & Wooldridge, M. J. (1998). *Agent technology: Foundations, applications and markets.* Springer-Verlag.

Lee C., & Talia, D. (2003). Grid programming models: Current tools, issues and directions. In F. Berman, G. Fox and T. Hey (Eds.), *Grid computing: Making the global infrastructure a reality* (pp. 555-578). John & Wiley Press.

Lieberman, H. (1997). Autonomous interface agents. *Proceedings of CHI Conf. on Human Factors in Computing Systems* (pp. 67-74).

Lopez, I., Follen, et al. (2000). *Using CORBA and Globus to coordinate multidisciplinary aeroscience applications.* Proceedings of the NASA HPCC/CAS Workshop.

Malone, T. W., & Crowston, K. (1995). The interdisciplinary study of coordination. *ACM Computing Survey, 26*(1), 87-119.

Moreau, L. (2002). Agents for the Grid: A comparison with Web services (Part I: transport layer). *Proceedings of 2nd IEEE/ACM International Symposium on Cluster Computing and the Grid* (pp. 220-228).

Moreau, L. (2003). On the use of agents in a bio-informatics Grid. *Proceedings of 3rd IEEE/ACM International Symposium on Cluster Computing and the Grid.*

MyGrid project. (2001). Retrieved from http://www.myGrid.org.uk/

Norman, T. J., et al. (2004). Agent-based formation of virtual organizations. *Knowledge-based Systems, 17*, 103-111.

Nwana, H. S., Rosenschein, J., et al. (1998). Agent-mediated electronic commerce: Issues, challenges and some viewpoints. *Proceedings of 2nd ACM International Conference on Autonomous Agents* (pp. 189-196).

Papazoglou, M.P., & Georgakopoulos, D. (2003). Service-oriented computing. *Communications of the ACM, 46*(10), 25-28.

Papazoglou, M. P., & van den Heuvel, W. J. (2005). *Service oriented architectures.* Retrieved from http://infolab.uvt.nl/pub/papazgloump-2005-81.pdf

Rana, O. F., & Pouchard, L. (2005). Agent based semantic Grids: Research issues and challenges. *Scalable Computing: Practice and Experience, 6*(4), 83-94.

Roure, D. D (2005). *Agents and the Grids: A personal view of the opportunity before us.* AgentLink Newsletter, 17.

Russell, S. J., & Norvig, P. (2003). *Artificial intelligence: A modern approach* (2nd ed.). Prentice Hall.

Schopf, J., & Nitzberg, B. (2003). *Grids: The top ten questions.* Retrieved from http://www.globus.org

Stone, P., & Veloso, M. (n.d.). *Multiagent systems: A Survey from a Machine Learning Perspective* (Tech. Rep. CMU-CS-97-193). Pittsburgh, PA: Carnegie Mellon University, School of Computer Science.

Watkins, C. J., & Dayan, P. (1992). Q-learning. *Machine Learning, 8*, 279-292.

Wijngaards, N. J. E., et al. (2002). Supporting internet-scale multi-agent systems. *Data & Knowledge Engineering, 41*(2-3).

Chapter X
MAITS:
A Multi-Agent-Based IT Security Approach

Dharmendra Sharma
University of Canberra, Australia

Wanli Ma
University of Canberra, Australia

Dat Tran
University of Canberra, Australia

Shuangzhe Liu
University of Canberra, Australia

Mary Anderson
University of Canberra, Australia

ABSTRACT

In this chapter, we propose a multi-agent-based information technology (IT) security approach (MAITS) as a holistic solution to the increasing needs of securing computer systems. Each specialist task for security requirements is modeled as a specialist agent. MAITS has five groups of working agents—administration assistant agents, authentication and authorization agents, system log *monitoring agents, intrusion detection agents, and pre-mortem-based computer forensics agents. An assessment center, which is comprised of yet another special group of agents, plays a key role in coordinating the interaction of the other agents. Each agent has an agent engine of an appropriate machine-learning algorithm. The engine enables the agent with learning, reasoning, and decision-making abilities. Each agent also has an agent interface, through which the agent interacts with other agents and also the environment.

INTRODUCTION

Computers pervade every aspect of human life, ranging from personal entertainment to critical defense and weaponry systems. These computers are connected via networks that enable resource sharing through the exchange of processing power or large amounts of data. The development and implementation of computer systems far out pace computer security advancements. Many of the systems currently in place are running critical business, yet little effort has been made to secure these systems. We are not in a position to readily answer questions such as (Saydjari, 2004):

- *Am I under attack?*
- *What is its nature and origin?*
- *What are the attackers doing?*
- *What might they do next?*
- *How does it affect my mission?*
- *What defences do I have that will be effective against this attack?*
- *What can I do about it; what are my options?*
- *How do I choose the best option?* or
- *How do I prevent such attacks in the future?*

A great deal of work needs to be done to develop and market security technologies and to supply users with the confidence they need to employ these technologies for their security needs.

In this chapter, we propose a multi-agent-based IT security approach (MAITS) to solve the increasing needs of securing computer systems in a fast-changing IT security landscape. Each specialist task required for security is modeled as a specialist agent task. To address the global security tasks, an environment is invoked in which multiple agents (a multi-agent system or MAS) execute their specialist skills and then communicate with each other to produce the desired behaviour. The discussion of agent roles is systemically integrated with research conducted

in several areas of security: system administration assistance, biometrics authentication, intrusion detection, and computer forensics. The proposed security system combines the various tasks of gathering security information, analysing the information using experiential knowledge, and generating alerts and actions to respond to any security breaches or attempts on breaches. The functionality is implemented in a distributed multi-agent environment.

This chapter commences with a look into the background of information technology (IT) security threats that inspire the need to protect computer systems, the process perpetrators may follow when making an attack, and an introduction into the agent technology that forms the basis for MAITS. This is then followed by a discussion of the current research work in the development of MAITS. The chapter concludes with a summary.

BACKGROUND

In this section, we will first briefly study security threats and agent technology. We will then discuss the motivation for MAITS.

Security Threats

Since 2000, several high-profile computer viruses/worms, such as CodeRed (Code Red, 2001), Slammer (Slammer Virus, 2003), and the LoveBug (Love Letter Worm, 2001), have caused havoc to IT infrastructure, resulting in millions of dollars in damages. According to an AusCERT survey, in 2004 alone, the average cost for IT crime- and IT security-related incidents was $116,212 per organization in Australia (Australian Computer Crime & Security Survey, 2004). On August 14, 2005, a new worm, Zobot, appeared (Zobot Worm, 2005). Zobot went beyond causing damage, indicating a new trend designed for financial gain (Krebs, 2005). Given the new motivation of money, we can only expect the IT security to get worse with time.

In general terms, a security threat is about undermining the confidentiality, integrity, and/or availability of IT infrastructure (Pfleeger & Pfleeger, 2003). Figure 1 shows a simplified logical illustration of an IT infrastructure that can represent any organisation.

All devices in the IT infrastructure, shown in Figure 1, are connected via a corporate network. The border router is where the infrastructure meets the wide world of the Internet, with firewalls inside the router to regulate the Internet traffic. The organization's Web server is located behind the first firewall; it provides the world with access to the organization's Web and e-mail services. The infrastructure servers, such as DNS, AD/LDAP, and DHCP servers, are responsible for the support of other computers and/or the network. Corporate application servers host core corporate business databases and applications, such as payroll and finance. The data on these servers are highly sensitive and can only be accessed by authorized employees. Another firewall might be in place to offer more protection to the corporate servers. Other devices such as desktop computers, printers, file servers, and print servers support day-to-day business operations.

Almost every point on the IT infrastructure diagram is subject to security threats. Threats may come from inside or outside of the organisation.

The following list details some examples of security risks:

- **Port scanning and hacking:** On the Internet, a computer is known by its Internet protocol (IP) address, and its services are provided via transmission control protocol (TCP) or user datagram protocol (UDP) ports (Comer, 2000). Port scanning is a technique by which a person deliberately tries to connect to all ports of a computer or all of the computers in an IP address range. This systematic port connections, or

Figure 1. IT infrastructure

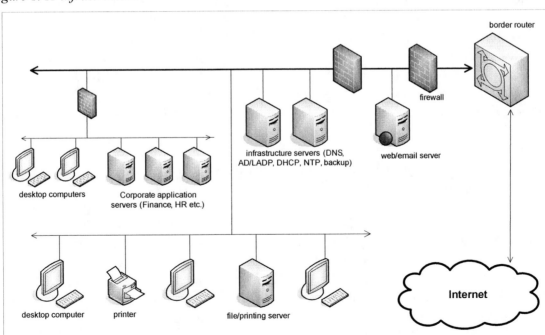

scanning, provides a clear picture of active computers, their running operating systems, applications (services provided), and their vulnerabilities.

- **Viruses and worms:** Viruses and worms are ordinary programs with two distinct characteristics. The first characteristic is that a virus or a worm is built to do harm; it may destroy files, create traffic jams, access confidential data, send local computer information outside the local environment, or even help its creator embezzle money. The second distinguishing characteristic is that a virus or a worm has the ability to reproduce itself and spread to other computer devices.

- **Denial of services attack:** If a number of computers visit a particular computer, say, a Web site, at the same time, they generate more Internet traffic and service requests than the targeted computer can serve. This constitutes a denial of services (DOS) attack. To orchestrate a large number of computers, the culprits may rely on viruses and worms to implant the attack program to these computers beforehand. At a specified time, all the computers request services from the target computer. CodeRed (CodeRed Worm, 2001) is just one of many examples in the category (Kienzle & Elder, 2003). Unfortunately, the denial of services attack is popular, and there is no effective defence.

- **Phishing:** "Phishing" is a phoney spelling of "fishing." As the name suggests, it is about phoney appearances and fishing. The phishing Web sites generally mimic financial institutions and other e-business operations. The perpetrators often send out inviting information by e-mail and then passively wait for gullible users to take the bait—like fishing.

- **SpyWare:** A piece of SpyWare is the same as a virus or a worm, except that it has a different purpose—collecting user data. SpyWare tries to be as stealthy as possible; it may be dropped by e-mail or Web downloading.

- **Spam e-mail:** Spam e-mail is the common name for "unsolicited bulk email." Although it does not sound as dangerous as the other security attacks described above, it is actually the most damaging one. There are two types of spam e-mail: *unsolicited commercial email* and *the email used as delivery agents for malware (malicious software)*. The former uses e-mail for commercial advertisement purpose, including illegal commercial activities. It costs staff time and IT resources. It is estimated that unsolicited commercial email "costs the world US$50 billion in lost productivity and other expenses" a year (Keizer, 2005). The latter has more sinister intentions. For any type of malware, be it virus, worm, or SpyWare, after being developed, it has to find a way to infect host computers. An easy and effective way to deliver malware is through unsolicited bulk e-mail. In the last a couple of years, several high-profile and successful virus/worm attacks were delivered via unsolicited bulk email, for example, LoveBug (Love Letter Worm, 2001) and Slammer (Slammer Virus, 2003). The Slammer worm alone "caused between US$950 million and US$1.2 billion" in its first five days worldwide (Lemos, 2003) and the LoveBug cost the world $8.8 billion (Lemos, 2003).

Security Solution

We start this section by looking at a possible sequence of a security attack and then generalize a security solution. In general, there are three steps an attacker may take.

- **Reconnaissance:** Attacking on computer systems is the same as attacking on battle fields; the first step is to gather intelligence.

In the context of computer system reconnaissance, the intelligence includes (1) the basic computer system information, such as manufacturers, models, hardware and software version, and similar information; (2) the local configuration, for example, the topological structure of network, services provided by the computer systems, and device population; (3) based on the intelligence collected, work out the possible vulnerabilities or security holes of this particular site. The reconnaissance process can be done automatically, semi-automatically, manually, or in a mix mode by a skilled attacker to maximize the intelligence. It normally starts with port scanning.

- **Attack:** After reconnaissance, the attackers now fully understand the vulnerabilities of the site. They can commence the attack. Depending on the skill level of the attacker, the nature of the vulnerabilities, and the availability of the attacking tools, the attacker may take attacking actions ranging from as simple as running an existing tool to orchestrating a number of different tools or crafting a new tool and then attacking. As the result of the attack, some computer systems are penetrated. In reality, reconnaissance and attack are often combined together, especially for the less-skilled attackers. Basically, the attackers will pick up an attack tool and run it against a site or several sites regardless of the computer system status of the site(s). That is why we see many attack attempts but little success.

- **Covering up:** After a successful attack, the attackers will normally install some kind of back door so that they can come back without going through the phases of attacking the vulnerabilities again. There are several reasons for this: firstly, the vulnerabilities may be patched by the local system administrators and no longer exist in the future; secondly, attacking the vulnerabilities and

then gaining access again are a long shot and require complicated operation; and thirdly, by going through the back door, the attacker actually legitimizes the access, as the back door access is the same as the other legitimate access but only open to the attackers. At this stage it is extremely hard to single out the perpetrators from the legitimate users. The perpetrators camouflage themselves into the environment, and their behaviours are similar to the legitimate users. Monitoring the network and examining the local host won't be enough to reveal unauthorized access through a back door. We will have better chance to catch the impostors if we can integrate the historical events.

Multi-Agent Systems

Agent technology originated from artificial intelligence research and can be traced back to the actor model by Hewitt (Hewitt, 1977) of 1970. The agent concept might be one of the most diverse topics among research communities. According to Bradshaw, a software agent is *"a software entity which functions continuously and autonomously in a particular environment"* (Bradshaw, 1997). Wooldridge and Jennings define agents by their characteristics. If a piece of software has the characteristics of autonomy, social ability, reactivity, and pro-activity, it is an agent in weak notion. On top of these characteristics, if the software has further characteristics of adaptability, mobility, veracity, and rationality then it is a agent in strong notion. Nwana suggests that agent is an umbrella term, under which many different types of agents exist (Nwana, 1996). Almost every agent system consists of multiple agents. A single-agent system may exist, but its ability as a system is in doubt. Multi-agent system (MAS) technology is another way of talking about agents; it emphasizes the multiple, perhaps distributed, agents and the communication among them. A multi-agent system (Stone & Veloso, 2000) could consist of:

- **Homogeneous agents:** With or without direct agent to agent communication
- **Heterogeneous agents:** With or without direct agent to agent communication

Communication among the agents can be achieved by either agent reacting with the environment or direct communication among the agents. The later involves a global naming scheme among the agents and can be done via point-to-point or broadcasting.

The nature of agents and the communication among these agents make them an excellent candidate for distributed computing and even general software applications. A breach of MAS study—agent-based software engineering (ABSE)—advocates using the agent technology for general software development. The basic idea of ABSE is to use agents as the fundamental building blocks for a software system, the same way that objects are the building blocks in object-oriented software engineering (Jennings, 2000; Petrie, 2001; Shoham, 1993; Wooldridge & Ciancarini, 2001).

In a general sense, an intelligent agent in MAS has two sets of behaviour, internal and external. The internal behaviour is the intrinsic operations of the agent. It consists of learning, reasoning, and decision-making abilities. We call this part of the agent an *agent engine*. The internal behaviour of an agent engine cannot be directly observed from outside of the agent. There are two broad approaches for agent engines – symbolic logic or statistical modeling. The former includes varieties of formal logic models, whereas the latter employs models such as hidden Markov model (HMM) (Rabiner & Juang, 1995), Gaussian mixture model (GMM) (Reynolds, Quatieri, & Dunn, 2000; Tran, Pham, & Wagner, 1999) and vector quantization (VQ) (Rabiner et al., 1983), and estimation methods such as maximum likelihood (ML) and quasi-likelihood estimation (QLE) methods (Dempster, Laird, & Rubin, 1977). In essence, the two different approaches serve

the same purpose—providing the agent with the required learning, reasoning, and decision-making abilities. In this chapter, we concentrate on the later approach for agent engines.

The external behaviour of an agent is comprised of the communications and the reactions with other agents and the environment. It is observable behaviour of this agent. This part of the agent is called *agent interface*. The interface is responsible for communicating with the other agents and the environment, for example, acquiring information from the environment or the other agents and exhibiting the results from the engine of this agent. The interface may follow some standard, for example, FIPA (FIPA, 2006), for the communication.

From BDI model (Rao & Georgeff, 1995; Wooldridge 2000) point of view, the behavior of an agent is driven by its beliefs, desires, and intention. Braubach, Pokahr, and Lamersdorf (2005) illustrated the ideas in programming terms: the beliefs reflect the environment where the agent resides, the desires are the goals for the agent, and the intentions are the operational or executable plans of the agents. The above-mentioned agent interface is responsible for communicating the beliefs of the agent with the environment and also formulating the goals for the agent. It then conveys the goals to the agent engine, which is responsible for achieving the goals.

The characteristics of MAS make it a primary candidate for the underlying framework in IT security. There are many advantages to taking the multi-agent approach:

- **Local knowledge:** Any security-related operation requires the knowledge of IT devices, such as firmware version, operating system type and version, patched levels, and the role of the device. It is virtually impossible to collect this information in a central repository, as information changes constantly. Some of the information is only useful to a local device, for example, the virus signature data on a particular computer, open ports and provided services on another computer, and the remote access to a network router.

- **Specialization:** An agent can be specialized in a specific area, for example, an intrusion detection agent, an authentication agent, or a traffic analysis agent. An agent may be programmed with pattern-matching skills; another agent may be programmed with neural network skills; yet the third agent may be programmed with the hidden Markov model.

- **Survivability:** From a system point of view, a large system consists of many components that only have a certain degree of reliability. These systems have to detect and deal with the possibility of component failure. Due to the distributed and autonomous nature of agents, a MAS can easily survive the loss of some agents.

- **Scalability:** Agents are autonomous. Therefore, cooperation among the agents may have varying levels of coupling; an agent may join in or drop out of cooperation at any time.

- **Extendibility:** Agents are heterogeneous. Different agents may be programmed with different skills. It is easy to program an agent with new technology and then introduce the agent into the agent system.

- **Communication and intelligence:** The intelligence of an agent is decided by its engine. We adopted a number of different machine learning and data mining algorithms as agent engines for MAITS. The communication among MAITS agents also provides an opportunity for the agents to gain knowledge from the other agents. The knowledge sharing is accomplished by either passing on the states of the engine of a particular agent to another or by receiving updated training data from the relevant agents and then retraining this agent.

MAITS APPROACH

Our current work concentrates on designing and developing agents to address four core areas in IT security: system administration assistants, authentication and authorization, intrusion detection, and computer forensics. This section provides an overview of the MAITS system, an explanation of the agent engines that provide the intelligence to the agents of MAITS, and a look at how MAITS is used in the four IT security areas.

Multi-Agent-Based IT Security Approach

- **The system:** The proposed system for MAITS (Figure 2) is implemented in a distributed multi-agent environment where each agent has specialized skills. The agents work together to gather and analyse security information and generate alerts and actions to respond to any security breaches or attempts on breaches. MAITS is a holistic security approach that provides security in the following areas: system administration assistants to help manage computers and collect security data, biometric authentication to protect access to systems, intrusion detection to monitor the system for suspicious activity, and computer forensics to gather evidence against the perpetrators in technological crimes. To provide security in these areas, agents work to gather local knowledge, which is sent to an assessment centre where the knowledge is collaborated and used to action security threats.

- **The agents:** The intellect of an agent comes from its processing engine. In this paper, we empower the agent engines with machine learning algorithms. The generic framework for machine learning-based agent engine can be illustrated in Figure 3.

Figure 2. Architecture of the multi-agent-based IT security approach

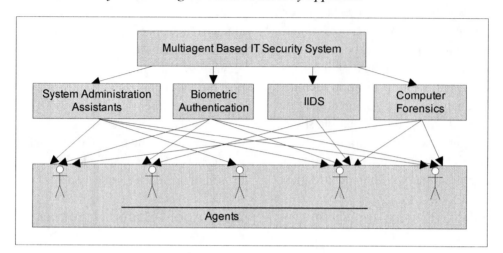

Figure 3. The generic framework for machine learning-based agents

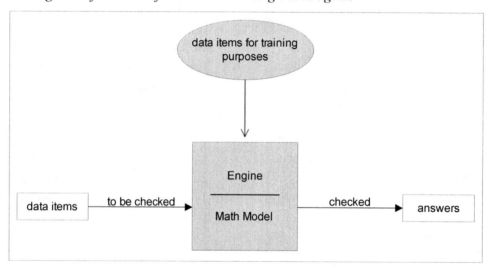

The three key features of the generic framework (Figure 3) are described below.

- **Engine:** The engine is constructed using a particular mathematical model; it is the intelligence part of the system. The engine is first trained via a specialized training data set and is then ready to make intelligent decisions on unknown test data items.
- **Data:** Neither training data nor test data can be in raw format; they have to be processed into a format that allows them to keep their original information intact. Domain knowledge and professional expertise in the field are essential for the data process. How successful the process is will decide how successful the engine is.

- **Answers:** Answers are the outcome of the engine's decision on the test data items.
- **The assessment centre:** The assessment centre consists of a number of agents specializing in data fusion and event correlation.

The assessment centre receives the information from all agents. It constructs the whole picture of the current activities. Based on the whole picture, the assessment centre will take one of the following actions:

- Raise intrusion alarm, if an intrusion can be identified, and instruct the relevant agents to take counter attack measures,
- Instruct some agents to pay attention to certain types of activities if there are suspicious activities,
- Instruct some agents to retrain their engines with specified parameters, and
- Ignore the information from a particular agent and do nothing etc.

System Administration Assistant

Nowadays, personal computers become more and more of a household necessity. Ironically, the management of the computers, for example, OS and application configuration, security updating, software upgrading, system fine-tuning, routine maintenance, and critical data backup and so forth, becomes more and more complicated. It is beyond the scope of ordinary users. Even IT professionals, who are experienced in this field, feel incapable of managing computer systems. The aim of our *Windows Autopilot* agent is to provide computer users with an automatic management facility and also to collect data for the security operation of MAITS. A system administration assistant agent, which has the knowledge of an experienced system administrator, is running on a computer and performing all the required system management and administration tasks. It will also answer the user's queries. The agent has the ability to check the security update, for example, security patches and virus signature data and so forth from software vendors. It will conduct or prompt the user to conduct the security updating operation. The agent also monitors the

system status of the computer, for example, CPU idle rate, memory usage, file accessing patterns, OS and application configuration changes, and so forth. If there are any suspicious events, it will contact the assessment centre for the relevant information. The assessment centre also receives the information of the other agents. By reconciling information, it has the big picture on what is going on at the moment.

Authentication and Authorization

User authentication (human-by-machine authentication) is the process of verifying the identity of a user: is this person really who he/she claims to be? Authentication systems can be categorized into three main types: knowledge-based authentication (what you know, e.g., passwords and PIN), object-based authentication (what you have, e.g., physical keys), and ID-based authentication (who you are, e.g., biometric ID such as voiceprint and signature, and physical ID such as passport and credit card) (O'Gorman, 2003).

Biometrics are useful to establish authenticity and for non-repudiation of a transaction, wherein a user cannot reject or disclaim having participated in a transaction. There has been a significant surge in the use of biometrics for user authentication in recent years due to the threat of terrorism and the increasing popularity of Web-enabling the world (Bolle, Connell, Pankanti, Ratha, & Senior, 2002). However, biometrics can be copied or counterfeited, so they cannot ensure authenticity or offer a guaranteed defence against repudiation. Different types of authenticators should be combined to enhance security and performance (Namboodiri & Jain, 2004, O'Gorman, 2003).

This section examines the agents that MAITS will use to verify users with verbal and written information and then looks at the logic models behind these agents. The enrollment (training) phase and the verification (testing) phase will also be presented in detail.

Multi-Agent-Based Biometric Authentication

We are applying a multi-agent-based user authentication and authorization system based on knowledge and biometric ID features. Our paradigm is a process of verifying the claimed identity of a user based on his/her handwriting and voice characteristics, as well as the information content of spoken and written phrases.

The multi-agent-based authentication system will consist of the following agents: voice (speaker) verification, verbal information verification (VIV), signature or handwriting (writer) verification, and written information verification (WIV). VIV (or WIV) is the process of verifying spoken (or written) words against personal information, such as the date of birth or the mother's maiden name. This personal information is stored in a personal data profile. The multi-agent-based user authentication system will be able to operate with any combination of these agents. A block diagram for the engine is shown in Figure 4. The agents for handwriting authentication are similar to those for voice authentication, so only the agents for voice verification are described in detail below.

The voice authentication agent involves two phases, enrollment and verification. During the *enrollment phase*, a key code, such as a user ID or an account number, is assigned to each *client* of the system. The client is then asked to provide a set of personal information items, such as date of birth, address and home telephone number. A dialogue agent leads the client through a series of questions and records the client's replies. Each question may be repeated several times in order to obtain a variety of acoustic productions for each reply. A microphone is set up to collect the speech waveforms. Speech data features, after feature extraction, are sent to the VIV agent to verify the utterance. The purpose of the VIV agent is to protect the system from incorrect training data in the event the user makes a mistake when repeating the utterances. Since the engine

knows the expected reply to each question, the corresponding sub-word models taken from the set of pre-trained speaker-independent sub-word HMMs are concatenated to obtain the phrase or keyword model.

During the *verification phase*, an identity claim is made by an unknown user. The dialog agent asks the user a series of questions related to the personal information of the claimed identity. The speech data obtained from the unknown speaker is sent to the VIV agent to verify the content of the utterances. Then the speech data from the unknown user is compared with the speaker models of the claimed user. The result is a similarity score that is compared with a given threshold to either accept or reject the unknown user's identity claim.

Logic Models for Biometric Authentication

Since user authentication is an area of pattern recognition, *probability* theory plays a very important role in providing quantitative, measurable parameters to measure the performance of a user authentication system. It is *a priori* fact that a person or identity can only be authenticated subject to the probability of making errors. For user authentication, there are two basic types of errors, namely *false acceptance* (FA) and *false rejection* (FR). False acceptance is the probability of accepting fake users and false rejection is the probability of rejecting true users (Bolle et al., 2002).

In order to measure the authentication error rates, determining the probability of a match of an input biometric with a biometric template or model is important. This probability is often translated into a similarity score S. A threshold θ can be explicitly set on the score S to directly control the error rates by authenticating a match if $S > \theta$. The probability of the input biometric coming from a fake user is significantly low (low FA) if a high similarity score is given. Conversely, if a low similarity score is given, the probability

Figure 4. Block diagram for the biometric authentication agent engine

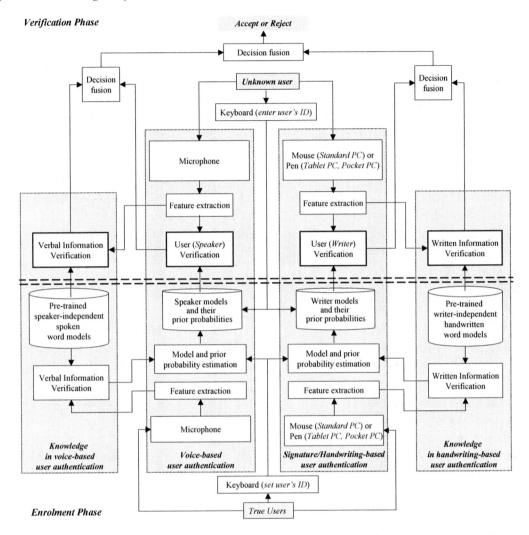

of the input biometric coming from a true user is significantly low (low FR).

The training data should be sufficiently broad and adequately represent the target population. For wide acceptance of biometrics, standards for interfaces and performance evaluation are needed. In this respect, the National Institute of Standards and Technology (NIST) in the U.S.A. is playing an important role in designing several fingerprint and voice databases.

The training method is based on a statistical pattern recognition approach. Statistical modeling

methods, especially the HMM approach, have become widely applied in speech recognition, voice authentication, online (dynamic) handwriting recognition, signature authentication, and face recognition systems. However, the HMM assumes that the occurrence of one feature is statistically *independent* of the occurrence of the others. This assumption is not appropriate for speech or handwriting recognition because a spoken or written word is represented as a time series of features and hence the features are correlated in time. The proposed temporal models can avoid this limitation of the HMM. Moreover, the HMM is trained using maximum likelihood estimation (MLE). The MLE method assumes the data sets have a statistical distribution. However, the statistical distribution of biometric or network data is unknown. To avoid these limitations of the current HMM, we use the temporal Markov modeling (TMM) method presented a later section. The TMM has an observed Markov chain where cluster indices are states to represent the dependence of each observation on its predecessor. The hidden Markov chain in the HMM is still employed in the TMM (Tran, 2004b; Tran & Pham, 2005).

We train the TMM using the quasi-likelihood estimation (QLE) method. The reason is that computer network data and biometric data do not have a statistical distribution, therefore the current MLE method is not appropriate. The QLE method requires only assumptions on the mean and variance functions rather than the full likelihood.

The method used to determine the similarity score S is usually formulated as a problem of statistical hypothesis testing. For a given input biometric X and a claimed identity, the problem formulation is to test the null hypothesis H_0: X is from the claimed identity, against the alternative hypothesis H: X is *not* from the claimed identity. If the probabilities of both the hypotheses are known exactly, according to Neyman-Pearson's Lemma, the optimum test to decide between these two hypotheses is a likelihood ratio test. Consider a false rejection of a claimed user caused in the current likelihood ratio-based scores because of the use of the background model set. The likelihood values of the background models are assumed to be equally weighted. However, this assumption is often not true as the similarity measures between each background model and the claimed model might be different. A likelihood transformation is proposed to overcome this problem. An alternative approach is the use of prior probabilities as mixture weights for background models.

On the other hand, a false acceptance of an untrue user can arise because of the relativity of the ratio-based values. For example, the two ratios of (0.06 / 0.03) and (0.00006 / 0.00003) have the same value. The first ratio can lead to a correct decision whereas the second one is not likely to because both likelihood values are very low.

Estimation of Prior Probabilities

The prior probabilities can be estimated directly from the training data. Let X be the training data set used to train the model set $\Lambda = \{\lambda_1, \lambda_2, ..., \lambda_M\}$. The prior probabilities $P(\lambda_i|\Lambda)$ satisfies:

$$\sum_{i=1}^{M} P(\lambda_i \mid \Lambda) = 1 \qquad (1)$$

Maximising $P(X|\Lambda)$ over $P(\lambda_i|\Lambda)$ using the Lagrangian method, the updated prior probabilities $\overline{P(\lambda_i \mid \Lambda)}$ is calculated from $P(\lambda_i|\Lambda)$ as follows:

$$\overline{P(\lambda_i \mid \Lambda)} = \frac{P(X \mid \lambda_i, \Lambda)P(\lambda_i \mid \Lambda)}{\sum_{k=1}^{M} P(X \mid \lambda_k, \Lambda)P(\lambda_k \mid \Lambda)}$$

or:

$$\overline{P(\lambda_i \mid \Lambda)} = \frac{1}{T}\sum_{t=1}^{T} \frac{P(x_t \mid \lambda_i, \Lambda)P(\lambda_i \mid \Lambda)}{\sum_{k=1}^{M} P(x_t \mid \lambda_k, \Lambda)P(\lambda_k \mid \Lambda)}$$

$$(2)$$

The second estimation method in (2) is called frame-level prior estimation to distinguish it from the first estimation.

Temporal Models

The use of codewords in a codebook as states of a Markov chain was developed by Dai (1995) for isolated word recognition. The proposed research extends this idea to a general framework, and hence it can apply to HMMs, GMMs, and their fuzzy versions.

Let $O = o_1, o_2, ..., o_T$ denote a stochastic process in discrete time. The probability that the t-th variable o_t takes the value w_t depends on the values taken by all the previous variables. Using the Markov assumption, the probability that the t-th variable o_t takes the value w_t depends on the immediately preceding value o_{t-1} as follows:

$$P(o_t = w_t \mid o_{t-1} = w_{t-1}, o_{t-2} = w_{t-2}, ..., o_1 = w_1) = P(o_t = w_t \mid o_{t-1} = w_{t-1})$$

(3)

The stochastic processes based on this assumption are termed Markov processes. Markov chains are Markov processes for which state variables are restricted to have a finite number of values, and the probability $P(o_t = w_t \mid o_{t-1} = w_{t-1})$ is assumed to be invariant in time. The sequence $W = w_1, w_2, ..., w_T$ represents a sequence of states. In order to apply Markov chains theory to temporal models, the feature vectors are considered outputs of Markov chains. Let $X = x_1, x_2, ..., x_T$ be a sequence of feature vectors that represents a spoken or written word, a feature vector x_t can be mapped to either a member of the set of codewords $V = \{v_1, v_2, ..., v_K\}$ obtained by vector quantisation (VQ) modelling or a member of the set of Gaussian components $G = \{g_1, g_2, ..., g_K\}$ by GMM. The state sequence W may be either a codeword sequence $w_1 = v_i, w_2 = v_j, ..., w_T = v_m$ or a Gaussian sequence $w_1 = g_i, w_2 = g_j, ..., w_T = g_m$, where $1 < i, j, m < K$. Therefore, each codeword in V or each Gaussian in G is a specific state of the Markov chain. The state-transition probabilities of the Markov chain are used to represent the dependence between acoustic features.

It should be noted that each observation in the sequence O is assumed to be statistically *dependent* on its predecessor in the proposed temporal model. In the HMM, observations in the sequence O are assumed to be *independent*. Therefore the temporal model has avoided the limitation of the HMM. There are 2 types of temporal models: *Temporal Gaussian Mixture Model* and *Temporal Hidden Markov Model*. The later can be further classified into discrete temporal hidden Markov model (DTHMM) and continuous temporal hidden Markov model (CTHMM) (Tran, 2004b).

Background Models for Verification Methods

Let λ_c be the claimed speaker model and λ be a model representing all other possible speakers, that is, impostors. Let $P(X \mid \lambda_c)$ and $P(X \mid \lambda)$ be the likelihood functions of the claimed speaker and impostors, respectively. For a given input utterance X and a claimed identity, a basic hypothesis test is between the null hypothesis H_0: X is from λ_c and the alternative hypothesis H_1: X is from λ. The optimum test to decide between these two hypotheses is a likelihood ratio test given by:

$$S(X) = \frac{P(X \mid \lambda_c)}{P(X \mid \lambda)} \begin{cases} > \theta & \text{accept } H_0 \\ \leq \theta & \text{reject } H_0 \end{cases}$$

(4)

$S(X)$ is regarded as the claimed speaker's similarity score. While the model for H_0 can be estimated using the training data from the claimed speaker, the model for impostors is less defined. The first approach is to use a subset of impostors' models that is representative of the population close (similar) to the claimed speaker. This subset has been called cohort set or background speaker set. Depending on the approximation of $P(X \mid \lambda)$ in (4) by the likelihood functions of the background model set $P(X \mid \lambda_i)$, $i = 1, ..., B$, we obtain different normalisation methods (Burileanu, Moraru, Bojan, Puchiu, & Stan, 2002). The second approach is to pool speech from several speakers to train a single universal background model (Reynolds et al., 2000). The third approach is the hybrid cohort-world model. The impostors' model is trained from impostors' utterances but the number of training utterances is the same as the number of utterances used to train the claimed model. The fourth approach is to use a virtual background speaker model. Assuming all speaker models are GMMs, the virtual model is regarded as a collection of Gaussian components from impostors' models close to the claimed speaker's model.

All of the above-mentioned background models were discovered by various considerations of the impostors' models. The proposed approach is quite different. The background speaker model can be directly generated from the claimed speaker model. Assuming there exists a model transformation that can be applied to the claimed model to generate a virtual model close to the claimed model, this virtual model can be regarded as the background speaker's model.

The proposed background speaker model has the following advantage. It is known that the speech signal is influenced by the speaking environment, the channel used to transmit the signal, and, when recording it, also by the transducer used to capture the signal. The proposed method can avoid such problems since both the claimed speaker's and background speaker's models are trained from the same training data. There are several open areas where future research can improve or build on the proposed approach. The first area is to find a good model transformation. Some transformations proposed are as follows:

- Using a subset of the claimed speaker's training set to train the background model,
- Using a "weaker" claimed speaker's model as the background model. For example, if the claimed model is a 64-mixture GMM, then the background model should be a 16-mixture GMM.
- Swapping values of a model parameter, that is, mixture values between GMM components in the claimed model to obtain the background model.

The second area is to find some invariant via the proposed transformations, that is, the decision threshold. The third area is the role of other speakers, which are far (dissimilar) from the claimed speaker in the acoustic space. A complete evaluation of background speaker models should be investigated.

Generalised Normalisation Method for Verification Systems

Applying the idea of the noise clustering (NC) method (Davé, 1991), we can obtain generalised scores that can reduce both false acceptance and false rejection errors. The general form of the generalised scores $S(X)$ is as follows:

$$S(X) = \frac{T[P(X \mid \lambda_c)]}{\frac{1}{B}\sum_{i=1}^{B} T[P(X \mid \lambda_i)] + P_c} \qquad (5)$$

where $T[.]$ is the likelihood transformation and P_c is a constant value.

System Log Monitoring

System logs provide rich information about the current system behavior and status. For any computer system, the operating system and applications keep detailed logs regarding the system, its security, and its applications. Operating system logs keep information ranging from user logon details, failed logon attempts, applications starting up and shutting down, system performance, and network activities. Although there is not a standard approach, well-written applications such as a Web server or a database server keep detailed logs about the application behaviors and operation checkpoints. When this information is put together it provides internal knowledge of the computer system's activities. This knowledge collaborated with the knowledge from other areas of the IT infrastructure helps to identify security breaches. Anderson and Khattak proposed to use information retrieval technology to comb through computer system logs to find clues of intrusion (Anderson & Khattak, 1998).

If we take the CodeRed worm (CodeRed, 2001) as an example, we can see the importance of the local knowledge. The CodeRed worm exploited a buffer overflow vulnerability of Microsoft's Internet Information Services (IIS) Web server; it sent the following request to an IIS server (the Xs in the request string can be Ns depending on the version of the worm):

```
GET/default.ida?XXXXXXXXXXXXXXXXXXXXXXXX
XXXXXXXXXXXXXXXXXXXXXXXXXXXXXXXXXXXX
XXXXXXXXXXXXXXXXXXXXXXXXXXXXXXXXXXXX
XXXXXXXXXXXXXXXXXXXXXXXXXXXXXXXXXXXX
XXXXXXXXXXXXXXXXXXXXXXXXXXXXXXXXXXXX
XXXXXXXXXXXXXXXXXXXXXXXXXXXXXXXXXXXX
XXXXXXXXXXXXXXXXXXXXXXXXXXXX%u9090%
u6858%ucbd3%u7801%u9090%u6858%ucbd3%u7801
%u9090%u6858%ucbd3%u7801%u9090%u9090%u8
190%u00c3%u0003%u8b00%u531b%u53ff%u0078%
u0000%u00=a
```

While a remote host may randomly try the request on many different targeted hosts, only those that are running vulnerable version of IIS will be compromised. A successful infection of a targeted host cannot be discovered by simply monitoring network traffic; local knowledge is needed to provide an accurate diagnosis.

We envisage that a group of agents will be specialized with the local knowledge of their resident hosts and closely monitor the behaviour and status of these hosts. At this stage, the agent will only monitor the operating system logs and the relevant application logs of the host computer system. We will expand the monitoring coverage into file system behaviour, system load, and system-related important information sources, such as the registry of a Windows operating system.

Intrusion Detection

In our opinion, there are three factors responsible for the high false alarm rate of current intrusion detection practice:

- Only a single information source is analyzed by an intrusion detection system
- Only a single method is used for the analysis
- The patterns of intrusions are not taken into consideration.

To reduce the volume of false alarms, we propose a multiple agent-based integrated intrusion detection system (IIDS) (Ma & Sharma, 2005). IIDS in itself can be regarded as a traditional intrusion detection system; it can be host, network, signature matching, or anomaly analysis based. Within IIDS, each of the multiple agents possesses a specialist skill to monitor a particular aspect of computer or network activities.

Any agent in IIDS will not raise any alarms by itself as it can only monitor part of computer or network activities. Unlike other standalone intrusion detection systems, when there are suspicious activities in an IIDS-protected system, the agent will pass the information back to the assessment centre.

An agent also has the knowledge of the local system, which helps it to make better decisions. For example, if an agent is running on a particular host, it would have the knowledge of the host: its operating system, patch level, services, and so forth. If it observes an attack attempt on a vulnerability that has already been patched on the system, it knows that there will be no damage to the system at all. Instead of alarming the assessment centre, it will just pass on the failed attempt as alerting information. The assessment centre, upon learning about the failed attack attempt, may further instruct the other agents to pay attention to this potential attack. We propose two types of engines for a host-based intrusion detection engine:

- **Data aggregation and clustering:** Network traffic records are converted into feature vectors. There are four types of aggregation on these vectors: local IP address-oriented incoming traffic, local IP address-oriented outgoing traffic, remote IP address-oriented incoming traffic, and remote IP address-oriented outgoing traffic. After the aggregation, the features vectors are fed into a clustering engine. A clustering engine is a data reduction method, which is used to convert a feature vector set into a small set of distinct vectors using a clustering technique. Advantages of this reduction are reduced storage, reduced computation, and efficient representation of network data.

- **Threading network traffic records and (hidden) Markov model:** Network traffic records are first converted into feature vectors and then threaded into sequences of vectors based on session activities. The dataset is a collection of sequences of vectors, and (hidden) Markov model is used to identify which sequences are not from legitimate operations.

An agent may also have the skills to take counter-attack measures. If an attacker successfully penetrates a system, there is virtually no time for a defender to take action manually. The penetration could happen at anytime, where the defenders cannot be on standby 24 hours a day, 7 days a week. If an intrusion is positively identified, the agent should be able to take some kind of counter measures, for example, changing firewall rules to stop traffic going to a host or stopping a particular type of traffic completely.

- **Computer forensics:** Digital evidence can be found anywhere from deleted files on hard drives and memory cards in mobile phones to databases that store e-mail on the Internet and even printers (Galves & Galves, 2004). Computer forensics (CF) techniques are used to discover this evidence, which is generally conducted by expert analysts in the field.

Most computer forensics literature and activities (Carvey, 2005; Davis, Philipp, & Cowen, 2005; Prosise, Mandia, & Pepe, 2003) are post-mortem based. By post-mortem we mean that the computer forensic techniques and operation are reactive: when an incident happens or there is enough suspicion, forensic investigation starts by following certain procedures. The investigation may start with freezing the computer system and then mirroring the data on this computer. After the data on the computer system is properly preserved, discovering, and perhaps recovering, the data of interest starts. The data is then correlated to restore the evidence of the events that happened before the incident.

For criminal investigation, including IT crime, we may not have any other choices but relying on post-mortem investigation. However, for IT security incident investigation, relying only on post-mortem investigation unnecessarily restricts our collection of evidence. One of the authors used to be responsible for the security operation in a medium-sized organization and was personally involved in several computer forensic investigations. Each time, the logs of previous days or weeks provided valuable information. The difficulty of keeping all the logs is that the volume of the data is enormous. It is not feasible to keep all the log records for a lengthy period of time. It is highly desirable if we can tell suspicious events and only keep the records for these events for potential investigation. On the other hand, some data evidence is transient, for example, the data packets on the network and the memory status of a computer system. It is impossible to keep the record of all transient data. However, again, if we can tell suspicious events and record only the data relevant to these events, we will have a much richer set of evidence for computer forensic investigation.

In MAITS, we propose pre-mortem based computer forensics agents. An agent of this type acquires the knowledge of possible suspicious events from the assessment centre. Upon being instructed, the agent starts to collect and correlate all possible evidences—system logs and also transient data. The processed data may further be fed back to the assessment centre. It is expected that the agents will increase the quality, validity, accuracy, and speed of gathering the evidence. The evidence also helps post-mortem investigation.

Preliminary Experiment Results

We have built one class of agents with two different agent engines based on statistical models for authentication purpose. The results are presented as follows.

For estimation of prior probabilities, a speaker identification experiment performed on the YOHO database using 16-mixture Gaussian mixture models (GMMs) showed that the identification error rate was 4.5% obtained by applying the MAP decision rule (with frame-level prior probabilities) compared with 5.0% obtained by applying the maximum likelihood decision rule only (Tran, 2004c).

For speaker background models, the claimed model was a 64-mixture GMM, and a "weaker" claimed speaker's model with 16-mixture GMM was used as the background model. The equal error rate obtained was of 2.5% on the 138-speaker YOHO corpus. The result was comparable with that obtained by using the five-background speaker set (Tran, 2004a).

For the generalised normalisation-based speaker verification, our speaker verification experiments using 32-mixture GMMs trained by 5 utterances only and tested by the generalised score with $T[P] = (-\log P)^{1/(1-m)}$ achieved the lowest equal error rate of 1.8% compared to 3.1% obtained by current normalization scores on 728640 test utterances of the YOHO corpus (Tran & Wagner, 2002).

CONCLUSION

The world is experiencing a surge in security breaches that vary from defacing Web sites and destroying files to accessing confidential data and embezzling money. This chapter first discussed the background of these malicious attacks to highlight the growing need for IT security. As a solution for the need to secure computer systems, this chapter presented the multi-agent-based IT security approach. MAITS proposed the use of agents to create a specialized security system that covers five core security areas: system administration assistants, authentication and authorization, system log monitoring, intrusion detection, and computer forensics. The chapter explained that MAITS is implemented in a distributed multi-agent environment where specialized agents gather local knowledge in their areas of expertise and send that knowledge to an assessment center where the knowledge is collaborated and used to generate alerts and take actions required to protect computer systems. MAITS is still under ongoing development. We anticipate a fully fledged system in the near future.

ACKNOWLEDGMENT

This research work is supported by the divisional grants from the *Division of Business, Law and Information Sciences, University of Canberra, Australia,* and the university grants from *University of Canberra, Australia.*

REFERENCES

Anderson, R., & Khattak, A. (1998). *The use of information retrieval techniques for intrusion detection.* Paper presented at the First International Workshop on Recent Advances in Intrusion Detection (RAID'98), Louvain-la-Neuve, Belgium.

Australian Computer Crime & Security Survey. (2004). *AusCERT.* Retrieved January 17, 2006, from http://www.auscert.org.au/download. html?f=114

Bigun, J., Aguilar, J. F., Ortega-Garcia, J., & Gonzalez-Rodriguez, J. (2003). Multimodal biometric authentication using quality signals in mobile communications. *International Conference on Image Analysis and Processing 2003* (pp. 2-12).

Bolle, R. M., Connell, J., Pankanti, S., Ratha, N. K., & Senior A. W. (2002). *Biometrics 101.* IBM Research Report. New York: T. J. Hawthorne.

Bradshaw, J. M. (1997). An introduction to software agents. In J. M Bradshaw (Ed.), *Software agents* (pp. 3-46). AAAI Press/The MIT Press.

Braubach, L., Pokahr, A., & Lamersdorf, W. (2005) Jadex: A BDI agent system combining middleware and reasoning. In M. Klusch, R. Unland, & M. Calisti (Eds.), *Software agent-based applications, platforms and development kits.* Birkhäuser.

Burileanu, C., Moraru, D., Bojan, L., Puchiu, M., & Stan, A. (2002). On performance improvement of a speaker verification system using vector quantisation, cohorts and hybrid cohort-word models. *International Journal of Speech Technology, 5,* 247-257.

Carvey, H. (2005). *Windows forensics and incident recovery.* Addison-Wesley.

CodeRed Worm. (2001). Retrieved November 22, 2005, from http://securityresponse.symantec. com/avcenter/venc/data/codered.worm.html

Comer, D. E. (2000). *Internetworking with TCP/IP* (4th ed., vol. 1). Prentice Hall.

Dai, J. (1995). Isolated word recognition using Markov chain models. *IEEE Transactions on Speech and Audio Processing, 3*(6).

Davé, R. N. (1991). Characterization and detection of noise in clustering. *Pattern Recognition Lett, 12*(11), 657-664.

Davis, C., Philipp, A., & Cowen, D. (2005). *Hacking exposed computer forensics (hacking exposed).* McGraw-Hill.

Dempster, A. P., Laird, N. M., & Rubin, D. B. (1977). Maximum likelihood from incomplete data via the EM algorithm. *Journal of the Royal Statistical Society, B*(39), 1-38.

FIPA. (2006). Retrieved May 22, 2005, from http://www.fipa.org/

Galves, F., & Galves, C. (2004). Ensuring the Admissibility of Electronic Forensic Evidence and Enhancing its Probative Value at Trial. *Criminal Justice Magazine*, 19. Retrieved March 18, 2006, from http://www.abanet.org/crimjust/cjmag/19-1/electronic.html

Hewitt, C. (1977). Viewing control structures as patterns of passing messages. *Artificial Intelligence, 8*(3), 323-364.

Jennings, N. R. (2000). On agent-based software engineering. *Artificial Intelligence, 117,* 277-296.

Keizer, G. (2005). Spam could cost businesses worldwide $50 billion. *InformationWeek.* Retrieved October 9, 2005, from http://www. informationweek.com/story/showArticle. jhtml?articleID=60403649

Kienzle, D. M., & Elder, M. C. (2003). *Recent worms: A survey and trends.* Paper presented at the ACM Workshop on Rapid Malcode, WORM'03, Washington, DC.

Krebs, B. (2005). Conversation with a worm author. *The Washington Post*. Retrieved September 20, 2005, from http://blogs.washingtonpost.com/securityfix/2005/08/a_couple_of_wee.html

Lemos, R. (2003). Counting the cost of slammer. *c|net News.Com*. Retrieved October 11, 2005, from http://news.com.com/2102-1001_3-982955.html?tag=st.util.print

Love Letter Worm. (2001). Retrieved November 22, 2005, from http://securityresponse.symantec.com/avcenter/venc/datat/vbs.loveletter.a.html

Ma, W., & Sharma, D. (2005, 14-16 September, 2005). *A multiple agents based intrusion detection system*. Paper presented at the Ninth International Conference on Knowledge-Based Intelligent Information & Engineering Systems (KES2005), Melbourne, Australia.

Namboodiri, A. M., & Jain, A. K. (2004). On-line handwritten script recognition. *IEEE Trans. on Pattern Analysis and Machine Intelligence, 26*(1), 124-130.

Nisenson, M., Yariv, I., El-Yaniv, R., & Meir, R. (2003). Towards behaviometric security systems: Learning to identify a typist. In N. Lavrač et al. (Eds.), *PKDD 2003, LNAI 2838* (pp. 363-374). Springer-Verlag, Berlin Heidelberg.

Nwana, H. S. (1996). Software agents: An overview. *Knowledge Engineering Review, 11*(3), 1-40.

O'Gorman, L. (2003). Comparing passwords, tokens, and biometrics for user authentication. *Proceedings of the IEEE: 91*(12), 2021-2040.

Petrie, C. (2001) Agent-based software engineering. In *The first International Workshop on agent-oriented software engineering (AOSE2000). LNCS 1957*, Springer-Verlag.

Pfleeger, C. P., & Pfleeger, S. L. (2003). *Security in computing* (3rd ed.). Prentice Hall.

Prosise, C., Mandia, K., & Pepe, M. (2003). *Incident response and computer forensics, 2nd ed.* McGraw-Hill.

Pusara, M., & Brodley, C.E. (2004). User ReAuthentication via Mouse Movements. In *VizSEC/DMSEC'04*. Washington, DC.

Rabiner, L. R., & Juang, B. H. (1995). *Fundamentals of speech recognition*. Prentice Hall PTR

Rabiner, L. R., Levinson, S. E., & Sondhi, M. M. (1983). On the application of vector quantisation and hidden Markov models to speaker-independent, isolated word recognition. *The Bell System Technical Journal, 62*(4), 1075-1105.

Rao, A. S., & Georgeff, M. P. (1995). *BDI agents: From theory to practice*, Australian Artificial Intelligence Institute.

Reynolds, D. A., Quatieri, T. F., & Dunn, R.B. (2000). Speaker verification using adapted Gaussian mixture models. *Digital Signal Processing, 10*, 19-41.

Rodrigues, R. N., Yared, G. F.G., Costa, C. R., Do N., Yabu-Uti, J. B. T., Violaro, F., et al . (2006). Biometric access control through numerical keyboards based on keystroke dynamics. In D. Zhang and A.K. Jain (Eds.), *ICB 2006, LNCS 3832* (pp. 640-646). Berlin/Heidelberg: Springer-Verlag.

Saydjari, O. S. (2004). Cyber defense: Art to science. *Communications of ACM, 47*(3), 53-57.

Shoham, Y. (1993). Agent-oriented programming. *Artificial Intelligence, 60*(1), 51-92.

Slammer Virus. (2003). Retrieved December 13, 2005 from http://securityresponse.symantec.com/avcenter/venc/data/w32.sqlexp.worm.html

Stone, P., & Veloso, M. M. (2000). Multiagent systems: A survey from a machine learning perspective. *Autonomous Robots, 8*(3), 345-383.

Tran, D. (2004a). New background models for pattern verification. *Proceedings of the INTER-SPEECH, ICSLP Conference, Korea, 4*, 2605-2608.

Tran, D. (2004b). Temporal hidden Markov models. *Proceedings of the International Symposium on Intelligent Multimedia, Video and Speech Processing* (pp. 137-140).

Tran, D. (2004c). Estimation of prior probabilities in speaker recognition. *Proceedings of the International Symposium on Intelligent Multimedia, Video and Speech Processing, Hong Kong* (pp. 141-144).

Tran, D., & Pham, T. (2005). Fuzzy estimation of priors in speaker recognition. *WSEAS Transactions on Circuits and Systems, 4*(4), 369-373.

Tran, D., Pham, T., & Wagner, M. (1999). Speaker recognition using Gaussian mixture models and relaxation labelling. *Proceedings of the World Multiconference on Systemetics, Cybernetics and Informatics/ The International Conference of Information Systems Analysis and Synthesis* (Vol. 6, pp. 383-389).

Tran, D., & Wagner, M. (2002). A fuzzy approach to speaker verification. *International Journal of Pattern Recognition and Artificial Intelligence (IJPRAI), 16*(7), 913-925.

Wooldridge, M. (2000). *Reasoning about rational agents.* Cambridge, MA: The MIT Press.

Wooldridge, M., & Ciancarini, P. (2001). Agent-oriented software engineering: The state of the art. *The First International Workshop on agent-oriented software engineering (AOSE2000), LNCS 1957.* Springer-Verlag.

Zobot Worm. (2005). Retrieved December 13, 2005 from http://securityresponse.symantec.com/avcenter/venc/data/w32.zotob.e.html

Section III
Agent-Based Intelligent Systems

Chapter XI
A Methodology for Modeling Expert Knowledge for Development of Agent–Based Systems

Michael Bowman
Murray State University, USA

ABSTRACT

For intelligent agents to become truly useful in real-world applications, it is necessary to identify, document, and integrate into them the human knowledge used to solve real-world problems. This article describes a methodology for modeling expert problem-solving knowledge that supports ontology import and development, teaching-based agent development, and agent-based problem solving. It provides practical guidance to subject matter experts on expressing how they solve problems using the task reduction paradigm. It identifies the concepts and features to be represented in an ontology; identifies tasks to be represented in a knowledge base; guides rule learning/refinement; supports natural language generation; and is easy to use. The methodology is applicable to a wide variety of domains and has been successfully used in the military domain. This research is part of a larger effort to develop an advanced approach to expert knowledge acquisition based on apprenticeship multi-strategy learning in a mixed-initiative framework.

INTRODUCTION

In order for multi-agent systems (MAS) to be truly useful in real-world applications and environments, it is necessary to identify, document, and integrate into the MAS the human knowledge people use to solve their real-world problems. This process has been found to be difficult and is a key part of the knowledge acquisition bottleneck.

This chapter presents a general methodology for collecting, modeling, and representing expert problem-solving knowledge for a given domain that supports ontology development and import, agent design, teaching-based intelligent agent development, and agent-based problem solving that is applicable to MAS. The methodology was developed as part of the George Mason University (GMU) Learning Agent Laboratory (LALAB) research funded by the Defense Advanced Research Projects Agency (DARPA) in the DARPA High Performance Knowledge Base (HPKB) and Rapid Knowledge Formation (RKF) programs (Bowman, 2002).

A methodology is a collection of methods, and methods are plans or systems of action consisting of procedures and guidelines for accomplishing tasks. The methodology described here was designed to address the necessity to identify and document expert problem-solving knowledge and facilitate its integration into a knowledge base, to support the design and creation of agents that solve real-world problems. It is applicable to a wide variety of domains and is natural and easy to use. It provides organized, effective, and repeatable methods with detailed procedures and guidelines for accomplishing these goals:

- Identification of the tasks to be represented in a knowledge base and a means of providing problem-solving examples
- Identification of necessary concepts and relationships to be represented in an ontology
- Guidance for rule learning and refinement
- Support for natural language generation for solutions and justifications

This methodology represents extensions of existing methods of knowledge modeling based on the task reduction paradigm. These extensions include a method that can be used to model how experts solve problems and are applicable to any domain in which task reduction is a suitable approach to problem solving. Further, a method is provided for creating an ontology specification that is a key early step in ontology development.

Other works (Mustafa, 1994; Schreiber et al., 2000; Tecuci, 1998) have included elements that describe the importance of knowledge acquisition, explain how knowledge engineers support the process, suggest ways knowledge can be represented, and provide examples. MAS-specific works (Hernandez, Gray, & Reilly, 2003; Maes, Tuyls, & Manderick, 2001) emphasize the importance of and describe methods for organizing or modeling MAS architecture. Neither of these groups of work, however, has concentrated on modeling expert problem-solving knowledge or providing specific methodologies for accomplishing it. This chapter documents a methodology for modeling expert problem-solving knowledge in support of agent development that can be used directly by an expert, knowledge engineers, or system designers for the design and implementation of MAS or individual agents.

BACKGROUND

A typical first step in the development of agent-based systems is modeling expert problem-solving processes and reasoning. Reasoning is the formulation of conclusions, judgments, or inferences from facts or premises. With respect to agent development, knowledge modeling is the conceptualization and representation of problem-solving knowledge in a knowledge base. It is potentially the most difficult aspect of developing knowledge-based systems. Knowledge conceptualization and representation are particularly difficult because the form in which experts expresses their knowledge is significantly different from how it should be represented in the knowledge base. Moreover, experts typically fail to specify the knowledge that is common sense or implicit in human communication but which needs to be explicitly represented in the knowledge base. After knowledge is conceptualized and represented, the representation must be verified for correctness and usefulness. This modeling and transfer of knowledge between the domain expert and the knowledge base is often a long, inefficient process. The methodology described here addresses these issues by allowing subject matter experts to directly model their problem-solving technique.

This methodology is based on the task reduction paradigm of problem solving. A task reduction solution diagram represents a logical set of steps that reduces a complex problem to a series of increasingly less-complex problems until the problem can be solved with the facts at hand. In this methodology, modeling is the process of creating an explicit yet initially informal representation of processes and reasoning an expert uses to solve a problem. That is, specifying a detailed sequence of problem-solving steps in the form of a task reduction solution diagram and expressing the problem-solving logic that justifies the reduction of each task to a subsequent sub-task or solution, in the form of a natural-language question and answer.

Task reduction as an element of system design has been a key concept in artificial intelligence and agent-based systems since the earliest days of the field. Allen Newell and Herbert A. Simon's seminal book on human intelligence and research directions for artificial intelligence, *Human Problem Solving*, (1972) emphasizes the importance of decomposition of complex problems into sub-problems. In his book *The Society of Mind* (1985), Marvin Minsky emphasizes the importance of problem decomposition in the design of agents. Task reduction remains a key element of modern agent development environments like Disciple (Tecuci, 1998), Protégé (Grosso et al., 1999), CommonKADS (Schreiber et al., 2000), and MIKE (Angele, Fensel, & Studer, 1998). Task reduction is also an essential element in the development of MAS as it serves as the basis for work allocation and cooperation among the agents comprising a system.

Despite its importance, the general concept of task-reduction is not sufficient for agent-based

system design. Newell, Minsky, and others have recognized the importance of dialog with domain experts to capture the essence of their problem-solving methods. This methodology takes advantage of a design concept generally alluded to by Newell, Simon, Minsky, and others and which can be called task reduction and dialog as metaphors for knowledge-based system design. In this methodology, the domain experts conduct a dialog through interaction with a computer or knowledge engineer, and by breaking down problem-solving methods into a series of tasks to be accomplished, questions to be addressed in the task, and the answers to those questions, the requisite problem-solving steps and logic, including ontological elements and state information, can be captured as a necessary first step in system design. The chapter includes both the "how to" steps and procedures of the methodology, and a structured, mathematical representation of the methodology.

A New Approach to Intelligent Agent Development: Direct Knowledge Modeling

The Learning Agents Laboratory at GMU has developed an apprenticeship, multi-strategy, learning approach for building intelligent agents called Disciple. A primary goal of Disciple is the creation of an environment in which subject matter experts (SME) develop and maintain their own problem-solving intelligent agents without the direct intervention of knowledge engineers (KE). In the Disciple approach, an SME teaches a learning agent how to perform domain-specific tasks in a manner that resembles the way the SME would teach a human apprentice, by giving the agent examples and explanations as well as by supervising and correcting the agent's behavior (Tecuci, 1998). The LALAB has developed a series of increasingly more capable learning agents from the Disciple family, which address very complex problems in the military domain.

While the principles, procedures, and formalization of the modeling methodology described here are very generally applicable to MAS development, it has been developed, tested, and externally evaluated over many years as an integrated element of the Disciple approach to agent development.

Task Reduction: A General Problem-Solving Paradigm

A fundamental and powerful concept for problem solving is that a complex problem can be successively reduced to simpler sub-problems until the sub-problems are simple enough to be solved immediately. The solutions to the sub-problems can then be successively combined to produce the solution to the initial problem.

A more formal representation of the task reduction concept is:

A problem P can be reduced to the simpler problems P_1, ... P_n. The solutions S_1, ... S_n of the problems P_1, ... P_n can be combined into a solution S of P.

For a simple example of this process from mathematics, see Box 1.

This general concept has been given many names, including problem or task decomposition, factorization, divide and conquer, and task reduction. In many works on problem solving, decision making, systems engineering and various aspects of artificial intelligence research, the process is described but not named. The term "task reduction" will be used for this concept throughout the

remainder of this chapter except where directly quoting other related works.

In an essay on human problem solving in *Society of Mind*, Minsky described human intelligence as a combination of simpler things, or agency through task reduction (Minsky, 1985). As an example of this concept, Minsky describes an agent for stacking a child's blocks to make a tower, called "builder," presenting the task and sub-tasks of builder with a simple task hierarchy diagram, similar to Figure 1. Task hierarchy diagrams are useful for most representations of problem solving with task reduction. This methodology uses the same principle to depict solutions graphically but calls the diagrams "solution trees."

Task Reduction in Multi-Agent Systems

Minsky described an agent as a process or entity that could accomplish some simple task (Minsky, 1985). Tecuci provides a general characterization of an intelligent agent as:

... a knowledge-based system that perceives its environment; reasons to interpret perceptions, draw inferences, solve problems and determine actions; and acts upon that environment to realize a set of goals or tasks for which it was designed. (Tecuci, 1998, p. 1)

Multi-agent systems are environments in which multiple, independently operating agents function, coexist, and cooperate to achieve goals. Although Minsky described theoretical multi-agent systems in detail as early as 1985, it has

Box 1.

P: Solve for x: $|x + 5| > 2$
Reduces to: P1: Solve for x: $x + 5 < -2$ S1: $x < -7$
And   P2: Solve for x: $x + 5 > 2$ S2: $x > -3$
S: S1 $\cup$ S2 $= (x < -7)$ or $(x > -3)$

Figure 1. Marvin Minsky's builder agent (Source: Minsky, 1985, p. 21)

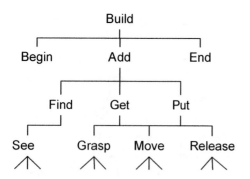

only been recently that research and computing advances have made systems of this type practical. Agent coexistence and cooperation are currently key research topics in artificial intelligence.

Task reduction is an essential element in the development of multi-agent systems, as it serves as the basis for work allocation and cooperation among the agents comprising the system. Four distinct phases have been identified for problem solving with multi-agent systems (Uma, Prasad, & Kumari, 1993):

- Problem decomposition
- Sub-problem allocation
- Sub-problem solution
- Sub-problem integration or result synthesis

Alvares, Menezes, and Demazeau (1998) identified two types of task reduction (using the term problem decomposition) necessary for multi-agent systems:

- Extrinsic decomposition, where each agent accomplishes the same type of tasks in parallel to speed up problem solving
- Intrinsic decomposition, where agents are specialized to solve particular sub-problems in parallel or serial manners

Basic investigation, development, and evaluation of MAS are major areas of emphasis in current artificial intelligence research. Luck, d'Inverno, Fisher, and FoMAS'97 Contributors (1998) described fundamental theory for MAS. Brazier, Jonker, and Van Treur (1998) described principles for MAS component reuse. Chavez, Moukas, and Maes (1997) developed and described Challenger, a MAS for resource allocation. All of these works include task reduction as an element of MAS development and operation.

Task Reduction and Dialog as Metaphors for Knowledge-Based System Design

As stated, a necessary first step in the development of knowledge-based systems is modeling expert problem-solving reasoning. Here, reasoning is the process of forming conclusions, judgments, or inferences from facts or premises. Task reduction is a natural and effective method for doing this. A key thesis of this methodology is that, done effectively, task reduction-based modeling of expert problem solving can contribute significantly to overcoming the knowledge acquisition bottleneck. This is also a general premise of the related agent development systems such as Protégé, CommonKADS, and MIKE.

The general concept of task reduction must be extended significantly to constitute a worthwhile component of a MAS development tool. A more comprehensive and repeatable methodology is needed for identifying and representing not only the problem-solving steps but also the background knowledge, state information, and problem-specific logic that explains the rationale of the problem-solving steps. Additionally, experts attempting to define, describe, and justify problem-solving steps for use in a knowledge-based system require guidance on how to organize supporting dialog and for what constitutes adequate definitions, descriptions, and justifications.

The importance of human-computer interaction and dialog for problem solving, and the use of dialog as a metaphor for system design, is a key component of mixed-initiative methods in artificial intelligence research (Cohen et al., 1998). The dialog metaphor is seen as a means of establishing context, goals, and current state information in knowledge-based problem solving.

What is missing from the general concepts of task reduction and dialog are mechanisms for documenting and translating the human dialog or narrative that explains the problem-solving steps into a usable knowledge base. The methodology described here combines the identification of problem-solving steps, background knowledge, state information, and problem-solving logic, as well as a language-to-logic translation mechanism in a single, multi-step process that can be used by both SMEs and KEs.

A GENERAL AND FORMAL PRESENTATION OF A METHODOLOGY FOR MODELING EXPERT KNOWLEDGE

Restating the concept of task reduction, a complex problem can be solved by successively reducing it to simpler problems, finding the solutions of the simplest problems, and successively composing these solutions until the solution to the initial problem is developed. Within the context of the task reduction paradigm, and the developed methodology, the phrase problem-solving task is used to convey the idea of a step or incremental procedure required to solve a given problem. To simplify the notation of this chapter, where appropriate, the term "task" will generally be used in place of problem, problem-solving task, sub-problem, or sub-task, which can be used interchangeably in most cases within the context of problem solving through task reduction. Figure 2 represents the task reduction concept.

To make task reduction useful for knowledge-based system development, it is necessary to do more than identify problem-solving steps. For the reduction from any task to any sub-task, and for each subsequent reduction between sub-tasks, it is necessary to identify the elements of knowledge that are relevant to solving each task.

One such element is background knowledge in the form of ontological structures (concepts, instances, and relationships) that are relevant to the current task and its reduction. Additionally, it is necessary to identify relevant, current, state information associated with the reduction between tasks and providing linkages to eventual solutions. For our purpose, state information is the collective relevant current characteristic conditions, or variable values within the system being modeled, at a particular point in time. Finally, the background knowledge and state information relevant to a given task must be combined with the appropriate problem-solving logic (reasoning) that justifies the reduction from a task to subsequent sub-tasks or solutions.

Modeling Expert Problem Solving as Tasks, Questions, and Answers

In this methodology, required problem-solving steps, background knowledge, state information,

Figure 2. Problem/task reduction diagram or tree

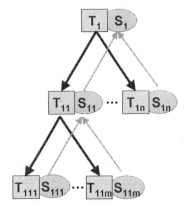

and logic is initially identified and represented in content-rich natural language expressions consisting of:

- A task name that corresponds to a problem or sub-problem
- A question relevant to the solution of the named task
- One or more answers to that question
- Sub-tasks or solutions identified by the preceding task, question, and answer

The process begins with the expert identifying the problem to be solved and generating a corresponding top-level task. Most problems are likely to have many potential solutions, and it is useful at this point to organize potential solutions into groups or categories. The expert may continue the modeling process by specifying a question that elicits categories of potential solutions, and as an answer, identify a category that corresponds to a particular example solution within the category to be modeled.

The modeling examples in this chapter come from the military domain and are examples of a process know as "*center of gravity (COG) analysis*." Carl von Clausewitz introduced the COG concept as "the hub of all power and movement, on which every thing depends" (von Clausewitz, 1832, p. 595). Modern military doctrine generally acknowledges that if a combatant can eliminate or influence an opponent's COG, the opponent will lose control of its power and resources and will eventually be defeated. Similarly, if a combatant fails to adequately protect its own strategic COG, it invites disaster (Giles & Galvin, 1996). This methodology has been used extensively to create COG analysis agents as part of the DARPA RKF project since 2002 (Bowman, Tecuci, Boicu, & Commello, 2004).

At the top of Figure 3 is an example of a top-level task (Identify a strategic COG candidate for the Sicily_1943 scenario). This top-level task is followed by a question relevant to solving that task (What is one of the opposing forces?). The question is followed by an appropriate answer (Anglo_allies_1943 is an opposing force), which leads to a new sub-task.

The process continues in the bottom half of Figure 3 as the sub-task (Identify a Strategic COG candidate in the Sicily_1943 scenario for Anglo_allies_1943) is followed by a new question (single member force or multi-member force?). This question is followed by the answer (multi-member force), which leads to a new sub-task.

The question following a task can have either a single answer leading to a single sub-task or solution, or multiple answers leading to multiple sub-tasks or solutions. Attempting to simultaneously model multiple branches of a solution tree down to multiple solutions can be extremely difficult. For any question resulting in more than one answer, the modeler selects the answer that corresponds to the example solution being modeled and continues down that branch of the solution tree, returning to the other branch(s) after the first branch is completed.

When an answer to a question appears to be complex, or includes an "and" condition, attempt to rephrase the question into a simpler, more incremental question that leads to a simpler answer. Figure 4 is a subtle variation on the top half of Figure 3, where the question is worded in a way that results in an answer containing an "and" condition (The Anglo_allies_1943 and European_axis_1943 are the opposing forces). Rephrasing of the question as in Figure 3 to ask "What is one of the opposing forces ..." results in two less-complex answers, (where the second answer is European_axis_1943, which was omitted from Figure 3 for simplicity).

If the question cannot be rephrased to result in a simpler answer, create branches as necessary, select a branch represented by a sub-task, and continue modeling down that branch. Return to the other branch(es) after the first branch is completed.

Figure 3. Example top-level modeling

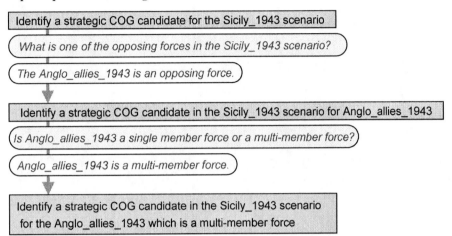

A different but common situation exists when two or more different subtasks must be completed to accomplish a parent task. For example, in the COG domain, if the parent task was to both identify a candidate and evaluate it in some fashion ("Identify and evaluate a strategic COG candidate for ..."), the two required sub-tasks might be "Identify a strategic COG candidate ..." and "Evaluate a strategic COG candidate ...". When this occurs, the required sub-tasks are identified and are circled, boxed, or linked in some other graphical manner to indicate an "and" condition, meaning all of the grouped tasks must be completed to accomplish the parent task. A branch represented by a sub-task is selected and modeling is continued down that branch. Return to the other branch(es) after the first branch is completed.

An effective manner of representing this situation in a question and answer is to phrase the question in a manner similar to "How does one X?" or "What actions must I complete to accomplish X?" where X is the action portion of the current task. This question would be followed by an answer with several sub-tasks such as "To do X, do A, B, and C" or "To accomplish X, I must complete A, B, and C." For example, if the current task was to emplace a bridge that involved multiple steps

that should be done concurrently, the question might be "How do I emplace this bridge?" The corresponding answer might then be "To emplace this bridge, I must prepare the banks, and relocate and construct a mobile military bridge." The steps or actions identified in the answer then form the basis of the new sub-tasks.

The task names, questions, and answers should be detailed and expressive because they serve five primary purposes:

- they identify the sequence of problem-solving steps;
- they identify the concepts, instances, and relationships necessary to represent the knowledge relevant to solving the problem;
- they identify the state information that is relevant at that particular point in the problem-solving process;
- they express the reasoning justifying the reduction from one task to the next sub-task, or to a solution;
- in their final form they serve as a script that directly supports agent training.

With these purposes in mind, it is important to express answers in complete sentences, re-

Figure 4. Mis-phrasing a question causing an "and" condition

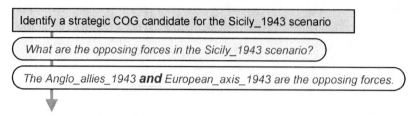

stating the key elements of the question in the answer. In Figure 3, for example, the answer to the first question is recorded as "The Anglo_allies_1943 is an opposing force," rather than just "Anglo_allies_1943." The expressiveness and thoroughness of the answers are very important to the language to logic translation process in MAS development.

The effects of this information gathering are cumulative. Subtasks generally contain the key information represented in preceding tasks, questions, and answers. The information necessary to solve a problem is the total of the information collected in each task reduction to a subsequent sub-task or solution. This holds true regardless of the problem type (planning, identification, analysis, etc.) or nature of the eventual solution (single-first adequate solution found, collection of partial solutions, or re-composition of partial solutions). This is truer in the larger sense that the goal of the methodology is to identify and represent the problem-solving knowledge necessary to teach an agent general problem-solving methods, rather than just solving any single given problem. For this broader goal, all information gathered is useful. Partial or even incorrect solutions, and the information that leads to them, contribute directly to producing more competent MAS.

To help the modeler maintain the problem-solving chain of thought while modeling complex solutions, and to portray the cumulative nature of the knowledge gathering, it is useful to express elements of preceding tasks in each sub-task. For example, the final sub-task shown in Figure 3 begins with the words of the preceding task and

adds the new relevant factor from the question and answer, "which is a multi-member force."

A final key guideline for the initial modeling phase of the developed methodology is that it should only be necessary to completely model solutions that are unique in their entirety. Entirely unique solutions are likely to be rare. Solutions can generally be organized within categories of solutions, and solutions within a category are often variations of, or branches off of, other solutions within the category. After completing a first solution tree, subsequent variations or branches off of that solution will reuse portions of the original solution tree. Figure 3 provides a very simple example of this. After identifying the top-level task and question, and generating the first answer in Figure 3 (Anglo_allies_1943), it is obvious that this top-level task and question can be reused when modeling solutions for the other opposing force in this scenario (European_axis_1943).

Creating the Ontology Specification

If complete and correct, the tasks, questions, and answers expressed during initial modeling should reveal the concepts, instances, and relationships that are necessary to represent the knowledge relevant to solving the problem. These objects represent a specification of the object ontology that must be developed. The role of tacit knowledge in expert problem solving makes this challenging. Experimental results collected indicate, however, that the cyclic nature of agent development and training compensates for this challenge, and the experience gained by experts in training an agent eventually overcomes the challenge (Bowman, 2002).

In most cases, initial ontology development with this methodology is a cyclic team effort between the SME using the methodology and a supporting KE. The expert models his or her problem-solving process as previously described and then sketches semantic nets of objects, instances, and relationships as described below. The basic idea is to draw the object ontology in the form of a graph in which the nodes represent objects and the arcs represent the relations between them. The supporting KE refines the sketches and then uses them as a basis for searching for useful, pre-existing object ontologies to be imported. If all of the necessary ontology elements cannot be found in knowledge repositories, which is likely to be the case, the SME or supporting KE can create them with ontology development tools. Once an initial object ontology is created, it is reviewed by the expert, who then updates the modeling to reflect the terminology used in the ontology. This, in turn, may generate additions to the ontology specification, which can cause another cycle of ontology import and extension.

Ontology specification is generally done after thoroughly modeling several example solutions in several solution categories. After completing solution trees for available examples in one or more categories, the expert selects a solution tree and begins ontology specification from the top of that tree. Examining each of the tasks, questions, and answers in the tree should reveal objects that must be represented in the ontology. By hand or with any available automated drawing tool, the expert draws simple, fragmentary semantic nets representing the objects that appear in the tasks, questions, and answers of the solution tree. More general objects are placed above their less-general subclasses and instances. Directed arcs are used to represent relationships between objects, with less-general objects pointing to their more general parent objects. Initial modeling may include objects whose relationship to other objects is not

initially clear. These objects are included in the semantic net with no arcs to other objects. These relationships may be worked out during ontology import and extension or by further modeling. Objects that are known by the SME to have been included in previous ontology specifications, or in the ontology itself, may be omitted from the semantic net for a newly modeled solution tree.

Nouns in a task, question, or answer are likely to be objects needed in the ontology specification. Questions are likely to contain objects that are more general than related objects that appear in the corresponding answer.

Figure 5 is an example of some of the ontology structure (force, opposing_force, multi_member_force) and state information (Anglo_allies_1943 is a multi_member_force and an opposing_force) that could be derived from the domain modeling from Figure 3.

The top-level task in Figure 5 clearly identifies at least two objects, *"strategic COG candidate"* and *"scenario."* These are included in the semantic net with no arcs since their relationship to other objects is not obvious at this time. The first question in Figure 5 includes something called an *"opposing force."* The answer to this question indicates that *"Anglo_allies_1943"* is an instance of an opposing force, so these objects are added to the semantic net with an arc from *Anglo_allies_1943*, which is less general, to *opposing_force*, which is more general. The second question and answer indicate that an *opposing force* can be subcategorized as either a *"single-member force"* or *"multi-member force,"* and that *Anglo_allies_1943* is an example of a *multi-member force*.

Given these new objects and relationships, *single_member_force* and *multi_member_force* are added to the semantic net with arcs to *opposing_force*, and the arc from *Anglo_allies_1943* is redrawn to point to *multi_member_force*. Finally, even without the object appearing anywhere in the modeling, the expert could reach the conclusion that a *"force"* may be a useful generalization of *opposing_force* as it corresponds to a well-established concept in the application domain. This and other objects the expert feels will be useful can be added to the semantic net with the corresponding arcs.

Modeling and ontology specification, as described above, can be complex non-linear processes. Figure 6 is a graphic representation of the first two steps of an agent development approach. Step 1, *initial domain modeling*, and step 2, *initial ontology development*, are done in a nearly concurrent, cyclic manner. Domain modeling produces informal solution trees. Initial ontology development produces an initial ontology specification. Both steps, 1 and 2, support and feed the next step, formalization, where the initial ontology is used to transform the informal solution trees into formalized solution trees as described next. Steps 1 and 2 are nearly concurrent in that once even a small collection of solutions trees is developed, an initial and partial semantic net of objects and relationships can be created.

The initial, partial semantic net can be used by a KE as a guide for object ontology import and extension while additional modeling is done. Steps 1 and 2 are cyclic in that modeling identifies the need for ontology development, and ontology development can identify the need for additional modeling. While ontology development can begin after a single-solution tree and corresponding semantic net of objects and relationships is cre-

ated, it is likely to be more effective to wait until a significant body of related trees and nets are created in order to limit the rework caused by later modeling.

When ontology elements are successfully identified and imported from pre-existing knowledge repositories, the names of imported objects and relationships are adopted into existing and future modeling where practical. Whether an imported name is adopted or an original name is preserved, a final decision is made as to which name to use, and a correspondence between the original and imported names is recorded and maintained.

Formalization of Modeled Tasks and Solutions

During task formalization, the expert rephrases the natural language description of each task into an equivalent formal description. A formal task description consists of an abstract phrase that represents its name, and a sequence of other phrases that represent its features. A general rule for creating the task name is to replace each specific object from the natural language description of the task with a general category. In the second task of the domain modeling in Figure 3, one could replace "*the Sicily_1943 scenario*" with "*a scenario,*" and replace "*Anglo_allies_1943*" with "*an opposing force,*" as in Figure 7.

Figure 5. Ontology specification derived from initial domain modeling

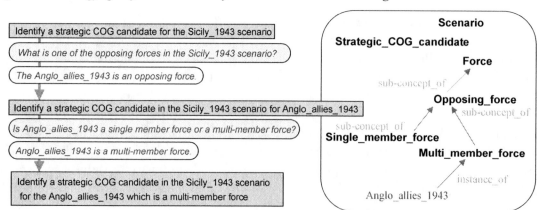

In this manner, the original task *"Identify a strategic COG candidate in the Sicily_1943 scenario for Anglo_allies_1943"* becomes this new task with two feature phrases:

Identify a strategic COG candidate in a <u>scenario</u> for an <u>opposing force</u>

The scenario is <u>Sicily_1943</u>
The opposing force is <u>Anglo_allies_1943</u>

The underlined words in the new task are general categories for the underlined words in the feature phrases, which are the objects that were removed from the original task. Feature phrases generally take the form: "The *general-category* is—object-removed-from-the-original-task-name."

When correctly formalized, a task name should not contain any specific object or constant. Each task feature is a sentence that describes one of the abstract categories introduced in the task name (e.g., *"a scenario"*) such that the task name and

the task features together are equivalent to the natural language description of the task.

Each feature sentence is independent of another. It is recommended that previously defined feature sentences should be re-used when it makes sense, rather than defining many variations that represent the same information. This limits the proliferation of task names and task features. Solutions must also be formalized with the same process.

There may be more than one way to correctly formalize a task or solution. Some formalizations are more versatile and useful that others. Figure 8 shows two different ways of correctly formalizing a solution. The first form follows the pattern specified above where each object is replaced with a general category. The second form is a more abstract representation of the task. Both forms are acceptable. However, the greater abstractness of the second form means it could be reused to formalize a larger number of solutions. It is up to the expert to determine the final form of the abstract names and features, selecting forms that he or she feels are most correct and natural.

Figure 6. A segment of an agent development process

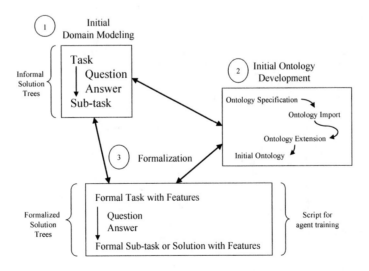

Language to Logic Translation Example from the Disciple Environment

The following section describes an example of how this modeling methodology supports the completion of the language to logic translation process. While the final formal representation of the logic is specific to the Disciple environment, the description of the general process should be useful in any MAS development environment.

After the expert formalizes a task or solution, Disciple forms a matching internal view that it uses in follow-on steps of the language to logic translation process, as depicted in Figure 9. The expert was responsible for first creating the natural language version of a specific task (A) and then formalizing it to create (B). The Disciple agent learns a general task from this specific task by replacing the instances, *Anglo_allies_1943*

and *US_1943*, with the variables *?O1* and *?O2*, respectively. From the natural language expression of the specific task (A), the agent learns the informal structure of the general task (C). From the formalized expression of the specific task (B), the agent learns the formal structure of the general task (D).

Completing the Natural Language to Logic Translation Through Agent Training

The questions and answers in Figure 7 provide the justification or explanation for the task reductions in the figure. While these explanations are very natural to a human expert, Disciple cannot understand them because they are written with unrestricted natural language. Figure 10 shows another task reduction, with both the initial and formalized tasks, which lead to a conclusion. The

Figure 7. Task formalization

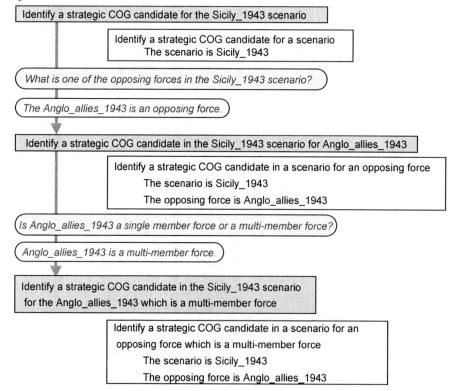

Figure 8. Variations of a formalized solution

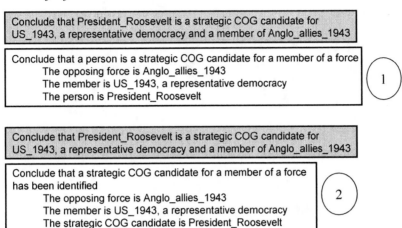

question and answer in this figure again provide a justification for this reduction that a human expert would understand. A translation of this justification that could be understood by Disciple is expressed in the three larger, un-boxed expressions, which consist of various relationships between relevant elements from the agent's ontology. When the agent's ontology is developed, it must include the objects, features, and relationships that will be part of these explanations.

In the agent-training process, the expert and the agent collaborate to identify the correct sequence of problem-solving steps in the form of the formalized tasks/sub-tasks/solutions. The expert and agent then establish the links between the steps by identifying the justifications for the reduction from one step to the next. This is done by performing the language to logic translation where the expert's expressive, natural language question and answer are converted to logic that can be understood by the agent, in the form of a sequence of object relationships that correspond to a fragment of the object ontology. The training process completes the natural language to logic translation and results in problem-solving rules that are understood and useable by the agent.

In agent training with Disciple, the expert uses a point and click interface to identify key concepts, instances, and types of relationships present in the question and answer. The agent uses analogical reasoning heuristics and general heuristics to generate a list of plausible explanations from these hints. The expert reviews the proposed explanations and selects those that match the logic in the natural language question and answer. If the desired explanations are not initially found, the expert can provide additional hints and prompt the agent to generate additional potential explanations until the necessary explanations are generated and selected by the expert.

Figure 11 is an example of a language-to-logic translation. The question and its answer on the left side of the figure represent the reasoning process of the expert. This natural language explanation must be translated to the ontology-based explanation on the right side of the figure, consisting of the following relations between relevant elements from the agent's ontology (see Box 2).

These lines state, in Disciple's language, that *US_1943* has as an industrial factor its industrial capacity, which is a major generator of war material and transports, which are strategically essential to the war effort. This thus matches the logic from the expert's question and answer that the industrial capacity of the U.S. in 1943 is a strategically critical element of its industrial civilization.

Figure 9. Disciple's internal view of a formalized task

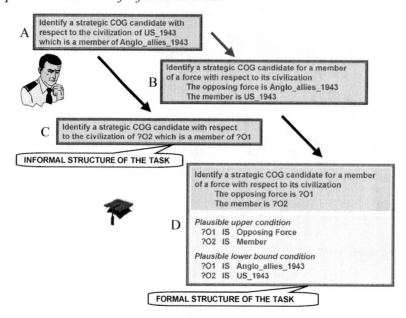

An expert is likely to be able to understand these formal expressions because they directly correspond to the natural language explanations generated by the expert during modeling. Not being a KE, however, the expert is not likely to be able to create them. For one thing, the expert would need to use the formal language of the agent. But this would not be enough. The expert would also need to know the names of the potentially many thousands of concepts and features from the agent's ontology (such as "*is_a_major_generator_of*").

While defining the formal explanation of this task reduction step is beyond the individual capability of the expert or the agent, it is not beyond their joint capabilities. Finding these explanation pieces is a mixed-initiative process involving the expert and the agent. Once the expert is satisfied with the identified explanation pieces, the agent generates the rule in Figure 12.

The learned rule in Figure 12 has both an informal structure and a formal structure. The formal structure contains the formal structures of the tasks, a general justification, and two applica-

bility conditions. The two applicability conditions approximate the exact applicability condition to be learned by the agent through rule refinement. During rule refinement, the agent will generalize the plausible lower bound condition and specialize the plausible upper bound condition until they essentially meet, allowing the variables to take on only values that produce correct reductions.

Agent Feedback to Domain Modeling

Figure 13 shows an entire agent development process, adding a fourth and fifth step and feedback loops to Figure 6. As stated earlier, domain modeling in support of agent development is a complex, non-linear process, involving many feedback loops. Domain modeling and ontology development go on in a nearly concurrent manner throughout the process. A significant amount of domain modeling and ontology development must be completed before formalization is practical and before agent training is possible.

Initial domain modeling and initial ontology development will drive and feed one another.

Figure 10. Disciple useable reduction justifications

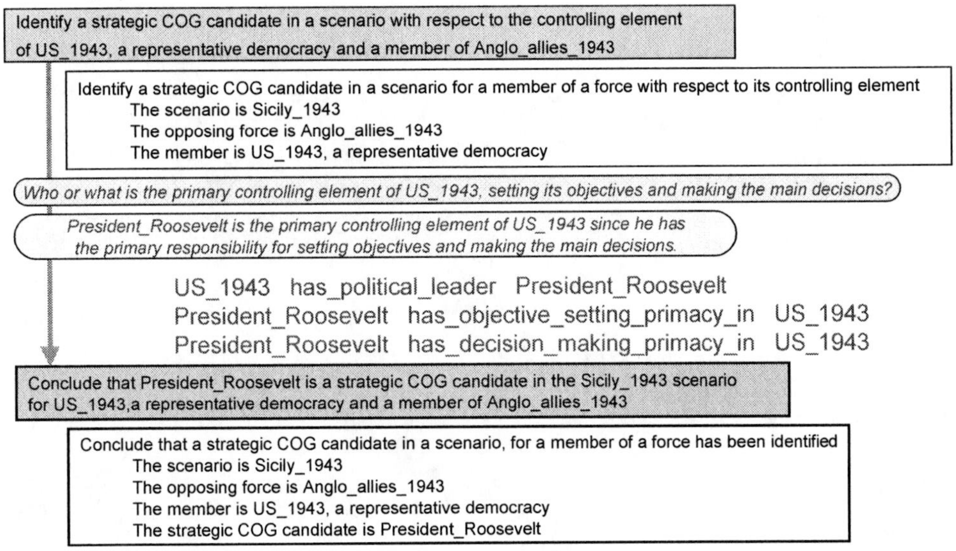

Box 2.

US_1943 → has_as_industrial_factor → Industrial_capacity_of_US_1943
Industrial_capacity_of_US_1943 → is_a_major_generator_of →
War_materiel_and_transports_of_US_1943
War_materiel_and_transports_of_US_1943 → is → Strategically_essential_goods_or_materiel.

Since even minor changes in the domain modeling or ontology could require major changes in formalized modeling, formalization and agent training should not be done until the domain model and ontology are relatively stable with regard to examples to be used for agent training.

As suggested by the feedback loops in Figure 13, changes and rework in the overall process cannot be avoided. It is unrealistic to expect that either the domain modeling or the ontology will ever be comprehensive for any real-world application domain.

A General Representation of the Developed Methodology

Modeling expert problem solving in the manner described above is a complex, cyclic, and iterative process, but it retains basic task-reduction properties. Figure 14 places the basic task reduction diagram from Figure 2 next to a new version where new constructs for questions, Q, and answers, A, are added.

Both diagrams in Figure 14 express the idea that problem-solving steps are represented in their structures. The new diagram on the right side of Figure 14 is expanded to express the idea that in addition to problem-solving steps, new information is represented in the form of the questions and answers portrayed. This new diagram, however, still falls short of representing the methodology. Still missing are representations for the ontology specification, state information, and expert reasoning that emerge from the content-rich natural language task names, questions, and answers

Figure 11. Agent training

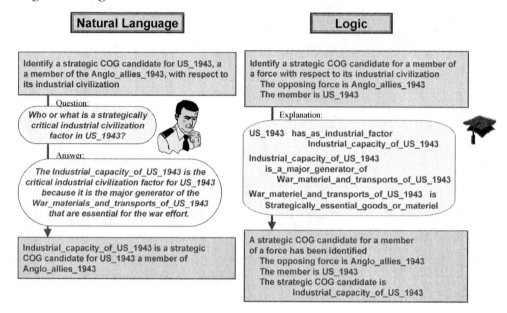

the methodology generates. Figure 15 builds on Figure 14 to more fully represent the product the methodology generates during the language to logic translation of problem-solving knowledge. The following expression summarizes the top half of Figure 15 and is followed by an explanation of the terms.

$$\{T_1Q_1\ \{(A_{11},OI_{11},T_{11}),\ \dots\ (A_{1n},OI_{1n},T_{1n})\}$$

T_1 is the top-level problem-solving task, and Q_1 is the first question asked. The answers to Q_1 are A_{11} to A_{1n}. Additionally, OI_{11} is the problem-solving knowledge generated through the language to logic translation of T_1, Q_1, and A_{11}, where:

- O is the set of ontological elements (objects and their relationships) revealed by the corresponding T, Q, and A and expressed in the ontology specification
- I is the set of state information (relevant current characteristic conditions, or variable values) and expert reasoning conceptually contained in the corresponding T, Q, and A

- T_{11} is the sub-problem of T_1 reduced by Q_1 and A_{11}, and accumulating OI_{11}.

In each case, the reduced problem-solving task T_{1i} generally accumulates the identified relevant facts from the preceding T, Q, and A. All of these expressions are free-form natural language sentences that include objects and relationships whose meaning remain consistent for a given problem-solving example.

The arrows from T_1 through Q_1 and A_{11} to T_{11} in Figure 15 are solid to denote a direct relationship between them. The arrows from the $T_1Q_1A_{11}$ set to OI_{11} are dotted because the identification and representation of the ontology structures and state information are closely related but separate processes that are begun during initial domain modeling, but not completed until the entire language to logic translation process is completed. The O of OI_{11} is captured initially in the construction of the ontology specification process described above, and completed in the ontology development process. The I of OI_{11} is conceptually contained in the logic of the natural language T_1, Q_1 and A_{11} but is not formally captured and expressed until

Figure 12. Informal and formal structure of a learned rule

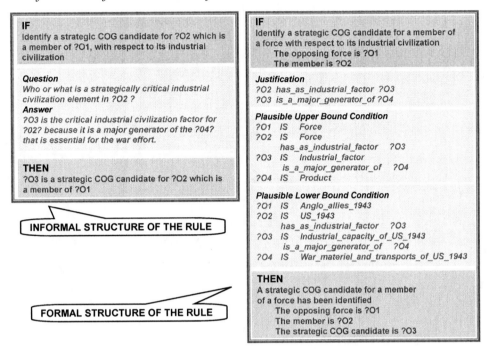

formal problem-solving rules are generated by the agent-training process.

Continuing the reduction in Figure 15 on T_{11} leads to a second level representation of:

$$T_{11}Q_{11} \{(A_{111}, OI_{111}, T_{111}), \dots (A_{11m}, OI_{11m}, T_{11m})\}$$

A chain of reductions is continued until a solution is obtained:

$$T_{1k}Q_{1k} \{(A_{1k}, OI_{1k}, S_{1k})\}$$

Whenever a reduction creates a result, that solution is back propagated and combined with other solutions through the solution tree substituting for the 3-tuple of answer, ontological element set/state information, and sub-task.

Thus a level of reasoning is concluded when:

$$T_{\delta}Q_{\delta} \{(A_{\alpha}, OI_{\alpha}, S_{\alpha}),(A_{\beta}, OI_{\beta}, S_{\beta}) \dots (A_{\eta}, OI_{\eta}, S_{\eta})\}$$

The entire problem is solved when:

$$\{TQ\{(S_1),(S_2), \dots (S_n)\}\}$$

This leads to a final expression for the methodology where the knowledge (K) necessary to solve a given problem within a class of problems is the total (T) of all the knowledge accumulated in task reduction and solution composition:

$$K_T = \{T_TQ_T (A_T, OI_T, S_T)\}$$

That is, the knowledge K_T required to solve a given task T is the union of the knowledge contained in all of the problem-solving tasks T_T, questions Q_T, answers A_T, and the solutions S_T. This knowledge is represented in all of the ontology elements generated in ontology development and conceptually contained in all of the state information and expert problem-solving logic contained in OI_T.

Figure 13. Agent development process with feedback loops

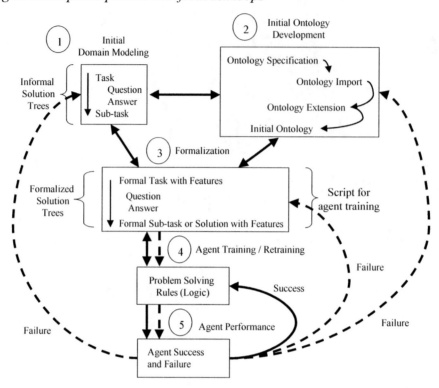

Initial Modeling Discussion and General Lessons Learned

Getting Started

When using this methodology to model expert problem solving for the first time with a new problem domain, or with a new class of problems within a domain, three general options are available to the modeler:

- **Depth first:** The expert begins with a depth-first analysis, modeling with great detail a complete solution to a specific example problem.
- **Breadth first:** The expert begins with a breadth-first analysis of the problem domain, brainstorming a wide range of potential solutions to many types of problems before examining any of those solutions in-depth.

- **Combination:** The third approach is a logical combination of the first two. In this Combination approach, the expert may begin with a fairly clear understanding of what the problem is and have in mind one or more potential solutions to the problem. After categorizing and prioritizing the potential solutions, the expert begins modeling the highest priority potential solutions but at each question considers branches and alternative solutions. The expert continues modeling the selected solution to completion, but as each new branch or alternative is considered, the expert makes notes to facilitate future modeling of that branch or alternative.

In practice, the Combination approach is likely to occur. This is because the complete set of all possible solutions to a given problem is not likely to be fully identified during a purely breadth-

Figure 14. Revised task reduction diagram with tasks, questions, and answers

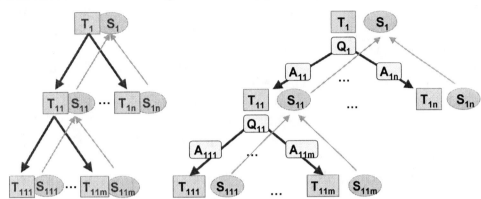

Figure 15. A general example of a partial solution tree

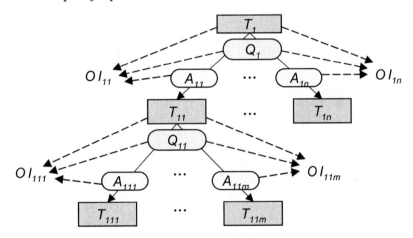

first examination, and a depth-first analysis of a single possible solution naturally identifies likely alternative solutions or branches to the solution being modeled.

Experimental results (Tecuci et al., 2000; Tecuci, Boicu, Bowman, & Marcu, 2001; Tecuci et al., 2005) show that a natural approach to the domain modeling process is to:

1. Brainstorm possible categories of solutions to the broad problem domain.
2. Identify a specific example problem to be solved.
3. Brainstorm potential solutions for that problem within a solution category.
4. Complete in-depth modeling of one or more promising solutions within a category.
5. Repeat steps as necessary.
6. Reevaluate/revise modeled solutions, adding levels of detail, based on lessons learned during subsequent modeling.

Task Reduction

A second major procedural issue is the manner in which a complete in-depth modeling of a solution is completed. Again, three approaches are possible:

- **Steps first:** The expert begins by identifying all the steps leading to a solution or conclusion without a detailed analysis of the logic that justifies the step-to-step progression. One or more solutions are modeled in this manner before each step is analyzed and modeled in detail.
- **Details first:** The expert begins by identifying one logical step along the solution tree, and then thoroughly identifies and documents all of the necessary knowledge elements and conditions necessary to justify the progression to the next step, before additional steps are identified.
- **Combination:** The third approach is a logical combination of the two pure approaches.

Experimental results strongly suggest that the two pure approaches to in-depth solution modeling are not practical. The first approach seems natural and can be productive, but it has serious drawbacks. In identifying all of the necessary steps before specifying any of the justifications for step-to-step progress, it is possible for the expert to lose track of the purpose or the reasoning behind a particular step by the time the end of the solution tree is reached. This approach also routinely produced steps that were too complex to adequately describe and justify later, which results in the steps being subsequently broken down into finer, simpler steps. Finally, this approach does not lend itself to incremental or team work. In long, complex solutions, it is difficult for the expert to stop work and efficiently pick it up again later, and extremely difficult for a development team member to understand the incomplete model when there is no documented justification for proceeding from one step to the next.

The second pure approach to in-depth modeling of a solution is also impractical. In this case,

the modeling proceeds much too slowly, and the task descriptions and justifications are very rarely actually complete until a solution has been modeled to a logical conclusion and has been looked at several times. Additionally, if analysis of a domain supports the import and reuse of an existing ontology much of the work done early in this approach will have to be revised to use the terminology from the imported ontology.

Finally, the level of detail actually necessary for productive work increases steadily during the stages of MAS development. Early, a minimal level of detail is necessary to support ontology development and import, and levels of detail beyond this are unnecessary and are likely to require major revision later. As work progresses to the later stages of knowledge base and agent development, additional levels of detail are necessary and are generated naturally in the cyclic feedback between modeling, agent training, and performance phases.

Modeling in Big vs. Small Steps

Another procedural issue for the methodology is the level of complexity or simplicity that is appropriate for each step in a solution tree. Experts often solve problems in what appears to be a "big bang" approach. They study a problem, collect relevant information, and announce a solution all in one, two or a few, complex steps. Asked to describe their process, they may write one very long, complex paragraph describing how they solved the problem. An expert may attempt to do domain modeling the same way. Using the proposed methodology, this may generate simple task names, but will require very complex questions and answers to adequately describe and justify the progression between these complex steps.

An alternate approach is to break down a problem solution into very simple, possibly tediously fine incremental steps. This approach results in more steps, possibly more complex task names, but generally produces much simpler questions and answers describing and justifying the progression between steps.

The first drawback to using complex steps is that as a problem-solving method, it does not scale up well to complex problems. When too much occurs in a single step, solutions and the justifications for moving from one step to the next easily become too complex to adequately describe or represent. This approach also disregards the primary goal of task reduction, which is breaking complex problems into simpler problems so that they may be more easily understood and solved. The primary drawback to this approach from the standpoint of knowledge acquisition and agent development is extremely important. The fundamental purpose for developing these representations of problem-solving knowledge is so they can be used to develop more general, re-useable problem-solving rules. Doing too much in a single step makes the step less general and much more difficult to turn into a re-useable problem-solving rule. The representation itself is also much more easily re-used for representing other problem-solving examples when it is broken down into finer steps. Most importantly, this incremental approach generates a representation that is more suitable for generating general, re-usable problem-solving rules.

CONCLUSION

The methodology described here provides a practical set of methods for modeling and representing an expert's problem-solving knowledge for an application domain, and supporting ontology development and import, teaching-based intelligent agent development, and agent-based problem solving. It is suitable for use in domains where task reduction can be used for problem solving. Detailed experimental results for using the methodology have been reported as part of the DARPA HPKB and RKF efforts (Bowman 2002, Tecuci, et al., 2005). In general, those results show that the methodology is both effective for modeling complex domains in support of agent development, and easy to use after minimal user training. While it was developed for and has been used extensively with a specific agent environment, the GMU LALAB Disciple system, it has very general applicability for MAS development. The methodology is only a first step in the development of agent-based systems. Research and experimentation in using the methodology to support the development of collaborative agents is ongoing. Use of the methodology to determine agent responsibilities in MAS is an excellent research opportunity.

REFERENCES

Alvares, L., Menezes, P., & Demazeau, Y. (1998). Problem decomposition: An essential step for multi-agent systems. *Proceedings of 10th International Conference on Systems Research, Informatics and Cybernetics (ICSRIC'98)*, Baden-Baden.

Angele, J., Fensel, D., & Studer, R. (1998). Developing knowledge-based systems with MIKE. *Journal of Automated Software Engineering.*

Bowman, M. (2002). *A methodology for modeling and representing expert knowledge that supports teaching-based intelligent agent development.* Doctoral dissertation, George Mason University, Fairfax, VA.

Bowman, M., Tecuci, G., Boicu, M., &Commello, J. (2004). Information age warfare—Intelligent agents in the classroom and strategic analysis center. *Proceedings of the 24th U.S. Army Science Conference,* Orlando FL.

Brazier, F., Jonker, C., & Van Treur, J. (1998). Principles of compositional multi-agent system development. In Cuena, J. (Ed.), *15th IFIP World Computer Congress, WCC'98, Conference on Information Technology and Knowledge Systems, Evaluating PSMs for Adaptive Design 23 (IT&KNOWS'98)* (pp. 347-360).

Chavez, A., Moukas, A., & Maes, P. (1997). Challenger: A multiagent system for distributed resource allocation. *Proceedings of the First International Conference on Autonomous Agents*, Marina Del Ray, CA.

Clausewitz, von C. (1832). *On war* (M. Howard & P. Paret, Trans.). Princeton, NJ: Princeton University Press.

Cohen, R., Allaby, C., Cumbaa, C., Fitzgerald, M., Ho, K., Hui, B., et al. (1998). What is initiative? *User Modeling and User-Adapted Interaction, 8*(3-4), 173.

Giles, P., & Galvin, T. (1996). *Center of gravity: Determination, analysis, and application.* Carlisle Barracks, PA: Center for Strategic Leadership.

Grosso, W., Eriksson, H., Fergerson, R., Gennari, J., Tu, S., & Musen, M. (1999, October 16-21). Knowledge modeling at the millennium, The design and evolution of protégé—2000. *Proceedings of the 12th Workshop on Knowledge Acquisition, Modeling and Management*, Banff, Alberta, Canada.

Hernandez, F., Gray, J., & Reilly, K. (2003). A multi-level technique for modeling agent-based systems. *Proceedings of 2nd International Workshop on Agent-Oriented Methodologies (OOPSLA-2003)* (pp. 33-42).

Luck, M., d'Inverno, M., Fisher, M., & FoMAS '97 Contributors. (1998). Foundations of multi-agent systems: Techniques, tools and theory. *Knowledge Engineering Review, 13*(3), 297-302.

Maes, S., Tuyls, K., & Manderick, B. (2001). Modeling a multi-agent environment combining influence diagrams. M. Mohammadian (Ed.), *Intelligent Agents, Web Technologies and Internet Commerce, IAWTIC2001*, Las Vegas, NV.

Minsky, M. (1985). *The society of mind.* New York: Simon and Schuster.

Mustafa, M. (1994). *Methodology of inductive learning: Structural engineering application.* Unpublished doctoral dissertation, Wayne State University, Detroit, MI.

Newell, A., & Simon, H. (1972). *Human problem solving.* Englewood Cliffs, NJ: Prentice Hall.

Schreiber, G., Akkermans, H., Anjewierden, A, de Hoog, R., Shadbolt, N., Van de Velde, W., et al. (2000). *Knowledge engineering and management; The commonKADS methodology.* Cambridge, MA: MIT Press.

Schreiber, A., Wielinga, B., & Breuker, J. (Eds.). (1993). KADS. A principled approach to knowledge-based system development, *Knowledge-Based Systems, 11.*

Simon, H., (1977). *The new science of management decision, rev. ed.* Englewood Cliffs: Prentice Hall. Quoted in Van Gundy Jr. (1981), *Techniques of Structured Problem Solving* (p. 5). New York: Van Nostrand Reinhold Company.

Tecuci, G., (1998). *Building Intelligent Agents*, San Diego, CA: Academic Press.

Tecuci, G., Boicu, M., Boicu, C., Marcu, D., Stanescu, B., & Barbulescu, M., (2005). The disciple-RKF learning and reasoning agent. *Computational Intelligence, 21*(4), 462-479.

Tecuci, G., Boicu, M., Bowman, M., & Marcu, D. (2001). An innovative application from the DARPA knowledge bases program, rapid development of a course of action critiquer. *AI Magazine, 22*(2), 43-61.

Tecuci, G., Boicu, M., Bowman, M., Marcu, D., Syhr, P., & Cascaval, C. (2000). An experiment in agent teaching by subject matter experts. *International Journal of Human-Computer Studies, 53*, 583-610.

Uma, G., Prasad, B., & Kumari, O. (1993). Distributed intelligent systems—Issues, perspectives and approaches. *Knowledge Based Systems, 6*(2), 77-96.

Chapter XII
Three Perspectives on Multi–Agent Reinforcement Learning

Yang Gao
Nanjing University, China

Hao Wang
Nanjing University, China

Ruili Wang
Massey University, New Zealand

ABSTRACT

This chapter concludes three perspectives on multi-agent reinforcement learning (MARL): (1) cooperative MARL, which performs mutual interaction between cooperative agents; (2) equilibrium-based MARL, which focuses on equilibrium solutions among gaming agents; and (3) best-response MARL, which suggests a no-regret policy against other competitive agents. Then the authors present a general framework of MARL, which combines all the three perspectives in order to assist readers in understanding the intricate relationships between different perspectives. Furthermore, a negotiation-based MARL algorithm based on meta-equilibrium is presented, which can interact with cooperative agents, games with gaming agents, and provides the best response to other competitive agents.

INTRODUCTION

Reinforcement learning (RL) dates back to the early days of cybernetics and work in statistics, psychology, neuroscience, and computer science.

Since the late 1980s, it has attracted increasing interests of researchers in the fields of machine learning (ML) and artificial intelligence (AI). Its promise is to find "*a way of programming agents by rewards and punishment without needing to specify how the task is to be achieved*" (Kaelbling & Littman, 1996, p. 237).

Multi-agent reinforcement learning (MARL) can be considered an extension of RL to the multi-agent domain. Also, it is a new paradigm of distributed artificial intelligence applications. This domain has many research issues. Many researchers have been chasing their own interests since the early 1990s, and they can be divided into two major research groups. One group studies MARL in the view of machine learning, while the other studies MARL in the view of multi-agent systems.

In our opinion, MARL has three main perspectives. The first perspective is cooperative MARL. It studies how to speed a learning process via mutual interaction. Consequently, there have been many discussions of interaction methods. The second perspective is equilibrium-based MARL. It has a mathematical foundation of game theory and takes some equilibrium solutions as the optimal policy. From this perspective, developing an algorithm to solve the game, namely to achieve the specified equilibrium, is of the most importance. The third perspective, best-response MARL, is to achieve a no-regret policy against other competitive agents.

In practice, as one may see from the descriptions above, these three perspectives of MARL have different features and different applicable domains. We must carefully distinguish between these three perspectives to apply MARL correctly. However, this task can sometimes be difficult due to the complexity of multi-agent systems. Therefore, we intend to develop a general method by combining these three main perspectives of MARL to deal with almost all the learning problems in multi-agent domain. We achieve our goal by examining the concept of *metagame* and *meta-equilibrium*. We then propose a general framework of MARL and a negotiation-based MARL algorithm later in this chapter.

The rest of the chapter is organized as follows. In the second section, we discuss three perspec-

tives of MARL technology and their state of arts. We compare these three perspectives of MARL and give the pseudo code for each of them. In the third section, we present a general framework of MARL and discuss negotiation-based MARL in detail. In the fourth section, we report some experiments conducted on the pursuit/prey grid world, and we investigate the performance of negotiation-based MARL. Finally, in the last section, we draw some conclusions and outline future work.

THREE PERSPECTIVES OF MARL

Cooperative MARL

One object of cooperative MARL is to solve the learning problem more effectively. Mutual interaction is the most important method in cooperative MARL. Tan (1993) gave three methods of exchanging information: exchanging states of environment, exchanging learning episodes (i.e., state, action, reward triplets), and exchanging policies or parameters. Nunes and Oliveira (2003) added the fourth method--exchanging advices. Later in 2005, this advice-exchange method was further used to cooperate between RL agents and agents using other learning methods such as evolutionary algorithm (Nunes & Oliveira, 2005).

The state-exchange method has been widely used in partially observable domains so that agents may have more complete information about the environment to improve their learning performance. Compared with state-exchange, episode-exchange often leads to a dilemma of how much information should be exchanged. Excessive exchange of information will result in poor exploration in search space. On the contrary, deficient exchange cannot help agents speed their learning. Another shortcoming of episode-exchange is that it needs high communication cost. Many researchers have indicated that the policy-exchange method is adequate for cooperative MARL. However, the best frequency of information exchange depends on the number of participating agents. Finally, in the recently developed advice-exchange method, an agent may ask for an advice when its performance drops below a certain threshold, which often relates to the average performance advertised by other agents.

All these information-exchange methods have proved that cooperative agents outperform independent agents by speeding their learning. As indicated by Plaza and Ontanon (2003), cooperative MARL is a distributed learning paradigm and can improve the performance like ensemble learning. Nowadays, the cooperative MARL technologies have been successfully applied to joint tasks such as coordination in multi-agent systems.

However, for the episode-exchange, policy-exchange, and advice-exchange methods, there are still some issues that have not been addressed properly. For example, when, why, and how to exchange information. Also, agents have little idea about the usefulness of a certain piece of information. Therefore, Nunes and Oliveira (2003) noted that:

A thorough analysis of the conditions in which this technique is advantageous is still necessary. It is important to discover how this technique performs when agents are not just communicating information about a similar learning problem, but attempting to solve the same problem in a common environment. (p. 45)

Cooperative MARL algorithms can be described by the pseudo code shown in Table 1, where I denotes the exchanged information and ξ is the generalized information exchanging operator. We define a new value function $Q_i'(s,a)$ in Step 2, after the agent has changed a piece of information. Then, in Step 3, we use this $Q_i'(s,a)$ to choose an action.

Equilibrium-Based MARL

Equilibrium-based MARL may be the most important MARL technology. Game theory provides us a powerful mathematical tool to model multi-agent systems and helps agents to make rational decisions. The notable idea of equilibrium-based MARL is to model multi-agent systems in Markov games.

Definition 1. An n-agent Markov game is a tuple $\langle N,S,(A_i(s))_{s\in S,1\leq i\leq n},T,(R_i)_{1\leq i\leq n}\rangle$. In this tuple, N is the set of n agents indexed from 1 to n; S is the set of the world's finite states; $A_i(s)$ is the set of agent i's finite strategies (actions) at state s; T is the state transition function in the form of $T(s,\vec{a},s')$, denoting the probability that event state s transits to state s' via joint strategy $\vec{a}$; and $T(s,\vec{a},s')$ is agent i's reward for taking a joint strategy $\vec{a}$ at state s.

In the n-agent Markov game, an agent's object is to find an optimal policy $\pi:S\rightarrow A$ to maximize its

Table 1. The pseudo code of cooperative MARL

<u>Step 1</u>. Agent i initializes $Q_i(s, a)$, learning factor α, discount factor γ, and exploration factor Pr;
<u>Step 2</u>. $Q_i'(s,a)\leftarrow\xi\left[Q_i(s,a),I\right]$;

Exchange information with other agents and modify value function.

<u>Step 3</u>. Select action $a\leftarrow\arg\max_a\left[Q_i'(s,a)\right]$ with probability Pr, select other actions with probability 1-Pr;
<u>Step 4</u>. Receive the experience $(s, \vec{a}, s', r)$;
<u>Step 5</u>. $Q_i(s,a)=(1-\alpha)Q(s,a)+\alpha\left[r+\gamma V_i(s')\right]$;
Modify current the state-action value according to the current reward and the value of next state;
<u>Step 6</u>. $V_i(s')\leftarrow\max_{a\in A_i}Q_i(s,a)$;
Use a greedy policy to update V-values.
<u>Step 7</u>. Return step 2.

expected total reward. Although the independent Q-learning algorithm can be directly applied to a multi-agent domain, it cannot reach an optimal solution in most cases due to the loss of stationarity. Therefore, it is necessary to introduce Nash equilibrium and other equilibria to describe an optimal policy in multi-agent systems.

Definition 2. The joint strategy $\vec{a}(s) = (a_1(s), \cdots, a_n(s))$ of n agents at state s is a Nash equilibrium if and only if $R_i(s, \vec{a}) = \max_{a' \in A_i(s)} R_i(s, a_1, \cdots, a_{i-1}, a', a_{i+1}, \cdots, a_n)$ holds for any $i \in \{1, 2, ..., n\}$. In other words, in the Nash equilibrium, each agent chooses a strategy that is a best response to the other agents' joint strategy, and no one can get a higher reward by changing its strategy alone. Here, a mixed strategy is a probability distribution over the agent's pure strategies.

There is no pure-strategy Nash equilibrium in many games, but it has been proven that there exists at least one mixed-strategy Nash equilibrium in any game. For example, the Nash equilibrium is a mixed strategy $(\frac{1}{3}, \frac{1}{3}, \frac{1}{3})$ in the rock-paper-scissors game (Figure 1). Now, most equilibrium-based MARL algorithms use some varieties of the Nash equilibrium. For example, Littman (1994) proposed the minimax solution for zero-sum stochastic games. Hu and Wellman (1998, 2003) made a pivotal contribution by introducing Nash Q-learning to general-sum games. Littman (2001) replaced Nash Q-learning by Friend-or-Foe Q-learning in some special stochastic games. Furthermore, Greenwald, Hall and Serrano (2003) introduced the concept of correlated equilibrium and proposed CE Q-learning to generalize both Nash Q-learning and Friend-or-Foe Q-learning methods.

Table 2 shows the general pseudo code of equilibrium-based MARL algorithms. In the table, Ξ is the function to achieve a certain equilibrium solution such as Nash equilibrium. In Step 2,

this equilibrium strategy is taken as an optimal strategy. Later, in Step 5, the equilibrium value of state s is used to update current V-value, which is much different from Step 6 in Table 1.

There are two essential properties for any equilibrium-based method: convergence and rationality. Generally speaking, a learning algorithm should achieve a stationary policy. And rationality means that the learning algorithm will converge to an optimal policy if other agents' policies become stationary.

One criticism for equilibrium-based MARL is why to focus on Nash equilibrium. In other words, is Nash equilibrium really optimal? Sometimes the answer is no. Figure 2 shows the famous Prisoners' Dilemma. There each prisoner has two alternative actions, either cooperate with his complicity or betray. Prisoners will receive different punishment for different joint action of course. It is well known that (*betray*, *betray*) is the only Nash equilibrium. However, intuitively, the optimal joint strategy should be (*cooperate*, *cooperate*) rather than (*betray*, *betray*) because prisoners might get a better reward if they cooperated. Clearly, this has shown a contradiction between individual rationality and collective rationality. Thus, we expect a better definition of *rationality* and *equilibrium*.

Best-Response MARL

Different from equilibrium-based MARL, best-response MARL aims to achieve optimal policies regardless of other agents' policies. The idea of best-response MARL is that an agent models its opponents' policies and then chooses its best policy according to the model.

As indicated by Bowling (2004), there are also two essential properties for a best-response MARL algorithm, convergence and no-regret. The property of convergence is the same as that of equilibrium-based MARL. A self-playing best-response MARL algorithm should converge to

Figure 1. Rock-paper-scissors

		Agent 2		
		rock	paper	scissors
Agent 1	rock	(0,0)	(-1,1)	(1,-1)
	paper	(1,-1)	(0,0)	(-1,1)
	scissors	(-1,1)	(1,-1)	(0,0)

some equilibrium solutions. Also, the no-regret property means that an algorithm has a non-positive average regret. Here the word *regret* is formally defined as follow.

Definition 3. In MARL, regret p_i that agent i feels for playing strategy ρ_i' rather than a pure strategy ρ_i is the difference between two rewards received by playing the above strategies, assuming that other agents play joint strategy ρ_{-i}.

$$p_i(\rho_i, \rho_i') = r_i(\rho_i \mid \rho_{-i}) - r_i(\rho_i' \mid \rho_{-i}) \tag{1}$$

For a given ρ_{-i}, best-response strategy ρ_i^* is a strategy that keeps the regret p_i non-positive against any pure strategy ρ_i. That is, formally, the following equation 2:

$$\forall \rho_i, \lim p_i(\rho_i, \rho_i^* \mid \rho_{-i}) \le 0 \tag{2}$$

So far, there are mainly three methods in best-response MARL. The first is PHC algorithm,

where PHC stands for policy hill climbing. It maintains and updates its own policy according to its learning history to maximize its rewards (Chang & Kaelbling, 2001). The second method is called opponent modeling. An agent estimates its opponents' joint policy according to its observation history, then it chooses a best response based on its estimation (Claus & Boutilier, 1998; Uther & Veloso, 1997; Weinberg & Rosenschein, 2004). The third method is IGA (infinitesimal gradient algorithm) and its variations such as GIGA, WoLF and GIGA-WoLf. These algorithms use the gradient technique to improve an agent's strategy so as to increase its expected reward (Bowling, 2004; Bowling & Veloso, 2002; Singh, Kearns & Mansour, 2000).

Table 3 shows the pseudo code of best-response MARL. In Table 3, $\alpha(s)$ is an agent's current strategy and $\beta(s)$ is other agents' joint strategy in state s. The agent chooses its action according to $Q(s, a)$, $\alpha(s)$ and the estimated $\beta(s)$. Function Y in Step 2 denotes this action selection process. After receiving its experience, a best-response agent must further optimize $\alpha(s)$ and reestimate $\beta(s)$. Functions Φ and ψ in Step 6 denote the optimization and estimation processes.

Now we can make a brief summary about these three perspectives of MARL. The problem space, frequently used algorithms, main criteria of MARL are listed in Table 4.

Table 2. The pseudo code of equilibrium-based MARL

<u>Step 1</u>: Initialization. $\forall s \in S, \forall i \in N, Q_i(s, \vec{a}) = 0$; Initialize α, γ, Pr;

<u>Step 2</u>: Select action $\vec{a} \leftarrow \Xi_{\vec{a}} [Q_1(s, \vec{a}), \cdots, Q_N(s, \vec{a})]$ with probability Pr, while select other actions with probability $1-Pr$;

<u>Step 3</u>: Receive the experience $(s, \vec{a}, s', r)$;

<u>Step 4</u>: $Q_i(s, \vec{a}) = (1-\alpha)Q_i(s, \vec{a}) + \alpha[r + \gamma V_i(s')]$;

Modify the current state-action value according to the current reward and the value of next state;

<u>Step 5</u>: $V_i(s) \leftarrow Q_i(s, \vec{a})$, where $\vec{a} = \Xi_{\vec{a}}[Q_1(s, \vec{a}), \cdots, Q_N(s, \vec{a})]$

Update the V-values based on some forms of equilibrium $\vec{a}$ in the game defined by the Q-values.

<u>Step 6</u>: Go to Step 2.

Figure 2. The prisoners' dilemma

$$
\begin{array}{c}
\quad\quad\quad\quad\quad Agent\ 2 \\
\quad\quad\quad\quad\quad betray \quad cooperate \\
Agent\ 1 \quad
\begin{array}{c}
betray \\
cooperate
\end{array}
\left(
\begin{array}{cc}
(-9,-9) & (0,-10) \\
(-10,0) & (-1,-1)
\end{array}
\right)
\end{array}
$$

A GENERAL FRAMEWORK OF MARL

A General Framework

We introduced three main perspectives of MARL in the second section. Clearly, there are many differences between them, which are illustrated by their pseudo codes. In our opinion, there are two major differences.

Firstly, different methods are employed to choose an action in a single learning cycle. Cooperative agents directly exchange information. Oppositely, best-response agents never exchange information. They model each other instead. Similar to equilibrium-based agents, they solve games. However, there is an implicit hypothesis

that each agent knows other agents' actual value functions. This hypothesis is necessary because it is the current Q-values that form a so-called *game*. In our opinion, this hypothesis actually means information exchange. That is, essentially, the same with cooperative MARL. Secondly, different methods are employed to update value functions. Cooperative agents and best-response agents use $\max_{a \in A_i} Q_i(s, a)$, namely the greedy policy. Equilibrium-based agents use a specified equilibrium in the current game. The discussion here is briefly summarized in Table 5.

Based on the discussion above, we integrate these three different methods into a general MARL framework in order to handle almost all learning problems in multi-agent systems. The general framework is illustrated in Figure 3. Note that the correct program flow should be determined at runtime. In section three, we propose a negotiation-based MARL algorithm as an instance of the general framework.

Metagame and Meta-Equilibrium

When the agents' rewards for different joint actions become common knowledge, one agent

Table 3. The pseudo codes of best-response MARL

Step 1: Initialization. $\forall s \in S, \forall i \in N, \forall a, Q_i(s,a) = 0$; Initialize $\alpha, \gamma, Pr; \alpha(s), \beta(s)$;
Step 2: $a \leftarrow \arg\max_a Y\left[Q_i(s,a), \alpha(s), \beta(s)\right]$.

Select action a with probability Pr, or select other actions with probability $1 - Pr$;

Step 3: Receive the experience $(s, a, -a, s', r)$;
Step 4: $Q_i(s,a) = (1-\alpha)Q_i(s,a) + \alpha\left[r + \gamma V_i(s')\right]$;

Update the current state-action value according to the reward and the value of the next state;

Step 5: $V_i(s) \leftarrow \max_{a \in A_i} Q_i(s,a)$;

Update the V-value according the greedy policy.

Step 6: $\alpha(s) \leftarrow \Phi\left[(s,a,-a,s',r), \alpha(s)\right]; \beta(s) \leftarrow \Psi\left[(s,a,-a,s',r), \beta(s)\right]$;

Further optimize $\alpha(s)$ and reestimate $\beta(s)$.

Step 7: Go to Step 2.

Table 4. Three perspectives of MARL

	Problem space	Algorithms	Criteria
Cooperative MARL	Distributive, homogenous, cooperative multi-agent system	Exchange states	Learning speed
		Exchange episodes	
		Exchange policies	
		Exchange advices	
Equilibrium-based MARL	Homogenous or heterogeneous, cooperative or competitive multi-agent system	Minmax-Q	Convergence to equilibrium
		Friend-or-Foe Q	
		Nash-Q	
		CE-Q	
Best-response MARL	Heterogeneous multi-agent system	PHC	No-regret
		NSCP-learner	
		IGA	

Table 5. Differences between three perspectives of MARL

Perspectives of MARL	Methods for choosing action	Updating methods
Cooperative MARL	Exchange information	Use the greedy policy
Equilibrium-based MARL	Exchange information	Use a specified equilibrium
Best-response MARL	Observe, model, and estimate	Use the greedy policy

will make its policy optimal if it deliberates its preference and predicts other agents' policies. This is the most important principle of metagame theory.

Metagame was first introduced by Howard (Thomas, 1984). It is a hypothetical game derived from the basic game by assuming that other agents have taken their actions first. Figure 4 represents a metagame derived from the Prisoner' Dilemma that is already illustrated in Figure 2.

In this metagame, agent 2 has four different strategies, or *reaction functions*, f_1, f_2, f_3, and f_4. $f_1(*) \equiv$ '*betray*', meaning that agent 2 always chooses action "*betray*" regardless of agent 1's action. Similarly, $f_2(*) \equiv$ '*cooperate*'. Then, $f_3(betray) = $ '*betray*', $f_3(cooperate) = $ '*cooperate*', $f_4(betray) = $ '*cooperate*', $f_3(cooperate) = $ '*betray*'. It is obvious that (*betray*, f_3) is a Nash equilibrium of the metagame, thus (*betray*, *betray*) is called a *meta-equilibrium* of the original game.

As a notation, if we extend agent i's strategies to reaction functions in a game G, then the metagame iG is constructed. Certainly, we can further extend agent j's strategies in iG, then we get metagame jiG. In general, for a n-person base game G, we can construct its metagame $k_1 k_2 \cdots k_m G$, where k_1, k_2, $\cdots k_m \in \{1, 2, \cdots, n\}$.

Definition 4. A joint strategy $\vec{s} = (s_1, s_2, \cdots, s_n)$ is called a meta-equilibrium of game G, if it can be derived from a pure Nash equilibrium $\vec{s}'$ of some metagame $k_1 k_2 \cdots k_m G$. Here, k_1, k_2, $\cdots k_m \in \{1, 2, \cdots, n\}$ and the word "derive" means to evaluate the reaction functions.

As a more direct criterion, Thomas (1984) proved a sufficient and necessary condition of meta-equilibrium, which can be considered as an identical definition of meta-equilibrium.

Figure 3. A general framework of MARL

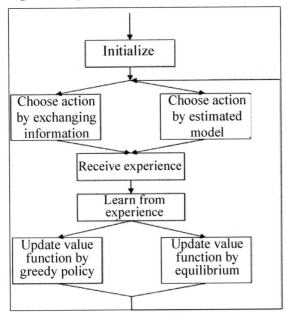

Definition 4'. A joint strategy $\vec{s} = (s_1, s_2, \cdots, s_n)$ is called a meta-equilibrium of game G from metagame $k_1 k_2 \cdots k_n G$ if for any i there holds:

$$\min_{s_{P_i}} \max_{s_i} \min_{s_{F_i}} R_i(s_{P_i}, s_i, s_{F_i}) \le R_i(\vec{s}) \qquad (3)$$

where P_i is the set of agents listed before sign i in prefixes $k_1 k_2 \cdots k_n$ and F_i is the set of agents listed after sign i.

Definition 5. For n-person Friend-or-Foe game G, metagame τG is also called a complete game if prefix τ is some permutation of 1, 2, $\cdots$, n.

Definition 6. A meta-equilibrium $\vec{s} = (s_1, s_2, \cdots, s_n)$ is said to be symmetric if it can be derived from all complete games.

Definition 7. A joint strategy $\vec{s}_1 = (s_{11}, s_{12}, \cdots, s_{1n})$ is said to be Pareto dominated by another joint strategy $\vec{s}_2 = (s_{21}, s_{22}, \cdots, s_{2n})$ if for any $i \in \{1, 2, \cdots, n\}$ there holds $r_i(\vec{s}_1) \le r_i(\vec{s}_2)$.

We proved several properties of meta-equilibrium.

Proposition 1. Every game has at least one meta-equilibrium.

Proposition 2. In any game G, if joint strategy $\vec{s}$ is a pure Nash equilibrium, then it is also a symmetric meta-equilibrium.

Proposition 3. In any game G, if $\vec{s}_1$ is a pure Nash equilibrium and Pareto dominated by joint pure strategy $\vec{s}_2$, then $\vec{s}_2$ is a symmetric meta-equilibrium.

The actual behavior of a meta-rational agent is that it considers other agents' interests as well as its own interest. As equation (3) tells us, a meta-rational agent will get quite satisfied if its interest is not less than a certain value. However, we can see from Definition 2 that a Nash-rational agent feels satisfied only if its interest goes to a maximum. It seems that meta-rational agents are somewhat foolish, but it is not true since the

Figure 4. Metagame 2G of prisoners' dilemma game G

		Agent 2			
		f_1	f_2	f_3	f_4
Agent 1	betray	$(-9, -9)$	$(0, -10)$	$(-9, -9)$	$(0, -10)$
	cooperate	$(-10, 0)$	$(-1, -1)$	$(-1, -1)$	$(-10, 0)$

Table 6. Negotiation algorithm for achieving meta-equilibrium

<u>Step 1</u>: Initialization. $J_1 \leftarrow NULL$

<u>Step 2</u>: Action 1 chooses a joint strategy $(a, b) \notin J_1$;

<u>Step 3</u>: If $Q_1(s, a, b) = \max\limits_{x \in A} Q_1(s, x, b)$, then $J_1 \leftarrow J_1 + (a, b)$, go to Step 1; else, $a' \leftarrow \arg\max\limits_{x \in A} Q_1(s, x, b)$, record (a', b) and go to Step 4;

<u>Step 4</u>: Agent 1 broadcasts a message to agent 2 and ask agent 2 to judge if $Q_2(s, a', b) = \max\limits_{y \in B} Q_2(s, a', y)$ is satisfied.

    <u>Step 4.1</u>: If yes, agent 2 sends a 'SUCCESS MESSAGE' to agent 1. Then agent 1 perform $J_1 \leftarrow J_1 + (a', b)$ and go to Step 1;

    <u>Step 4.2</u>: If no, agent 2 sends a 'FAIL MESSAGE' to agent 1. After receiving this message, agent 1 records the (a', b') where $b' = \arg\max\limits_{y \in B} Q_2(s, a', y)$, then go to Step 5;

<u>Step 5</u>: Agent 1 judges whether $Q_1(s, a', b') \geq Q_1(s, a, b)$. If the relation is satisfied, then go to Step 1, else $J_1 \leftarrow J_1 + (a, b)$ and then go to Step 1.

<u>Step 6</u>: When all agents get their rational joint action sets, the meta-equilibria can be obtained by performing $J_1 \cap J_2$.

Table 7. Algorithm for negotiation-based MARL

<u>Step 1</u>: Initialization. $\forall s \in S, \forall i \in I, \forall \vec{a}$, initialize $Q_i(s, \vec{a}), \alpha, \gamma, Pr, Be$;

<u>Step 2</u>: Select action. Agent i chooses action $a_{i,m}$ with probability $Pr \times Be$, chooses the greedy action with probability $Pr \times (1 - Be)$, or chooses a random action with probability $1 - Pr$;

<u>Step 3</u>: Observation. Agent i observes reward r_i, other agents' action a_{-i}, and next state s';

<u>Step 4</u>: Negotiation. Agents negotiate with each other to get meta-equilibrium $\vec{a}_m(s')$ at s';

<u>Step 5</u>: Learning. Agents update their Q-values:

$$Q_i(s, \vec{a}) = Q_i(s, \vec{a}) + \alpha [r_i(s, \vec{a}) + \gamma Q_i(s', \vec{a}_m(s')) - Q_i(s, \vec{a})]$$

<u>Step 6</u>: Measure other agents' belief. If $a_{-i} = a_{-i,m}$, $Be = Be + \delta$. Else, $Be = Be - \delta$.

<u>Step 7</u>: Modify learning rate α and selection factor Pr, and then go to step 2.

propositions above guarantee a better collective rationality.

In case of cooperation, agents may exchange their Q-values and compute meta-equilibrium directly according to Definition 4. However, in many cases, it is improper to assume that agents exchange their Q-values. In these cases, a negotiation process can be used to achieve meta-equilibrium. We discuss this algorithm in the case of two-person game for convenience.

Based on this negotiation algorithm and the general framework of MARL, we have a MetaQ learning algorithm, shown in Table 7. Here we simply assume that both agents are meta-rational, so they negotiate with each other to achieve a meta-equilibrium. In other cases, for example, if the opponent is a best-response agent, a slight modification to the algorithm is needed, so that the negotiation process degenerates to a best-response process.

Figure 5. A pursuit problem in a grid world

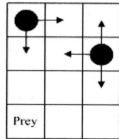

EXPERIMENTS AND DISCUSSION

Pursuit Problem

The pursuit problem has been widely examined in multi-agent learning domain. We employ a simple pursuit test-bed to compare negotiation-based MARL with other algorithms. In a 4×3 grid

Figure 6. The average success steps of three learning algorithms

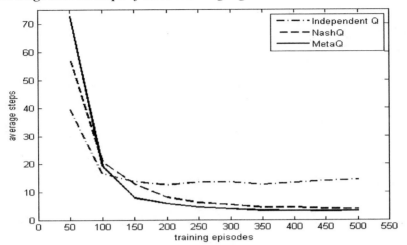

world, there are two predator agents and one prey agent. The initial positions of the three agents are set shown in Figure 5, and the prey agent is immovable in this test-bed. A predator has five possible actions: left, right, up, down, and stay. We assume that the predators capture the prey when they occupy two of its neighbor positions.

At each step, each predator simultaneously chooses and performs one action. When it tries to run against the wall of the grid world, it will fail and get a reward of -0.2. If both predators attempt to occupy the same position, they both fail and get a reward of -0.5. When predators capture the prey, they both receive a reward of 1. In other cases, predators' rewards are 0. Obviously, the optimal solution to this problem takes three moving steps.

In our experiment, we compare our negotiation-based MARL with Nash Q-learning algorithm and independent Q-learning algorithm. We conduct 10 tests. In each test, the game is played 500 times. We record the medium value and average value of capture steps in each learning episodes.

The results are shown in Figure 6. MetaQ and NashQ approximate the optimal steps after 500 episodes. However, the independent Q-learner will finally take more than 10 steps to capture the

prey. Thus, we can conclude that a negotiation-based learner and NashQ learner can converge to an optimal policy for self-play, which is much better than independent Q-learning.

Moreover, we can see, from the figure, that the curves of MetaQ and NashQ are very close in this experiment. NashQ behaves better than MetaQ in earlier learning episodes, but after about 100 episodes, MetaQ becomes better. Though the difference between MetaQ and NashQ is not remarkable, it is very important to note that MetaQ approximates the performance of NashQ without solving Nash equilibria. In fact, solving Nash equilibria is such an arduous task it may take an exponential complexity in the worst case (Murty, 1978).

A Grid-World Game

We also test our MetaQ algorithm in a grid-world game described by Hu and Wellman (2003). In this grid-world game, as shown in Figures 7 and 8, two agents start from positions 0 and 2. Their destinies are positions 8 and 6, respectively. Each agent moves one step a time, and there are only four possible actions in all: left, right, up, and down. Reaching the destiny brings an agent a reward of 100. Both agents will be rewarded if

Figure 7. The grid-world game

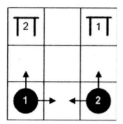

Figure 8. Indices of the grid-world

6	7	8
3	4	5
0	1	2

Figure 9. The performance of MetaQ vs. Independent Q, NashQ, and MetaQ

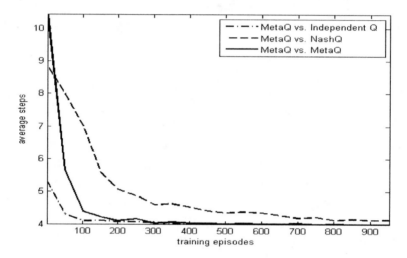

both agents reach their destinies at the same time. However, agents will be punished with a reward of -1 and bounced back to their previous positions if they attempt to enter the same position. In other cases, agents just make their movements and get a reward of 0. Learning algorithms are therefore expected to acquire a winning strategy with least steps and no collisions.

We train those agents by episodes. In each episode, the training process stops as soon as one agent reaches its destiny, then the game restarts. In this experiment, agent 1 always uses MetaQ algorithm, whereas agent 2 may use independent Q-learning, NashQ, or MetaQ. It is easy to see that in this game the optimal strategy will take exactly four steps.

For each combination of algorithms we repeated 10 experiments with an initial learning rate of 0.1. Each experiment is composed of 250 episodes. Our results are shown in Figure 9.

The figure shows that all three curves are convergent to the theoretic optimal value. There is a slight deviation between the optimum and dashed curve (MetaQ vs. NashQ), which is caused by the lower speeds of convergence. In fact, if we increase the number of training episodes, for example, to 1,500, this dashed curve will reach the optimum as well.

For further discussion, we then focus on the solid curve (MetaQ vs. MetaQ). This curve decreases rapidly during the first 100 episodes, and after 400 episodes it stays stably at optimum. This can be considered as an illustration of the outstanding performance of MetaQ algorithm.

The dash-dot curve (MetaQ vs. Independent Q) is somewhat special. In this curve, the maximal value is about 5.5, which is much smaller than those of other curves. Also, the dash-dot curve decreases rapidly, too. It stays at optimum after about 300 episodes. We think it is because independent Q-learning is simple and naive, so MetaQ can easily understand its opponent and then make correct decisions.

On the contrary, NashQ algorithm and its Nash rationality are much more complex compared to Independent Q-learning. Therefore, it is expected that MetaQ takes more time to understand its opponent. We think that this is one reason for the relatively low speed of decrease and convergence of the dashed curve in Figure 9.

CONCLUSION

In this chapter, we conclude the principles and features of three perspectives of MARL. Then, we integrate three perspectives of MARL into a general framework. Based on this general framework and metagame theory, we propose a negotiation-based MARL. In the experiment section, we compare the performances of three MARL algorithms, independent Q, NashQ, and MetaQ, in a pursuit problem and a grid world game. Our results show that the negotiation-based MARL, MetaQ algorithm, has the best convergence performance when self-played, and it can relate well to other two learning algorithms.

Two important directions remain to be pursued in the future. One includes further investigation of this negotiation-based method, especially in some competitive multi-agent systems. The other direction is to compare MetaQ to other learning methods theoretically.

ACKNOWLEDGMENT

We would like to acknowledge support for this project from the National Science Foundation of China (NSFC grant No.60475026 and No.60325207) and the National Grand Fundamental Research 973 Program of China (grant No.2002CB312002).

REFERENCES

Bowling, M. (2004). Convergence and no-regret in multiagent learning. *Advances in Neural Information Processing Systems, 17*, 209-216.

Bowling, M., & Veloso, M. (2002). Multiagent learning using a variable learning rate. *Artificial Intelligence, 136*(2), 215-250.

Chang, Y. H., & Kaelbling, L. P. (2001). Playing is believing: The role of beliefs in multi-agent learning. *Advances in Neural Information Processing Systems, 14*, 1483-1490.

Claus, C., & Boutilier, C. (1998). The dynamics of reinforcement learning in cooperative multiagent systems. In *Proceedings of the 15th National / 10th Conference on Artificial Intelligence / Innovative Applications of Artificial Intelligence* (pp. 746-752). Madison, WI: American Association for Artificial Intelligence Press.

Greenwald A., Hall K., & Serrano, R. (2003). Correlated-q learning. In T. Fawcett and N. Mishra (Eds.), *Proceedings of the 20th International Conference on Machine Learning* (pp. 242-249). Washington, DC: American Association for Artificial Intelligence Press.

Hu, J., & Wellman, M. (1998). Multiagent reinforcement learning: theoretical framework and an algorithm. In J. Shavlik (Ed.), *Proceedings of the 15th International Conference on Machine Learning* (pp. 242-250). Madison, WI: Morgan Kaufmann Publishers.

Hu, J., & Wellman, M. (2003). Nash q-learning for general-sum stochastic games. *Journal of Machine Learning Research, 4*(11), 1039-1069.

Kaelbling, L. P., & Littman, M. L. (1996). Reinforcement learning: A survey. *Journal of Artificial Intelligence Research, 4,* 237-285.

Littman, M. L. (1994). Markov games as a framework for multi-agent reinforcement learning. In W. Cohen and H. Hirsh (Eds.), *Eleventh International Conference on Machine Learning* (pp. 157-163). New Brunswick: Morgan Kaufmann Publishers.

Littman, M. L. (2001). Friend-or-foe q-learning in general-sum games. In C. E. Brodley & A. P. Danyluk (Eds.), *Proceedings of the 18ᵗʰ International Conference on Machine Learning* (pp. 322-328). Williamstown, MA: Morgan Kaufmann Publishers.

Murty, K. G. (1978). Computational complexity of complementary pivot methods. In *Mathematical programming study: vol. 7. Complementary and fixed point problems* (pp. 61-73). Amsterdam: North-Holland Publishing Co.

Nunes, L., & Oliveira, E. (2003). Cooperative learning using advice exchange. In E. Alonso (Ed.), *Adaptive agents and multiagent systems, lecture notes in computer science: Vol. 2636* (pp. 33-48). Berlin, Heidelberg, Germany: Springer-Verlag.

Nunes, L., & Oliveira, E. (2005). Advice-exchange between evolutionary algorithms and reinforcement learning agents: Experiments in the pursuit domain. In D. Kudenko, D. Kazakov, & E. Alonso (Eds.), *Adaptive agents and multi-agent systems:*

vol. 2. Adaptation and multi-agent learning (pp. 185-204).

Plaza, E., & Ontanon, S. (2003). Cooperative multiagent learning. In E. Alonso (Ed.), *Adaptive agents and MAS, Lecture Notes on Artificial Intelligence: Vol. 2636* (pp. 1-17). Berlin, Heidelberg: Springer-Verlag.

Singh, S., Kearns, M., & Mansour, Y. (2000). Nash convergence of gradient dynamics in general-sum games. In C. Boutilier and M. Goldszmidt (Eds.), *Proceedings of the 16ᵗʰ Conference on Uncertainty in Artificial Intelligence* (pp. 541-548). San Francisco: Morgan Kaufmann Publishers.

Tan, M. (1993). Multi-agent reinforcement learning: Independent vs. cooperative agents. In M. N. Huhns and M. P. Singh (Eds.), *Proceedings of the Tenth International Conference on Machine Learning* (pp. 330-337). Amherst, MA: Morgan Kaufmann Publishers.

Thomas, L. C. (Ed.). (1984). *Games, theory and applications.* Chichester: Halsted Press.

Uther, W., & Veloso, M. (1997). *Adversarial reinforcement learning* (Tech. Rep. CMU-CS-03-107). Pittsburgh, PA: Carnegie Mellon University, School of Computer Science.

Weinberg, M., & Rosenschein, J. (2004). Best-response multiagent learning in non-stationary environments. In *The Third International Joint Conference on Autonomous Agents and Multi-Agent Systems: Vol. 2* (pp. 506-513). Washington, DC: IEEE Computer Society.

Chapter XIII
Modeling Knowledge and Reasoning in Conversational Recommendation Agents

Maria Salamó
University College Dublin, Ireland

Barry Smyth
University College Dublin, Ireland

Kevin McCarthy
University College Dublin, Ireland

James Reilly
University College Dublin, Ireland

Lorraine McGinty
University College Dublin, Ireland

ABSTRACT

This chapter introduces conversational recommender agents that facilitate user navigation through a product space, alternatively making concrete product suggestions and eliciting the user's feedback. Critiquing is a common form of user feedback, where users provide limited feedback at the feature-level by constraining a feature's value-space. For example, a user may request a cheaper product, thus critiquing the price feature. One of the most important objectives in a recommender agent is to discover, with minimal user feedback, which are the user's product preferences. For this purpose, the chapter includes recent research on critiquing-based recommendation and a comparison between standard and recent proposals of recommendation based on critiquing.

INTRODUCTION

Recommender systems help users to navigate through complex product spaces as they search for their preferred products. They do this by drawing on ideas and technologies from areas such as information retrieval, artificial intelligence, and user modeling, among others, to provide users with more proactive and personalized information services. *Conversational, case-based recommender systems* (Aha, Breslow, & Muñoz-Avila, 2000), in particular, are set to play an increasingly important role in many e-commerce applications. This type of recommender system helps user navigation as part of an extended recommendation process. During each *recommendation cycle*, the recommender agent suggests a new product (or products) to the user and solicits feedback in order to refine its search during subsequent cycles. In this way, conversational recommender systems seek to incrementally learn about a user's product preferences. Subsequent cycles prioritize products among the available options that best satisfy these evolving preferences. Ideally, each recommendation cycle relocates the user to a part of the product space that is closer to their target product. The conversational approach provides users with greater control over the navigation process and has the potential to deliver more efficient recommendation dialogs that involve minimal interaction with the user (Burke, Hammond, & Young, 1997; McGinty & Smyth, 2002; Shimazu, 2002).

Survey of Related Work

Considerable research effort has been invested in developing and evaluating different forms of feedback for conversational recommender agents, and a variety of feedback alternatives have become commonplace. For example, *value elicitation* approaches ask the user to provide details relating to specific features (e.g., "what is your target price?") while *preference-based* feedback and *ratings-based* methods simply ask the user to indicate which product they prefer when presented with a small set of alternatives (McGinty & Smyth, 2002; McGinty & Smyth, 2003a; Smyth & McGinty, 2003b) or to provide ratings for these alternatives (Smyth & Cotter, 2000). It is well known that different forms of feedback introduce different types of trade-offs when it comes to recommendation efficiency and user-effort. For instance, value elicitation is a very informative form of feedback, but it requires the user to provide very specific feature-level information. In contrast, preference-based feedback is a far more ambiguous form of feedback but it requires only minimal user effort. One form of feedback that strikes a useful balance, in this regard, is *critiquing* (Burke, Hammond, & Young, 1996; Burke et al., 1997). The user expresses a *directional preference* over the value-space for a particular product feature. For example, in a travel vacation recommender, a user might indicate that they are interested in a vacation that is *longer* than the currently recommended option; in this instance, *longer* is an example of a critique over the *duration* feature.

Within the recommender systems literature, the basic idea of critiquing can be traced back to the seminal work of Burke et al. (1995, 1997). For example, Entrée is the quintessential recommender system that employs critiquing (also sometimes referred to as *tweaking*) in the restaurant domain, allowing users to critique restaurant features such as *price, style, atmosphere,* and so forth. The advantage of critiquing is that it is a fairly lightweight form of feedback, in the sense that the user does not need to provide a specific *feature value* in order to refine their search towards relevant recommendations (McGinty & Smyth, 2003). In recent years, researchers have highlighted the importance of investigating techniques for reasoning of implicit preference knowledge while requiring minimal information input from the user (McSherry & Stretch, 2005). As recommender systems have become more commonplace, there has been a major focus on increasing the efficiency of recommendation dialogues that rely on critiquing as the primary mode of user feedback (Burke, 2002; Faltings, Pu, Torrens, & Viappiani, 2004; McCarthy, Reilly, McGinty, & Smyth, 2004a; Nguyen, Ricci, & Cavada, 2004; Pu & Kumar, 2004; Sherin & Lieberman, 2001).

Description of the Chapter

The aim of this chapter is two-fold: (1) to provide an introduction to case-based conversational recommendation techniques, and (2) to describe recent research in critiquing-based recommendation as a means to introduce our novel conversational recommendation agent-based architecture (see Figure 1). In addition, we will also provide details on the various sources of knowledge used in the recommendation process and the individual agents that are used to make product suggestions (i.e., the *recommend* agent), capture user feedback (i.e., the *review* agent), and update the user model (i.e., the *revise* agent).

One of the critical factors determining the success of conversational recommendation sys-

tems is the degree to which they can help users to navigate to satisfactory products in an efficient manner, with minimal user feedback (Aha, Maney, & Breslow, 1998; Doyle & Cunningham, 2000; McGinty & Smyth, 2002; McSherry, 2003a). In other words, all other things being equal, *short* recommendation sessions are more desirable than *long* recommendation sessions. However, critiquing-based feedback does not always lead to short recommendation sessions (McGinty & Smyth, 2003b). In this work, we propose to use a user's critiquing history as a vital form of user knowledge to guide the recommendation process. Unlike standard forms of critiquing where only the most recent feedback is used to filter and decide on the retrievals for the next recommendation cycle, we describe the notion of *incremental critiquing* where a user's prior critiquing history recorded over a sequence of cycles is also used to influence subsequent recommendations (Reilly, McCarthy, McGinty, & Smyth, 2004a).

We discuss *three* further improvements to the incremental critiquing model that leverages the critiquing history of a user in different ways to promote more efficient recommendation (i.e., reduce the length of the recommendation session

Figure 1. The conversational recommendation agent-based architecture

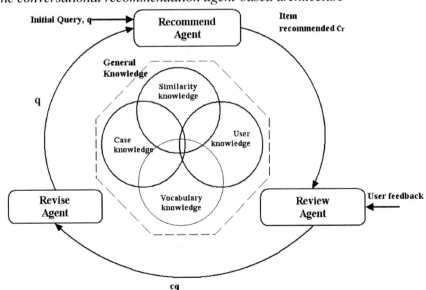

that a user needs to engage in). These are described briefly below:

- One of the shortcomings of standard critiquing is that an individual critique may result in a relatively minor progression through the product space. For instance, invoking a *cheaper* critique over a price value of $7000 could result in a product recommendation that is only *slightly cheaper* (e.g., $6990). If the value-space is large (e.g., $500 up to $10,000), this can lead to long recommendation sessions. We will describe a new technique for interpreting critiques that facilitates larger jumps through the product space by adopting a binary search of the value-space of a critiqued feature.

- We also describe a new technique for selecting a product to recommend in the next recommendation cycle, which looks at how compatible the available products are with the past critiques of the user.

- Finally, we introduce a feature weighting model that is tuned to a user's preferences and that facilitates a more personalized notion of product similarity during recommendation.

Importantly, this chapter will also present experimental evidence in support of the above three techniques, in isolation and in combination, when compared to the standard and the incremental models of critiquing. We will conclude with a discussion on the lessons that have been learned during this work, identifying some interesting areas for future work in agent-based recommender systems.

A REVIEW OF CRITIQUING

Recently researchers have begun to look more closely at critiquing and have suggested a number of ways that this form of feedback can be improved.

For example, McCarthy, McGinty, Smyth, and Reilly (2005a), McCarthy, Reilly, McGinty, and Smyth (2005b), McGinty and Smyth (2003a), McGinty and Smyth (2003b), and McSherry (2002) show how the efficiency of critiquing can be improved in a variety of ways, as discussed in the next section. However, a number of challenges remain when it comes to the practicalities of critiquing. Certainly, the lack of any continuity-analysis of the critiques provided in successive cycles means that recommender systems could be misled by inconsistent feedback provided by an uncertain user, especially during early recommendation cycles, as they broaden their understanding of the product domain.

Unit vs. Compound Critiques

Standard approaches to critiquing rely on so-called *unit critiques*. That is, they express preferences over a single feature: in Entrée, *cheaper* critiques a *price* feature, *more formal* critiques a *style* feature, for example. This ultimately limits the ability of the recommender to narrow its focus, because it is guided by only single-feature preferences from one cycle to the next.

An alternative strategy is to consider the use of what we call *compound critiques* (McCarthy et al., 2004a; Reilly, McCarthy, McGinty, & Smyth, 2004b). These are critiques that operate over multiple features. This idea of compound critiques is not novel per se. In fact, the seminal work of Burke et al. (1996) refers to critiques for manipulating multiple features. They give the example of the *sportier* critique, in a car navigator recommender, which operates over a number of different car features; (i.e., engine size, acceleration and price are all increased). Similarly, we might use a *high-performance* compound critique in a PC recommender to simultaneously increase processor speed, RAM, hard-disk capacity, and price features. Obviously compound critiques have the potential to improve recommendation efficiency because they allow the recommender

Figure 2. *Unit critiques and compound critiques in a sample digital camera recommender*

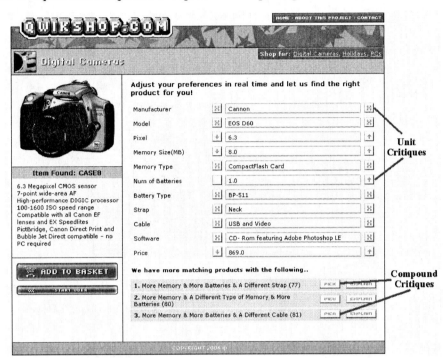

system to focus on multiple feature constraints within a single cycle. In addition, it has also been argued that they carry considerable explanatory power because they help the user to understand feature trade-offs (McCarthy, Reilly, McGinty, & Smyth, 2004b; Reilly et al., 2004b); in the PC example above, the user can easily understand that increased CPU speed and memory come at an increased price.

In the past when compound critiques have been used, they have been hard-coded by the system designer so that the user is presented with a fixed set of pre-defined compound critiques in each recommendation cycle. These compound critiques may, or may not, be relevant depending on the products (also known as *cases* in conversational recommendation literature) that remain at a given point in time. Recently, we have argued the need for a more dynamic approach to critiquing in which compound critiques are generated *on the fly*, during each recommendation cycle, by mining commonly

occurring patterns of feature characteristics that exist amongst the remaining cases (McCarthy et al., 2004a; Reilly et al., 2004b). Figure 2 shows a digital camera recommender system that we have developed to explore usability and efficiency issues in a real-world setting. The screenshot shows two types of critiques. Standard unit critiques are presented alongside each individual feature, while a set of k (where k=3) dynamically generated compound critiques appear below the *current case* description.

Regardless of the type of critiquing used (*unit* versus *compound*, or a mixture of both), or the manner in which the critiques have been generated (fixed versus dynamic), it is important to keep in mind that *strict filtering* policy is usually not employed by conversational recommender systems in practice. Instead of permanently filtering out incompatible cases, irrelevant cases for a particular cycle tend to be *temporarily removed* from consideration but may come to be reconsidered during future cycles as appropriate. Of course, this strategy introduces the related problem of how past critiques should influence future recommendations, especially if they conflict or strengthen the current critique.

KNOWLEDGE MODELING

The recommendation strategies presented in this chapter are built upon the *incremental critiquing* concept (Reilly et al., 2004a), where the idea is to consider a user's critiquing history as well as the current critique when making new recommendations. The incremental critiquing implementation assumes a conversational recommender system in the style of standard critiquing, as used by Burke et al. (1996).

From Standard Critiquing to Incremental Critiquing

The standard critiquing algorithm assumes a conversational recommender system in the likeness of Entrée (Burke et al., 1996). Each recommendation session starts with an initial user query, and this will result in the retrieval of the most similar case available in the first recommendation cycle. The user will have the opportunity to accept this case, thereby ending the recommendation session, or to critique this case as a means to influence retrievals in the next cycle. A simplified version of the basic algorithm is given in Figure 3 and consists of 3 key agents: (1) a new case c_r is *recommended* to the user based on the current query; (2) the user *reviews* the recommendation and applies a directional feature critique, cq; (3) the query, q is *revised* for the next cycle. The recommendation process terminates either when the user is presented with a suitable case, or when they give up.

A critique is a directional feature preference (e.g., *[price, <, $1000]* the user prefers a product with a *price* lower than $1000). Importantly, in the **Recommend_Agent**, when the user critiques

a case, the critique itself acts as a filter over the remaining cases (see line 11 in Figure 3), and the case chosen for the next cycle is that case that is compatible with the critique and which is maximally similar to the query, q (lines 12 and 13). The chosen case will be the next query (line 20). In other words, once a critique has been selected, the recommender first eliminates any items that are incompatible with this critique, and then selects the next recommendation from those that remain.

The incremental critiquing implementation (Reilly et al., 2004a) extends the standard critiquing algorithm (see Figure 4). The algorithm presents the key steps of the standard critiquing algorithm, but it adds an extra key step that consists of updating the user model. The algorithm maintains a critique-based user model that is made up of those critiques that have been chosen by the user so far. This model is used during recommendation to influence the choice of a new product case, along with the current critique. Our basic intuition is that the critiques that a user has applied so far provide a representation of their evolving requirements. Thus the set of critiques that the user has applied constitutes a type of user model ($U = \{U_1,..., U_n\}$, where U_i is a single unit critique) that reflects their current preferences. At the end of each cycle, after the user has selected a new critique, we add this critique to the user model.

The **UpdateModel_Agent** maintains an accurate user model. Nevertheless, is not quite as simple as storing a list of previously selected critiques; some critiques may be *inconsistent* with earlier critiques.

For example, in the case of a PC recommender, a user selecting a critique for *more memory* beyond the *512MB* of the recommended case during one cycle, may later *contradict* themselves by indicating a preference for *less memory* than the *256 MB* offered during a subsequent cycle. In addition, a user may *refine* his or her requirements over time. They might start, for example, by indicating a preference for more than *128 MB* of RAM

Figure 3. The standard critiquing algorithm

```
Input: < q: query, CB: CaseBase, cq: critique, c_r : current recommendation >

1.   define Standard_Critiquing(q, CB)          15.  define Review_Agent(c_r , CB)
2.   cq:= null                                  16.    cq ← user critique for some f ∈ c_r
3.   begin                                      17.    CB ← CB - c_r
4.      do                                      18.  return cq
5.         c_r ← Recommend_Agent(q, CB, cq, U)
6.         cq ← Review_Agent(c_r, CB)           19.  define Revise_Agent(q, c_r)
7.         q  ← Revise_Agent(q, c_r)            20.    q ← c_r
8.      until UserAccepts(c_r)                   21.  return q
9.   end

10.  define Recommend_Agent(q, CB, cq)
11.     CB' ← {c ∈ CB | Satisfies(c, cq)}
12.     CB' ← sort cases in CB' in decreasing order
              of their similarity to q
13.     c_r ← most similar case in CB'
14.  return c_r
```

Figure 4. The incremental critiquing algorithm

```
q: query, CB: CaseBase, cq: critique, c_r : current recommendation, U : User model

1.   define Incremental_Critiquing(q, CB)       17.  define Review_Agent(c_r , CB)
2.   cq:= null                                  18.    cq ← user critique for some f ∈ c_r
3.   U:= null                                   19.    CB ← CB - c_r
4.   begin                                      20.  return cq
5.      do
6.         c_r ← Recommend_Agent(q, CB, cq, U)  21.  define Revise_Agent(q, c_r)
7.         cq ← Review_Agent(c_r, CB)           22.    q ← c_r
8.         q  ← Revise_Agent(q, c_r)            23.  return q
9.         U  ← UpdateModel_Agent(U, cq, c_r)
10.     until UserAccepts(c_r)                   24.  define UpdateModel_Agent(U, cq, c_r)
11.  end                                        25.    U ← U - contradict(U, cq, c_r)
                                                26.    U ← U - refine(U, cq, c_r)
12.  define Recommend_Agent(q, CB, cq, U)       27.    U ← U + (<cq, c_r>)
13.     CB' ← {c ∈ CB | Satisfies(c, cq)}       28.  return U
14.     CB' ← sort cases in CB' in decreasing Quality
15.     c_r ← highest quality case in CB'
16.  return c_r
```

(with a *more memory* critique on a current case that offers *128 MB*). Later they might indicate a preference for more than *256 MB* of RAM with a *more memory* critique on a case that offers *256 MB*. In consideration of the above, our incremental critiquing strategy updates the user model by adding the latest critique only after pruning previous critiques of the same feature so as to eliminate these sorts of inconsistencies (see lines 24-28 in Figure 4). Specifically, prior to adding a new critique all existing critiques that are inconsistent with it are removed from the user model. Also, all existing critiques, for which the new critique is a refinement, are removed from the model.

The incremental critiquing implementation also modifies the **Recommend_Agent**. Instead of ordering the filtered cases on the basis of their similarity to the recommended case, it also computes a compatibility score for each candidate case, which is essentially the percentage of critiques in the user model that this case satisfies (see equation 1 and note that *satisfies* (U_i, c') returns a score of 1 when the critique U_i satisfies the filtered case, c, and returns 0 otherwise. Thus, a case that satisfies 3 out of the 5 critiques in a user model obtains a compatibility score of 0.6.

$$Compatibility(c',U) = \frac{\sum_{\forall i} satisfies(U_i, c')}{|U|}$$

Compatibility score (1)

$$Quality(c', c_r, U) =$$
$$Compatability(c', U) * Similarity(c', c_r)$$

Quality score (2)

This compatibility score is then combined with the candidate's (c') similarity to the recommended case, (c_r), in order to obtain an overall quality score; see equation 2. This quality score is used to rank-order the filtered cases prior to the next recommendation cycle, and the case with the highest quality is then chosen as the new recommendation (see lines 14-15 in Figure 4).

Sources of Knowledge in Recommender Systems

A recommender system can be seen from the point of view of the type of knowledge used for reasoning. The knowledge sources in a recommender system are divided in four main parts, or *containers* (Richter, 1998) as known on case-based reasoning literature. We adapt these containers to recommender systems, although we also consider four knowledge containers, as depicted in Figure 5. The relationship of the knowledge

containers with the recommender cycle can be seen in Figure 1.

A knowledge container is a collection of knowledge that is relevant to many tasks rather than to one. It is important to note that a knowledge container is not enough to complete the process of an agent. The four knowledge containers can be shared by different agents for several subtasks. They give some structure to the knowledge but can also be dependent on each other. For example, when the user knowledge is changed, this may also impact on the similarity function.

The four *knowledge containers* are: the *user knowledge*, the *vocabulary knowledge*, the *case knowledge,* and finally the *similarity knowledge*. The *user knowledge* contains all the information of the user preferences during the session, and it can be used by the **recommend** and **review** agents. It is used during recommendation to influence the choice of a new product case, along with the current critique. Maintaining accurate user knowledge, however, is not quite as simple as storing a list of previously selected critiques. Users may not always provide consistent feedback; sometimes they make mistakes or change their mind, which will manifest itself in the form of a sequence of conflicting critiques. To eliminate such preference inconsistencies, the *revise agent* updates the user knowledge by adding the latest critique only after pruning previous incompatible critiques (see lines 24-28 in Figure 4 and example in previous section).

The *vocabulary knowledge* covers everything that defines the system, for example, attributes, predicates, and the structure of the domain schema. In a recommender system, it is commonly based on a description of the attributes. For example, the personal computer (PC) dataset contains nine features like *price, type* of *manufacturer,* or *memory size.*

The *case knowledge*—also known as case base in case-based reasoning (Aamodt & Plaza, 1994; Kolodner, 1993; Riesbeck & Schank,

Figure 5. Knowledge containers in a recommender system

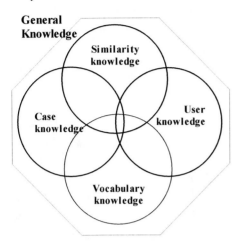

1989)—contains a description of each one of the products available to recommend. Each product is represented as a single *case,* and it is common to define each *product case* in terms of attribute-value pairs.

The knowledge that defines how the most useful case is retrieved and by what means the similarity is calculated is held by the *similarity knowledge.* The similarity knowledge in a recommender system identifies the most useful case between the recommended case and all the cases available for recommendation in the case knowledge. It is usually computed using equation 3, where the similarity between the candidate case (c') and the recommended case (c_r) for each feature f is combined with the weight for this feature. The weight is computed using equation 7.

$$Similarity(c',c_r) =$$

$$\sum_{\forall_f} weight(c'_f) \times similarity(c'_f, c_{r_f})$$

Computation of similarity inside the recommend agent (3)

Each knowledge container can be changed locally. Changes in one container have little ef-fect on the other containers. For example, adding new cases to the case base does not change the similarity measures. Of course, changing one knowledge container will have some impact on the other knowledge containers, but the knowledge containers view helps keeping changes local.

For this reason, efficiency of a recommend system usually depends on improving reasoning in one of the knowledge containers. In this chapter, the reasoning strategies focus on the use of user knowledge by the similarity and case knowledges.

REASONING WITH THE SOURCES OF KNOWLEDGE

We will argue that by its very nature there is a tendency for the standard form of critiquing to lead to relatively minor changes in the value of the critiqued feature from cycle to cycle.

For example, in a holiday recommender, the user might have received a recommendation for a luxury 2-week package in Spain for $2,000. She might be interested in something around the $1000 mark and so may indicate that they want something *cheaper.* However, the next recommendation might be for a $1,750 holiday and so they might again select the *cheaper* critique again and continue like this until a $1000 holiday is presented. This can lead to the type of repetitive feedback observed in live user trials (McCarthy et al., 2005a; Salamó, Smyth, McCarthy, Reilly, & McGinty, 2005c) and also to longer sessions. There is little to be gained from this type of in-teraction, and we present a simple modification to the traditional form of critiquing that facilitates larger jumps through the product space in order to focus in more rapidly on satisfactory product cases. Our response to these issues is to give due consideration to the past critiques during future recommendation cycles reasoning in a different way with knowledge of the recommender.

Using Range Values to Reduce Repetition

In this section, we describe how the standard critiquing algorithm can be easily altered to facilitate *larger jumps* through the value space for a given feature by taking a more efficient binary search approach.

Figure 6 demonstrates how the standard algorithm can be easily extended to support our proposed approach. The only procedure that is affected is the **Revise_Agent** step. Just as before, the new query is updated with all of the features from the current recommendation, c_r. In addition three new steps are added. First, the recommender agent gathers all of the available cases to the current feature critique (see line 4 of Figure 6). The second step focuses on one important point that concerns previous critiques on the same feature (see line 5 of Figure 6).

For example, to illustrate it, imagine that the user has asked in a previous cycle for a *less-expensive* vacation than a $2,500 recommendation. Thus, as detailed in line 6 of Figure 6, we compute the mean or the median with all those cases that satisfy a price lower than $2,500. Nevertheless, suppose that in the current cycle on the same session the user indicates that she prefers a *more expensive* vacation than the current $1,000 recommendation. Accordingly to the last critique, all

the cases, including those that exceed a $2,500 vacation, will satisfy the current critique *more expensive* than $1,000. Considering this situation, if we compute the mean or the median value to jump larger in the search space, we also include those cases rejected previously by the user. To avoid these situations, we maintain a history with all the critiques applied by the user in order to cut off the search space correctly. The history of critiques constitutes a type of *user model* (Reilly et al., 2004a) that reflects all the user preferences in the current session. The previous critiques stored in the user model are treated as a set of *soft constraints* (Stolze, 2000) that allow us to control the number of remaining cases that will be used to compute the mean or median values. Put differently, we use prior critiques to decide what cases should be covered by *CB'*, and to ultimately set the value selection bounds for f_{cq}. So, following the earlier example, we compute the mean or median of those cases that are *more expensive* than $1,000 and *less expensive* than $2,500.

Finally, the third step of the algorithm (see lines 6 and 7 of Figure 6) involves determining the value change the critiqued feature will take on in the revised query, *q*, used for retrieval of the next recommendation. Importantly, in our approach all the remaining cases, *CB'*, influence the final value. There are many approaches that could be used to compute this value. Here, we examine

Figure 6. Adapting the standard critiquing algorithm Revise_Agent to reduce critique repetition

```
Input: <q: query, CB: CaseBase, cq: critique, c_r : current recommendation>

1.    define Revise_Agent(q, cq, CB, c_r)
2.    begin
3.        q    ← c_r
4.        CB'  ← {c ∈ CB | Satisfies(c, cq)}
5.        CB'  ← eliminate cases that conflict with prior critiques
6.        f_cq ← Compute value for critiqued feature f ∈ cr by Eq. 4 or 5
7.        q    ← Set value f_cq in q
8.    return q
9.    end
```

two possibilities -- by computing the mean (see equation 4) or the median (see equation 5) for all cases in *CB'*. Note that f_{cq} is the value used in the algorithm of Figure 6.

$$f_{cq} = \frac{\sum_{\forall c} CB'_c (\text{feature } f \text{ critiqued by } cq)}{n}$$

Mean equation (4)

For both approaches the recommender agent collects all of the alternative value possibilities for the critiqued feature from the cases covered by *CB'*. For instance, if the critiqued feature were [price, <, $2,000] the recommender would gather all value options that were less than $2000 from the set of remaining cases (e.g., $1,800, $1,650, $1,600, $1,570, $1,460, $1,350, etc.). Equation 4 assigns a value for the critiqued feature $f_{cq} \in q$ by calculating the average feature value over all the relevant cases.

For equation 5 (see bottom of the page) it is assumed that the remaining case options, *CB'* are first sorted in ascending order. Here CB'_i (*f of cq*) is the feature value critiqued by *cq* in the ith case. The median value corresponds to a cumulative percentage of 50% (i.e., 50% of the values are below the median and 50% of the values are above the median).

Discovering Satisfactory Cases: Highest Compatibility Selection

A key problem with the standard incremental critiquing (Reilly et al., 2004a) approach is that there are no guarantees that the recommendations

it returns will completely satisfy a user's preferences. As detailed in Salamó Reilly, McGinty, and Smyth (2005a), this is largely due to the underlying case selection strategy, which averages the compatibility (with past critiques) and similarity (with the current preference case), see equation 2. Put differently, incremental critiquing treats all user-model critiques equally when computing case compatibility. A second problem is that the compatibility values produced are highly dependant on the size of the user-model, which can make it difficult to adapt to different domains. Ideally, we would like a compatibility score that does not have these problems.

For example, as an illustration of these problems, consider a user session that has contributed 10 critiques to the user model. A candidate case that satisfies all of the first 5 of these critiques, but none of the last 5, receives a compatibility score of 0.5, as does a candidate case that satisfies none of the first 5 critiques but all of the last 5. However, the later critiques have been added as a result of more recent critiques by the user, and thus we can reasonably suppose that they reflect a more up-to-date picture of the user's preferences. We believe that the more recent critiques should hold more sway than earlier critiques because over time, the critiques will become more refined, better expressing user preferences than earlier critiques.

We propose an alternative strategy for product recommendation, *highest compatibility selection* (HCS), which allows the recommender to select cases that are most compatible with the recorded user preferences. This maximum compatibility strategy can be easily introduced into

Equation 5. Median equation

$$f_{cq} = \begin{cases} CB'_{n+1/2} (f \text{ of } cq) & \text{if odd \#cases} \\ \dfrac{CB'_{n+1/2} (f \text{ of } cq) + CB'_{(n+1/2)+1} (f \text{ of } cq)}{2} & \text{if even \#cases} \end{cases}$$

Figure 7. Adapting the Recommend_Agent of the incremental critiquing algorithm to improve focus on recommendation by using highest compatibility selection strategy

```
Input: <q: query, CB: CaseBase, cq: critique, c_r : current recommendation, U: User Model>

1.    define Recommend_Agent(q, CB, cq, U)
2.      CB' ← {c ∈ CB | Satisfies(c, cq)}
3.      CB' ← sort cases in CB' in decreasing compatibility score
4.      CB'' ← selects those with highest compatibility
5.      CB'' ← sort cases in CB'' in decreasing order of their sim to q
6.      c_r ← most similar case in CB''
7.    return c_r
```

the incremental critiquing algorithm as shown in Figure 8.

Figure 7 demonstrates that the only agent that is affected in the critiquing algorithm is the **Recommend_Agent**. As before, the list of remaining cases is filtered out using the current critique (*cq*). In addition, two new steps are added. First, the recommender computes the compatibility score. It is important to note that the compatibility function has also been modified, as explained below in equation 6. Instead of averaging the compatibility and the similarity, as is done with incremental critiquing, our second step assembles the cases with the highest compatibility from the list of remaining cases. Importantly, in our approach, only the remaining cases with highest compatibility value, *CB''*, influence the product recommendation.

We have considered case discovery to be an *optimization* problem in which we are trying to recommend cases that maximally satisfy the user preferences. For this reason, we evaluate the remaining cases as if they were a set of states in a *reinforcement learning problem* (RLP) (Harmon & Harmon, 1996), which consists of maximizing the sum of future rewards in a set of states. Reinforcement learning theory is usually based on *finite Markov decision processes* (FMDP). In our strategy each case is treated as a state whose compatibility score is updated at each cycle using a Monte–Carlo value function (see equation

6). This function evaluates the *goodness* of each state—for us the possible states are the complete set of remaining cases we want to enhance—according to the critiques the user has selected.

Our goal is to maximally satisfy all the user preferences. Thus, we are looking for a set of maximally compatible cases (i.e., those cases which have the highest compatibility *(comp)* value considering all the user preferences (*U*) or past critiques). At the beginning of each session, each candidate case, *c'*, has a default compatibility value (i.e., *comp(c') = 0.5*). This value is updated over cycles taking into account the satisfaction or not of the current critique. The α parameter in **equation 6** (see above) is the learning rate, which is usually set up to 0.1 or 0.2 values; a larger value leads to a larger gap between cases in early stages. In our case, the learning rate is not important since we are looking for levels of satisfaction. In other words, we are not trying to obtain a set of states that arrive as quickly as possible to a 1.0 value, as usually is done in RLP.

For example, Table 1 shows the evolving compatibility score using equation 6 for the previous example, where two cases have an equal number of critiques satisfied at critique 10 in the session.

It is important to point out the last critique score (*Crit. 10*), which illustrates a difference in compatibility between case 1 and case 2, thus showing how the Monte-Carlo compatibility is able to enhance those cases that best satisfy the last critiques.

Equation 6. Compatibility function using Monte-Carlo approach

$$Compatibility(c',U_f) = \begin{cases} comp(c') + \alpha \times (1 - comp(c')) & \text{if } c' \text{ satisfies } U_f \\ comp(c') + \alpha \times (0 - comp(c')) & \text{if } c' \text{ dissatisfies } U_f \end{cases}$$

Importantly, note that equation 6 updates the compatibility value stored by each case according to the last user critique (U_f). The *Compatibility* (c', U_f) value computed in the current cycle will be the *comp(c')* in the next cycle.

Local User Preference Weighting

The previous strategy highlights the case dimensionality problem. In other words, it is focused on discovering cases that maximally satisfy user preferences. Now, we present a strategy that concentrates on the feature dimensionality (Salamó, Reilly, McGinty, & Smyth, 2005b). We propose a *local user preference weighting* (LW) strategy that discovers the relative importance of each feature in each case as a weighting value for computing the similarity, taking into account user preferences.

Our LW strategy for the discovery of feature knowledge is basically motivated by the previous knowledge discovery strategy. The discovery of case knowledge is based on maximizing user preferences, which means we are looking for the most compatible cases. These cases are quite similar on their critiqued features, and their differences mainly belong to those features that have not yet been critiqued. So, the aim of LW strategy is to prioritize the similarity of those features that have not yet been critiqued.

We generate a feature weight vector for each case, as shown in equation 7 (see above). A feature that has not been critiqued will assume a weight value of 1.0, and a decrement will be applied when a critique is satisfied by the case. As such, the feature weight will be proportional to the number of times a critique on this feature is satisfied by the case. However, as it can be seen in equation 7, the weight never decreases to a 0 value.

For example, in a travel vacation recommender with a user model that contains two critiques [price, >, $1000] and [price, >, $1500], a case with two features {*duration, price*} whose price is $2000 will have a price weight value of 0.5 because it satisfies both critiques whereas the duration weight will be 1.0 because there is no critique on this feature. It is important to recap that the key idea here is to prioritize the similarity of those features that have not yet been critiqued in a given session.

Our proposal is to discover the best product to recommend by exploiting the similarity of those features that best differentiate the highest compatible cases. To achieve this, a candidate's (c') similarity to the recommended case (c_r) is computed at each cycle in the *stand*ard recommender system as shown by equation 3. For example, to illustrate it, consider the weight vector *{1.0, 0.5}* of the example above and two cases with the same compatibility score and close value for the price

Table 1. Example of the compatibility scores for two cases with the same number of critiques satisfied but in different time (setup α= 0.1)

Candidate Cases	Initial Value	Crit. 1	Crit. 2	Crit. 3	Crit. 4	Crit. 5	Crit. 6	Crit. 7	Crit. 8	Crit. 9	Crit. 10
case 1	0,5	0,55	0,60	0,64	0,67	0,70	0,63	0,57	0,51	0,46	*0,42*
case 2	0,5	0,45	0,41	0,36	0,33	0,30	0,37	0,43	0,49	0,54	*0,58*

Equation 7. Weighting equation

$$\text{for each feature } f \text{ in case } c' \text{ compute:}$$
$$weight(c',f) = 1 - \left(\frac{\#\text{critiques in } U \text{ that satisfy } feature_f \text{ in case } c'}{\#\text{total critiques } feature_f \text{ in } U} \times 0.5 \right)$$

but different value for the duration feature. In such a situation, without weighting, both cases could be close enough to the current case and the result will depend on the feature values. However, when considering the weight vector, the similarity score will prioritise the case for which duration is closer to the current case.

EVALUATION

In this chapter, we have argued that the traditional form of critiquing is limited by its tendency to attract sequences of repeat critiques from users as they respond to incremental changes in case features during subsequent recommendation cycles. Furthermore, the standard approach to critiquing does not consider the history of critiques when recommending new products to the user.

We have presented an algorithm that encourages larger changes in the values of critiqued features during recommendation. We also have presented a strategy for selecting cases and weighting features by considering the history of critiques. In this section, we describe the results of an evaluation that demonstrates that these approaches have the ability to lead to a significant reduction in average recommendation session length.

Setup and Methodology

The evaluation was performed using the standard travel dataset (available from http://ww.ai-cbr.org), which consists of 1024 vacation cases; this dataset is a common benchmark used in recommender systems research. Each case is described in terms of nine features including price, duration, etc. The dataset was chosen because it contains numerical and nominal features, and it also provides a wide search space.

We evaluate the highest compatibility selection (*HCS*), the local user preference weighting (*LW*), the binary search (*BS*) and also all three strategies combined (*ALL*) in our recommender over standard critiquing (*standard*) and over incremental critiquing (*incremental*).

We would like to have carried out an online evaluation with live users, but unfortunately this was not feasible. As an alternative we opt for an offline evaluation similar to the one described by (Smyth & McGinty, 2003b); again it is worth highlighting that this *leave-one-out* evaluation methodology is standard practice among recommender systems researchers. Accordingly, each case (referred to as the *base*) in the case-base is temporarily removed and used in two ways. First, it serves as a basis for a set of queries by taking random subsets of its features. We focus on subsets of one, three, and five features to allow us to distinguish between hard, moderate, and easy queries, respectively. Second, we select the case that is most similar to the original base. These cases are the recommendation *targets* for the experiments. Thus, the base represents the ideal query for a "user", the generated query is the initial query provided by the "user', and the target is the best available case for the user. Each generated query is a test problem for the recommender, and in each recommendation cycle the "user" picks a critique that is compatible with the known target case; that is, a critique that, when applied to the remaining cases, results in the target case being left in the filtered set of cases. Each leave-one-out pass through the case-base is repeated 10 times, and the recommendation sessions terminate when the target case is returned.

The artificial user models we use for our evaluations (Salamó et al., 2005c) are informed by real-user studies (McCarthy et al., 2005a). In particular, our artificial user model repeats critique selections during recommendation sessions until its target feature values are met.

Recommendation Efficiency

We analyse the recommendation efficiency—by which we mean average recommendation session length—when comparing the new strategies to *standard* and *incremental* critiquing. Figure 8(a) presents a graph comparing the average session

length of the incremental critiquing approach to the combination of all the strategies (ALL) for three different initial query lengths. The three strategies combined consistently reduce average session length when compared to the incremental critiquing approach, demonstrating the potential to improve recommendation efficiency. For example, for the hard queries, the incremental recommender results in an average session of 12.46 cycles, while the combined recommender results in an average of 11.47 cycles.

Figure 8(b) shows the benefit of each strategy (HCS, LW, and BS) separately and the combined strategies (ALL) in our recommender when compared to the incremental critiquing. We find that all strategies separately result in a relative session length reduction of between 2.65% and fewer

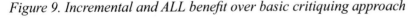

Figure 8. Average session length and benefit over incremental critiquing

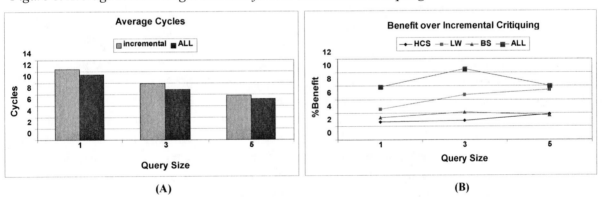

Figure 9. Incremental and ALL benefit over basic critiquing approach

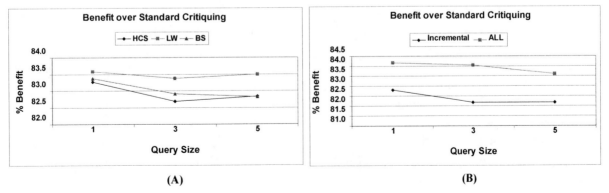

than 7.5%, with some variation in the relative benefit due to the HCS, LW, and BS approaches. The lowest benefit is for the highest compatibility selection (HCS) approach, which ranges between 2.65% and 3.81%, because it does the same process as the incremental critiquing approach with two little modifications that consist of using a different compatibility measure and a different strategy for discovering the set of cases available for recommendation.

Similarly, a 3% to 4% benefit is found using the binary search (BS) strategy. On the other hand, the local weighting approach (LW) gives the highest benefit, ranging from 4.5% to 6.73%, when applied alone. These results show that the strategy to promote uncritiqued features is able to discover and detect differences between cases that are maximally compatible to the user's critiques.

We have found that the combined strategies in our recommender result in a reduction in session length that ranges from nearly 8% to 10.5%. Combining all of the strategies further enhances recommendation performance, resulting in the discovery of better recommendations for all queries (hard, moderate, and easy).It seems that the recommender ability to learn user preferences is greater when combining information from these three distinct knowledge discovery resources. An important point to note is that all results show a lower benefit for easy queries. This is to be expected perhaps, since the easy queries naturally result in shorter sessions, and thus there are fewer opportunities to find good lower and upper critique bounds to focus the search space properly in the BS strategy, and hence fewer opportunities for the benefit to be felt.

It is worth noting the benefit of the proposed strategies over the standard critiquing algorithm; see Figure 9. We can see in Figure 9(a) that all strategies separately result in benefit on the recommendation efficiency over 82.5% of the standard critiquing algorithm. Nevertheless, as it can be seen in Figure 9(b), our combination of approaches

has the potential to deliver further reductions in session length (from 83.5% to upper 84%) even with short sessions where the BS approach does not have much of an opportunity to affect the recommendations.

To summarise, a significant efficiency benefit is enjoyed by HCS, LW, and BS strategies, when compared to the standard and incremental critiquing approaches. Importantly, the proposed strategies assist in the discovery of useful recommendation knowledge, allowing the system to prioritize products that best satisfy the user. We have demonstrated that this approach is highly effective, even in situations where only a minimal knowledge of user preferences is available (e.g., critiquing approach).

CONCLUSION

In order to be useful, conversational recommender systems should be able to guide users through a product space in the most efficient manner possible, making the most of elicited user feedback to find suitable products in the least number of recommendation cycles.

Critiquing is a form of user feedback that is ideally suited to many conversational case-based recommender scenarios. In this chapter, we have made some observations about the different knowledges and how the recommender interacts and reasons with them. A summary of lessons learned in this chapter are described below:

- The standard and incremental critiquing algorithms, as showed in a live-user evaluation (McCarthy et al., 2005a; Salamó et al., 2005c), can lead to protracted recommended sessions as there is a tendency toward relatively minor changes in the values of the critiqued features from cycle to cycle. We have presented a *binary search* strategy that facilitates larger jumps through the product space (*case knowledge*) in order to focus in more rapidly on satisfactory cases.

- Traditional implementations of critiquing can also lead to protracted recommendation sessions as they tend to focus only on last critique ignoring preferences supplied earlier. To address this issue, Reilly et al. (2004a) introduced an algorithm called *incremental critiquing*, which maintains a model of user preferences over the course of a recommendation session and uses this model to make better recommendations by taking into account *all* the preferences. This approach has shown significant improvement on recommendation efficiency over standard critiquing. We have also presented an alternative case priorization strategy, called *highest compatibility selection*, to incremental critiquing that maximizes the user preferences (*user knowledge*) over time by combining the user profiling and reinforcement learning to good effect.

- A more personalized notion of product similarity (*similarity knowledge*) during recommendation can be done by introducing a weighting strategy that is tuned to user preferences. It is well known in case-based reasoning that weighting helps improving the system performance when computing similarity. We have presented a local weighting strategy that prioritizes features locally to each case and adapting them to the preference of each user.

The three strategies presented in this chapter aim to improve recommendation efficiency by using one or more of the knowledge containers: *case knowledge, user knowledge,* and/or *similarity knowledge*. The discovery of implicit knowledge is necessary to decide which product recommendations are the most suitable for each user during a live customer interaction.

Our experiments indicate that the three proposals have the potential to deliver worthwhile efficiency benefits. Reductions in the average length of recommendation sessions were noted in all of the proposals, both separately and combined, when compared to the incremental and standard critiquing setups. Importantly, the presented strategies are sufficiently general to be applicable across a wide range of recommendation scenarios. In particular, those that assume a complex product space where recommendation sessions are likely to be protracted, and/or domains where only minimal user feedback is likely to be available.

Looking to the future, we are continuing our research in the area of critiquing based recommenders but are now moving from recommending products for individuals to recommending products for groups of users. Group recommendation (Jameson, 2004; McCarthy & Anagnost, 1998; Plua & Jameson, 2002; Prada & Paiva, 2005) brings with it many new challenges that are not present in single-user recommenders, such as competing preferences between users, collaborative navigation and feedback, and dealing with group versus individual recommendations (Jameson, 2005). Research in the area of group recommendation includes: MusicFX (McCarthy & Anagnost, 1998) is a group preference arbitration system that adjusts the selection of music playing in a fitness center to best accommodate the musical preferences of the people working out at any given time; PolyLens (O'Connor, Cosley, Konstan, & Riedln, 2001) is a generalization of the MovieLens system that recommends movies to a group of users; and Travel Decision Forum (Jameson, 2004) is a prototype that helps a group of users to agree on the desired features of a vacation that they are planning to take together.

Our approach to group recommendation is called CATS (Collaborative Advisory Travel System) (McCarthy et al., 2006a), which helps groups of users to find appropriate ski holidays. We propose to use the DiamondTouch device (Kobourov et al., 2005) to showcase our new simultaneous collaborative group recommender system. The DiamondTouch (Dietz & Leigh, 2001) consists of a touch-sensitive table connected to a computer whose display is projected onto the table. The table can detect and distinguish between simultaneous touch events, allowing the development of innovative and intuitive collaborative and cooperative applications. CATS is based on this collaborative recommender framework, assumes the availability of individual and group interaction spaces, and uses a conversational recommendation engine that is able to record and manage personal, as well as group, profiles as the basis for its recommendations. In fact, we utilize the user knowledge agent in the same way that the incremental critiquing strategy does to model the preferences of the individual. We then combine the individual user's knowledge to form a group knowledge container. This knowledge is then used to help with case recommendation, navigation, awareness of preferences of other users, and eventually, convergence on a single product recommendation (McCarthy, Salamó, McGinty, & Smyth, 2006b).

REFERENCES

Aamodt, A., & Plaza, E. (1994). Case-based reasoning: Foundations issues, methodological variations, and system approaches. *AI Communications, 7*, 39-59.

Aha, D. W., Breslow, L. A., & Muñoz-Avila, H. (2000). Conversational case-based reasoning. *Applied Intelligence, 14*, 9-32.

Aha, D. W., Maney, T., & Breslow, L. A. (1998). Supporting dialogue inferencing in conversational case-based reasoning. *Proceedings of EWCBR 98: Proceedings of the 4th European Workshop on Advances in Case-Based Reasoning* (pp. 262-273). Springer.

Burke, R. (2002). Interactive critiquing for catalog navigation in e-commerce. *Artificial Intelligence Review, 18*(3-4), 245-267.

Burke, R., Hammond, K., & Kozlovsky, J. (1995). Knowledge-based information retrieval for semi-structured text. *Proceedings of the AAAI Fall Symposium on AI Applications in Knowledge Navigation and Retrieval* (pp. 19-24). Menlo Park, CA: AAAI Press.

Burke, R., Hammond, K., & Young, B. (1996). Knowledge-based navigation of complex information spaces. *Proceedings of the 13th National Conference on Artificial Intelligence* (pp. 462-468). Menlo Park, CA: AAAI Press.

Burke, R., Hammond, K., & Young, B. C. (1997). The findme approach to assisted browsing. *Journal of IEEE Expert, 12*(4), 32-40.

Dietz, P., & Leigh, D. (2001). DiamondTouch: A multi-user touch technology. *Proceedings of the 14th Annual ACM Symposium on User Interface Software Technology* (pp. 219-226). New York: ACM Press.

Doyle, M., & Cunningham, P. (2000). A Dynamic approach to reducing dialog in on-line decision guides. In E. Blanzieri & L. Portinale (Ed.), *Proceedings of the Fifth European Workshop on Case-Based Reasoning* (pp. 49-60). Springer-Verlag.

Faltings, B., Pu, P., Torrens, M., & Viappiani, P. (2004). Design example-critiquing interaction. *Proceedings of the International Conference on Intelligent User Interface* (pp. 22-29). New York: ACM Press.

Harmon, M., & Harmon, S. (1996). *Reinforcement learning: A tutorial.*

Jameson, A. (2004). More than the sum of its members: Challenges for group recommender systems. *Proceedings of the International Working Conference on Advanced Visual Interfaces* (pp. 48-54).

Jameson, A. (2005). User modeling meets usability goals. In L. Ardissono, P. Brna, & A. Mitrovic

(Ed.), *User Modeling: Proceedings of the Tenth International Conference* (pp. 1-3). Springer.

Kobourov, S. G., Pavlou, D., Cappos, J., Stepp, M., Miles, M., & Wixted, A. (2005). Collaboration with DiamondTouch. *Proceedings of the 10th International Conference on Human-Computer Interaction* (pp. 986-990).

Kolodner, J. (1993). *Case-based reasoning*. Morgan Kaufmann.

McCarthy, J., & Anagnost, T. (1998). Musicfx: An arbiter of group preferences for computer supported collaborative workouts. *Proceedings of Conference on Computer Supported Cooperative Work* (pp. 363-372).

McCarthy, K., McGinty, L., Smyth, B., & Reilly, J. (2005a). On the evaluation of dynamic critiquing: a large-scale user study. *Proceedings 20th National Conference on Artificial Intelligence*, (pp. 535-540). Menlo Park, CA: AAAI Press / The MIT Press.

McCarthy, K., Reilly, J., McGinty, L., & Smyth, B. (2004a). On the dynamic generation of compound critiques in conversational recommender systems. In P. De Bra (Ed.), *Proceedings of the Third International Conference on Adaptive Hypermedia and Web-Based Systems (AH-04)* (pp. 176-184). Springer.

McCarthy, K., Reilly, J., McGinty, L., & Smyth, B. (2004b). Thinking positively—Explanatory feedback for conversational recommender systems. *Proceedings of the European Conference on Case-Based Reasoning (ECCBR-04) Explanation Workshop* (pp. 115-124). Springer.

McCarthy, K., Reilly, J., McGinty, L., & Smyth, B. (2005b), Generating diverse compound critiques. *Artificial Intelligence Review, 24*(3-4), 339-357.

McCarthy, K., Salamó, M., Coyle, L., McGinty, L., Smyth, B., & Nixon, P. (2006a). Group recommender systems: A critiquing based approach. In C. Paris & C. Sidner (Eds.), *Proceedings of*

the 10th *International Conference on Intelligent User Interfaces* (pp. 267-269). New York: ACM Press.

McCarthy, K., Salamó, M., McGinty, L., & Smyth, B. (2006b). CATS: A synchronous approach to collaborative group recommendation. *Proceedings of the 19th International Florida Artificial Intelligence Research Society Conference* (pp. 86-91). Menlo Park, CA: AAAI Press.

McGinty, L., & Smyth, B. (2002). Comparison-based recommendation. In Susan Craw (Ed.), *Proceedings of the 6th European Conference on Case-Based Reasoning* (pp. 575-589). Springer.

McGinty, L., & Smyth, B. (2003a). On the role of diversity in conversational recommender systems. In K. Ashley & D. Bridge (Eds.), *Proceedings 5th International Conference on Case-Based Reasoning* (pp. 276-291). Springer.

McGinty, L., & Smyth, B. (2003b). Tweaking critiquing. *Proceedings of the Workshop on Personalization and Web Techniques at the International Joint Conference on Artificial Intelligence* (pp. 20-27). Morgan Kaufmann.

McSherry, D. (2002). Diversity-conscious retrieval. *Proceedings of the 6th European Conference on Case-Based Reasoning* (pp. 219-233). Springer.

McSherry, D. (2003). Increasing dialogue efficiency in case-based reasoning without loss of solution quality. *Proceedings of the 18th International Joint Conference on Artificial Intelligence* (pp. 121-126). Morgan Kaufmann.

McSherry, D., & Stretch, C. (2005). Automating the Discovery of Recommendation Knowledge. In *Proceedings of the 19th International Joint Conference on Artificial Intelligence* (pp. 9-14). Morgan Kaufmann.

Nguyen, Q. N., Ricci, F., & Cavada, D. (2004). User preferences initialization and integration in critique-based mobile recommender systems. *Proceedings of Artificial Intelligence in Mobile*

Systems 2004, in conjunction with UbiComp 2004 (pp. 71-78). Universitat des Saarlandes Press.

O'Connor, M., Cosley, D., Konstan, K., & Riedln, J. (2001). Polylens: A recommender system for Groups of Users. In *Proceedings of European Conference on Computer-Supported Cooperative Work* (pp. 199-218).

Pu, P., & Kumar, P. (2004). Evaluating example-based search tools. *Proceedings of the ACM Conference on Electronic Commerce (EC 2004)* (pp. 208-217). New York: ACM Press.

Plua, C., & Jameson, A. (2002). Collaborative preference elicitation in a group travel recommender system. *Proceedings of the AH 2002 Workshop on Recommendation and Personalization in eCommerce* (pp. 148-154).

Prada, R., & Paiva, A. (2005). Believable groups of synthetic characters. *Proceedings of the 4th International Joint Conference on Autonomous Agents and Multi-Agent Systems* (pp. 37-43).

Reilly, J., McCarthy, K., McGinty, L., & Smyth, B. (2004a). Incremental critiquing. In M. Bramer, F. Coenen, & T. Allen (Eds.), *Research and development in intelligent systems XXI: Proceedings of AI-2004* (pp. 101-114). Springer.

Reilly, J., McCarthy, K., McGinty, L., & Smyth, B. (2004b). Dynamic critiquing. In P. A. Gonzalez Calero & P. Funk (Eds.), *Proceedings of the European Conference on Case-Based Reasoning*, (pp. 763-777). Springer.

Richter, A. (1998). Case-based reasoning technology from foundations to applications. *Introduction chapter* (pp. 1-15). Springer.

Riesbeck, C. K., & Schank, R. C. (1989). *Inside case-based reasoning.* Lawrence Erlbaum Associates.

Salamó, M., Reilly, J., McGinty, L., & Smyth, B. (2005a). Improving incremental critiquing. *16th Artificial Intelligence and Cognitive Science* (pp. 379-388).

Salamó, M., Reilly, J., McGinty, L., & Smyth, B. (2005b). Knowledge discovery from user preferences in conversational recommendation. In *Knowledge Discovery in Databases: 9th European Conference on Principles and Practice of Knowledge Discovery in Databases* (pp. 228-239). Springer.

Salamó, M., Smyth, B., McCarthy, K., Reilly, J., & McGinty, L. (2005c). Reducing critiquing repetition in conversational recommendation. *Proceedings IX Workshop on Multi-agent Information Retrieval and Recommender Systems at the International Joint Conference on Artificial Intelligence* (pp. 55-61).

Sherin, S., & Lieberman, H. (2001). Intelligent profiling by example. *Proceedings of the International Conference on Intelligent User Interfaces (IUI 2001)* (pp. 145-152). New York: ACM Press.

Shimazu, H. (2002). ExpertClerk: A conversational case-based reasoning tool for developing salesclerk agents in e-commerce Webshops. *Artificial Intelligence Review, 18*(3-4), 223-244.

Smyth, B., & Cotter, P. (2000). A personalized TV listings service for the digital TV age. *Journal of Knowledge-Based Systems, 13*(2-3), 53-59.

Smyth, B., & McGinty, L. (2003a). An analysis of feedback strategies in conversational recommender systems. In P. Cunningham (Ed.), *Proceedings of the 14th National Conference on Artificial Intelligence and Cognitive Science* (pp. 211-216).

Smyth, B., & McGinty, L. (2003b). The power of suggestion. *Proceedings of the International Joint Conference on Artificial Intelligence* (pp. 127-132). Morgan-Kaufmann.

Stolze, M. (2000). Soft navigation in electronic product Catalogs. *International Journal on Digital Libraries, 3*(1), 60-66.

Chapter XIV
Task Allocation in Case–Based Recommender Systems:
A Swarm Intelligence Approach

Fabiana Lorenzi
Universidade Federal do Rio Grande do Sul, Brazil
Universidade Luterana do Brasil, Brazil

Daniela Scherer dos Santos
Universidade Federal do Rio Grande do Sul, Brazil

Denise de Oliveira
Universidade Federal do Rio Grande do Sul, Brazil

Ana L. C. Bazzan
Universidade Federal do Rio Grande do Sul, Brazil

ABSTRACT

Case-based recommender systems can learn about user preferences over time and automatically suggest products that fit these preferences. In this chapter, we present such a system, called CASIS. In CASIS, we combined the use of swarm intelligence in the task allocation among cooperative agents applied to a case-based recommender system to help the user to plan a trip.

INTRODUCTION

In the tourism branch, travel agencies have a hard task to plan a trip because there are dependencies on information that changes over time. Besides, this information is distributed on the Internet (in sites of flight companies, hotels, city's attractions etc.). Another difficulty is that frequently the trip destination is not fixed. Finally, it is hard to plan according to the user's preferences when one does not have all the necessary information.

Thus, a tool is necessary to retain the knowledge about the most popular destinations (e.g., within a season) and the travel agency experience. To solve those questions, we propose an approach that combines case-based recommender and multi-agent systems. The overall system has two different layers (with different goals): to search the case base and to search new information on the Internet. This work focuses on the former, proposing a metaphor from swarm intelligence to help the negotiation process among agents.

A multi-agent system (MAS) needs to deal with dynamic problems such as variation in the number of agents and changes in the environment and in the system's goals. These organizational issues depend on the system's goals, the perceived environment, and the relationships among agent's activities, as well as their interactions.

There have been many propositions to tackle these issues, whose discussion is outside the scope of this paper. However, we are interested in the use of swarm-based approach. In Ferreira, Oliveira, and Bazzan, (2005), for instance, the authors proposed the use of swarm-based approach to adapt organizations in a MAS. This approach is useful because it deals with dynamic organizations, the same kind of problem posed by the tourism scenario just described.

This chapter is organized as follows: The second section presents a background of case-based recommender systems, negotiation among agents, and swarm intelligence. The third section shows the CASIS system, and the fourth section presents some experiments and the results. Finally, the future trends and the conclusions are discussed.

BACKGROUND

Case-Based Recommender Systems

Case-based reasoning (CBR) is a problem-solving methodology that deals with a new problem by first retrieving a past, already-solved similar case and then reusing that case for solving the new problem (Kolodner, 1993). A case models a past experience, storing both the problem description and the solution applied in that context. All the cases are stored in the case base. When the system is presented with a new problem to solve,

it searches for the most similar case(s) in the case base and reuses an adapted version of the retrieved solution to solve the new problem.

CBR is a cyclic and integrated problem solving process that supports learning from experience (Aamodt & Plaza, 1994) and has four main steps: retrieve, reuse, adaptation, and retain. The adaptation phase is split into two sub-steps: revise and review. In the revise step, the system adapts the solution to fit the specific constraint of the new problem, whereas in the review step the constructed solution is evaluated by applying it to the new problem, understanding where it fails, and making the necessary corrections. CBR is one of the most successful machine learning methodologies that exploits a knowledge-rich representation of the application domain (Aamodt & Plaza, 1994; Watson, 1997).

In a CBR recommender system (CBR-RS), a set of suggestions or recommendations is retrieved from the case base by searching for cases similar to a case described by the user (Burke, 2000). In the simplest application of CBR to recommend, the user is supposed to look for some product to purchase. He/she inputs some requirements about the product and the system searches the case base for similar products (by means of a similarity metric) that match the user requirements. A set of cases is retrieved from the case base, and these cases can be recommended to the user.

If the user is not satisfied with the recommendation, he/she can modify the requirements, that is, build another query, and a new cycle of the recommendation process is started. The case retrieval is typically the main step of the CBR cycle, and the majority of CBRRS can be described as sophisticated retrieval engines. For example, in the order-based retrieval (Bridge & Ferguson, 2002), the system uses special operators to retrieve a partially-ordered set, whereas in the compromise-driven retrieval (McSherry, 2003), the system retrieves similar cases from the case base but also groups the cases, putting together those offering to the user the same compromise, and presents just a representative case for each group.

Negotiation Among Agents and Swarm Intelligence

In a MAS, it is necessary that agents coordinate their actions because they do not have a global view, and so the goals and knowledge are local, making it difficult for agents to cooperate. Besides, the system should be able to deal with global constraints, which are not perceived by the individual agents' local view and with inter-agents dependencies.

In a more general way, coordination increases the MAS performance. There are many ways to coordinate agents in a MAS, classified by Nwana, Lee, and Jennings (1996) in four categories: organizational structuring, contracting, multi-agent planning, and negotiation.

Negotiation is a process where two or more parties make a joint decision. The negotiation can be classified as competitive or cooperative. We are interested here in the cooperative negotiation that can be viewed as a distributed search process where the agents try to reach the maximum global utility.

The negotiation process starts when the agent realizes that the agent is not able to perform a given task. This can happen for many reasons: the agent can be overloaded, the agent does not have capacity to perform the task, or maybe the agent knows that another agent can perform the task with a higher quality. When the agent has to perform the task, it calculates the task's utility (e.g., cost and time) and decides if it is necessary to start negotiation process.

One way to achieve cooperation without explicit communication is to use swarm intelligence, an artificial intelligence technique based around the study of collective behavior in decentralized, self-organized systems. The use of the social insect metaphor to solve computer problems such as combinatorial optimization, communications

networks, or robotics is increasing (Bonabeau, Theraulaz, & Dorigo, 1999).

Social insects living in colonies, e.g., ants, termites, bees, and wasps distinguish themselves by their organization skill without any centralized control (Camazine et al., 2003; Gordon, 1996). This self-organization emerges from interactions among individuals, between the individuals and the environment, and from behaviors of the individuals themselves (Bonabeau et al, 1999).

Models based on self-organization assume that it might be possible to explain something apparently complex in terms of simple interacting processes (Bonabeau et al., 1999). There are several approaches inspired by social insects' behavior; the complete list is outside the scope of this paper. However, one example of the self-organization can be seeing in the way in which ants travel to and from a food source. They deposit a certain amount of pheromone while walking, and each ant prefers to follow a direction rich in pheromone. This enables the ant colony to quickly find the shortest route. In Dorigo and Caro (1998), the AntNet, an adaptive, distributed routing algorithm for telecommunication networks, is described, which was inspired by the ant colony behavior described above.

Another important behavior related to ant colony is the division of labor, which is fundamental to the organization of insect societies (Robinson, 1992). Colonies respond to changing internal and external conditions by adjusting the ratios of individual workers engaged in the various tasks. Based on this behavior, some models were proposed. Ferreira (2005), for instance, applied one of these models to task allocation in dynamic environments where the agents adapt to changes in the organization, just as social insects do.

Another example of self-organization is found in bees. Bees travel up to 10 kilometers away from the hive to collect nectar. They return with nectar and information about the nectar source (Camazine et al., 2003). This process of dispatching bees into the surrounding countryside to gather the colony's food is called foraging.

In Seeley, Camazine, and Sneyd (1991), the authors presented an experiment showing the recruitment of nectar forager bees to feeders containing sugar solutions. Two food sources are presented to the colony at 8 a.m. at the same distance from the hive: source A is characterized by a sugar concentration of 1.00 mol and source B by a concentration of 2.5 mol. At the noon, the sources are exchanged: source A is now characterized by a sugar concentration 2.5 mol and source B by a concentration of 0.75 mol. In both situations, the better source is more visited. This experiment showed that the foraging decision of each bee is based on very limited information of its own particular visited source. This simple behavior allows the colony to select the best quality source of nectar.

Based on these experiments, Camazine and Sneyd (1991) developed a mathematical model, which shows that he colony is capable to select the best nectar source available through three simple probabilistic behavioral rules:

- f_d^a and f_d^b : are the probability of sharing the nectar source information, A and B respectively, by dancing, a behavior in which a bee communicates to other bees the direction, distance, and desirability of the food source, trying to recruit new bees to that food source;

- f_x^a and f_x^b : are the probability of abandoning the food source A and B, respectively, and going to the area inside the hive called the dance floor to observe dancing bees and select a next food source;

- $A(f_l^a)$ and $B(f_l^b)$: is the probability of following a dancer for A and B, respectively.

The probability of following a dancer for source A and B is estimated by:

$$A(f_l^a) = \frac{D_a d_a}{D_a d_a + D_b d_b}$$

and

$$B(f_l^b) = \frac{D_b d_b}{D_a d_a + D_b d_b}$$

Where:

- D_a and D_b are the number of bees dancing for source A and B, respectively

- d_a and d_b are the time spent dancing to source A and B, respectively.

Camazine and Sneyd's model shows how the properties of the system emerge automatically from the dynamic interactions among the constituent components.

THE CASIS SYSTEM

Many researches are generating new solutions to show how e-commerce can be used for travel and tourism, trying to reproduce the traditional travel agents' advice. In Ricci et al. (2003), the authors describe an intelligent recommender system developed with Case-Based Reasoning approach that helps a traveler to select a tourist destination, building a set of products and composing a plan for the travel. Dietorecs (Fesenmaier, Ricci, Schaumlechner, Wober, & Zanella, 2003) is also a recommender system that incorporates a human decision model that stresses individual differences in decision styles.

In this chapter, we present a case-based swarming intelligence recommender system (called CASIS) to the forfeit's[1] planning task using agents to recommend travel packages to the user. The process starts with the user's query (that we call demand) and the metaphor of the honey bees is used to select the most similar cases to the user's demand. Similar works were not found in the literature to recommend travel packages based on swarm intelligence and case-based reasoning.

Camazine and Sneyd's mathematical model (1991) was adapted and used in the negotiation process. Each agent represents a bee with the following behaviors: probability of abandoning the nectar source i (P^i_X); probability of recruiting more bees by dancing (P^i_D) to source i and probability of following the source i (P^i_F). P^i_F was adapted in our approach because we are not taking into account the time the bee spend dancing. Thus:

$$P^i_F = \frac{D_i}{\sum_{j=1}^{M} D_j}$$

where D_i is the number of dancer bees to the source i and M is the total number of sources. Notice that P^i_F is the proportion of bees dancing to the source i related to all the bees that are dancing to the other sources.

There is a case base with past travel cases, and the agents search in this case base for possible travel to recommend according to the user's preferences or the user's profile. Each case is viewed as a nectar source for the bees. Given a new user query, the metaphor calls for honey bees leaving the nest looking for nectar sources. In our system, the original model was modified and the bee can forage for several different sources (not only two as in the original model).

According to Camazine and Sneyd's model, each bee's choice is calculated by using probabilities. The most important one is the abandon probability (P^i_X), where the bee checks the quality of the nectar source and decides whether or not to continue in this source. This probability was adapted in our model. In a traditional case-based recommender system, the new query is compared with all cases in the case base, and the most similar is shown to the user. However, in CASIS, the similarity is used to help the bee to make its decision to continue in the nectar source or not. Randomly, the bee visits a case in the case base, comparing the query with this case, and it calculates P^i_X. P^i_X calculates the euclidean distance between the new query and the cases. The cases with the smallest distance to the new query are the most similar, that is, they represent the best nectar sources.

Figure 1 shows the model with the hive having two compartments (*dancing for case* and *observing a dancer*), the case base (representing the available nectar sources), and also the bee's decision possibilities. As we can see, the bee can decide to visit the compartment *dancing for case* to perform recruitment's dance before returning to its case C_i or to continue to forage at the case without recruiting other bees. Another possibility is to abandon the case and then visit the compartment *observing a dancer* (that has bees dancing for different cases). Here the bee selects (randomly) a dancer bee and decides to follow C_j (the case visited by the dancer bee) or to select a different dancer bee. In each one of these possibilities, the respective probabilities are calculated.

To improve CASIS, allowing that several passengers can request a recommendation at the same time, we found inspiration in Bonabeau's allocation task model. This adapted model allows the recommender system to have several bees working in different demands.

The bee picks a demand to solve and calculates the *tendency* (T) that is the probability to visit a specific case, instead of visiting all cases from the case base. A bee will visit a case stored in the case base according to the tendency associated to this case. It means that the bee has a tendency associated to each pair of case/demand. This tendency is inspired on Bonabeau et al.'s mathematical model (1999), and it is calculated using the following equation:

$$T_{ij} = \frac{S_{ij}^2}{S_{ij}^2 + \theta_{ij}^2}$$

Figure 1. Dancing metaphor (Adapted from Camazine and Sneyd)

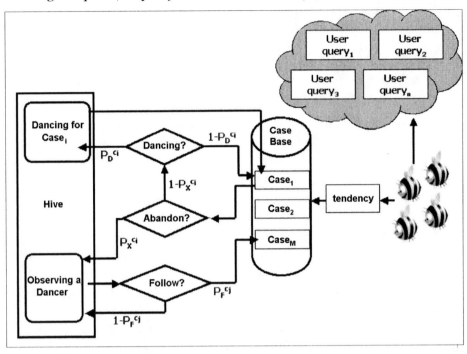

where:

- S_{ij} represents the stimulus associated with the case i and the demand j
- θ_{ij} is the bee's answer threshold associated with the case i and the demand j

θ_{ij} and S_{ij} are updated as follow:

- if the bee dance to recruit new bees to the case it is visiting:

$$\theta_{ij} = \theta_{ij} - \alpha, \ \text{if } \theta_{ij} > 0$$
$$\theta_{ij} = 0, \text{ otherwise}$$
$$S_{ij} = S_{ij} + \alpha$$

- if the bee does not dance and abandons the case:

$$\theta_{ij} = \theta_{ij} + \alpha$$
$$S_{ij} = S_{ij} - \alpha$$

where α is a constant.

θ_{ij} and S_{ij} work as a reinforcement to those cases that are most similar to the user query, ensuring that the bees do not visit cases not relevant to the demand that is being solved.

The tendency helps the bee to decide which case it should visit, depending on the demand it is solving, reducing the search space and avoiding waste of time. In the moment the bee is working on a demand, it will continue in that demand until the recommendation appears. This behavior guarantees that a recommendation is always given to the user, since the bees will work until the best possible recommendation shows up.

As shown in the recommendation's algorithm, when the user informs his/her preferences (a new request), the negotiation process is called. All the bees that are not busy (unemployed), that is, the bees that are not working in any demand, are candidates to work this new demand.

Table 1. Example of the user preferences

Destination	Transportation	Hotel	Local	Period	Price
Ibiza	Plane	Five-star hotel	Beach	10/01/2007 to 20/01/2007	Up to U$ 3.000,00

Let us assume a specific demand, shown in Table 1. When the user informs all his/her preferences, the random process of allocation task (which bees will work in this demand) starts. Each bee now has to select (randomly) which case it will visit. To decide about this, the bee calculates the tendency (T) for that case (i) given demand (j).

Following the recommendation cycle, the bee visits a case i (according to the calculated tendency) and now it has to calculate the probabilities (which means choose an option): abandon the case, follow a case, or dance for a case. The first probability calculated is the *abandon* - P^{cij}_X. With this probability, the bee decides if it has to abandon the case or not. It means that a low P^{cij}_X value indicates a low probability of the bee to abandon the case and a greater similarity between the visited case and the user's preferences.

If the bee decides to abandon case i, then it will randomly select a dancer bee to observe. There are always bees in the *dancing for case* compartment, dancing to recruit new bees to a specific case (case j). When observing the dancer bee, the bee calculates P^{cxj}_F, which represents the probability of visiting case j. If it decides to visit it, the whole cycle restarts. The bee visits case j, calculates the probability of abandoning the case, and so on. On the other hand, if the bee decides not to visit case j, it will select a different dancer bee until P^{cxj}_F is satisfied. When the probability P^{cij}_X leads the bee to decide not to abandon the case it is visiting, it goes to the *dancing for case* compartment to recruit new bees to this case. So: $P^{cij}_D = 1 - P^{cij}_X$.

See Box 1.

The process is repeated until the most similar case regarding the user's preferences emerges, and it is immediately recommended to the user in a textual form.

The tourism scenario is a dynamic domain, and the recommendation demands are seasonal. As an example, we can say that the travel packages can be divided in two different clusters. In the summer, users prefer beaches and sunny places, while in winter, usually the users prefer ski resorts. Following this idea, we can see that, using the honey bee dance metaphor, this clustering behavior emerges, and if the user starts a query asking for some beach package, the bees will concentrate in cases that have summer travel packages, avoiding the cases with winter packages. The advantage of this behavior is that the bees can specialize themselves in some cases, according to the demands. However, it is important to mention that the bees can surprise the user with different cases if he/she does not define some preferences. The bees can use both clusters in this situation.

The advantage of using this metaphor is that the bees always return something to recommend. Despite the controversy over whether it is sometimes better not to recommend instead of recommending wrong products, this is not true in the tourism context, especially in the frequent case where the client does not know exactly where to go or what to do. Our approach always returns some recommendation, which is specific for the current season, given the dynamic nature of the approach (bees adapting to the environmental changes, which is here the travel demands of the current season).

Box 1.

```
Recommendation's algorithm
N: number of bees
M: number of cases (sources)
CB: case base -(where CB = C₁, C₂, …, Cₘ)
D: number of demands
DB: demand base -(DB = D₁, D₂, …, Dᵣ)
q: user's query
θᵢⱼ = 1
Sᵢⱼ = 1
for b = 1, ..., N do
   dⱼ = random (DB)
   cᵢ = random (CB)
   Tᵢⱼ = S²ᵢⱼ / S²ᵢⱼ + θ²ᵢⱼ
   if (Tᵢⱼ met) then
   begin
      //the bee goes to the case cᵢⱼ
      repeat
         Pᶜⁱʲₓ = Euclidean Distance (q, cᵢⱼ)
         if ((Pᶜⁱʲₓ) not met) then
         begin
            Pᶜⁱʲ_D = 1 - Pᶜⁱʲₓ
            if (Pᶜⁱʲ_D met) then
            begin
               //visit the compartment Dancing for Case
               θᵢⱼ = θᵢⱼ - α
               Sᵢⱼ = Sᵢⱼ + α
            end
            else keep foraging
            end if
         end
         else begin
            //visit the compartment Observing a dancer
            θᵢⱼ = θᵢⱼ + α
            Sᵢⱼ = Sᵢⱼ - α
            repeat
               //choose a random dancer bee
               Pᶜˣʲ_F = D_cxj / Σᴹ_y=1 D_y //D_cxj is the number of bees
                                    //dancing to pair Cₓ and demand dⱼ
               if (Pᶜˣʲ_F met) then
                  cᵢ = cₓ //bee will forage cₓ
               end if
            until (cᵢ = cₓ)
         end
         end if
      until (number of bees working in case i and demand j ≥ 80%
            of the total number of bees working in the demand j)
   end
   end if
end for
return Most_danced_case //The case with the highest number of
                     //bees dancing.
```

EXPERIMENTS AND RESULTS

To validate the algorithm proposed, we have performed some experiments with different users' queries and also different parameters such as number of bees and number of cases in the case base. This section shows some experiments done in CASIS and the results achieved.

Parameters

The experiments were performed with 50 and 100 cases in the base case. A different number of bees was used to evaluate the performance of the system, such as 200, 500, 1000, 2000, and 2500. However, the variation of these parameters did not present differences in the results.

We report results related to the experiments with 2500 agents, 50 cases, and with α set to 0.05. The system was allowed to run for 1000 iterations, a time considered enough to analyze the bees' behavior in performing the tasks randomly asked by different users.

Figure 2 shows the variations of the number of bees working in a demand in a part of the simulation. In the moment that some demand is

Figure 2. Number of bees vs. time, for different demands

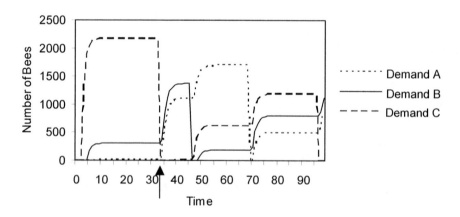

Figure 3. Number of bees dancing for given cases vs. time (N = 200; M = 50)

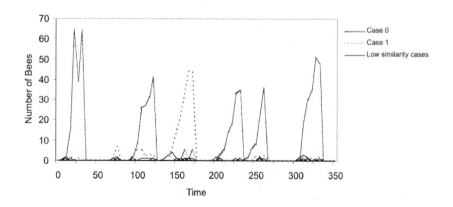

Figure 4. Number of bees dancing for given cases vs. time (N = 2500; M = 50)

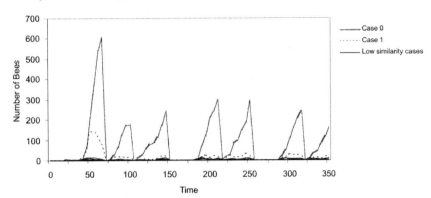

Figure 5. Number of cases that were visited by bees in demand A

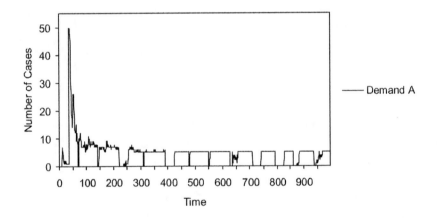

performed (some travel package is recommended to the user), the bees abandon that demand and are idle until a new demand appears. The arrow indicates this situation in Figure 2 (between time 30 and 40). When the demand C is performed, there is a considerable increase of bees to demand B. This demand is then quickly finished between time step 40 and 50.

It is important to notice that, after a demand has been performed and returned to the user, any user can request it again. This situation can be seen in figure 2 between time step 40 and 50,

when demand C, after has been performed once, is requested by another user's query. During the recommendation process, bees are allocated to the demands at the moment they get into the system.

Figures 3 and 4 show the number of bees dealing with demand A. In Figure 3, N is equal to 200, and in Figure 4 N is equal to 2500. The arrows indicate the moments the recommendation was returned to the user. In Figure 3, between the time steps 50 and 100, and also between 150 and 200, it is possible to see that Case 1 was the most-danced case, that is, the case that was recommended to the user, but the most similar was Case 0. This situation shows that the model behaves better (i.e., recommends the most similar case) with a big number of bees. However, this recommendation cannot be considered as a totally wrong recommendation because Case 1 is the second most similar.

Figure 5 shows the number of cases visited by bees when they were working in the demand A, that is, this figure shows how the tendency changes. In the beginning of the simulation, when the tendency of all cases was nearly equal, the bees have visited a high number of cases. However, within time, bees do not waste time in cases not relevant to the demands they are working in. It means that the bees focus on the more similar (appropriate) cases only.

FUTURE TRENDS AND CONCLUSION

This chapter presented an approach inspired by swarm intelligence applied to a case-based recommender system in the tourism domain. This is justified by the success such agents (social insect inspired) have in dynamic environments. The task of planning travel needs dynamic information that is not always available to the travel agent. The use of agents combined to case-based recommender systems can help the travel agent in this task. Our experiments' results have shown that using this metaphor, the system always return some recommendation to the user, avoiding the user's disappointment with the recommender system.

In future work, we intend to improve the case representation of CASIS, storing the previous queries as cases. Depending on the similarity of the new query, the bees can start not completely randomly. Instead, they may use the information gathered regarding the previous query.

Recommender systems are being used in e-commerce to help users to find better prod-ucts according to their needs and preferences. A new kind of recommender system is arising: distributed multi-agent recommender system. In these systems, the agents work together to search information that fits the user's preferences. Each agent has its own knowledge base, and all agents communicate with each other to exchange information only when they do not have it in their knowledge base.

REFERENCES

Aamodt, A., & Plaza, E. (1994). Case-based reasoning: Foundational issues, methodological variations, and system approaches. *AI Communications, 7*(1), 39-59.

Bonabeau, E., Theraulaz, G., & Dorigo, M. (1999). *Swarm intelligence: From natural to artificial systems*. Oxford University Press.

Bridge, D., & Ferguson, A. (2002). Diverse product recommendations using an expressive language for case retrieval. In S. Craw and A. Preece (Eds.), *Advances in Case-Based Reasoning, Proceedings of the 6th European Conference on Case Based Reasoning, ECCBR* (pp. 43-57). Springer Verlag.

Burke, R., (2000). Knowledge-based recommender systems. In J. E. Daily, A. Kent, & H. Lancour (Eds.), *Encyclopedia of library and information science, vol. 69*. Marcel Dekker.

Camazine, S., Deneubourg, J. L., Franks, N. R., Sneyd, J., Theraulaz, G., & Bonabeau, E. (2003). *Self-organization in biological systems*. Princeton.

Camazine, S., & Sneyd, J. (1991). A model of collective nectar source selection by honey bees: Self-organization through simple rules. *Journal of Theoretical Biology, 149*(4), 547-571.

Dorigo, M., & Caro, G. D. (1998). AntNet: Distributed stigmergetic control for communications network. *Journal of Artificial Intelligence Research JAIR, 9,* 317-365.

Ferreira, P. R., Jr., Oliveira, D., & Bazzan, A. L. (2005). A swarm based approach to adapt the structural dimension of agents' organizations [Special issue]. *Journal of Brazilian Computer Society JBCS,* 101-113.

Fesenmaier, D., Ricci, F., Schaumlechner, E., Wober, K., & Zanella, C. (2003). DIETORECS: Travel advisory for multiple decision styles. In A. J. Frew, M. Hitz, & P. O'Connors (Eds.), *Information and communication technologies in tourism* (pp. 232-241).

Gordon, D. (1996). The organization of work in social insect colonies. *Nature, 380,* 121-124.

Kolodner, J. (1993). *Case-based reasoning.* San Mateo, CA: Morgan Kaufmann Publishers.

McSherry, D. (2003). Similarity and compromise. In A. Aamodt, D. Bridge, & K. Ashley (Eds.), *ICCBR 2003, 5ᵗʰ International Conference on Case-Based Reasoning* (pp. 291-305). Trondheim, Norway.

Nwana, H. S., Lee, L. C., & Jennings, N. R. (1996). Coordination in software agent systems. *The British Telecom Technical Journal, 14*(4), 79-88.

Robinson, G. E. (1992). Regulation of division of labor in insect societies. *Annual Review of Entomology, 37,* 637-665.

Ricci, F., Venturini, A., Cavada, D., Mirzadeh, N., Blaas, D., & Nones, M. (2003) Product recommendation with interactive query management and twofold similarity. In A. Aamodt, D. Bridge, and K. Ashley (Eds.), *ICCBR 2003, 5ᵗʰ International Conference on Case-Based Reasoning* (479-493). Trondheim, Norway.

Seeley, D., Camazine, S., & Sneyd, J. (1991). Collective decision-making in honey bees: How colonies choose nectar sources. *Behavioral Ecology Sociobiology, 28,* 277-290.

Watson, I. (1997). *Applying case-based reasoning: Techniques for enterprise systems.* Morgan Kaufmann.

ENDNOTE

[1] Forfeit is a special travel package created by the travel agent with flights, hotels, and further services that match with the customer's preferences.

Section IV
Applications of Multi-Agent Systems

Chapter XV
A Multi–Agent System for Optimal Supply Chain Management

Hyung Rim Choi
Dong-A University, Korea

Hyun Soo Kim
Dong-A University, Korea

Yong Sung Park
Catholic University of Busan, Korea

Byung Joo Park
Dong-A University, Korea

ABSTRACT

Supply chain management recently has been developing into a dynamic environment that has to accept the changes in the formation of the supply chain. In other words, the supply chain is not static but varies dynamically according to the environmental changes. Therefore, under this dynamic supply chain environment, the priority is given not to the management of the existing supply chain but to the selection of new suppliers and outsourcing companies in order to organize an optimal supply chain. The objective of this research is to develop a multi-agent system that enables the effective formation and management of an optimal supply chain. The multi agent system for optimal supply chain management developed in this research is a multi agent system based on the scheduling algorithm, a cooperative scheduling methodology, which enables the formation of an optimal supply chain and its management. By means of active communications among internal agents, a multi-agent system for optimal supply chain management makes it possible to quickly respond to the production environment changes such as the machine failure or outage of outsourcing companies and the delivery delay of suppliers. This research has tried to suggest a new direction and new approach to the optimal supply chain management by means of a multi-agent system in dynamic supply chain environment

INTRODUCTION

Many companies have tried to introduce SCM (supply chain management) in an effort to enhance competitiveness amid severe competition caused by market globalization. Now, the participating companies in the supply chain are not fixed but rather are dynamically being changed in response to the environmental changes. Under such a dynamic SCM, it is very important to determine with whom to cooperate in order to solve these problems coming from environmental changes. Instead of seeking to optimize the existing supply chains, this study has focused on optimizing the supply chain itself. The optimization of an existing supply chain can be efficient to a fixed supply chain, but it is difficult for a dynamic supply chain to respond flexibly under the environment that its member is always changing. When a company joins an existing optimal supply chain, or when a company, which is currently joining a supply chain, has to transfer to another supply chain, they have to change their systems or processes in order to join in the new supply chain. However, this is not an easy job. The optimization of a supply chain is not made only once. Rather, it is to be made continually in response to diverse environmental changes. That is, it needs to be made on a real-time basis.

By the way, the supply chain, which consists of a lot of companies, is likely to meet with various complex problems for entire optimization, and these problems bring a significant influence on making the optimal supply chain. For example, machine failure of one participating company affects not only its related member companies but also the whole supply chain that the company belongs to. Therefore, this problem must be coordinated or adjusted not as a problem of one company, but as a problem of whole supply chain. To this end, each member of the supply chain has to cooperate and exchange information between members on a real-time basis. A multi-agent system can provide a useful tool for this purpose.

Many preceding studies have emphasized that the multi-agent system is the best way in solving many complicated problems under diverse environmental changes (Bussmann, 1999; Choi, Kim, Park, & Park, 2004; Fox, Barbuceanu, & Teigen, 2000; Julka, Karimi, & Srinivasan, 2002; Shen & Norrie, 1998; Shen, Norrie, & Kremer, 1999). Also, this is an efficient way of exchanging and sharing information without integration of its applications among companies. That is to say, it enables relevant companies to move smoothly to another supply chain without changing their systems and processes. Accordingly, only by the transfer of the agent alone, which represents the relevant company, cooperation, and information exchange among members within the supply chain can this be made possible.

In this study, we developed an integrated scheduling method in order to organize and manage an optimal supply chain and a multi-agent system in order to solve the various problems occurring on a real-time basis in the optimal supply chain. The integrated scheduling method enables the scheduling for the entire supply chain in cooperation with related members in a supply chain, thus it is possible for a manufacturing company to make scheduling by taking into consideration the production environments of outsourcing companies and the delivery status of suppliers. And the multi-agent system shares the information on production environment and supply capacity of both outsourcing companies and suppliers, making it possible to respond to the dynamic environmental changes such as a delay in supplying parts or raw materials, power stoppage, or machine failure of the outsourcing companies for an optimal supply chain management.

BACKGROUND

A multi-agent system has been considered the best way to solve complicated problems under the diverse environmental changes (Shen et al., 1999).

In fact, it is not easy for manufacturing companies to be flexible for dynamic changes. A number of researchers have attempted to apply agent technology to manufacturing enterprise integration, supply chain management, manufacturing planning, scheduling, and control (Bussmann, 1999; Maturana & Norrie, 1996; Parunak, 1987; Parunak, Baker, & Clark, 1997). This trend is well described in Shen et al.'s studies on agent-based production system (1999). Shen et al. developed in their studies many production-related agents with diverse functions and configurations. Their studies mainly focused on making new a manufacturing system using an agent technology for automation and efficiency in the process planning and scheduling. Also, the AARIA (Autonomous Agents for Rock Island Arsenal) project of Intelligent Automation company (Baker, Parunak, & Erol, 1997), ABCDE (Agent-Based Concurrent Design Environment) system developed by KSI (Knowledge Science Institute) of University of Calgary (Balasubramanian & Norrie, 1995), a virtual manufacturing agent made by LIPS institute of the University of Texas at Austin (Chuter, Ramaswamy, & Baber, 1995) and MASCOT (Multi-Agent Supply Chain cOordination Tool) agent of Intelligent Coordination and Logistics team of Carnegie-Mellon University (Norman, David, Dag, & Allen, 1999) are representative studies that have used a multi-agent system for development of intelligent manufacturing system.

While making intensive studies on the intelligent manufacturing system by means of an agent system, the scope of this research has been extended to the study on a multi-agent system for supply chain management. Shen et al. (1999) emphasized that there are a lot of complexities and changes in the manufacturing environment under supply chain, and that the agent system can be the best way for effective supply chain management. Also, they said that a multi-agent system can be the best method to integrate the activities of suppliers, customers, and business partners with internal activities of a company (Shen & Norrie,

1998). Meanwhile, more active research has been done on the agent-based supply chain models. Wu, Cobzaru, Ulieru, and Norrie (2000) suggested a new method that one participating member is connected via a Web system to the agents of its related business partners in the manufacturing, distribution, and service field. When an event happens, each agent cooperates to organize a virtual cluster to solve a specified problem. Julka et al. (2002) suggested an SCM model based on an agent while emphasizing the importance of a more flexible and efficient system. Shen et al. (1999) divided production management into five divisions such as design, process planning, scheduling, marketing, and coordination. And then they established a mediator agent for each division and a mediator agent for each mediator agent. Through this mediator-based multi-agent system, they suggested the possibility that if the scope of manufacturing activities within a factory is extended to its suppliers or business partners, an effective SCM could be established. MetaMorph II system suggested by ISG has a mediator-based multi agent structure, suggesting a supply chain network model where the agents for suppliers, business partners, and customers are connected to the mediator of the system via Internet (Shen et al., 1999).

Most existing research has tried to solve the complex and difficult problems, which cannot be solved by individual application programs, by means of mutual cooperation among agents. That is to say, the existing studies have focused on solving various problems occurring within a supply chain by way of communicating among agents. But this study has tried to organize an optimal supply chain by means of communicating among agents, while focusing on maintaining and managing the optimal supply chains. The existing studies and this study are similar in the sense that both have made use of a multi-agent system, but differences between them are in where and how the multi-agent system has been used. Also, it can be said that the studies on the optimization of supply chain by means of a multi-agent system have not yet been made much.

A METHOD FOR OPTIMAL SUPPLY CHAIN MANAGEMENT

Organization of Optimal Supply Chain

This study focuses on the following problems: How to organize an optimal supply chain under the dynamic supply chain environment? When environmental changes have occurred to the optimal supply chain, how to respond to it? As an object of our research, this study chose a molding company among many make-to-order manufacturers. When a molding company tries to select a supplier and an outsourcing company, such factors as delivery date, cost, and productivity are to taken into consideration. In particular, owing to its industrial characteristics, the due date is the most important factor. A molding company is a typical make-to-order manufacturer, and so if it fails to meet the due date required by a customer, it is impossible for the company to sell its product. Also, as most products of the molding companies are standardized, their price and quality are almost the same, thus showing no much difference. Because of this, instead of the price and quality, the delivery date becomes a critical factor in choosing a supplier or an outsourcing company.

When there are many outsourcing companies and suppliers, as illustrated in Figure 1, this study has selected the supplier and outsourcing company that can meet the due date demanded by customers in order to organize an optimal supply chain.

If an outsourcing company participating in the optimal supply chain is unable to perform operation due to its machine failure, or a supplier fails to provide the specified parts on the due date, the manufacturer has to reorganize the supply chain. Like this, when environmental changes occur, it is absolutely necessary to automatically obtain, exchange, or share information in order to speedily respond to the sudden environmental changes.

An Integrated and Dynamic Scheduling Method for Optimal Supply Chain Management

This research uses genetic algorithm to establish integrated and dynamic scheduling. This algorithm integrates process planning and scheduling in order to consider alternative machines of outsourcing companies and operation sequences, and also can perform rescheduling in response to the changes in the production environment. Traditionally, process planning and scheduling were achieved sequentially. However, the integration of process planning and scheduling brings not only best effective use of production resources but also practical process planning without frequent changes. Choi, Kim, Park, and Park (2004) have

Figure 1. Optimal supply chain

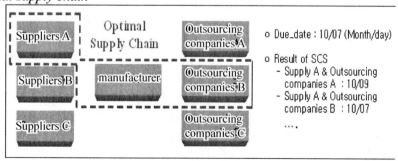

proved that this integration of process planning and scheduling is far superior to the sequential process of planning and scheduling in the aspect of completion time of jobs.

We used a genetic algorithm with flexible representation structure for the integrated and dynamic scheduling method. Genetic algorithm enables integrated scheduling, considering alternative machines of outsourcing companies and operation sequences. Also, it enables rescheduling when changes have been made to the suppliers, outsourcing companies, and producer. In order to design genetic algorithm, first of all, the attribute of the problem should be analyzed, and then the presentation proper to the problem, performance measure, genetic operator, and genetic parameter should be decided. The following is genetic algorithm for the establishment of integrated scheduling considering alternative machines and operation sequence under the dynamic situation.

Representation

To achieve integrated production plan through genetic algorithm considering alternative machines and operation sequences, first of all, the problem should be represented in chromosome. The representation should be made in the way that all the processing sequence, alternative operation sequences, and alternative machines could be decided. First, to represent processing sequence, the pattern to repeat the number of the job as many as the number of operation is used. One gene means one operation, and in the represented order it will be allocated to the machines. For example, the problem of three jobs and three machines is represented in sequence as shown in Figure 2. The threefold repeated number in the first row is the number of the job, and the reason that each job number has been repeated three times is that each job has three operations. The first repeat of the job number means the first operation of the job, and the second repeat means the second job operation. If the job number continues to represent

the number of job operation, this chromosome will always maintain its feasibility. The second row is the random numbers that will be used to decide alternative operation sequence. As each job is done in the one-operation sequence, each job produces the same random number within the number of maximum alternative operation sequence. For example, as job 2 in Table 1 has three alternative operation sequences, the random figure has to be produced within three. The third row has the random numbers to decide the alternative machine, producing them within the number of maximum alternative machines. In Table 1, the second operation of job 1 is to be done in the M2 but also can be done in the M1 and M3. In this case, the number of machines that can handle the second operation of job 1 is 3. As there are no more alternative machines than this in Table 1, the random figures for all alternative machines will be produced within three. The index in the last row means the repeat number of job numbers, namely showing the ordinal operation of each job.

Selection Method

The seed selection is used as a way of selection (Park, Choi, & Kim, 2001). Seed selection, as a way of individual selection that is used in the propagation of cattle and the preservation of the individual, has been introduced to the evolution of genetic algorithm. If the random value of the individual, which belongs to the father among parents, comes within the figure of probability (0.9), the best individual will be selected from within superior individuals from ranking population. But, if not, the individual will be randomly selected from among the entire group. The mother will be selected randomly among the entire group, but in this case, first two individuals will be selected randomly, and then the better individual based on the value of probability will be selected. These will be used as parents, and then returned to the individual groups, so that they will be used again later.

Genetic Operator

Crossover operator should maintain and evolve the good order relationship of chromosome. The crossover operator used in this research has a process as follows:

① Produce a random section

② Insert all the genes inside the random section into parent 2

③ All genes with the same index as the genes in the random section will be deleted in parent 2

④ It will be corrected according to the alternative operations sequence of the initial job number to make alternative operation sequence coincide to the same job number

⑤ These processes will be performed alternating parent 1 and parent 2

The position of insertion is just before the gene where the random section has started. If in parent 1 the random section starts in the fourth place, then the position of insertion will be before the fourth gene in parent 2. This crossover operator produces two children. After two offspring are evaluated, the better one will be sent as a next generation. The mutation operator gives a change to the chromosome, thus maintaining diversity within the group. This research uses the mutation operator based on the neighborhood searching method (Park et al., 2001).

Objective Function and Replacement

The minimum makespan in the scheduling often means the highest efficiency of a machine. When a chromosome is represented as a permutation type, the makespan is produced by the process

Table 1. Alternative machines and alternative operation sequences of each job

		M1	M2	M3
Job 1	Operation sequence 1 (alternative machine)	M1	M2	M3
		(M3)	(M1)	
			(M3)	
	Operation sequence 2 (alternative machine)	M1	M3	M2
		(M3)		(M1)
				(M3)
Job 2	Operation sequence 1 (alternative machine)	M1	M2	M3
		(M3)		(M1)
				(M2)
	Operation sequence 2 (alternative machine)	M1	M3	M2
		(M3)	(M1)	
			(M2)	
	Operation sequence 2 (alternative machine)	M3	M1	M2
		(M1)	(M3)	
		(M2)		
Job 3	Operation sequence 1 (alternative machine)	M1	M3	M2
		(M3)	(M1)	
			(M2)	
	Operation sequence 2 (alternative machine)	M1	M2	M3
		(M3)		(M1)
				(M2)

Figure 2. Chromosome representation

```
3 2 2 2 3 1 1 1 3
2 3 3 3 2 1 1 1 2
3 2 2 1 1 2 1 1 2
```
(1 1 2 3 2 1 2 3 3) ... (Index)

that assigns operations to the machines according to sequence of gene from left to right, while maintaining the technological order of jobs and considering its alternative operation sequence and alternative machine. The process is shown in Figure 3. The next generation will be formed by the selection among the current generation and with the help of genetic operator. The new individuals will be produced as many as the number of initial population and form the next generation. By using elitism, bad individuals will be replaced with good individuals. Also, because of crossover rate and mutation rate, some individuals will be moved to the next generation without getting through the genetic operator.

Genetic Algorithm for Dynamic Scheduling

The genetic algorithm suggested in this paper reflects the dynamic changes in the suppliers and outsourcing companies along with the production changes of the producer. When the changes of production environment have happened in suppliers or outsourcing companies—the acceptance of new orders, machine failure, outage, and the absence of the worker in duty—all these changes will be reflected in the rescheduling. For example, when a machine cannot be operated for 10 hours because of its failure, or a supplier cannot keep the lead-time, thus delaying 10 hours, the integrated scheduling will reflect the usable

time of each machine and the possible starting time of each job. Figure 4 shows the process of rescheduling when a new order has been accepted at the time of t1.

In the process of rescheduling, the remaining jobs and the new jobs to be done by the new orders will be considered in the new production planning. It also considers the starting time of jobs and the usable time of machines. The starting time of jobs can be changed by the delay of supply or the operation delay of its prior process. The usable time of machines, as shown in the black shade of Figure 4, can be changed by when the machine has already been allotted to other job, machine failure, and the absence of the worker on duty. All these dynamic changes will be reflected in the rescheduling (Park, 1999). In the rescheduling process, the chromosome is to be modified, and a new objective function is to be produced in response to the environmental changes. Based on this rescheduling, a new supplier or an outsourcing company is to be selected, and the information of rescheduling is to be transmitted through the multi-agent system. In order to solve several problems simultaneously, the genetic algorithm in this study has been represented in a chromosome and has been designed for better evolution, so that it can more effectively solve the complex problems of integrated scheduling. Like this, the strong point of genetic algorithm lies in its approach based on the problem-centered chromosome design. Also, thanks to its flexible representation, speedy performance, and excellent performance capability, the genetic algorithm makes it possible to reflect in the rescheduling all the information about suppliers and outsourcing companies, which comes from the multi-agent system on a real-time basis. In this respect, the genetic algorithm is considered to be best suited to the dynamic supply chain management.

Figure 3. The example of crossover

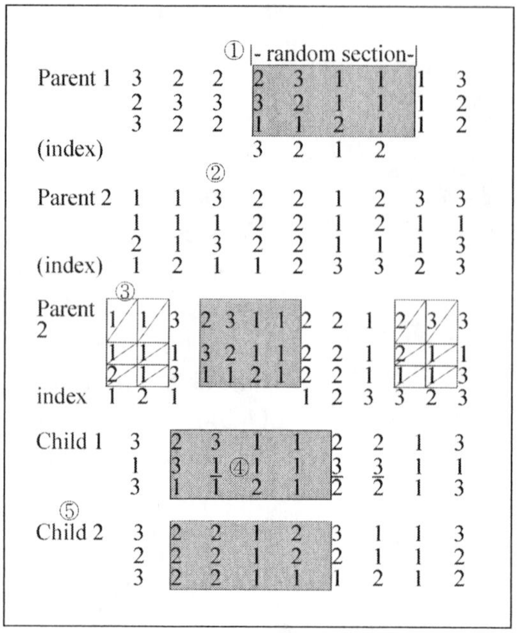

A MULTI-AGENT SYSTEM FOR OPTIMAL SUPPLY CHAIN MANAGEMENT

The Whole Structure of a Multi-Agent System

The key factor in the development of a multi-agent system is how the roles should be assigned to each agent. In the multi-agent system, one agent doesn't perform all functions. Rather, each agent has an individual function, and so they mutually communicate with each other to jointly solve complicated matters. Because of this reason, how to classify each agent is a key factor to designing a multi-agent system. For the development of a multi-agent system, all the activities from a customer's order to manufacturing were reviewed, and then these activities were assigned to each agent. Each agent is given a specified function so as not to have many functions.

As illustrated in Figure 5, the multi-agent system can be divided in two subsystems: vir-

tual manufacturing system and SCM system. The virtual manufacturing system is composed of an inventory analysis agent, manufacturability analysis agent, process planning agent, and scheduling agent. This system makes a decision on whether it will be able to manufacture or not, makes scheduling in consideration of the production environments of both suppliers and outsourcing companies, and makes a decision on the necessity of parts or materials through inventory analysis. This activity is directly related to the selection of suppliers. The SCM system consists of an outsourcing management agent, supplier management agent, outsourcing company communication agent, supplier communication agent, and registry server agent. This system organizes and manages the optimal supply chain based on the integrated scheduling that is the result of virtual manufacturing.

Based on the exact scheduling, the virtual manufacturing system makes a decision on whether it can manufacture within the due date. The SCM system's main function is to respond to the manu-

Figure 4. Example of dynamic scheduling

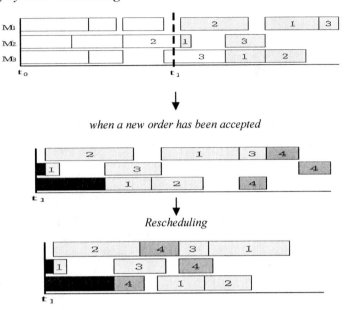

facturing environment changes occurring in the optimal supply chain. To this end, the mediator of the manufacturing company has to exchange information on a real-time basis with both the supplier's and outsourcing company's agent. The multi-agent system has a mediator-centered structure. All the agents are connected to the mediator, which takes control of each agent, and also are responsible for smooth information exchange with suppliers and outsourcing companies.

Function of Each Agent

All agents own their basic function to communicate with each other, and each one has diverse kinds of engines according to his role.

Mediator

The mediator plays the role of controlling and coordinating the message exchange among agents within the system. The agent in charge of controlling and coordination is necessary in order to perform harmoniously the various jobs of many agents, to remove the bottlenecks occurring within the system, and to prevent the collision between each agent. For this purpose, the mediator has a knowledge base for agent coordination and message exchange as well as information on each agent.

For example, when the SMA (supplier management agent) received from the SCA (supplier communication agent) the information on production environment change, that is, "The material delivery from the supplier is delayed," the mediator is to send this information speedily to the SA (scheduling agent) so that it may make rescheduling according to the production environment changes. The roles of mediator are as follows:

- Message transmission between internal agents
- Function control of internal agents
- Function of filtering the messages
- Knowledge of mediator's behaviors
- Knowledge of internal agents

The mediator is in charge of controlling and coordinating each agent, and has diverse knowledge base to help the message exchanges between agents, which are illustrated in Table 2.

As illustrated, the knowledge is expressed in the form of rules. Case 1 shows that when OMA (order management agent) receives an order, the mediator is to send the message asking the MAA (manufacturing analysis agent) to make a decision whether it can be produced or not. See Case 1.

Case 2 shows that when it receives the message that it can produce the ordered product from MAA, the mediator is to send PPA (process planning agent) the message asking for scheduling. See Case 2.

Diverse messages from internal agents converge to the mediator. The mediator is to perform the function of operating its system smoothly, so that it can remove bottlenecks and prevent collisions between each agent. This study adopted the FIFO (first in first out) method in handling the messages. If messages from the agents come to the message queue, those messages will be handled in sequence.

Registry Server Agent

Buyer agent, outsourcing company agent, and supplier agent are to be registered in the registry server agent (RSA). Registered agents are

Figure 5. Structure of multi-agent system of an optimal supply chain

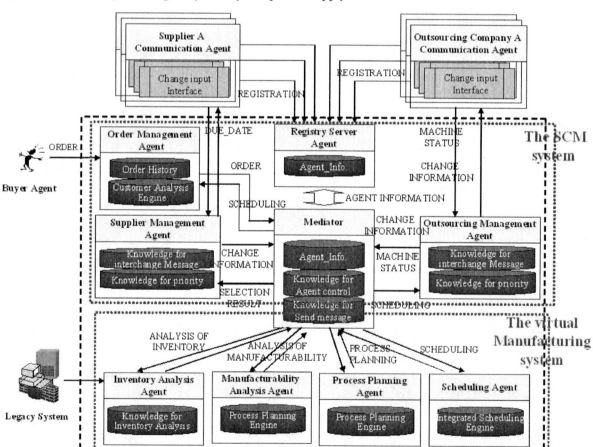

to obtain position information from RSA so as to be able to communicate to his or her partner agent. The agents registered in the RSA can be candidates for the participating member of the optimal supply chain. In principle, the optimal supply chain needs to be organized through communication with the agents of all the suppliers and outsourcing companies. But in reality, for mutual communication among agents, each agent has to obtain information about his or her partner agent. For this reason, only the agents who can communicate via RSA can be candidates for the optimal supply chain organization.

The outsourcing companies and suppliers have to register the information on their agent's position and basic data of their companies. The basic data of the companies includes their name and role. Their role is whether they are outsourcing companies or suppliers. Outsourcing company and supplier have a different role. Because of this, they have to register additional information besides basic data. That is, the outsourcing company has to provide information on machines and facilities, and the supplier has to include information on the parts and materials that it can provide. In particular, in case of an outsourcing company, as an outsourcing company executes some parts of an ordered product, information on its production facilities such as a mill or a drill has to be registered.

Order Management Agent (OrderMA)

An order management agent receives orders and confirms them. It keeps order information and analyzes and classifies buyers through data mining and statistic analysis.

Supplier Management Agent

A supplier management agent provides the information on the environmental changes in the suppliers to the inside system and also transmits the information on supply schedule to the suppliers. This agent also keeps the suppliers' priority on the basis of their capability and confidence. This data will be used at the time of selecting suppliers when they all can keep the same due date.

Outsourcing Management Agent (OMA)

An outsourcing management agent provides the information on the machine situation of outsourcing companies for the sake of scheduling, and also, based on the scheduling, it makes a decision on the necessity of outsourcing. The criteria for the decision-making are whether the outsourcing company can keep the due date or not. When the producer cannot keep the due date for itself, this agent sends the message containing the necessity of outsourcing. The following is the agent's action knowledge represented in the form of IF-THEN, saying, "If the due date based on the production planning is not satisfactory, inform the mediator of the necessity of outsourcing." Here, Last_time is the finishing time of the last operation in the production planning.

Table 2. The knowledge in the mediator

Knowledge of agent role	Knowledge of subagent composition Knowledge of subagent role
Knowledge of message exchange	Knowledge of job handling procedures Knowledge of how to handle the contents of message
Knowledge of problem solution	Knowledge of how to handle message in case of no answer Knowledge of how to express in time of trouble

Case 1.

```
[ case 1 ]
 rule name  Accept Order
 if   contents_name = order
 then send product_width and product_length and product_height and raw_material and part_width and part_length and
 part_height to ManufacturabilityAnalysisAgent
```

Case 2.

```
[ case 2 ]
 rule name  Accept ManufacturabilityAnalysisResult
 if  contents_name = ManufacturabilityAnalysisResult and
 ManufacturabilityAnalysisResult = yes
 then send use_for and model_name and number_of_part and process_time and product_width and product_length and
 product_height and raw_material and part_width and part_length and part_height to Process Planning Agent.
```

```
IF  Last_time > due_date
Then send  yes_message  to Mediator
```

This agent has the priority information on outsourcing companies, and this information will be used for selecting outsourcing companies.

Inventory Analysis Agent (IAA)

An inventory analysis agent analyzes the inventory level and makes a decision on the purchase of materials. The information on the inventory level is to be secured from the inside of the system. The inventory analysis agent makes a decision based on the purchase necessity analysis knowledge.

Manufacturability Analysis Agent (MAA)

Based on the information on products and parts, MAA checks up the constraints related to the manufacturing process in order to make a decision on its manufacturability. Constraints usually come from the size and weight. In case the size of an ordered product is too large or the weight is too heavy, the small manufacturer cannot produce it. For example, if the size and weight surpass the capacity of the cranes of the manufacturer, it cannot execute the order. The judgment on manufacturability can be made by the knowledge base. This knowledge base includes information on various kinds of size and weight as well as the cases making it impossible to execute an order. The knowledge in Box 1 shows how the judgment on manufacturability can be expressed in JESS, that is, a language of java-based rule expression.

Process Planning Agent (PPA)

A process planning agent performs the role of process planning. This paper used CBR (case-based reasoning) based on a process planning engine. The reason is that if the products of order-based producers are similar, the same process will be used (Kolodner, 1993). Choi, Kim, and Park (2002) have proved the availability of this methodology by applying it to molding industry.

Box 1.

```
"The mold size of cavity plate is a>600, b>270, c>400, it is impossible to execute the order."
(constraint_rule_002
        (size_a    ?a)
        (size_b    ?b)
        (size_c    ?c)
    =>
    (if (&& (>=?a600) (>=?b270) (>=?c400)))
    then (assert (manufacturability  no)))
```

Scheduling Agent

A scheduling agent performs the role of scheduling based on a genetic algorithm-based engine, considering alternative machines and operation sequence. This agent plays the critical role in the multi-agent system, and based on this scheduling, the supplier and outsourcing company will be selected.

Supplier and Outsourcing Company Communication Agent

A supplier and outsourcing company communication agent performs the role of communications between multi-agent system and suppliers and outsourcing companies. For the establishment of scheduling, the supplier communication agent provides the possible due date of raw materials, and the outsourcing company communication agent provides the information on the machine situation. These two agents provide multi-agent systems with the information on the production environment changes through user interface.

The Process of the Multi-Agent System

The process of the multi-agent system is composed of the followings: the process of scheduling for self-production, the process of scheduling for selecting outsourcing company, the process of scheduling for selecting supplier, and the process for rescheduling in case the production environments of suppliers and outsourcing companies have been changed. If necessary, based on the rescheduling, the supplier and outsourcing company should be reselected.

The Process of Scheduling for Self-Production

Figure 6 shows the case that a producer can make for order-based products at his own factory without the help of suppliers and outsourcing companies. The producer establishes the scheduling for accepted orders, and provides the result to the buyer agent.

The Process of Scheduling for Selecting Outsourcing Company

Figure 7 shows the case that if a producer cannot meet the required due date by self-production, he has to select an outsourcing company.

The outsourcing management agent analyzes the necessity of outsourcing based on the scheduling, and if necessary, it asks for the information on the machine situation of outsourcing companies. Based on this information on machine situation, the scheduling agent establishes rescheduling. Based on this rescheduling and outsourcing company priority, the outsourcing management agent selects an outsourcing company.

The Process of Scheduling for Selecting Supplier

Figure 8 shows how to select the supplier in case that the producer doesn't have enough inventory of raw materials. The inventory analysis agent analyzes the inventory of the inside system and required raw materials for orders. If it thinks the supplier should be selected, the supplier management agent will ask the suppliers for a possible due date, and based on this information, it will select a supplier.

The Process of Rescheduling for Production Environment Changes

Figure 9 shows how to respond to the changes in the production environment. When there are changes in the production environments of outsourcing companies, the outsourcing communication agent provides this information to the outsourcing management agent. And based on this changed production environment, the scheduling agent achieves rescheduling, and the outsourcing management agent analyzes this rescheduling. However, if this rescheduling cannot meet the required due date, other outsourcing company should be selected.

To testify to the availability of the above processes of the multi agent system, this research adopts a molding company as a case study.

CASE STUDY OF MULTI-AGENT SYSTEM

Case Definition

In order to test the validity and practicality of the multi-agent system developed by this study, we made a prototype and applied it to real field cases. We visited the small "J molding company," the domain of this study, and reviewed and analyzed the facilities of the factory and its field situation. J molding company has such machines as a large mill, medium and small mill, drill, and lathe to perform milling, drilling, grinding, and electric discharge machining. Meanwhile, due to the constraint of facility of this company, there are some molds that cannot be manufactured. That is, the cranes of this company cannot handle the mold exceeding the weight of five tons. But there are no other difficulties in the resources, like manpower or machines, and in technologies. The knowledge base of MMA defines the constraints and uses them in judging manufacturability. The J molding company was maintaining a close relationship with its outsourcing companies and suppliers while outsourcing some part of milling and electric discharge machining.

As illustrated in Figure 10, J molding company has a supply chain consisting of material suppliers, outsourcing companies, and customers. Also, in order to meet the due date of the order, it tries to organize an optimal supply chain. The company keeps a good business relationship with three outsourcing companies and three suppliers. This case study is for the mold production of a "cake box."

Case Study

The case study has two stages: The first stage is how to organize an optimal supply chain according to the procedures as illustrated in Figure 11. The second stage is how to respond to the environmental changes such as a machine failure or power stoppage after organizing an optimal supply chain.

As illustrated in Figure 11, the organization of an optimal supply chain needs two steps: The first step is to perform virtual manufacturing for an ordered product. The second step is to select an optimal supplier and outsourcing company according to the result of virtual manufacturing.

Figure 6.The process of scheduling for self-production

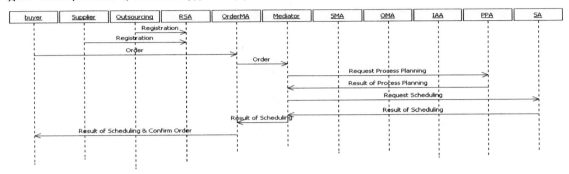

Figure 7. The process of scheduling for selecting outsourcing company

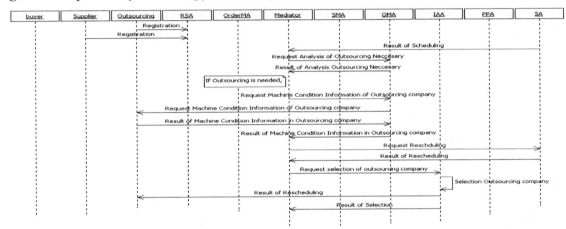

Figure 8. The process of scheduling for selecting supplier

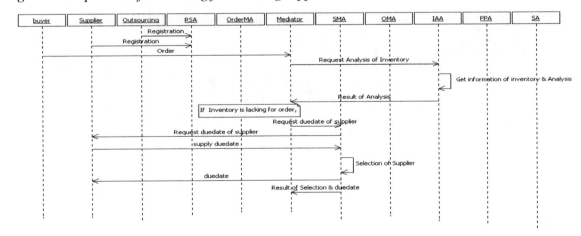

Figure 9. The process of rescheduling for production environment changes

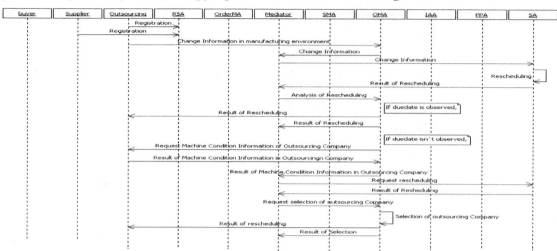

Figure 10. Supply chain of J molding company

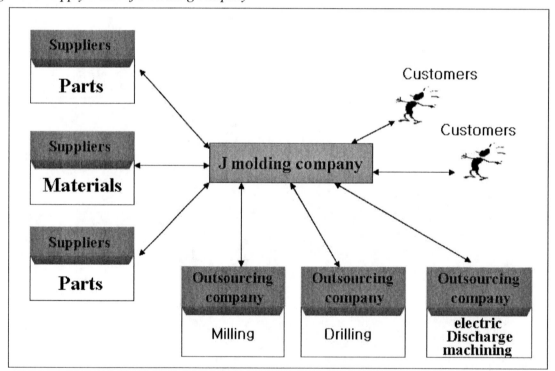

Step 1. Virtual manufacturing

If the mediator receives from OMA a message that a client order "cake box" within six days from order date, it sends necessary information to the MAA so as to make judgment on manu-facturability.

If the mediator receives a "yes" message from MAA, it sends order-related information to the PPA and SA so that both agents may prepare for process planning and scheduling respectively.

The mediator sends scheduling information from SA to the OMA to make a decision on whether there it is necessary to outsource.

"Makespan 61" is the result of scheduling for an ordered "cake box" mold. This means that if the factory operates eight hours per day, it takes eight days. In this case, as the customer's due date request is within six days from his or her order date, J molding company cannot satisfy the customer's due date. Accordingly, the OMA sends the message of outsourcing necessity to the mediator.

Step 2. The organization of an optimal supply chain

In order to select an optimal outsourcing company that can meet the due date, the mediator asks OMA for the information on the machine situation of outsourcing companies registered in the RSA.

OMA asks the OCCA (outsourcing company communication agent) of each outsourcing com-pany for the information on machine situation, which includes the machine schedule. If the ma-chine is now in operation, that machine cannot be used for another order until the current operation is over. When the mediator receives the following information on machine schedule from outsourc-ing companies, it sends this information to the SA so that it may prepare for rescheduling.

- A outsourcing company: two units of mill are now not in operation. (AM 1 0, AM 2 0)

- B outsourcing company: one unit of mill can be used after six hours. (BM 6)
- C outsourcing company: one unit of mill can be used after three hours, and another one unit is now not in operation. (CM 3, CM 0)

As illustrated in Figure 17, rescheduling was made by considering outsourcing companies' machine situation. As a result of rescheduling, in case of A and C outsourcing companies, pos-sible due date is October 18, 2005, thus satisfying customer's request. But B outsourcing company's possible due date is October 20, consequently not meeting the requested due date. This means that A and C can be a participating member of the optimal supply chain. Therefore, the media-tor asks OMA to choose one company between these two outsourcing companies. Based on the priority information, OMA chooses A outsourc-ing company, and then notifies the mediator and OCCA of it.

By selecting A outsourcing company, the optimal supply chain for a "cake box" mold was organized. In this case study, the case of selecting a supplier was excluded, but the supplier also can be selected in the same way as the above-mentioned outsourcing company. Meanwhile, the optimal supply chain is not fixed, rather it can be changed in response to the changes of a manufacturing environment. But even if such environmental changes take place repeatedly, an optimal supply chain can be organized in the same way as the first organization of an optimal supply chain. As illustrated in Figure 19, this study performed the tests for two kinds of environmental changes. The first environmental change is: A outsourcing company, which is chosen as a member of the optimal supply chain, is unable to work because of milling machine failure. The second one is: A supplier becomes unable to provide the parts within the requested date. Figure 19 shows the process to solve the environmental changes.

The above two environmental changes can affect J molding company in the following two

Figure 11. Procedure for organizing an optimal supply chain

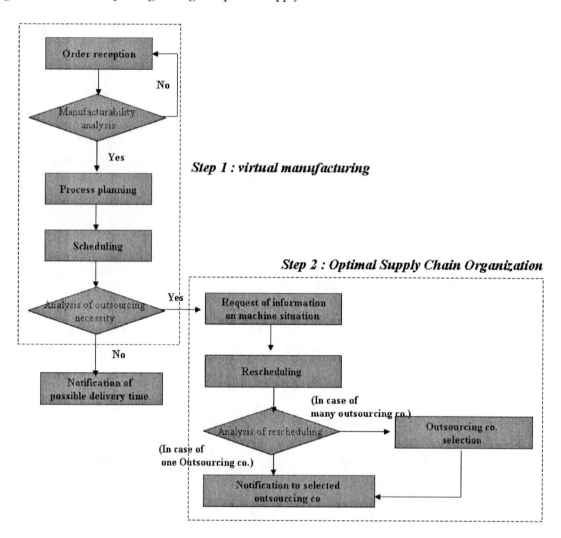

Figure 12. Manufacturability analysis-related message interface

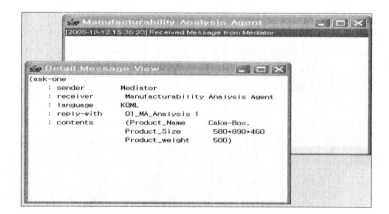

Figure 13. Process planning-related message interface

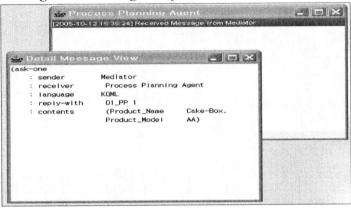

Figure 14. Scheduling-related message interface

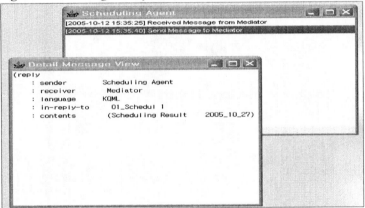

ways: one is that the delay of work doesn't directly affect the due date requested by the customer, and the other is that it affects the due date. In the first case, the company's manufacturing activity will be continued according to the rescheduling, but in the second case, it has to reselect a new outsourcing company or supplier.

As shown in the above tests, the optimal supply chain can be reorganized in response to the dynamic changes in the manufacturing environment, so that the manufacturing company may smoothly maintain and manage its optimal supply chain.

Review of Case Study

In order to test the validity and practicality of the developed multi-agent system, this study produced a prototype performing key functions and applied it to the field for case study. Unfortunately, the multi-agent system has not yet commercialized because of many difficulties in realizing its knowledge base. Likewise, the multi agent system's prototype made by this study is not enough to be commercialized, and so we couldn't measure the performance and effect by means of application. Instead, as a way to test its validity and practical-

Figure 15. Outsourcing necessity-related message interface

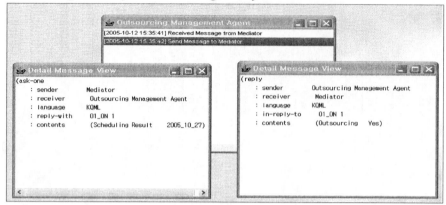

Figure 16. Message interface asking for information on the machine situation of outsourcing companies

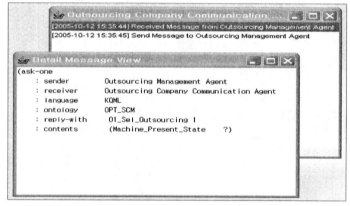

Figure 17. Rescheduling-related message interface in consideration of outsourcing companies' situation

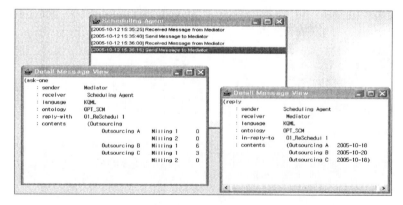

Figure 18. Message interface related to the notification of the result of outsourcing company selection

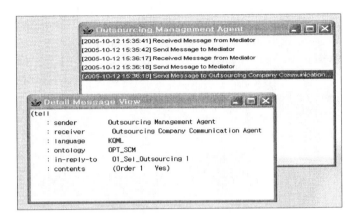

Figure 19. The test procedures of optimal SCM cases

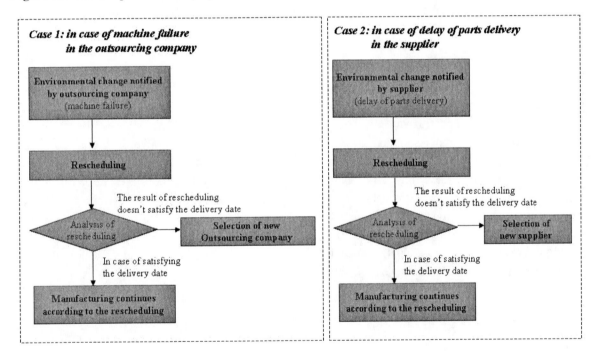

ity, we had interviews with the experts in charge of scheduling at the make-to-order manufacturing companies, including the J molding company and 15 software developers related to agent development. The experts in charge at the make-to-order manufacturing companies testified to the validity of the multi-agent system, and those software developers evaluated the systemic performance of the multi-agent system. Evaluation was performed on a five-point scale on the next major items.

- *Experts in charge at the make-to-order manufacturers*
  - Is the scheduling of this system correct and accurate?
  - Is it reasonable that the optimal supply chain consisting of suppliers and outsourcing companies focused on due date for supply chain organization?

○ Does the work process for calculating the possible due date reflect well the reality?

○ Does this system smoothly react to the environmental change occurring in the supply chain?

• *Software developers*

○ Is communications among agents smoothly performing?

○ Is the role of each individual agent well assigned? And is the multi-agent structure appropriate?

○ Is the handling speed of the system satisfactory?

○ Is the agent development method reasonable?

○ Is there any serious mistake in the system?

As a result of evaluation, the experts in charge at the make-to-order manufacturers gave a score of 3.8 on the overage, and software developers gave a score of 4.2. The experts in charge gave a relatively higher score to the capability to react to the environmental changes and well-reflected work process, but a somewhat low score to the accuracy of scheduling. This seems to come from the fact that the current algorithm is not fully enough, because of the complex scheduling of the molding industry. However, they put a high value on the automation of scheduling and the possibility of job handling without human intervention and believed that commercialization of the multi-agent system will be able to bring cost reduction and productivity improvement. They also added that many efforts were being made to maintain a solid relationship with outsourcing companies and suppliers that satisfy the due date. These efforts mean that the core point of satisfaction of due date in the organization of optimal supply chain has validity. The agent software developers, who gave a higher score, seem to value the current high level of agent development. The evaluation team as a whole rated the validity and practicality of the multi-agent system very high. In particular, they have paid attention to the new approach to SCM.

FUTURE TRENDS

Owing to the characteristics of the domain of this research, we organized an optimal supply chain based on the satisfaction of due date. From now on, however, further research on the optimal supply chain, which has two different objectives, or considers two key factors simultaneously, will be made. Many companies consider the problem of price to be very important as well as due date.

Figure 20. Evaluation of due date and price

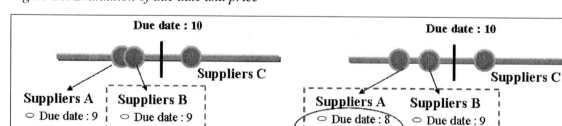

For example, when we consider the two factors of price and due date simultaneously, as the due date is the same but the price is different like Figure 20, it is easy to select its business partner. But as shown on the right side of Figure 20, if the price and due date are respectively different, it is not easy to evaluate them because the two have different worth. Therefore, the method to evaluate due date and price simultaneously has to be developed.

Furthermore, as due date and price have a trade-off relationship, negotiation is possible. That is, the following negotiation can be made: Instead of lowering the price, the due date can be lengthened, or if an earlier due date is required, the price will be higher. In these cases, a new negotiation protocol as well as a new negotiation method needs to be developed.

CONCLUSION

Owing to the increasing importance of quick response to the rapid changes of business environments, the supply chain also needs dynamic changes according to its environmental changes. In the dynamic supply chain environment, it is a key factor to decide who to cooperate with for effective manufacturing. This study developed a system to efficiently select an optimal business partner under the dynamic supply chain environment. To this end, this study developed an algorithm for both scheduling and rescheduling, which is to be made by taking into consideration the manufacturing environments of both suppliers and outsourcing companies. Also, by using a multi-agent system, this study made it possible to organize and manage an optimal supply chain on a real-time basis in response to the dynamic changes in the supply chain environment.

Like this, instead of trying to optimize an existing, fixed supply chain, we have tried to organize a new supply chain that can dynamically respond to the environmental changes, so that it can bring diverse effects such as cost saving, productivity enhancement, and speedy job handling. These effects are well presented in the results of our case study.

Finally, we expect that this multi-agent system will be usefully applied to the complex supply chain environment and also have expectations that the agents realized in the wrapper method through a new development framework will be used in diverse fields.

REFERENCES

Baker, A. D., Parunak, H. V. D., & Erol, K. (1997). *Manufacturing over the Internet and into your living room: Perspectives from the AARIA project* (Tech. Rep. TR208-08-97). ECECS Dept.

Balasubramanian, S., & Norrie, D. H. (1995). A multi-agent intelligent design system integrating manufacturing and ship-floor control. *Proceedings of the First International Conference on Multi-Agent Systems*. San Francisco: The AAAI press/The MIT Press.

Bussmann, S. (1999). An agent-oriented architecture for holonic manufacturing control. *Proceedings of the First International Workshop on IMS*, Lausanne, Switzerland.

Choi, H. R., Kim, H. S., & Park, Y. S. (2002). Intelligent injection mold process planning system using case-based reasoning. *Journal of Korea Intelligent Information Systems Society*, 8(1), 159-171.

Choi, H. S., Kim, H. S., Park, B. J., & Park, Y. S. (2004). Multi-agent based integration scheduling system under supply chain management environment. *Lecture Notes in Artificial Intelligence, 3029*, 249-263.

Chuter, C. J., Ramaswamy, S., & Baber, K. S. (1995). *A virtual environment for construction and analysis of manufacturing prototypes*. Retrieved from http://ksi.cpsc.ucalgaly.ca/projects/mediator

Fox, M. S., Barbuceanu, M., & Teigen, R. (2000). Agent-oriented supply chain management. *The International Journal of Flexible Manufacturing Systems, 12*, 165-188.

Julka, N., Karimi, I., & Srinivasan, R. (2002). Agent-based supply chain management-2: A refinery application. *Computers and Chemical Engineering, 26*, 1771-1781.

Kolodner, J. (1993). *Case-based reasoning.* Morgan Kaufmann Publishers.

Maturana, F., & Norrie, D. H. (1996). Multi agent mediator architecture for distributed manufacturing. *Journal of Intelligent Manufacturing, 7,* 257-270.

Norman, M. S., David, W. H., Dag, K., & Allen, T. (1999). MASCOT: an agent-based architecture for coordinated mixed-initiative supply chain planning and scheduling. *Proceedings of the Third International Conference on Autonomous Agent (Agents '99)*, Seattle, WA.

Park, B. J. (1999). *A development of hybrid genetic algorithms for scheduling of static and dynamic job shop.* Unpublished doctoral thesis, Dong-A University, Busan, Korea.

Park, B. J., Choi, H. R., & Kim, H. S. (2001). A hybrid genetic algorithms for job shop scheduling problems. *Computers & Industrial Engineering, 45*(4), 597-613.

Parunak, V. D. (1987). Manufacturing experience with the contract net. In M. N. Huhns (Ed.), *Distributed artificial intelligence* (pp. 285-310). Pitman.

Parunak, V. D., Baker, A. D., & Clark, S. J. (1997). The AARIA agent architecture: An example of requirements-driven agent-based system design. *Proceedings of the First International Conference on Autonomous Agent*, Marina del Rey, CA.

Shen, W., & Norrie, D. H. (1998). An agent-based approach for distributed manufacturing and supply chain management. In G. Jacucci (Ed.), *Globalization of manufacturing in the digital communications era of the 21st century: Innovation* (pp. 579-590). Kluwer Academic Publisher.

Shen, W., & Norrie, D.H. (1999a). Developing intelligent manufacturing systems using collaborative agents. *Proceedings of the Second International Workshop on Intelligent Manufacturing Systems* (pp. 157-166).

Shen, W., & Norrie, D. H. (1999b). Agent-based systems for intelligent manufacturing: A state-of-the-art survey. *The International Journal of Knowledge and Information System*

Shen, W., & Norrie, D. H. (1999c). *An agent-based approach for manufacturing enterprise integration and supply chain management.*

Shen, W., Norrie, D. H., & Kremer, R. (1999). *Implementing Internet enabled virtual enterprises using collaborative agents, infrastructures for virtual enterprises.* Kluwer Academic Publisher.

Shen, W., Ulieru, M., Norrie, D. H., & Kremer, R. (1999). Implementing the Internet enabled supply chain through a collaborative agent system. *Proceedings of Workshop on Agent Based Decision-Support for Managing the Internet-Enabled Supply-Chain*, Seattle.

Wu, J., Cobzaru, M., Ulieru, M., & Norrie, D. H. (2000). SC-web-CS: Supply chain Web-centric systems. *Proceedings of the IASTED International Conference on Artificial Intelligence and Soft Computing* (pp. 501-507).

Xue, D., Yadav, S., & Norrie, D. H. (1999). Development of an intelligent system for building product design and manufacturing - Part I: Product modeling and design. *Proceedings of the 2nd International Workshop on Intelligent Manufacturing Systems* (pp. 367-376).

Chapter XVI
Macroscopic Modeling of Information Flow in an Agent–Based Electronic Health Record System

Ben Tse
University of Regina, Canada

Raman Paranjape
University of Regina, Canada

ABSTRACT

This chapter presents an architecture, or general framework, for an agent-based electronic health record system (ABEHRS) to provide health information access and retrieval among different medical services facilities. The agent system's behaviors are analyzed using the simulation approach and the mathematical modeling approach. The key concept promoted by ABEHRS is to allow patient health records to autonomously move through the computer network uniting scattered and distributed data into one consistent and complete data set or patient health record. ABEHRS is an example of multi-agent swarm system, which is composed of many simple agents and a system that is able to self-organize. The ultimate goal is that the reader should appreciate the benefits of using mobile agents and the importance of studying agent behaviors at the system level and at the individual level.

INTRODUCTION

Health information is the heart of any electronic health record (EHR) application, and the management of this growing and complex information has become a huge and complicated task for every health care organization. Moreover, much of this health information is fragmented and scattered among different medical service facilities, mainly because a patient is usually seen by many different health care providers in many different medical service facilities. So, the patient is likely to have at least one relevant health document or record in each medical facility he/she visits. Over time, the patient's medical record becomes fragmented, inaccurate, and inconsistent. This is the complex environment in which EHR management must operate.

Fortunately, a large part of today's health information is already available in electronic form, and the primary task of the EHR system is to communicate this information electronically anywhere in the world. Based on this vision, the need to move the patient's health information among different health care facilities grows in parallel with the need to centralized health information across numerous EHR systems within the health care domain (Silverman, Andonyadis, & Morales, 1998). Therefore, in order to allow rapid and accurate access of patients' health record, the creation of a digital health information network is essential to our modern health care system.

Mobile agent technology can be an essential tool in creating this system, because of fundamental mobile agent attributes including: autonomy, mobility, independence, pro-activity, reactivity, communicability, swarm, and group intelligence. Because of these attributes, mobile agents can provide solutions to address the challenges of health information systems in the health care domain, as suggested in Nealon and Moreno (2003) and Crow and Shadbolt (2003). Later section in the chapter, we will present an architecture or general framework for ABEHRS to provide health information access and retrieval among different medical services facilities.

As shown in Lerman and Galstyan (2001), a swarm agent system (simple agents with a distributed controller) that exhibits collective behaviors has demonstrated advantages in robustness, scalability, and cost, over a traditional agent system (intelligent agents with a centralized controller) that exhibits individualized behaviors. Moreover, self-organization is one of the interesting collective behaviors that appears in a swarm system. This concept of self-organization manifests itself

in our ABEHRS, which allows the patient's health record to self-organize. In the background section, basic definitions of swarm and intelligence will be presented, and the definition of self-organization will also be presented. Later sections in the chapter will present the reasons why the swarm paradigm is chosen over the traditional paradigm and the process of self-organization used in our ABEHRS.

In order for our ABEHRS to be useful, a study of the system-level behavior must be performed. This allows a greater understanding of the system dynamics, so that if such a system was actually implemented, the dangers of unexpected system behavior could be limited. Smith, Paranjape, and Benedicenti (2001) show that the full potential of individual agents is not obtained during unexpected/unwanted agent-group behaviors (for example, oscillation of agents between hosts). Therefore, we believe that the behavior of agents in a multi-agent system must be completely understood before the completion of actually system design, so as to minimize the chances of system failure and to achieve superior system and individual agent performance. In the proceeding sections, we present a study of agent behaviors in ABEHRS using simulation and mathematical models, as well as the comparison between the simulation and numerical results.

BACKGROUND

The Electronic Health Record

As defined in Grimson, Grimson, and Hasselbring (2000) and the Web site of the Healthcare Information and Management Systems Society (http://www.himss.org), an electronic health record is an electronic version of patient's health record, which includes prescriptions, lab results, evaluations by doctors, and so forth. Since the EHR is in an electronic format, so it can be easily accessed by a health information system within an electronic health network. Around the world, people are recognizing the value of EHR systems. Their advantages include increasing effectiveness and efficiency of clinical staff and health practitioner, providing seamless care for patients with timely, appropriate, and secure access to the right information whenever and wherever they are, and increasing the profitability of the practice or facility.

Although EHR appears to hold great promise, there are many challenges that need to be addressed before they can be fully integrated in a health care system. As described in Nealon & Moreno (2003), Huston (2001), and Walczak (2003), these challenges include scattered and fragmented health information, security and confidentiality, delay in availability of information, complexity of medical data, heterogeneous health information system, and network bandwidth consumption.

Mobile Agent Technology

A mobile agent (MA) is a software object that can migrate to different computers over an Internet protocol (IP) network, or the Internet, to perform user-assigned and self-initiated tasks in heterogeneous computing environments (Gray, Kotz, Nog, Rus & Cybenko, 1997). An MA is a representation of its owner, and it inherits the owner's authority and acts on behalf of the owner. By adding artificial intelligence modules to a MA, it can have the ability to select the best set of activities to perform until it reaches the goal specified by the owner, or the ability of reacting to specific events in its surrounding environment to provide flexible, dynamic, and intelligent solutions. Mobile agents exhibit a number of characteristics, and they include:

- **Modularity:** Mobile agents are diverse in nature; different services can be distributed among a set of agents or encapsulated into a single complex agent. In this way, the

required algorithms can be embedded into the agent system to perform the service
- **Mobility:** Agents can migrate to the resource they need instead of accessing these resources remotely, which reduces network bandwidth usage tremendously
- **Interactivity:** Agents can communicate to other agents using a specified message format
- **Autonomy:** Agents are typically independent entities and have the ability to choose the best actions to perform to achieve specific goals

Mobile agents do not operate independently; they required extensive supporting infrastructure to provide communication services, mobility services, management services, security, and monitoring services. This infrastructure is commonly called an agent execution environment, or AEE. The AEE must be installed and running on a host computer before the mobile agent program can run. TEEMA (TRLabs execution environment for mobile agents) is an AEE that was developed by the faculty, staff, and graduate students at TR-Labs Regina and Electronic Systems Engineering at the University of Regina. More information related to TEEMA can be found in Gibbs (2000) and Martens (2001). TEEMA is the experimental platform used in this work.

There are various software applications that are uniquely suited for development using mobile agent technology. Typically, these applications take advantages of the intrinsic characteristics of mobile agents, including autonomy, re/proactivity, modularity, interaction, and/or mobility. And our ABEHRS is one of the applications that take advantage of these intrinsic characteristics of agent to facilitate the process of retrieving/accessing fragmented and scattered patient health information across different medical service sites. So, each mobile agent has the ability to "move" around different medical service facilities across IP networks, the ability to "automate" tasks on behalf of the patient, the ability to act in a "re/pro-active" bases to respond to the patients or medical providers, the ability to "interact" with other agents, and the ability to "embed" partial or whole patient information as a function. After the health information is encapsulated by the agent, it can be moved to different medical sites within our ABEHRS, we can define these behaviors/actions as information flow within ABEHRS.

Swarm and Its Intelligence

The idea of an intelligent agent swarm takes its inspiration from insect societies in biology and nature. Swarm consists of a large group of small insects (such as bees or ants), and each insect has a simple role, with limited capability (for example, moving around). The swarm as a whole (such as a colony of ants or a hive of bees), however, is able to do many complex and sophisticated tasks (such as finding the shortest distance between the nest and the food source). Furthermore, each insect works autonomously, and essentially their teamwork is self-organized. Coordination and cooperation between individual insects arises from the interactions between insects, or the interactions between insects and the environment. Through these interactions (such as stigmergy), collective behavior emerges, and efficient and effective outcomes are generated.

As defined in Bonabeau, Dorigo and Theraulaz (1999), swarm intelligence is the concept of using the collective behavior arising from a group of relatively simple objects in a decentralized and self-organized system to solve complex and distributed problems. Artificial swarm intelligence can be demonstrated using relatively simple and autonomous agents. The agents are distributed, self-organized, and there is no central controller to direct how each agent should behave. Agents may be dynamically added or removed, making the system highly flexible and scalable. Examples of agent swarm systems are Truszkowski, Hinchey,

Rash, and Rouff (2004), Wu (2003), and Charles, Menezes, and Tolksdorf (2004).

Self-Organization Definition

According to Camazine et al. (2001), self-organization is a key feature in a swarm system. It refers to the process that describes a system as it moves from a chaotic state to a well-ordered state by using the interactions at the lowest-level components of the system. Camazine et al. also pointed out the four characteristics of self-organization in a swarm system, and they are: positive feedback, amplification of fluctuations, multiple interactions, and negative feedback. When the system is in the chaotic state, the positive feedback signals will influence certain properties of the system, and these properties will be amplified by the many random interactions between the individual components. These interactions can be seen as a combination of exploitation and exploration of new solutions from the components. The negative feedback serves as a regulatory control mechanism of the system's properties, and is used to direct the system back to a well-ordered state. In fact, the self-organization of a system can be seen as a formulated feedback control loops between the individual components in the system. An example of a self-organized swarm system is Kadrovach and Lamont (2002).

By combing the concept of self-organization with agent technology, we are able to allow individual health record to self-organize themselves in our ABEHRS.

Agent Behaviours Modeling

In order to ensure that a useful and effective mobile agent system is constructed, it is important to study, examine, and analyze the system-level behaviors, as well as the agent-level behaviors. There are several approaches used to study behavior in multi-agent systems; most include simulation and mathematical modeling. Using the simulation approach to evaluate agent behaviours in multi-agent systems is a traditional approach for agent designers and researchers. In this approach, the simulation consists of a set of agents that encapsulate the behaviours (for example, rules of movement, strategies) of various individuals that interacted with the local environment and with other individuals. Usually, these behaviours, as well as external forces (for example, resource fluctuation), are represented using different stochastic processes, and so, by executing these behaviours during the simulation, a global dynamic model of the system and of the agents can be created. The simulation model provides reasonable design ideas to the agent designers when developing a real multi-agent system. Simulations of agent behaviour in multi-agent system are shown in Tecchia, Loscos, Conroy, and Chrysanthou (2001), Smith et al. (2001), and Heine, Herrier and Kirn (2005).

The mathematical modeling approach is an alternate way of evaluating agent behaviours. The mathematical model usually consists of a set of equations that describe the process of the behaviours being modeled, and these behaviours are represented by a set of stochastic probabilities that are used in the equations. In order for the mathematical model to be useful and realistic, relevant details of the process must be accounted for. Generally, two different levels of mathematical modeling are used to describe a multi-agent system, and the levels are microscopic and macroscopic. In general, a microscopic model describes the agent-level behaviours in a multi-agent system, for example, interactions between two agents. On the other hand, a macroscopic model describes the system level behaviours in a multi-agent system, for example, collective or global behaviour emerged from the agent's interactions. Studies of agent behaviours using microscopic or macroscopic mathematical models are shown in Agassounon and Martinoli (2002), Lerman and Galstyan (2001), Lerman and Shehory

(2000), Sugawara and Sano (1997), and Wang, Liu, and Jin (2003).

In this work, we choose the approach of agent system evaluation using simulation and mathematical modeling. For the simulation, a prototype of ABEHRS model was developed using TEEMA platforms, and simulation results were obtained. For the mathematical modeling, we choose a macroscopic model to analyze system behavior in ABEHRS. The reasons to use a macroscopic model are that global dynamic behaviors of the system can be readily observed, and macroscopic modeling is computationally more efficient than microscopic model, since only a few parameters are used. Moreover, among the mathematical modeling approaches mentioned above, Lerman and Galstyan (2001) have presented a general mathematical macroscopic approach to analyze the global dynamic behaviors of multi-agent swarm system. In our mathematical model, a set of differential equations based on the Lerman and Galstyan (2001) model are determined and numerical results are obtained by solving these equations. We can compare and contrast these results in the context of our ABEHRS. It is our belief that a simple multi-agent swarm system will exhibit complex and unexpected behaviors, and unless we model these behaviors using a macroscopic mathematical model and simulation, unpredictable system behavior will result.

THE AGENT-BASED ELECTRONIC HEALTH RECORD SYSTEM

Our main objective in this work is to propose a general framework or architecture that incorporates the use of mobile agent technology to facilitate the flow of health records among various medical service facilities, and combines all scattered and fragmented health records into one consistent and complete data set.

To accomplish the system objective, agents must exhibit the following characteristics: autonomy, re/pro-activity, mobility, modularity, and interaction. With the presence of autonomy and re/pro-activity, agents can monitor any changes in the patient's electronic health record. Whenever a change is identified to the patient's electronic record, the agent will automatically perform necessary tasks to ensure the electronic record of the patient is up-to date and is consistent. Thus the ABEHRS agents are highly autonomous. Another important characteristic of agents is mobility. With this characteristic, agents are able to migrate to different medical service facilities to perform necessary data collection tasks. Interaction between agents is mandatory in our system, and it is used in identity verification of patients and agents at different medical service facilities. It is also used in the co-ordination of other agents' activities. Agents can encapsulate health information, communication protocols, or medical data en/decoding formats as embedded functions. By using mobile agents and their fundamental and intrinsic characteristics, many of the challenges of the EHR systems can be overcome. In the subsequent sections, we will present system concepts, design concept, and the system components for the ABEHRS.

System Concepts

By using mobile agent technology, we add mobility and autonomy to the health record, which allows the record to automatically move anywhere within the health information network. This system can be colloquially described as "putting a mobile agent wrapper" around an electronic health record and instructing the agent to move to other medical facilities for its owner (the patient).

There are two important aspects of the system, which are shown below:

1. A complete health record is defined as every pieces of information in a patient's health record (which may be generated by different

medical facilities within the health care system) united into one consistent and complete set of information. The health record may include doctor's evaluations, test results, prescriptions, and so forth.

2. The ABEHR system is described as self-completing, self-regulating, and self-organizing. We define these capabilities for the system as the mechanism by which it automatically (without any supervision or guidance) makes each patient health record complete.

Therefore, we wish to apply the idea of self-organization through agents to facilitate the concept of self-completing patient's health records. The following subsections will provide an overview of how self-organized health record is achieved, and how agent cloning is used in ABEHRS.

Self-Organized Health Record

As defined above, self-organization refers to the process of a system moving from a chaotic state to a well-ordered state by using the interactions between the lowest-level components of the system. From the perspective of the individual patient's health record, an individual health record is in a well-ordered state, when the record is complete and consistent. If the health record is not complete and consistent (for example, newly created record), then the record is in a chaotic state. Mobile agents are effectively the lowest-level component, which autonomously interact with other agents in the system to move a chaotic health record into a well-ordered state (for example, update health record in HRC and in patient's health storage device). Once initiated, agents perform the necessary actions to have the health records system self-organize. All the actions and interactions related to self-organized health record performed by the agents are presented in the section of Typical Actions of Patient Agent in Different Medical Sites.

Agent Cloning

In order to facilitate the process of self-organization and to provide needed information in a timely fashion, agent cloning is used in our ABEHRS. By using the agent-cloning approach, the agents are able to perform parallel tasks at different medical sites. Also, when inheriting sensitive information (for example, health card number, access control permissions) from the initiator (the agent who initiates the cloning process), more secure control of data may be achieved than passing the information to other agents using messaging. Therefore, cloning of mobile agents is the process typically used in the ABEHRS. The events that trigger the cloning process depend on the medical services required by the patient. Medical services could be record update/retrieval services, prescription-filling services, lab test services, and so forth. Using this agent-cloning approach, a group of agents can be easily generated, and their direct and group actions work, to keep the health record complete and consistent for the individual patient.

Design Concepts

As previously stated, multi-agent systems are either developed using the traditional paradigm with centralized control and deliberative agents or the swarm paradigm with distributed control and simple agents. There are various factors that influence the decisions as to which design paradigm to adopt for the development of ABEHRS, and Lerman and Galstyan (2001) had shown us that the swarm paradigm is a more suitable approach than the traditional paradigm for the development of our ABEHRS. Reasons supporting this decision are the following:

- Health information systems are diverse in nature. This diversity makes it almost impossible to develop a centralized controller for a large group of health information systems.

- Deliberative agents are smarter, autonomous, and more individualized than swarm agents. Deliberative agents contain deeper knowledge about the system and have higher capabilities to perform more complicated tasks. In order to get the full potential out of the deliberative agents, agent designers must have detailed coordination and complete plans of actions for the agents. These robust mechanisms simply do not exist. Conversely, agents in the swarm are simple and task-oriented, so agent designers can easily develop mechanisms to coordinate and plan the actions of agents. Also, swarm agents require only the knowledge necessary to perform the specified task. Thus, designing and coding swarm agents is more simple and less error prone than deliberative agents.

- In general, health information organizing is conceptually simple but it requires collective effort from a large group of agents to accomplish. When the task is performed in a collective way, the operation is more effective and efficient than if an individual complex agent attempts to perform it. Coalition formation of deliberative complex agents is not easily achieved, while for swarm agents, coalition forming can scale up to thousands of agents easily.

- The health care industry is very dynamic and rapidly changing (for example, standard of health information, medical protocols). The adaptation to a changing process for swarm agents is less complex than the adaptation for deliberative agents. This is mainly due to the deliberative agents containing a large amount of knowledge about the system that is hard to substitute. Swarm agents, on the other hand, contain only the necessary knowledge to perform a specific task, and coordination between swarm agents is self-directed. So a swarm agent system will be able to tolerate changes in the health care industry more effectively.

Thus, we see that the properties of swarm agents (simple, interchangeable, distributed, dynamically add/delete) and the features of the agent swarm system (self-organization, self-regulation, collective action, ant forging) can be effectively applied to real-world problems in the health care domain.

System Components

The agent-based electronic health record system is developed using the TEEMA platform. A system overview is shown in Figure 1. Each TEEMA platform represents a certain physical location, such as a clinic or laboratory. In each platform, there are a single stationary and mobile agent. The system contains five different types of stationary agents and one mobile agent.

Stationary agents

- Clinic agent (CA) is responsible for verifying the identity of the patient, and creating a mobile patient agent if a patient arrives at a clinic and requests medical services. It can be seen as an agent interface between the patient, clinical staff, and the patient agent.
- Doctor agent (DA) is responsible for managing the doctor's evaluation of the patient. It can be seen as an agent interface between the patient agent and the doctor.
- Pharmacy agent (PhA) is responsible for verifying the identity of the patient agent, retrieves prescriptions from the patient agent, and sends notification to the patient agent when the patient or owner wishes to pickup his/her prescription. It can be seen as an agent interface between the patient agent and the pharmacist.
- Lab agent (LA) is responsible for verifying the identity of the patient agent, retrieves lab work orders from the patient agent, sends notification to the patient agent when the patient or owner arrives at the lab, and

sends notification to the patient agent when the test result for its owner is prepared. It can be seen as an agent interface between the patient agent and the laboratory technicians.
- Health record central agent (HRCA) is responsible for controlling access to the health record database that holds the personal and medical information of all patients. It can be seen as an agent interface between the patient agent and the central database.

Mobile agents

- Patient agent (PA) is responsible for updating the patient health record that is stored in the patient's storage device card, transferring records to the health record central, and if there is a prescription and/or lab test needed, the patient agent will clone itself and migrate to pharmacy and/or laboratory. It can migrate to all of the different platforms in the simulation.

Typical Actions of Patient Agent in Different Medical Sites

The process begins when a patient visits the medical clinic. The patient places his/her health storage device card (SC) into a card reader, and the clinic agent performs verification (for example, fingerprint) on the patient's identity. If the verification is successful, a patient agent is created, and the PA copies the patient's entire health record from the SC into its payload area. If the verification fails or any other incidents (for example, the patient forgets to bring his/her SC) take place, then the clinical staff will be involved to resolve the incidents. The first operation of the PA is to review the medical service request log (for example, request lab work order) from the patient's record. By doing this, the PA will have enough data to decide what actions to perform next. If the patient's record is not up to date (for example, missing lab test result), then the PA will

Figure 1. An overview of the ABEHRS architecture

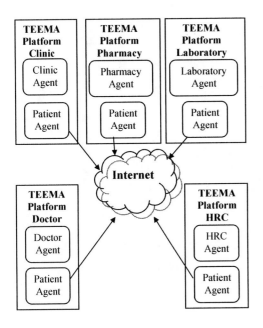

clone itself. The PA clone will migrate to health record central (HRC), retrieve the latest record from HRC database, migrate back to the clinic with the record, send the new record to the original PA, insert the record into the patient's SC, and finally destroy itself. After the cloning process, the original PA will migrate to the platform of the doctor that has been chosen by the patient, and inform the doctor agent about its owner/patient who needs the consultation service. The original PA will then wait at the doctor platform for the examination to be finished.

During the examination of the patient, which is performed by the doctor, the doctor is able to review the patient's completed and consistent health record. This access to the complete health record will allow the doctor to provide a diagnosis quickly and effectively. After the doctor finishes the examination of the patient, the DA will save the results of the medical evaluation into a specific location on the doctor's storage device, and then the DA will send a notice to the PA to retrieve the medical evaluation (for example, diagnosis,

prescription form, lab work order form) of the patient from that specific location. After the PA retrieves the evaluation, it will migrate back to the clinic platform to perform actions required to serve the patient.

Once the PA migrates back to the clinic, it will check the doctor's evaluation for any medical services requested by the doctor. If the medical services are requested, then the PA will clone itself, and the clone will migrate to the platform of the medical service provider that is chosen by the patient. For example, if the requested service is filling a prescription, then the PA clone will migrate to the platform of the pharmacy that is chosen by the patient. This cloning process will be repeated until all requested medical services have been looked after. At the end of the process, the original PA will save the medical evaluation to the patient's SC. Finally, the original PA migrates to HRC and appends the newest medical evaluation to the complete set of the patient's health record in the database, and then destroys itself.

When the cloned PA arrives at the platform of the patient's chosen pharmacy, it will first verify itself to the pharmacy agent at the pharmacy service site. If the verification is successful, then the PA will send the prescription content to the PhA and hibernate. If the verification fails, then the PA will destroy itself. When the patient visits the pharmacy and wishes to pickup his/her prescription, then the PhA will inform the PA about the arrival of the patient, and this will trigger the PA to de-hibernate. Once the PA de-hibernates, it will perform verification on the patient's identity and the prescription content inside the patient's SC, and the cloned PA will destroy itself after a successful verification. If the verification fails, then a notice will send to PhA, which in turn sends a notice to pharmacy staff. And the process of verification will be repeated until a successful verification occurs or a verification override is executed by the facility staff. At the end, the PA will be forced to act as if there is a successful verification and destroys itself.

When the cloned PA arrives at the platform of the patient's chosen laboratory, it will first verify itself to the laboratory agent at the laboratory service site. If the verification is successful, then the PA will hibernate. If the verification fails, then the PA will destroy itself. When the patient visits the laboratory and wishes to go through the lab testing procedures, the LA will inform the PA about the arrival of the patient, and it will trigger the PA to de-hibernate. Once the PA de-hibernates, it will perform verification on the patient's identity and the work order form in the patient's SC. If the verification fails, then a notice will be sent to the LA, which will in turn send a notice to laboratory staff. And the process of verification will be repeated until a successful verification occurs or verification override is executed by the facility staff. After a successful verification, the PA will send the lab work order to LA and re-hibernate until the lab test results are ready to be retrieved. After the lab technician generates the test results for the patient, the LA will inform the PA, and it will trigger the PA to de-hibernate again. Once the PA is de-hibernated, it will retrieve the results and go through the process of cloning. The clone of the PA will migrate to HRC, update/append the lab test result to the complete set of the patient's health record, and then destroy itself. After the cloning process, the PA will migrate back to the clinic where it was originally formed, store the test results into a specific location, inform the doctor (whom the patient consulted with) via the doctor's DA about the test results and the location of where the test result is stored, and finally destroy itself.

Once the PA arrives at the HRC, it will verify itself to the heath record central agent before it can access the centralized health information database. If the verification fails, the PA will destroy itself. If there is a successful verification, the PA can either retrieve or update health information from or to the complete set of patient's health record. If the operation of PA is updating, then it will destroy itself after completion. If the opera-

tion of PA is to retrieve information, then after the information is retrieved, it will migrate back to the clinic's platform where it originated.

The actions of PA in different locations within ABEHRS can be summarized by the following flowcharts, as shown in Figures 2 through 6. Based on the above actions and interactions, the concepts of self-completing, self-regulating and self-organizing can be achieved in our proposed system architecture.

SIMULATION SETUP

In order to demonstrate that the architecture of ABEHRS presented above can achieve the concept of health record self-organization, a simulation approach has been applied to ABEHRS. We chose to use the simulation approach because actual physical prototype will have a greater potential to exhibit unexpected or unplanned system behaviors related to the self-organization processes. At the same time, we examine the global system dynamics for the self-organized processes, so agent population at each medical site can be measured. The parameters of the simulation also help formulate our macroscopic mathematical model of the system. Therefore, the simulation results will be used as a contrasting representation for the comparison to the numerical results we generate from the mathematical model. In this section, the structure and conditions of the simulation are presented, as well as the results and the discussion.

Structure and Conditions

A simple computer environment was setup to simulate the necessary scenario. Several computers were used in our simulation, and they are interconnected via 100Mbps Ethernet. Each computer executed at least one TEEMA platform, and each TEEMA platform represented one specific physical medical site; the number of platforms used depends on the structure of the simulation. For this simulation run presented in this work, we used: one clinic, two doctors in the clinic, one pharmacy, one laboratory, and one HRC; thus a total of six TEEMA platforms were used, and they are executed on two computers: TEEMA platforms for one clinic and two doctors are executed on the first computer, and TEEMA platforms of one HRC, one lab, and one pharmacy are executed on the second computer.

Basic conditions and assumptions used in the simulation are listed next:

Figure 2. Clinic actions flowchart (flowchart representation of the actions of patient agents at the clinic platform)

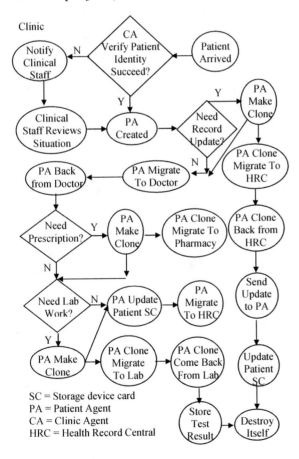

SC = Storage device card
PA = Patient Agent
CA = Clinic Agent
HRC = Health Record Central

1. Doctor evaluation, prescription content, and lab test results are predefined to be fixed-length text. The combination of this content is considered the health record of a patient.

2. Even though the health records are randomly generated, records in the storage device card and records in the HRC are correlated. If the record in the storage device card indicates there is an absent of lab test result, then the record in the HRC must contain the lab test result, and it must be ready for the patient agent to retrieve.

3. There are several random behaviours used in the simulation, and they are represented by different kinds of random numbers. The behaviours are shown below:

    o   **Patient preference behavior:** This behavior describes a patient's wish to choose a specific doctor. For simplicity, a uniform distributed random number is used to represent this behavior.

    o   **Patient necessitated behavior:** This behavior describes the need for a specific medical action. This includes the need for prescriptions and lab work. A Bernoulli random number was used to describe this type of behavior. Since the need for a prescription/lab work is binary, the chance that a patient will need this type of medical service when he or she visits the clinic is 50/50.

    o   **Patient arrival behavior:** This behavior describes the rate of patient arrival at the clinic. For simplification, a constant mean rate of arrival was used and set to one patient arrival at the clinic every minute.

    o   **Professional service behavior:** This behavior describes the service time of any medical services provided to the patients. This includes physicians, pharmacists, and lab technician patient processing time. For simplicity, a uniform distributed random numbers between one and five was used to represent this type of behavior in the experiment.

Simulation Result

The results of a typical simulation run are shown in Figure 7. From Figure 7, we see that there are many events occurring in each platform, especially for Clinic_1. These events are the indication of agent actions/interactions at different platforms or medical service sites. To show that ABEHRS does achieve health record self-organization as defined in the section of self-organized health record, we first examine the health information files in HRC at the end of the simulation and all the self-organization related events occurring during the simulation. By reviewing the files, we are able to see that each patient's health record does contain the newly created record, and it was appended to the complete set of patient history of health information. This indicated that every piece of health record generated at different medical sites did indeed combine into one complete and consistent data set for the patient.

Although the results in Figure 7 do not represent the entire range of behaviours exhibited by the system, it is possible to identify some relevant observations, and they are:

- We notice there are several cluster formations at Doctor_A, Doctor_B, Pharmacy_1 and Lab_1 platforms. It seems that the cluster size of PAs at Doctor_B has the same cluster size of PAs at Doctor_A, which is ~ 5. Cluster formations at the Pharmacy_1 and the Lab_1 platforms are also similar to the cluster sizes at both doctor platforms. Each PA arriving at those medical service platforms waits for an event (for example, patient arrives at the lab) to trigger the action of the next task, and this causes the size of the cluster to grow continuously. Even though there are events (for example, patient picks up his/her prescription) to cause the PAs to either destroy themselves or migrate to other platforms, the occurrences of these events were not high enough to limit the cluster growth due to the arrival of PAs at those platforms. Clearly, we can solve this problem by changing the patient's arrival rate and/or the service rates of these facilities to overcome the increase of the cluster size. Conversely, we can take advantage of this growing cluster size of PAs, since cluster formation is a valuable behaviour in a system where a group of agents can perform a task more effectively than a single agent can. So, a large cluster size means a large number of PAs grouping together, and there could be tremendous

Figure 3. Doctor actions flowchart (flowchart representation of the actions of patient agents at the doctor platform)

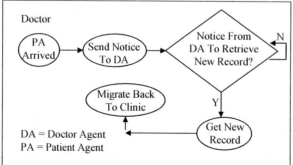

Figure 4. Pharmacy actions flowchart (flowchart representation of the actions of patient agents at the pharmacy platform)

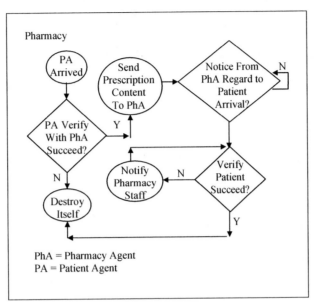

Figure 5. Lab actions flowchart (flowchart representation of the actions of patient agents at the lab platform)

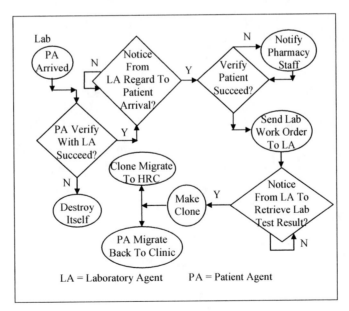

Figure 6. Health record central actions flowchart (flowchart representation of the actions of patient agents at the health record central platform)

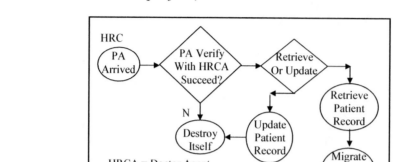

gains for group or batch processing from the agent cluster.

- We observe the total number of clones produced by the PAs during simulation period, since an agent-cloning approach is used to replicate agents into a group of agents to perform the self-organizing health record-related tasks, as mentioned in the section on agent cloning. Generally, each PA can clone itself zero, one, two, or four times during the process of self-organization. Maximum clones produced for each PA are four, which is counted as follows: one for HRC update, one for prescription, and two for lab work (the clone created in the lab platform will be included as the clone produced by the original PA). So, for the period of 30 minutes, 30 unique PAs are created (since the patient's arrival rate is ~1 per each minute, PA's creation rate is also ~1 per each minute), and there could be a maximum of 120 clones produced during the simulation period. As stated above for patient necessitates behaviours, if there are 30 PAs, then the number of clones produced for pharmacy and lab should be 15 and 15, respectively. Therefore, the cloning effect can be easily model by a Bernoulli random

variable, which in turn we can apply it to our mathematical model. Moreover, by observing the number of clones produced, we are able to observe any overpopulation of PAs at each medical service site.

DYNAMIC MODEL

Using the flowcharts as a guide, we are able to construct a macroscopic model that treats agent population at each medical site as the fundamental unit, hence directly describing the characteristic of the system. The mathematical model captures the dynamics of the self-organization process by examining agent population at each platform. This model contains a set of coupled rate equations that describe how the agent population at each platform evolves over time. The following is our general mathematical model of ABEHRS that contains n number of clinics, m number of doctors in each clinic, x number of pharmacies, y number of laboratories, and one health record central. See Box 1.

The dynamic variables in the model are:

- $N_{Cn}(t)$ is the number of agents in clinic n, where $n \geq 1$

Figure 7a-b. Evolution of agent populations. Typical traces showing movements of patient agents in the ABEHRS between six TEEMA platforms for the first 30 minutes (x-axis is time, y-axis is agent population).

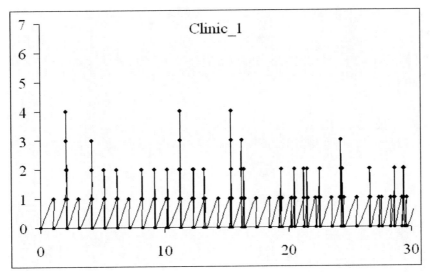

(a) Evolution of Agent Population in Clinic_1 Platform

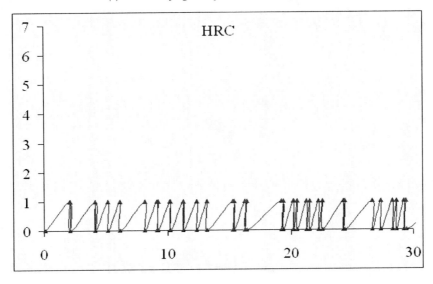

(b) Evolution of Agent Population in HRC Platform

319

Figure 7c-d. Evolution of agent populations. Typical traces showing movements of patient agents in the ABEHRS between six TEEMA platforms for the first 30 minutes (x-axis is time, y-axis is agent population).

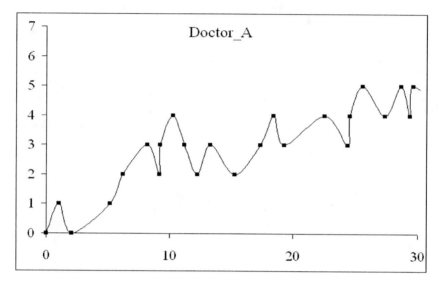

(c) Evolution of Agent Population in Doctor_A Platform

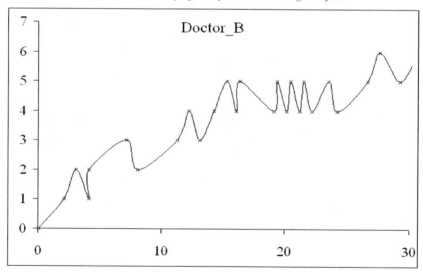

(d) Evolution of Agent Population in Doctor_B Platform

Figure 7e-f. Evolution of agent populations. Typical traces showing movements of patient agents in the ABEHRS between six TEEMA platforms for the first 30 minutes (x-axis is time, y-axis is agent population).

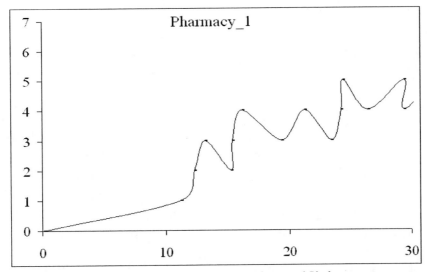

(e) Evolution of Agent Population in Pharmacy_1 Platform

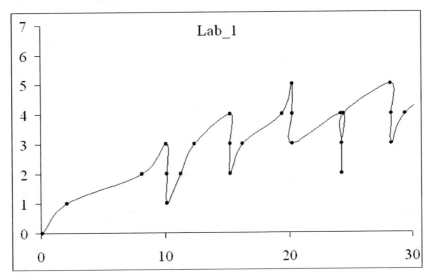

(f) Evolution of Agent Population in Lab_1 Platform

- $N_{CnDm}(t)$ is the number of agents in the doctor m in clinic n, where $m \geq 1$
- $N_{Px}(t)$ is the number of agents in pharmacy x, where $x \geq 1$
- $N_{Ly}(t)$ is the number of agents in laboratory y, where $y \geq 1$
- $N_{HRC}(t)$ is the number of agents in the health record central

And the definitions of the parameters used in the model are:

- λ is the patient's arrival rate at the clinic, which is equivalent to the creation rate of agent
- δ is the rate of agent cloning occur at the clinic platform, which is $\sim \lambda * \beta_A + (\Sigma (1/\tau_{CnDm}) * (\beta_B + \beta_C)) *$
- τ_{CnDm} is the examination time of a doctor on a patient
- τ_{AvgD} is the average of all τ_{CnDm}
- τ_{Px} is the service time for an individual agent in a pharmacy service site (prescription fill time + prescription pickup time)
- τ_{Ly} is the service time for an individual agent in a lab service site (time for a patient to come to the lab + test result production time).
- τ_{SPC} is the service time for an individual agent to perform necessary task in the clinic platform
- τ_{SPL} is the service time for an individual agent to perform necessary task in the lab platform
- τ_{HRC} is the service time for an individual agent in a HRC
- β_A, β_B, β_C are the probability of a patient who needs an update or a prescription or a lab work, respectively
- β_{Dm} is the probability of a specific doctor being chosen by a patient; it is set to 1/(# of doctors in the clinic), since we assume each doctor is to be chosen equally
- β_{PPx} is the probability of a specific pharmacy chosen by a patient; it is set to 1/(number of

Table 1. Average number of clone produced for the first 30 PAs in 30 trials

Clone Type	Number of clone produced
Update	13
Pharmacy	15
Lab	14
Total	56

pharmacies in the system), since we assume each pharmacy is to be chosen equally
- β_{PLy} is the probability of a specific lab chosen by a patient; it is set to 1/(# of labs in the system) and we assume each lab is to be chosen equally
- α is the transition rates of agents between different medical platforms, for example, α_{CnPx} is the rate at which PAs leave the clinic n platform to the pharmacy x platform. α_{CnR} is the rate at which PAs leave the clinic n platform to the HRC platform
- $\theta_{(t-\tau)}$ is a unit step function to ensure certain variables are zero during $t < \tau$

Instead of providing a detailed explanation of what each team in each equation means, we will only provide a general explanation. For the terms with a minus sign in front, they are describing the patient agents (PAs) that leave the platform for other platforms. The terms having the plus sign in front describe PAs who enter the platform from other platform. In addition, in most of the terms, there is a time delay inside a dynamic variable (for example, $N(t-\tau)$), which illustrates that some of the agents that entered a platform at $(t-\tau)$ time are now exiting this platform and migrating to other platform. For example, $N_{Cn}(t-\tau_{HRC})$ illustrates that there are several patient agents that entered the HRC platform at $(t-\tau_{HRC})$ time and which are now exiting the HRC platform and migrating to the clinic platform.

The number of terms in each equation in the above model is too large and the equations are

Box 1.

$$\frac{d}{dt}N_{Cn}(t) = \lambda + \delta + \sum_{i=1}^{m} 1/\tau_{CnDm} + \beta_A * \alpha_{CnR} * N_{Cn}(t-\tau_{HRC})$$
$$+ \beta_C * \alpha_{CnLy} * N_{Cn}(t-\tau_{AvgD}-\tau_{Ly}) * \theta(t-\tau_{AvgD}-\tau_{Ly}) - \sum_{i=1}^{m} 1/(\tau_{CnDm}+\tau_{SPC}) - \alpha_{CnD} * N_{Cn}(t+\tau_{SPC})$$
$$- \beta_A * \alpha_{CnR} * N_{Cn}(t) - \beta_B * \alpha_{CnPx} * N_{Cn}(t-\tau_{AvgD}) - \beta_C * \alpha_{CnLy} * N_{Cn}(t-\tau_{AvgD})$$
$$- \beta_A * \alpha_{CnR} * N_{Cn}(t-\tau_{HRC}+\tau_{SPC}) - \beta_C * \alpha_{CnLy} * N_{Cn}(t-\tau_{AvgD}-\tau_{Ly}+\tau_{SPC}) * \theta(t-\tau_{AvgD}-\tau_{Ly})$$
$$(1)$$

$$\frac{d}{dt}N_{CnDm}(t) = \alpha_{CnD} * N_{Cn}(t) * \beta_{Dm} - 1/\tau_{CnDm} \tag{2}$$

$$\frac{d}{dt}N_{Px}(t) = (\beta_{PPx} * \sum_{i=1}^{n} \alpha_{CiPx} * N_{Ci}(t-\tau_{AvgD}) * \beta_B - 1/\tau_{Px}) * \theta(t-\tau_{AvgD}) \tag{3}$$

$$\frac{d}{dt}N_{Ly}(t) = (\beta_{PLy} * \sum_{i=1}^{n} \alpha_{CiLy} * N_{Ci}(t-\tau_{AvgD}) * \beta_C + 1/(\tau_{Ly}-\tau_{SPL}) - 2/\tau_{Ly}) * \theta(t-\tau_{AvgD}) \tag{4}$$

$$\frac{d}{dt}N_{HRC}(t) = \sum_{i=1}^{n} \alpha_{CiR} * N_{Ci}(t) * \beta_A + \theta(t-\tau_{AvgD}-\tau_{Ly}) * \sum_{j=1}^{y} 1/\tau_{Lj} - 1/\tau_{HRC} + \sum_{j=1}^{n} \sum_{i=1}^{m} 1/(\tau_{CjDi}+\tau_{SPC}) \tag{5}$$

too complex to be solved numerically. In order to further minimize the number of terms, we assume τ_{SPC} and τ_{SPL} are negligibly small. So, the equations in the above model will change to a general minimized model, as shown in Box 2.

Using the minimized model above, we can represent the same number of platforms as in our simulation, and we have six dynamic variables, $N_{C1}(t)$, $N_{C1D1}(t)$, $N_{C1D2}(t)$, $N_{P1}(t)$, $N_{L1}(t)$, and $N_{HRC}(t)$. The equations in Box 2 will be changed to those in Box 3.

The equations in Box 3 illustrate the self-organized health record process in the sense that each term in the equations is modeling part of the process that are required to achieve self-organized health record.

Numerical Result

This is an initial investigation of the model focused on the self-organized health record by examining the agent population at each medical site. The results have shown that mathematical analysis is not only robust but yields obvious results. For simplicity, we assume the following when solving the equations:

- All α to be uniformly distributed in some space, which is set to 1.
- All β to be a constant value 0.5, except for β_{PP1} and β_{PL1}, which is set to 1.
- τ_{C1D1} and τ_{C1D2} are set to be a constant value of 3, τ_{P1} and τ_{L1} are set to a constant value of 6. These values are the expected value of the uniform distributed random number in our parameters used in the simulation. τ_{HRC} is set to be a constant of 0.787.
- $\lambda = 1$ and $\delta = 7/6$.

We use a built-in function named "dde23" in Matlab to solve the time-delay differential equations in our model. The following is the solution of solving the differential equations (11-16) in our macroscopic model, and the solution is shown in Figure 8.

From Figure 8, we see that there is a small oscillatory effect that occurs in the value of $N_{C1}(t)$ at the beginning of the result. The reason may be that there are many PAs being created, and they are cloning themselves at the same time, causing an increase in $N_{C1}(t)$. As the PAs leave the Clinic_1 platform to either Doctor_A or Doctor_B platform, this situation causes $N_{C1}(t)$ to decrease. Thus there are forces increasing and decreasing the agent population in the Clinic_1 platform. As time goes by, the number of agents in each platform becomes stable or predictable in the form of an upward straight line. This suggests that the system is adjusting itself to the changes of PA population in each platform. To show that this solution is reasonable, we calculate the number of agents in each platform at the end of 30 minutes. If the patient arrival rate is 1 patient/minute, then there will be 30 PAs created in the 30-minute simulation. The agents will divide themselves up between the Doctor_A and Doctor_B platforms, since there are only two doctors they can choose from. As indicated above, each doctor's examination time is three minutes on average. So, at the end of 30 minutes, Doctor A and Doctor B platform should have five PA left, on average, which is only slightly different from what we observe in Figure 8. Similar calculations for the pharmacy and lab platform indicate that there should be six PAs in Lab_1 and six PAs in Pharmacy_1. It is very similar to what we observe in Figure. 8.

The above numerical results are subject to our initial assumption of setting all the parameters to some constants that we used in the simulation. Many parameters in the model are free parameters, such as λ, β_A, β_B, β_c, τ_{C1D1}, τ_{C1D2}, τ_{P1}, τ_{L1}. These free parameters are tied to the process

of self-organized health records in a sense that they are affecting the time it takes an individual health record to recover from a chaotic state and back to a well-ordered state. For example, if $\tau L1$ is large, then the time it takes for the test result to be appended to the HRC database will also be long. Therefore, the values for these parameters are up to the agent designer to choose. Note that all the parameter values used in the model must be positive.

RESULTS COMPARISON BETWEEN MODELS

Since the numerical results give us the dynamics of average quantities of agent population at each medical site, the simulation results must also be formulated as an average. Therefore, we executed 30 simulation runs and the average of these simulation results, and then compare them to the numerical results obtained from the macroscopic mathematical model. The mean square error (MSE) is calculated to indicate the difference between the simulation results and the numerical results. We proposed that an acceptable value for the MSE for our study would be 10 (for now); however, this value can be set arbitrarily by agent designers. As shown in Figure 9, we can clearly

Box 2.

$$\frac{d}{dt}N_{Cn}(t) = \lambda + \delta - \alpha_{CnD}*N_{Cn}(t) - \beta_A*\alpha_{CnR}*N_{Cn}(t) - \beta_B*\alpha_{CnPx}*N_{Cn}(t-\tau_{AvgD}) - \beta_C*\alpha_{CnLy}*N_{Cn}(t-\tau_{AvgD})$$
(6)

$$\frac{d}{dt}N_{CnDm}(t) = \alpha_{CnD}*N_{Cn}(t)* \beta_{Dm} - 1/\tau_{CnDm}$$
(7)

$$\frac{d}{dt}N_{Px}(t) = (\beta_{PPx}* \sum_{i=1}^{n} \alpha_{CiPx}*N_{Ci}(t-\tau_{AvgD})* \beta_B - 1/\tau_{Px}) * \theta(t-\tau_{AvgD})$$
(8)

$$\frac{d}{dt}N_{Ly}(t) = (\beta_{PLy}* \sum_{i=1}^{n} \alpha_{CiLy}*N_{Ci}(t-\tau_{AvgD})* \beta_C - 1/\tau_{Ly}) * \theta(t-\tau_{AvgD})$$
(9)

$$\frac{d}{dt}N_{HRC}(t) = \sum_{i=1}^{n} \alpha_{CiR}*N_{Ci}(t)* \beta_A + \theta(t-\tau_{AvgD}-\tau_{Ly}) * \sum_{j=1}^{y} 1/\tau_{Lj} - 1/\tau_{HRC} + \sum_{j=1}^{n} \sum_{i=1}^{m} 1/(\tau_{CjDi})$$
(10)

Box 3.

$$\frac{d}{dt}N_{C1}(t) = \lambda + \delta - \alpha_{C1D}*N_{C1}(t) - \beta_A*\alpha_{C1R}*N_{C1}(t) - \beta_B*\alpha_{C1P1}*N_{C1}(t-\tau_{AvgD}) - \beta_C*\alpha_{C1L1}*N_{C1}(t-\tau_{AvgD})$$

(11)

$$\frac{d}{dt}N_{C1D1}(t) = \alpha_{C1D}*N_{C1}(t)*\beta_{D1} - 1/\tau_{C1D1}$$

(12)

$$\frac{d}{dt}N_{C1D2}(t) = \alpha_{C1D}*N_{C1}(t)*\beta_{D2} - 1/\tau_{C1D2}$$

(13)

$$\frac{d}{dt}N_{P1}(t) = (\beta_{PP1}*\alpha_{C1P1}*N_{C1}(t-\tau_{AvgD})*\beta_B - 1/\tau_{P1}) * \theta(t-\tau_{AvgD})$$

(14)

$$\frac{d}{dt}N_{L1}(t) = (\beta_{PL1}*\alpha_{C1L1}*N_{C1}(t-\tau_{AvgD})*\beta_C - 1/\tau_{L1}) * \theta(t-\tau_{AvgD})$$

(15)

$$\frac{d}{dt}N_{HRC}(t) = \alpha_{C1R}*N_{C1}(t)*\beta_A + \theta(t-\tau_{AvgD}-\tau_{L1})* 1/\tau_{L1} + 1/\tau_{C1D1} + 1/\tau_{C1D2} - 1/\tau_{HRC}$$

(16)

see that both models for Clinic_1 and HRC platforms have settled to a steady state, and the MSE for Clinic_1 is 1.59, and MSE for HRC is 0.58, and this indicates our parameter values for these sites in our macroscopic model are acceptable. The clusters of PAs (or agent population) in both doctor platforms increase linearly, and in both simulation and numerical results. However, the MSE between simulation and numerical results for Doctor_A is 24.63, and MSE for Doctor B is 20.37. This indicates our parameter values for the both doctor's equations in our macroscopic model need to re-adjust. The cluster of PAs in pharmacy and lab platforms are also exhibited linear aviation. We have only MSE = 6.63 for the pharmacy and MSE = 9.58 for the lab, and this indicates our parameter values for these sites in our macroscopic model are barely acceptable.

FUTURE TRENDS

Mobile agent technology has been used to solve most of the problems in health care domain for more than a decade, and its reputation and popularity have only increased. There are numerous studies on applying mobile agent architecture to different fields in the health care domain. For example, medical image retrieval (Liu, Martens, Paranjape, & Benedicenti, 2001), organ and tissue transplant and management (Moreno, 2003), health services scheduling and collaboration (Kirn, 2002), and optimization and management of clinical processes (Heine et al., 2005) all examine the application of mobile agent technology. We believe that in the near future, the mobile agent paradigm will become a dominated force in telemedicine application and in the telemedicine industry. This trend will likely keep increasing until new network computing technology that is even more flexible than mobile agent technology is developed.

There are several challenges, not mentioned in the section of The Electronic Health Record but presented in Moreno (2003), that also need to be addressed before we can expect useful multi-agent systems to the real health care domain. One such challenge is the slow in adoption of new information technology by medical professionals. Many medical professionals feel a loss of control when the information technology becomes too central to the access and retrieval of medical data

Figure 8a-b. Numerical results of the macroscopic model of ABEHRS (x-axis is time, y-axis is agent population)

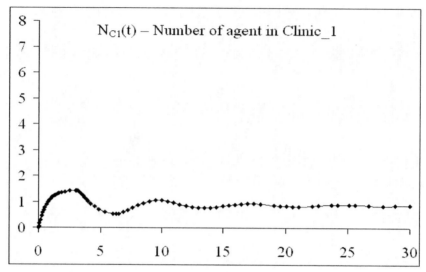

(a) Numerical Solution for NC1(t)

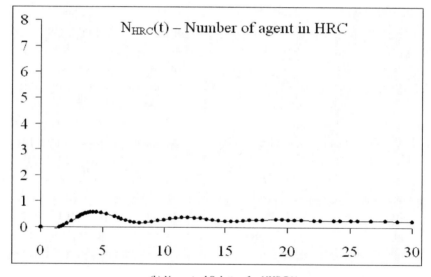

(b) Numerical Solution for NHRC(t)

Figure 8c-d. Numerical results of the macroscopic model of ABEHRS (x-axis is time, y-axis is agent population)

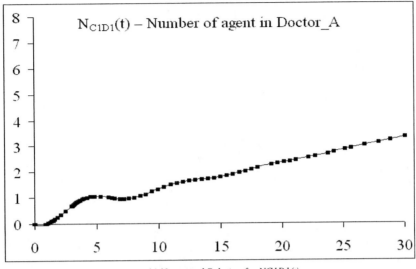

(c) Numerical Solution for NC1D1(t)

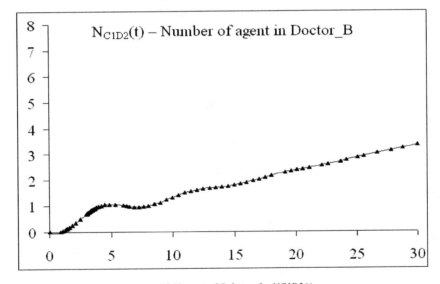

(d) Numerical Solution for NC1D2(t)

Figure 8e-f. Numerical results of the macroscopic model of ABEHRS (x-axis is time, y-axis is agent population)

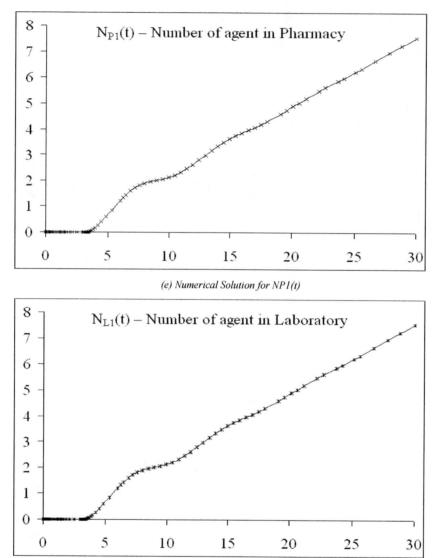

(e) Numerical Solution for NP1(t)

(f) Numerical Solution for NL1(t)

Figure 9a-b. Results comparison between models (x-axis is time, y-axis is number of agent)

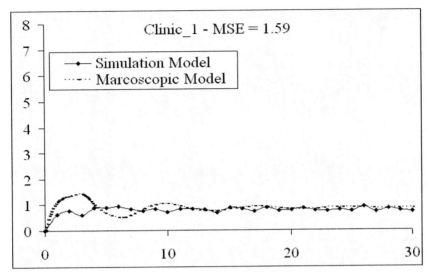

(a) Comparison Between Models for Clinic_1

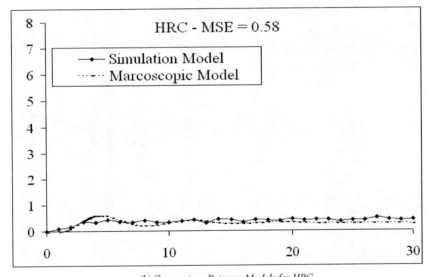

(b) Comparison Between Models for HRC

Figure 9c-d. Results comparison between models (x-axis is time, y-axis is number of agent)

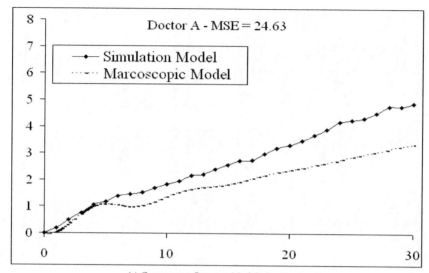

(c) Comparison Between Models for Doctor_A

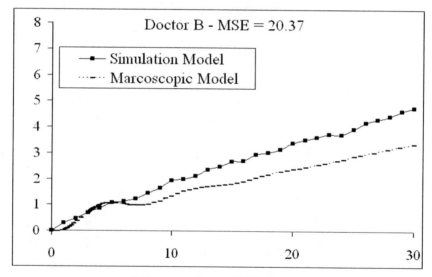

(d) Comparison Between Models for Doctor_B

Figure 9e-f. Results comparison between models (x-axis is time, y-axis is number of agent)

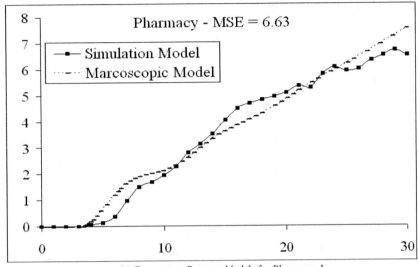

(e) Comparison Between Models for Pharmacy_1

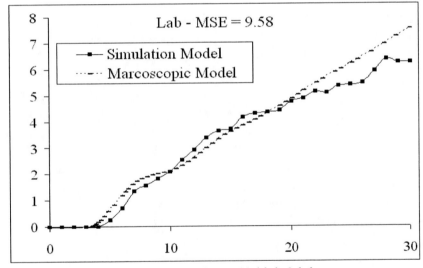

(f) Comparison Between Models for Lab_1

(Moore, 1996). This is more critical, especially for the technologies that contain a high level of automation, like mobile agents. Before we can see an increase in the rate of adoption by medical professionals, we need to see an acceptance by the general public. Thus, if we see mobile agent enabled cellular phones or PDAs and services (such as agent-controlled appliances, agent-based stock exchange) in our normal day lives, as shown in Kirn (2002), then only will we see acceptance in the medical community.

Intelligent swarms have given the agent designers a new perspective of developing multi-agent system. If an agent system consists of thousands of simple autonomous and distributed agents, then their collective power arising from the interactions between the agents is tremendous. The intrinsic properties of the swarm system can be very significant. We believe that swarm intelligence and multi-agent systems will have a strong impact of solving problems in health care domain.

CONCLUSION

In this chapter, we have presented a general framework and the basic concepts behind ABEHRS. These concepts encapsulated the fundamental principles of self-completing, self-regulating, and self-organizing data sets by using the strength of agent mobility and automation. Based on the principles of the swarm paradigm, we have designed and implemented an ABEHRS model using the TEEMA system. Initial simulation results from modeling ABEHRS have been presented, and from these results it is shown that the fundamental goals of ABEHRS are achieved. It also shown that cluster formations occur in specific sites of the health care system (for example, doctor, pharmacy, and lab platforms). The existence of these clusters, and their growth rate, identifies new challenges and new opportunities for the health care system. These cluster formations can identify valuable

collective behaviour in the system, as also seen in Lerman and Galstyan (2001).

In addition to the design and simulation of ABEHRS, we also presented a macroscopic mathematical model of the ABEHRS, which contains a set of differential equations. These equations describe the global dynamics of mobile agents in the ABEHRS. Our numerical analysis of these equations strongly matches our simulation results. However, both the numerical and simulation results are subject to the initial conditions and assumptions, which can significantly alter the behaviour of the system. Further work using different initial conditions and assumptions should be used to help better understand the macroscopic behaviour of the ABEHRS. Also, we may want to look for some parallel to the current health record system to demonstrate that there is a relationship between what we propose in this work and the actual health system in use today.

Finally, our current simulation and numerical work on the ABEHRS does not show any extraordinary or catastrophic collective swarm behaviour. The global simulation dynamics of ABEHRS compares well to the mathematical model. However, our work is only very preliminary, and we have not attempted to push the system to any extremes. This type of testing and analysis is critical in order to ensure that the system will always be stable.

REFERENCES

Agassounon, W., & Martinoli, A. (2002). A macroscopic model of an aggregation simulation using embodied agents in groups of time-varying sizes. *Proceedings of the 2002 Institute of Electrical and Electronics Engineers Systems, Man and Cybernetics Conference* (pp. 250-255). Retrieved April 3, 2005, from http://swis.epfl.ch/backup_caltech/coro/People/alcherio/papers/SMC02.pdf

Bonabeau, E., Dorigo, M., & Theraulaz, G. (1999). *Swarm intelligence: From natural to artificial systems*. New York: Oxford University Press.

Camazine S., Deneubourg, J. L., Franks, N., Sneyd, J., Theraulaz, G., & Bonabeau, E. (2001). *Self-organization in biological systems*. Princeton, NJ: Princeton University Press.

Charles, A. A., Menezes, R., & Tolksdorf, R. (2004). On the implementation of SwarmLinda. *Proceedings of the 42nd Association for Computing Machinery Southeast Regional Conference* (pp. 297-298). Retrieved July 15, 2006, from Association for Computing Machinery Digital Library Database.

Crow, L., & Shadbolt, N. (2001). Extracting focused knowledge from the Semantic Web. *International Journal of Human Computer Studies, 54*(1), 155-184. Retrieved December 27, 2003, from Association for Computing Machinery Digital Library Database.

Gray, R., Kotz, D., Nog, S., Rus, D., & Cybenko, G. (1997). Mobile agents: The next generation in distributed computing. *Proceedings of the Second Aizu International Symposium on Parallel Algorithms and Architectures Synthesis* (pp. 8-24). Retrieved November 15, 2002, from Institute of Electrical and Electronics Engineers Digital Library Database.

Gibbs, C. (2000). *TEEMA reference guide version 1.0*. Regina, Saskatchewan, Canada: TRLabs.

Grimson, J., Grimson, W., & Hasselbring, W. (2000). The SI challenge in health care. *Communications of the Association for Computing Machinery, 43*(6), 49-55. Retrieved May 27, 2003, from Association for Computing Machinery Digital Library Database.

Heine, C., Herrier, R., & Kirn, S. (2005). ADAPT@AGENT.HOSPITAL: Agent-based optimization and management of clinical processes. *International Journal of Intelligent Information Technologies, 1*(1). Retrieved July 10, 2006, from http://wi2.uni-hohenheim.de/team/documents/public/heine/%5BHeHK2005%5D.pdf

Huston T. (2001). Security issues for implementation of e-medical records. *Communications of the Association for Computing Machinery, 44*(9), 89-94. Retrieved January 9, 2005, from Association for Computing Machinery Digital Library Database.

Kadrovach, B. A., & Lamont, G. B. (2002). A particle swarm model for swarm-based networked sensor systems. In *Proceedings of the 2002 ACM Symposium on Applied Computing* (pp. 918-924). Retrieved June 19, 2004, from Association for Computing Machinery Digital Library Database.

Kirn, S. (2002). *Ubiquitous healthcare: The OnkoNet mobile agents architecture*. Paper presented at the 2002 Mobile Computing in Medicine, Heidelberg, Germany. Retrieved September 23, 2004, from http://www.old.netobjectdays.org/pdf/02/papers/node/0278.pdf

Lerman, K., & Galstyan, A. (2001). *A methodology for mathematical analysis of multi-agent systems* (Tech. Rep. No. ISI-TR-529). University of California Information Sciences Institute. Retrieved November 20, 2004, from http://www.isi.edu/%7Elerman/papers/isitr529.pdf

Lerman, K., & Shehory, O. (2000). Coalition formation for large-scale electronic markets. *Proceedings of the Fourth International Conference on Multiagent Systems* (pp. 167-175). Retrieved November 20, 2004, from http://www.isi.edu/%7Elerman/papers/LerShe99.pdf

Liu, A., Martens, R., Paranjape, R., & Benedicenti, L. (2001). Mobile multi-agent system for medical image retrieval. *Proceedings of the 2001 Institute of Electrical and Electronics Engineers Canadian Conference on Electrical and Computer Engineering Conference*, Ontario, Canada. Retrieved October 15, 2003, from Institute of

Electrical and Electronics Engineers Digital Library Database.

Martens, R. (2001). *TEEMA TRLabs execution environment for mobile agents.* Regina, Saskatchewan, Canada: TRLabs.

Moore, B. (1996). Acceptance of information technology by health care professionals. *Proceedings of the 1996 Symposium on Computers and the Quality of Life* (pp. 57-60). Retrieved August 9, 2003, from Association for Computing Machinery Digital Library Database.

Moreno, A. (2003). *Medical applications of multi-agent systems.* Paper presented at the 2003 Intelligent and Adaptive Systems in Medicine Workshop, Praha, Czech Republic. Retrieved September 21, 2004, from http://cyber.felk.cvut.cz/EUNITE03-BIO/pdf/Moreno.pdf

Nealon, J., & Moreno, A. (2003). *Agent-based applications in health care.* Paper presented at the 2003 EU-LAT Workshop, Mexico. Retrieved September 21, 2004, from http://www.etse.urv.es/recerca/banzai/toni/MAS/papers.html

Silverman, B., Andonyadis, C., & Morales, A. (1998). Web-based health care agents; The case of reminders and todos, too (R2Do2). *Artificial Intelligence in Medicine, 14*(3), 295-316. Retrieved May 29, 2003, from Science Direct Database.

Smith, K., Paranjape, R., & Benedicenti, L. (2001). Agent behavior and agent models in unregulated markets. *Association for Computing Machinery SIGAPP Applied Computing Review, 9*(3), 2-12. Retrieved May 27, 2003, from Association for Computing Machinery Digital Library Database.

Sugawara, K., & Sano, M. (1997). Cooperative acceleration of task performance: Foraging behavior of interacting multi-robots system. *Physica*

D, 100(3-4), 343-354. Retrieved November 27, 2004, from Association for Computing Machinery Digital Library Database.

Tecchia, F., Loscos, C., Conroy, R., & Chrysanthou, Y. (2001). Agent behaviour simulator (ABS): A platform for urban behaviour development. *Proceedings of the First International Game Technology Conference and Idea Expo (GTEC'01) in co-operation with ACM SIGGRAPH and EUROGRAPHICS* (pp. 17-21). Retrieved January 9, 2005, from http://www.equator.ac.uk/var/uploads/TecchiaGTEC2001.pdf

Truszkowski, W., Hinchey, M., Rash, J., & Rouff, C. (2004). NASA's swarm missions: The challenge of building autonomous software. *Institute of Electrical and Electronics Engineers Information Technology Professional, 6*(5), 47-52. Retrieved August 5, 2006, from Institute of Electrical and Electronics Engineers Digital Library Database.

Walczak, S. (2003). A multiagent architecture for developing medical information retrieval agents. *Journal of Medical Systems, 27*(5), 479-498. Retrieved July 29, 2005, from Association for Computing Machinery Digital Library Database.

Wang, Y., Liu, J., & Jin, X. (2003). Modeling agent-based load balancing with time delays. *Proceedings of the 2003 Institute of Electrical and Electronics Engineers/WIC International Conference on Intelligent Agent Technology,* 189+. Retrieved December 15, 2004, from Institute of Electrical and Electronics Engineers Digital Library Database.

Wu, J. (2003). Towards a decentralized search architecture for the Web and P2P systems. *Proceedings of the 2003 Adaptive Hypermedia and Adaptive Web-Based Systems Workshop.* Retrieved August 5, 2006, from http://wwwis.win.tue.nl/ah2003/proceedings/paper18.pdf

Chapter XVII
Robust Intelligent Control of Mobile Robots

Gordon Fraser
Institute for Software Technology, Graz University of Technology, Austria

Gerald Steinbauer
Institute for Software Technology, Graz University of Technology, Austria

Jörg Weber
Institute for Software Technology, Graz University of Technology, Austria

Franz Wotawa
Institute for Software Technology, Graz University of Technology, Austria

ABSTRACT

An appropriate control architecture is a crucial premise for successfully achieving truly autonomous mobile robots. The architecture should allow for a robust control of the robot in complex tasks, while it should be flexible in order to operate in different environments pursuing different tasks. This chapter presents a control framework that is able to control an autonomous robot in complex real-world tasks. The key features of the framework are a hybrid control paradigm that incorporates reactive, planning and reasoning capabilities, a flexible software architecture that enables easy adaptation to new tasks and a robust task execution that makes reaction to unforeseen changes in the task and environment possible. Finally, the framework allows for detection of internal failures in the robot and includes self-healing properties. The framework was successfully deployed in the domain of robotic soccer and service robots. The chapter presents the requirements for such a framework, how the framework tackles the problems arising from the application domains, and results obtained during the deployment of the framework.

INTRODUCTION

An appropriate control architecture is a crucial premise for successfully achieving truly autono-mous mobile robots. The architecture should allow for a robust control of mobile robots during the execution of a wide range of different tasks. Moreover, it should be flexible enough to facilitate different control strategies and algorithms. In addition, the architecture should be adaptable in order to handle more complex tasks and to be able to operate in different environments.

Finding an appropriate architecture for a specific purpose is a challenging task. In fact, no single architecture can be sufficient for all purposes. There is always a trade-off between general applicability and usability. The issue of determining an appropriate architecture suitable to robustly control an autonomous mobile robot can be divided into several sub-problems:

- The first and easier one is the question of which control paradigm to choose. In this chapter the different control paradigms are introduced. It is then motivated why a hybrid paradigm is the most appropriate for applications where robots carry out complex and non-trivial tasks.

- The second problem is more related to software engineering and concerns the software architecture. The software architecture determines how the functionality of the software is physically organized. Several projects working on an architecture sufficient for the needs of mobile robots are introduced. For an in-depth discussion of the issue of choosing or implementing an appropriate software framework, the reader is referred to Orebäck (2004). Finally, an example of a successful solution to this issue is illustrated.

- A more or less strong, deliberative component is part of every hybrid control paradigm. The use of symbol-based abstract decision making has two major drawbacks. First, in general, planning techniques are insufficiently reactive for unpredictable and highly dynamic environments. A solution to this problem is presented, which enables the deliberative component to react more

quickly to such effects. Second, if an abstract deliberative component is used, then some kind of connection between the quantitative world of the sensors and actors and the qualitative world of planning and reasoning is necessary. If sensors and actors are prone to uncertainties, then this abstraction of knowledge is difficult. Unfortunately, such uncertainties are nearly always adherent to sensors and actors. Therefore, a novel symbol grounding mechanism is presented, which significantly relaxes this problem.

- The final problem is especially important in the area of autonomous mobile robots. Tolerance of the robot and its control system against faults is crucial for long-term autonomous operation. It is shown how a model-based fault-diagnosis and repair system improves the overall robustness of the control architecture.

Consideration of all these features and requirements has resulted in a control architecture that serves as a platform for research in several areas in autonomous mobile robots, for example, RoboCup robot soccer and service robots. This robust and flexible architecture will serve as a running example and as a guideline throughout this chapter.

SOFTWARE FRAMEWORKS FOR MOBILE ROBOTS

This section addresses the problem of software frameworks for autonomous mobile robots. For this, the applicable control paradigms are introduced. Control paradigms describe how control is organized. Then, general requirements for software architectures in order to be usable for autonomous robots are identified. Finally, popular publicly available software frameworks are reviewed.

Robot Control Paradigms

A robot control paradigm guides the organization of the control of a mobile robot, which enables the robot to carry out given tasks. It structures how the robot maps its sensor readings to actions via a more or less intelligent decision-making module.

One of the first attempts to structure control was the *sense-plan-act* (SPA) paradigm, depicted in Figure 1. This paradigm was inspired by the research on artificial intelligence (AI) of the late '60s and was first successfully used by Nilsson in the robot *Shakey* (Nilsson, 1984). It was guided by the early view on artificial intelligence. The paradigm divides the control into three different functionalities. *SENSE* is responsible for the perception of the robot's internal state and its environment. The data provided by the robot's sensors are interpreted and combined in a central abstract model of the world. Based on the information contained in the world model, a description of the capabilities of the robot and the goal of the task the *PLAN* module tries to find a plan (i.e., a sequence of actions) that will lead to a given goal. The *ACT* module executes this plan in order to achieve the goal. Although the SPA paradigm is powerful and flexible, it suffers from a set of drawbacks. First of all, planning takes a lot of time even on very powerful computers. Therefore, the reaction to dynamic environments is slow. Another drawback is caused by the fact that planning algorithms generally work on a qualitative and abstract representation of the world. The design of such a representation and the transformation of quantitative sensor data into this representation is far from trivial.

In contrast, the reactive *sense-act* (SA) control paradigm provides a different organization of control. Figure 2 depicts the SA paradigm. The paradigm is biologically inspired by the mechanism of reflexes, which directly couple the sensor input with the actor output. Such a reflex of the robot is commonly called a behavior. More com-

plex behaviors emerge through the combination of different reflexes.

A system that follows this paradigm was first proposed in the mid 1980s with the subsumption architecture by Brooks (1986). This architecture achieved significant progress in the research on mobile robots and is still popular and widely used. Brooks argued that abstract knowledge about the world and reasoning is not necessary for the control of a mobile robot. The paradigm is able to control a robot also in dynamic environments because the reaction time is very quick due to the encoding of the desired behavior into reflexes and the tight coupling of the sensors and actors. Although relatively complex behaviors can be achieved by blending different reflexes, the paradigm is prone to fail for more complex tasks. This arises from the fact that neither explicit information about the internal state of the robot nor about the world, nor additional knowledge about the task, are used. Therefore, for complex tasks a goal-driven approach seems much more appropriate than a simple instinct-driven one.

Even though the choice of an appropriate control paradigm sometimes seems to be rather a question of faith than of science, there is a relatively clear commitment within the robotics research community that the most appropriate architecture is hybrid architecture (see Figure 3). Hybrid systems combine the advantages of the planning approach and the reactive paradigm while avoiding most of their drawbacks. Such systems use reactive behaviors where reactivity

Figure 1. The sense-plan-act control paradigm

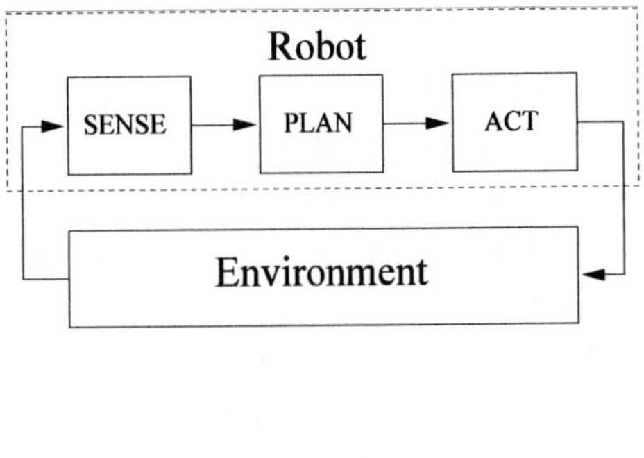

Figure 2. The reactive sense-act control paradigm

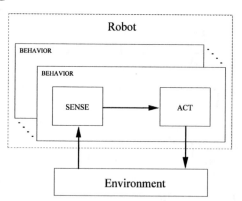

Figure 3. The hybrid control paradigm

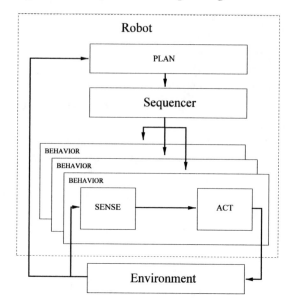

is needed (e.g., avoiding a dynamic obstacle) and use planning and reasoning where complex decisions have to be made and a limited amount of delay is not critical.

Commonly, hybrid systems consist of three layers. The *reactive layer* uses reactive behaviors to implement a fast coupling of the sensors and the actors in order to be reactive to a dynamic environment. Often this layer implements the basic skills of a robot, that is, basic movement primitives and obstacle avoidance. The *deliberative layer* has a global view on the robot and its environment, and is responsible for high-level planning in order to achieve a given goal. Typical functionalities that are located in this layer are mission planning, reasoning, localization, path planning, and the interaction with humans or other robots. The *sequence layer* is located between the reactive and the deliberative layer and bridges the different representations of the two layers. The sequencer generates a set of behaviors in order to achieve a sub-goal submitted by the deliberative layer. It is also responsible for the correct execution of such a set of behaviors and should inform the higher layer if the sub-goal was successfully achieved or the execution failed for some reason.

A more detailed introduction to the different control paradigms can be found in the book by

Kortenkamp, Bonasso, and Murphy (1998) and the book by Murphy (2002).

Requirements for the Software Architecture of an Autonomous Robot

The control paradigm guides the functional decomposition of the robot control on a more abstract view. The software architecture, on the other hand, guides the modular decomposition of the system into different components and the implementation of such components. Furthermore, it concerns the encapsulation of different functionalities into manageable modules.

A well-designed software architecture should provide, among others, the following features:

- Robustness
- Flexibility
- Sensor and actor interface abstraction
- Easy exchange and reuse of components
- Reliable communication between components

- Easy adaptation of the system for new purposes
- Easy portability to other hardware platforms
- Support of a defined development process
- Support for test and evaluation

For a long time the above requirements and principles have been neglected during the development of many prototype control systems. This is because the issue of software architecture design is not tightly coupled to pure robotic research. As a result, most of the research software is hard to maintain and to adapt and therefore lacks general usability. Fortunately, many of the best-practice principles and processes from the software development community are now widely accepted by the robotic research community. These principles are, amongst others, object-oriented design, the incorporation of well-known design patterns, the reuse of established libraries, the compliance to widely accepted standards, and the use of test and evaluation frameworks. This leads to higher quality and to improved adaptability of the software. Furthermore, a great pool of software frameworks for robotic research has been developed. Most of these frameworks can be used out of the shelf and fulfil most of the requirements proposed by robotic research.

Existing Frameworks for Mobile Robots

There exists a number of popular frameworks for mobile robot research. Some of them are more general and flexible than others while some of them are closely related to specific robots or tasks. Examples for such frameworks are: task control architecture (TCA) (Simmons, 1994), Saphira (Konolige & Myers, 1998), *Carnegie Mellon Robot Navigation Toolkit* (Carmen) (Montemerlo, Roy, & Thrun, 2003), and Player/Stage (Gerkey et. al, 2001). A very good overview and a more formal and detailed evaluation of existing frameworks

is given in (Orebäck & Christensen, 2003). In the next section, we will discuss the framework named *Middleware for Robots* (Miro), on which our own developments are based.

Miro is a distributed object-oriented software framework for robot applications. It has been developed at the Department of Computer Science at the University of Ulm (Utz, 2005; Utz, Sablatnüg, Enderle, & Kraetzschmar, 2002). The aim of the project is to provide an open and flexible software framework for applications on mobile robots. In general, Miro is a software framework and not a ready-to-use robotic application. The goals for the design of Miro are:

- Full object-oriented design
- Client/server system design
- Hardware and operating system abstraction
- Open architecture approach
- Multi-platform support, communication support, and interoperability
- Software design patterns
- Agent technology support

Miro achieves these goals by adopting an architecture that is divided into three layers. Figure 4 depicts the architecture of Miro. The use of the *Adaptive Communication Environment* (ACE) and CORBA for the communication between the layers and other applications enables a flexible, transparent, and platform-independent development. Miro uses *the ACE Object Request Broker* (TAO) (Schmidt, 2000) as CORBA framework. The implementation of this object-oriented framework is completely done in the C++ language.

The *Miro device layer* provides object-oriented interface abstractions for all sensory and actuatory facilities of a robot. This is the platform-dependent part of Miro. The *Miro communication and service layer* provides active service abstractions for sensors and actuators via CORBA *interface definition language* (IDL) descriptions and implements these services as network-transparent

Figure 4. The architecture of Miro (Figure from Utz, 2005)

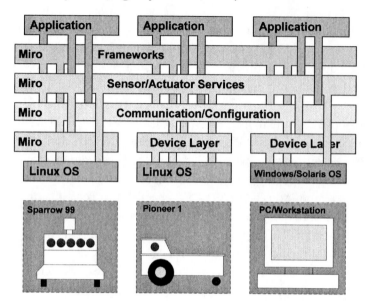

objects in a platform-independent manner. The programmer uses standard CORBA object protocols to interface to any device, either on the local or a remote robot. Miro provides a number of often-used functional modules for mobile robot control, like modules for mapping, self-localization, behaviour generation, path planning, logging and visualization facilities.

A complete description of Miro and many useful examples can be found in The Miro Developer Team (2005). The use of Miro as a basis for further development has the following advantages:

- **Object-oriented design:** The design of the framework is fully object-oriented, elaborated, and easy to understand. Moreover, there are a whole bunch of ready-to-use design patterns that provide, for example, multi-threading, device reactors, and so forth.
- **Multi-platform support and reuse:** Miro comprises a great number of abstract interfaces for numerous different sensors and actors, for example, odometry, bumper, sonar,

laser, and differential drives. Moreover, for all of these interfaces Miro already provides implementations for many different robot platforms. Due to the clear design and the use of CORBA and IDL, the implementation of interfaces for a new robot platform and the integration of new interfaces is straightforward. Miro currently supports many different common robot platforms like the B21, the Pioneer family, and some RoboCup MSL (Middle-Size League) robots.

- **Communication:** For the communication between different components of the robot control software, Miro provides two main mechanisms:

Direct CORBA method calls are used in a client/server manner for a 1-1 communication of components. This mechanism is commonly applied to actor and sensor interfaces. Due to the use of CORBA, the user does not have to deal with the internals of such a communication, for example, marshalling or memory management. Furthermore, the communication is completely transparent even if the client and the server run on different computers or use different programming languages.

The *event channel,* on the other hand, provides 1-n communication. The event channel follows the producer/consumer paradigm. The producer simply pushes an event of a certain type to the channel. All consumers who are subscribed for this event are automatically informed when this specific event is available. Although this mechanism has a lot of advantages, it has to be mentioned that a heavy use of this mechanism leads to a poor run-time performance because of the computational overhead in the event channel.

- **Behaviour engine:** Miro contains a complete module for the modeling and the implementation of reactive behaviours. The *behaviour engine* follows the behavioural control paradigm introduced by Brooks (1986). The module uses a hierarchical decomposition of behaviours. On the base of the hierarchy, there are different atomic *behaviors* like, for example, "dribble ball" for a soccer robot. These behaviors can be grouped in *action patterns.* Such action patterns may be comprised of, for example, a dribble action and a local obstacle avoidance behavior. Different action patterns can be combined to a *policy.*

Once the behaviours are implemented, action patterns and policies are built up by describing them in an XML-file. Therefore, experiments with different action patterns and policies are easy and straightforward.

Unfortunately, Miro does not provide any paradigms and implementations for a deliberative layer. Therefore, extension of the Miro framework by a planning system is described in the third section.

A MODULAR ARCHITECTURE FOR AUTONOMOUS MULTI-PURPOSE ROBOTS

In order to fulfil as many of the requirements for an appropriate framework stated in the second part of the second section as possible, a novel design approach for mobile autonomous robots was developed (Fraser, Steinbauer, & Wotawa, 2004). The approach is based on a consequent modularization of both the robot's software and its hardware.

It is possible to distinguish between the functional view on the software and the software architecture. The functional view provides a decomposition of functionality into layers with increasing levels of abstraction. Therefore, the functionality is organized into different layers ranging from an abstract top layer with planning and reasoning capabilities down to a layer with direct hardware access. The software architecture represents a physical view on the software system.

The framework presented in this section is built upon the Miro framework and was deployed and evaluated in the RoboCup middle-size league team (MSL) of the Graz University of Technology. Besides using the robots for soccer games, the robots are also used for research in the area of service robotics.

Figure 5 shows the modularized robot platform, which was developed and used as a target system for the proposed control architecture. The hardware of the robot is divided into five layers. Each layer provides one particular skill. The layers are stacked to build up the robot platform.

Functional View on the Software

The functional view on the software is guided by a consequent modularization. The functionality of the software is divided into three layers with

Figure 5. The modularized robot platform

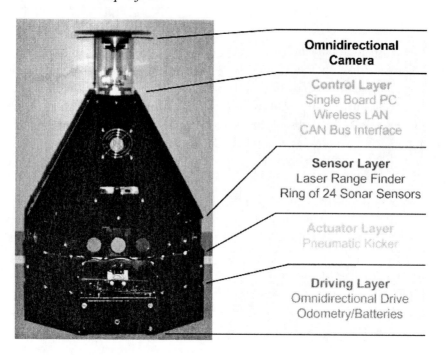

Omnidirectional Camera

Control Layer
Single Board PC
Wireless LAN
CAN Bus Interface

Sensor Layer
Laser Range Finder
Ring of 24 Sonar Sensors

Actuator Layer
Pneumatic Kicker

Driving Layer
Omnidirectional Drive
Odometry/Batteries

an increasing level of abstraction. The layers are shown in Figure 6. Note that the functionality of a layer fully relies on the layer below.

The idea of functional layers with different levels of abstraction is similar to the idea of cognitive robotics (Castelpietra, Guidotti, Iocchi, Nardi, & Rosati, 2002). As mentioned above, a combination of reactive behaviors, explicit knowledge representation, planning, and reasoning capabilities promises to be more flexible and robust. Furthermore, such an approach will be able to fulfil far more complex tasks. Note that this functional design is inspired by the hybrid control paradigm.

Hardware Layer

The hardware layer implements the interfaces to the sensors and actuators of the robot. This layer delivers raw continuous sensory data to the next layer and performs a low-level control of the actuators.

Continuous Layer

The continuous layer implements a numerical representation (quantitative view of the world) of the sensing and acting of the robot. This layer performs the processing of range data and the image processing. This processing computes possible positions of objects in the environment, including the robot's own *pose*. A pose consists of position and orientation of an object. These positions, together with the motion information from the odometry, are fused into a continuous world model by Kalman Filters (other objects) (Dietl, Gutmann, & Nebel, 2001) or Monte Carlo methods (own pose) (Fox, Burgard, Dellaert, & Thrun, 1999). Of course, all sensing and acting of a real mobile robot is afflicted with uncertainty. Therefore, sensor fusion is done using the above probabilistic methods. The world model represents the continuous world by estimating the most likely hypothesis for the positions of objects and the position of the robot itself.

Figure 6. Functional view of the software (robot soccer example)

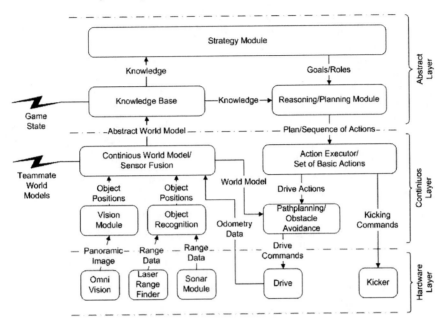

Furthermore, this layer is responsible for the low-level execution of actions. Execution is based on a set of actions implemented as patterns of prioritized simple reactive behaviors. To take an example from robot soccer, suppose that the abstract layer (see next section) chooses to execute the high-level action DribbleBall. This action could be implemented by the following reactive behaviors: *dribble, kick,* and *obstacle_avoidance (oa). Dribble* will have the lowest priority, *oa* the highest. That is, if an obstacle is detected, only *oa* is executed in order to avoid a collision with the obstacle. However, as long as there is no obstacle, this behavior will be inactive, and so behaviors with lower priorities can be executed. *Kick* is inactive most of the time; it becomes active only when the robot is in a proper distance and angle to the opponent goal. Then this behavior will emit a kick command, which is sent to the hardware layer, and become inactive again. *Dribble* is executed at those times when the other behaviors are inactive. This action execution forms the reactive part of the

hybrid control paradigm and is similar to Brooks' subsumption architecture (Brooks, 1986).

Abstract Layer

The abstract layer contains a symbolic representation (qualitative view of the world) about the knowledge of the robot and a planning module for the decision making. A detailed description of the planning system can be found in Fraser et al. (2005). A similar approach also has been proven to work in the RoboCup MSL domain (Dylla, Ferrein, A., Lakemeyer, 2002). The abstract layer allows for an easy implementation of a desired task by specifying the goals, actions, and knowledge as logical sentences.

The core of this layer is the knowledge base. It contains a symbolic representation of the entire high-level knowledge of the robot. This knowledge consists of predefined domain knowledge, of a qualitative world model, which is an abstracted representation of the continuous world model, and of an abstract description of the actions the robot is able to perform.

The qualitative world model is represented by a set of logical propositions. The knowledge about actions is represented using a STRIPS-like representation language (Fikes & Nilsson, 1972) enriched by quantifiers from first-order logic. That is, an action is described by means of a precondition and an effect, where precondition and effect are represented by conjunctions of logical propositions. An action can be executed only if its precondition holds, and the effect states which conditions hold after the action has been executed successfully. Note that those propositions that are not included in the effect are not changed by the action.

Based on the agent's domain knowledge, the strategy module chooses the next goal the robot has to achieve for fulfilling the long-term task. In a simplified view, the strategic knowledge could be regarded as a set of condition-goal pairs, where the condition is a logical sentence, and the goal can only be chosen if this condition is fulfilled. The planning module generates a plan that is supposed to achieve this goal. Any planning algorithm can be used within the planning module. Currently a simple regression planner (Russell & Norvig, 2003) or the more effective Graphplan is used (Blum & Furst, 1995). It has to be mentioned that the use of planning suffers from two drawbacks. First, planning takes time. Decisions that are made by planning are not feasible for time-critical tasks where a tight schedule have to be maintained. Furthermore, planning needs a significant amount of computational resources. Therefore, planning is only feasible for systems with enough resources or for systems where the time needed for the decision making is not that important.

The calculated plan is communicated to the action executor, which implements the actions by means of simple behaviors. Note that a plan is monitored permanently for its validity during execution. The plan is canceled or updated if preconditions or invariants of the plan or its actions are no longer valid. This concept will be explained below.

Software Architecture

The software architecture, which is based on Miro (Utz et al., 2002), is shown in Figure 7. All software modules are implemented as autonomous services. Each service runs as an independent task. The communication between services primarily employs two mechanisms, the CORBA-interfaces and the event channel, which were described in the second section.

Hence, the services are independent of each other and an adaptation of software modules or the integration of new services is very easy and transparent to the rest of the system. It has to be mentioned that the event channel has a major drawback beside its advantages. The problem is that the Event channel needs significantly more computational resources than, for instance, a simple CORBA-interface. This fact is caused by its more complex communication mechanism and results in greater communication delays. Therefore, the use of the event channel is limited to only the necessary communications. Furthermore, time-critical communications like the connection between the action-execution with its behaviours and actuators are implemented by the faster CORBA method-calls.

ROBUST PLAN EXECUTION

In this section, an extension to hybrid architectures is presented that improves the quality of the plan execution in unpredictable and dynamic environments. First, it is illustrated how a plan is created, which fulfils a chosen goal. Then issues related to the plan execution and monitoring are discussed. Finally, it is shown how a quantitative world model can be transformed to a qualitative symbolic representation and which problems arise.

Figure 7. Software architecture. Solid connections represent remote invocations to CORBA IDL interfaces. Dashed connections denote an event-based communication.

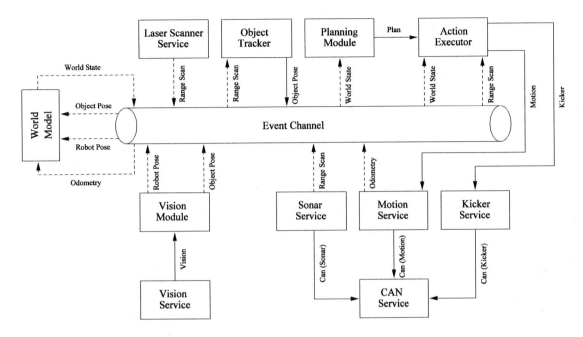

Examples in this section are based on a RoboCup scenario, which is the original intent of the architecture presented in the previous section.

A Simple Example

Suppose that the following predicates are used for a qualitative representation of the world:

InReach(x)	true iff object *x* is in reach, i.e., within a small distance
KickDistance(x)	true iff the object *x* is close enough to be reachable by a ball which is kicked by this robot
HasBall	true iff the robot has the ball
IsAt(x,y)	true iff object *x* is at position *y*

where *x* and *y* can be one of the object constants *Ball* or *OppGoal* (opponent goal).

A classical AI-planning problem (Fikes & Nilsson, 1972) is defined by an initial state, a goal state, and the available actions. In the example, the initial state refers to the current state of the world,

that is, the state of the environment and the robot itself. Suppose that initially all predicates are false and that the agent wants to achieve that a goal is scored. Furthermore, the knowledge base contains four high-level actions described in first-order logic, which the robot is able to perform.

1. Initial state s_{init} = ¬*InReach(Ball)* ∧ ¬*InReach(OppGoal)* ∧ ¬*HasBall* ∧ ¬ ...
2. Goal state *g = IsAt(Ball,OppGoal)*
3. Actions schemas: Λ^A ={*GrabBall,MoveTo ,Score,DribbleTo*}. The schema definitions are given below.

As already explained, an action is defined by a precondition and an effect. The precondition denotes which conditions must hold before the action can be started, and the effect states how the qualitative world state is changed by the action. Consider the following example actions, where *target* is a placeholder for object constants. See Box 1.

Box 1. A set of example actions

action:	precondition:	effect:
GrabBall	¬*HasBall* ∧ *InReach*(*Ball*)	*HasBall*
MoveTo(*target*)	-	*InReach*(*target*)
Score	*HasBall* ∧ *KickDistance*(*OppGoal*)	¬*HasBall* ∧ ¬*InReach*(*Ball*) ∧ *IsAt*(Ball,*OppGoal*)
DribbleTo(*target*)	*HasBall*	*KickDistance*(*target*)

A planning algorithm (Weld, 1999) searches for a sequence of actions that fulfils a given goal. In this example, the algorithm can find the following plan that achieves the goal *IsAt*(*Ball,OppGoal*):

1. *MoveTo*(*Ball*)
2. *GrabBall*
3. *DribbleTo*(*OppGoal*)
4. *Score*

Figure 8 depicts the qualitative states that appear during the execution of this plan. The nodes of the graph represent states, while the labels of the edges are actions. Only those predicates that are true are shown in the states; all other predicates are false. The state on the top of the graph is the initial state, in which all predicates are false. The last state at the bottom satisfies the goal *g*. In the initial state, only the action *MoveTo*(*Ball*) can be executed, as the preconditions of the other actions are not fulfilled in this state. After the execution of this action, the ball is in reach. Thus, action *GrabBall* can begin. If this action succeeds, *DribbleTo*(OppGoal) can be executed, and finally *Score* is supposed to achieve the goal. Please note that the term "goal" is twofold in the robot soccer domain.

Plan Execution and Monitoring

The classical AI planning theory makes some simplifying assumptions. Actions are consid-

Figure 8. An example plan that aims at scoring a goal

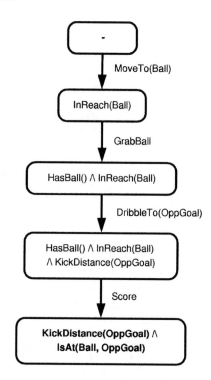

ered atomic, their effects are deterministic, and they do always succeed. Furthermore, all world changes are caused by actions of this agent only, therefore the environment is fully deterministic. Finally, it is assumed that the environment is fully observable.

While these assumptions are convenient for the planning theory, they often do not hold in real-world applications. In practice, robots operate in dynamic and uncertain environments. Actions are not atomic, as their execution needs time, and unpredictable things can happen during the execution. Thus, actions may fail or their effect may be non-deterministic. Another issue is to determine when an action is finished, that is, when the effect is achieved. Moreover, the world is not only influenced by actions of this agent but also by other agents, for example, by other robots, by humans, or by other influential factors. In addition, due to the limitations of the sensors, the environment is not fully observable.

This discussion shows that permanent execution monitoring is required in real domains. The execution monitoring has to deal, among other things, with the following issues:

- Has the current action already achieved its effect?
- When is it necessary to abort the ongoing action due to unforeseen changes of the environment?
- Can the next action of the plan be executed in the current world state? It might be the case that its precondition is no longer fulfilled due to a change of the environment.
- Is the plan still valid? Under which conditions is it necessary to abort a plan?

In order to be able to perform a permanent monitoring of the plan execution, the qualitative world state has to be re-computed each time a continuous world state is created. After the computation of the truth values of the predicates, the preconditions and effects of the action in the plan can be re-evaluated. Action invariants are also used, that is, conditions that must hold as long as the action is executed. In most cases, the action invariant is equal to the action precondition. Let us come back to the example plan in Figure 8. Suppose the first action, *MoveTo(Ball)*, has succeeded, and therefore the robot executes

GrabBall. The invariant and the effect of this action are permanently re-evaluated.

Traditional approaches to plan execution and monitoring only take the preconditions of actions into account. In Fraser, Steinbauer, and Wotawa (2005), the use of plan invariants is proposed as a means to supervise plan execution. When a violation of the plan invariant is detected, the plan is aborted immediately. A plan invariant is a condition that refers to the plan as a whole and thus can include conditions that are not present in the action preconditions and invariants. The use of plan invariants is proposed in order to define conditions such that a violation indicates that it is no longer desirable to pursue this plan, although the plan is feasible according to the action preconditions and invariants, and its goal could be achieved. This allows the agent to adapt its behaviour to unforeseen changes in the environment.

In Fraser et al. (2005) the *extended planning problem* was defined, which extends the original definition in Fikes and Nilsson (1972). It consists of:

1. An initial state s_{init}
2. A goal state g
3. A set A that contains all possible actions
4. The plan invariant inv

A plan invariant can be defined for each goal and thus is assigned to plans that are created for this goal. In the example, one could define that the goal *IsAt(Ball,OppGoal)* should no longer be pursued when two or more players of the opponent team have moved between the ball and the opponent goal, no matter whether or not this robot already owns the ball. The idea is that in this case it is not reasonable to attempt to score a goal, as the chances of success are low, and that it may be better to change the tactics. Therefore, a new predicate *Blocked(Ball,OppGoal)* is introduced, and its negation is part of the plan invariant.

This robust method of plan execution has been deployed and successfully evaluated in the RoboCup middle-size league.

From the Quantitative World to a Symbolic Representation

As already explained, the perceptions from different sensors are fused in order to create the most probable continuous model of the real environment. The resulting model contains the robots' own pose and the positions of objects in the world.

This purely quantitative model is transformed to an abstract world model, which consists of logical predicates that are true or false. The example predicate *InReach*(*x*) has already been introduced, which is true if and only if the object *x* is within a certain distance of the robot. The truth value of a predicate is re-computed each time a new quantitative world model is available. For each type of predicate, an evaluation function is defined, which determines the truth value. For example, the value of *InReach*(*x*) is computed as follows:

```
COND_InReach(x, m): boolean
    return (dist(r, x) < t)
```

where *m* is the continuous world model, *r* is the robot, and *t* is a threshold.

This approach has, compared to reasoning based on continuous data, many advantages. Amongst others, a qualitative model has only a finite number of possible states, and qualitative models are implicitly able to cope with uncertain and incomplete knowledge. Another reason is the fact that the programming of the robot is simplified and can also be done by human operators who have no programming skills. The knowledge and the strategy of a robot can be neatly expressed in logical formulas on a more abstract level. Such programming appears more intuitive.

The mapping from a quantitative model to symbolic predicates in a dynamic and uncertain environment leads to two major problems: First, the truth value of predicates is calculated using thresholds, that is, there are sharp boundaries. Thus slight changes of the environment can cause truth value changes and result in abortion of plans due to a violation of the invariant, even if the plan still could be finished successfully. The consequence is instability in the high-level decision-making process. A longer-lasting commitment to a plan, once it is chosen, is desired. Second, sensor data is inherently noisy. Hence, due to the sharp boundaries, sensor noise leads to unstable knowledge, that is, to undesired oscillation of truth values, even if the environment does not change.

In Steinbauer, Weber, and Wotawa (2005a) a predicate hysteresis was proposed as an attempt to reduce the problems described above. The term hysteresis is well known from electrical engineering. It means that the current state is influenced by a decision that has been made previously. This concept was adapted in order to improve the robustness of the decision making process. The basic idea is that once a predicate evaluates to a certain truth value, only significant changes of the environment can cause a change of this truth value.

In an example, an improved evaluation function for *InReach*(*x*) is introduced:

```
COND_InReach(x, m, l): boolean
    if l then
        return (dist(r, x) < t + h)
    else
        return (dist(r, x) < t – h)
```

where the variable *l* represents the current truth value of *p* and *h* is the hysteresis size.

Such an evaluation function has the advantage that at the boundary only a significant change in the quantitative world causes a change of the truth value. This leads to a stabilization of the evaluation. However, it has to be mentioned that hysteresis is always a trade-off between stability and reactivity.

RUNTIME FAULT DETECTION AND REPAIR

Even if the control software of a mobile robot is carefully designed, implemented, and tested, there is always the possibility of faults in the system. Generally, faults are the deviation of the current behaviour of a system from its desired behaviour. Carlson and Murphy (2003) presented a quantitative evaluation of failures on mobile robots. The situation gets even worse if one thinks about autonomous robots, which operate for a long time without the possibility of human intervention, for example, nuclear inspection robots, space probes, or planetary rovers. Therefore, control architectures that are robust and fault-tolerant are crucial for truly autonomous robots.

Because faults are not totally avoidable, it is desirable that mobile robots are able to autonomously detect and repair such faults. When a permanent fault, that is, a broken hardware component, is identified, then the robot should at least provide basic functionality or should be able to switch to a safe state. These requirements can be fulfilled if a dedicated diagnosis system is attached to the robot control software. Usually, a diagnosis system is comprised of three modules: (1) a monitoring module, (2) a fault detection and localization module, and (3) a repair module. The first module observes the actual behaviour of the hardware and software of the robot system. The fault detection uses observations and a model of the system's desired behaviour to detect deviations between them. A deviation is equivalent to a detected fault. However, in practice the detection of a fault is not enough. The module should also identify the hardware or software component that caused the fault. If a fault and its location are identified, the repair module tries to resolve the fault.

This could happen by a restart or reconfiguration of the affected components.

There are many proposed and implemented approaches for fault diagnosis and repair in autonomous systems. The Livingstone architecture by Williams, Muscettola, Nayak, and Pell (1998) was used on the space probe *Deep Space One* in order to detect failures in the probe's hardware and to recover from them. The fault detection and recovery is based on model-based reasoning. Model-based reasoning uses a logic-based formulation of the system model and the observations. Verma, Gordon, Simmons, and Thrun (2004) used particle filter techniques to estimate the state of the robot and its environment. These estimations together with a dynamic model of the robot were used to detect faults. Rule-based approaches were proposed by Murphy and Hershberger (1996) to detect failures in sensing and to recover from them. Additional sensor information was used to generate and test hypotheses to explain symptoms resulting from sensing failures. Roumeliotis, Sukhatme, and Bekey (1998) used a bank of Kalman filters to track specific failure models and the nominal model.

In this section, a solution for real-time fault diagnosis and repair of control software of autonomous robots is presented. The fault diagnosis follows the model-based diagnosis paradigm (Reiter, 1987). It is based on observations of the current behaviour of the control system's components, a model of the desired behaviour of the control system's components, and the dependencies between them. A monitoring module continuously observes the behaviour of the control software. If a deviation of the desired behaviour is observed, a diagnosis kernel derives a diagnosis, that is, a set of malfunctioning software components explaining the deviation. Based on this diagnosis and on a model of the software components and their connections, a repair module executes appropriate repair actions to recover the system from the fault. The proposed diagnosis system has been implemented and tested as part of the proposed control architecture on RoboCup MSL robots within the robotic soccer scenario (Steinbauer & Wotawa, 2005).

Robot Control Software

Figure 9 shows an overview of the robot control software framework, the features of which have been presented in the preceding sections. In Figure 9, remote CORBA calls are shown as solid lines directed to the server. The data-flow between server and client is shown as chain dotted lines. The figure also shows the dependencies between services. Remote CORBA calls are called *strongly dependent* because a fault in the server directly affects the client. Connections using the event channel are shown as dashed lines, and the data-flow direction is always directed from the producer to the consumer. Connections that rely on this communication mechanism impose a *weak dependency*, that is, the services are loosely

coupled and a failure of the server does not cause a failure of the client. The distinction between strong and weak dependencies is later important for the diagnosis and repair process.

The above described structure of the control software, the different types of connections, and the dependencies between the services are used to build a model of the desired behaviour of the control software. In the next section it is described how this model together with various observations of the behaviour of services and connections are combined to form a diagnosis system for the control software of the robots.

Diagnosis System

Monitoring

The task of the monitoring module of the diagnosis system is to observe the actual behaviour of the control system. For this purpose, the concept of observers was introduced. An observer monitors

Figure 9. Dependencies and data-flow within the robot control software

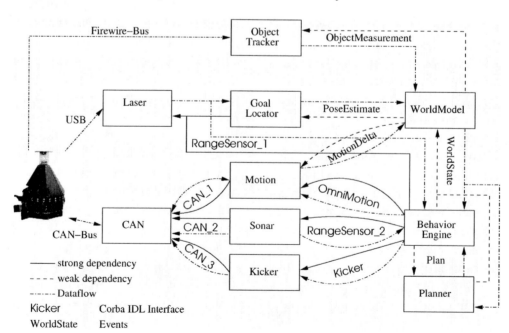

the behaviour of a service or the communication between services. The observer determines a misbehaviour of the control system if the observed behaviour deviates from the specified behaviour. In the current implementation, the following observers are used:

- **Periodic event production:** This observer checks whether a specific event *e* is at least produced every *n* milliseconds.
- **Conditional event production:** This observer checks whether an event e_1 is produced within *n* milliseconds after an event e_2 occurred.
- **Periodic method calls:** This observer checks whether a service calls a remote method *m* at least every *n* milliseconds.
- **Spawn processes:** This observer checks whether a service spawns at least *n* threads.

There are several requirements for the monitoring module. First, if observers are used, there should be no, or at least only a minimum necessity for, changes in the control system. Furthermore, the monitoring component should not significantly reduce the overall performance of the control system. Both requirements can be met easily by using mechanisms provided by CORBA (Henning & Vinoski, 1999) and the Linux operating system (OS). The first two observers are implemented using the CORBA event channel. The third observer is implemented using the CORBA portable interceptor pattern. The last observer is implemented using the information provided by the *proc* file-system of the Linux OS. For all these observers, no changes are necessary in the control system. Furthermore, the computational power requirements for all the observers are negligible.

Diagnosis

A fault is detected if an observer belonging to the monitoring module recognizes a deviation between the actual and the specified behaviour of the system. However, so far one does not know which misbehaving service causes this fault. The model-based diagnosis (MBD) paradigm (de Kleer & Williams, 1987; Reiter, 1987) is used to locate the faulty service.

Figure 10 shows an example for the diagnosis process in case of a malfunctioning CAN-Service. First, an abstract model of the correct behaviour of the CAN sonar and motion service is built. Therefore, two predicates are introduced: *AB(x)* becomes true if a service *x* is abnormal, meaning *x* is malfunctioning. *Ok(y)* becomes true if a connection *y*, either a remote call or an event, shows a correct behaviour. The model for the correct behaviour of the example could contain the following clauses:

1. $\neg AB(CAN) \rightarrow ok(CAN\_1)$
2. $\neg AB(CAN) \rightarrow ok(CAN\_2)$
3. $\neg AB(Sonar) \wedge ok(CAN\_1) \rightarrow$ $ok(RangeSensor\_2)$
4. $\neg AB(Motion) \wedge ok(CAN\_2) \rightarrow$ $ok(MotionDelta)$

The principles of MBD will be explained with a simple example. Lines 1 and 2 specify that, if the CAN-Service works correctly, then also the connections *CAN_1* and *CAN_2* work correctly. Line 3 specifies that if the sonar service and its input connection *CAN_1* work correctly, the connection *RangeSensor_2* has to show a correct behaviour. Line 4 specifies similar facts for the motion service.

If there is a deadlock in the CAN-Service, the motion and sonar services cannot provide new events or calls, as they get no more data from

Figure 10. Diagnosis of a fault in the Can-Service. The upper figure shows the desired behaviour. The lower figure shows the behaviour after a deadlock in the Can-Service.

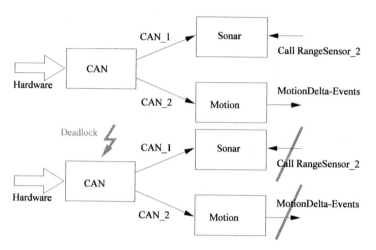

CAN. This fact is recognized by the corresponding observers and can be expressed by the clause: $\neg ok(RangeSensor\_2) \wedge \neg ok(MotionDelta)$. If a correct behaviour of the system is assumed (expressed by the clause $\neg AB(CAN) \wedge \neg AB(Sonar) \wedge \neg AB(Motion)$), then a logical contradiction is observed. This means a fault was detected.

Finding the service that caused the fault is equivalent to finding the set of predicates $AB(x)$ with $x \in \{CAN, Motion, Sonar\}$ that resolves the contradiction. These sets are called *diagnoses*, Δ. Sets with minimal cardinality are preferred, that is, a single faulty service. These diagnoses are in general sufficient as multiple faults are unlikely. In this example, the set $\{AB(CAN)\}$ with only one element is able to resolve the contradiction. Therefore, the faulty CAN-Service is located.

Repair

Once the diagnosis system has found one or more malfunctioning services responsible for a detected fault, it should be able to recover the control system from this fault. Therefore, the repair module determines an appropriate repair action based on the described diagnosis and the dependencies between the services. The repair action consists of a stop and a restart of the malfunctioning services.

The appropriate repair action is derived in the following way: Put all members of the diagnosis D in a set R. The members of this set R are scheduled for restart. In the next step insert all services into R, which strongly depend on a member of R. Repeat this step until no more services are added to R. R now contains all services which that to be restarted. But first of all the scheduled services have to be stopped in an ordered way. This means to first stop all services that no other service strongly depends on. Afterward, stop all services for which no more services are running that depend on them. This process is necessary to avoid additional crashes of services caused by a sudden stop of a service another service depends on. Hereafter, restart all affected services in the reverse order. Services that were restarted because of a strong dependency on the malfunctioning services should be able to retain data that it had gained so far or they should be able to recover such data after a restart. Otherwise, the control system may become inconsistent. After this repair action took place, the robots control system is again in the desired state.

CONCLUSION

In this work, a successful control architecture for autonomous mobile robots was presented. The proposed architecture is comprised of four major parts that give the architecture the power to control an autonomous mobile robot in complex tasks in difficult environments while still maintaining a great amount of flexibility. The four parts answer the questions that were posed in the introduction:

- **Control paradigm:** It has been motivated that only a hybrid control paradigm that combines the advantages of reactive and deliberative control enables a robot to perform complex tasks robustly. A three-layered paradigm was used to organize the control of the presented architecture.

- **Framework:** The experiences in building a mobile robot have shown that the adoption of modular frameworks for software and hardware can significantly reduce the development time and costs. At the same time, it increases the flexibility and robustness of the robot. By using this design approach, it was possible to develop four soccer robots from scratch with limited human and financial resources within less than one year.

The quality and robustness of the robots were demonstrated during a number of RoboCup tournaments where the hardware and software of the robots operated in a stable manner. Moreover, the adaptability and flexibility of the proposed control solution were impressive. For example, a RoboCup player's strategy could be modified within a few minutes on the field by simply adapting the knowledge base; no re-compilation of the software was necessary. Furthermore, the same framework is also applied successfully for the control of a delivery robot within the office domain.

However, the framework suffers from two major drawbacks. For one, the extensive use of the event channel as a flexible communication mechanism slows down the system and reduces the reactivity of the robot in dynamic environments. In addition, the system's reactivity is limited because of the incorporated classical AI planning techniques, which have a high computational complexity. However, this is necessary because only due to this abstract decision making module is the robot able to deal with very complex tasks. This drawback can be reduced by the increasing power of the used on-board computers and further achievements in the research on AI planning.

- **Robust plan execution:** The deliberative components have been enriched by a robust plan execution and symbol grounding mechanism. These extensions enhance the deliberative component, which plays a crucial part within an architecture aiming at the execution of complex tasks. The enhancements increase the applicability for unpredictable, noisy, and dynamic environments. Plan invariants and a hysteresis-based symbol grounding are used to achieve this.

- **Runtime fault diagnosis and repair:** The presented diagnosis system is capable of real-time fault detection, localization, and repair for the control software of autonomous mobile robots. The proposed system follows the model-based diagnosis paradigm. It uses a general abstract model of the correct behaviour of the control system together with observations of the actual behaviour of the system to detect and localize faults in the software. Furthermore, a repair method was presented that is able to recover the software from a fault. Because of its general methods, the proposed system is also applicable to software other than robot control software.

The presented overall control architecture solves a couple of problems that arise from the deployment of autonomous mobile robots in complex tasks in dynamic and unpredictable domains. It is an excellent example for a general flexible architecture for robust intelligent control.

ACKNOWLEDGMENT

This research has been funded in part by the Austrian Science Fund (FWF) under grant P17963-N04.

REFERENCES

Blum, A., & Merrick, F. (1995). Fast planning through planning graph analysis. *Proceedings of the 14th International Joint Conference on Artificial Intelligence (IJCAI 95)* (pp. 1636-1642).

Brooks, R. A. (1986). A robust layered control system for a mobile robot. *IEEE Journal of Robotics and Automation, RA-2*(1), 14-23.

Carlson, J., & Murphy, R. R. (2003). Reliability analysis of mobile robot. *Proceedings of the 2003 IEEE International Conference on Robotics and Automation, ICRA 2003.* Taipei, Taiwan.

Castelpietra, C., Guidotti, A., Iocchi, L., Nardi, D., & Rosati, R. (2002). Design and implementation of cognitive soccer robots. In *RoboCup 2001: Robot soccer World Cup V,* vol. 2377 of *Lecture Notes in Computer Science.* Springer.

de Kleer, J., & Williams, B. C. (1987). Diagnosing multiple faults. *Artificial Intelligence, 32*(1), 97-130.

Dietl, M., Gutmann, J. S., & Nebel, B. (2001). Cooperative sensing in dynamic environments. *Proceedings of the IEEE/RSJ International Conference on Intelligent Robots and Systems (IROS'01),* Maui, HI.

Dylla, F., Ferrein, A., & Lakemeyer, G. (2002). Acting and deliberating using golog in robotic soccer - A hybrid approach. *Proceedings of the 3rd International Cognitive Robotics Workshop (CogRob 2002).* AAAI Press.

Fikes, R., & Nilsson, N. (1972). Strips: A new approach to the application of theorem proving to problem solving. *Artificial Intelligence, 2*(3-4), 189-208.

Fox, D., Burgard, W., Dellaert, F., & Thrun, S. (1999). Monte Carlo localization: Efficient position estimation for mobile robots. In *AAAI/IAAI,* 343-349.

Fraser, G., Steinbauer, G., & Wotawa, F. (2004). A modular architecture for a multi-purpose mobile robot. In *Innovations in Applied Artificial Intelligence, IEA/AIE, vol. 3029, Lecture notes in artificial intelligence* (pp. 1007-1014). Ottawa, Canada: Springer.

Fraser, G., Steinbauer, G., & Wotawa, F. (2005). Plan execution in dynamic environments. *Proceedings of the 18th Conference on Industrial and Engineering Applications of Artificial Intelligence and Expert Systems, IEA/AIE, LNAI 3029,* (pp. 208-217). Bari, Italy: Springer.

Gerkey, B. P., Vaughan, R. T., Stroy, K., Howard, A., Sukhatme, G. S., & Mataric, M. J. (2001). Most valuable player: A robot device server for distributed control. *Proceedings of the IEEE/RSJ International Conference on Intelligent Robots and Systems (IROS 2001)* (pp. 1226-1231).

Henning, M., & Vinoski, S. (1999). *Advanced CORBA©Programming with C++* (1st ed.). Addison Wesley Professional.

Kortenkamp, D., Bonasso, R. P., & Murphy, R. (Ed.). (1998). *Artificial intelligence and mobile robots. Case studies of successful robot systems.* MIT Press.

Montemerlo, M., Roy, N., & Thrun, S. (2003). Perspectives on standardization in mobile robot programming: The Carnegie Mellon navigation (CARMEN) toolkit. *Proceedings of the Conference on Intelligent Robots and Systems (IROS)*.

Murphy, R. R. (2002). *Introduction to AI Robotics*. MIT Press.

Murphy, R. R., & Hershberger, D. (1996). Classifying and recovering from sensing failures in autonomous mobile robots. *AAAI/IAAI, 2*, 922-929.

Nilsson, N. (1984). *Shakey the robot*. (Tech. Rep. No. 325). Menlo Park, CA: SRI International.

Orebäck, A. (2004). *A component framework for autonomous mobile robots*. Unpublished doctoral thesis, KTH numerical and computer science.

Orebäck, A., & Christensen, H. I. (2003). Evaluation of architectures for mobile robotics. *Autonomous Robots, 14*, 33-49.

Reiter, R. (1987). A theory of diagnosis from first principles. *Artificial Intelligence, 32*(1), 57-95.

Roumeliotis, S. I., Sukhatme, G. S., & Bekey G. A. (1998). Sensor fault detection and identification in a mobile robot. *Proceedings of IEEE Conference on Intelligent Robots and Systems* (pp. 1383-1388).

Russell, S., & Norvig, P. (2003). *Artificial intelligence: A modern approach* (2nd ed.). Englewood Cliffs, NJ: Prentice-Hall.

Schmidt, D. C. (2000). *TAO developer's guide* (1.1a ed.). Object Computing Inc.

Simmons, R. (1994). Structured control for autonomous robots. *IEEE Transactions of Robotics and Automation, 10*, 34-43.

Steinbauer, G., Weber, J., & Wotawa, F. (2005a). From the real-world to its qualitative representation - Practical lessons learned. *Proceedings of the 18th International Workshop on Qualitative Reasoning (QR-05)* (pp. 186-191).

Steinbauer, G., & Wotawa, F. (2005b). Detecting and locating faults in the control software of autonomous mobile robots. *Proceedings of the 16th International Workshop on Principles of Diagnosis (DX-05)* (pp. 13-18).

Steinbauer, G., & Wotawa, F. (2005c). Detecting and locating faults in the control software of autonomous mobile robots. *Proceedings of 19th International Joint Conference on Artificial Intelligence (IJCAI-05)*, Edinburgh, UK.

The Miro Developer Team (2005). *Miro Manual, 0.9.4 ed.* University of Ulm: Department of computer science.

Utz, H. (2005). *Advanced Software Concepts and Technologies for Autonomous Mobile Robotics*. Unpublished doctoral dissertation, University of Ulm.

Utz, H., Sablatnüg, S., Enderle, S., & Kraetzschmar, G. (2002). Miro: Middleware for mobile robot applications [Special issue]. *IEEE Transactions on Robotics and Automation, 18*(4), 493-497.

Verma, V., Gordon, G., Simmons, R., & Thrun, S. (2004). Real-time fault diagnosis. *IEEE Robotics & Automation Magazine, 11*(2), 56-66.

Weld, D. S. (1999). Recent advances in AI planning. *AI Magazine, 20*(2), 93-123.

Williams, B. C., Muscettola, N., Nayak, P. P., & Pell, B. (1998). Remote agent: To boldly go where no AI system has gone before. *Artificial Intelligence, 103*(1-2), 5-48.

Chapter XVIII
RiskMan:
A Multi-Agent System
for Risk Management

Manolya Kavakli
Macquarie University, Australia

Nicolas Szilas
Macquarie University, Australia

John Porte
Macquarie University, Australia

Iwan Kartiko
Macquarie University, Australia

ABSTRACT

The purpose of this chapter is to discuss the use of multi-agent systems to develop virtual reality training systems. We first review these systems and then investigate the architectures used. We demonstrate an example of our own (RiskMan) and then discuss the advantages and drawbacks of using multi-agent agent approaches in the development of virtual reality training systems. The chapter describes the system architecture of a multi-agent system for risk management (RiskMan) to help train police officers to handle high-risk situations. RiskMan has been developed using a high-level scripting language of a game engine, Unreal Tournament 2004. The major modules are a scenario-based expert system, a narrative engine, a game engine, and a graphics engine. The system integrates a simulation agent, trainee agent, communication agent, interface agent, and scripted agents communicating using games technology.

INTRODUCTION

The purpose of this chapter is to discuss the use of multi-agent systems in the development of virtual reality training systems. We first review these systems overall and then investigate the architectures used. We demonstrate an example of a multi-agent virtual reality training system

(RiskMan) and then discuss the advantages and drawbacks of using multi-agent agent approaches in the development of virtual reality training systems.

A *multi-agent simulation* consists of intelligent agents competing or co-operating with each other, with a view to achieving system objectives (Rzevski, 2003). There are a number of multi-agent architectures designed for interactive learning. Some of these work on a generic platform of agents (Capuano, Marsella, & Salerno, 2000; Silveira & Vicari, 2002). Some address the use of pedagogical agents (Johnson, Rickel, & Lester, 2000) and learning companion agents (Chan, 1996), socially intelligent agents (Conati & Klawe, 2000), and tutor agents (Ritter & Kodinger, 1996). Some explore software engineering techniques based on the multi-agent-oriented analysis for agent, environment, interactions, and organizations (Petsy & Webber, 2004) proposing that the educational function of a system will be an emerging property of the interactions organized between agents and humans.

In this chapter, we investigate agents as a paradigm for software engineering and discuss how a virtual reality training system, which draws on research in the areas of computer games (Kavakli et al., 2004; Kavakli & Thorne, 2002), knowledge acquisition (Kavakli & Thorne, 2003; Richards & Busch, 2003), agent technology (Pelachaud & Poggi, 2001; Richards & Busch, 2003) and natural language processing (Dras, 1998; Rudra, Kavakli, & Bossomaier, 2003), can provide a safe learning experience to assist knowledge acquisition. Tacit knowledge is practical know-how as defined by Wagner and Sternberg (1991). Tacit knowledge cannot be read from a procedures manual in a training simulation. Tacit knowledge can be acquired through interacting with the world and objects. We call this process *interactive learning.*

Interaction is probably the most important single characteristic of complex software (Wooldridge, 2002). As a complex system, we will explore the interrelationships between the components of a multi-agent system for risk management. RiskMan is an ARC Discovery project carried out by Macquarie University (Barles, Dras, Kavakli, Richards, & Tychsen, 2005, Dras, Kavakli, & Richards, 2005). The project's goal is to train emergency police and defense personnel to handle high-risk situations that can be costly and even dangerous. RiskMan has been developed using a high-level scripting language of a game engine, Unreal Tournament 2004.

RiskMan links three research projects carried out by the department of computing, Macquarie University, and sponsored by the Australian Research Council (ARC):

- ARC Discovery Grant (DP0558852 titled "Risk Management Using Agent Based Virtual Environments") to Richards, Kavakli, and Dras,
- ARC Linkage International Grant (LX0560117 titled "An Interactive Drama Engine in Virtual Reality") to Kavakli, Pelachaud, and Szilas, and
- ARC Linkage Grant (LP0216837 titled "Cognitive Modelling of Computer Game Pidgins") to Kavakli, Bossomaier, and Cooper.

RiskMan comprises these three projects in a unique system architecture integrating risk management, desktop and immersive virtual reality, and agent-based natural language systems, using game engineering. In the following section, we will review these systems.

Virtual reality training simulations for risk management: The satisfactory management of risk situations (Decker, 2001) involves risk identification, the development of risk handling strategies and plans (Kavakli & Gao, 2005; Kavakli, Kavakli, & Gao, 2004c; McCamley, 2000), and the conduct and monitoring of those plans. Risk management requires the use of both codified and tacit knowledge. Recognizing the importance of tacit knowledge, scenario-based training has gained momentum in recent years. For example, the U.S.A. General Accounting Office (GAO) released a report on homeland security (Decker, 2001) that provides a list of risk assessment measurements for contingency plan development and a matrix for risk-based scenario development. As an example of a risk assessment system, Kavakli and Gao (2005) developed a "Virtual Crime Prevention through Environmental Design Kit" (Virtual CPTED). The Virtual CPTED kit enables trained and experienced police officers to identify and quantify the crime risk, situational hazards, and social conditions that are believed to attract and/or facilitate criminal behavior. Another example of a risk management system is ExpertCop (Furtado & Vasconcelos, 2004). ExpertCop is a training simulation for police officers who configure and allocate an available police force for a selected urban region and then interact with the simulation. The goal of the training in ExpertCop is to induce members of the police force to reflect on resource allocation to prevent crime. The training simulator receives a police resource allocation plan as input, and it generates simulation scenarios of how the crime rate would behave in a certain period of time.

Desktop virtual reality systems: The use of game engineering as desktop virtual reality systems to develop training simulations is widely employed by the U.S. military (Kavakli, 2005). In 1999, the U.S. Army established the Institute for Creative Technology (ICT) to explore the use of commercial entertainment technology and content for military training and education (Kennedy, 2002). The ICT is working with STRICOM and commercial game development companies to create training simulations. The Naval War College, in Newport, has worked with Sonalysts Inc., of Waterford, CT, to create more than 500 games (Prensky, 2001). For example, the Army Command and General Staff College in Kansas uses a strategy game called Decisive Action, originally

developed for corps-level operations. The Naval Postgraduate School in Monterey, CA, and the Modeling, Virtual Environment and Simulation (MOVES) Institute also developed a number of games (Prensky, 2001) similar to commercial games Counter Strike, Delta-Force, Rainbow Six, and America's Army. Most of these games accurately depict military equipment, training, and the real-life movements of soldiers.

Immersive virtual reality systems: More recently, the Army's Soldier Systems Center, in Natick, MA, has decided to use immersive virtual reality (VR) systems in training and commissioned games developer Novalogic California to modify the popular Delta Force 2 game to help familiarize soldiers with the service's experimental Land Warrior system (Kennedy, 2002). The Land Warrior system includes a self-contained computer and radio unit, a global-positioning receiver, a helmet-mounted liquid-crystal display, and a modular weapons array that adds thermal and video sights and laser ranging to the standard M-4 carbine and M-16A2 rifle. A customized version of another computer game, Microsoft Flight Simulator, is issued to all U.S. Navy student pilots and undergraduates enrolled in Naval Reserve Officer Training Courses at 65 colleges around the U.S.A. (Prensky, 2001).

Agent-based natural language systems: The use of VR for training has become a major focus in academic communities as well. Two noteworthy projects are the Net Environment for Embodied Conversational Agents (NECA) (Klesen, 2002), supported by the European Commission in order to develop conversational agents that are able to speak and act like humans, and the mission rehearsal exercise system (MRE) (Swartout et al., 2001) supported by the U.S. Army in order to develop an immersive learning environment where the participants experience the sights, sounds, and circumstances, as they encounter real-world scenarios. While both projects seek to build intelligent agents that are able to respond and adapt to their environment in natural and believable ways, NECA's primary focus is on natural language and emotional agents whereas MRE's primary focus is on movie-like realism. Commercial simulation environments that are currently available offer minimal user interaction cannot be used to define complex training scenarios and use scripted characters that cannot react appropriately to the user or the events.

HUMAN AND SOFTWARE AGENTS

An *agent* is a software object capable of communicating with other agents, as well as with humans, with a view to achieving a given task. We categorize agents in three groups:

- **Believable** (one able to show emotions and has a personality)
- **Interactive** (one interacting with a user by following the rules of face-to-face interaction) and
- **Embodied** (Cassell, 2000) (one able to interact with the user in all modalities a human agent may use: through words, voice, gesture, gaze, facial expression, body movements, posture, etc.)

At the current stage, the agents in RiskMan are interactive agents but we have been moving to implement embodied agents in the future stages of the system development. Poggi and Pelachaud (2000) have explored emotional meaning and expressions, as well as how the cognitive and expressive analyses of communicative acts could be applied in the construction of expressive animated faces. Cappella and Pelachaud (2001) have defined rules for responsive robots, using human interactions to build virtual interaction. We integrate these to create social agents in a training system for risk assessment.

Agents can be used to simulate the behavior of human societies (Wooldridge, 2002). Hybrid social spaces such as virtual environments are social spaces where human agents and artificial agents co-exist. In order for these agents to be able to co-exist, various types of agents have to have a working model of the other agents that enables them to correctly interact.

Architecture of Multi-Agent Systems

There are a number of architectures proposed in the literature for multi-agent systems: Some consider a *multi-agent simulation* a distributed system in which the entities are agents (Gervais & Muscutariu, 2001). Gervais and Muscutariu (2001) propose the use of the UML-standardized notation for specifying agent based systems according to open distributed processing (ODP) semantics and define an architecture description language (ADL) for modeling the system both in analysis and design phases.

Some focus on providing an interactive learning environment using pedagogical agents (e.g., JADE project by Peña, Marzo, & de la Rosa, 2002; Silveira and Vicari, 2002). One of the major problems of computer-aided training simulations is how to provide adaptive teaching. Mathoff, Van Hoe, and Apeall (1996) describe the minimum requirements necessary for an interactive learning environment: interactivity, adaptable instruction, robustness, direct monitoring of the learning process, empirical evaluation, and parsimony. JADE system contains a special pedagogical agent responsible for each teaching strategy and for the domain knowledge retrieval. The student model agent monitors all actions of the student accessing data. The pedagogical agent updates the student history, when required, and sends the data to be updated to the student model agent, as well as changes in the students' cognitive state, as demonstrated in Figure1.

Furtado and Vasconcelos (2004)'s training simulation ExpertCop performs the interactions

Figure 1. An architecture of multi-agent systems using pedagogical agents (Source: Silveira & Vicari, 2002)

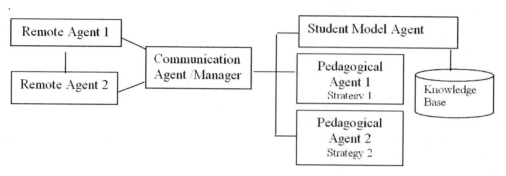

of police teams and criminals in a game-based virtual environment, including a pedagogical tool that implements and explains interaction strategies between the police officer and the simulator. The simulations occur in a learning environment with graphical visualizations that help the police officers learning. The system allows the student to manipulate parameters dynamically and analyze results. The ExpertCop system uses problem solving methods to support the development of KBSs by using the unified problem-solving method description language (UPML) (Fensel et al., 2003).

In these systems, *knowledge base* contains the specification of domain knowledge of the system. The knowledge may be structured in terms of classes of *objects, properties, attributes, scripts, and relationships* resembling an augmented semantic network. The performance of agents depends on the quality of the domain knowledge stored in the knowledge base and associated databases. Knowledge base can be modified by the users of the system and may evolve through internal processes eliminating its own useless components and experimenting with new ones. Rzevski (2003) suggested a similar architecture to this, using the term ontology instead of a knowledge base. Rzevski's architecture consists of a virtual world, runtime engine, and an interface, in addition to the knowledge base. *Virtual world* is the place where software agents are created when needed, where they interact with each other and are destroyed when their useful life comes to an end. The virtual world is a dynamic model of the real world. Each software agent represents a person or a physical object from the domain. The challenge is to design a virtual world that will reflect all relevant situations observable in the real world and all changes of these situations. Rzevski (2003) also includes a *runtime engine* that contains all the algorithms and protocols required for proper functioning of agents. The engine supports parallel running of a number of agents and enables their interaction. *Interface* links the multi-agent system with users and other software.

System Architecture of RiskMan

In this section, our purpose is to highlight how RiskMan system components interface with each other using a hybrid agent architecture. The hybrid agent architecture integrates a rapid response mechanism with the pro-active behavior enabled by planning. RiskMan is composed of modules that separate the data models and functionality. The major modules are an agent and scenario-based expert system, a narrative engine, a game engine, and a graphics engine (Kavakli, 2006). Our architecture is given in Figure 2.

There are five types of agents in RiskMan as follows:

Figure 2. Risk management training system architecture

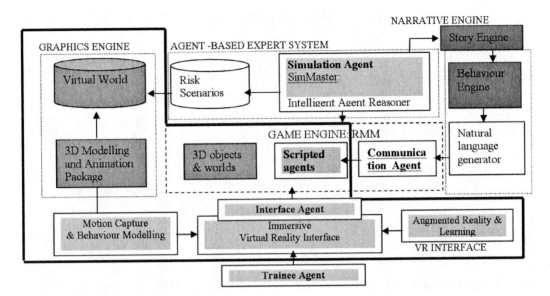

- The *simulation agent (SimMaster)* is given the task of deciding and maintaining the optimal training of a trainee in risk assessment procedures. SimMaster monitors the immediate environment, making sure that trainee is properly trained regarding risk situations in a potential crime zone. Simulation agent takes all actions of trainee's data accessing, communicating with the trainee agent. In the current version of the system, SimMaster controls story engine.

- The *scripted agents* are programmed to initiate a negotiation with the trainee whether to terminate the process, slow down, or continue, and initiate an action at the next opportune time, depending on the commands of the SimMaster.

- The *trainee agent* is the trainee using the system in either a local or remote location. Trainee agent negotiates with the scripted agents in potential risk situations. The trainee agent updates the user profile of the system and sends messages to the simulation agent, interface agent, and communication agent.

- The *interface agent* proposes an adaptive and intuitive gesture/mouse/keyboard-based interface using the profile of the trainee agent. The user may communicate with the system using datagloves, head-mounted display, semi-cylindrical projection system, stereoscopic goggles, keyboard, mouse, or any other interface available.

- The *communication agent* is responsible for the speech-based communication with the scripted agents using a natural language generator and a speech synthesizer.

RiskMan uses socket connections to feed information between the narrative engine and SimMaster to Unreal Tournament game engine (UT2004) and vice versa. In this case, both the narrative engine and the SimMaster are external client programs controlling the decisions of the scripted agents' (NPCs: non-player characters) actions such as walk, run, turn, and talk. Socket communication has been set up having Unreal as the server application and a Java application as the client connecting to Unreal over a transmission control protocol (TCP) connection.

Narrative Engine

One of the major components of RiskMan is narrative engine, since it directly controls scripted agents (NPCs). Noel LeJeune (2003) defines a story engine as *"a software environment in which unsophisticated developers, known as authors, can create a story."* Figure 3 demonstrates the system architecture of the interactive story engine developed by Fairclough and Cunningham (2002).

Using UT2004 game engine, we integrated two main modules: the story engine and the behavior engine within a narrative engine. The behavior engine (BE) is a middle layer between the narrative engine and the game engine. It transforms the high level actions produced by the former into a set of low-level animations played by the latter. The narrative engine (NE) is responsible for generating narrative events, including NPC actions as well as possible player actions. The narrative engine also includes a graphical interface for selecting an action and the text generation module in an interactive drama environment (Szilas & Kavakli, 2006). The data related to the story is stored as external files that allow modification of the story without having to enter into the program code. In particular, XML (extensible markup language) files are used to store the structures of the narrative. In computer games, the narrative is generally limited to a graph of possibilities predetermined by an author. An interactive drama engine provides the users of the system a fully immersive interactive dramatic experience in a virtual world. Integration of interactive narrative and virtual reality hardware and software is a novel approach to the current problems in digital media. It is expected to lead to the development of new-generation interactive films and computer games.

The general architecture of our story engine (Figure 4) can be divided into five modules (Szilas, 2003):

Figure 3. The architecture of a story engine (Source: Fairclough & Cunningham, 2002)

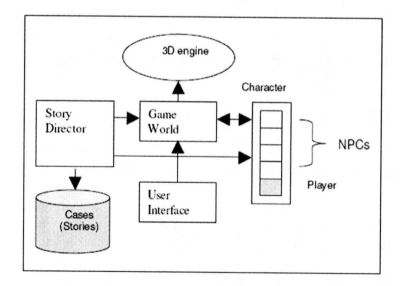

- The world of the story contains basic entities in the story (characters, goals, tasks, sub-tasks or segments, obstacles), the states of the characters (defined with predicates), and facts concerning the material situation of the world of the story.
- The narrative logic calculates the set of all the possible actions of the characters from the data stored in the world of the story.
- The narrative sequencer filters the actions calculated by the narrative logic in order to rank them from the most valuable to the least valuable. For this purpose, the sequencer tries to provide some narrative effects.
- The user model contains the state of the user at a given moment in the narrative. It provides to the narrative sequencer an estimation of impact of each possible action on the user.
- The theatre is responsible for displaying the action(s) and manages the interaction between the computer and the user.

Depending on the narrative mode chosen for the narrative sequencer, there are several ways to activate these five modules. Currently, we have two modes:

- **Automatic generation:** The narrative sequencer chooses one action among the best actions, which is sent to the theatre;
- **First person:** The user is responsible for all of the actions of one character. The user and the computer alternate their actions.

By *action*, we mean a dialog act or a performance act in the virtual world, which has a narrative signification.

The choice of the set of generic actions comes from narratology. These actions constitute the basic units of the narrative sequence. Current actions in narrative engine are (Szilas, 2003): *decide, inform, encourage, dissuade, accept, refuse, perform, condemn, and congratulate.* (*Decide* concerns the goals, while *accept* concerns the tasks.)

These actions contain parameters, which are elements of the world of the story:

- characters, goals, obstacles, tasks, attributes,
- state of characters: WISH, CAN, KNOW, WANT, etc. (WISH concerns a goal, while WANT concerns a task)

A set of 35 rules produces the possible actions. For example, the following rule describes the possibility of triggering an encouragement:

Figure 4. The general architecture of the narrative engine (Source: Szilas, 2003)

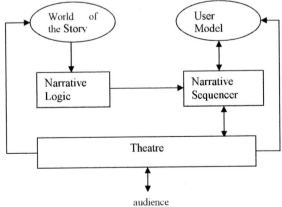

IF

    CAN (x , t , p)

    KNOW(x , CAN (x , t , p))

    KNOW(y , CAN (x , t , p))

    ~ KNOW (y , WANT(x , t , p))

    ~ KNOW (y , HAVE_BEGUN (x , t , p))

    ~ KNOW (y , HAVE_FINISHED(x , t , p))

    x ≠ y

THEN

    ENCOURAGE (y , x , t , p)

x and y are characters, t is a task and p is its optional parameters.

In this case, we stated that encouragements only occurred before the agent's decision (hence the multiple negative preconditions).

In the current version of RiskMan, individual agents have been designed to be relatively simple. They act within rules, guidelines, and constraints stored in knowledge base. There is evidence to claim that the larger the number of agents within a multi-agent system, the greater its emergent intelligence. In the following stages of system development, we are especially interested in creating intelligent interactive agents being capable of:

- Comprehending tasks that need to be performed
- Choosing the most effective strategy and tactics for the task in hand
- Selecting relevant correspondents (other agents or humans)
- Composing meaningful messages and sending them to selected correspondents
- Interpreting received messages
- Making decisions on how to respond to the content of received messages making sure that the decision contributes to the achievement of system goals
- Acting upon these decisions

Behavior Engine

The behavior engine (BE) is a module transforming high-level actions calculated by the story engine (SE) into low-level animation commands for the game engine. Unreal Tournament game engine provides us with an animation engine, able to execute basic commands like "*X* walk toward *Y*," "*X* says *content* to *Y*," and so forth. A story engine provides us with a high-level actions generator, which outputs commands like "*X* encourages *Y* to perform *t*," "*X* insults *Y*," and so forth. Between these two engines, there is a behavior engine. Such an engine should be capable of solving the following AI (artificial intelligence) issues in a simple framework:

- Composing sequences of animations into a behavior
- Provide alternative animations, depending on the context
- Provide alternative animations in case of failure
- Run animations in parallel (gestures and speech, typically)
- Manage priorities between competing behaviors (those who share the same resources)
- blend behaviors
- Interrupt behaviors and restart them
- Synchronize parallel running behaviors
- Synchronize joint behaviors between several characters

For example, SE sends the action Inform (Paul, Daryl, "I want to check Mrs. Kim's bag") to the BE, which outputs a set of coordinated animations: Paul walks toward Daryl, Daryl looks at Paul when Paul is getting close, Paul says "I want to check Mrs. Kim's bag;" in parallel, Daryl looks at Paul. The module is an independent Java program communicating via sockets with the SE and the GE.

The BE developed for the project combines three features:

- Ability to trigger and synchronize animations, both in sequence and in parallel
- Simple priority management between conflicting behaviors
- Easily authored behaviors

In BE, an action is associated with a behavior coded as a list of parallel graphs. Each node corresponds to an animation. Graphs are synchronized through events generated by GE during the execution of the animation. These graphs, stored as XML files, can be visually represented, making the authoring easier.

Natural Language Generator

When building agents that must interact with humans, it is important to achieve a rational balance between the beliefs, goals, and intentions of the agents. As we are interested in creating realistic risk situations, we cannot ignore the natural communication channel between the agents using speech (e.g., Cohen & Levesque, 1990). The virtual worlds developed include speech modules. Natural language generation systems start from an underlying representation of content; their task is to decide between various realizations (e.g., syntactic, such as full sentence versus relative clause; lexical, the choice of vocabulary; or register) in order to express this content. The representations of existing systems (e.g., Jing, Netzer, Elhadad, & McKeown, 2000; Stone & Doran, 1997) allow for some variation depending on speaker intention and so on; however, generation is quite underspecified, not capable of producing the nuances found in speech between humans, for example, the use of short clipped sentences and blunt vocabulary to express annoyance. These can be viewed as

more complex constraints of the type investigated in Dras (1998). There are research studies on the creation of specialized game slang, which we refer to as game pidgins. Game pidgins have a potential to be considered another rich source of data for cognitive and social linguists (Kavakli & Thorne, 2002; Rudra et al., 2003). Slang and dialects also serve to bond communities or subgroups.

In the project RiskMan, we have attempted animating faces using RUTH (Rutgers University Talking Head) (DeCarlo & Stone, 2001) and GPL (game pidgin language) that we have developed (Rudra et al., 2003). Animation of RUTH affords interactive agents the opportunity to reproduce the functions and behaviors of natural face-to-face conversation. It also offers a methodological tool for developing and testing psycholinguistic theories of those functions and behaviors. The integration of RUTH with RiskMan is still in the preliminary stages.

Game Engine

The term "game engine" refers to a software platform on which game developers can produce computer games. A game engine provides real-time rendering of virtual 3D scenes with a high level of interactivity. A modification (mod) in the game world is the alteration to a game. RiskMan is a mod to the game Unreal Tournament 2004, which is originally expected to work as a first-person shooter game. Instead, RiskMan modifies UT2004 so that it can be used as a first-person training simulation. A list of the functionalities of RiskMan includes:

- The ability to spawn and control non-playable characters through an external client program
- Allows for any map to be used
- Allows for import of custom characters
- Allows for the activation of custom animations

Unreal Tournament game engine comes with a number of game types. Each game type has its own rules for the player and sometimes its own systems of actors that must be implemented by the mapper. A computer-controlled player character is called Bot in Unreal Tournament. *Bot Support* and *Botplay* are both terms used to describe a map's support system for bots: artificially intelligent players that can act as if they were human. The term botplay is often used the same way the term gameplay is used to describe the playability of a particular map. One of the reasons for the success of the Unreal engine games is the realistic AI, which includes bots that appear to play as if they are human. This is accomplished with the coordination of two elements: the bot support of the map as created by the level designer and the Bot class AI construct.

Each map should contain a system of waypoints called the *Bot Path Network*. This bot path network defines the safe areas for a bot player to occupy in the map. Bots are able to walk, run, and jump to get to a desired point of the map with the help of the bot path network. Special objects within the map can also provide more complex behavior beyond navigation. The AI code that drives bots doesn't have the power to interpret the 3D maps.

Instead, a map has to have a set of waypoints, joined together to make a network, which the bots follow. PathNodes are special actors specifically designed to tell bots of places that are safe and easy to travel. These nodes make up the bulk of most bot path networks. Other types allow bots to tackle more complex things, such as lifts, jumping, translocation, and camping. Unless specifically told so, bots assume they can simply walk, run or jump through the entire bot path network. Simple obstacles like doors, lifts, and ladders pose problems for bots and require special nodes to help them navigate as players do.

To spawn and control bots in Unreal requires three classes. The first is an extension of the xDeathMatch class. The second class is an extension of the xPawn class, and the last class, is a controller class. This section provides a diagrammatic view of the code as well as brief descriptions of each of the classes. Figure 5 portrays how the classes of RiskMan interact with each other. The arrows indicate class dependencies. In the diagram, RiskServerMain depends on RiskDeathMatch.

A brief description of each of RiskMan classes is as follows:

Figure 5. RMM class diagram

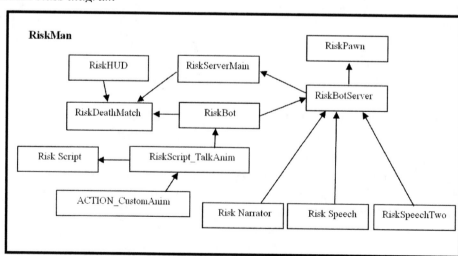

- **RiskDeathMatch:** This class inherits the functions from DeathMatch, and it is where training begins. Before the gameplay/simulation begins, RiskServerMain is started so that incoming socket connections are listened for. The original AddBot function of DeathMatch has been replaced with an AddRiskBot function so that control of the NPCs can be carried out by an external client program.

- **RiskServerMain:** This class inherits the functions from TCPLink. It listens for events on an address and port number, which has been specified in the RiskConf.ini file. Once a connection is accepted, it gets passed on to RiskBotServer, which handles the incoming messages.

- **RiskBotServer:** This class inherits functions from TCPLink. The NPCs get loaded into the simulation upon acceptance of a connection. The AddRiskBot function from RiskDeathMatch is called to initialize the NPCs. The received messages from an external client get processed. These messages are commands that modify the behavior of the NPCs, therefore giving control over the NPCs from an external client program.

- **RiskBot:** This class inherits functions from Bot. The AddRiskBot function of RiskDeathMatch returns an NPC of type RiskBot. The behaviors of an NPC, such as walking, running, and turning, are specified here.

- **RiskNarrator:** This class inherits functions from GUIPage. Once started, RiskNarrator brings up a narrator's speech bubble.

- **RiskSpeech:** This class inherits functions from GUIPage. Once started, RiskSpeech brings up an NPC's speech bubble.

- **RiskSpeechTwo:** This class inherits functions from GUIPage. Once started, RiskSpeechTwo brings up the trainee's speech bubble.

- **RiskPawn:** This class inherits functions from xPawn. This class allows for the customization of pawn/avatar of an NPC. The mesh, textures, and the animations associated with the NPC can be customized. The mesh and textures are specified in the RiskConf.ini file.

- **RiskHUD:** This class inherits functions from HUDBase. All standard messages and other heads-up-display items normally associated with the UT2004 gameplay are not displayed.

- **RiskScript:** This class inherits functions from ScriptedSequence. This class is the base class for custom scripted sequences.

- **RiskScript_TalkAnim:** This class subclasses RiskScript. This class specifies the sequence of actions to be carried out by the NPC.

- **ACTION_CustomAnim:** This class inherits functions from ScriptedAction. It will play any animation you assign to the Anim variable. One can activate custom animations using this class.

SimMaster Interface

SimMaster is an alternative to narrative engine. In the current version of the program, SimMaster is a human agent. SimMaster (SM) (Figure 6) coordinates and runs the simulation, controlling the NPCs and organizing the events that take place throughout the simulation through the Sim Master Interface (SMI). We developed a Python program that runs a command-line SMI. The SMI is an external program to Unreal that can be run on a networked PC. More information on SimMaster can be found in Tychsen, Hitchens, Brolund, and Kavakli (2005).

The SimMaster sheet portrays a top-down view of the game map/world. This top-down view also presents the location coordinates that are possible for an NPC to move to. Some of the commands for the SMI are as follows:

- sp/<actor>/<speech>
  Actor – is the NPC that will be doing the talking.
  Speech – is the text that will appear in the speech bubble.
- wk/<actor>/<location>
  Actor – is the NPC that will do the walking. Location – is the symbolic coordinate to where the NPC will walk toward. This symbolic coordinate is specified in the LocationCoordinates file and can be viewed in the SimMaster sheet.
- tn/<actor>/<position>
  Actor – is the NPC that will do the turning. Position – is a compass co-ordinate being either n, s, e, w, ne, se, sw, or nw.

Trainee Interface

The trainee interface (TI) (Figure 7) is a GUI for the user that is being trained. This interface currently allows for users to input what they want to say to the NPCs in the simulation, using a keyboard. We developed a Python program to run TI.

We run the training simulation on an immersive semi-cylindrical projection system (CAVE) in our VR Lab to test the level of immersion. The system consists of three projectors, which display the virtual world onto a semi-cylindrical screen canvas. The user is positioned slightly off centre toward the canvas to allow a 160° field of view (FOV), which simulates almost the maximum of 180° of the natural human FOV to achieve immersion in this virtual environment. We use a "Matrox TripleHead2Go" device (Fassbender, Richards, & Kavakli, 2006), which is an external device that receives a monitor signal of 3840×1024 and splits this signal into three segments on a hardware level to project the scene on the canvas. It then sends three segments of 1280×1024 to the appropriate monitors (center, left, right). In the next version of the system, we are planning to use Vizard Virtual Reality Software and datagloves to interact with the NPCs, developing a gesture and speech-based interface (Figure 8) as an improvement over the keyboard interface.

Figure 6. RiskMan interface using narrative engine

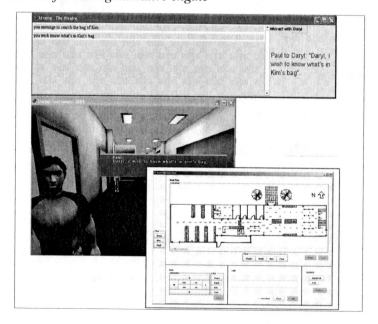

Figure 7. Trainee interface

Figure 8. Immersive interface in prospect

Graphics Engine

As a CAD package, we used 3D Studio Max, a 3D modeling and animation program, to generate game characters/agents and a series of behavioral animations. We were able to transfer these models and animations into Unreal Tournament game engine using a special exporter for 3D Studio Max developed by Unreal developers.

Maps

RiskMan works with any map created for UT2004. The only thing that needs to be done in order for the map to be usable for the mod is to determine all the path node locations. Once determined, these locations can be used by the SimMaster or narrative engine controller to navigate the bots/NPCs around the map. PathNode properties demonstrate the coordinates of a specific location (Figure 9).

To navigate an NPC around the map, a message has to be sent from an external client program to RiskMan. The current command for navigating an NPC includes:

#MOVETO::<actor>::<location>::<walk>

Actor is the NPC's name. Location is the path node location. Walk is a Boolean stating whether the NPC is to walk or run; when true the NPC walks. An example on how to use the #MOVETO command is:

#MOVETO::Daryl::823.33|582.91|350.80::True

Other ways of navigating an NPC include telling Daryl to walk to Paul. Such commands are more complex to program because Paul's location could be behind a wall, for instance, which would require AI for path node navigation so that Daryl does not just bump into the wall that leads to Paul.

Figure 9. PathNode properties

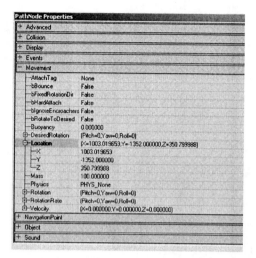

Custom Animations

Avatars for the NPCs can be included in Risk-Man just like any other GameType of Unreal. RiskMan also allows the control of an avatar's custom animations. For instance, if the avatar has a coughing animation, which is not part of the standard set of animations, RiskMan allows the player to activate it. RiskPawn, which is the custom pawn class utilized by RiskMan, contains the section where the custom animations of an avatar can get activated. Facilities provided by Unreal engine are as follows:

1. **Modifying an animation**
   One can modify an avatar's animation, for instance, from holding a weapon to being idle. Simply changing the following line in defaultproperties, we changed the avatar's animation as follows:

   IdleWeaponAnim=Idle_Rest

Thus, whenever the NPC is holding a weapon and not doing anything, it will instead carry out the animation for resting.

2. **Adding a custom walk animation**
   To make an avatar to walk without holding the weapon, we created this animation. The animation name associated with the animation can be used instead of the default animation; for instance, if custom forward walk is called Walk_Forward, then changing this line in defaultproperties is required as follows:

   WalkAnims(0)=Walk_Forward

3. **Adding and activating a custom animation**
   In the bot's controller class (in the RMM it is called RiskBot), we activated a scripted sequence (a set of animations) by adding following lines to the bot's controller class:

   rs_TalkAnim = Spawn(Class'RiskScript_TalkAnim',self,,Pawn.Location);
   SetNewScript(rs_TalkAnim); // Tell bot that it has new orders

   RiskScript_TalkAnim is the scripted sequence class that will be invoked.

The *placeable* keyword allows for this scripted sequence to be placed into the level by a level editor. Action_WAITFORTIMER is a class that already exists in UT2004 and has the property of PauseTime, which defines how long the character should wait before starting the next animation. Action_CUSTOMANIM is a class that does not exist in UT2004. It is a generic class that allows the activation of any of your own animations. The Anim property gets assigned the custom animation that you created for your character.

The actions array specifies the order in which to carry out the actions.

Limitations of Game Engineering

Although the game engineering approach provides a successful vehicle for interactive learning, there are a number of enhancements that could be made to the current training simulation, some of which are described in this section. Future enhancements do not entail limitations, rather things that have been implemented and can be improved.

- The SimMaster interface (GMI) can be made easier to use by allowing for voice activations[1] of the NPCs rather than a command-line interface. Voice activations can be carried out by using a third-party program or using the built-in voice recognizer in the Unreal game engine.

- The current trainee interface is an external application. This can be improved by making it part of UT2004's interface; for instance, the in-game chat feature of UT2004, activated by pressing F3, allows users to type what they want to say and output it to the screen. The TI can be modified to act similarly to the in-game chat feature.

- Currently, there are only a few commands available. In future, more commands are required to be added to activate each of the possible actions of a character; for instance, mouth movements for talking, raising of arms for a frisk, and so on. Currently animations exist for mouth synching and hand movements, which have yet to be activated via the code.

- Although the GMI can be run on a networked PC, the GM currently cannot be in another room. This limitation occurs because the GM cannot see what the trainee sees without actually looking onto the trainee's monitor. A program has to be created so that a networked PC can view another PC's monitor, otherwise known as mirroring. It is not possible to run the current mod in network mode to resolve the problem of SimMaster confinement. The mod requires drastic changes to the code to enable network play.

- The user is randomly spawned around the map according to where the spawn points/playerstarts are located. It is currently limited to spawn only in one location by having only one playerstart inside the entire airport map. Unlike the NPCs, the player's spawn point cannot be customized by using the RiskConf.ini file. Fixing this is a matter of altering the login function inside the GameInfo class. Since the current version of RiskMan begins with a subclass of the DeathMatch class, beginning with the GameInfo class would require major changes to the code, and it is not worthwhile to spend lots of time just to have a customized player spawn.

- RiskMan is created as a GameType mod and therefore has to be executed inside the UT2004 menus. In future, a total conversion mod would be ideal.

Figure 10. Panoramic view of RiskMan in the immersive display system

Advantages of Using Desktop and Immersive Virtual Reality

Using computer games for training relies first of all on the assumption that people are able to learn from a game, in particular, that they do not find an animation distracting or in some way inappropriate for training. In an initial study conducted in 2005 involving 74 third-year computer graphics students, we compared the accuracy of answers to watching a training video to watching a game demonstration of the same content. We found that participants' perception, memory, and reasoning were not significantly different using different forms of media (video versus game demo). A key outcome of that study (Richards, Barles, Szilas, Kavakli, & Dras, 2006) was that the participants believed that interactivity was critical for using the game environment successfully for learning.

We developed a virtual environment applying the CPTED guidelines from McCamley's kit and assessed the usability of the virtual risk assessment kit (Kavakli & Gao, 2005). Our experimental results indicate no significant differences in crime risk assessment within the physical and virtual representations of the world. Virtual CPTED kits provide a suitable ground for making appropriate decisions before the physical construction of the proposed environment. We used EON Reality, a virtual reality system, to integrate various components within a compact system. These components include a database, a CAD package, and virtual reality hardware and software. We are currently in the process of moving RiskMan to Vizard Virtual Reality Package to test the system in immersive virtual environments.

CONCLUSION

Interaction is the key element not only for computer games but also for multi-agent systems in software engineering context. Researchers working on collaborative virtual environments (e.g.,

Cagdas, Kavakli, Ozsoy, Esin Altas, & Tong, 2000; Kavakli, Akca, & Thorne, 2004a, 2004b) found that a virtual environment may reinforce learning of an event with the presentation of a proactive and *interactive learning* environment that is suitable for legitimate peripheral participation. Lave and Wenger (1990) argue that learning is a function of the activity, context, and culture in which it occurs (i.e., it is situated). Social interaction is a critical component of situated learning. Situations might be said to co-produce knowledge through activity. We are currently working on producing various models of interaction.

Multi-agent simulation of social processes can have a number of benefits (Conte & Gilbert, 1995): They provide facilities for the observation of properties of a model, exploration of alternatives to a phenomenon observed in nature, investigation of properties at leisure in isolation, and an explicit demonstration of sociality. Moss and Davidson (2001) further support a case for multi-agent simulation. They state that designing such systems requires a different approach to software engineering and mechanism design. In this chapter, we have demonstrated the use of game engineering to explore its potential for interactive learning and agent interaction for social simulation.

ACKNOWLEDGMENT

This project links three research projects sponsored by the Australian Research Council (ARC): ARC Discovery Grant (DP0558852 entitled "Risk Management Using Agent Based Virtual Environments") to Dr. Debbie Richards, Dr. Manolya Kavakli, and Dr. Mark Dras; an ARC Linkage International Grant (LX0560117 entitled "An Interactive Drama Engine in Virtual Reality") to Dr. Manolya Kavakli, Prof. Catherine Pelachaud, and Dr. Nicolas Szilas; and an ARC Linkage Grant (LP0216837 entitled "Cognitive Modelling of Computer Game Pidgins") to Dr.

Manolya Kavakli, Prof. Terry Bossomaier, and Dr. Mike Cooper. The authors acknowledge the support of all of these researchers who provided the grants. This project was also sponsored by the Macquarie University New Staff Research Grant to Dr. Manolya Kavakli entitled "Gesture Recognition and Motion Capture as a Precursor for Behavioral Biometrics." Special thanks to Jason Barles, who took active role in the implementation of RiskMan.

REFERENCES

Barles, J., Dras, M., Kavakli, M., Richards, D., & Tychsen, A. (2005, July 25-26). An overview of training simulation research and systems, proceedings of the agent based systems for human learning (ABSHL). *Proceedings of Workshop held in conjunction with the Fourth International Joint Conference on Autonomous Agents and Multi Agent Systems*, Utrecht, The Netherlands. Retrieved from http://agents.cs.columbia.edu/abshl

Cagdas, G., Kavakli, M., Ozsoy, A., Esin Altas, N., & Tong, H. (2000) Virtual design studio VDS2000 as a virtual construction site: Game-like learning versus traditional design education. *International Journal of Design Computing, 3, 1-20.*

Cappella, & Pelachaud, C. (2001). Rules for responsive robots: Using human interactions to build virtual interactions. In Reis, Fitzpatrick, & Vangelisti (Eds.), *Stability and change in relationships.*

Capuano, N., Marsella, M., & Salerno, S. (2000). ABITS: An agent based intelligent tutoring system for distance learning. *Proceedings of the International Workshop in Adaptive and Intelligent Web-Based Educational Systems.*

Cassell, J. (2000). More than just another pretty face: Embodied conversational interface agents. *Communications of the ACM, 43*(4), 70-78.

Chan, T. W. (1996). Learning companion systems, social learning systems, and intelligent virtual classroom [Invited talk]. Conference on Artificial Intelligence in Education. *Journal of Artificial Intelligence in Education, 7*(2), 125-159.

Cohen, P. R., & Levesque, H. J. (1990). Rational interaction as the basis for communication. In P.R. Cohen, J. Morgan, & M.E. Pollack (Eds.), *Intentions in communication* (pp. 221-256). Cambridge, MA: MIT Press.

Conati, C., & Klawe, M. (2000). Socially intelligent agents to improve the effectiveness of educational games. *Proceedings of AAAI Fall Symposium on Socially Intelligent Agents, The Human in the Loop.*

Conte, & Gilbert (1995). Computer simulation for social theory. In N. Gilbert & R. Conte (Eds.), *Artificial societies: The computer simulation of social life* (pp. 1-15). London: UCL Press.

Decker, R. J. (2001). Homeland Security: A Risk Management Approach Can Guide Preparedness Efforts, USA General Accounting Office, report no GAO-02-208T, October 31Carbonell, J. R. (1970) AI in CAI: An artificial intelligence approach to computer-assisted instruction. *IEEE Transactions on Man-Machine Systems, 11*(4), 190-202.

Dras, M. (1998). Search in constraint-based paraphrasing. *Proceedings of the Second International Conference on Natural Language Processing and Industrial Applications* (pp. 213-219).

Dras, M., Kavakli, M., & Richards, D. (2005, July 25-26). Training for high-risk situations. *Proceedings of The Agent Based Systems for Human Learning (ABSHL), Workshop to be held in conjunction with the Fourth International Joint Conference on Autonomous Agents and Multi Agent Systems*, Utrecht, The Netherlands. Retrieved from http://agents.cs.columbia.edu/abshl

Fairclough, C., & Cunningham, P. (2002). *An interactive story engine*. Computer Science Department, Trinity College, Dublin.

Fassbender, Richards, & Kavakli (2006, December 4-6). Usage of a 3D game engine to evaluate different styles of music and their effect on learning in virtual-immersive environments. *Proceedings of the Joint International Conference on CyberGames and Interactive Entertainment 2006 (CGIE2006)*, Perth, Western Australia

Fensel, D., et al. (2003). The unified problem-solving method development language UPML. *Knowledge and Information Systems, An International Journal, 5*, 83-127.

Furtado, V., & Vasconcelos, E. (2004). Geosimulation in education: The ExpertCop system. *Proceedings of Agent-based Simulation Workshop, SCS European Publisher,* Lisbon, Portugal.

Gervais, M. P., & Muscutariu, F. (2001). Towards an ADL for designing agent-based systems. *Proceedings of 2nd International Workshop on Agent-Oriented Software Engineering (AOSE'01)*, Montreal, Canada. To appear in *Lecture Notes in Computer Science*, Springer Verlag

Jing, H., Netzer, Y. D., Elhadad, M., & McKeown, K. (2000). Integrating a large-scale, reusable lexicon with a natural language generator. *Proceedings of the 1st International Conference on Natural Language Generation* (pp. 209-216).

Kavakli, M. (2005, June 27-July 1). Games of soldiers: A survey of military training & computer games. *Proceedings of ISAGA 2005, 36th Annual Conference for the International Simulation and Gaming Association*, Atlanta, GA.

Kavakli, M. (2006, July 10-13). Training simulations for crime risk assessment. *Proceedings of ITHET 2006: 7th International conference on Information Technology Based Higher Education and Training*, Sydney, Australia.

Kavakli, M., Akca, B., & Thorne, J. (2004a). The role of computer games in the education of history. *Mugla University Journal of Institute of Social Sciences (Muğla Üniversitesi Sosyal Bilimler Enstitüsü Dergisi), 13,* 66-78.

Kavakli, M., Akca, B., & Thorne, J. (2004b, February 13). The role of computer games in learning history. *Proceedings of Australian Workshop on Interactive Entertainment*, University of Technology, Sydney, Australia. Retrieved from http://research.it.uts.edu.au/creative/ie

Kavakli, M., & Gao, Y. F. (2005, June 15-18). Consistency of risk assessment in physical and virtual environments. *Proceedings of INISTA 2005, Innovations in Intelligent Systems and Applications, IEEE Computational Intelligence Society Turkey Chapter*, Istanbul, Turkey.

Kavakli, M., Kavakli, K., & Gao, Y. F. (2004c, September 13-16). Crime prevention through environmental design in virtual reality. *Proceedings of the 9th Crime Prevention Through Environmental Design (CPTED) Conference*, Brisbane, Australia.

Kavakli, M., & Thorne, J. (2002, November 25-29). A cognitive modelling approach to capturing the context of complex behaviour in gameplay. *Proceedings of The First International Conference on Information Technology & Applications (ICITA2002)*, Bathurst, Australia.

Kavakli, M., & Thorne, J. (2003, July 5-10). Knowledge acquisition in distance education. *Proceedings of the 6th International Conference on Computer Based Learning in Science (CBLIS2003) Conference*, Nicosia, Cyprus.

Kennedy, H. (2002). Computer games liven up military recruiting, training. *National Defense Magazine,* November.

Klesen, M. (2002). *Report on affective reasoning and cultural diversity* (Tech. Rep. DFKI).

Lave, J., & Wenger, E. (1990). *Situated learning: Legitimate peripheral participation.* Cambridge, UK: Cambridge University Press.

LeJeune, N. (2003). Story engine, software engineering practices project. Metropolitan State College, Denver.

Johnson, W., Rickel, J., & Lester, J. (2000). Animated pedagogical agents: Face-to-face interaction in interactive learning environments. *International Journal of Artificial Intelligence in Education, 11,* 47-78.

Mathoff, J., Van Hoe, R., & Apeall. (1996). A multi agent approach to interactive learning environments. *Proceedings of European Workshop on Modelling Autonomous Agents, MAAMAW, 6.* Berlin: Springer Verlag.

McCamley, P. (2000). *Companion to safer by design.* Evaluation, Document 2, NSW Police Service, p.36.

Moss & Davidson. (Eds.). (2001). *Multi agent based simulation, LNAI Vol. 1979.* Berlin: Springer.

Noma, T., Zhao, L., & Badler, N. (2000). Design of a virtual human presenter. *IEEE Journal of Computer Graphics and Applications, 20*(4), 79-85.

Pelachaud, C., & Poggi, I., (2001). *Multimodal Embodied Agents.* ACM.

Peña, C. I., Marzo, J. L., & de la Rosa, J. L. (2002). Intelligent agents in a teaching and learning environment on the Web. *Proceedings of the 2nd IEEE International Conference on Advanced Learning Technologies, ICALT2002.*

Pesty, S., & Webber, C. (2004). The Baghera multiagent learning environment: An educational community of artificial and human agents. *Upgrade, Journal of CEPIS (Council of European Professional Informatics Societies), 4,* 40-44.

Poggi, I., & Pelachaud, C. (2000). Emotional meaning and expression in animated faces. In A. Paiva (Ed.), *Affect in interactions.* Berlin: Springer-Verlag.

Prensky, M. (2001). *Digital game-based learning.* New York: McGraw Hill.

Richards, D., Barles, J., Szilas, N., Kavakli, M., & Dras, M. (2006, May 9). Human and software agents learning together. *Proceedings of Agent Based Systems for Human Learning (ABSHL), workshop to be held at the 5th International Joint Conference on Autonomous Agents and Multiagent Systems (AAMAS 2006),* Hakodate, Japan.

Richards, D., & Busch, P. (2003) Acquiring and applying contextualised tacit knowledge. *Journal of Information and Knowledge Management, 2*(2), 179-190.

Ritter, S., & Kodinger, K. R. (1996). An architecture for plug-in tutor agents. *Journal of Artificial Intelligence in Education, 7,* 315-347.

Rudra, T., Kavakli, M., & Bossomaier, T. (2003, September 10-12). A game pidgin language for speech recognition in computer games. *Proceedings of 3rd International Conference on Computational Semiotics for Games and New Media,* Middleborough, Tees Valley, UK.

Rzevski, G. (2003). On conceptual design of intelligent mechatronic systems. *Mechatronics 13,* 1029-1044.

Silveira, R. A., & Vicari, R. M. (2002). Developing distributed intelligent learning environment with JADE – Java agents for distance education framework. *Proceedings of International Conference on Intelligent Tutoring Systems, ITS 2002* (LNCS 2362, pp. 105-118).

Stone, M., & Doran, C. (1997). Sentence planning as description using tree-adjoining grammar. *Proceedings of ACL 1997* (pp. 198-205).

Swartout, W., Hill, R., Gratch, J., Johnson, W. L., Kyriakakis, C., & LaBore, et al. (2001). Toward the holodeck: integrating graphics, sound, character and story. *Proceedings of the 5th International Conference on Autonomous Agents* (pp. 409-416). Retrieved from http://citeseer.nj.nec.com/447724.html

Szilas, N. (2003). IDtension: A narrative engine for interactive drama. In Göbel et al. (Eds.), *Technologies for interactive digital storytelling and entertainment (TIDSE'03).*

Szilas, N., & Kavakli, M. (2006, January 29-February 1). PastMaster@Storytelling: A controlled interface for interactive drama. *Proceedings of*

IUI 2006: International Conference on Intelligent user Interfaces, CSIRO ICT Centre, Macquarie University, Sydney, Australia.

Tychsen, A., Hitchens, M., Brolund, T., & Kavakli, M. (2005, December). The game master. *Proceedings of 2nd International Workshop on Interactive Entertainment (IE2005),* Sydney, Australia.

Wagner, R., & Sternberg, R. (1991). *TKIM: The common sense manager: Tacit knowledge inventory for managers: Test Booklet The Psychological Corporation Harcourt Brace Jovanovich San Antonio.*

Wooldridge, M. (2002). *An introduction to multiagent systems.* West Sussex, UK: John Wiley & Sons.

Compilation of References

Aamodt, A., & Plaza, E. (1994). Case-based reasoning: Foundational issues, methodological variations, and system approaches. *AI Communications, 7*(1), 39-59.

Abdennadher, S., & Schlenker, H.(1999). Nurse scheduling using constraint logic programming. *Proceedings of the 11ᵗʰ Conference on Innovative Applications of Artificial Intelligence (IAAI-99)* (pp. 838-843).

About.com (2003). *Definition of Java runtime environment (JRE)*. Retrieved April 27, 2006, from http://java.about.com/library/glossary/bldef-jre.htm

Access Grid. (2001). Retrieved from http://www.accessgrid.org/

Agassounon, W., & Martinoli, A. (2002). A macroscopic model of an aggregation simulation using embodied agents in groups of time-varying sizes. *Proceedings of the 2002 Institute of Electrical and Electronics Engineers Systems, Man and Cybernetics Conference* (pp. 250-255). Retrieved April 3, 2005, from http://swis.epfl.ch/backup_caltech/coro/People/alcherio/papers/SMC02.pdf

Aglets Project Homepage (2006). Retrieved April 27, 2006, from http://sourceforge.net/projects/aglets

Aha, D. W., Breslow, L. A., & Muñoz-Avila, H. (2000). Conversational case-based reasoning. *Applied Intelligence, 14*, 9-32.

Aha, D. W., Maney, T., & Breslow, L. A. (1998). Supporting dialogue inferencing in conversational case-based reasoning. *Proceedings of EWCBR 98: Proceedings of the 4ᵗʰ European Workshop on Advances in Case-Based Reasoning* (pp. 262-273). Springer.

Ahuja, S., Carriero, N., & Gelernter, D. (1986). Linda and friends. *IEEE Computer*, 26-34.

Albers, S. (2003). Online algorithms: A survey. *Mathematical Programming, 97*(1), 3-26

Allen, G., Dramlitsch, T., et al. (2001). Supporting efficient execution in heterogeneous distributed computing environments with Cactus and Globus. *Proceedings of International Conference of Supercomputing.*

Allen, G., Goodale T., Russell M., Seidel E., & Shalf, J. (2003). Classifying and enabling grid applications. In F. Berman, G. Fox, & T. Hey (Eds.), *Grid computing: Making the global infrastructure a reality* (pp. 601-614). John &Wiley Press.

Alvares, L., Menezes, P., & Demazeau, Y. (1998). Problem decomposition: An essential step for multi-agent systems. *Proceedings of 10ᵗʰ International Conference on Systems Research, Informatics and Cybernetics (ICSRIC'98)*, Baden-Baden.

Anderson, A., Tenhunen, M., & Ygge, F.(2000). Integer programming for combinatorial auction winner determination. *Proceedings of the 4ᵗʰ International Conference on Multi-Agent Systems (ICMAS2000)* (pp. 39-46).

Anderson, R., & Khattak, A. (1998). *The use of information retrieval techniques for intrusion detection.* Paper presented at the First International Workshop on Recent Advances in Intrusion Detection (RAID'98), Louvain-la-Neuve, Belgium.

Angele, J., Fensel, D., & Studer, R. (1998). Developing knowledge-based systems with MIKE. *Journal of Automated Software Engineering.*

Arumugam, S., Helal, A., & Nalla, A. (2002). aZIMAs: Web mobile agent system. *Proceedings of 6th International Conference on Mobile Agents (MA'02)* (LNCS 2535). Barcelona, Spain: Springer-Verlag.

Atkins, D. E., et al. (1996). Toward inquiry-based education though interacting software agents. *IEEE Computer, 29*(5), 69-76.

Australian Computer Crime & Security Survey. (2004). *AusCERT.* Retrieved January 17, 2006, from http://www.auscert.org.au/download.html?f=114

Azar, Y. (1998). On-line load balancing. In A. Fiat & G. Woeginger (Eds.), *Online algorithms: The state of the art* (pp. 178-195). Springer.

Baker, A. D., Parunak, H. V. D., & Erol, K. (1997). *Manufacturing over the Internet and into your living room: Perspectives from the AARIA project* (Tech. Rep. TR208-08-97). ECECS Dept.

Bakker, R.R., Dikker, F., Tempelman, F.,& Wognum, P. M. (1993). Diagnosing and solving over-determined constraint satisfaction problems. *Proceedings of the 13th International Joint Conference on Artificial Intelligence (IJCAI93)* (pp. 276-281).

Balasubramanian, S., & Norrie, D. H. (1995). A multi-agent intelligent design system integrating manufacturing and ship-floor control. *Proceedings of the First International Conference on Multi-Agent Systems.* San Francisco: The AAAI press/The MIT Press.

Banâtre, J. P. (1996). Parallel multiset processing: From explicit coordination to chemical reaction. In P. Ciancarini & C. Hankin (Eds.), *Coordination languages and models, first international conference, COORDINATION'96* (pp. 1-11). Springer-Verlag.

Banâtre, J. P., & Métayer, D. L. (1990). The GAMMA model and its discipline of programming. *Science of Computer Programming, 15,* 55-77.

Banâtre, J. P., & Métayer, D. L. (1993). Programming by multiset transformation. *Communications ACM, 36*(1), 98-111.

Banâtre, J. P., Coutant, A., & Métayer, D. L. (1988). A parallel machine for multiset transformation and its programming style. *Future Generation Computer System, 4,* 133-144.

Baratloo, A., et al. (1998, April 27-30). Filter fresh: Hot replication of Java RMI server objects. *Proceedings of 4th USENIX Conference on Object-Oriented Technologies and Systems (COOTS),* Santa Fe, NM.

Barles, J., Dras, M., Kavakli, M., Richards, D., & Tychsen, A. (2005, July 25-26). An overview of training simulation research and systems, proceedings of the agent based systems for human learning (ABSHL). *Proceedings of Workshop held in conjunction with the Fourth International Joint Conference on Autonomous Agents and Multi Agent Systems,* Utrecht, The Netherlands. Retrieved from http://agents.cs.columbia.edu/abshl

Bartal Y., Fiat, A., & Rabani, Y. (1992). Competitive algorithms for distributed data management. *Proceedings of the 24th Annual ACM Symposium on Theory of Computing* (pp. 39-50; pp. 51-58). Retrieved March 20, 2003, from http://portal.acm.org

Barto, A. G. (1992). Reinforcement learning and adaptive critic methods. In D. A. White and D. A. Sofge (Eds.), *Handbook of intelligent control: Neural, fuzzy, and adaptive approaches* (pp. 469-491). New York: Van Nostrand Reinhold.

Bass, L., Klein, M., & Bachmann, F. (2001, October 4). Quality attribute design primitives and the attribute driven design method. *Proceedings of 4th Conference on Product Family Engineering,* Bilbao, Spain.

Bauer, B., Muller, J. P., & Odell, J. (2001). Agent UML: A formalism for specifying multi-agent software systems. *International Journal of Software Engineering and Knowledge Engineering, 11*(3), 207-230.

Bazaraa, M., & Shetty, C. (1979). *Non-linear programming*. New York: John Wiley and Sons.

Beck, K. (1999). *eXtreme programming explained: Embrace change*. Addison-Wesley.

Bellavista, P., Corradi, A., & Stefanelli, C. (1999). A secure and open mobile agent programming environment. *Proceedings of the 4th International Symposium on Autonomous Decentralized Systems (ISADS'99)*, Tokyo, Japan.

Bellifemine, F., Poggi, A., & Rimassi, G. (1999). JADE: A FIPA-compliant agent framework. *Proceedings of Practical Applications of Intelligent Agents and Multi-Agents* (pp. 97-108).

Berenji, H. R., & Khedkar, P. (1992). Learning and tuning fuzzy logic controllers through reinforcement. *IEEE Transactions on Neural Networks, 3*(5), 724-740.

Bergenti, F., Poggi, A., Rimassa, G., & Turci, P. (2000). *Middleware and programming support for agent systems*. Telecom Italia Labs.

Berry, G., & Boudol, G. (1992). The chemical abstract machine. *Theoretical Computer Science, 96*, 217-248.

Bigun, J., Aguilar, J. F., Ortega-Garcia, J., & Gonzalez-Rodriguez, J. (2003). Multimodal biometric authentication using quality signals in mobile communications. *International Conference on Image Analysis and Processing 2003* (pp. 2-12).

Biswas, P. K. (2005, April 18-21). Architecting multi-agent systems with distributed sensor networks. *Proceedings of IEEE International Conference on Integration of Knowledge Intensive Multi-Agent Systems (KIMAS)*, Waltham, MA.

Biswas, P. K. (in press). Towards an agent-oriented approach to conceptualization. *Applied Soft Computing*.

Blum, A., & Merrick, F. (1995). Fast planning through planning graph analysis. *Proceedings of the 14th International Joint Conference on Artificial Intelligence (IJCAI 95)* (pp. 1636-1642).

Bolle, R. M., Connell, J., Pankanti, S., Ratha, N. K., & Senior A. W. (2002). *Biometrics 101*. IBM Research Report. New York: T. J. Hawthorne.

Bonabeau, E., Dorigo, M., & Theraulaz, G. (1999). *Swarm intelligence: From natural to artificial systems*. New York: Oxford University Press.

Bonabeau, E., Theraulaz, G., & Dorigo, M. (1999). *Swarm intelligence: From natural to artificial systems*. Oxford University Press.

Boudol, G. (1993). Some chemical abstract machines. In J. W. d. Bakker, W. P. d. Roever & G. Rozenberg (Eds.), *A decade of concurrency: Reflections and perspectives* (pp. 92-123). Springer-Verlag.

Bowling, M. (2004). Convergence and no-regret in multiagent learning. *Advances in Neural Information Processing Systems, 17*, 209-216.

Bowling, M., & Veloso, M. (2002). Multiagent learning using a variable learning rate. *Artificial Intelligence, 136*(2), 215-250.

Bowman, M. (2002). *A methodology for modeling and representing expert knowledge that supports teaching-based intelligent agent development*. Unpublished doctoral dissertation, George Mason University, Fairfax, VA.

Bowman, M., Tecuci, G., Boicu, M., &Commello, J. (2004). Information age warfare – Intelligent agents in the classroom and strategic analysis center. *Proceedings of the 24th U.S. Army Science Conference*, Orlando FL.

Box, D. (1997). *Essential COM*. Addison-Wesley.

Bradshaw, J. M. (1997). An introduction to software agents. In J. M. Bradshaw (Ed.), *Software agents* (pp. 3-46). AAAI Press/The MIT Press.

Braubach, L., Pokahr, A., & Lamersdorf, W. (2005) Jadex: A BDI agent system combining middleware and reasoning. In M. Klusch, R. Unland, & M. Calisti (Eds.), *Software agent-based applications, platforms and development kits*. Birkhäuser.

Brazier, F. M., Dunin-Keplicz, B. M., Jennings, N. R., & Treur, J. (1997). DESIRE: Modeling multi-agent systems in a compositional formal framework. *International Journal of Cooperative Information Systems, 6*(1), 67-94.

Brazier, F. M., Keplicz, B. D., Jennings N. R., & Treur, J. (1995, June 12-14). Formal specification of multi-agent systems: A real-world case. *Proceedings of the 1st International Conference on Multi-agent Systems (ICMAS '95),* San Francisco.

Brazier, F., Jonker, C., & Van Treur, J. (1998). Principles of compositional multi-agent system development. In Cuena, J. (Ed.), *15th IFIP World Computer Congress, WCC'98, Conference on Information Technology and Knowledge Systems, Evaluating PSMs for Adaptive Design 23 (IT&KNOWS'98)* (pp. 347-360).

Bridge, D., & Ferguson, A. (2002). Diverse product recommendations using an expressive language for case retrieval. In S. Craw and A. Preece (Eds.), *Advances in Case-Based Reasoning, Proceedings of the 6th European Conference on Case Based Reasoning, ECCBR* (pp. 43-57). Springer Verlag.

Britton D., Cass A. J., et al. (2005). GridPP: Meeting the particle physics computing challenge. *Proceedings of UK e-Science All Hands Conference.*

Brooks, R. A. (1986). A robust layered control system for a mobile robot. *IEEE Journal of Robotics and Automation, RA-2*(1), 14-23.

Brown, M. C. (2005). *What is the semantic grid.* Retrieved from http://www-128.ibm.com/developerworks/grid/library/gr-semgrid/

Brunett, S., et al. (1998). Implementing distributed synthetic forces simulations in metacomputing environments. *Proceedings of IPPS/SPDP Heterogeneous Computing Workshop.*

Buchanman, W.J., Naylor, M., & Scott, A.V. (2000). Enhancing network management using mobile agents. *The 7th IEEE International Conference and Workshop on the Engineering of Computer Based Systems* (pp. 218-228). Retrieved April 5, 2002, from http://ieeexplore.ieee.org

Burileanu, C., Moraru, D., Bojan, L., Puchiu, M., & Stan, A. (2002). On performance improvement of a speaker verification system using vector quantisation, cohorts and hybrid cohort-word models. *International Journal of Speech Technology, 5,* 247-257.

Burke, R. (2000). Knowledge-based recommender systems. In J. E. Daily, A. Kent, & H. Lancour (Eds.), *Encyclopedia of library and information science, vol. 69.* Marcel Dekker.

Burke, R. (2002). Interactive critiquing for catalog navigation in e-commerce. *Artificial Intelligence Review, 18*(3-4), 245-267.

Burke, R., Hammond, K., & Kozlovsky, J. (1995). Knowledge-based information retrieval for semi-structured text. *Proceedings of the AAAI Fall Symposium on AI Applications in Knowledge Navigation and Retrieval* (pp. 19-24). Menlo Park, CA: AAAI Press.

Burke, R., Hammond, K., & Young, B. (1996). Knowledge-based navigation of complex information spaces. *Proceedings of the 13th National Conference on Artificial Intelligence* (pp. 462-468). Menlo Park, CA: AAAI Press.

Burke, R., Hammond, K., & Young, B. C. (1997). The findme approach to assisted browsing. *Journal of IEEE Expert, 12*(4), 32-40.

Bussmann, S. (1999). An agent-oriented architecture for holonic manufacturing control. *Proceedings of the First International Workshop on IMS,* Lausanne, Switzerland.

Butnariu, D., & Klement, E. P. (1993). *Triangular norm based measures and games with fuzzy coalitions.* Dordrecht, Netherlands: Kluwer Academic Publishers.

Cagdas, G., Kavakli, M., Ozsoy, A., Esin Altas, N., & Tong, H. (2000) Virtual design studio VDS2000 as a virtual construction site: Game-like learning versus traditional design education. *International Journal of Design Computing, 3, 1-20.*

Camazine S., Deneubourg, J. L., Franks, N., Sneyd, J., Theraulaz, G., & Bonabeau, E. (2001). *Self-organiza-*

tion in biological systems. Princeton, NJ: Princeton University Press.

Camazine, S., & Sneyd, J. (1991). A model of collective nectar source selection by honey bees: Self-organization through simple rules. *Journal of Theoretical Biology, 149*(4), 547-571.

Camazine, S., Deneubourg, J. L., Franks, N. R., Sneyd, J., Theraulaz, G., & Bonabeau, E. (2003). *Self-organization in biological systems.* Princeton.

Cao, J. (2001). *Agent-based resource management for grid computing.* Unpublished doctoral dissertation, University of Warwick, Coventry, UK.

Cao, J., Javis, S. A., & Asini S. (2002). An agent-based resource management system for grid computing. *Scientific Programming, 10*(2), 135-148.

Cappella, & Pelachaud, C. (2001). Rules for responsive robots: Using human interactions to build virtual interactions. In Reis, Fitzpatrick, & Vangelisti (Eds.), *Stability and change in relationships.*

Capuano, N., Marsella, M., & Salerno, S. (2000). ABITS: An agent based intelligent tutoring system for distance learning. *Proceedings of the International Workshop in Adaptive and Intelligent Web-Based Educational Systems.*

Cardelli, L. (1995). A language with distributed scope. *Computing Systems Journal, 8*(1).

Carlson, J., & Murphy, R. R. (2003). Reliability analysis of mobile robot. *Proceedings of the 2003 IEEE International Conference on Robotics and Automation, ICRA 2003.* Taipei, Taiwan.

Carriero, N., & Gelernter, D. (1989). Linda in context. *Communication ACM, 32*(4), 444-458.

Carriero, N., Gelernter, D., Mattson, T., & Sherman, A. (1994). The Linda alternative to message-passing systems. *Parallel Computing, 20*, 632-655.

Carvey, H. (2005). *Windows forensics and incident recovery.* Addison-Wesley.

Cassell, J. (2000). More than just another pretty face: Embodied conversational interface agents. *Communications of the ACM, 43*(4), 70-78.

Castelfranchi, C., Miceli, M., & Cesta, A. (1992). Dependence relations among autonomous agents. *Proceedings of the 3rd European Workshop on Modeling Autonomous Agents and Multi-Agent Worlds* (pp. 215-231). Amsterdam, The Netherlands: Elsevier Science Publishers.

Castelpietra, C., Guidotti, A., Iocchi, L., Nardi, D., & Rosati, R. (2002). Design and implemantation of cognitive soccer robots. In *RoboCup 2001: Robot soccer World Cup V*, vol. 2377 of *Lecture Notes in Computer Science.* Springer.

Castro, J. (1995). Fuzzy logic controllers are universal approximators. *IEEE Trans. On Systems, Man, and Cybernetics, 25*(4), 629-635.

Cattell, R., & Inscore, J. (2001). *J2EE technology in practice.* Addison-Wesley.

Chan, T. W. (1996). Learning companion systems, social learning systems, and intelligent virtual classroom [Invited talk]. Conference on Artificial Intelligence in Education. *Journal of Artificial Intelligence in Education, 7*(2), 125-159.

Chang, Y. H., & Kaelbling, L. P. (2001). Playing is believing: The role of beliefs in multi-agent learning. *Advances in Neural Information Processing Systems, 14*, 1483-1490.

Charles, A. A., Menezes, R., & Tolksdorf, R. (2004). On the implementation of SwarmLinda. *Proceedings of the 42nd Association for Computing Machinery Southeast Regional Conference* (pp. 297-298). Retrieved July 15, 2006, from Association for Computing Machinery Digital Library Database.

Chavez, A., Moukas, A., & Maes, P. (1997). Challenger: A multiagent system for distributed resource allocation. *Proceedings of the First International Conference on Autonomous Agents*, Marina Del Ray, CA.

Chaw, D. L. (1981). Untraceable electronic mail, return addresses, and digital pseudonyms, *Communications of the ACM, 24*(2), 84-90.

Chess, D., Grossof, B., Harrison, C., Levine, D., Parris, C., & Tsudik, G. (1994). *Mobile Agents: Are they are good idea?* (RC19887). IBM Research.

Chess, D., Harrison, C., & Kershenbaum, A. (1995). *Mobile agents: Are they a good idea.* IBM Research Report RC 19887. Retrieved from http://mega.ist.utl. pt/~ic-arge/arge-96-97/artigos/mobile-ibm-7929.ps.gz

Choi, H. R., Kim, H. S., & Park, Y. S. (2002). Intelligent injection mold process planning system using case-based reasoning. *Journal of Korea Intelligent Information Systems Society, 8*(1), 159-171.

Choi, H. S., Kim, H. S., Park, B. J., & Park, Y. S. (2004). Multi-agent based integration scheduling system under supply chain management environment. In *Innovations in applied artificial intelligence.* Ottawa, Canada: Springer Verlag.

Chun, J. K., Cho, K. Y., & Cho, S. H. (2002). Network management based on pc communication platform with SNMP and mobile agents. *Proceedings of the 22nd International Conference on Distributed Computing Systems Workshops* (pp. 222-227). Retrieved May 16, 2003, from http://ieeexplore.ieee.org

Chuter, C. J., Ramaswamy, S., & Baber, K. S. (1995). *A virtual environment for construction and analysis of manufacturing prototypes.* Retrieved from http://ksi. cpsc.ucalgaly.ca/projects/mediator

Clarke, E. M., Grumberg, O., & Hiraishi, H. (1993). Verifying of the Futurebus+ cache coherence Protocol. In L. Claesen (Ed.), *Proceedings of the Eleventh International Symposium on Computer Hardware Description Languages and Their Applications.* North-Holland.

Clarke, E., Grumberg, O., & Long, D. (1993). Verification tools for finite-state concurrent systems. In J. W. de Bakker, W. P. d. Roever, & G. Rozenberg (Eds.), *A decade of concurrency: Reflections and perspectives* (pp. 125-175). Springer-Verlag.

Claus, C., & Boutilier, C. (1998). The dynamics of reinforcement learning in cooperative multiagent systems. In *Proceedings of the 15th National / 10th Conference on Artificial Intelligence / Innovative Applications of Artificial Intelligence* (pp. 746-752). Madison, WI: American Association for Artificial Intelligence Press.

Clausewitz, von C. (1832). *On war* (M. Howard & P. Paret, Trans.). Princeton, NJ: Princeton University Press.

Clement, B. J., & Durfee, E. H. (1998). Scheduling high-level tasks among cooperative agents. *International Conference on Multi Agent Systems* (pp. 96-103). Retrieved March 3, 2002, from http://ieeexplore.ieee.org

CodeRed Worm. (2001). Retrieved November 22, 2005, from http://securityresponse.symantec.com/avcenter/ venc/data/codered.worm.html

Cohen, P. R., & Levesque, H. J. (1990). Rational interaction as the basis for communication. In P.R. Cohen, J. Morgan, & M.E. Pollack (Eds.), *Intentions in communication* (pp. 221-256). Cambridge, MA: MIT Press.

Cohen, R., & Molinari, B. (1991). Implementation of C-Linda for the AP1000. Proceedings of the 2nd ANU/ Fujitsu CAP Workshop.

Cohen, R., Allaby, C., Cumbaa, C., Fitzgerald, M., Ho, K., Hui, B., et al. (1998). What is initiative? *User Modeling and User-Adapted Interaction, 8*(3-4), 173.

Comer, D. E. (2000). *Internetworking with TCP/IP* (4th ed., vol. 1). Prentice Hall.

Conati, C., & Klawe, M. (2000). Socially intelligent agents to improve the effectiveness of educational games. *Proceedings of AAAI Fall Symposium on Socially Intelligent Agents, The Human in the Loop.*

Conchon S., & Fessant, F. (1999). Jocaml: Mobile agents for objective-caml. *Proceedings of the Joint Symposium on Agent Systems and Applications/Mobile Agents (ASA/ MA'99),* Palm Springs, CA.

Condor System (1998). Retrieved from http://www. cs.wisc.edu/condor/

Condor-G System (2001). Retrieved from http://www.cs.wisc.edu/condor/condorg/

Conoise-G project. (2005). Retrieved from http://www.conoise.org

Conte, & Gilbert (1995). Computer simulation for social theory. In N. Gilbert & R. Conte (Eds.), *Artificial societies: The computer simulation of social life* (pp. 1-15). London: UCL Press.

Cooke, D. J., & Bez, H. E. (1984). *Computer mathematics.* Cambridge: Cambridge University Press.

Cossentino, M., & Potts, V. (2002, June 24-27). A CASE tool supported methodology for the design of multi-agent systems. *Proceedings of International Conference on Software Engineering Research and Practice (SERP'02),* Las Vegas, NV.

Coulouris, G., Dollimore, J., & Kindberg, T. (2000). *Distributed systems: Concepts and design* (3rd ed.). Addison-Wesley.

Coveney, P. (2005). Simulated pore interactive computing environment (SPICE): Using grid computing to understand DNA translocation across protein nanopores embedded in lipid membranes. *Proceedings of International Conference on Supercomputing.*

Crow, L., & Shadbolt, N. (2001). Extracting focused knowledge from the Semantic Web. *International Journal of Human Computer Studies, 54*(1), 155-184. Retrieved December 27, 2003, from Association for Computing Machinery Digital Library Database.

Curry, H. B. (1963). *Foundations of mathematical logic.* McGraw-Hill.

Czajkowski, K., Ferguson, D. F., Foster, I., et al. (2003). *The WS-resource framework.* Retrieved from http://www.globus.org

Dahl, O.-J., Dijkstra, E. W., & Hoare, C. A. R. (1972). *Structured programming.* Academic Press.

Dai, J. (1995). Isolated word recognition using Markov chain models. *IEEE Transactions on Speech and Audio Processing, 3*(6).

Dale, J., & Mamdani, E. (n.d.). Open standards for interoperating agent-based systems. *Software Focus, 2*(1), 1-8.

Davé, R. N. (1991). Characterization and detection of noise in clustering. *Pattern Recognition Lett, 12*(11), 657-664.

Davis, C., Philipp, A., & Cowen, D. (2005). *Hacking exposed computer forensics (hacking exposed).* McGraw-Hill.

de Kleer, J., & Williams, B. C. (1987). Diagnosing multiple faults. *Artificial Intelligence, 32*(1), 97-130.

Decker, R. J. (2001). Homeland Security: A Risk Management Approach Can Guide Preparedness Efforts, USA General Accounting Office, report no GAO-02-208T, October 31 Carbonell, J. R. (1970) AI in CAI: An artificial intelligence approach to computer-assisted instruction. *IEEE Transactions on Man-Machine Systems, 11*(4), 190-202.

Delamaro, M., & Picco, G. (2002). Mobile code in .NET: A porting experience. *Proceedings of 6th International Conference on Mobile Agents (MA'02)* (LNCS 2535). Barcelona, Spain: Springer-Verlag.

DeLoach, S. A. (2001, May 28 - June 1). Specifying agent behavior as concurrent tasks: Defining the behavior of social agents. *Proceedings of the 5th Annual Conference on Autonomous Agents*, Montreal, Canada

DeLoach, S. A., Wood, M. F., & Sparkman, C. H. (2001). Multiagent systems engineering. *The International Journal of Software Engineering and Knowledge Engineering, 11*(3).

Dempster, A. P., Laird, N. M., & Rubin, D. B. (1977). Maximum likelihood from incomplete data via the EM algorithm. *Journal of the Royal Statistical Society, B*(39), 1-38.

Dennett, D. C. (1987). *The intentional stance.* Cambridge, MA: MIT Press.

Denning, A. (1997). *ActiveX controls inside out* (2nd ed.). Redmond, WA: Microsoft Press.

Dennis, J. B., & Misunas, D. P. (1975). A preliminary architecture for a basic dataflow processor. *Proceedings of 2nd Symposium on Computer Architectures* (pp. 126-132).

Dennis, J. B., Gao, G. R., & Todd, K. W. (1984). Modeling the weather with dataflow supercomputers. *IEEE Transactions on Computer, 33*, 592-603.

Di Stefano, A., & Santoro, C. (2002). *Locating mobile agents in a wide distributed environment.* Retrieved April 27, 2006, from http://www.cs.albany.edu/~mhc/Mobile/leena_Presentation1.ppt

Dietl, M., Gutmann, J. S., & Nebel, B. (2001). Cooperative sensing in dynamic environments. *Proceedings of the IEEE/RSJ International Conference on Intelligent Robots and Systems (IROS'01)*, Maui, HI.

Dietz, P., & Leigh, D. (2001). DiamondTouch: A multi-user touch technology. *Proceedings of the 14th Annual ACM Symposium on User Interface Software Technology* (pp. 219-226). New York: ACM Press.

Dijkstra, E. W. (1976). *A discipline of programming.* Prentice-Hall.

Distributed Net. (2006). *Distributed net, node zero.* Retrieved April 27, 2006, from http://www.distributed.net/

Dogherty, P., Driankov, D., & Heffendorn, H. (1993). Fuzzy if then unless rules and their implementation. *International Journal of Uncertainty, Fuzziness and Knowledge Based Systems 1*(2), 167-182.

Dorigo, M., & Caro, G. D. (1998). AntNet: Distributed stigmergetic control for communications network. *Journal of Artificial Intelligence Research JAIR, 9*, 317-365.

Doyle, M., & Cunningham, P. (2000). A Dynamic approach to reducing dialog in on-line decision guides. In E. Blanzieri & L. Portinale (Ed.), *Proceedings of the Fifth European Workshop on Case-Based Reasoning* (pp. 49-60). Springer-Verlag.

Dras, M. (1998). Search in constraint-based paraphrasing. *Proceedings of the Second International Conference on Natural Language Processing and Industrial Applications* (pp. 213-219).

Dras, M., Kavakli, M., & Richards, D. (2005, July 25-26). Training for high-risk situations. *Proceedings of The Agent Based Systems for Human Learning (ABSHL), Workshop to be held in conjunction with the Fourth International Joint Conference on Autonomous Agents and Multi Agent Systems,* Utrecht, The Netherlands. Retrieved from http://agents.cs.columbia.edu/abshl

Dubois, D. & Prade, H. (1992). Gradual inference rules in approximate reasoning. *Information Sciences, 61,* 103-122.

Dunne, C. R. (2001). Using mobile agents for network resource discovery in peer-to-peer networks. *ACM SIGecom Exchanges, 2*(3), 1-9.

Duvigneau, M., & Moldt, D. (2002, July). Concurrent architecture for a multi-agent platform. *Proceedings of the 3rd International Workshop on Agent-Oriented Software Engineering (AOSE-2002),* Bologna, Italy.

Dylla, F., Ferrein, A., & Lakemeyer, G. (2002). Acting and deliberating using golog in robotic soccer - A hybrid approach. *Proceedings of the 3rd International Cognitive Robotics Workshop (CogRob 2002).* AAAI Press.

Earth System Grid. (2001). Retrieved from https://www.earthsystemgrid.org/http://e-science.ox.ac.uk/oesc/projects/test/projects.xml.ID=body.1_div.12

Elammari, M., & Lalonde, W. (1999). An agent-oriented methodology: High-level view and intermediate models. *Proceedings of AOIS Workshop,* Seattle, WA.

Fairclough, C., & Cunningham, P. (2002). *An interactive story engine.* Computer Science Department, Trinity College, Dublin.

Faltings, B., Pu, P., Torrens, M., & Viappiani, P. (2004). Design example-critiquing interaction. *Proceedings of the International Conference on Intelligent User Interface* (pp. 22-29). New York: ACM Press.

Farmer, W., Guttman, J., & Swarup, V. (1996). Security for mobile agents: Issues and requirements. *Proceedings of the 19th National Information Systems Security Conference (NISSC'96),* Baltimore.

Farooq Ahmad, H., Ali, A., Suguri, H., Abbas Khan, Z., & Rehman, M. U. (2003). Decentralized multi agent system: Basic thoughts. *Proceedings of 11ᵗʰ Assurance System Symposium* (pp. 9-14).

Farooq Ahmad, H., Iqbal, K., Ali, A., & Suguri, H. (2003). Autonomous distributed service system: Basic concepts and evaluation. *Proceedings of the 2ⁿᵈ International Workshop on Grid and Cooperative Computing, GCC 2003* (pp. 432-439).

Farooq Ahmad, H., Suguri, H., Ali, A., Malik, S., Mugal, M., Omair Shafiq, M., et al. (2005, July 25-29). Scalable fault tolerant Agent Grooming Environment: SAGE. *Proceedings of the 4ᵗʰ International Joint Conference on Autonomous Agents and Multiagent Systems (AAMAS) 2005*, The Netherlands.

Farooq Ahmad, H., Suguri, H., Omair Shafiq, M. & Ali, A. (2004, September). Autonomous distributed service system: Enabling Webs services communication with software agents. *Proceedings of 16ᵗʰ International Conference on commuters and Communication (ICCC 2004)*, Beijing, China.

Farooq Ahmad, H., Sun, G., & Mori, K. (2001). Autonomous information provision to achieve reliability for users and providers. *IEEE Proceedings of the 5ᵗʰ International Symposium on ADS (ISADS01)* (pp. 65-72).

Fassbender, Richards, & Kavakli (2006, December 4-6). Usage of a 3D game engine to evaluate different styles of music and their effect on learning in virtual-immersive environments. *Proceedings of the Joint International Conference on CyberGames and Interactive Entertainment 2006 (CGIE2006)*, Perth, Western Australia

Fensel, D., et al. (2003). The unified problem-solving method development language UPML. *Knowledge and Information Systems, An International Journal, 5*, 83-127.

Ferrante J., Ottenstein K. J., & Warren J. D. (1987). The program dependence graph and its use in optimization. *ACM Transactions on Programming Languages and Systems, 9*(3), 319-349.

Ferreira, P. R., Jr., Oliveira, D., & Bazzan, A. L. (2005). A swarm based approach to adapt the structural dimension of agents' organizations [Special issue]. *Journal of Brazilian Computer Society JBCS*, 101-113.

Fesenmaier, D., Ricci, F., Schaumlechner, E., Wober, K., & Zanella, C. (2003). DIETORECS: Travel advisory for multiple decision styles. In A. J. Frew, M. Hitz, & P. O'Connors (Eds.), *Information and communication technologies in tourism* (pp. 232-241).

Fiat, A., & Mendel, M. (2000). Better algorithms for unfair metrical task systems and applications. *Proceedings of the 32ⁿᵈ Annual ACM Symposium on Theory of Computing* (pp. 725-734). Retrieved June 20, 2003, from http://portal.acm.org

Fikes, R., & Nilsson, N. (1972). Strips: A new approach to the application of theorem proving to problem solving. *Artificial Intelligence, 2*(3-4), 189-208.

Finin, T., Labrou, Y., & Mayfield, J. (n.d.). KQML as an agent communication language. In J. Bradshaw (Ed.), *Software agents* (pp. 291-316). Cambridge, MA: MIT Press.

FIPA (1998a). *FIPA 97 specification Part 2: Agent communication language, Version 2.0.* Foundation for Intelligent Physical Agents. Retrieved from www.fipa.org

FIPA (1998b). *FIPA 97 specification Part 1: Agent management, Version 2.0.* Foundation for Intelligent Physical Agents. Retrieved from www.fipa.org

FIPA (1998c). FIPA *98 specification part 13: FIPA97 developers guide, Version 1.0.* Foundation for Intelligent Physical Agents. Retrieved from www.fipa.org

FIPA (1998d). FIPA *specification 11 V1.0: Agent management support for mobility specification.* Retrieved from www.fipa.org

FIPA (2003). *FIPA Methodology: Glossary rel. 1.0.* Retrieved from http://www.pa.icar.cnr.it/~cossentino/FIPAmeth/glossary.htm

FIPA. (2000). *FIPA agent management support for mobility specification.* DC000087C. Geneva, Switzerland: Foundation for Intelligent Physical Agents.

FIPA. (2002). *FIPA abstract architecture specification.* SC00001L. Geneva, Switzerland: Foundation for Intelligent Physical Agents.

FIPA. (2006). Retrieved May 22, 2005, from http://www.fipa.org/

FIPA. (n.d.) *The Foundation for Intelligent Physical Agents.* Retrieved from http://www.fipa.org

FIPA-OS. (n.d.) Retrieved from http://fipa-os.sourceforge.net/features.htm

Fonseca1, S. P., Griss, M. L., & Letsinger, R. (2001). *Agent behavior architectures, A MAS framework comparison* (Tech. Rep.HPL-2001-332). Hewlett-Packard Laboratories.

Ford, B., Hibler, M., Lepreau, J., Mccgrath, R., & Tullmann, P. (1999). Interface and execution models in the Fluke kernel. *Operating Systems Design and Implementation,* 101-115.

Foster, I. (2002). *What is the grid? A three point checklist.* GRIDToday.

Foster, I., & Kesselman, C. (2005). *The Grid: Blueprint for a new computing infrastructure,* Morgan Kaufmann Publisher.

Foster, I., Frey, J., Graham, S, & Tuecke, S. (2004). *Modeling stateful resources with Web services, Version 1.1.*

Foster, I., Geisler, J., et al. (1997). Software infrastructure for the I-WAY high performance distributed computing experiment. *Proceedings of IEEE Symposium on High Performance Distributed Computing* (pp. 562-571).

Foster, I., Jenning, M., & Kesselman, C. (2004). Brain meets brawn: Why grid and agents need each other. *Proceedings of Autonomous Agents and Multi-Agent Systems.*

Foster, I., Kesselman, C., & Nick, J. M. (2002). Grid services for distributed system integration. *IEEE Computer, 35*(6), 37-46.

Foster, I., Kesselman, C., & Tuecke, S. (2001). The anatomy of the grid. *International Journal of Supercomputer Applications,* 15(3).

Foster, I., Kesselman, C., & Tuecke, S. (2002). *The physiology of the grid: An open grid services architecture for distributed systems integration.* Open Grid Service Infrastructure WG, Global Grid Forum.

Foundation for Intelligent Physical Agents. (2000). *Agent Management specification.* Retrieved from http://www.fipa.org/

Foundation for Intelligent Physical Agents. (2001). FIPA interaction protocol library, Retrieved from http://www.fipa.org/repository/ips.html

Fowler, M., & Scott, K. (2001). *UML distilled* (2nd ed.). Addison-Wesley.

Fox, D., Burgard, W., Dellaert, F., & Thrun, S. (1999). Monte Carlo localization: Efficient position estimation for mobile robots. In *AAAI/IAAI,* 343-349.

Fox, M. S., Barbuceanu, M., & Teigen, R. (2000). Agent-oriented supply chain management. *The International Journal of Flexible Manufacturing Systems, 12,* 165-188.

Fraser, G., Steinbauer, G., & Wotawa, F. (2004). A modular architecture for a multi-purpose mobile robot. In *Innovations in Applied Artificial Intelligence, IEA/AIE, vol. 3029, Lecture notes in artificial intelligence* (pp. 1007-1014). Ottawa, Canada: Springer.

Fraser, G., Steinbauer, G., & Wotawa, F. (2005). Plan execution in dynamic environments. *Proceedings of the 18th Conference on Industrial and Engineering Applications of Artificial Intelligence and Expert Systems, IEA/AIE, vol. 3533. Lecture notes in artificial intelligence* (pp. 208-217). Bari, Italy: Springer.

Furtado, V., & Vasconcelos, E. (2004). Geosimulation in education: The ExpertCop system. *Proceedings of Agent-based Simulation Workshop, SCS European Publisher,* Lisbon, Portugal.

Galstyan, A., Czajkowski, K., & Lerman, K. (2004). Resource allocation in the grid using reinforcement learning. *Proceedings of International Conference on Autonomous Agents and Multi-agent Systems.*

Galves, F., & Galves, C. (2004). Ensuring the Admissibility of Electronic Forensic Evidence and Enhancing its Probative Value at Trial. *Criminal Justice Magazine, 19*. Retrieved March 18, 2006, from http://www.abanet.org/crimjust/cjmag/19-1/electronic.html

Geldof, M. (2004). *The semantic grid: Will semantic Web and grid go hand in hand?* Retrieved from http://www.semanticgrid.org/documents/Semantic%20Grid%20report%20public.pdf

Gelernter, D., & Carriero, N. (1992). Coordination languages and their significance. *Communication ACM, 35*, 96-107.

Genesereth, M. R., & Ketchpel, S. P. (1994). Software agents. *Communications of the ACM, 37*(7), 48-53.

Gerkey, B. P., Vaughan, R. T., Stroy, K., Howard, A., Sukhatme, G. S., & Mataric, M. J. (2001). Most valuable player: A robot device server for distributed control. *Proceedings of the IEEE/RSJ International Conference on Intelligent Robots and Systems (IROS 2001)* (pp. 1226-1231).

Gervais, M. P., & Muscutariu, F. (2001). Towards an ADL for designing agent-based systems. *Proceedings of 2nd International Workshop on Agent-Oriented Software Engineering (AOSE'01)*, Montreal, Canada. To appear in *Lecture Notes in Computer Science*, Springer Verlag

Ghafoor, A., Rehman, M.U., Abbas Khan, Z., Farooq Ahmad, H., & Ali, A. (2004). SAGE: Next Generation multi-agent system. *Proceedings of IEEE International Conference on Parallel and Distributed Processing Techniques and Applications (PDPTA'04)* (Vol. 1, pp. 139-145).

Gibbs, C. (2000). *TEEMA reference guide version 1.0*. Regina, Saskatchewan, Canada: TRLabs.

Giles, P., & Galvin, T. (1996). *Center of gravity: Determination, analysis, and application*. Carlisle Barracks, PA: Center for Strategic Leadership.

Giunchiglia, F., Mylopoulos, J., & Perini, A. (2002). The Tropos software development methodology: Processes, models and diagrams. *Proceedings of AOSE Workshop*

(pp. 162-173). Retrieved from http://www.jamesodell.com/AOSE02-papers/aose02-23.pdf

Glass, G. (1997). *ObjectSpace voyager core package technical overview*. ObjectSpace.

Gordon, D. (1996). The organization of work in social insect colonies. *Nature, 380*, 121-124.

Gordon, M. J. C. (1979). *The denotational description of programming languages: An introduction*. Springer-Verlag.

Gotzhein, R. (1992). Temporal logic and application: A tutorial. *Computer Networks and ISDN Systems, 24*, 203-218.

Gray, R., Kotz, D., Nog, S., Rus, D., & Cybenko, G. (1997). Mobile agents: The next generation in distributed computing. *Proceedings of the Second Aizu International Symposium on Parallel Algorithms and Architectures Synthesis* (pp. 8-24). Retrieved November 15, 2002, from Institute of Electrical and Electronics Engineers Digital Library Database.

Greenberg, M., Byington, J., & Harper, D. (1998). Mobile agents and security. *IEEE Communications Magazine, 36*(7).

Greenwald, A., Hall, K., & Serrano, R. (2003). Correlated-q learning. In T. Fawcett and N. Mishra (Eds.), *Proceedings of the 20th International Conference on Machine Learning* (pp. 242-249). Washington, DC: American Association for Artificial Intelligence Press.

Grimson, J., Grimson, W., & Hasselbring, W. (2000). The SI challenge in health care. *Communications of the Association for Computing Machinery, 43*(6), 49-55. Retrieved May 27, 2003, from Association for Computing Machinery Digital Library Database.

Grosso, W., Eriksson, H., Fergerson, R., Gennari, J., Tu, S., & Musen, M. (1999, October 16-21). Knowledge modeling at the millennium, The design and evolution of protégé – 2000. *Proceedings of the 12th Workshop on Knowledge Acquisition, Modeling and Management*, Banff, Alberta, Canada.

Gschwind, T., Feridun, M., & Pleisch, S. (1999). ADK: Building mobile agents for network and systems management from reusable components. *Proceedings of the Joint Symposium on Agent Systems and Applications/Mobile Agents (ASA/MA'99),* Palm Springs, CA.

Guessoum, Z., & Briot, J. P. (1999). From active objects to autonomous agents. *IEEE Concurrency, 7*(3), 68-76.

Guttman, E., Perkins, C., Veizades, J., & Day, M. (1999). *RFC 2608: Service location protocol, Version 2.* Retrieved April 27, 2006, from http://www.ietf.org/rfc/rfc2608.txt

Hagan, M. T., Demuth, H. B., & Beale, M. (1995). *Neural network design.* Boston: PWS Publishing Company.

Hankin, C., Métayer, D. L., & Sands, D. (1992). *A calculus of GAMMA programs.* Springer-Verlag.

Harel, D., & Pnueli, A. (1985). On the development of reactive systems. In K. R. Apt (Ed.), *Logics and models of concurrent systems* (pp. 477-498). Springer-Verlag.

Harmon, M., & Harmon, S. (1996). *Reinforcement learning: A tutorial.*

Harvey, W. D., & Ginsberg, M. L. (1995). Limited discrepancy search. *Proceedings of the 14th International Joint Conference on Artificial Intelligence (IJCAI-95)* (pp. 607-613).

Haykin, S. (1994). *Neural networks: A comprehensive foundation.* Macmillan College Publishing.

Heine, C., Herrier, R., & Kirn, S. (2005). ADAPT@ AGENT.HOSPITAL: Agent-based optimization and management of clinical processes. *International Journal of Intelligent Information Technologies, 1*(1). Retrieved July 10, 2006, from http://wi2.uni-hohenheim.de/team/documents/public/heine/%5BHeHK2005%5D.pdf

Hellendoorn, H., & Thomas, C. (1993). Defuzzification in fuzzy controllers. *Journal of Intelligent and Fuzzy Systems, 1*(2), 109-123.

Henning, M., & Vinoski, S. (1999). *Advanced CORBA©Programming with C++* (1st ed.). Addison Wesley Professional.

Hernandez, F., Gray, J., & Reilly, K. (2003). A multi-level technique for modeling agent-based systems. *Proceedings of 2nd International Workshop on Agent-Oriented Methodologies (OOPSLA-2003)* (pp. 33-42).

Hernandez, G., El Fallah-Seghrouchni, A., & Soldano, H. (2004, January 6-7). Learning in BDI multi-agent systems. *Proceedings of 4th International Workshop on Computational Logic in Multi-Agent Systems (CLIMA IV),* Florida.

Hewitt, C. (1977). Viewing control structures as patterns of passing messages. *Artificial Intelligence, 8*(3), 323-364.

Hill, F. (n.d.). *JESS- Java expert system shell.* Retrieved from http://herzberg.ca.sandia.gov/jess

Hinton, G. E., & Sejnowski, T. S. (1986). Learning and relearning in boltzmann machines. In D. E. Rumerhart, J. L. Mclelland, and the PDP Research Group (Eds.). Parallel distributed processing (pp. 282-317). Cambridge, MA: MIT Press.

Hofe, H. M. (1997). ConPlan/SIEDAplan: Personnel assignment as a problem of hierarchical constraint satisfaction. *Proceedings of the 3rd International Conference on Practical Applications of Constraint Technologies* (pp. 257-272).

Hohl, F. (1998). A model of attack of malicious hosts against mobile agents. In *Object-Oriented Technology, ECOOP'98 Workshop Reader / Proceedings of the 4th Workshop on Mobile Object Systems (MOS'98): Secure Internet Mobile Computations* (LNCS 1543). Brussels, Belgium: Springer-Verlag.

Hsia, T. C. (1977). *System identification: Least square methods.* D.C. Heath and Company.

Hu, J., & Wellman, M. (1998). Multiagent reinforcement learning: theoretical framework and an algorithm. In J. Shavlik (Ed.), *Proceedings of the 15th International Conference on Machine Learning* (pp. 242-250). Madison, WI: Morgan Kaufmann Publishers.

Hu, J., & Wellman, M. (2003). Nash q-learning for general-sum stochastic games. *Journal of Machine Learning Research, 4*(11), 1039-1069.

Hunsberger, L., & Grosz, B. J. (2000). A combinatorial auction for collaborative planning. *Proceedings of the 4ᵗʰ International Conference on Multi-Agent Systems (ICMAS2000)* (pp. 151-158).

Huston, T. (2001). Security issues for implementation of e-medical records. *Communications of the Association for Computing Machinery, 44*(9), 89-94. Retrieved January 9, 2005, from Association for Computing Machinery Digital Library Database.

IBM Software. (n.d.). *IBM Lotus Notes.* Retrieved April 27, 2006, from http://www.lotus.com/products/product4. nsf/wdocs/noteshomepage

Ingber, L. (1989). Very fast simulated re-annealing. *Mathematical and Computer Modeling, 12*(8), 967-973.

IPG project (1998). Retrieved from http://www.ipg. nasa.gov/

Ito, T., Yokoo, M., Matsubara, S., & Iwasaki, A. (2005). A new strategy proof greedy-allocation combinatorial auction protocol and its extension to open ascending auction protocol. *Proceedings of the 20ᵗʰ National Conference on Artificial Intelligence (AAAI-05)* (pp. 261-266).

JADE – Java Agent DEvelopment Framework. (n.d.) Retrieved from http://jade.tilab.com/

Jameson, A. (2004). More than the sum of its members: Challenges for group recommender systems. *Proceedings of the International Working Conference on Advanced Visual Interfaces* (pp. 48-54).

Jameson, A. (2005). User modeling meets usability goals. In L. Ardissono, P. Brna, & A. Mitrovic (Ed.), *User Modeling: Proceedings of the Tenth International Conference* (pp. 1-3). Springer.

Jang, J. S. R. (1991). Fuzzy modeling using generalized neural networks and kalman filter algorithm. *Proceedings of the Ninth National Conference on Artificial Intelligence (AAAI-91),* 762-767.

Jang, J. S. R. (1993). ANFIS: Adaptive network based fuzzy inference systems. *IEEE Transactions on Systems, Man, and Cybernetics, 23*(03), 665-685.

Jang, J. S. R., Sun, C. T., & Mizutani, E. (1997). *Neuro-fuzzy and soft computing.* NJ: Prentice Hall.

Java Agent Development Framework. (1998). http://sharon.cselt.it/projects/jade

Java. (1998). *Programming Java threads in the real world: A Java programmer's guide to threading architectures.* Retrieved from http://www.javaworld/jw-09-1998/jw-09-threads_p.html

Jennings, N. R. (2000). On agent-based software engineering. *Artificial Intelligence, 117,* 277-296.

Jennings, N. R. (2001). An agent-based approach for complex software systems. *Communications of the ACM,* 35-41.

Jennings, N. R., & Wooldridge, M. J. (1998). *Agent technology: Foundations, applications and markets.* Springer-Verlag.

Jennings, N. R., et al. (2000). Autonomous agents for business process management. *International Journal of Applied Artificial Intelligence, 14*(2), 145-189.

Jennings, N. R., Sycra, K., & Wooldridge, M. (1998). A roadmap of agent research and development. In M. Wooldridge (Ed.), *Autonomous agents and multi-agent systems* (pp. 275-306). Boston: Kluwer Academic Publisher.

Jing, H., Netzer, Y. D., Elhadad, M., & McKeown, K. (2000). Integrating a large-scale, reusable lexicon with a natural language generator. *Proceedings of the 1st International Conference on Natural Language Generation* (pp. 209-216).

Johnson, W., Rickel, J., & Lester, J. (2000). Animated pedagogical agents: Face-to-face interaction in interactive learning environments. *International Journal of Artificial Intelligence in Education, 11,* 47-78.

Jones, P. B., Blake, M. A., & Archibald, J. K. (2002). A real-time algorithm for task allocation. *IEEE International Symposium on Intelligent Control,* 672-677. Retrieved September 1, 2003, from http://ieeexplore.ieee.org

Julka, N., Karimi, I., & Srinivasan, R. (2002). Agent-based supply chain management-2: A refinery application. *Computers and Chemical Engineering, 26*, 1771-1781.

Kadrovach, B. A., & Lamont, G. B. (2002). A particle swarm model for swarm-based networked sensor systems. In *Proceedings of the 2002 ACM Symposium on Applied Computing* (pp. 918-924). Retrieved June 19, 2004, from Association for Computing Machinery Digital Library Database.

Kaelbling, L. P., & Littman, M. L. (1996). Reinforcement learning: A survey. *Journal of Artificial Intelligence Research, 4*, 237-285.

Kavakli, M. (2005, June 27-July 1). Games of soldiers: A survey of military training & computer games. *Proceedings of ISAGA 2005, 36th Annual Conference for the International Simulation and Gaming Association*, Atlanta, GA.

Kavakli, M. (2006, July 10-13). Training simulations for crime risk assessment. *Proceedings of ITHET 2006: 7th International conference on Information Technology Based Higher Education and Training*, Sydney, Australia.

Kavakli, M., & Gao, Y. F. (2005, June 15-18). Consistency of risk assessment in physical and virtual environments. *Proceedings of INISTA 2005, Innovations in Intelligent Systems and Applications, IEEE Computational Intelligence Society Turkey Chapter*, Istanbul, Turkey.

Kavakli, M., & Thorne, J. (2002, November 25-29). A cognitive modelling approach to capturing the context of complex behaviour in gameplay. *Proceedings of The First International Conference on Information Technology & Applications (ICITA2002)*, Bathurst, Australia.

Kavakli, M., & Thorne, J. (2003, July 5-10). Knowledge acquisition in distance education. *Proceedings of the 6th International Conference on Computer Based Learning in Science (CBLIS2003) Conference*, Nicosia, Cyprus.

Kavakli, M., Akca, B., & Thorne, J. (2004a). The role of computer games in the education of history. *Mugla University Journal of Institute of Social Sciences (Muğla Üniversitesi Sosyal Bilimler Enstitüsü Dergisi), 13*, 66-78.

Kavakli, M., Akca, B., & Thorne, J. (2004b, February 13). The role of computer games in learning history. *Proceedings of Australian Workshop on Interactive Entertainment*, University of Technology, Sydney, Australia. Retrieved from http://research.it.uts.edu.au/creative/ie

Kavakli, M., Kavakli, K., & Gao, Y. F. (2004c, September 13-16). Crime prevention through environmental design in virtual reality. *Proceedings of the 9th Crime Prevention Through Environmental Design (CPTED) Conference*, Brisbane, Australia.

Keizer, G. (2005). Spam could cost businesses worldwide $50 billion. *InformationWeek*. Retrieved October 9, 2005, from http://www.informationweek.com/story/showArticle.jhtml?articleID=60403649

Kennedy, H. (2002). Computer games liven up military recruiting, training. *National Defense Magazine*, November.

Kephart, J. O., & Chess, D. M. (2003). The vision of autonomic computing. *Computer, 36*(1), 41-52.

Khalique, S., Jamshed, M., Farooq Ahmad, H., Ali, A., & Suguri, H. (2005, September). Significance of semantic language in multi agent systems. *Proceedings of 8th Pacific Rim Workshop on Agents and Multi-Agent Systems (PRIMA, 2005)*, Kuala Lumpur, Malaysia.

Khan, Z. A., Farooq Ahmad, H., Ali, A., & Suguri, H. (2005, April 5-7). Decentralized architecture for fault tolerant multi agent system. *Proceedings of International Symposium on Autonomous Decentralized Systems*, China.

Kienzle, D. M., & Elder, M. C. (2003). *Recent worms: A survey and trends.* Paper presented at the ACM Workshop on Rapid Malcode, WORM'03, Washington, DC.

Kirn, S. (2002). *Ubiquitous healthcare: The OnkoNet mobile agents architecture.* Paper presented at the 2002 Mobile Computing in Medicine, Heidelberg, Germany. Retrieved September 23, 2004, from http://www.old.netobjectdays.org/pdf/02/papers/node/0278.pdf

Klein, M., & Dellarocas, C. (1999, May 1-5). Exception handling in agent systems. *Proceedings of the Third*

International Conference on Autonomous Agents, Seattle, WA.

Klesen, M. (2002). *Report on affective reasoning and cultural diversity* (Tech. Rep. DFKI).

Klir, G. J. & Yuan, B. (1995). *Fuzzy sets and fuzzy logic. Theory and applications*. NJ: Prentice Hall.

Kobourov, S. G., Pavlou, D., Cappos, J., Stepp, M., Miles, M., & Wixted, A. (2005). Collaboration with Diamond-Touch. *Proceedings of the 10th International Conference on Human-Computer Interaction* (pp. 986-990).

Koehler, J., Giblin, C., Gantenbein, D., & Hauser, R. (2003). *On autonomic computing architectures* (Research Report). IBM Research Zurich Research Laboratory.

Kolodner, J. (1993). *Case-based reasoning*. Morgan Kaufmann Publishers.

Kona, M. K., & Xu, C. Z. (2002). A framework for network management using mobile agents. *Proceeding of the International Parallel and Distributed Processing Symposium* (pp. 227-234). Retrieved October 15, 2002, from http://ieeexplore.ieee.org

Kortenkamp, D., Bonasso, R. P., & Murphy, R. (Ed.). (1998). *Artificial intelligence and mobile robots. Case studies of successful robot systems*. MIT Press.

Kosko, B. (1991). *Neural networks for signal processing*. NJ: Prentice Hall.

Kotz, D., Gray, R., & Rus, D. (2002). Future directions for mobile agent research. *IEEE Distributed Systems Online, 3*(8).

Kotz, D., Gray, R., Nog, S., Rus, D., Chawla, S., & Cybenko, G. (1997). AGENT TCL: Targeting the needs of mobile computers. *IEEE Internet Computing, 1*(4).

Krebs, B. (2005). Conversation with a worm author. *The Washington Post*. Retrieved September 20, 2005, from http://blogs.washingtonpost.com/securityfix/2005/08/a_couple_of_wee.html

Kröger, F. (1987). *Temporal logic of programs*. Springer-Verlag.

Kumar, S., Cohen, P. R., & Levesque, H. J. (2000, July). The adaptive agent architecture: Achieving fault-tolerance using persistent broker teams. *Proceedings of the 4th International Conference on Multi-Agent Systems (ICMAS 2000)*, Boston.

Labrou, Y., Finin, T., & Peng, Y. (1999). Agent communication languages: The current landscape. *IEEE Intelligent Systems*, 45-52.

Lamport, L. (1993). Verification and specification of concurrent programs. In J. W. d. Bakker, W. P. d. Rover, & G. Rozenberg (Eds.), *A decade of concurrency: Reflections and perspectives* (pp. 347-374). Springer-Verlag.

Lange, D. B., & Oshima, M. (1998). Mobile agents with Java: The Aglet API. *World Wide Web (Journal), 1*(3), 111-121.

Lange, D. B., & Oshima, M. (1999). Seven good reasons for mobile agents. *Communications of the ACM, 42*(3), 88-89.

Lave, J., & Wenger, E. (1990). *Situated learning: Legitimate peripheral participation*. Cambridge, UK: Cambridge University Press.

Lee C., & Talia, D. (2003). Grid programming models: Current tools, issues and directions. In F. Berman, G. Fox and T. Hey (Eds.), *Grid computing: Making the global infrastructure a reality* (pp. 555-578). John & Wiley Press.

Leeuwen, J. V. (1990). *Handbook of theoretical computer science: Formal models and semantics* (Vol. B). Elsevier, The MIT Press.

LeJeune, N. (2003). Story engine, software engineering practices project. Metropolitan State College, Denver.

Lemos, R. (2003). Counting the cost of slammer. *c|net News.Com*. Retrieved October 11, 2005, from http://news.com.com/2102-1001_3-982955.html?tag=st.util.print

Lerman, K., & Galstyan, A. (2001). *A methodology for mathematical analysis of multi-agent systems* (Tech. Rep. No. ISI-TR-529). University of California Information Sciences Institute. Retrieved November 20, 2004, from http://www.isi.edu/%7Elerman/papers/isitr529.pdf

Lerman, K., & Shehory, O. (2000). Coalition formation for large-scale electronic markets. *Proceedings of the Fourth International Conference on Multiagent Systems* (pp. 167-175). Retrieved November 20, 2004, from http://www.isi.edu/%7Elerman/papers/LerShe99.pdf

Lieberman, H. (1997). Autonomous interface agents. *Proceedings of CHI Conf. on Human Factors in Computing Systems* (pp. 67-74).

Lind, J. (2000). *General concepts of agents and multi-agent systems.* Retrieved from www.agentlab.de

Littman, M. L. (1994). Markov games as a framework for multi-agent reinforcement learning. In W. Cohen and H. Hirsh (Eds.), *Eleventh International Conference on Machine Learning* (pp. 157-163). New Brunswick: Morgan Kaufmann Publishers.

Littman, M. L. (2001). Friend-or-foe q-learning in general-sum games. In C. E. Brodley & A. P. Danyluk (Eds.), *Proceedings of the 18th International Conference on Machine Learning* (pp. 322-328). Williamstown, MA: Morgan Kaufmann Publishers.

Liu, B., Luo, J., & Li, W. (2005). Multi-agent based network management task decomposition and scheduling. *The 19th International Conference on Advanced Information Networking and Applications* (pp. 41-46). Retrieved December 1, 2005, from http://ieeexplore.ieee.org

Liu, A., Martens, R., Paranjape, R., & Benedicenti, L. (2001). Mobile multi-agent system for medical image retrieval. *Proceedings of the 2001 Institute of Electrical and Electronics Engineers Canadian Conference on Electrical and Computer Engineering Conference,* Ontario, Canada. Retrieved October 15, 2003, from Institute of Electrical and Electronics Engineers Digital Library Database.

Lloyd, J. W. (1987). *Foundations of logic programming.* Springer Verlag.

Lopez, I., Follen, et al. (2000). *Using CORBA and Globus to coordinate multidisciplinary aeroscience applications.* Proceedings of the NASA HPCC/CAS Workshop.

Loureiro, S. (2001). *Mobile code protection.* Unpublished doctoral dissertation, Institut Eurecom, ENST, Paris.

Love Letter Worm. (2001). Retrieved November 22, 2005, from http://securityresponse.symantec.com/avcenter/venc/datat/vbs.loveletter.a.html

Lübke, D., & Marx Gómez, J. (2003). Designing a framework for mobile agents in peer-to-peer Networks. *Proceedings of SCI 2003.*

Lübke, D., & Marx Gómez, J. (2004). Applications for mobile agents in peer-to-peer-networks. *Proceedings of the 11th IEEE International Conference and Workshop on the Engineering of Computer-Based Systems.*

Luck, M., d'Inverno, M., Fisher, M., & FoMAS '97 Contributors. (1998). Foundations of multi-agent systems: Techniques, tools and theory. *Knowledge Engineering Review, 13*(3), 297-302.

Luck, M., McBurney, P., & Preist, C. (2002). *Agent technology: Enabling next generation computing.* AgentLink, software report.

Lugmayr, W. (1999). *Gypsy: A component-oriented mobile agent system.* Unpublished doctoral dissertation, Technical University of Vienna, Austria.

Luo, X., Huang, Z., & Li, L. (1995). A method for partitioning a sequential program into parallel tasks. *Journal of HarBin Institute of Technology, 27*(5), 46-50.

Ma, W., & Orgun, M. (1996). Verifying multran programs with temporal logic. In M. Orgun & E. Ashcroft (Eds.), *Intensional programming I* (pp. 186-206). World-Scientific.

Ma, W., & Sharma, D. (2005, 14-16 September, 2005). *A multiple agents based intrusion detection system.* Paper presented at the Ninth International Conference on Knowledge-Based Intelligent Information & Engineering Systems (KES2005), Melbourne, Australia.

Ma, W., Johnson, C. W., & Brent, R. P. (1996a). Concurrent programming in T-Cham. In K. Ramamohanarao (Ed.), *Proceedings of the 19th Australasian Computer Science Conference (ACSC '96),* 291-300).

Ma, W., Johnson, C. W., & Brent, R. P. (1996b). Programming with transactions and chemical abstract machine. In G.-J. Li, D. F. Hsu, S. Horiguchi, & B. Maggs (Eds.), *Proceedings of Second International Symposium on Parallel Architectures, Algorithms, and Networks (I-SPAN'96)* (pp. 562-564).

Ma, W., Krishnamurthy, E. V., & Orgun, M. A. (1994). On providing temporal semantics for the GAMMA programming Model. In C. B. Jay (Ed.), *CATS: Proceedings of computing: The Australian Theory Seminar* (pp. 121-132). Sydney, Australia: University of Technology.

Ma, W., Orgun, M. A., & Johnson, C. W. (1998). Towards a temporal semantics for frame. *Proceedings SEKE'98, Tenth International Conference on Software Engineering and Knowledge Engineering* (pp. 44-51).

Mabuchi, S. (1993). A proposal for a defuzzification strategy by the concept of sensitivity analysis. *Fuzzy Sets and Systems, 55*(1), 1-14.

Maes, S., Tuyls, K., & Manderick, B. (2001). Modeling a multi-agent environment combining influence diagrams. M. Mohammadian (Ed.), *Intelligent Agents, Web Technologies and Internet Commerce, IAWTIC2001*, Las Vegas, NV.

Malone, T. W., & Crowston, K. (1995). The interdisciplinary study of coordination. *ACM Computing Survey, 26*(1), 87-119.

Mamdami, E. H. (1977). Applications of fuzzy logic to approximate reasoning using linguistic systems. *IEEE Trans. On Systems, Man, and Cybernetics, 26*(12), 1182-1191.

Mamdami, E. H., & Gaines, B. R. (Eds.). (1981). *Fuzzy reasoning and its applications.* London: Academic Press.

Mangina, E. (2002). *Review of software products for multi-agent systems.* AgentLink, software report 2002.

Manna, Z., & Pnueli, A. (1983). How to cook a temporal proof system for your pet language. *Proceedings of 10th Ann. ACM Symp. on Principles of Programming Language* (pp. 141-154).

Manna, Z., & Pnueli, A. (1992). *The temporal logic of reactive and concurrent systems: Specification.* Springer-Verlag.

Marques, P. (2003). *Component-based development of mobile agent systems.* Unpublished doctoral dissertation, Faculty of Sciences and Technology of the University of Coimbra, Portugal.

Marques, P., Fonseca, R., Simões, P., Silva, L., & Silva, J. (2002a). A component-based approach for integrating mobile agents into the existing Web infrastructure. In *Proceedings of the 2002 IEEE International Symposium on Applications and the Internet (SAINT'2002)*. Nara, Japan: IEEE Press.

Marques, P., Santos, P., Silva, L., & Silva, J. G. (2002b). Supporting disconnected computing in mobile agent systems. *Proceedings of the 14th International Conference on Parallel and Distributed Computing and Systems (PDCS2002)*. Cambridge, MA.

Marques, P., Simões, P., Silva, L., Boavida, F., & Gabriel, J. (2001). Providing applications with mobile agent technology. *Proceedings of the 4th IEEE International Conference on Open Architectures and Network Programming (OpenArch'01)*, Anchorage, AK.

Martens, R. (2001). *TEEMA TRLabs execution environment for mobile agents.* Regina, Saskatchewan, Canada: TRLabs.

Mathoff, J., Van Hoe, R., & Apeall. (1996). A multi agent approach to interactive learning environments. *Proceedings of European Workshop on Modelling Autonomous Agents, MAAMAW*, 6. Berlin: Springer Verlag.

Maturana, F., & Norrie, D. H. (1996). Multi agent mediator architecture for distributed manufacturing. *Journal of Intelligent Manufacturing, 7*, 257-270.

McCamley, P. (2000). *Companion to safer by design.* Evaluation, Document 2, NSW Police Service, p.36.

McCann, J. A., & Huebscher, M. C. (2004, October). Evaluation issues in autonomic computing. *Proceedings of the 3rd International Conference on Grid and Cooperative Computing (GCC)*.

McCarthy, J., & Anagnost, T. (1998). Musicfx: An arbiter of group preferences for computer supported collaborative workouts. *Proceedings of Conference on Computer Supported Cooperative Work* (pp. 363-372).

McCarthy, K., McGinty, L., Smyth, B., & Reilly, J. (2005a). On the evaluation of dynamic critiquing: a large-scale user study. *Proceedings 20th National Conference on Artificial Intelligence*, (pp. 535-540). Menlo Park, CA: AAAI Press / The MIT Press.

McCarthy, K., Reilly, J., McGinty, L., & Smyth, B. (2004a). On the dynamic generation of compound critiques in conversational recommender systems. In P. De Bra (Ed.), *Proceedings of the Third International Conference on Adaptive Hypermedia and Web-Based Systems (AH-04)* (pp. 176-184). Springer.

McCarthy, K., Reilly, J., McGinty, L., & Smyth, B. (2004b). Thinking positively – Explanatory feedback for conversational recommender systems. *Proceedings of the European Conference on Case-Based Reasoning (ECCBR-04) Explanation Workshop* (pp. 115-124). Springer.

McCarthy, K., Reilly, J., McGinty, L., & Smyth, B. (2005b). Generating diverse compound critiques. *Artificial Intelligence Review, 24*(3-4), 339-357.

McCarthy, K., Salamó, M., Coyle, L., McGinty, L., Smyth, B., & Nixon, P. (2006a). Group recommender systems: A critiquing based approach. In C. Paris & C. Sidner (Eds.), *Proceedings of the 10th International Conference on Intelligent User Interfaces* (pp. 267-269). New York: ACM Press.

McCarthy, K., Salamó, M., McGinty, L., & Smyth, B. (2006b). CATS: A synchronous approach to collaborative group recommendation. *Proceedings of the 19th International Florida Artificial Intelligence Research Society Conference* (pp. 86-91). Menlo Park, CA: AAAI Press.

McConnell, S. (1996). *Rapid development: Taming wild software schedules*. Redmond, WA: Microsoft Press.

McGinty, L., & Smyth, B. (2002). Comparison-based recommendation. In Susan Craw (Ed.), *Proceedings of the 6th European Conference on Case-Based Reasoning* (pp. 575-589). Springer.

McGinty, L., & Smyth, B. (2003a). On the role of diversity in conversational recommender systems. In K. Ashley & D. Bridge (Eds.), *Proceedings 5th International Conference on Case-Based Reasoning* (pp. 276-291). Springer.

McGinty, L., & Smyth, B. (2003b). Tweaking critiquing. *Proceedings of the Workshop on Personalization and Web Techniques at the International Joint Conference on Artificial Intelligence* (pp. 20-27). Morgan Kaufmann.

McSherry, D. (2002). Diversity-conscious retrieval. *Proceedings of the 6th European Conference on Case-Based Reasoning* (pp. 219-233). Springer.

McSherry, D. (2003). Increasing dialogue efficiency in case-based reasoning without loss of solution quality. *Proceedings of the 18th International Joint Conference on Artificial Intelligence* (pp. 121-126). Morgan Kaufmann.

McSherry, D. (2003). Similarity and compromise. In A. Aamodt, D. Bridge, & K. Ashley (Eds.), *ICCBR 2003, 5th International Conference on Case-Based Reasoning* (pp. 291-305). Trondheim, Norway.

McSherry, D., & Stretch, C. (2005). Automating the Discovery of Recommendation Knowledge. In *Proceedings of the 19th International Joint Conference on Artificial Intelligence* (pp. 9-14). Morgan Kaufmann.

Mendel, J. M. (2001). *Uncertain rule-based fuzzy logic systems*. NJ: Prentice Hall.

Microsoft. (2006). *Microsoft exchange server*. Retrieved April 27, 2006, from http://www.microsoft.com/exchange/

Milojicic, D., Chauhan, D., & la Forge, W. (1998). Mobile objects and agents (MOA), design, implementation and lessons learned. *Proceedings of the 4th USENIX Conference on Object-Oriented Technologies (COOTS'98)*, Santa Fe, NM.

Minsky, M. (1985). *The society of mind*. New York: Simon and Schuster.

Mizutani, E., & Jang, J. S. R. (1995). Coactive neural fuzzy modeling. *Proceedings of the International Conference on Neural Networks*, 760-765.

Mizutani, E., Jang, J. S. R., Nishio, K., Takagi, H., & Auslander, D. M. (1994). Coactive neural networks with adjustable fuzzy membership functions and their applications. *Proceedings of the International Conference on Fuzzy Logic and Neural Networks*, 581-582.

Montemerlo, M., Roy, N., & Thrun, S. (2003). Perspectives on standardization in mobile robot programming: The Carnegie Mellon navigation (CARMEN) toolkit. *Proceedings of the Conference on Intelligent Robots and Systems (IROS)*.

Moore, B. (1996). Acceptance of information technology by health care professionals. *Proceedings of the 1996 Symposium on Computers and the Quality of Life* (pp. 57-60). Retrieved August 9, 2003, from Association for Computing Machinery Digital Library Database.

Moreau, L. (2002). Agents for the grid: A comparison with Web services (Part I: transport layer). *Proceedings of 2nd IEEE/ACM International Symposium on Cluster Computing and the Grid* (pp. 220-228).

Moreau, L. (2003). On the use of agents in a bioinformatics grid. *Proceedings of 3rd IEEE/ACM International Symposium on Cluster Computing and the Grid.*

Morel, B., & Alexander, P. A. (2003). Slicing approach for parallel component adaptation. *The 10th IEEE International Conference and Workshop on the Engineering of Computer-Based Systems* (pp. 108-114). Retrieved May 20, 2003, from http://ieeexplore.ieee.org

Moreno, A. (2003). *Medical applications of multi-agent systems.* Paper presented at the 2003 Intelligent and Adaptive Systems in Medicine Workshop, Praha, Czech Republic. Retrieved September 21, 2004, from http://cyber.felk.cvut.cz/EUNITE03-BIO/pdf/Moreno.pdf

Mori, K. (1993). Autonomous decentralized systems: Concept, data field architecture and future trends. *Proceedings of the 1st International Symposium on Autonomous Decentralized Systems (ISADS93)* (pp. 28-34). IEEE.

Morreale, P. (1998, April). Agents on the move. *IEEE Spectrum.*

Moss & Davidson. (Eds.). (2001). *Multi agent based simulation, LNAI Vol. 1979.* Berlin: Springer.

Murphy, R. R. (2002). *Introduction to AI Robotics.* MIT Press.

Murphy, R. R., & Hershberger, D. (1996). Classifying and recovering from sensing failures in autonomous mobile robots. *AAAI/IAAI, 2*, 922-929.

Murty, K. G. (1978). Computational complexity of complementary pivot methods. In *Mathematical programming study: vol. 7. Complementary and fixed point problems* (pp. 61-73). Amsterdam: North-Holland Publishing Co.

Mustafa, M. (1994). *Methodology of inductive learning: Structural engineering application.* Unpublished doctoral dissertation, Wayne State University, Detroit, MI.

MyGrid project. (2001). Retrieved from http://www.mygrid.org.uk/

Namboodiri, A. M., & Jain, A. K. (2004). On-line handwritten script recognition. *IEEE Trans. on Pattern Analysis and Machine Intelligence, 26*(1), 124-130.

Nealon, J., & Moreno, A. (2003). *Agent-based applications in health care.* Paper presented at the 2003 EU-LAT Workshop, Mexico. Retrieved September 21, 2004, from http://www.etse.urv.es/recerca/banzai/toni/MAS/papers.html

Nelson, J. (1999). *Programming mobile objects with Java.* John Wiley & Sons.

Newell, A., & Simon, H. (1972). *Human problem solving.* Englewood Cliffs, NJ: Prentice Hall.

Nguyen, Q. N., Ricci, F., & Cavada, D. (2004). User preferences initialization and integration in critique-based mobile recommender systems. *Proceedings of Artificial Intelligence in Mobile Systems 2004, in conjunction with UbiComp 2004* (pp. 71-78). Universitat des Saarlandes Press.

Nilsson, N. (1984). *Shakey the robot.* (Tech. Rep. No. 325). Menlo Park, CA: SRI International.

Nisenson, M., Yariv, I., El-Yaniv, R., & Meir, R. (2003). Towards behaviometric security systems: Learning to identify a typist. In N. Lavrač et al. (Eds.), *PKDD 2003, LNAI 2838* (pp. 363-374). Springer-Verlag, Berlin Heidelberg.

Noma, T., Zhao, L., & Badler, N. (2000). Design of a virtual human presenter. *IEEE Journal of Computer Graphics and Applications, 20*(4), 79-85.

Norman, M. S., David, W. H., Dag, K., & Allen, T. (1999). MASCOT: an agent-based architecture for coordinated mixed-initiative supply chain planning and scheduling. *Proceedings of the Third International Conference on Autonomous Agent (Agents '99)*, Seattle, WA.

Norman, T. J., et al. (2004). Agent-based formation of virtual organizations. *Knowledge-based Systems, 17*, 103-111.

Nunes, L., & Oliveira, E. (2003). Cooperative learning using advice exchange. In E. Alonso (Ed.), *Adaptive agents and multiagent systems, lecture notes in computer science: Vol. 2636* (pp. 33-48). Berlin, Heidelberg, Germany: Springer-Verlag.

Nunes, L., & Oliveira, E. (2005). Advice-exchange between evolutionary algorithms and reinforcement learning agents: Experiments in the pursuit domain. In D. Kudenko, D. Kazakov, & E. Alonso (Eds.), *Adaptive agents and multi-agent systems: vol. 2. Adaptation and multi-agent learning* (pp. 185-204).

Nwana, H. S. (1996). Software agents: An overview. *Knowledge Engineering Review, 11*(3), 1-40.

Nwana, H. S., Lee, L. C., & Jennings, N. R. (1996). Coordination in software agent systems. *The British Telecom Technical Journal, 14*(4), 79-88.

Nwana, H. S., Rosenschein, J., et al. (1998). Agent-mediated electronic commerce: Issues, challenges and some viewpoints. *Proceedings of 2nd ACM International Conference on Autonomous Agents* (pp. 189-196).

Nwana, H., Nduma, D., Lee, L., & Collis, J. (1999). ZEUS: A toolkit for building distributed Multi-Agent Systems. *Artificial Intelligence Journal, 13*(1), 129-186.

O'Connor, M., Cosley, D., Konstan, K., & Riedln, J. (2001). Polylens: A recommender system for Groups of Users. In *Proceedings of European Conference on Computer-Supported Cooperative Work* (pp. 199-218).

O'Gorman, L. (2003). Comparing passwords, tokens, and biometrics for user authentication. *Proceedings of the IEEE: 91*(12), 2021-2040.

Odell, J., & Burkhart, R. (1998). *Beyond objects: Unleashing the power of adaptive agents*. Tutorial presented at OOPSLA, Vancouver, B.C.

Odell, J., Paranuk, H. V., & Bauer, B. (2000). Extending UML for agents. *Proceedings of the AOIS Workshop at the 17th National Conference on Artificial Intelligence* (pp. 3-17). Retrieved from http://www.jamesodell.com/extendingUML.pdf

Odell, J., Van Dyke, Parunak, H., & Bauer, B. (2001). Representing, agent interaction protocols in UML. *Proceedings of the 1st International Workshop, AOSE 2000 on Agent Oriented Software Engineering* (pp. 121-140).

Omair Shafiq, M., Ali, A., Tariq, A., Basharat, A., Farooq Ahmad, H., Suguri, H., et al. (2005). A distributed services based conference planner application using software agents, grid services and Web services. *Proceedings of the Fourth International Joint Conference On Autonomous Agents and Multi Agent Systems (AAMAS)* (pp. 137-138).

OMG. (1997). *OMG mobile agent systems interoperability facilities specification (MASIF)*. OMG TC Document ORBOS/97-10-05. Retrieved from http://www.camb.opengroup.org/RI/MAF

OMG. (2000). *Mobile agent facility, version 1.0*. Formal/00-01-02: Object Management Group.

OR. (2002). Sense and respond business scenarios. *OR/MS Today*, April 2002. Retrieved from http://lionhrtpub.com/orms/orms-4-02/frvaluechain.html

Orebäck, A. (2004). *A component framework for autonomous mobile robots*. Unpublished doctoral thesis, KTH numerical and computer science.

Orebäck, A., & Christensen, H. I. (2003). Evaluation of architectures for mobile robotics. *Autonomous Robots, 14*, 33-49.

Orgun, M., & Ma, W. (1994). An overview of temporal and modal logic programming. In D. M. Gabbay & H. J. Ohlbach (Eds.), *The first international conference on temporal logic* (pp. 445-479). Springer-Verlag.

Ousterhout, J. K. (1996). Why threads are a bad idea (for most purposes). *Proceedings of USENIX Technical Conference.*

Overeinder, B., & Brazier, F. (2003). Fault tolerance in scalable agent support system: Integrating DARX in the agentscape framework. *Proceedings of the 3rd International Symposium on Cluster Computing and the Grid*, Tokyo, Japan.

Padgham, L., & Winikoff, M. (2002, July 15-19). Prometheus: A methodology for developing intelligent agents. *Proceedings of the 3rd AOSE Workshop at AAMAS'02*, Bologna, Italy. Retrieved from http://www.cs.rmit.edu.au/agents/Papers/oopsla02.pdf

Panti, M., et al. (2000). A FIPA compliant agent platform for federated information systems. Computer Science Department – University of Ancona – 60131- Ancona –Italy. *International Journal of Computer & Information Science*, RY Lee and H. Fouchal (eds.), *1*(3).

Papaioannou, T. (2000). *On the structuring of distributed systems: The argument for mobility.* Unpublished doctoral dissertation, Loughborough University, Leicestershire, UK.

Papazoglou, M. P., & van den Heuvel, W. J. (2005). *Service oriented architectures.* Retrieved from http://infolab.uvt.nl/pub/papazgloump-2005-81.pdf

Papazoglou, M.P., & Georgakopoulos, D. (2003). Service-oriented computing. *Communications of the ACM, 46*(10), 25-28.

Park, B. J. (1999). *A development of hybrid genetic algorithms for scheduling of static and dynamic job shop.* Unpublished doctoral thesis, Dong-A University, Busan, Korea.

Park, B. J., Choi, H. R., & Kim, H. S. (2001). A hybrid genetic algorithms for job shop scheduling problems. In E. Goodman (Ed.), *Genetic and evolutionary computation conference late-breaking papers* (pp. 317-324). San Francisco: ISGEC Press.

Parkes, D. C., & Kalagnanam, J. (2005). Models for iterative multiattribute Vickrey auctions. *Management Science, 51*, 435-451.

Parkes, D. C., & Ungar, L. H. (2001). An auction-based method for decentralized train scheduling. *Proceedings of the 5th International Conference on Autonomous Agents (Agents-01)* (pp. 43-50).

Parunak, H., Brueckner, S., Fleischer, M., & Odell, J. (2002, July 15-19). Co-X: Defining what agents do together. *Proceedings of AAMAS '02*, Bologna, Italy.

Parunak, V. D. (1987). Manufacturing experience with the contract net. In M. N. Huhns (Ed.), *Distributed artificial intelligence* (pp. 285-310). Pitman.

Parunak, V. D., Baker, A. D., & Clark, S. J. (1997). The AARIA agent architecture: An example of requirements-driven agent-based system design. *Proceedings of the First International Conference on Autonomous Agent*, Marina del Rey, CA.

Pedrycz, W., & Gomidt, F. (1998). *An introduction to fuzzy sets analysis and design.* Cambridge, MA: The M.I.T. Press.

Pelachaud, C., & Poggi, I., (2001). *Multimodal Embodied Agents*. ACM.

Peña, C. I., Marzo, J. L., & de la Rosa, J. L. (2002). Intelligent agents in a teaching and learning environment on the Web. *Proceedings of the 2nd IEEE International Conference on Advanced Learning Technologies, ICALT2002.*

Peng Xu, E., & Deters, R. (2005). Fault-management for multi-agent systems. *Proceedings of SAINT 2005* (pp. 287-293).

Perini, A., Pistore, M., Roveri, M., & Susi, A. (2003, 2004). *Agent-oriented modeling by interleaving formal and informal specification.* Paper presented at the 4th International Workshop on agent-oriented software engineering, AOSE 2003, LNCS 2935, Melbourne, Australia.

Pesty, S., & Webber, C. (2004). The Baghera multiagent learning environment: An educational community of artificial and human agents. *Upgrade, Journal of CEPIS (Council of European Professional Informatics Societies), 4,* 40-44.

Petrie, C. (2001) Agent-based software engineering. In *The first International Workshop on agent-oriented software engineering (AOSE2000). LNCS 1957,* Springer-Verlag.

Pfleeger, C. P., & Pfleeger, S. L. (2003). *Security in computing* (3rd ed.). Prentice Hall.

Picco, G. (1998). *Understanding, evaluating, formalizing, and exploiting code mobility.* Unpublished doctoral dissertation, Politecnico di Torino, Italy.

Plaza, E., & Ontanon, S. (2003). Cooperative multiagent learning. In E. Alonso (Ed.), *Adaptive agents and MAS, Lecture Notes on Artificial Intelligence: Vol. 2636* (pp. 1-17). Berlin, Heidelberg: Springer-Verlag.

Plua, C., & Jameson, A. (2002). Collaborative preference elicitation in a group travel recommender system. *Proceedings of the AH 2002 Workshop on Recommendation and Personalization in eCommerce* (pp. 148-154).

Poggi, I., & Pelachaud, C. (2000). Emotional meaning and expression in animated faces. In A. Paiva (Ed.), *Affect in interactions.* Berlin: Springer-Verlag.

Pokahr, L., Braubach, & Lamersdorf. (2003). Jadex: Implementing a BDI-Infrastructure for JADE Agents. *EXP: In search of innovation, 3*(3), 76-85.

Poslad, S., Buckle, P., & Hadingham, R. (2000). The FIPA-OS agent platform: Open source for open standards. *Proceedings of the 5th International Conference and Exhibition on the Practical Application of Intelligent Agents and Multi-Agents* (pp. 355-368).

Prada, R., & Paiva, A. (2005). Believable groups of synthetic characters. *Proceedings of the 4th International Joint Conference on Autonomous Agents and Multi-Agent Systems* (pp. 37-43).

Pras, A. (1995). *Network management architectures.* Unpublished doctoral dissertation, Netherlands: Centre for Telematics and Information Technology of the University of Twente.

Prensky, M. (2001). *Digital game-based learning.* New York: McGraw Hill.

Prosise, C., Mandia, K., & Pepe, M. (2003). *Incident response and computer forensics, 2nd ed.* McGraw-Hill.

psearch (n.d.). Retrieved April 27, 2006, from http://www.people.iup.edu/vmrf/

Pu, P., & Kumar, P. (2004). Evaluating example-based search tools. *Proceedings of the ACM Conference on Electronic Commerce (EC 2004)* (pp. 208-217). New York: ACM Press.

Pusara, M., & Brodley, C.E. (2004). User ReAuthentication via Mouse Movements. In *VizSEC/DMSEC '04.* Washington, DC.

Rabiner, L. R., & Juang, B. H. (1995). *Fundamentals of speech recognition.* Prentice Hall PTR

Rabiner, L. R., Levinson, S. E., & Sondhi, M. M. (1983). On the application of vector quantisation and hidden Markov models to speaker-independent, isolated word recognition. *The Bell System Technical Journal, 62*(4), 1075-1105.

Rana, O. F., & Pouchard, L. (2005). Agent based semantic grids: Research issues and challenges. *Scalable Computing: Practice and Experience, 6*(4), 83-94.

Rao, & Georgeff, M. (1991). Modeling rational agents within a BDI architecture. *Proceedings of the Second International Conference on Principles of Knowledge Representation and Reasoning* (pp. 473-484).

Rao, & Georgeff, M. (1995). BDI agents: From theory to practice. *Proceedings of the First International Conference on Multi-Agent Systems (ICMAS-95)* (pp. 312-319).

Rao, A. S., & Georgeff, M. P. (1995). *BDI agents: From theory to practice*. Australian Artificial Intelligence Institute.

Rassenti, S., Smith, V., & Bulfin, R. (1982). Combinatorial auction mechanism for airport time slot allocation. *Bell Journal of Economics, 13*(2), 402-417.

RBD. (2000). Retrieved from http://www.reliabilityblock-diagram.info/http://www.staff.brad.ac.uk/ckarazai/Reliability Modelling/Reliability%20Block%20Diagrams.pdf

Reilly, J., McCarthy, K., McGinty, L., & Smyth, B. (2004a). Incremental critiquing. In M. Bramer, F. Coenen, & T. Allen (Eds.), *Research and development in intelligent systems XXI: Proceedings of AI-2004* (pp. 101-114). Springer.

Reilly, J., McCarthy, K., McGinty, L., & Smyth, B. (2004b). Dynamic critiquing. In P. A. Gonzalez Calero & P. Funk (Eds.), *Proceedings of the European Conference on Case-Based Reasoning*, (pp. 763-777). Springer.

Reiter, R. (1987). A theory of diagnosis from first principles. *Artificial Intelligence, 32*(1), 57-95.

Rescher, N., & Urquhart, A. (1971). *Temporal logic*. Springer-Verlag.

Reynolds, D. A., Quatieri, T. F., & Dunn, R.B. (2000). Speaker verification using adapted Gaussian mixture models. *Digital Signal Processing, 10*, 19-41.

Ricci, F., Venturini, A., Cavada, D., Mirzadeh, N., Blaas, D., & Nones, M. (2003) Product recommendation with interactive query management and twofold similarity. In A. Aamodt, D. Bridge, and K. Ashley (Eds.), *ICCBR 2003, 5th International Conference on Case-Based Reasoning* (479-493). Trondheim, Norway.

Richards, D., & Busch, P. (2003) Acquiring and applying contextualised tacit knowledge. *Journal of Information and Knowledge Management, 2*(2), 179-190.

Richards, D., Barles, J., Szilas, N., Kavakli, M., & Dras, M. (2006, May 9). Human and software agents learning together. *Proceedings of Agent Based Systems for Human Learning (ABSHL), workshop to be held at the 5th International Joint Conference on Autonomous Agents and Multiagent Systems (AAMAS 2006)*, Hakodate, Japan.

Richter, A. (1998). Case-based reasoning technology from foundations to applications. *Introduction chapter* (pp. 1-15). Springer.

Riesbeck, C. K., & Schank, R. C. (1989). *Inside case-based reasoning*. Lawrence Erlbaum Associates.

Ritter, S., & Kodinger, K. R. (1996). An architecture for plug-in tutor agents. *Journal of Artificial Intelligence in Education, 7*, 315-347.

Robinson, G. E. (1992). Regulation of division of labor in insect societies. *Annual Review of Entomology, 37*, 637-665.

Rodrigues, R. N., Yared, G. F.G., Costa, C. R., Do N., Yabu-Uti, J. B. T., Violaro, F., et al . (2006). Biometric access control through numerical keyboards based on keystroke dynamics. In D. Zhang and A.K. Jain (Eds.), *ICB 2006, LNCS 3832* (pp. 640-646). Berlin/Heidelberg: Springer-Verlag.

Roumeliotis, S. I., Sukhatme, G. S., & Bekey G. A. (1998). Sensor fault detection and identification in a mobile robot. *Proceedings of IEEE Conference on Intelligent Robots and Systems* (pp. 1383-1388).

Roure, D. D (2005). *Agents and the grids: A personal view of the opportunity before us*. AgentLink Newsletter, 17.

Rudra, T., Kavakli, M., & Bossomaier, T. (2003, September 10-12). A game pidgin language for speech recognition in computer games. *Proceedings of 3rd International Conference on Computational Semiotics for Games and New Media*, Middleborough, Tees Valley, UK.

Russell, S. J., & Norvig, P. (1995). *Artificial intelligence, A modern approach*. NJ: Prentice-Hall.

Russell, S. J., & Norvig, P. (2003). *Artificial intelligence: A modern approach* (2nd ed.). Prentice Hall.

Rzevski, G. (2003). On conceptual design of intelligent mechatronic systems. *Mechatronics 13*, 1029-1044.

Saaty, T. L. (1980). *The analytic hierarchy process*. New York: McGraw Hill.

Sakurai, Y., Yokoo, M., & Kamei, K. (2000). An efficient approximate algorithm for winner determination in combinatorial auctions. *Second ACM Conference on Electronic Commerce*.

Salamó, M., Reilly, J., McGinty, L., & Smyth, B. (2005a). Improving incremental critiquing. *16th Artificial Intelligence and Cognitive Science* (pp. 379-388).

Salamó, M., Reilly, J., McGinty, L., & Smyth, B. (2005b). Knowledge discovery from user preferences in conversational recommendation. In *Knowledge Discovery in Databases: 9th European Conference on Principles and Practice of Knowledge Discovery in Databases* (pp. 228-239). Springer.

Salamó, M., Smyth, B., McCarthy, K., Reilly, J., & McGinty, L. (2005c). Reducing critiquing repetition in conversational recommendation. *Proceedings IX Workshop on Multi-agent Information Retrieval and Recommender Systems at the International Joint Conference on Artificial Intelligence* (pp. 55-61).

Saltzer, J., Reed, D., & Clark, D. (1984). End-to-end arguments in system design. *ACM Transactions in Computer Systems, 2*(4).

Sandholm, T. (1999). An algorithm for optimal winner determination in combinatorial auctions. *Proceedings of the 16th International Joint Conference on Artificial Intelligence (IJCAI-99)* (pp. 542-547).

Sandholm, T., Suri, S., Gilpin, A., & Levine, D. (2001). Cabob: A fast optimal algorithm for combinatorial auctions. *Proceedings of the 17th International Joint Conference on Artificial Intelligence (IJCAI-01)* (pp. 1102-1108).

Satoh, I. (2002). A framework for building reusable mobile agents for network management. *IEEE/IFIP Network Operations and Management Symposium* (pp. 51-64). Retrieved May 20, 2005, from http://ieeexplore.ieee.org

Saydjari, O. S. (2004). Cyber defense: Art to science. *Communications of ACM, 47*(3), 53-57.

Schmidt, D. C. (2000). *TAO developer's guide* (1.1a ed.). Object Computing Inc.

Schopf, J., & Nitzberg, B. (2003). *Grids: The top ten questions*. Retrieved from http://www.globus.org

Schreiber, A., Wielinga, B., & Breuker, J. (Eds.). (1993). KADS. A principled approach to knowledge-based system development, *Knowledge-Based Systems, 11*.

Schreiber, G., Akkermans, H., Anjewierden, A, de Hoog, R., Shadbolt, N., Van de Velde, W., et al. (2000). *Knowledge engineering and management; The commonKADS methodology*. Cambridge, MA: MIT Press.

Seeley, D., Camazine, S., & Sneyd, J. (1991). Collective decision-making in honey bees: How colonies choose nectar sources. *Behavioral Ecology Sociobiology, 28*, 277-290.

Sen, A., & Srivasta, M. (1990). *Regression analysis: Theory, methods, and applications*. London: Springer Verlag.

seti@home. (2006). *Seti@home project*. Retrieved April 27, 2006, from http://setiathome.ssl.berkeley.edu/

Shen, W., & Norrie, D. H. (1998). An agent-based approach for distributed manufacturing and supply chain management. In G. Jacucci (Ed.), *Globalization of manufacturing in the digital communications era of the 21st century: Innovation* (pp. 579-590). Kluwer Academic Publisher.

Shen, W., & Norrie, D. H. (1999a). Developing intelligent manufacturing systems using collaborative agents. *Proceedings of the Second International Workshop on Intelligent Manufacturing Systems* (pp. 157-166).

Shen, W., & Norrie, D. H. (1999b). Agent-based systems for intelligent manufacturing: A state-of-the-art survey. *The International Journal of Knowledge and Information System*

Shen, W., & Norrie, D. H. (1999c). *An agent-based approach for manufacturing enterprise integration and supply chain management*.

Shen, W., Norrie, D. H., & Kremer, R. (1999). *Implementing Internet enabled virtual enterprises using collaborative agents, infrastructures for virtual enterprises.* Kluwer Academic Publisher.

Shen, W., Ulieru, M., Norrie, D. H., & Kremer, R. (1999). Implementing the Internet enabled supply chain through a collaborative agent system. *Proceedings of Workshop on Agent Based Decision-Support for Managing the Internet-Enabled Supply-Chain*, Seattle.

Sherin, S., & Lieberman, H. (2001). Intelligent profiling by example. *Proceedings of the International Conference on Intelligent User Interfaces (IUI 2001)* (pp. 145-152). New York: ACM Press.

Shimazu, H. (2002). ExpertClerk: A conversational case-based reasoning tool for developing salesclerk agents in e-commerce Webshops. *Artificial Intelligence Review, 18*(3-4), 223-244.

Shoham, Y. (1993). Agent-oriented programming. *Artificial Intelligence, 60*(1), 51-92.

Silva, L., Simões, P., Soares, G., Martins, P., Batista, V., Renato, C., et al. (1999). James: A platform of mobile agents for the management of telecommunication networks. *Proceedings of the 3rd International Workshop on Intelligent Agents for Telecommunication Applications (IATA'99)* (LNCS 1699). Stockholm, Sweden: Springer-Verlag .

Silveira, R. A., & Vicari, R. M. (2002). Developing distributed intelligent learning environment with JADE – Java agents for distance education framework. *Proceedings of International Conference on Intelligent Tutoring Systems, ITS 2002* (LNCS 2362, pp. 105-118).

Silverman, B., Andonyadis, C., & Morales, A. (1998). Web-based health care agents; The case of reminders and todos, too (R2Do2). *Artificial Intelligence in Medicine, 14*(3), 295-316. Retrieved May 29, 2003, from PubMed Database.

Simmons, R. (1994). Structured control for autonomous robots. *IEEE Transactions of Robotics and Automation, 10*, 34-43.

Simões, P., Reis, R., Silva, L., & Boavida, F. (1999). Enabling mobile agent technology for legacy network management frameworks. *Proceedings of the 1999 International Conference on Software, Telecommunications and Computer Networks (SoftCOM1999)*, FESB-Split, Split/Rijeka Croatia, Trieste/Venice, Italy.

Simões, P., Rodrigues, J., Silva, L., & Boavida, F. (2002). Distributed retrieval of management information: Is it about mobility, locality or distribution? *Proceedings of the 2002 IEEE/IFIP Network Operations and Management Symposium (NOMS2002)*, Florence, Italy.

Simon, H., (1977). *The new science of management decision, rev. ed.* Englewood Cliffs: Prentice Hall. Quoted in Van Gundy Jr. (1981), *Techniques of Structured Problem Solving* (p. 5). New York: Van Nostrand Reinhold Company.

Singh, A., & Pande, S. (2002). Compiler optimizations for Java aglets in distributed data intensive applications. *The 17th ACM Symposium on Applied Computing, with a Neuro-Fuzzy Applications Track* (pp. 87-92). Retrieved March 20, 2003, from http://portal.acm.org

Singh, M. P. & Huhns, M. N. (2005). *Service-oriented computing.* Wiley.

Singh, S., Kearns, M., & Mansour, Y. (2000). Nash convergence of gradient dynamics in general-sum games. In C. Boutilier and M. Goldszmidt (Eds.), *Proceedings of the 16th Conference on Uncertainty in Artificial Intelligence* (pp. 541-548). San Francisco: Morgan Kaufmann Publishers.

Slammer Virus. (2003). Retrieved December 13, 2005 from http://securityresponse.symantec.com/avcenter/venc/data/w32.sqlexp.worm.html

Sleator, D. D., & Tarjan, R. E. (1985). Amortized efficiency of list update and paging rules. *Communications of the ACM, 28*, 202-208.

Small, P. (1996). *Lists, objects and intelligent agents.* Retrieved from www.obsolete.com/dug/sorcery/loops

Smith, K., Paranjape, R., & Benedicenti, L. (2001). Agent behavior and agent models in unregulated markets. *As-*

sociation for Computing Machinery SIGAPP Applied *Computing Review, 9*(3), 2-12. Retrieved May 27, 2003, from Association for Computing Machinery Digital Library Database.

Smyth, B., & Cotter, P. (2000). A personalized TV listings service for the digital TV age. *Journal of Knowledge-Based Systems, 13*(2-3), 53-59.

Smyth, B., & McGinty, L. (2003a). An analysis of feedback strategies in conversational recommender systems. In P. Cunningham (Ed.), *Proceedings of the 14th National Conference on Artificial Intelligence and Cognitive Science* (pp. 211-216).

Smyth, B., & McGinty, L. (2003b). The power of suggestion. *Proceedings of the International Joint Conference on Artificial Intelligence* (pp. 127-132). Morgan-Kaufmann.

Socolofsky, T., & Kale, C. (1991). *A TCP/IP tutorial.* Retrieved April 27, 2006, from http://www.cis.ohio-state.edu/cgi-bin/rfc/rfc1180.html

Srini, V. P. (1986). An architecture comparison of dataflow systems. *Computer*, 68-88.

Stallings, W. (2000). *Operating systems: Internals and design principles* (4th ed). Alan Apt.

Steinbauer, G., & Wotawa, F. (2005b). Detecting and locating faults in the control software of autonomous mobile robots. *Proceedings of the 16th International Workshop on Principles of Diagnosis (DX-05)* (pp. 13-18).

Steinbauer, G., & Wotawa, F. (2005c). Detecting and locating faults in the control software of autonomous mobile robots. *Proceedings of 19th International Joint Conference on Artificial Intelligence (IJCAI-05)*, Edinburgh, UK.

Steinbauer, G., Weber, J., & Wotawa, F. (2005a). From the real-world to its qualitative representation - Practical lessons learned. *Proceedings of the 18th International Workshop on Qualitative Reasoning (QR-05)* (pp. 186-191).

Stolze, M. (2000). Soft navigation in electronic product Catalogs. *International Journal on Digital Libraries, 3*(1), 60-66.

Stone, M., & Doran, C. (1997). Sentence planning as description using tree-adjoining grammar. *Proceedings of ACL 1997* (pp. 198-205).

Stone, P., & Veloso, M. (n.d.). *Multiagent systems: A Survey from a Machine Learning Perspective* (Tech. Rep. CMU-CS-97-193). Pittsburgh, PA: Carnegie Mellon University, School of Computer Science.

Stone, P., & Veloso, M. M. (2000). Multiagent systems: A survey from a machine learning perspective. *Autonomous Robots, 8*(3), 345-383.

Stoy, J. E. (1977). *Denotational semantics: The Scott-Strachey approach to programming language theory.* The MIT Press.

Strobach, P. (1990). *Linear prediction theory: A mathematical basis for adaptive systems.* London: Springer Verlag.

Sugawara, K., & Sano, M. (1997). Cooperative acceleration of task performance: Foraging behavior of interacting multi-robots system. *Physica D, 100*(3-4), 343-354. Retrieved November 27, 2004, from Association for Computing Machinery Digital Library Database.

Suguri, H. (1998). Integrated meta media environment based on FIPA agent platform (in Japanese). *Proceedings of Symposium on Creative Software and E-Commerce Promotion* (pp. 279-282).

Suguri, H., Farooq Ahmad, H., Omair Shafiq, M., & Ali, A. (2004, October). Agent Web gateway -enabling service discovery and communication among software agents and Web services. *Proceedings of Third Joint Agent Workshops and Symposium (JAWS2004)*, Karuizawa, Japan.

Sun Microsystems. (1995-2003a). *JAR files.* Retrieved April 27, 2006, from http://java.sun.com/docs/books/tutorial/jar/index.html/

Sun Microsystems. (1995-2003b). *Java™ 2 platform.* Retrieved April 27, 2006, from http://java.sun.com/java2/whatis

Sun Microsystems. (1995-2003c). *The source for Java technology.* Retrieved April 27, 2006, from http://java.sun.com

Swartout, W., Hill, R., Gratch, J., Johnson, W. L., Kyriakakis, C., & LaBore, et al. (2001). Toward the holodeck: integrating graphics, sound, character and story. *Proceedings of the 5th International Conference on Autonomous Agents* (pp. 409-416). Retrieved from http://citeseer.nj.nec.com/447724.html

Szilas, N. (2003). IDtension: A narrative engine for interactive drama. In Göbel et al. (Eds.), *Technologies for interactive digital storytelling and entertainment (TIDSE'03)*.

Szilas, N., & Kavakli, M. (2006, January 29-February 1). PastMaster@Storytelling: A controlled interface for interactive drama. *Proceedings of IUI 2006: International Conference on Intelligent user Interfaces*, CSIRO ICT Centre, Macquarie University, Sydney, Australia.

Takagi, H., & Hayashi, I. (1991). Nn-driven fuzzy reasoning. *Proceedings of the International Journal of Approximate Reasoning, 5*(3), 191-212.

Tan, M. (1993). Multi-agent reinforcement learning: Independent vs. cooperative agents. In M. N. Huhns and M. P. Singh (Eds.), *Proceedings of the Tenth International Conference on Machine Learning* (pp. 330-337). Amherst, MA: Morgan Kaufmann Publishers.

Tanenbaum, A., & Steen, M. (2002). *Distributed systems: Principles and paradigms*. Prentice Hall.

Tariq, A., Basharat, A., Farooq Ahmad, H., Ali, A., & Suguri, H. (2005). A hybrid agent architecture for modeling autonomous agents in SAGE. *Proceedings of Sixth International Conference on Data Engineering and Automated Learning (IDEAL 2005)*, Brisbane, Australia.

Tariq, A., Amna, B., Farooq Ahmad, H., Ali, A., & Suguri, H. (2005, April 12). SAgents: Next generation autonomic entities for FIPA-compliant multi-agent system. *Proceedings of IADIS Virtual Multi Conference on Computer Science and Information Systems (MCCSIS 2005) under Intelligent Systems and Agents (ISA 2005)*.

Tecchia, F., Loscos, C., Conroy, R., & Chrysanthou, Y. (2001). Agent behaviour simulator (ABS): A platform for urban behaviour development. *Proceedings of the First International Game Technology Conference and Idea Expo (GTEC'01) in co-operation with ACM SIGGRAPH and EUROGRAPHICS* (pp. 17-21). Retrieved January 9, 2005, from http://www.equator.ac.uk/var/uploads/TecchiaGTEC2001.pdf

Tecuci, G., (1998). *Building Intelligent Agents*, San Diego, CA: Academic Press.

Tecuci, G., Boicu, M., Boicu, C., Marcu, D., Stanescu, B., & Barbulescu, M., (2005). The disciple-RKF learning and reasoning agent. *Computational Intelligence, 21*(4), 462-479.

Tecuci, G., Boicu, M., Bowman, M., & Marcu, D. (2001). An innovative application from the DARPA knowledge bases program, rapid development of a course of action critiquer. *AI Magazine, 22*(2), 43-61.

Tecuci, G., Boicu, M., Bowman, M., Marcu, D., Syhr, P., & Cascaval, C. (2000). An experiment in agent teaching by subject matter experts. *International Journal of Human-Computer Studies, 53*, 583-610.

Tesauro, G., Chess, D. M., Walsh, W. E., Das, R., Segal, A., Whalley, I., et al. (2004, July 19-23). A multi-agent systems approach to autonomic computing. *Proceedings of AAMAS '04*. New York.

The Internet Society. (1998). *RFC 2440: OpenPGP message format*. Retrieved April 27, 2006, from http://www.ietf.org/rfc/rfc2440.txt

The Internet Society. (1999a). *RFC 2459: Internet X.509 public key infrastructure, certificate and CRL profile*. Retrieved April 27, 2006, from http://www.ietf.org/rfc/rfc2459.txt

The Internet Society. (1999b). *RFC 2633: S/MIME version 3 message specification*. Retrieved April 27, 2006, from http://www.ietf.org/rfc/rfc2633.txt

The Miro Developer Team (2005). *Miro Manual, 0.9.4 ed.* University of Ulm: Department of computer science.

Thomas, L. C. (Ed.). (1984). *Games, theory and applications*. Chichester: Halsted Press.

Tong, R. M. (1985). An annotated bibliography of fuzzy control. In M. Sugeno (Ed.). *Industrial applications of fuzzy control* (pp. 249-269). New York: North Holland.

Tran, D. (2004a). New background models for pattern verification. *Proceedings of the INTERSPEECH, ICSLP Conference, Korea, 4,* 2605-2608.

Tran, D. (2004b). Temporal hidden Markov models. *Proceedings of the International Symposium on Intelligent Multimedia, Video and Speech Processing* (pp. 137-140).

Tran, D. (2004c). Estimation of prior probabilities in speaker recognition. *Proceedings of the International Symposium on Intelligent Multimedia, Video and Speech Processing, Hong Kong* (pp. 141-144).

Tran, D., & Pham, T. (2005). Fuzzy estimation of priors in speaker recognition. *WSEAS Transactions on Circuits and Systems, 4*(4), 369-373.

Tran, D., & Wagner, M. (2002). A fuzzy approach to speaker verification. *International Journal of Pattern Recognition and Artificial Intelligence (IJPRAI), 16*(7), 913-925.

Tran, D., Pham, T., & Wagner, M. (1999). Speaker recognition using Gaussian mixture models and relaxation labelling. *Proceedings of the World Multiconference on Systemetics, Cybernetics and Informatics/ The International Conference of Information Systems Analysis and Synthesis* (Vol. 6, pp. 383-389).

Tripathi, A., Karnik, N., Ahmed, T., Singh, R., Prakash, A., Kakani, V., et al. (2002). Design of the Ajanta system for mobile agent programming. *Journal of Systems and Software, 62*(2).

Truszkowski, W., Hinchey, M., Rash, J., & Rouff, C. (2004). NASA's swarm missions: The challenge of building autonomous software. *Institute of Electrical and Electronics Engineers Information Technology Professional, 6*(5), 47-52. Retrieved August 5, 2006, from Institute of Electrical and Electronics Engineers Digital Library Database.

Tsuruta, T., & Shintani, T. (2000). Scheduling meetings using distributed valued constraint satisfaction algorithm. *Proceedings of the 14th European Conference on Artificial Intelligence (ECAI-00)* (pp. 383-387).

Turchin, V. (1993). The cybernetic ontology of action. *Kybernetes, 22*(2), 10-30.

Tychsen, A., Hitchens, M., Brolund, T., & Kavakli, M. (2005, December). The game master. *Proceedings of 2nd International Workshop on Interactive Entertainment (IE2005),* Sydney, Australia.

Uma, G., Prasad, B., & Kumari, O. (1993). Distributed intelligent systems – Issues, perspectives and approaches. *Knowledge Based Systems, 6*(2), 77-96.

Uther, W., & Veloso, M. (1997). *Adversarial reinforcement learning* (Tech. Rep. CMU-CS-03-107). Pittsburgh, PA: Carnegie Mellon University, School of Computer Science.

Utz, H. (2005). *Advanced Software Concepts and Technologies for Autonomous Mobile Robotics.* Unpublished doctoral dissertation, University of Ulm.

Utz, H., Sablatnüg, S., Enderle, S., & Kraetzschmar, G. (2002). Miro: Middleware for mobile robot applications [Special issue]. *IEEE Transactions on Robotics and Automation, 18*(4), 493-497.

Venners, B. (1997). *Java security: How to install the security manager and customize your security policy.* Retrieved April 27, 2006, from http://www.javaworld.com/javaworld/jw-11-1997/jw-11-hood.html

Verma, V., Gordon, G., Simmons, R., & Thrun, S. (2004). Real-time fault diagnosis. *IEEE Robotics & Automation Magazine, 11*(2), 56-66.

Vitaglione, F., Quarta, E., & Cortese. (2002, July 16). Scalability and performance of JADE message transport system. *Proceedings of AAMAS Workshop on AgentCities,* Bologna, Italy. Retrieved from http://sharon.cselt.it/projects/jade

W3C (1996). *W3C: On mobile code.* Retrieved April 27, 2006, from http://www.w3.org/MobileCode/

Wagner, R., & Sternberg, R. (1991). *TKIM: The common sense manager: Tacit knowledge inventory for managers: Test Booklet The Psychological Corporation Harcourt Brace Jovanovich San Antonio.*

Walczak1, S. (2003). A multiagent architecture for developing medical information retrieval agents. *Journal of Medical Systems, 27*(5), 479-498. Retrieved July 29, 2005, from Association for Computing Machinery Digital Library Database.

Wang, Y., Liu, J., & Jin, X. (2003). Modeling agent-based load balancing with time delays. *Proceedings of the 2003 Institute of Electrical and Electronics Engineers/WIC International Conference on Intelligent Agent Technology, 189+.* Retrieved December 15, 2004, from Institute of Electrical and Electronics Engineers Digital Library Database.

Watkins, C. J., & Dayan, P. (1992). Q-learning. *Machine Learning, 8*, 279-292.

Watson, I. (1997). *Applying case-based reasoning: Techniques for enterprise systems.* Morgan Kaufmann.

Weber, S. (1983). A general concept of fuzzy connections, negations and implications based on t-norms. *Fuzzy Sets and Systems 11*, 115-134.

Weinberg, M., & Rosenschein, J. (2004). Best-response multiagent learning in non-stationary environments. In *The Third International Joint Conference on Autonomous Agents and Multi-Agent Systems: Vol. 2* (pp. 506-513). Washington, DC: IEEE Computer Society.

Weld, D. S. (1999). Recent advances in AI planning. *AI Magazine, 20*(2), 93-123.

White, J. (1996). Telescript technology: Mobile agents. In J. Bradshaw (Ed.), *Software agents.* AAI/MIT Press.

Wijngaards, N. J. E., et al. (2002). Supporting internet-scale multi-agent systems. *Data & Knowledge Engineering, 41*(2-3).

Williams, B. C., Muscettola, N., Nayak, P. P., & Pell, B. (1998). Remote agent: To boldly go where no AI system has gone before. *Artificial Intelligence, 103*(1-2), 5-48.

Winikoff, M., Padgham, L., Harland, J., & Thangarajah, J. (2002, April 22-25). Declarative & procedural goals in intelligent agent systems. Paper presented at the *Proceedings of the 8th International Conference on Principles and Knowledge Representation and Reasoning (KR-02),* Toulouse, France.

Wojciechowski, P., & Sewell, P. (1999). Nomadic pict: Language and infrastructure design for mobile agents. *Proceedings of the Joint Symposium on Agent Systems and Applications/Mobile Agents (ASA/MA'99),* Palm Springs, CA.

Wooldridge, M. J. (2002). *An introduction to multi-agent systems.* John Wiley & Sons.

Wooldridge, M. (1997). Agent-based software engineering. *IEE Proceedings of Software Engineering 144* (pp. 26-37).

Wooldridge, M. (2000). *Reasoning about rational agents.* Cambridge, MA: The MIT Press.

Wooldridge, M. (2002). *An introduction to multiagent systems.* West Sussex, UK: John Wiley & Sons.

Wooldridge, M., & Ciancarini, P. (2001). Agent-oriented software engineering: The state of the art. *The First International Workshop on agent-oriented software engineering (AOSE2000), LNCS 1957.* Springer-Verlag.

Wooldridge, M., & Jennings, N. (1999). Software engineering with agents: Pitfalls and pratfalls. *IEEE Internet Computing, 3*(3).

Wooldridge, M., & Jennings, N. R. (1995). Intelligent agent: Theory and practice. *Knowledge Engineering Review, 10*(2), 115-152.

Wooldridge, M., & Jennings, N. R. (2000). Agent-oriented software engineering. In J Bradshaw (Ed.), *Handbook of agent technology.* AAAI/MIT Press.

Wooldridge, M., Jennings, N. R., & Kinny, D. (1999). Methodology for agent-oriented analysis and design. *Proceedings of the 3rd International conference on Autonomous Agents* (pp. 69-76).

Wooldridge, M., Jennings, N. R., & Kinny, D. (2000). The Gaia methodology for agent-oriented analysis and design. *Journal of Autonomous Agents and Multi-agent Systems, 3*(3), 285-312.

Wu, J. (2003). Towards a decentralized search architecture for the Web and P2P systems. *Proceedings of the 2003 Adaptive Hypermedia and Adaptive Web-Based Systems Workshop.* Retrieved August 5, 2006, from http://wwwis.win.tue.nl/ah2003/proceedings/paper18.pdf

Wu, J., Cobzaru, M., Ulieru, M., & Norrie, D. H. (2000). SC-web-CS: Supply chain Web-centric systems. *Proceedings of the IASTED International Conference on Artificial Intelligence and Soft Computing* (pp. 501-507).

Xue, D., Yadav, S., & Norrie, D. H. (1999). Development of an intelligent system for building product design and manufacturing - Part I: Product modeling and design. *Proceedings of the 2nd International Workshop on Intelligent Manufacturing Systems* (pp. 367-376).

Yager, R. (1984). Approximate reasoning as a basis for rule-based expert systems. *IEEE Trans. On Systems, Man, and Cybernetics, 14*(4), 636-643.

Yager, R., & Filer, D. P. (1993). On the issue of defuzzification and selection based on a fuzzy set. *Fuzzy Sets and Systems, 55*(3), 255-272.

Yamakawa, T. (1989). Stabilization of an inverted pendulum by a high speed logic controller hardware system. *Fuzzy Sets and Systems, 32*(2), 161-180.

Yan, W., & Wu, W. (Eds.). (2000). *Data structure.* Beijing, China: Tsinghua University Press.

Yang, X., Ma, W., & You, J. (2002). On the dynamic allocation of mobile Agents by on-line task scheduling.

The 16th Proceedings of the International Parallel and Distributed Processing Symposium (pp. 217-224). Retrieved April 19, 2003, from http://ieeexplore.ieee.org

Zadeh, L. A. (1975a). Fuzzy logic and approximate reasoning. *Synthese 30*(1), 407-428.

Zadeh, L. A. (1975b). The concept of a linguistic variable and its application to approximate reasoning i, ii, iii. *Information Sciences, 8*, 199-251; 9, 43-80.

Zambonelli, F., & Jennings, N. R. (2003). Developing multi-agent systems: The Gaia methodology. *ACM Transactions on Software Engineering and Methodology, 12*(3), 317-370. Retrieved from http://www.ecs.soton.ac.uk/~nrj/download-files/tosem03.pdf

Zenith, S. E. (1991). A rationale for programming with ease. In J. P. Banâtre & D. L. Mètayer (Eds.), *Research directions in high-level parallel programming languages* (pp. 147-156). Springer-Verlag.

Zhang, F., Luh, P.B., & Santos, E. Jr. (2004). Performance study of multi-agent scheduling and coordination framework for maintenance networks. In K. Deguchi (Ed.), *Sendai, Japan: Vol. 3. Proceedings of 2004 IEEE/RSJ International Conference on Intelligent Robots and Systems* (pp. 2390-2395). Sendai: Kyodo Printing Co.

Zhuang, X., & Pande, S. (2003). Compiler scheduling of mobile agents for minimizing overheads. *Proceedings of the 23rd International Conference on Distributed Computing Systems* (pp. 600-607). Retrieved September 1, 2003, from http://ieeexplore.ieee.org

Zobot Worm. (2005). Retrieved December 13, 2005 from http://securityresponse.symantec.com/avcenter/venc/data/w32.zotob.e.html

About the Contributors

Hong Lin received his PhD in computer science from the University of Science and Technology of China (1997). He is currently an assistant professor of computer science at the University of Houston-Downtown and the chairperson of the Computer Science Curriculum Committee. His research interests include multi-agent systems, parallel/distributed computing, and formal methods. He has recently studied the application of the chemical reaction model in multi-agent system specification and derivation. His research results have been published in several papers in professional journals and conference proceedings.

* * *

Arshad Ali is a professor and director general at NUST Institute of Institute of Information Technology (NIIT), Pakistan, which he co-founded in 1999. He received his PhD from the University of Pittsburgh in 1992. His main research topics are multi-agent systems, Grid computing, network monitoring, and management and Semantic Grid. He is playing a key role in collaboration of NIIT with Stanford Linear Accelerator Center (SLAC), Center of European Nuclear Research (CERN) in Switzerland, University of the West of England (UWE) in the UK, and the California Institute of Technology (CalTech). He is a member of Institute of Electrical and Electronics Engineers (IEEE) and ACM.

Mary Anderson is a research assistant with the School of Information Sciences and Engineering at the University of Canberra. She has a Master of Information Technology.

Amna Basharat is a research associate in the multi-agent systems research group at NUST Institute of Information Technology (NIIT), Pakistan. She received a BS in software engineering from National University of Sciences and Technology (NUST), Pakistan (2005). Her research interests include multi-agent systems frameworks, agent architectures, and real-world application development via synergy of agents. She is working as a key member for collaborative research work among NUST Institute of Information and Technology (NIIT), Pakistan, and Communication Technologies (Comtec), Japan.

Ana L. C. Bazzan is an adjunct professor at the University of Rio Grande do Sul (UFRGS), Brazil, in the Department of Computer Science. She has a PhD from the University of Karlsruhe, Germany, with a thesis on an evolutionary game-theoretic approach to coordination of traffic signal agents. Currently, she coordinates a project on intelligent traffic systems and is a member of the board of the International Foundation of Autonomous Agents and Multi-Agent Systems (IFAAMAS), as well as of several program committees.

Pratik K. Biswas is currently a senior member of the technical staff at Avaya Inc. in New Jersey. Prior to this, he was a senior research faculty at the Applied Research Laboratory (ARL) of The Pennsylvania State University, where he led and managed a Defense Advanced Research Projects Agency (DARPA)-funded, multi-university (The Pennsylvania State University, Duke University, University of Wisconsin-Madison, University of California at Los Angeles, Cornell University, and Louisiana State University) research initiative (MURI) project, known as the *Emergent Surveillance Plexus*, on the surveillance capabilities of sensor networks. Earlier, he held senior technical/research positions at Lucent/Bell Laboratories, AT&T Bell Laboratories/AT&T, IBM, and *Krupp Forschungsinstitut* (Germany), among others. His current interests include autonomic systems, sensor networks, VoIP networks, artificial intelligence, intelligent agents, distributed systems, software architecture, and conceptual modeling. Dr. Biswas received his MS and PhD in computer science from Florida State University (1988 and 1991, respectively).

Liu Bo is a PhD candidate in the School of Computer Science and Engineering, Southeast University, China. Her current research interests include multi-agent technology and distributed network management.

Michael Bowman is an assistant professor of telecommunications systems management at Murray State and a retired U.S. Army colonel. He teaches graduate and undergraduate courses in telecommunications, information assurance, and computer science. During his military career, Dr. Bowman directed development, acquisition, fielding, and life-cycle management for military intelligence, surveillance and reconnaissance (ISR) architectures. Dr. Bowman earned a PhD in 2002 from George Mason University with study and research for the Defense Advanced Research Projects Agency investigating advanced methods in artificial intelligence, knowledge engineering, and intelligent agents for real-world, complex problem solving in the military domain. Dr. Bowman is a member of ITERA, IEEE, ACM, AAAI, and AFCEA.

Hyung Rim Choi is a professor of management information systems at Dong-A University, Korea. He received his BBA from Seoul National University and an MS and PhD in management science from the Korea Advanced Institute of Science and Technology. His major research interests include artificial intelligence (AI) for electronic commerce, automation of process planning, and scheduling in manufacturing systems. Currently, he is interested in the research area of port and logistics systems. He is a member of the American Association for Artificial Intelligence.

Andre de Korvin received a PhD in mathematics from the University of California Los Angeles (1967). He is currently a professor with the Department of Computer and Mathematical Sciences and assistant chair for research at the University of Houston – Downtown. His research interests include fuzzy logic, neuro-fuzzy systems, stochastic processes, business applications, the mathematical theory of evidence, and measure and integration theory. He has published 200 refereed papers and received grants from NASA, National Science Foundation (NSF), and the Army. He is the owner of the Excellence in Scholarship Award (1999), the Enron Excellence in Teaching Award (1993), the Excellence in Scholarship Award (1992), and the Excellence in Professional Service Award (1990) at the University of Houston – Downtown.

H. Farooq Ahmad is a specialist engineer in communication technologies (Comtec), Sendai, Japan, with joint appointment as an associate professor at NUST Institute of Information Technology (NIIT), Pakistan. He received a PhD from the Tokyo Institute Technology, Japan, in 2002. His main research domains are autonomous decentralized systems, multi-agent systems, autonomous Semantic Grid, and Semantic Web. He has played an instrumental role in developing collaborative research linkage between NIIT, Pakistan, and Comtec, Japan. He is a member of IEEE.

Gordon Fraser received a master's degree in computer engineering (Telematik) in 2003 from Graz University of Technology. He joined the robotic community as member of the university's RoboCup team, focusing on automated planning. Currently, he is a PhD student at the Institute for Software Technology at Graz University of Technology, working on software test automation.

Yang Gao is an associate professor in the Department of Computer Science at Nanjing University, China. He received a master's degree from Nanjing University of Science and Technology (1996) and a PhD in computer science from Nanjing University (2000). His current research interests include agent and machine learning.

Jorge Marx Gómez studied computer engineering and industrial engineering at the University of Applied Science of Berlin (Technische Fachhochschule). He was a lecturer and researcher at the Otto-von-Guericke-Universität Magdeburg, where he also obtained a PhD in business information systems with the work "Computer-based Approaches to Forecast Returns of Scrapped Products to Recycling." In 2004, he received his habilitation for the work "Automated Environmental Reporting through Material Flow Networks" at the Otto-von-Guericke-Universität Magdeburg. From 2002-2003, he was a visiting professor for business informatics at the Technical University of Clausthal. In 2004, he became a full professor of business information systems at the Carl von Ossietzky University, Oldenburg. His research interests include business information systems, e-commerce, material flow management systems, federated ERP-systems, data warehousing, recycling program planning, disassembly planning and control, simulation, and neuro-fuzzy-systems.

Hiromitsu Hattori received a BE, ME, and doctor of engineering from Nagoya Institute of Technology (1999, 2001, and 2004, respectively). He has been a research fellow of the Japan Society for the Promotion of Science (JSPS) since 2004. From 2004-2005, he was a visiting researcher at University of Liverpool. Since 2006, he has been a visiting researcher at Massachusetts Institute of Technology. His main research interests include multi-agent systems, agent argumentation, agent-mediated electronic commerce, and intelligent group decision support.

Luo Junzhou is a professor and dean of the School of Computer Science and Engineering, Southeast University. As a principal investigator, he completed 20 national and provincial projects in the past 18 years. He published more than 270 journal and conference papers on computer networking. His research interests are protocol engineering, network management, network security, and grid computing.

Iwan Kartiko works as a research fellow at the Department of Computing, Macquarie University. His work focuses on digital content creation for games and virtual reality applications. His interest is particularly in 2D illustration and 3D modeling. He graduated from University of New South Wales in 2001 with a degree in mechatronics engineering. His interest in 3D design and modeling outweigh his interest in artificial intelligence. Kartiko is also working as a freelance illustrator for an international company.

Manolya Kavakli earned a BSc (1987), MSc (1990), and PhD (1995) from Istanbul Technical University. She worked as an associate professor in design science at Istanbul Technical University until 1999. In 1996, Dr. Kavakli was awarded a NATO Science Fellowship in the UK. In 1998, she received a postdoctoral fellowship from the University of Sydney, Australia. Dr. Kavakli worked as the course coordinator of the first computer science (games technology) degree in Australia until 2003 at the School of Information Technology, Charles Stuart University. She has been working as a senior lecturer in computer graphics at the Department of Computing, Macquarie University since 2003. Dr. Kavakli established a virtual reality (VR) lab for fostering graphics research in 2003 and brought researchers together as a multidisciplinary and international research team with the establishment of VISOR (visualisation, interaction and simulation of reality) research group.

Hyun Soo Kim is a professor of management information systems at the Dong-A University in Korea. He received his BBS from Seoul National University, and an MS and PhD in management science from the Korea Advanced Institute of Science and Technology. His current research interests lie in agent-mediated commerce and collaboration in supply chain and virtual market.

Shuangzhe Liu is a senior lecturer at the University of Canberra. He holds a PhD in econometrics from the University of Amsterdam/Tinbergen Institute, The Netherlands, and has previously worked at Northeastern University, University of Amsterdam, University of Basel, and Australian National University. He has published a number of papers in top mathematical and statistical journals and book chapters contributed to books and proceedings. He has also authored a monograph and jointly edited proceedings for an international statistics workshop. Currently, he conducts research on some issues in multivariate statistics and data mining with applications to financial, medical, and other areas.

Fabiana Lorenzi is a PhD student at the Federal University of Rio Grande do Sul (UFRGS), and she teaches at the Lutheran University of Brazil (ULBRA). Her current research interests include multi-agent recommender systems, case-based reasoning, swarm intelligence, and knowledge management.

Daniel Lübke achieved his diploma degree in business informatics at the TU Clausthal in 2004. He worked in software development and coaching. Currently, he is a research assistant at the software engineering group at the Leibniz University Hannover. Areas of interest include modern approaches for distributed applications like mobile agents and Web service technologies and the software engineering paradigms behind them.

Wanli Ma is a lecturer in the School of Information Sciences and Engineering, University of Canberra. His research interests include computer security (intrusion detection, biometrics, and computer forensics) and multi-agent system (system structure, applications, and agent-based software engineering). Ma also has six years of first-hand experience in running information technology (IT) infrastructure and IT security operations.

Paulo Marques (pmarques@dei.uc.pt) is a researcher at the Center for Informatics and Systems of the University of Coimbra and an assistant professor at its Department of Informatics Engineering. He holds a PhD in informatics engineering from the same university earned in 2003. His main research interests are distributed systems, software reliability, virtual machines, and modern programming languages. He was the main developer of the M&M mobile agent framework. More recently, he has lead the RAIL and RAIL2 projects on code instrumentation for virtual machines and is currently leading the LeonVM project on dynamic code translation for the LEON2 processor.

Kevin McCarthy is a PhD student, studying in the School of Computer Science and Informatics at University College Dublin (UCD). He graduated from University College Dublin in 2003 and holds a BSc (Hons) in computer science. McCarthy's research is funded by the Science Foundation Ireland (SFI), and his current research focuses on the aggregation of user preferences in group recommendation scenarios. He has published more than 25 peer-reviewed papers and has received two best paper awards to date. His research interests include group collaboration, critiquing, diversity, user feedback, personalization, recommender systems, and case based reasoning.

Lorraine McGinty received both her BSc in computer science (1998) and her PhD (2002) from University College Dublin (UCD), and is currently a lecturer in the School of Computer Science and Informatics at UCD. Her primary research interests include adaptive retail, recommender systems, case-based reasoning, personalization, and e-commerce. She has in excess of 40 peer-reviewed scientific publications (including book chapters and papers in leading international conference and journals) and holds membership on a wide number of program committees for several international conferences and journal boards. Most recently, she served as chair of the doctoral consortium for the 2006 International Conference on Adaptive Hypermedia and Adaptive Web-Based Systems (AH 2006).

Denise de Oliveira is a PhD student at the University of Rio Grande do Sul (UFRGS), Brazil, in the Department of Computer Science. Her main interests are agent-based simulation, swarm intelligence, reinforcement learning, Markov decision processes, and coordination in multi-agent systems.

Tadachika Ozono received his bachelor's degree in engineering from the Nagoya Institute of Technology, his master's degree in engineering from Nagoya Institute of Technology, and his PhD in engineering from Nagoya Institute of Technology. He is a research associate of the Graduate School of Computer Science and Engineering at Nagoya Institute of Technology. His research topic is Web intelligence using multi-agent and machine learning technologies.

Raman Paranjape's main research interests are in mobile agent-based systems for scheduling and modeling, as well as the extraction of meaningful information from signals and images using methods of digital signal processing, computer vision, statistical analysis, and neural networks. Dr. Paranjape received a PhD in electrical engineering from the University of Alberta in 1989. He worked as post-doctoral fellow and research associate in the department of electrical and computer engineering at the University of Calgary for two years. Dr. Paranjape worked as research scientist, software engineer and project manager in Canadian industry for five years in metro Toronto. Dr. Paranjape joined the University of Regina in 1997, where he was the chair of the Electronic Systems Engineering Program between 1998-2004 and is currently professor of electronic systems engineering. Dr. Paranjape is a professional engineer and is the chair of the IEEE South Saskatchewan Section.

Byung Joo Park is a research professor of BK21 at the Dong-A University in Korea. He received his BS, MS, and PhD in industrial engineering from the Dong-A University. His major research area is application of optimization method, scheduling in manufacturing systems, logistics, and intelligent agent system.

Yong Sung Park is a professor of distribution management information systems at the Catholic University of Busan, Korea. He received his BS, MS, and PhD in management information systems from the Dong-A University. His major research areas are multi-agent systems, intelligent systems, and supply chain management. Now he is interested in the research area of ubiquitous computing and logistics systems.

John Porte is a member of the VISOR (Visualisation, Interaction and Simulation of Reality) Research Group, Department of Computing, Macquarie University. He is currently the virtual reality lab manager. His studies focused on software development, he completed a diploma in systems analysis and programming in 1999. He has undertaken various projects in software development (e.g., AuxTrack, audio mastering software for the Australian Caption Centre). Pursuing an interest in computer-generated graphics and interactive entertainment, he has found himself collaborating with artists, developing graphics engines with productions on the fringes of the underground graphics demo scene and the Indy games industry.

James Reilly is a PhD student in the School of Computer Science and Informatics at the University College Dublin. He graduated with a BSc (Hons) in computer science from the University College Dublin in 2003. Reilly works as part of the adaptive information cluster research group, which is funded by SFI. His research interests include recommender systems, user modeling, case-based reasoning, personalization, and e-commerce. James has published more than 20 peer-reviewed papers in the area of critiquing and conversational recommender systems. He has received best paper awards at the International Conference on Adaptive Hypermedia and Adaptive Web-Based Systems (AH) and a distinguished paper at the SGAI International Conference on Innovative Techniques and Applications of Artificial Intelligence.

Maria Salamó held a postdoctoral researcher post in the School of Computer Science and Informatics at University College Dublin (2005-2006). She is currently a lecturer in the department of matemàtica aplicada i anàlisi and is also a member in the volume visualization and artificial intelligence research group at the University of Barcelona. She received a PhD (2004) from Ramon Llull University, Barcelona, Spain. Her research covers a broad set of topics within artificial intelligence, including conversational recommendation, case-based reasoning, user modeling, and personalization techniques. She has published more than 30 peer-reviewed papers and has received an award for her PhD project on information and communication technologies and a best paper award.

Daniela Scherer dos Santos graduated in computer science at the University of Santa Cruz do Sul (UNISC), Brazil. Nowadays, she is a collaborative student of the Multi-Agent Systems Laboratory at the Computer Science Institute of the University of Rio Grande do Sul (UFRGS). Her main interests are in swarm intelligence, self-organization, clustering, and agent-based simulation.

Dharmendra Sharma is an associate professor in computer science and head of the School of Information Science and Engineering at the University of Canberra, Australia. His PhD is from the Australian National University, and his research interest is mainly in artificial intelligence and applying AI technology to real-world problems and developing computational models for complex problems. His areas of research expertise include distributed artificial intelligence, multi-agents, data mining, fuzzy reasoning, security, health/medical informatics, intelligent applications, and ICT applications to education. Dr Sharma has supervised many research students and has published widely.

Toramatsu Shintani received a BE, MS, and doctor of engineering from the Science University of Tokyo (1980, 1982, and 1993, respectively). From 1982-1994, he was a research staffer at the International Institute for Advanced Study of Social Information Science (IIAS-SIS), FUJITSU LABORATORIES LTD. Since 1994, he has been a professor in the Department of Intelligence and Computer Science, Nagoya Institute of Technology. From 2000-2001, he was a visiting professor at the Robotics Institute at Carnegie Mellon University (CMU). His research interests include logic programming, decision support systems, multi-agent systems, and intelligent Web systems.

Luís Silva (luis@dei.uc.pt) is a researcher at the Center for Informatics and Systems of the University of Coimbra and an associate professor at its Department of Informatics Engineering. He holds a PhD in informatics engineering from the same university received in 1997. Over the years, he has published more than 80 scientific papers at international conferences and journals, as well as led several major research projects in distributed systems and software reliability. His main research interests are dependable computing, in particular software aging and rejuvenation, autonomic computing, reliable Web services, as well as distributed systems and desktop grid computing. He is currently responsible for the reliability package of the European Network of Excellence "Core Grid."

Plamen Simeonov received an MS in mathematics from Sofia State University, Bulgaria (1992) and a PhD in mathematics from the University of South Florida (1997). His research interests are in the areas of analysis, approximation theory, orthogonal polynomails, special functions, and, most recently, fuzzy logic and its applications. Dr. Simeonov is an associate professor of mathematics at the University of Houston-Downtown.

Barry Smyth received a BSc in computer science from University College Dublin in 1991 and a PhD from Trinity College Dublin in 1996. He is an ECCAIf and is currently the head of the School of Computer Science at University College Dublin, where he holds the digital chair in computer science. His research interests include artificial intelligence, case-based reasoning, information retrieval, and user profiling and personalization. He has published more than 200 scientific articles in journals and conferences and has received a number of international awards for his research.

Gerald Steinbauer received an MSc in computer engineering (Telematik) in 2001 from Graz University of Technology. He is currently a researcher at the Institute for Software Technology at the Graz University of Technology and works on his PhD thesis focused on intelligent robust control of autonomous mobile robots. His research interests include autonomous mobile robots, sensor fusion, world modeling, robust robot control and RoboCup. He built up the RoboCup Middle-Size League team of Graz University of Technology and works as its project leader. He is a member of the IEEE Robotics and Automation Society, the IEEE Computer Society, and the Austrian Society for Artificial Intelligence. Moreover, he is co-founder and member of the Austrian RoboCup National Chapter.

Hiroki Suguri is a vice president and chief technology officer at Communication Technologies in Sendai, Japan, which he co-founded in 2000. He received his PhD from Iwate Prefectural University in 2004. His main research topics are multi-agent systems, autonomous Semantic Grid, and Semantic Web. He received a certificate of appreciation from the Foundation for Intelligent Physical Agents in 2002 and an award for key role in developing research linkages between Pakistan and Japan by the Pakistan Software Export Board in 2004. He is a member of Information Processing Society of Japan (IPSJ), IEEE, and ACM.

Nicolas Szilas entered a video game studio in 1997 in order to manage the newly created research and development (R&D) program on AI for video games, after the completion of his PhD in cognitive science in 1995 (Grenobe, France), and two postdoctoral positions (in Montreal). Between 1999-2001, he was chief scientist at the Department of Innovation of a European software integration company. In parallel, he conducted his own research program on interactive drama called Idtension, and continued working on this project at the University of Paris 8, then at the Macquarie University in Sydney, before entering the University of Geneva in 2006 as an associate professor. His research areas include games, narrative, and learning.

Amina Tariq is a research associate in multi-agent systems research group at NUST Institute of Information Technology (NIIT) in Pakistan. She received a BS in software engineering from National University of Sciences and Technology in Pakistan (2005). Her research interests include multi-agent systems frameworks, agent architectures, and real-world application development via synergy of agents.

She is working as key member for collaborative research work among NUST Institute of Information and Technology in Pakistan and Communication Technologies (Comtec) Japan.

Dat Tran received a BSc and MSc from University of Ho Chi Minh City, Vietnam (1984 and 1994, respectively), and a PhD in information sciences and engineering from University of Canberra (UC), Australia (2001). He is currently senior lecturer in software engineering at UC. Dr. Tran has published 70 research papers, has been awarded nine research grants, and has served as reviewer for *IEEE Transactions, Pattern Recognition*, and *Bioinformatics* journals. He is IEEE senior member and WSEAS board member. His biography has been included in Marquis' Who's Who in the World and in Sciences and Engineering.

Ben Tse is a graduate student at the University of Regina. He is majoring in electronic system engineering and convocated with great distinction. One year after his graduation, he decided to pursue a masters degree. Later, he became a student of TRLabs Regina, and obtained NSERC IPS. His research interests are mainly mobile agent technology, health information access and retrieval, and image processing. He is currently employed by Streamlogics Inc., as an application developer for Web casting and Web conferencing applications.

Hao Wang is a master's student in the Department of Computer Science at Nanjing University, China. His current research interest is multi-agent systems and reinforcement learning.

Lizhe Wang received a BE and ME from Tsinghua University in China (1998 and 2001, respectively), and will earn his PhD from University of Karlsruhe in Germany 2007 in applied computer science. Dr. Wang worked as a research staffer in the Institute of Computing Technology, Chinese Academic of Science (2001), School of Computer Engineering, Nanyang Technological University (2001-2003), and INRIA, France (2004-2005). His research interests include parallel computing, cluster computing, and Grid computing.

Ruili Wang is a lecturer in the Institute of Information Sciences and Technology at Massey University, New Zealand. He received a PhD in computer science from Dublin City University. His research interests include mathematical modeling and artificial intelligence. He is a member of the editorial board of the *International Journal of Business Intelligence and Data Mining*. He is currently supervising several PhD students and holds several research grants.

Jörg Weber is a PhD student at the Institute for Software Technology at Graz University of Technology (Austria). His general research interests include model-based diagnosis, qualitative reasoning, robotics, and the application of AI planning to the deliberative control of autonomous robots. His current research focuses on self-healing systems and, in particular, on model-based diagnosis and repair in mobile autonomous robots. He is a member of the "Mostly Harmless" RoboCup team at his university. He received an MSc degree from the Graz University of Technology.

Li Wei is a PhD candidate in the School of Computer Science and Engineering, Southeast University, China. His current research interests include distributed network management, traffic engineering, and e-learning.

Franz Wotawa received a PhD in 1996 from Technical University of Vienna. Since 2001, he has been a professor for software engineering at the Graz University of Technology, where he heads the Institute for Software Technology. His research interests include verification, testing, debugging, and model-based reasoning. Wotawa has written more than 100 papers, has been member of several program commitees, and has organized several workshops and special issues for journals in his field. He is a member of ACM, IEEE Computer Society, and AAAI.

Index